Anonymous

City of Hamilton Directory

Alphabetical, General, Street, Miscellaneous and Subscribers' ...

Anonymous

City of Hamilton Directory
Alphabetical, General, Street, Miscellaneous and Subscribers' ...

ISBN/EAN: 9783744756822

Printed in Europe, USA, Canada, Australia, Japan

Cover: Foto ©Andreas Hilbeck / pixelio.de

More available books at **www.hansebooks.com**

See Back Cover for **"ROYAL"** DAVID McLELLAN'S **"STANDARD"** Advertisement

›THE CELEBRATED

COOK'S FRIEND

TRADE MARK.

BAKING POWDER

THE FAVORITE OF THE PEOPLE OF CANADA.

Manufactured only by

W. D. McLAREN,

55 College Street, MONTREAL.

THE TRADE LIBERALLY DEALT WITH.

WILLIAM STEWART,

ARCHITECT.

Heating and Ventilating Engineer,

AND

Practical Superintendent.

Offices in Wentworth Chambers.

Cor. JAMES AND MAIN STS., HAMILTON, ONT.

Over 25 Years Experience as an Architect throughout the United States and Canada

N. B. Plans, Specifications and Superintendence of Steam Heating, Hot Water **Heating**, Ventilation and Sanitary Plumbing a Specialty.

ESTABLISHED IN 1863.

VICTORIA MUTUAL

FIRE INSURANCE COMPANY.

Head Office, Wentworth Chambers, 25 James St. South, Hamilton, Ontario.

The aim of the Company is by careful and economical management to afford perfect security to its members at actual cost.

Confined to property within range of hydrants in Hamilton. Business conducted on strictly mutual principles.

BOARD OF DIREECTORS.

GEO. H. MILLS, Esq.,
President.

JAMES CUMMINGS, Esq.,
Vice-President.

PETER BALFOUR, ESQ.
W. KAVANAGH, ESQ.

REGINALD KENNEDY, ESQ.
GEORGE SHARP, ESQ.

PETER BALFOUR, jr.,
AGENT, HAMILTON.

W. D. BOOKER,
SECRETARY.

McILWRAITH & McMASTER,

Importers of

Staple and Fancy Dry Goods.

MANUFACTURERS OF

MILLINERY AND MANTLES.

ALSO

Dress-Making in First-Class Style.

12 JAMES ST. NORTH,

HAMILTON, - - ONTARIO.

ADVERTISEMENTS. 3

MALCOLM & SOUTER,
MANUFACTURERS OF
FINE FURNITURE.
IMPORTERS AND DEALERS IN
Carpets, Oil Cloths & General House Furnishings

A Complete Stock of Every Description of Furniture on Hand and Made to Order

FIRST CLASS CABINET AND **UPHOLSTERED WORK A SPECIALTY**

67 and 69 King Street West, (Cor Park), HAMILTON, ONT

HANNAFORD BROS.,
Contractors
—AND—
Plasterers.

CENTRE FLOWERS, BRACKETS
ENRICHMENTS.
PANEL CEILINGS, CORNICES,
CAPITOLS,
BOSSES, BLACKBOARS, ETC.

Modelling executed to order

Every Description of Plain and Ornamental Plastering Done to Order.

76 MERRICK STREET, HAMILTON, ONT.

HAMILTON COFFEE TAVERN COMPANY,

(Incorporated)

GORE COFFEE TAVERN

13 Hughson St. north, next Times Office,

ARCADE COFFEE ROOM

Alexandra Arcade, adjoining the Market.

EAST END COFFEE ROOM

King St. East, adjoining N. & N. W. R'y Station.

—— MEALS AT ALL HOURS ——

With Tea, Coffee and Cocoa, Etc., at low prices.

ADAM BROWN,   ALFRED POWIS,
President.   *Secretary*

R. PRAY & SON

UNDERTAKERS

29 King St. West, Hamilton

TELEPHONE NO. 641.

☞ Patrons will please observe that all orders for the Hamilton City Directory bear our name, and that our agents are not authorized to receive money or goods in advance payment for subscriptions.

City of Hamilton.

FOURTEENTH ANNUAL

Alphabetical, General, Street, Miscellaneous, and Subscribers' Classified Business

DIRECTORY

FOR THE YEAR, MARCH, 1887, TO MARCH, 1888.

PRICE, - - $2.50.

W. H. IRWIN & CO., Compilers and Publishers

HAMILTON, - - ONTARIO.

Printed at the Office of A. McPherson, 51 North James St., Hamilton.

PREFACE.

The publishers, in presenting their FOURTEENTH ANNUAL EDITION of the City of Hamilton Directory, gratefully acknowledge the support awarded them, and assure their patrons, the great majority of whom they are happy to know are personal friends or acquaintances, that as in the past, so in the future, every means in their power will be exerted to make the work as thorough and reliable as it is possible for a compilation of this kind to be. Every house has been visited by our agents, and if errors are discovered we solicit a lenient criticism. The present volume contains about 14,000 names and addresses which is in excess, considering the population of the city, of the average Directory number. Wishing our patrons a favorable year, we take our leave, hoping in due time to request their support for the FIFTEENTH edition of this book.

☞ Several of our patrons complain that certain persons are in the habit of constantly borrowing Directories, and when most needed they are not to be found. The best remedy for this evil is not to permit the book to leave your premises. Every business man requires the book and can afford to purchase it.

W. H. IRWIN & CO.,
March 1st, 1887.   Hamilton, Ont.

NOTICE TO THE PUBLIC.

We deem it our duty to warn our patrons against certain "Directory publishers" who have recently appeared in the province, and who by the most disreputable representations obtain orders for their imperfect and often almost worthless publications. Several parties in this city have been victimized in this manner. Please see that all orders for the City of Hamilton Directory bear our name and address. Maps, calenders, business charts and other so called first-class advertising mediums will also bear investigation.

W. H. IRWIN & CO.

GENERAL INDEX.

	PAGE		PAGE
Addenda	8	Knights of Pythias	428
Banks and officials	430	Law Society	425
Benevolent Institutions	426	Literary Societies	425
Board of Trade	422	Masonic	427
Catholic Mutual Benefit Ass'n	426	Medical Society	425
Changes, Removals, etc	8	Military	426
Church Directory	422	National Societies	426
City Government	421	Odd Fellows	428
Classified Business Directo'y	394	Orange Association	430
Colleges and Schools	424	Post office and officials	421
County officials	414	Railways	431
Customs & Inland Revenue	422	Roman Catholic Institutions	426
Division Courts and Clerks	431	St Andrews's Society	426
Dundas, Town of	415	St George's Society	426
Educational	424	St Jean Baptiste Society	426
Emerald Beneficial Ass'n	426	Street Directory	428
Fire Alarm	421	Temperance Organizations	426
Foresters	429	United Workmen	429
Irish Protestant Benevolent Society	426	Waterworks	421
		Wentworth, County of	414

ADVERTISERS' INDEX.

	PAGE		PAGE
Ambrose Walter, insurance	405	McIlwraith & McMaster, dry goods	2
Anderson & Bates, oculists	104	Mackay Bros, dry goods	104
Barristers' cards	395-7-9	McKeand Geo, steamship agent	405
Bell T S, civil engineer	399	McLellan David, Royal Insurance Co	back cover
Brass Peter, architect	152	McMeekin John, insurance	408
Bruce Wm, patents	399	Malcolm & Souter, furniture	3
Clohecy Robt, architect	399	Notice to the public	6
Cook's Friend Baking Powder, *front cover* and page	408	Payne Elford F, insurance	405
Findlay W F, accountant	405	Pray R & Son, undertakers	4
Goering W & Co, wine and spirits	408	Ralston & Irwin, real estate	152
Hamilton Coffee Tavern Co	4	Raymond Montagu, piano tuner	399
Hannaford Bros, plasterers	3	Royal Insurance Co	back cover
Herron Joseph, tailor	104	Stewart Wm, architect	front cover
Ing Henry, watchmaker	152	Strong Wm, insurance	405
Irwin Thos & Son, roofers	413	Townsend Sherman E, accountant	395
Irwin W H & Co, directory publishers	247-432	Townsend W G, custom broker	234
Jones Seneca, insurance	405	Victoria Mutual Fire Ins Co	2
Kennedy R D, civil engineer	399		
Macdonald John & Co, wh dry goods, *inside back cover*			

ADDENDA.

NAMES RECEIVED TOO LATE FOR REGULAR INSERTION, CHANGE OF RESIDENCE, AND BUSINESS LOCALITIES, NEW ARRIVALS, ETC.

Asbourne Mills, Geo Fox, manager, 91 John s
Bankier P M, M A, (Crear & Bankier), res Hamilton Provident and Loan Chambers
Barker Edward, book and job printer, 10 John n, h 68½ Wellington n
Beasley R S, agent Toronto *Mail*, Arcade, h 103 Main e
Biggar & Lee, barristers, Canada Life Chambers, 1 James s
Booth Mrs Thompotone, servants registry, 109½ King w
Bowering & Pain, butchers, 89 King w
Boyd Julian R F, agent The *Mail* newspaper, Toronto, bds 80 James s
Bridgewood C A, boots and shoes, 103 John s
Bull Richard, insurance agent, 12 Hughson s
Carrol Cyrus P L S, civil engineer, 9 King w
Carscallan & Cahill, barristers 2½ James s
Cook & Seaver, (Wm Cook, Wm Seaver), east end wood yard, 143 King e
Crerar & Bankier, (P D Crerar, M A, P M Bankier, M A,) barristers, 24 Main e
Crerar P D, M A, (Crear & Bankier), h 14 James s
Culp & Tinling Mfg Co, (J H Culp, H J Tinling,) 185 King e
Dean W H, com traveler, 14 Emerald s
Ellicott John, plumber, 234 King e
Goodwin William, watchmaker and jeweller, 99 John s
Hamilton Whip Co, (limited) John Patterson, pres, John H Tilden, T D Murphy, sec-treas, 81 Mary
Hesse J R & Co, auctioneers, 76 James n
Mackay Richard, real estate agent, 29 King e
McKeand J C, marriage license issuer, Landed Banking and Loan Co, 3 James s, h s s Concession between Locke and Garth
Mackelcan & Mewburn, barrister, 20 Main e, *see card.*
Martin Thomas A, wood dealer, Lower Cathcart cor Kelly
Merchants Protcetive and Collecting Association, J Bidwell Mills, manager, 55 James n
Midgley George, jr, book and job printer, bookseller and stationer, 172 James n
Mills J Bidwell, manager Merchants Protective and Collecting Association, 55 James n
Murphy Charles, bookkeeper, 31 Wellington s
Murphy T D, sec-treas Hamton Whip Co, 31 Wellington s
Ogg Bros, (Alex and Charles), grocers, 177 Mary
Osborne & Co, scale manfrs, Barton e
Patten L H, barrister, Chancery Chambers, 18-20 Hughson s
Reeves A L, jr, grocer, 212 King e
Robinson E F, druggist, 36 James n
Shannon Samuel, restaurant, 112 James n
Wholton Wm, jr, stoves and tinware, 162 West ave n
World, The (Daily), Toronto, R S Beasley, agent, Arcade, 33 James n

HAMILTON DIRECTORY, 1887-8.

FOURTEENTH ANNUAL EDITION.

W. H. IRWIN & Co., Compilers.

Abbs, John A, salesman, 45 Wellington s
Abell, Mrs Elizabeth (with Daniel) 27 Wellington n
Abel, Frederick, Tailor, 126 Rebecca
Abbey, Jarvis, violin maker, 169 Queen n
Abraham, C J, stocks, grains, and provisions, 18 **James** s, h 19 Park s
Abraham, Edward A, bookkeeper 17 Park s
Accident of North America Insurance Co, Seneca Jones, Agent, 6 James s
Acheson John, 91 Wellington n
Acland, Robert, carpenter, 61 Steven
Ackland, **Robert, pattern** maker, 140 John n
Ackland, Mrs Laura, 145 John s
Acomb, Henry, laborer, 104 Macnab n
Acres, Wm hats, caps and furs, 12 King e, h 44 Hunter w
Actworth, Mrs Mary, (wid John P) 182 Napier
Adam, James, plumber, 22 Hughson n
Adam, James R, bookkeeper, h 22 Hughson n

Adam, **Mrs** Mina, **(wid** James) 16 Hunter e
Adams, Frederick, machinist, 98 Victoria ave n
Adams, George, stovemounter, 107 East ave n
Adams, James, shipper, 83 Mary
Adams, James, machinist, 79 Hannah e
Adams, Mrs Margaret, (wid Warren) 79 Hannah e
Adams, Peter, tailor, 135 Hunter e
Adams, Thomas, mariner, 164 James n
Adams, Thomas, carpenter, 14 Inchbury n
Adamson, Edward, grain inspector, 8 John n
Adcock, Mrs, Robinson n s, near Garth
Addison, George, carpenter, **78** Hughson **s**
Addison **Mrs** Grace, (wid John) 113 Rebecca
Addison, Miss Janet 78 Hughson s
Addison, John, real estate agent, 94 Wellington s
Addison, William, jr **(W W** Addison) **90** Wellington s
Addison, William, sr (W W Addison) 94 Wellington s

2

Addison, W & W, builders, Young
Addlay, Thomas, laborer, 10 Railway
Alderholz. Henry, laborer, 48 Cherry
Adley, Mrs Ellen, 256 Hughson n
Adrian, Mrs Harriet G (wid Mark) 13 Wood Market
Ætna, of Hartford, Fire Insurance Co, W F Findlay, agent, Wentworth Chambers, 25 James s
African Methodist Episcopal Church, Rev J A Johnson, pastor, 80 John n
Aged Women's Home, Miss Margaret McFarlane, matron, 115 Wellington s
Agricultural Insurance Co, of Watertown, N Y, M A Pennington, agent, 51 James n
Agutter, Charles Alfred, carpenter, 16 Jones
Ahrens, Nelson, potter, bds 103 Main w
Aikin, James, carpenter, 182 Emerald n
Aiken William, blacksmith, 34 Wellington n
Aikins, Mrs Mary, (wid James) 65 Catharine n
Aikins, Robert, scalemaker, 38 Stuart e
Aikins, Samuel, driver, 64 Market
Aikins, William, machinist, 65 Catharine n
Ailes, James, mechanic, 80 Bay n
Ailles, Richard, bricklayer, 2 Margaret
Ainsborough, John H, moulder, 367 Catharine n
Ainslie, James, tanner, 171 King William
Ainslie, William, trunk maker, 25 Markland
Ainsworth, A L S, poultry dealer, 100 Young

Aitchison, A W, chief fire brigade, 15 West ave n
Aitchison & Co, (Wm & David) planing mills, 56-58 Main w
Aitchison, David, (Aitchison & Co) 9 Bay s
Aitchison, James W, com traveller, 33 Caroline n
Aitchison, Joseph laborer, 20 Lower Cathcart
Aitchison, Thomas A, bookkeeper, 68 Hannah w
Aitchison, Wm, (Aitchison & Co) 33 Caroline n
Aitchison, Wm, Royal Oak Hotel, 93 Bay n
Aitchison, Wm J, carpenter, 9 Bay s
Aitken, Mrs Christina, (wid Samuel M) 39 Jackson w
Aitken, E P, clerk, 139 Jackson, w
Albert Chambers, 20-22 Main e
Albins, Wm, machinist, 195 East ave n
Albrecht, Ferdinand, machinist, 61 Steven
Alexander, A E, salesman, Concession, cor Hilton
Alexander, Andrew, clerk customs, Wentworth s
Alexander, Ernest, clerk, Wentworth s
Alexander, Frederick, laborer, rear 20 Strachan w
Alexander, Henry, machinist, 91 Picton e
Alexander, Mrs Isabella, 153 John s
Alexander, James, 45 Queen n
Alexander, John, leather and findings, 13 King w, h, Concession, cor Hilton
Alexander, S H, clerk, Wentworth s
Alexander, W D, bartender, Royal Hotel
Alexander —, railway man, bds 206 Macnab n

CITY OF HAMILTON.   11

Alexandra Hall, 33 James n
Alderman, Charles, laborer, r
  11 Tom
Alderman, Wm, blacksmith, 5
  Harriet
Anderson George W, plasterer,
  30 Bay n
Aldous J E P, B A, professor of
  music, 84 James s
Aldrich Wm, laborer, 141 Wood e
Aldridge Fredk A, foreman R
  Raw & Co, 47 Ferguson ave
Aldridge James, shoemaker, 7
  Ferguson ave
Aldridge Robt, teamster, 186
  King Wm
Aldridge Wm, 261 King Wm
Alford Mrs, 138 Rebecca
Alingham Robt, mechanic, 82
  Bay n
Allardice Geo R, stonecutter,
  229 Main w
Allardice Robt A, (R A Allardice
  & Co), bds St Nicholas Hotel
Allardice R A & Co, wholesale
  furniture manufacturers, 86-88
  Merrick
Allardice Thomas, cabinetmaker,
  bds 44 Vine
Allan Mrs Agnes, (wid James),
  25 Florence
Allen Mrs Ann, (wid Osborne),
  Main e of Wentworth
Allen Mrs Catharine, (wid Wm),
  107 Hunter w
Allan Edward, blacksmith, 135
  Wood e
Allan Miss Eliza, 163 King Wm
Allan Frank, foreman, 80 Catharine s
Allan Fredk A, laborer, 88 Simcoe e
Allan George, telegraphist, 138
  Cannon e
Allan George, machinist, 136
  King Wm
Allan Mrs George, 84 John n
Allan Mrs George, 104 Barton e

Allan George R, printer, 24
  Locomotive
Allan Geo T, confectioner, 56
  John s
Allan Mrs Helen, (wid Thos), 64
  Queen s
Allan Henry, boilermaker, 28
  Simcoe e
Allan James, laborer, 178 York
Allan James R, city agent *Spectator*, 39 Magill
Allan John, lithographer, 64
  Queen s
Allan John, machinist, 128 Park n
Allan Mrs Maggie, (wid Adam),
  60 Robert
Allen Martin, laborer, 128 East
  ave n
Allan Mrs Mary, (wid George),
  84 John n
Allen Michael, laborer, 128 East
  ave n
Allen Michael, shoemaker, 55
  Hunter e
Allen, Mrs Michael, grocer, 55
  Hunter e
Allen Patrick, 75 Catharine n
Allen Paul L, bds 13 Bold
Allen Richard, bootmaker, 116
  King w
Allen Robt, carter, 11 Kinnell
Allen Robert, weekly payment
  store, 14 King Wm, h 13 King
  Wm
Allan Steamship Line, J B
  Fairgrieve, agent, 6 James s
Allen Thos, machinist, 10 Simcoe e
Allen Thomas, cutter, bds 45
  Hess n
Allan Thomas, shirtcutter, 66
  Queen s
Allen Thos, builder, 143 West Ave
Allan William, carpenter, 136
  King Wm
Allan William, contractor, 14
  Barton w
Allan Wm C, Fireman GTR. 51
  Florence

CITY OF HAMILTON.

Allan Wm R, blacksmith, 48 Caroline s
Allan ——, laborer, 247 Catharine n
Allberry Wm, shoemaker, 166 John n
Allis Joseph, laborer, 228 James n
Allison House, Wm Y Allison proprietor, 51 Stuart w
Allison Mrs, 182 Emerald n
Allison Thos, machinist, 100 Ferguson ave
Allison William Y, proprietor Allison House, 51 Stuart w
All Saints' Church, Rev Geo Forneret, rector, King cor Queen
Almas Adam, 57 Catharine n
Almas Albert, hair dresser, 119 James n, h 57 Catharine n
Almas Harris, laborer, 58 Ray n
Almas John, agent, 200 Cannon e
Almond Mrs Mary, (wid David) dairy, 200 King w
Ambold Thos, gas laborer, bds 24 Mulberry
Ambridge H A, accountant Molson's Bank, 147 John s
Ambrose Mrs Charles, 27 Maria
Ambrose Mrs E, 199 Hughson n
Ambrose E H. law student, 20 Augusta
Ambrose E S, teller Bank of Hamilton, 27 Maria
Ambrose R. S. music teacher, 20 Augusta
Ambrose Walter, insurance agent, 14 Hughson s, h 92 Bay s *see card*
American Express Co, J P Johnson, agent, 18 James s
American Hotel, F W Bearman propr, 61 King w
American Suspender Factory, A G Taylor propr, 6 Macnab n
Ames John, laborer, 18 Strachan w
Ames Jonathan, L D Sawyer & Co, h 6 West ave s

Amey Thomas, laborer, 90 Elgin
Amiss Jeremiah, gardener, 88 East ave n
Amor Mrs James, 3 Queen s
Amor John, bds Victoria Hotel, King e
Amor Wm, inland revenue, 15 Queen n
Amos James, builder, 125 King e
Amos James S, 48 Catharine n
Amos Robert, salesman, 155 Bay n
Amos Samuel, contractor, bds 153 King e
Anchor Hotel (A, S. Hills. prop) cor Hughson & King Wm
Anchor Steamship Line, Geo McKeand, agent, 57 James n
Ancient Order United Workman Hall, 14 Macnab s
Anders John, foreman Meakins & Sons, 12 Steven
Anderson A, boilermaker, 42 Ferrie w
Anderson Alex, blacksmith, 25 Florence
Anderson Alexander, laborer, 55 Maria
Anderson Alexander, teamster, 121 Hannah e
Anderson Alex, 42 Hunter w
Anderson & Bates (J N Anderson, M D, Frank D W Bates, M D) oculists and aurists, 34 James n *See card*
Anderson Charles, stonecutter, Nelson
Anderson David, draughtsman G T R, bds 285 York
Anderson E G, clerk, 7 O'Rielly
Anderson Mrs Eliza (wid Samuel) 58 East ave n
Anderson Geo, accountant, 66 Stinson
Anderson, Geo, moulder, ft Wentworth n
Anderson Rev Geo, Baptist, ft Wentworth n

CITY OF HAMILTON. 13

Anderson Geo, carpenter, 69 Queen n
Anderson Geo, carpenter, 15 Murray e
Anderson Henry, machinist, Herkimer s s, w Locke
Anderson James, M D, 25 Bay n
Anderson James, stonecutter, 4 Emerald n
Anderson Jas, carpenter, bds 98 Queen s
Anderson **James**, mechanic, bds 92 Hess n
Anderson James, patterncleaner, 146 Emerald n
Anderson James, laborer, 99 Victoria ave n
Anderson Jas, blacksmith, 61 West ave n
Anderson James, bricklayer, 32 Smith ave
Anderson James, carpenter, 69 **Vine**
Anderson J N, M D, (Anderson & Bates) 34 James n, res Burlington village
Anderson John, heater, **113 Hess** n
Anderson John, machinist, 44 Catharine s
Anderson John, bricklayer, 267 Barton e
Anderson John, boot crimper, 34½ Mulberry
Anderson John, barber, 91 York, bds 46 Market
Anderson John, sr, 46 Market
Anderson Joseph, polisher, bds 87 **John** s
Anderson Mrs Martha, 164 Main w
Anderson Mrs Mary A (wid Wm) 17 Liberty
Anderson Peter, laborer, 32 **Strachan** e
Anderson Robt, bookkeeper, 164 Main w
Anderson Thos, machinist, 33 Lower Cathcart

Anderson Thomas, baker, 8 Oak ave
Anderson Thos K, cutter, bds 39 Main w
Anderson Walter, bookkeeper, **114 Market**
Anderson **Wm**, machinist, 97 Victoria ave n
Anderson Wm, clerk, 110 Market
Anderson Wm, boot crimper, 7 O'Reilly
Anderson Wm J, carpenter, 17 Liberty
Anderson Wm J, butcher, **King** e of Wentworth
Anderson W R, clerk, 164 Main w
Andrew Geo **H**, laborer, 17 Sophia n
Andrew J W, printer, 55 Lower Cathcart
Andrews Andrew, 12 Murray e
Andrews Mrs Annie, 7 Picton w
Andrews Mrs Eliza (wid **John**) laundress, 75 **Peter**
Andrews Geo, civil engineer, bds 100 Park n
Andrews James, carpenter, **264** Macnab n
Andrews **Mrs** Jane (wid Herbert) 47 Hunter e
Andrews ——, blacksmith, bds **206 Macnab** n
Andrup, Hans, tinplater, 41 Tisdale
Angold Henry, machinist, 66 East ave n
Angus Andrew (R Evans & Co) 42 Duke
Angus Henry, mangr **China** Palace, 13 West ave s
Angus Hugh M, bookkeeper, **13** West ave s
Angus James, jr, hats, caps and furs, 24 King w, h 44 Duke
Angus James, **sr**, 42 Duke
Angus Mrs Margaret, boarding, **79** Cannon **w**

Angus Wm, letter carrier, St Paul's cottage, James s
Anketell Mrs Margaret (wid John) 89 Young
Anstey Chas W, letter **carrier**, 31 Alanson
Anstey Wm, shoemaker, 103 Victoria ave n
Anthony Alfred J, plasterer, 137 Picton e
Ante Gustave, moulder, 197 East ave n
Ante Otto, watchmaker, 80 Robert e
Appleby Mrs Helen E (wid Edward) 49 Hannah w
Applegate Thos, laborer, 156 Hughson n
Applegate Thos, sr, **hackdriver**, 170 **Hughson n**
Applegath J K, dry goods, 20 James n, h 186 King w
Applegath Thos G, 120 York
Applegath Walter, hats and caps, 62 King w, h 16 Colborne
Applegath Wm, **salesman**, 129 York
Appleton Thos, **gardener**, 88 Wilson
Appleton Thos, pawnbroker, 89 James n
Appleyard John, mechanic, r103 Catharine n
Appleyard Mrs Susan (widow Thos) r 103 Catharine n
Arcade Coffee Rooms, Hamilton Coffee Tavern Co, props, Alexandra Arcade
Archer Genis C, cutter, 25 Hess n
Archer T G, tuner, 9 Bay n
Archibald Mrs Christina (wid Wm) 88 Peter
Archibald **Robert**, mechanic, 48 Murray w
Archibald Robt, jr, fireman, 226 Macnab n
Archibald Thos, millwright, 66 Hannah e

Arde Wm, shoemaker, 227 Cannon e
Ardini Julian, image maker, 58 Robert
Ardini Pietro, **image maker**, 58 Robert
Argent James, blacksmith, bds 7 Ferguson ave
Argyll Terrace, 14 18 Herkimer
Arkison Robt, shoemaker, 195 Wellington n
Arland H & Bro (Henry & Patrick) boots and shoes, 62 King e, h 67 Park n
Arland Michael, laborer, 119 Bay n
Arland Wm A, mail clerk H & N W, 81 Emerald n
Armitage Mrs Ann, 38 Strachan e
Armitage Mrs Harriet (wid Geo) 140 Jackson e
Armitage Mrs Mary (wid Wm) 168 King w
Armitage Mrs Thos, grocer, cor Emerald and Cannon
Armitage Thos, machinist, 212 Cannon e
Armour John, 147 James s
Armor Robt, civil engineer G T R, 79 Jackson w
Armshaw **Geo**, laborer, 54 Stuart e
Armstrong Miss Anna H, 109 Main w
Armstrong Chas, cartage agt N & N W, Wentworth s
Armstrong Edward, clerk, 66 King w
Armstrong Edward, 181 John n
Armstrong Fergus, stationmaster G T R, 16 Park s
Armstrong Geo, cotton dyer, 181 John n
Armstrong Geo H, 109 Main w
Armstrong Mrs Hannah H (wid Geo H) 109 Main w
Armstrong Henry, bookkeeper, bds 100 Park n

Armstrong H N, 36 Bay n
Armstrong Isaac, grain buyer, 95 Market
Armstrong James, painter, 6 Liberty
Armstrong James, 213 James n
Armstrong Miss Jane, dressmaker, 130 Park n
Armstrong J J, quarryman, 29 Alanson
Armstrong John, wireweaver, Sophia n
Armstrong John, 36 Bay n
Armstrong John, carpenter, 7 Walnut n
Armstrong John, jr, plumber, 36 Bay n
Armstrong Joseph, grain buyer, 95 Market
Armstrong M A, bartender St Charles Restaurant
Armstrong Mathew, clerk, 49 Robinson
Armstrong Mrs Mary (wid Thos) 319 Macnab n
Armstrong Miss, 194 John n
Armstrong Peter, carriagemaker, 33 Mary, h 22 Catharine n
Armstrong Richard, confectioner, bds 174 King e
Armstrong R J, clerk, 66 King w
Armstrong Robert, foreman B G & Co., 153 West ave n
Armstrong Mrs Ruth (wid Arthur) 70½ Ferguson ave
Armstrong Mrs Sarah (wid Matthew) 130 Park n
Armstrong Mrs Sarah M (wid Allan) 107 West ave n
Armstrong Thos, prop Russell House, 66-68 King w
Armstrong Thos, mariner, 258 James n
Armstrong Wm, laborer, 20 Florence
Armstrong Wm, clerk, bds 89 Hess n
Armstrong Wm, mangr Cotton Mills, 181 John n
Armstrong Wm, tailor, 290 York
Arnedt Bernard, tailor, 18 Oak ave
Arnedt Frank, tailor, 18 Oak ave
Arnold Mrs Caroline (wid Frank) 186 Robert
Arnold Stanley, upholsterer, 45 Wilson
Arnold Wm, polisher, 148 Cannon e
Arrol James, moulder, 317 Macnab n
Arrol Robert, second-hand deal'r, 25 York, h 309 Macnab n
Arthur Colin, butcher, King, e of Wentworth
Arthur Humphrey M, r 81 Caroline n
Arthur James, 20 Mary
Arthur John, polisher, 25 Oak ave
Arthur John M, shipper, Wentworth n
Arthur Mrs Mary (wid John) 347 James n
Arthur Mrs, second-hand store, 93 York
Arthur Samuel, builder, 16 Elgin
Arthur T, carpenter, 250 King e
Ascott Wm, bds 37 Macaulay w
Ashbaugh Frederick A, com traveller, 5 Peter
Ashborne Wm, laborer, 56 Tom
Ashby George, cabinetmaker, 115 John s
Ashby Wm, laborer, 110 Bay n
Ashton Walter, salesman, bds 45 Hess n
Ashworth John, moulder, bds 37 Catharine n
Askew George, shoemaker 256 Mary n
Askin Robert, asst undertaker, bds 49 King w
Aspet William, 118 Maria
Astle Samuel, machinist, 32 Railway

Asylum for the Insane, J Mc L Wallace, medical supt, mountain top
Athawes Charles, bookkeeper, 43 Inchbury n
Atkin Samuel, salesman, 25 Victoria ave n
Atkins James, hair dresser, 83 James n
Atkins Jesse, cotton weaver, 48 Ferrie e
Atkinson Mrs Anna, (wid Thomas, 75 Hunter e
Atkinson Bros, (W G & W H) wh card manfrs, 13 King e, h, 3 Bay s
Atkinson James, shoemaker, Mills' block, Merrick
Atkinson James, carpenter, bds 67 Stuart w
Atkinson John, machinist, George n s, near Locke
Atkinson John T, com traveller, 42 Jackson w
Atkinson Joseph, painter, 32 Wilson
Atkinson Richard, shoemaker, 99½ Wellington n
Atkinson Wm, 3 Bay s
Atlantic House, A Ruthven, prop, 29 Macnab n
Atwater T S, 73 York
Attle John, tinsmith, 90 Florence
Attwood M W & Sons, jewelers, (M W, C W, J A Attwood) 77 John s and 88 King w, h 17 Pearl s
Atwell Harry, warehouseman, Burlington n
Audette David, clerk 5 Ferrie e
Audette Isaiah, blacksmith, 38 Barton e
Audette Mrs Margaret (wid Joshua) 25 Inchbury s
Audley Mrs Ellen, 8 Locke s
Auld Wm, laborer, Robinson s s w Locke
Aussem G H, confectioner, 75 James n

Austin Edward H, painter, 192 Emerald n
Austin James, blacksmith, 15 Park n
Austin Peter, carpenter, 114 Strachan e
Austin Thomas B S, letter carrier, 84 Emerald n
Avis Richard, driver, 100 Queen s
Awrey Peter, farmer, 30 Walnut
Awty Arthur, shipper, 23 Nelson ave
Axford George, butcher, 149 Wilson
Axtell Wm, upholsterer, bds 56 Park n
Ayers Wm, carpenter, 179 Emerald n
Aylett Samuel, gardener, 77 Caroline s
Aylwin Mrs Fanny T (wid Horace) 24 Macnab s
Aylwin H C, clerk, 24 Macnab
Back Arthur, porter, bds 222 Macnab n
Backhouse Hiram, weaver, 272 Macnab n
Backus Thos, barber. 63 John s
Babb James, melter, 70 West ave n
Baby W A D, excise officer, 115 Macnab n
Babcock Devardo, barber, 23 Napier
Badeau John A, tinsmith, bds 144 Catharine n
Badeau Joseph, shoemaker, 101 Ferrie e
Badger James, shoemaker, 37 Crooks
Baghott Mrs Hannah (wid Samuel F) 53 Hess n
Baglin Vincent, laborer, 50 Locomotive
Bagnall Robert, foreman H & N W, 105 Victoria ave n
Bagster ——, law student, bds 80 James s

Bagwell G M, mangr job dept *Times*, 29 Robinson
Bagwell John B, 21 Park n
Baikie C F, hairdresser, **150** King e
Baikie Mrs Elizabeth, r 51 Young
Bailey Alfred, gardener, Wentworth n
Bailey Mrs Annie (wid Henry) **162** Market
Bailey Mrs Annie (wid Henry) 74 Peter
Bailey Mrs Charlotte, **47** Peter
Bailey George, laborer, 90 Emerald n
Bailey John, blacksmith, 114 Picton e
Baillie John, bookkeeper, 82 Merrick
Baillie John, salesman, 58 Walnut s
Bailey Joseph, shipper, 55 **Robinson**
Baillie Mrs M E (wid J S) 192 Macnab n
Bailey Wm G, miller, 11 Park s
Bainbridge John, policeman, bds 39 John **n**
Bain Alex, **hackman**, 214 Main e
Bain Alex, **stableman**, 11 Market
Bain **Alexander**, miller, 1 Ferguson ave
Bain Andrew G, salesman, 19 Spring
Bain Mrs Annie (wid Alex) 32 Peter
Bain & Colville (J D Bain, C A Colville) engineering machinists, 68 Mary
Baine Henry, grocer, 60 Cherry
Bain James D (Bain & Colville) **151** West ave **n**
Baine John, laborer, **201** Mary n
Baine **Miss** Mary, 185 Main **e**
Baine Mrs Marjory (wid Thos) 14 Wellington **n**
Baine Matthew, carpenter, 185 Main e

Bain Thos, grocer, etc, 60 Cherry
Baine T J, organ manfr and dealer in pianofortes, general musical merchandise, 84 King w
Baines James, fitter, 40 Magill
Baird C C, grocer, Wellington, cor Rebecca, h 34 Mary
Baird David, laborer, 70 Catharine s
Baker A **H**, watchmaker, 64 Herkimer
Baker Albert **E**, jeweler, 66½ East ave n
Baker **Alexander**, painter, 144 Emerald n
Baker **Alfred**, brickmaker, 318 King **w**
Baker D H, salesman, 28 James s
Baker Edgar (Pennington & Baker) bds Walnut
Baker Edward, gas fitter, 90 Park n
Baker Frank, fitter, 7 Devonport
Baker Geo, driver, 176 Hunter w
Baker George W, ins agent, **149** Main w
Baker Geo W, brickmaker, 318 King w
Baker H D, Standard Whip Co, **175** James n, h 130 Catharine n
Baker Hugh C, mangr Ont Dept Bell Telephone Co, 1 Hughson s, h **3** Herkimer
Baker James, **55** Napier
Baker James, **laborer**, bds Locke s, w s, nr Robinson
Baker John W, laborer, **154** Hughson n
Baker Josiah, carpenter, 14 Blyth
Baker J P, stationmaster G T R, bds 44 Murray w
Baker Ralph, **salesman**, 14 Blyth
Baker Robert, engineer, **123** Catharine n
Baker Thos, baker, **81** Walnut s

3

Baker Thomas, clerk, bds 44 Main w
Baker Rev Thos, s w cor Jackson and Macnab
Baker Wm, laborer, 318 King w
Baker W C, wholesale and retail fruiterer, 26-28 James s
Bakie Mrs James, 59 George
Baldwin John, carpenter, 36 Wellington n
Bale Chas, coachman, 31 Hunter w
Bale James, bookkeeper, h 83 Emerald n
Bale J C, bookkeeper, 130 Victoria ave n
Bale Thos, 153 Mary
Bale Thos, com traveler, 83 Emerald n
Bale Thos, machinist, 72 Hughson n
Bale Walter, bookkeeper, 116 Victoria ave n
Balfour James, architect and building superintendent, Wentworth Chambers, 25 James s, h 130 Bay s
Balfour Peter, jr, agent Victoria Mutual Ins Co, Markland s s, w Queen
Balfour Peter, sr, city assessor, Hannah w, n s, w Bay
Balfour St Clair (Brown, Balfour & Co) h 33 Bold
Ball Alexander, moulder, bds 37 Catharine n
Ball Edward, laborer, 34 Macauley e
Ball Frederick, moulder, 82 Locke n
Ball J A, brass finisher, 251 Hughson n
Ball John W, baker, 108 Rebecca
Ball Robert, laborer, 310 Hughson n
Ballentine Adam (A Ballentine & Bros) 119 John s

Ballentine Adam & Bros (Adam, R B, A L Ballentine) grocers, 117-19 John s
Ballentine A L (A Ballentine & Bros) 119 John s
Ballentine R B (A Ballentine & Bros) 23 Young
Ballantyne Thos, plumber, 162 Victoria ave n
Ballentine W J, grocer, 97 James s, h 119 John s
Ballantine Wm, laborer, 52 Caroline s
Ballard John F, school teacher, bds 135 King e
Ballard W H, M A, inspector of schools, 241 King w
Balmer Stephen, laborer, 41 Peter
Balsh Thomas, fitter, 5 Picton w
Bambrick John, foreman Tuckett & Son, 37 Park s
Bamford Mrs Ann (wid John) r 1 Evans
Bampfylde Chas H, clerk, 39 Bay s
Bampfylde John T, bottler, 38 Victoria ave n
Bampfyld Robt Jas, com trav, 102 Cannon w
Bainhart Chas, barber, 132 Macnab n
Bangarth Mrs Pauline (wid Wm) confectionery, 14 York
Bank of British North America, D G Magregor, manager, 5 King e
Bank of Hamilton, E A Colquhoun, cashier, 17-19 King w
Bank of Montreal, J N Travers, manager, James cor Main
Bankes Wm, artist, 15 Inchbury n
Banks Louis, laborer, 145 Duke
Baptist Church (colored) 106 Macnab n
Baptist Mission Church, Herkimer, n s, w Locke

CITY OF HAMILTON. 19

Baptist Mission Church, Wentworth n
Barber Abraham N, 55 Emerald s
Barber Bristol, laborer, 8 New
Barber B F, clerk P O, King, e of Wentworth
Barclay Robert, laborer, 308 Macnab n
Barclay Wm, carpenter, 206 Victoria ave n
Bard Andrew, glassblower, 267 John n
Bard Thomas, glassblower, 283 James n
Bardwell James, machinist, 51 Ray s
Barker Daniel, carpenter, 57 Burlington w
Barker Edward, printer, 68½ Wellington n
Barker Holden, laborer, 357 James n
Barker James, fruiterer, 83½ John s
Barker James H, 207, Wellington n
Barker Robert, carriage maker, 207 Wellington n
Barker Samuel, general manager N & N W, h John s
Barker Wm R, fireman, 144 Jackson w
Barling Frank, machinist, 73 Colborne
Barnard Alfred, bookkeper, 15 Head
Barnard A W, ledger keeper Molsons' bank, 36 Bay s
Barnard Henry, rubber stamp maker, 5 Rebecca, h 110 Catharine s
Barnard James T, sec-treas Hart Emery Wheel Co, 10 Park s
Barnard John N, bracket manfr, 169 Main w
Barnard P B, (Barnard, Murdoff & Co) h 44 George

Barnard, Murdoff & Co, P B
Barnard, M W Murdoff, staple and fancy dry goods, 36 King w
Barnard Robert, laborer, end Ferrie e
Barnes Mrs Ann E (wid Thomas) 60 Wellington n
Barnes Ebenezer P, (Gillesby & Barnes) 26 Liberty
Barnes Henry, moulder, 20 Pearl s
Barnes & Haskins, native wines, 7 Arcade
Barnes Mrs, 22 Elgin
Barnes Philander, Main e of Wentworth
Barnes Thomas, laborer, 22 Elgin
Barnes Thomas, (Barnes & Haskins) h Main east Hamilton
Barnes W C, (W C Barnes & Son) 146 King William
Barnes W C & Son, stained glass works, 49 King William street, 1st flat
Barnfather Wm C, engineer, 92 Barton e
Barlow Charles, carpenter, 76 Catharine s
Barlow George, grocer, cor Wilson and Emerald
Barlow John, belt repairer, 24½ Inchbury n
Barr Mrs Barbara (wid Peter) 133 Ferguson ave
Barr Miss Eliza, 124 Jackson e
Barr Fred, railroader, 161 Park n
Barr George, carpenter, 52 West ave n
Barr Mrs George, 34 Cartharine n
Barr Geo A, glassblower, 43 Picton w
Barr George D, salesman, 5 Ontario
Barr Herbert, clerk, 161 Park n
Barr John, clerk, 161 Park n
Barr John A (John A Barr & Co) 38 Victoria ave s

Barr John A & Co, druggists, York cor Macnab
Barr Capt Litellus B, 20 Ray n
Barr Mrs Margaret, 317 James n
Barr William, 188 Main e
Barr Wilson, 161 Park n
Barrett Daniel, fireman, 88 Maria
Barrett Mrs E (wid William) 117 Mary
Barrett Mrs Ellen (wid Richard) 68 Vine
Barrett Frank, confectioner, 117 Mary
Barrett Patrick, tinsmith, 143 Catharine n
Barrett Robt, laborer, 81 Young
Barrett Robert, laborer, r 51 Young
Barrett Thomas, baker, 47 Cannon w
Barrett Thomas, paper hanger, 118 Jackson e
Barrett T J, excise officer
Barron James, policeman, 59 East ave n
Barrow Ernest G, surveyor, end Wilson
Barry Daniel, lithographer, 18 Hunter e
Barry James, clerk G T R, 103 Locke n
Barry John, laborer, 201 Catharine n
Barry John, barrister, 18 Hunter e
Barry Martin, laborer, 47 Strachan e
Barry Mrs Mary (wid Daniel) 88 Jackson e
Barry Michael, iron worker, bds r 143 Locke n
Barry Michael J, shoemaker, 66 West ave n
Barth Theodore, cigar packer, 113 West Ave n
Bartle James, laborer, 43 Alanson
Bartlett C, accountant Bank of Hamilton, 117 Macnab s
Bartlett, John, 52 Hughson n

Bartley Mrs Ann, (wid John) 46 Hannah e
Bartley William J, piano maker, 75 Wellington s
Bartholomew James, moulder, 183 Hughson n
Bartmann Adam, tailor, 80 Macnab n
Bartman George, tailor, 1 Walnut s, h 169 Hughson n
Bartmann George W, cutter, 84 Wellington s
Bartmann John, tailor, 10 King William, 3rd flat, h 84 Wellington s
Barton David, bookkeeper. 76 West ave n
Barton Mrs Elizabeth (wid William) 104 Wellington s
Barton G M, barrister, 2 James n
Barton Terrace, east side Wellington, near Barton
Barwell Egbert, saw filer, 81 Pearl n
Basquill Michael, moulder, 174 Rebecca
Basquill Mrs, 174 Rebecca
Bassett Henry D, machinist, 99 King e
Bastedo Walter, gardener, 156 Cannon e
Bastien H L, boatbuilder, 265 Bay n
Bastien Louis H, boatbuilder, 269 Bay n
Bateman Mrs Cynthia E, 43 Main w
Bateman E W, baker, 250 King e, h 27 Victoria ave n
Bateman Patrick S, blacksmith, 33 York, h 71 Wellington s
Bateman Thomas, baker, 11 Spring
Bates Alfred, carpenter, 270 Mary n
Bates David, teamster, 92 George
Bates Edward, upholsterer, 136-138 King w

Bates Frank, D W, M D, (Anderson & Bates), 34 James n, res Burlington Village
Bates James P, clerk, 28 Gore
Bates Mrs Mary, (wid James), 28 Gore
Bates Thos P, clerk, 158 John n
Batterton, Richard, bricklayer, 4 Little Market
Battram E, fruiterer, 122 King e
Battram Charles, merchant, 18 West ave n
Battram Sylvester, **geocer,** 18 West ave n
Battram William, fruiterer, 54 James n, h 18 West ave n
Batty Mrs Mary Jane, 248 Barton e
Batty Peter, fireman, 104 Simcoe e
Batty Robert, moulder, 104 Simcoe e
Baur Mrs Henry, **saloon,** 10 Main e
Baugh James, **laborer,** bds 65 Park n
Baumstark, John, agent, bds 144 King w
Bautz Miss Lucy, 36 Main w
Bawden Aaron, brick manfr, end Canada n s
Bawden Harry, hotelkeeper, s e cor **Locke** and Peter
Bawden John, brickmaker, 64 Canada
Baxter **Andrew B,** (James Baxter & **Son), 54 Caroline** s
Baxter David T, dentist, 2 Gore
Baxter D W, lawstudent, res Burlington
Baxter George, driver, 66 Lock s
Baxter James, (James Baxter & Son), 96 Bold
Baxter James & Son, (James & Andrew B), wood and coal dealers, 91 Bold
Baxter John, driver, 76 Market
Baxter John, teamster, 17 Bay n

Baxter Thomas, wireworker, 169 King e
Bagley John, salesman, 58 Walnut s
Bagley Thos, carpenter, 14 Smith ave
Baylie William, fitter, bds 83 King w
Baylie Alfred H, grocer, 148 King e
Bayles John, **gardner** Wentworth n
Byliss **Walter,** coachman, s e cor Robinson and Park
Bayne John, moulder, 188 Napier
Bayne Peter, carpenter, 25 Queen n
Bazzard George, railway agent, 3 Arcade, h 20 Main w
Beal John, baker, 6 Augusta
Beal Samuel, laborer, bds 92 George
Beard Edward, asst messenger Canada **Life** Assurance Co
Beardmore Thomas, brassfinisher 37 Oak Ave
Beardwell James carpenter 4 Main w
Beare Henry moulder 102 West avenue north
Beare Josiah, moulder, 81 **West** ave n
Beare Wm, dairyman, **42** Markland
Bearman F W, prop American hotel, 61 King w
Beasley A C, Furlong & Beasly, h Main e of Wentworth
Beasley David C, broom-maker 282 King w
Beasley Richard S, 103 Main e
Beasley Sylvester, agt Toronto World, 103 Main e
Beasley Thomas, City Clerk, Main e of Wentworth
Beasley Thomas, conductor N N W, 76 Elgin
Beatty Charles, customs broker, **251** Macnab n

Beatty Edward, laborer, 15 Upper Cathcart
Beattie Hugh M, printer, 31 Robinson
Beattie John, clerk G T R, bds 51 Hess n
Beattie John A, clerk, 31 Robinson
Beatty Oliver, hotel, 300 James n
Beatty Oliver, jr, clerk, 7 Ferrie e
Beatty Thomas, laborer, 111 Jackson e
Beatty Thomas, boilermaker, 300 Hughson n
Beattie Wm, engine driver, 141 Ferguson ave
Beaufort John, carpenter, 167 Catharine n
Beaver George, hotel, 225-7 York
Beavers Thomas, laborer, 40 Macauley w
Beavis Samson, gas stoker, 152 Bay n
Beck Mrs Elizabeth, (wid Geo), 22 Ray n
Beck Lewis, wire weaver, 22 Ray n
Beckerson Elijah, teamster, 8 Mill
Beckerson John, teamster, 66 John n
Beckerson Matthew, maildriver, 79 Main e
Beckerson Richard, 48½ Walnut s
Beckett, the F G Engine Co, engines, boilers and general machinery, cor York and Bay
Beckett Frederick G (F G Beckett Engine Co) bds 9 Peter
Beckett Henry, clerk, 26a West ave s
Beckett John, 9 George
Beckett Thos, driver, 9 George
Beckingham Edward, marble polisher, 43 Little Wm
Beckman Frederick, shoemaker, 160 Hunter w

Beckman Mrs Johanna P (wid Fredk) r 281 King w
Beckman John, laborer, r 281 King w
Beckman Wm, laborer, 94 Florence
Beddie Alexander, stonecutter, 156 West ave n
Beddoe Thos D, mangr Hamilton Iron Forging Co, 159 James s
Bedlington Henry, com trav, 3 Victoria ave n
Bedwell Daniel A, cutter, 2 Hilton
Bees Arthur, laborer, bds 208 Macnab n
Beer Frank, butcher, 123 King e
Beer John S, butcher, Burlington n
Beer Isaiah, contractor, 35 Murray e
Beer Wm, clerk, 170 Victoria ave n
Beers Wm G, salesman, 170 Victoria ave n
Beeston Samuel, laborer, 31 Kelly
Begg Alex, polisher, bds 11 Colborne
Begg Andrew, laborer, 83 East ave n
Begg George, bartender, 41 Wilson
Begley Alex, blacksmith, 9 Tom
Begley James, laborer, 95 Simcoe e
Begley James, fireman, 283 Hughson n
Begley Mrs Mary Jane (wid Andrew) 9 Strachan e
Begley Maurice, brakesman, Main e of Wentworth
Begley ——, laborer, 358 John n
Behan Jeremiah, glassblower, 8 Simcoe
Behrens Geo, tinsmith, bds 35 Catharine n
Belau Antoine, tailor, 81 Caroline s

Belknap Charles N, lumber merchant, 17 Colborne
Belknap William, tinsmith, 100 John n
Bell Adam, tailor, 22 Cannon w
Bell Mrs Agnes (wid Matthew) 57 Wilson
Bell C, tailor, bds 60 James s
Bell Mrs Ella (wid Alex) 43 Ray n
Bell Geo F, law student, 100 Market
Bell Geo M, locksmith, 20 Macnab n, h 51 Ray s
Bell John, machinist, Maple
Bell John, trustee Ontario Cotton Mills, 35 Hannah w
Bell Miss L C, teacher, 46 Duke
Bell Mrs Mary A (wid Nathaniel) 67 Colborne
Bell Samuel, county constable, 29 East ave
Bell Telephone Co (Ontario depart) Hugh C Baker, mgr, 1 Hughson s
Bell Telephone Co, K J Dunstan, agent, city office 1 Hughson s
Bell & Thomson (Wm Bell, G C Thomson) barristers, 25 James s
Bell T S, C E, civil engineer, 4 Main e, h 100 Market *see card*
Bell Wm, machinist, Robinson s s nr Garth
Bell Wm, moulder, bds 142 Cannon e
Bell Wm, core repairer, 62 Locomotive
Bell Wm (Bell & Thomson) h head Wentworth s
Bell Wm & Co, R A Hutchison, mangr, pianos and organs, 44 James n
Bell Wm T, confectioner, 174 King e
Bellfoy Abraham, bricklayer, 43 John n

Bellhouse W A, accountant, Merchants' Bank, 115 Catharine s
Belling Chas, jeweler, 114 Cannon w
Belling Geo, carpenter, 99 Florence
Belling James, watchmaker, 21 York, h 114 Cannon w
Belleville Evangelist, tobacco roller, 30 Poulette
Bellivelle Peter, tobacco roller, end Barton e
Belroche John, 42 Canada
Belz Adam, cutter, 4 Henry
Belz Lawrence, tailor, 20 Upper Cathcart
Benedict C L, receiving teller Bank of Montreal, 48 Hunter w
Benner R, ins agt and general broker, 17 Main e, h 6 Main e
Bennett Mrs Charles, 138 Macnab n
Bennett F, messenger Bank of Hamilton, 17 King w
Bennett Henry, printer, 40 Victoria ave n
Bennett Henry, foreman Tubkett & Son, 20 Napier
Bennett James, carpenter, 31 Elgin
Bennett John J, engine driver, 165 West ave n
Bennett Lewis, waiter, 57 Gore
Bennett Patrick, laborer, 10 Guise
Bennett Robert, moulder, 39 Barton e
Bennett Robert, blacksmith, 328 King Wm
Bennett Samuel, brass finisher, 268 Bay n
Bennett Samuel, wood turner, 3 George
Bennett Thos H, miller, 172 King w
Benson Mrs Alice (wid Wm) nurse, 87 Hess n

Benson Beter, billiardist, 51 James n
Benson Thos, laborer, Nightingale
Benwelle J O, ledger keeper, Bank B N A bds 80 James s
Bernard Isaac, laborer, end Ferrie e
Bernger Mrs Sarah (wid Wm) 135 Rebecca
Bernhardt Charles, barber, 132 Macnab n
Berry Charles, pattern maker, 39 Oak ave
Berry Henry, laborer, 164 Vic ave n
Berry James, teamster, 32 and 34 Guise
Berry Samuel, carpenter, 58 Guise
Berrie W A C, chief clerk, Royal Hotel
Berry William, stockfitter, 155 King William
Berryman Albert, telegraph operator, 147 Bay n
Berryman Jas E, shoemaker, 7 Park s
Berryman Richard, machinist, 126 cannon w
Berryman Robert, wool dealer, 1 Market, h 122 Catharine s
Berryman William, painter, 20 Guise
Bertram James, laborer, n e cor Pine and Locke
Bessey Alonzo E, huxter, 298 James n
Bessey George, butter and egg merchant, 44 Cannon w
Bessey Maurice Edgar, butcher, 75 Park n
Bessey Vernon, butter and egg merchant, 44 Cannon w
Bessey Webber, produce dealer, 71 Merrick
Best Albert C, salesman, 145 Hunter w
Best Alfred, gardener, 140 Duke

Best Thos, student, bds 99 York
Bethune Edward, bookkeeper, 63 Catharine n
Betts Joseph Y, bookkeeper, bds 80 Market
Betzner David, stableman, 86 Mulberry
Betzner William, glassblower, 49 Macaulay w
Beulah Suburb, mountain foot south of Concession
Bevan Chas, laborer, Maple s s near Locke
Bevan Wm. saddler, bds 94 John s
Beveridge Chas, carpenter, 10 New
Beveridge John, shoemaker, 234 Barton e
Bevis William, machinist, 259 Cannon e
Bews Bros, (W D and J Y) merchant tailors, 74 King e
Bews James, shipper, 168 Emerald n
Bews Mrs Mary (wid James) 25 Victoria ave n
Bews J Y, 25 Victoria ave n
Bews William, 52 Hunter e
Bews W D, (Bews Bros) 278 King e
Bewicke David, printer, 22 Macnab s, h mountain top
Bezanson Elgin, artist, 14 Jones
Bible George, contractor, 155 Main w
Bible Robt, bds 15 Margaret
Bickell George, feather dyer, 74 Merrick
Bickle Mrs Hattie B (wid Wm) 1 Bay s
Bickell John, carpenter, 5 Inchbury s
Bickle John W, broker, 12 Main e, h 37 Bold
Bicknell George, moulder, bds 41 John n
Bicknell James, bookkeeper, 43 Queen s

Blandford Henry, picture framer and artists' material, 50 King e, h Main cor Wentworth
Blandford Raymond, bookkeeper 66 Stinson
Blaney Mrs Johanna (wid Robt W) 45 Park n
Blankstein Henry, carpenter, **154** Duke
Blasdell John W (J W Blasdell & Co) s w cor Locke and Robinson
Blasdell J W & Co (John W Blasdell, John Stonehouse) **grocers, s w cor** Locke and **Robinson**
Blatz Leo, tailor, 1 O'Reilly, h 81 Hannah e
Bleckhart Mrs, 136 Bay n
Bleeze Mrs R, 201 John n
Blevin Marshal, fireworks, **bds** 134 King Wm
Bliss Henry C, patent medicines. 117 Catharine s
Blockley E H, civil engineer, 23 West ave n
Blondin Moses, engineer, 351 Hughson n
Bloodsworth **John,** 26 Hannah e
Bloomer Mrs Ann, 9 Picton w
Bloomer **Andrew,** laborer, **34** Picton e
Bloomfield Abraham, cigarmaker, bds 42 Kelly
Blows Isaac, laborer, 344 James n
Blows Mrs James, 364 James n
Blows Samuel, sailor, 6 Wood e
Blue Henry, laborer, 35 George
Blumensteil Isaac, (Blumensteil & **Karsten**) 249 John s
Blumensteil Joseph, second hand **dealer,** 49 John s
Blumensteil & Karsten, **cigar** manfs 73 King e
Blunder Chas **A,** laborer, **1** Garth
Boan Mrs Francis E, (wid A P) 140 Wellington n

Board Arthur, **stove mounter,** 227 Mary n
Board Geo S, blacksmith, **42** Florence
Board John, tobacco roller, bds 9 Hess n
Bodden W **H,** bricklayer, **129** Macaulay e
Boden ——, brickmaker, **194** Hunter w
Boehm Frederick, tailor, 80 **Main** e
Boggess James Hy, furniture dealer, 97 Lower Cathcart
Boggess Mrs Mary Ann (wid Thos) **97 Lower** Cathcart
Boggess **Robert,** second hand dealer, 152½ Rebecca
Boggess Thomas, furniture dealer and broker, **19** King Wm, h **130** King Wm
Boggs Nathaniel, machinist, **bds** 173 **East ave n**
Boice **Mrs Elizabeth A,** (wid Wm) 50 John n
Boisfeuillet W H, manager Hamilton Electric Light Co, 29 Wellington n
Bolger John, bartender, 87 John s
Boligan John C, grocer, s w cor Main and Locke
Bolingbroke Chas, cabinetmaker, 68 Cherry
Bolt Richard, machinist, **s w cor Locke s s**
Bolton Chas, carpenter, 199 **John n**
Bolton George, laborer, 312 John n
Bolton **Richard,** laborer, 109 Caroline n
Bolton Thos, porter, 120 Jackson e
Bolton Wm, carpenter, 199 Catharine n
Bolus, Edward, patternfitter, 57 King Wm
Bolus George, moulder. bds 79 Robert

Bolus Harold, decorator, 57 King Wm
Boond Arthur, file cutter, 2 Erie ave
Bond Edgar, clerk, 303 King Wm
Bond F, bds Walker House
Bond George, grocer, 125 Hunter w
Bond John, coachman, n e cor Herkimer and Kent
Bond Mrs Maria, 99 Macnab n
Bonifice Pedro, tinsmith, bds 150 Rebecca
Bonney Anthony, laborer, 109 Strachan e
Bonny Henry P, clerk, 308 King e
Bonney Lewis, laborer, 112 Strachan e
Bonny Stephen, laborer, Ferguson ave
Booker Albert H, bookkeeper, 88 Jackson w
Booker Chas, tinsmith, bds 65 Park n
Booker Charles G, merchant tailor and importer, h 88 Jackson w, 2 King Wm, 1st flat
Booker Henry A, machinst, South w s s near Locke
Booker John, com traveller, end Wilson
Booker Newman, ledger keeper, 88 Jackson w
Booker W D, sec-treasurer Victoria Mutual Fire Insurance Co, h 88 Jackson w
Booth Chas C, heater, 37 Magill
Booth Francis, clerk, 54 Tisdale
Booth John T, butcher, 126 King Wm
Booth Patrick, shoemaker, 33 Liberty
Booth Robert, spoke turner, 179 East ave n
Booth Mrs Thompstone, milliner, 126 King Wm
Boothby Henry, draughtsman, 112 Bay n
Boothman & Hutchison, painters 128½ King e
Boothman John, painter, bds 128 Cannon e
Borland John, laborer, Barton w s s nr Locomotive
Bordley Wm J, upholsterer, 116 John s
Bosselman Henry, laborer, 54 Burlington w
Boston James, spice manfr, 69 Queen n
Boswell George, painter, bds 109 King Wm
Boswell Philip, stovemounter, bds 41 John n
Boswell Wm, clerk, Herkimer w Garth
Bouchier Wm, blacksmith, bds 165 Bay n
Boughner Wm W, insurance agent, 280a King e
Bolter Thos, druggist, 97 John s
Bougnet Chas, teamster, 119 Cannon e
Bourque Alfred, burnisher, 67 Steven
Bourque Chas, brushmaker, 174 Wilson
Bovaird James, carriagemaker, 82½ Stinson
Bowditch A E, shipper, 28 Main w
Bowditch Alfred, clerk, 28 Main w
Bowe James, ironworker, bds r 143 Locke n
Bowe Robert, tinsmith, 85 Hughson n
Bowen Mrs Annie, fancy goods, 13 York, h 290 Macnab n
Bowen Elijah, engineer, 290 Macnab n
Bowen James, tobacco roller, 86 Hess n
Bowering & Pain, (Robert Bowering & Albert Pain) butchers, 89 King w

Bowering Robert, (Bowering & Pain) h 89 King w
Bowers Mrs Margaret, **24 Strachan** e
Bowes Mrs Caroline, (wid John), 23 Augusta
Bowes, Jamieson & Co, stove founders, (J G Bowes, J Jamieson) cor King and Tisdale
Bowes John G, (Bowes & Jamieson), 40 East ave s
Bowes Miss Lucy, **teacher, 36 Herkimer**
Bowes Samuel, machinist, **36** East ave n
Bowes Miss Sarah, 36 Herkimer
Bowker Anthony, laborer, 211 Hughson n
Bowker Thomas C, fruiterer, 46½ York
Bowman Mrs Annie, **(wid** Joseph C), **44 Jackson w**
Bowman J W, **salesman, 44 Jackson w**
Bowman & Moore, (Wm Bowman, John H Moore) hardware **54 King e**
Bowman N, commission **merchant,** 3 Market
Bowman Peter, boarding **house, 12** Wood Market
Bowman Willam, (Bowman & Moore), h 46 Hunter w
Bowron Addison, tinsmith, **52** Wellington n
Bowran Boulton D, foreman P J & Co, **53** Victoria ave n
Bowron John, tinsmith, 52 Wellington n
Bowstead Edward, broker, 95 Catharine n
Bowstead Wm, manfr at D Moore & Cos foundry, 95 Catharine n
Bowstead W W, ship carpenter, 95 Catharine n
Boyd Alex, varnisher, 2 Elgin
Boyd David, cooper, 27 Catharine n

Boyd E W, bookkeeper, **bds 80** James s
Boyd James, 3 West ave n
Boyd James, hatter, 27 **Catharine n**
Boyd James, **tobacco presser,** 18½ Elgin
Boyd Julian R F, agent **Mail** newspaper, 16 James s, **h 80** James s
Boyd Mrs Mary, (wid Alex) 40 Wellington n
Boyd Robert, hatter, 2 Elgin
Boyd W E, manager Levy Bros, h 80 James s
Boyd ——, blacksmith, 14 Simcoe e
Boylan Wm, driver, 41 Ray n
Boyle A, shoemaker, **44** Hannah w
Boyle Arthur, druggist, cor York and Magill
Boyle Mrs Ellen (wid Timothy) 177 Bay n
Boyle Geo, moulder, bds **35** Hughson n
Boyle Hilda, 43 Catharine n
Boyle Mrs Johanna, dairy, 319 York
Boyle John, hotel, 73 Stuart **w**
Boyle Martin, machinist, **bds** 166 Bay n
Boyle ——, blacksmith, r 208 John n
Boyle Francis D, clerk G T R, 80 George
Boys' Home, Mrs M Shaw, matron, Stinson
Boyter Richard, tinsmith, **bds** 35 Hughson n
Bracken, Hugh **C,** spinner, 137 Victoria ave n
Bracken James, shoemaker, 291 King Wm
Bradburn Edward, cutter, **bds** Simcoe hotel
Bradfield, Chas, laborer, r 109 Macnab n
Bradfield **C** W, manager London China House, **h 7** Market Sq

Bradfield Wm, laborer, 137 John n
Bradford Henry, laborer, 69 Park n
Bradley, Mrs Carlisle, 219 Barton e
Bradley Edward, lumber inspector, 237 Cannon e
Bradley John, Flatt & Bradley, h 62 Catharine n
Bradley John, sewer contractor, 13 Mulberry
Bradley John, carpenter, Markland n s w Queen nr Locke
Bradley John H, cabinet maker, 113 Macnab s
Bradley Patrick, 8 York
Bradley Mrs Sarah, fancy dry goods, 6½ York
Bradley Thos, butcher, 77 East ave n
Bradley Wm, cooper, 13 Tiffany
Bradley Wm, blacksmith, 298 King W
Bradshaw, George, 89 York
Bradt Geo, lather, 142 Emerald n
Bradt Jacob, grain buyer, bds Union Hotel
Bradt Mrs Rhoda (wid Samuel) 78 Victoria ave n
Brady John, laborer, 24 O'Reilly
Brady Michael, laborer, 120 Queen n
Brady Thos, coal inspector, h 235 Hughson n, Macnab n
Bragg George, broommaker, bds 23 Napier
Bragg Wm, yardsman, 221 Catharine n
Braid Alex, shoemaker, 53 Pearl s
Braid Henry, shoemaker, 96 Emerald n
Braid Wm, com traveler, bds 98 James s
Braidwood Wm, bookkeeper, h 15 Wood w
Brand Fredk, hackdriver, 9 Margaret

Brand George, laborer, 14 Florence
Brand Mrs Margaret (wid Edwd) 5 Margaret
Brannigan Geo, brickmaker, Main w, s s, w Garth
Bransby Henry A, clerk, 129 York
Brant Geo, foreman Gurney & Co, bds 55 York
Brantford Wm, plasterer, 26a Liberty
Branton Albert, asst undertaker, bds 29 King w
Brass Benjamin, printer, 27 Markland
Brass James, watchman, 127 Hess n
Brass John, tinsmith, 56 Canada
Brass Mrs Margaret (wid Peter) 27 Markland
Brass Peter, architect, 52 Hunter w, h 50 Bay s
Brass William, carpenter, 92 Market
Braston James T, bricklayer, 52 Hunter w
Brayley Frederick F, agent, bds 37 Catharine n
Brayles James, (Brayley & Dempster) h Mountain top
Brayley & Dempster, (Jas Brayley, Chas H Dempster) saddlers and builders, wrought iron hardware, 47-49 King Wm
Brazier Henry, barber, 19 York
Breay Henry P, baggage express, 112 King w, h 84 Caroline n
Bredin Egerton R, music teacher, bds 54 Park n
Breheny Mrs Annie (wid William) 7½ Walnut s
Breheney Edward, shoemaker, 155 King e, h 7½ Walnut s
Breheny John, shoemaker, 220 Macnab n
Bremen Steamship Line, Wm Herman, agent, 16 James s

Bremner Chas, grocer, 115 King e, h Herkimer cor Hess
Bremner James, commission merchant, 250 King w
Bremner Wm, com traveler, 102 Jackson w
Brend Henry J, gilder, 177 Main
Brend William C, fitter, 177 Main w
Brennan C J (J & C J Brennan, h 5 Market sq
Brennan Edward, tinsmith, 285 Macnab n
Brennen H S (M Brennen & Sons) 192 Main e
Brennan J (J & C J Brennan, 160 Napier
Brennan J & C J, grocers, 5 Market sq
Brennen J S (M Brennen & Sons) 34 Victoria ave n
Brennan John, 192 Main e
Brennan John, carpenter, 208 Hughson n
Brennan **John**, laborer, 2 Emerald n
Brennen Michael (M Brennen & Sons) 192 Main e
Brennen M & Sons (Michael, H S & J S) planing mills, sash and doors, 67 King Wm
Brennan Mrs Sarah (wid James) 202 John n
Brennan **Peter**, machinist, 208 Hughson n
Brent Geo W, receiving **teller** Bank of Hamilton, 61 George
Brent John, stove plater, 144a Cannon e
Brenton Sydney, polisher, 107½ Simcoe e
Breternitz Julius, tailor, 114 Napier
Bretherton E **V**, clerk Bank of Montreal
Brethour & Co, merchant tailors, 190½ King e
Brethour C J (Brethour & Co) 190½ King e

Brettingham Geo, fitter, 8 Greig
Brewer Louis, coachman A T Wood, 151 James s
Brick John, dog inspector, 104 Jackson e
Brick Mrs **Sarah** (wid Timothy) 105 Hunter e
Brick Thomas, carter, 22 Cherry
Bridges Charles, laborer, 204 East ave n
Bridges Edward, laborer, 130 Jackson w
Bridges George, porter, bds 166 **Bay** n
Bridges John, laborer, 337 King w
Bridgewater Mrs Jane (wid Thomas) 60 Hess n
Bridgman **A**, lawstudent, 39 West ave n
Bridgwood Geo, carriagemaker, 20 Jackson e
Bridgwood John, teamster, Hannah w, s s, nr Locke
Bridgwood William, driver, 74 Ray s
Brierley Richard, druggist, 14 King e, h 83 Jackson w
Briers Thos, painter, 41 Markland
Briggs G C & Sons **(G** C, Walter S, Wm A) patent medicines, 25 King w, h 1 Bay s
Briggs **Mrs** Hannah K (wid Edmund) 87½ Jackson w
Briggs Miss Mary Ann 87½ Jackson w
Briggs Samuel, supt Hart Emery Wheel Co, Park s, w s nr Robinson
Briggs Thos, watchman, 89 Ferrie e
Bristol G E (Lucas Park & Co) h 51 Bay s
British American Assurance Wm Strong, agent, 15 Arcade
British and Foreign Marine Insurance Co (Liverpool) W F Findlay, agent, Wentworth Chambers, 25 James s

Britt E, labor and real estate agent, 109½ King w
Britt D, com traveler, 109½ King w
Britt William, shoemaker, 110 Macnab n
Britt Wm, merchant tailor, 146½ York, h 109½ King w
Britton George, painter, 93 Emerald s
Britton Mrs, laundry, 64 Robert
Britton Robert, machinist, 86 Florence
Brizzi Gustave, moulder, 22 East ave n
Broadbent Geo (T & G Broadbent) 191 Cannon e
Broadbent Hiram, machinery dealer, 164 King w
Broadbent Matthew, fireman Court House
Broadbent T & G (Thos & Geo) machinery brokers, 164 King w
Broadbent Thos (T & G Broadbent) bds Pioneer hotel
Broadfield George E (McMahon, Broadfield & Co), h Emerald cor Hunter
Broadfield Mrs H, 60 Emerald s
Broadie John, shipper, 189 Wellington n
Broatch William D, engineer, 36 Tisdale
Brock George, driver, 81 Market
Brock James, whipmaker, 90 Wilson
Brockelsby Mrs Ann, confectioner, 112 James n
Brockelsby Richard, moulder, 83 Elgin
Broderick Edward, laborer, bds 66 John n
Broderick Mrs H, grocer, cor Barton and John
Brohman Frank, malster, 14½ Harriet
Bromley John, barber, 48 John n
Bronson J T, prop Beaver Saloon, 52 John s

Brooke Thos, 68 Ray s
Brooking Alfred, dry plate mkr, 96 West ave n
Brooking Philip A, 96 West Ave
Brooks Mrs Charlotte (wid L H) 133 James s
Brooks Egbert, brakeman, 144 Cannon e
Brooks Geo W, laborer, 139 John s
Brooks John, woodturner, 116 Catharine n
Brookes William, machinist, 52 Hess n
Brooks Wm, dairyman, Beulah
Broughton Wm, fireman G T R, 18 Inchbury s
Brow Harris, teamster, 35 Barton w
Brown Adam (Brown, Balfour & Co) 13 Duke
Brown Alfred, machinist, Wentworth n
Brown Mrs Annie, 11 Charles
Brown Arthur, gardener, Wentworth n
Brown A W, forwarder, etc, 61 East ave s
Brown, Balfour & Co (Adam Brown, St Clair Balfour) wholesale grocers, 5 James s
Brown Benjamin, laborer, Robert w
Brown Mrs Catharine (wid John) r 358 John n
Brown Chas B, roll turner, 38 Magill
Brown Mrs Christina (wid And) 199 Main w
Browne Mrs Bridget, 155 Macnab n
Brown Crosier, 10 Elgin
Brown David, builder, 14 Mulberry
Brown Duncan, bookkeeper, 157 Mary
Browne E, coal merchant and forwarder, ft Macnab n, h Arkledum, hd John s

CITY OF HAMILTON. 33

Brown Edmund, builder, 45 George
Brown Mrs E G (wid Chas P) Wentworth n
Browne Mrs Eliza (wid Michael W) 12 Park s
Brown Mrs Eliza (wid John) 83 **Pearl n**
Brown Mrs Elizabeth (wid Jas) Robinson s s, w Locke
Brown Frank, watchmaker, bds 17 Cannon w
Brown Frederick, laborer, 116 John n
Brown George, 17 Vine
Brown George, packer, 73 **Park n**
Brown Geo, polisher, **bds 35 Hughson n**
Browne Geo W, inland revenue, 109 Catharine s
Brown George Mc L, clerk **G T R**, 13 Duke
Brown H, clerk Bank of Hamilton, 13 Duke
Brown Harry K, shipper, 13 Duke
Brown Herbert, machinist, 27 Little Wm
Brown Hugh, bds 11 Barton e
Brown J, bartender, h 143 Ferguson ave
Brown James, hide inspector, 5a Victoria ave **n**
Brown James, engineer, 36 **Macauley w**
Brown James, foreman **Murton & Reid, 140** Mary
Browne James, hd York, s s nr Dundurn
Browne J B, grocer, **56-58 King w, h** 46 Herkimer
Brown Mrs Jessie, 36 Macauley w
Brown J H, clerk, **13** Duke
Brown John, bds 159 James **n**
Browne John, blacksmith, 116 York, h 68 Caroline **n**
Brown John E, tannery and whip lash maker, **r** 9 East ave **n**

5

Brown John M, machinist, **33** Railway
Brown John L, machinist, **81** Hess n
Brown Joseph, laborer, **40 Emer-ald n**
Brown Josesh, bartender, **bds** 261 Bay n
Brown Joseph, stonemason, 204 Robert
Brown O J, **M A**, **teacher Collegiate Institute, 48 York**
Brown Picton **C**, mangr Ham Sewer Pipe Co, s w cor Barton **and Wentworth**
Brown R B, com traveler, **21 King w**
Brown Robert, stonemason, bds **95 York**
Brown Robt J, machinist, **79 Hess n**
Brown Samuel, laborer, 41 **East ave n**
Brown Sydney H, laborer, **40** Locomotive
Brown Thomas, **teamster, 65** Canada
Brown Thos E, checker, 94½ Catharine n
Brown Thomas **H**, clerk, 13 Duke
Browne's Wharf, E Browne, prop, foot Macnab n
Brown Wm, brakeman, 176 Bay
Brown Wm, tailor, 18 Pearl n
Brown Wm E, clerk, **32** Jackson w
Brown Wm T, machinist, 107 Market
Bruce Alex, Q C, M A, (Bruce, Burton & Culham) h 36 Duke
Bruce. Burton & Culham, (Alex Bruce, Q C, M A, Warren F Burton, J A Culham M A) barristers, Canada Life Chambers, James s
Bruce David, Aikman Ave
Bruce F C (John A Bruce & Co) h **39** George

Bruce John A (John A Bruce & Co) bds Royal hotel
Bruce John A & Co (John A & F C) seedsmen, 37-39 King w
Bruce Mrs **Margaret Louise, 89** Park n
Bruce R R, law student, 36 **Duke**
Bruce Walter, brakeman, 30 Mulberry
Bruce Wm, solicitor of patents and engrosser, 14½ King e, h mountain top
Brugge James, cabinetmaker, **72** Hess n
Brugge Wm J, grocer, **68 Hess** n, h 72 Hess n
Brundle John, tinsmith, **283** King w, h 104 Market
Brundle Joshua, letter collector, **97** Hess n
Brunke Albert, furrier, 30-32 York
"Brunswick, The" saloon (James Crooks, prop) 7-9 King Wm
Brunt A S, hairdresser, 92 King e
Brunt Edward, carpenter, **92** King e
Brunt Mrs Sarah A (wid Samuel) 92 King e
Brush William J, prop St James saloon, 19 Hugbson n
Bryant Harry, grocer, 131-3 **John s**
Bryant James F, plasterer, **85 Victoria ave n**
Bryant John, barber, bds **88** Hughson
Bryant Thos W, upholsterer, **7** Hunter w
Bryce Robt, mechanic, 12 Railway
Bryce Thos, baker, 34 Augusta
Brydges Mrs Catharine (wid Thos) 211 Robert
Bryer Jas, lather, 154 King Wm
Buchanan C H, printer, bds 44 **Hunter e**

Buchanan Henry, sausage maker, 56 Kelly
Buchanan Mrs Isaac, 95 James s
Buchanan Joshua G, city editor, *Times*, 18 Young
Buchanan Samuel, carpenter, 174 Emerald n
Buchanan Wm G, packer, 47 Augusta
Buchanan W W, managing editor *International Royal Templar*, 97 James n, h 90 James s
Buck Nicholas, tailor, 89 Catharine n
Buck John J, clerk, 89 Catharine n
Buck ——, agent, bds 132 John n
Buckingham Anderson, plasterer, r 86 Macnab
Buckingham Ed, laborer, 43 Little William
Buckingham George, painter, 231 King e
Buckingham **Geo**, tanner, 57½ Mary
Buckingham **Isaac**, plasterer, 108 Macnab n
Buckingham James **W**, laborer, 93 Wilson
Buckingham John, laborer, 32 Lower Cathcart
Buckingham John B, bookkeeper, **32 Lower** Cathcart
Buckingham Levi, Metropolitan Hotel, 49 Stuart w
Buckingham **Thos**, boiler maker, 242 Mary
Buckingham **Wm**, butcher, 276 James n
Bucklen H **E** & Co, patent medicine dealers, **94** Macnab n
Buckley Daniel, laborer, Duke n s nr **Locke**
Budd Wm, cabinetmaker, bds 50 Wilson
Budge Mrs James (wid Peter) **101 Bay n**
Budge Robt, laborer, 81 Canada

Bugghy Arthur, tobacco roller, 34 Peter
Buck David, laborer, 329 Barton e
Bull Geo H, clerk P O, 77 Jackson w
Bull Harcourt E O, salesman, bds 42 Main w
Bull Henry, heater, bds 56 Locomotive
Bull J Eldon, salesman, 38 Wellington s
Bull **John,** **hostler,** Franklin House
Bull Richard, insurance and real estate agent, 55 James n. h 14 Hunter e
Bull Stephen, laborer, 213 Main w
Bullen C F, clerk, 64 Hannah w
Bullen Mrs Edith, (wid Chas F) 64 Hannah w
Bullen Frank, com traveller, James cor Bold
Bulley Robert, jr, 95 York
Bulley Robert, sr, tailor, 95 York
Bunbury H T, clerk 1st div court, 12 James s, h 110 Park s
Bunt Wm, laborer, r 81 Caroline n
Buntin, Gillies & Co, wholesale stationers, 41-3 King w
Bunting James, painter, **172** Caroline n
Burbeck Thos, teamster, **23 Sim**coe w
Burchill **Samuel,** laborer, **61** Peter
Burdett Edward, brushmaker, **44** Robinson
Burdett Frank, brushmaker, 103 Macnab n
Burdett Joseph, brush manfr, bds 72 Queen s
Burdon Chas A, agt Silver Creek Brewery, **18** James s
Burger **J,** baker, 64 King e
Burgess Alex, hotel keeper, hd York nr toll gate

Burgess Alfred, laborer, 5 Wentworth n
Burgess Chas, laborer, Duke n s w Locke
Burgess George, laborer, 140 Robert e
Burgess Hiram, pedler, 126 Maria
Burgess James, prop Union Hotel, cor Hughson and Hay Market
Burgess Jacob, **fish dealer,** 82 Catharine s
Burgess James, agent, 34 Walnut s
Burgess John, canvasser, hd York w, nr toll gate
Burgess John, music teacher, 83 Hunter e
Burgess Wm, machinist, 108 East ave n
Burgess Wm, laborer, 94 Maria
Burke A W, prop Simcoe hotel, 153 King e
Burke Miss Bridget, 54 Cherry
Burke Mrs Ellen (wid John) 70a East ave n
Burke Geo, agent, 50 Ray s
Burke John, laborer, 6 Walnut **n**
Burke Miss Maggie, tailoress, 160 Jackson w
Burke Michael, laborer, r 7 Picton w
Burke Patrick, laborer 283 Macnab n
Burke Patrick, hackman, 160 Jackson w
Burkholder Chas E, law student, King, **e** Hamilton
Burkholder Elijah, 5 Baillie
Burkholder David J, carpenter, 51 Tisdale
Burkholder Geo W, 5 Baillie
Burkholder Herbert, machinist, 56 Cartharine s
Burkholder James, laborer, 253 James n
Burkholder J G Y, bookkeeper E & C Gurney Co

Burkholder John, laborer, 50 Gore
Burkholder Michael B, Wentworth n
Burlington Glass Works, Burlington w
Burn Mrs **Frederica, 21 West ave** s
Burn & Robinson, The Manfr Co [limited] (W S Burn, mangr) lanterns, bird cages, etc, 5 Walnut n
Burn Valentine, laborer, s e cor Barton & Locke
Burn W S, (mangr Burn & Robinson Mfg Co) "Chedoke" Mountain top. Telephone connection
Burnelle Frank, shoemaker, bds 34½ Mulberry
Burner Samuel, gardener, King e of Wentworth
Burnett **James**, laborer, **10** Picton e
Burnett **Louis**, carpenter, 205 Hughson n
Burnett **Robert, laborer, 6 Hunter** e
Burnette **Wm**, glassblower, **342** James n
Burnie **Mrs Grace I** (wid Arch D) 46 Duke
Burniston Edward, carpenter, 58 Burlington w
Burns Adam, 16 Hannah w
Burns Rev Alex, D D, LL D, governor Wesleyan Ladies' College, 57 King e
Burns Arthur C, laborer, **r Duke** w Locke
Burns Mrs Bridget [wid **John**] 44 Jackson e
Burns Mrs Catharine [wid **Daniel**] 46 Peter
Burns Chas W, 31 West ave s
Burns Edward, builder, 54 Jackson e
Burns Mrs Eliza [wid Edward] 107 Catharine s

Burns Mrs Elizabeth [wid And] nurse, Florence w Dundurn
Burns E Napier R, law student, 14 Herkimer
Burns Felix, employe **Express Co**
Burns Fred, salesman, 31 **West ave** s
Burns G D, clerk, 16 Hannah w
Burns Hugh **A**, salesman, **31** West ave s
Burns James, expressman, **38** Ray n
Burns James, machinist, s e cor Locke and Herkimer
Burns James, teamster, Sherman
Burns Mrs Jane (wid John) 17 East ave n
Burns J M, manager Molson's Bank, Argyll terrace, 14 Herkimer
Burns John, teamster, Sherman
Burns John, moulder, **17** East **ave n**
Burns John, laborer, 35 Little Wm
Burns John, assessor, 54 Jackson e
Burns John, printer, 96 Elgin
Burns John, laborer, 35 Little Wm
Burns John R, carriage trimmer, 116½ Locke n
Burns Mrs Margaret (wid Wm) **r 61** Jackson e
Burns Matthew, teamster, 77 Bay n
Burns Patrick, laborer, 56 Wood e
Burns Patrick, glassblower, **51 Ferrie**
Burns Robt, heater, 46 Peter
Burns Robt, blacksmith, Wentworth n
Burns Robt, moulder, **17** East ave n
Burns Samuel, 245 York
Burns M S, grocer, s e **cor Locke** and Herkimer

Burns Thos, clerk **P O, 96** Victoria ave s
Burns Thos, bookkeeper, 195 Mary
Burns Thos, laborer, 79 Cherry
Burns Wm, laborer 52 Robinson
Burns Wm, tailor, 139 Victoria **ave n**
Burnstone John, teamster, **bds 88** Park n
Burnstone Wm, carpenter, **bds** 88 Park n
Birrell James, **boiler** maker, **bds** 144 Cannon e
Burrell Thos, fireman G T R, 11 Tom
Burrow Wm (Burrow, Stewart & Milne) h 197 Hughson n
Burrow, Stewart & Milne, (Wm Burrow, Chas Stewart, John Milne) manfrs of stoves, scales, **malleable** and gray iron castings, etc, Cannon cor John
Burrowhuff Jacob, **laborer**, 24 Wood w
Burrows Fred, clerk, 75 West ave n
Burrows Henry, laborer, r **177 Bay n**
Burrows Henry, bookkeeper, 29a Wellington n
Burrows Capt J C, 260 Bay n
Burrows John, laborer, 54 Hughson s
Burrows John, laborer, 209 York
Burrows John C, contractor, 32 Hunter w
Burrows Thos, auctioneer, **78** James n, h 38 West ave n
Burrows Thos, jr, clerk, 287 King Wm
Burrows Wm, tailor, 162 Rebecca
Burrows Wm C, carpenter, 48 **Markland**
Burshaw Peter, laborer, **134** Victoria ave n
Burt John, moulder, 45a Wellington n
Burt Mrs Mary, 223 Barton e

Burt R B (Davis & Burt) **Barton** cor Victoria ave
Burt Wm, boiler maker, 36 Locomotive
Burtch Brock, stone mason, **165** Bay n
Burtchall, Wm E, hatter, **21** Spring
Burton Edwin, brakeman, **99** Lower Cathcart
Burton George, engraver, **20** Murray e
Burton James, cabinetmaker, **226** Cannon e
Burton John, carpenter, 27 Peter
Burton Warren F, (Bruce, Burton & Culham) h 238 King e
Burwell Wm, railroader, 92 Hess
Burwell ——, **gardener,** hd York w canal
Busby Robert, brakeman, bds **89** Cannon e
Buscombe Edwin, builder, 52 Inchbury n
Buscombe Frederick, corn traveller, 71 Herkimer
Buscombe John, contractor, **r** synagogue, Hughson s
Buscombe John, hackman, 58 Tisdale
Buscomb Richard, bricklayer, 31 Inchbury n
Buscombe Samuel, shoemaker, 58 Tisdale
Buscomb Wm, moulder, 50 Tom n s w Dundurn
Bush Chas, grocer, **280** Cannon e
Bush Hiram E, manager Bush **windmill** and pump Co, 89 Market
Bush Thos, Beulah
Bush Windmill and Pump Co, Hiram **E** Bush, manager, 16 Market
Buskard Alfred, carriagemaker, 31 Simcoe e
Buskard Jeremiah, blacksmith, **105** Ferrie **e**

Buskard Robt, carriagemanfr, 124 King w, h 8 Bay n
Bustin Hy, piano maker, 101 Robinson
Butler David, Markland n s nr Garth
Butler Dennis, laborer, 141 John
Butler Mrs Ellen (wid Partrick) 51 Caroline s
Butler Patrick, hachman, 51 Caroline s
Butler Mrs Sarah (wid Geo) laundress, Markland n s nr Garth
Butler Mrs Susanna (wid James) 30 Augusta
Butler Thos, hackman, 17 Pearl n
Butler Thos H, manager Thorley Cattle Food Co, 18 Wilson
Butler Wm, machinist, 30 Augusta
Butler Walter, wood turner, 37 Tisdale
Butler Wm, brakeman, 17 Mill
Buttenham Wm, teamster, 169 Mary
Butterfield John, stonecutter, 112 Jackson e
Butterfield Mrs John, grocer, 110 Jackson e
Butterworth John, carpenter, 16 Blyth
Buttle Thos, 84 Hughson n
Buttrey Leonard H, finisher, 73½ West ave n
Byrne Miss Maggie, dressmaker 98 Park n
Byrne Martin, machinist, 197 Mary n
Byrne Mrs Mary (wid Andrew) 81 Bay n
Byrne Mrs Mary, 51 Ferguson ave
Byrne Jas, laborer, 221 York
Byrens Jas M, builder, 79 Catharine n
Byrens Geo C, carpenter, 36 Magill
Byron Thomas, broommaker, 126 Hannah e

Cable Joseph, policeman, 104 Catharine s
Caddy Edward F, civil engineer, bds 47 Peter
Caddy John H, 22 Main w
Caffrey John, furnaceman, 27 Cannon e
Caffery John, moulder, 128 John n
Cahill A R, ledger keeper Merchants' Bank, 101 King e
Cahill Edwin D, (Carscallen & Cahill) h 101 King e
Cahill James, police magistrate 101 King e
Cahill John, blacksmith, 10 Barton e, h 187 Bay n
Cahill Joseph, glassblower, 306 Hughson n
Cahill Michael, 125 Ferrie e
Cahill Patrick, boilermaker, 13 Wood e
Cain Robert, coremaker, 58 Florence
Cain Thomas, shoemaker, 136 Emerald n
Calback George, hotel, 352 John n
Calder A & Co, chemist and druggist, 60-62 York
Calder Alex (A Calder & Co) h 90 Merrick
Calder John, John Calder & Co, h 98 Hughson s
Calder John & Co, wholesale clothiers, Macnab cor Merrick
Caldwell ——, bds 122 Cannon
Caldwell Mrs Belle (wid James) 91 Market
Caldwell Chas B, moulder, 58 John s
Caldwell Mrs C B, tobacconist, 58 John s
Caldwell George, machinist, 21 Gore
Caldwell John, Barton Terrace, Wellington n
Caldwell Wm J, moulder, Albert Road

Caledonia Hall, 33 James n
Call Frederick, moulder, 43 Bay n
Callaghan Misses Annie & Minnie, Hamilton laundry, 32 Merrick, h 52 Maria
Callaghan Edmund, laborer, Albert road
Callaghan Hugh, block paver, 22 Napier
Callaghan John, watchman, 231 Catharine n
Callaghan John, laborer, 12 Picton w
Callaghan John, laborer, 14 Guise
Callaghan Margaret, 14 Guise
Callan Mrs Kate. r 185 Bay n
Callanane John, 86 Park n
Callanane J, hotel, 81 Stuart w
Callaghan ——, laborer, 41 Caroline n
Callon Mrs Honora (wid Thos) 25 Barton e
Callon John, laborer, bds 67 Stuart
Callowhill Henry, tinsmith, 78 Maria
Callum ——, 52 Maria
Calvert John, shoemaker, 17 West ave n
Cambden J R, butcher, 97 King e
Camp Charles, laborer, 100 John n
Camp Solomon, coachman, 96 Main e
Cameron A D (Cameron & Witherspoon) h 58 East ave s
Cameron Andrew, conductor G T R, 109 Hess n
Cameron Charles, bds 16 Hughson s
Cameron Charles, laborer, 16 Strachan w
Cameron D M, stenographer, 123 King w
Cameron Duncan, com traveler, 155 York

Cameron H D, treasurer Ham Provident & Loan Society, 74 Emerald s
Cameron James, laborer, 229 Cannon e
Cameron James, moulder, 73 Tisdale
Cameron John, consulting acturay, Canada Life Building
Cameron John, shipper, 88 Ray s
Cameron John, laborer, 219 Wellington n
Cameron John, moulder, 153 York
Cameron John A, engine fitter, 193 Wellington n
Cameron J R, managing editor Spectator, mountain top
Cameron Wm, prop Mechanics' hotel, 153 Catharine n
Cameron & Witherspoon. (A D Cameron, LL B, R W Witherspoon) barristers, Hamilton Provident Chambers, 1 Hughson s
Campaign Francis, blacksmith, 74 Oak ave
Campaign James, laborer, 29 Simcoe w
Campaign Wm, policeman, 238½ Bay n
Campbell Albert, moulder, 131 Park n
Campbell Alex, grocer, 54 York
Campbell Alex, policeman, 9 Oxford
Campbell Alexander, druggist, 146 West ave n
Campbell Calvin, cook dining car GTR, 43 Park s
Campbell Mrs Catharine, 131 King Wm
Campbell Colin, tailor, 52 Jackson e
Campbell Colin C, salesman, Wellington s
Campbell Colin C, bookkeeper, 120 Jackson w
Campbell D, detective, 52 Magill

Campbell Donald, woodcarver, 131 King Wm
Campbell Donald, cabinetmaker, 120 Locke n
Campbell Donald, livery, 11 Market, h 53 York
Campbell Donald D, clerk P O, 80 Hunter w
Campbell Douglas, moulder, 35 Catharine s
Campbell Dougald J, inspector Canada Life Co, 162 Main w
Campbell D W, M D, 268 King e
Campbell Ed, moulder 198 Barton e
Campbell Geo, 39 Hannah e
Campbell Geo, coachman "Oak Hall," West ave s
Campbell Henry, printer, 152¾ Rebecca
Campbell Jas, moulder, 86 West ave n
Campbell Jas, contractor, 105 Emerald n
Campbell Jas, lather, 10 Upper Cathcart
Campbell Mrs James, 50 West ave s
Campbell John, boilermaker, 324 John n
Campbell John, (Campbell & Pentecost) h 55 Jackson w
Campbell John, packer, 378 James n
Campbell John, fireman, 4 Harriet
Campbell John, collector, 47 Caroline n
Campbell John, machinist, 59 Wellington n
Campbell John D, enameller, 20 Canada
Campbell Kenneth, laborer, 114 Bold
Campbell Mrs Lilly (wid Daniel) 53 Jackson w
Campbell Mitchell, laborer, bds 55 York

Campbell & Pentecost, (John Campbell, Albert L Pentecost) importers of **staple and** fancy dry goods, 43 Macnab n
Campbell Peter S, B A, principal collegiate institute, 40 Emeral s
Campbell R, Hamilton Pottery, 46-52 **Locke**, h 108 Jachson w
Campbell **Robt**, laborer, 156 Rebecca
Campbell **Robt**, carpenter, 6 Picton w
Campbell **Robt**, 111 **Main w**
Campbell Sewer Pipe Co, A E Carpenter, Pres, H New, sec-treas, end Jackson w
Campbell, Mrs Sarah (wid Alex) 117 Wellington n
Campbell Mrs Susan (wid **Wm**) 41 Queen s
Campbell Thos, moulder, 119 Wellington n
Campbell Walter P, **foreman** *Times* **78** John n
Campbell West, potter, 19 **Lock s**
Campbell **Wm**, boilermaker, **bds** 21 Florence
Campbell Wm, freight checker, 256 Bay n
Campbell Wm, spipper, 276b King e
Campbell Wm C, teacher, 275 King e
Canada Business College, R E Gallagher, principal, 33 James n
Canada Furniture Co, Thos Hill, manager, 30 Merrick
Canada Life Assurance Co, A G Ramsay, Managing Director and President, R Hills, Secretary, King e cor James s
Canada Glass House, J C Smyth, Manager, 52 King e
Canadian Bank of Commerce, Edward Mitchell Manager, 15 King e

Canadian Millers' Mutual Fire Insurance Company, Senaca Jones, Sec., 6 James s
Canadian Oil Co, C J Williams, prop, 18 Macuab n
Canadian Pacific R'y, W J Grant, agent, 33 James n
Canadian Pacific R'y, Arch Frew, agent, 31 King e
Canadian Pacific Railway's Telegraph, C J Jones, agent, 8 James s
Canary Jas, laborer, r 69 Cherry
Canary Michael, laborer, 84 Simcoe e
Canary Michael, laborer, r 69 Cherry
Canary Patrick, laborer, 67 Strachan e
Canary Thos, fireman, 52 Emerald n
Canary Wm, pedlar, r 69 Cherry
Canavan John, moulder, bds 82 Hughson n
Canham Alfred, laborer, 147 Jackson w
Cann Adolphus E, com traveller 4 Tisdale
Cann Mrs Samuel, 77 Hughson n
Canning Geo, plasterer, 49 Wellington s
Canning Geo jr, plasterer, 2 Grove
Cannon Geo N, plater, 155 East ave n
Cant Jos, ledger keeper Bank B N A, 61 George
Canute Geo, teamster. bds 34 Colborne
Canute Jacob, teamster, bds 34 Colborne
Canute Wm John, teamster, 34 Colborne
Canute Mrs Rosa A, 34 Colborne
Capes John, tailor, 46 Maria
Carbery Right Rev James Joseph, D D, O P, S T M, Bishop of Hamilton, the palace, 25 Sheaffe

Cardwell John, plasterer, Wentworth n
Cardwell John, laborer, 15 Greig
Cardwell Wm, laborer, 89 Picton e
Carey Geo W, groceries, 6 York
Carey Miss Mary, 26 Young
Carey Wm, (Carey & Southam) h 132½ Bay s
Carless Wm E, carter, 136 Macaulay e
Carleton Charles S, 12 Concession
Carling Thos, machinist, 93 Hughson n
Carlisle Geo, refrigerator manfr, 44 Caroline n, h 46 Caroline n
Carlisle Wm, weaver, 5 Strachan w
Carlson Carl G, merchant tailor, 44 York, h 106 Robinson
Carlyon Walter, blacksmith, 21 Queen n
Carlyon Wm, painter, 135 John n
Carmichael Geo, cabman, 182 Hughson n
Carmichael Rev Hartley, M A, Dublin, rector Church of Ascension, Hannah w s s near Macnab
Carmichael John, conductor, 221 Victoria ave n
Carmichael John H, shoemaker, 9 York
Carnahan John, brushmaker, 74 Bay s
Carnegie Peter, tailor, 57 York
Carpenter Albert E, pres Campbell Sewer Pipe Co, end Jackson w, h 111 Hughson n
Carpenter Bryan. carpenter, 9 Upper Cathcart
Carpenter Bros, (John O and Thos B) family grocers, 9 Market square
Carpenter Chas, hardware merchant. 12 Hess s

6

Carpenter Chas & Co, hardware merchant, 53½ York
Carpenter Henry, student, 12 Hess s
Carpenter Henry, 35 Canada
Carpenter J H, milk dealer, 63 Victoria ave n
Carpenter Jonathan, Mountain ave
Carpenter John O, (Carpenter Bros) h 128 King Wm
Carpenter Thomas B (Carpenter Bros) h 89 Napier
Carr Aaron, messenger Meriden Britannia Co, 89 Napier
Carr E H, clerk Bank of Montreal, 14 Caroline s
Carr E & D, flour and feed, 91-93 King w
Carr Geo W, plater, 46 Steven
Carr's Direct Hamburg Steamship Line, Wm Herman, agent, 16 James s
Carr Miss H, millinery and fancy goods, 152 King e
Carr John, patternmaker, 52 Victoria ave n
Carr Mrs M A E (wid Samuel) 1 Hunter e
Carr Robert, laborer, 66 Maria
Carre Rev Eugene M, Roman Catholic, 25 Sheaffe
Carrier Nicholas, shoemaker, 1 Wellington Terrace, Wellington n
Carroll Chas, carriagemaker, 267 Macnab n
Carroll James M, bricklayer, 76 Bold
Carroll John, stovemounter, 225 James n
Carroll John, engineer, 14 Harriet
Carroll John D, Union hotel, 7 Market
Carrol John M, moulder, 94 West ave n
Carroll Joseph, laborer, 158 Hughson n
Carroll Mrs Mary (wid John) 5 Bruce
Carroll Matthew, lumberman, 267 Macnab n
Carroll Matthew J, bricklayer, 128 Bold
Carroll Maurice, barber, 234 James n
Carroll Maurice, 80 Young
Carroll Michael, heater, 147 Locke n
Carroll Michael, shoemaker, 80 Young
Carroll Mrs, 3 Bruce
Carroll Nicholas, teamster, 28 Ferguson ave
Carroll Patrick, laborer, 13 Strachan e
Carroll Peter, carpenter, 276 Mary n
Carroll P J, clerk Traders' Bank, s e cor Jackson and Walnut
Carroll Mrs Sarah (wid James) 102 Bold
Carroll T J (A M Foster & Co) h 104 Rebecca
Carroll Wm, tobacconist, 98 James n
Carroll ———, bds 43 John n
Carruthers John, flour and feed, 15 King Wm, h 76 Mary
Carruthers W, salesman, 1 53 King Wm
Carry James, laborer, 53 Strachan
Carscallen & Cahill (Henry Carscallen, Edwin D Cahill) barristers, 7 King w
Carscallen Henry (Carscallen & Cahill) h 243 Main e
Carse John, employee Hamilton club
Carse John, stonecutter, 1 57½ York
Carse J M, waiter, Hamilton club
Carse P D, gents' furnisher, 126 King e, h 38 West ave n
Carson Mrs Amelia, 329 and 331 James n

Carson George, wood dealer, bds 134 King Wm
Carson George, laborer, 9 Devonport
Carson Henry, shoemaker, 3 Mill
Carson **James, moulder**, Maple ave
Carson James, boarding, **105 King w**
Carson **James**, jr, varnisher, Maple ave
Carson Rice, laborer, 17 Railway
Carson **Wm**, moulder, bds 63 Ferguson ave
Carter **Charles, scale maker**, 5 Kelly
Carter Chas, laborer, 75 James s
Carter Esau, harnessmaker, 107 King Wm
Carter James, 53 Lower Cathcart
Carter James, plasterer, South w, n s, nr Garth
Carter Stephen, blacksmith, 56 Florence
Carter Thomas, laborer, end Ferrie e
Carter **Wm, plasterer, 80 Cannon w**
Cartmell Henry, tailor, 55 Kelly
Cartney Mrs Henora, 203 Hughson n
Cartney John, blacksmith, **203** Hughson n
Cary Wm **T, ice dealer**, Wentworth n
Case Adolphus C, farmer, King e of toll gate
Case A J, dairymen, 42 Stuart e
Case Albert, cardriver, 222 Macnab n
Case Edward, bartender Atlantic House, 29 Macnab n
Case Edwin J, laborer, 54 Walnut s
Case George, blacksmith, 13 George
Case **Henry N**, postmaster, res old P O building

Case H Spencer, druggist, **50** King w, h 171 Main e
Case William H, M D, 113 King e
Case William I A, M D, 113 King e
Casey James B, manufacturer, 86 Main e
Casey John P, manufacturer, 86 Main e
Casey M E, manfr, 86 Main e
Casey Mrs **Sanford**, **72 Oak ave**
Casey & Sons (Wm, J P, J B, M E Casey) planing mill, 70-72 Main e
Casey William, manfr, 86 Main e
Cashion David, moulder, 70 Locomotive
Cashman Timothy, laborer, **64** Hannah **e**
Cashin Thomas, **moulder, bds** 17 Pearl n
Cassells Thos, gardener, n e cor Bay and Concession
Cassford Wm, melter, Garth e s nr Duke
Cassidy Amos, carpenter, 99 Hess n
Cassidy Hugh, moulder, r 53 Kelly
Cassidy Hugh, laborer, **31** Strachan e
Castell James, sergeant police, 73 Duke
Catchpole Mrs Ann, 114 East ave n
Catchpole **Arthur, laborer, 114** East ave **n**
Catchpole Chas, cigarmaker, **114** East ave n
Catchpole Geo, jr, salesman, 30 Nelson ave
Catchpole Geo, umbrella maker, 15 Rebecca
Catchpole Richard, umbrellas and crockery, 99 King w
Catchpole Samuel G, bookkeeper, 40 Oxford

Catchpole Samuel, bookkeeper, 99 King w
Cathcart Thomas, baker, 4 **Ferguson ave**
Cathro E M, bookkeeper, 24 Hunter e
Cathro, Kent & Rogers, contractors, Arcade
Cathro William, contractor, bds 24 Hunter e
Catlin James, laborer, 41 Little **Wm**
Catlin James, laborer, 41 Little Wm
Catton Walter, car inspector, 123 Ferguson ave
Caughell Alonzo (Caughell & Weaver) Dominion hotel
Caughell & Weaver, prop's Dominion hotel, 80-86 King w
Caughlin Daniel, carpenter, 113 Park n
Cauley Brian, cigar **manfr**, 29 John n, h 112 King e
Cauley John, 77 Young
Ceasar John F, driver, 5 Florence
Centenary Methodist Church Rev S J Hunter, pastor, Main w
Central Drug Store, n e cor York and Hess
Central Fire Station, A W Aitchison chief, 34 Hughson n
Central Hotel, Peter Meegan, prop, 135 King e
Central Presby'n Church, Rev Samuel Lyle, B D, pastor, n w cor Jackson and Macnab
Central School, Hunter w, between Bay and Park
Chadwick Arthur H, manfr, 56 Hughson n
Chadwick John A, manfr spun sheet metal goods, 171 James n, h 56 Hughson n
Chadwick Thomas, railway man, 197 Bay n
Chagnon Emory, metal spinner, 114 Victoria ave n

Challice Samuel, butcher, 64 West ave n
Chambers Mrs Elizabeth (wid David) 173 Bay n
Chambers Mrs Elizabeth (wid James) dressmaker, 202 King w
Chambers James, conductor G T R, 121 Macnab n
Chambers Mrs Sarah (wid Wm) 22 Spring
Champ Wm S, **paymaster** G T R 36 Wellington s
Champagne Chas, **moulder**, bds 10 Picton e
Champagne Joseph, harness maker, 96 Mulberry
Champagne Louis, moulder, bds 10 Picton e
Chancery Chambers, 8-10 Hughson s
Chandler George, stovemounter, 120 Hannah e
Channell Wm, **bartender, the Hub, 6½** James n
Chanter Robert, engineer, Robinson n s, nr Locke
Chanter Robt W, carpenter, Robinson n s, nr Locke
Chapman Mrs A T, 18 Herkimer
Chapman Jesse, (W M Chapman's Sons) h 49 King w
Chapman John, machinist, 9 Walnut n
Chapman John, 109 King William
Chapman Joseph, chair repairer, 288 King e
Chapman Josh M, Grand Opera Saloon, 94 James n
Chapman Samuel, druggist, 284 King e
Chapman Walter, bread pedler, 91 Jackson e
Chapman Walter, laborer, 114 Wood e
Chapman Wm, boilermaker, bds 165 Bay n

Chapman Wm, fish dealer, bds Street Car Inn, King e
Chapman W M, funeral emporium, 49 King w
Chappel Horatio, tinsmith, 38 Picton e
Chappel Horatio **C**, tinsmith 188 James n
Chapple Thomas, foreman pork factory, 170 Rebecca
Chappel Wm, **tinsmith, bds 144** Catharine n
Chappell Wm, 131 Cannon e
Charles **Dew**, Clyde Hotel, **49** McNab n
Charles Frederick, fitter, 12½ Crooks
Charles Geo, moulder, **79 East ave n**
Charter Wm, moulder, bds 236 Macnab n
Charteris James, letter carrier, 57 Victoria ave n
Charlton B E, (Pres of Ham Vinegar Works Co, limited) **Cor** John and Gore
Charlton Jos, glassblower, **274 Bay n**
Chatley Mrs Elizabeth **(wid** Jesse) **32** Crooks
Chatts Robt, teamster, 5 Vine
Cheeseman Alfred, laborer, **34 Little Wm**
Cheeseman Jas, brickmaker, 338 King **w**
Cheeseman John, brickmaker, 308 King w
Cheeseman Samuel, brickmaker, West
Cheeseman Thos, brickmaker, 330 King w
Cherrier E, butcher, 303 and 305 James n
Cherrier F L, grocer, 15 Market Square, h Barton cor Mary
Chesnut Herbert, clerk Bank of Hamilton, 143 James s
Chesnut Mrs Jane, ladies' boarding school, 143 James s

Chessum Arthur C, painter, 37 Tom
Chessum **Thos** S, painter, 37 Tom
Cheyne Jas, carpenter, 9 Hunter e
Children's Home, Rev **J S** Evans, Governor, Main **e of** Wentworth
Childs Frederick, brick manfr, Garth w s opp Duke h **27** Stuart e
Childs Geo, carpenter, 18 Harriet
Child ———, moulder, 75 Cannon w
Chilman Mrs Celia **(wid** Isaac **C** sr) 48 Hannah w
Chilman I C, baker and confectioner, 119 King w
Chilman Mrs Margaret **(wid** Isaac C jr, 74 Napier
Chilman Reuben E, **clerk, 119** King w
Chilman Wm H, (I C Chilman), h 20 George
Childs Wm H, machinist 7 Mill
China Arcade, 182 King e
China and Japan Tea Merchant Samuel Wilkinson, manager, **4** King Wm
China Palace, 9-11 King e
Chine Jos, laborer, 51 Mary
Chisholm James B A, (McQuesten & Chisholm) **107** Hughson n
Chisholm Jas, contractor, 114 Macnab n
Chisholm Mrs Janet (wid Wm) 80 Caroline s
Chisholm Robt, contractor, 20 Ray s
Chisholm **Wm** P, student, **80** Caroline s .
Chisnell Roderick, emery wheel moulder, 15 Hunter w
Chisnell Wm, moulder, 125 Emerald n
Chittenden C S, D D S, dentist, 8½ King e, h 69 Bay s

Choate Miss Augusta, 143 Main e
Choate Zacchaeus, carpenter, 30 Hughson s
Christ Church Cathedral, Rev C H Mockridge D D, rector in charge, 68 James n
Christian Isaac, pressman, 88 Stinson
Christian Mrs Jane, 187 Main e
Christian John, porter, Burton
Christie Alex, blacksmith, bds 174 Bay n
Christie John, 11 Macaulay w, h 235 Catharine n
Christie Robt, Supt L D Sawyer & Co, 54 East ave n
Christopher Oliver, laborer, 194 Robert
Chubb Thos, railwayman, 119 Cannon e
Chudley James, laborer, bds 26 Ray n
Church Alex, blacksmith, 76 Lower Cathcart
Church Mrs Sarah, (wid James) 173 Mary
Church Samuel, laborer, 221 Macnab n
Church of the Ascension, Rev Hartley Carmichael, M A Rector, John cor Maria
Church of the Evangelical Association, 98 Market
Churchill Hugh, laborer, 77 Mucaulay e
Citizen's Insurance Co, Jas Walker, agent, 29 Main e
Citizen's Insurance Co (Accident Branch) Richard Bull, agent, 55 James n
City Hall, James n
City Hospital, Barton cor Victoria ave n
City of London Fire Insurance Co, Richard Bull, agent, 55 James n
City Mutual Fire Insurance Co, Walter Ambrose, agent, 14 Hughson s

City Steam Laundry, Joseph Jeffrey, proprietor, 60 Main w
City Weigh Scales, James Hammond, weigh inspector, John n
Celophan John, plasterer, 7 Pine
Celophan Samuel, plasterer, 143 Jackson w
Clappison Thos, bookseller and stationer, 66 James n, h 87 Market
Claringbowl Fred, watchmaker and jeweller, 150 King e
Claringbowl Wm jr, 77 Wellington s
Claringbowl Wm, carpenter, 77 Wellington s
Clark Adam, fitter, 262 James n
Clark Adam, machinist, 102 Queen n
Clark Adam, plumber and gas fitter, 36 James s, h 142 Main w
Clark Alex, stonecutter, 78 Emerald n
Clark Alvin, engineer, 56 Burlington w
Clark A W, teller, Traders' Bank, 41 Main w
Clark Benjamin, engineer, 182 Victoria ave n
Clark Chas, laborer, Herkimer n s nr Garth
Clark Chas, clerk, bds 44 Main w
Clark Chas, bricklayer, Hess s, w s nr Markland
Clark Christopher, hatter, 215 Hughson n
Clark Mrs Elizabeth (wid Hutchinson) 77 Hughson n
Clark Frederick, laborer, 110 Maria
Clark Geo, machinist, 5 Hess n
Clark George, stableman, 12 Simcoe e
Clark George, brushmaker, 182 Victoria ave n
Clark Henry A, publisher, 168 West ave n

Clark James, stovemounter, 190 Park n
Clark James, carpenter, 256½ Macnab n
Clarke John, student, 73 Main w
Clark John, painter, 182 Victoria ave n
Clark John A, druggist, 34 King e, h 30½ Jackson w
Clark John B, heater, 11 Greig
Clarke John D, assistant editor, 104 Jackson w
Clark Joseph, clerk, 73 Cannon w
Clarke Joseph, laborer, 75 Canada
Clarke Joseph, salesman, 72 Park n
Clark Mrs Maria (wid David) 30½ Jackson w
Clarke Miss Mary, dressmaker, 127 King e
Clark Nelson, carter, 198 Robert
Clarke O S, clerk Bank of Hamilton, 17 King w
Clark Lawrence, shipper, 118 King w
Clark Peter, laborer, 131 Simcoe e
Clark Richard, moulder, 193 Cannon e
Clark Thos, painter, 182 Victoria ave n
Clark Thos, laborer, 302 Macnab n
Clark Thos, butcher, 212 James n
Clark Wm M, packer, 104 Catharine s
Clark Wm, carriage builder, 72 Park n
Clarke Wm H, laundry prop, 178 King w
Clark ——, rougher, bds 56 Locomotive
Clarkson Mrs Grace, 264 James n
Clarkson Harry, cotton weaver, 293 James n

Claus Peter, tinsmith, bds 35 Hughson n
Clayton Mrs Harriet (wid Wm E) laundress, 88 Ray s
Clayton John, painter, 18 Hughson n, h 23 Crooks
Clayton Mrs Sarah, 36 Main w
Cleary Edward, shoemaker, 82 Hughson n
Cleary James, laborer, 50 Jackson e
Cleary Mrs Margaret (wid Dennis) 50 Jackson e
Clegg John, laborer, 17 Tom
Cleghorn Mrs Sarah A (wid Wm) 32 George
Clement Miss Mary E, 44 Catharine n
Clements Thomas, rougher, bds 23 Magill
Clements Thomas, mechanic, bds 143 Bay n
Clendening A B, R R and S S ticket clerk, 33 James n
Cleves John, salesman, bds 44 Hess n
Cliff William H, printer, 55 Ray n
Clifford John, driller, 34 Queen n
Clifford Miss Margaret, dressmaker, 107 Macnab n
Clifton John W, engineer G T R, 26 Locomotive
Climie J D, boots and shoes, 28 King e, h 33 East ave s
Cline Arthur, hackman, 135 Locke n
Cline John J, 101 Emerald n
Cline John P, marble yard, 16 Cherry, h 10 Baillie
Cline R M, fish dealer, 244 King e
Cline Thos, 99 Emerald n
Cline William, hatmaker, 99 Emerald
Clinton Joseph, printer, 103 Catharine n
Clinton Wm, pattern fitter, 103 Catharine n

Clohecy Robert, architect, 2½ James s. h 18 Emerald n *See card*
Clohecy Thos, harnessmaker, 59 Merrick h, 105 Macnab n
Cloke J G, (John Eastword & Co) h 193 Main e
Cloney James, laborer, 46 Picton w
Close Francis R. bookkeeper, 169 King Wm
Close John, 169 King Wm
Club Chambers, W J Lovering, prop, 16 Hughson s
Clucas Chas, carpenter, bds 125 Cannon w
Clucas John, carpenter, bds 125 Cannon w
Clucas William, builder, 125 Cannon w
Clucas Wm, machinist, 68 Locomotive
Clushman John, moulder, 57 Tisdale
Coates Henry M, letter carrier, 142 Hughson n
Cobb David, laborer, 120 Macnab n
Coburn H P, (L D Sawyer & Co) h cor Hannah and Park
Cochenour Frank, mechanic, bds 54 Park n
Cochrane C S, photographer, 124 King e, h 28 Liberty
Cochrane James, laborer, 30 Colborne
Cochrane Michael, laborer, bds 35 Hughson n
Cochrane W F, bds 16 Hughson s
Cockburn Lestock W, M D, physician and surgeon, n e Jackson and Caroline
Cockburn Thos, wire worker, 26 Canada
Coddington W H, hat manfr, 176 King e
Code Jas, law student, bds 36 Bay s

Coffey John Wm, lather, 37 Kailway
Coghlan Thos, laborer, 110 Walnut
Cohen Mark, ins agent, 50 Victoria ave s
Cohen Morris, pedlar, 66 Emerald n
Cohen Wolfe, dealer, 66 Hess n
Coil Thos, laborer, 66 Locke s
Coiley Wm, lithograper, 61 Pearl n
Colbeck Henry, asist post master, mountain top
Cole Henry, hostler, 105 John s
Cole John, bookkeeper, 105 Hughson s
Cole Jos, 16 Oak ave
Cole Wm, barber, 311 James n
Cole Wm, butcher, 111 Napier
Cole Wm W, com traveller, 202 Cannon e
Coleman Chas, teamster, bds 43 John n
Coleman Chas, laborer, 108 George
Coleman Rev Francis, 121 Napier
Coleman Geo, painter, 126 East ave n
Coleman Jas, laborer, 46 John n
Coleman Richard, com traveller, 90 Jackson w
Coles, Frederick S, boiler fitter, Princess
Collegiate Institute, n e cor Main and Caroline
Collett Ernest A, engineer, 1½ Queen s
Collett Geo T, machinst 21 Florence
Collier Geo, operator, h 115 Bay n
Collier Wm, restaurant, 4 King w
Collingwood Henry, tripe dresser, 184 James n
Collingwood and Lake Superior Steamship Line, W J Grant, agent, 33 James n

Collingwood Robt, reporter, Main w s s w Garth nr King
Collingwood ——, pedlar, 184 James n
Collins Daniel, laborer, 87 Rebecca
Collins E S, sign painter, 28 Hughson s, h 317 York
Collins Geo, carpenter, 154 Wilson
Collins Geo W, bricklayer, 7 Herkimer n s w Locke
Collins John, culler, 38 Locomotive
Collins Jos, glassblower, 308½ John n
Collins Miss Maggie, 154 Market
Collins Mrs, laundress, 98 Bold
Collins Thos, coachman, Aikman ave
Collins Thos, potter, 68 Canada
Collis Edward, laborer, Chesnut ave
Collis Geo, coppersmith, 76 Markland s s w Locke
Collyer Augustus T (Imperial Straw Works) h mountain top
Collyer Edward, miller, 122 Maria
Collyer **Samuel**, laborer, 337 York
Colquhoun E A, cashier Bank of Hamilton, h mountain top
Colton Mrs Mary, (wid Thos) 66½ East ave n
Coltrust John, laborer, 80 **Wal**nut s
Colville Chas A (Bain & Colville) 6 Wilson
Columbia Hotel, Wm McIver, prop, King cor Park
Colville Miss Margaret, 22 **Hess** n
Colvin J, grocer, 136 James n
Colvin Mrs Margaret, 24 Wood e
Colvin Mrs Margaret, 338 Hughson n
Colvin Peter, grocer, hd York s s nr cemetry

Comfort John, laborer, 21 Inchbury s
Commercial Union Fire, Life and Marine Assurance Co, Elford G Payne, agent, 97 James n
Commerford Peter, 259 **James n**
Conde Alfred, fireman, 159 West ave n
Confederation Life Association, Senaca Jones, agent, 6 James s
Congo David, porter, 57 Lower Cathcart
Congregational **Church**, Rev John Morton, pastor, Hughson cor Cannon
Conkle Wilfurn, laborer, bds 70 Wellington n
Conklin Mrs Sarah A (wid Thos D) 127 Hunter w
Conian Jos, con N & N W 18 Walnut s
Conley **Chas E**, printer, 10 West Ave n
Conley Christopher, boilermaker, 282 Mary n
Conley Wm, teamster, 30 Murray
Conlon Partrick, laborer, 93 Macaulay e
Connan Lawrence H, **clerk bds** 124 Rebecca
Conneticut Fire Insurance Company, J T Routh, agent, 16 James s
Connell Dennis, gardener, 103 Cherry
Connell James, tobacco roller, 50 Napier
Connell John J, bricklayer, 2 Clark ave
Connell Miss Louisa, dressmaker, 34 Hunter e
Connell Mrs Mary (wid Thos) 50 Napier
Connell Maurice, laborer, 105 Hess n
Counell Owen, laborer, 117 Walnut s

Connell Patrick, laborer, 67 Hannah e
Connell Timothy, stovemounter, 67 Hannah e
Connell Wm, finisher, 10 Wellington n
Connell ——, laborer, 106 Maria
Connolly Bernard, mechanic, 13 Kelly
Connolly Bernard J, brakeman, 245 James n
Connolly James, grocer, 13 Elgin
Connolley James, laborer, bds 116 Queen n
Connolly Lawrence, laborer, 39 Burlington w
Connolly Mrs Maggie (wid Thos) boarding house keeper, 26 Main w
Connelly Michael, laborer, r 153 Cannon e
Connolly Philip, piano finisher, 13 Kelly
Connelly Wm, laborer, 49 Locomotive
Connor Frank, wagon maker, 146 Duke
Connor Henry, laborer, 79 Caroline n
Connor James, machinist, 88 Park n
Connor John, carpenter, 9 Oak ave
Connor Kennedy, shoemaker, 36 Margaret
Connor Mrs Mary (wid Wm) 65 York
Connor Peter, teamster, 233 Mary n
Connor Thomas, carpenter, 121 Jackson w
Connor Wm H, fruiterer, 65 York
Connors James, laborer, 30 Alanson
Connors James, burnisher, 62 Tisdale
Connors Jeremiah, laborer, 30 Alanson

Connors John, laborer, 54 Erie ave
Connors John, conductor GTR, 120 Hess n
Connors John, laborer, 215 Mary n
Connors John, jr, carter, 50 Jackson w
Connors John, sr, dairyman, 50 Jackson w
Connors Mrs Margaret, r 358 John n
Connors Patrick, laborer, 325 John n
Connors Patrick, teamster, 5 Maple
Constable Lewis T, supt Ontario Rolling Mills, 18 Florence
Continental Hotel, Wm Proper, prop, 162-4 Bay n
Convent, Mount St Mary, King cor Ray
Conway Bartholemew J, excise officer, 133½ Park n
Conway Jas, machinist, 239 Wellington n
Conway M W, glassblower, 80 Macauley e
Conway Robert, moulder, 125 Locke n
Cook Adam (Ennis & Cook) h Mountain top
Cook David, bartender, 75 Bay n
Cooke Edward A P, painter, 168 York
Cook George, carpenter, 81 Locke n
Cook George, watchman, 22 Crooks
Cook Henry T, baker, 53 Peter
Cook James, painter, Duke, s s, nr Locke
Cook John, plumber, 126 Hunter w
Cook John, painter, 113 Wellington n
Cook John B, 118 Market
Cook Joseph, butcher, 222 James n

Cook Mrs Kenneth, 251 Catharine n
Cook Lewis, moulder, 175 King Wm
Cook Nicholas, moulder, 169 John n
Cook Robert L, mechanic, 5 Mill
Cook Samuel, carpenter, 34 Steven
Cook Thomas, engineer, 47 Sheaffe
Cook Thomas, clerk, 40 Main w
Cook Thomas (James Stewart & Co) 40 Main w
Cook William, weaver, 325 James n
Cook Wm, painter, 168 York
Cook Wm, caretaker market, 126 Hunter w
Cook Wm, coachman, 10 Concession
Cook Wm (J M Williams & Co) 40 Main w
Cook Wm E, plumber, 116 Hunter w
Cook Wm L, mechanic, 163 West ave n
Cookman Fred, grocer, 221 James n
Cookson Thos, machinist, 107 Napier
Coombe George, builder, 119 Rebecca
Coombs Benjamin, laborer, 27 Macnab s
Coombs David, 82 Queen s
Coombes Ephraim, nickle plater, 47 George
Coombs George, moulder, Markland s s, nr Garth
Coombs Isaac, pattern maker, hd Queen s
Coombs Jabez, nickle plater, 27 Macnab s
Coombes Jesse, laborer, Duke n s, nr Garth
Coombs Richard J, clerk, 28 Queen s
Coombs Richard S, clerk, 82 Queen s
Coombs Samuel, mechanic, 24 Jones
Coombs Wm, moulder, Markland s s, nr Garth
Cooper Albert R, printer, 41 George
Cooper Christopher, carriage painter, 41 George
Cooper Edward, laborer, 3 Garth
Cooper Mrs Eliza J (wid Henry G) 6 Park s
Cooper George, laborer, 92 Picton e
Cooper Mrs Geo, 289½ King w
Cooper Geo jr, laborer, 289½ King w
Cooper Geo W, blacksmith, 39 Alanson
Cooper Hamilton (H G Cooper & Co) 109 Market
Cooper H G & Co [W H & Hamilton Cooper) carriage builders 6 Park s
Cooper James, hair dresser, 82½ King w, h 25 Augusta
Cooper James H, 44 Hess n
Cooper John C, baby carriage manfr, 4-6 Magill
Cooper Mrs Lydia (wid Hugh) 73 Victoria ave n
Cooper Matthew, glassblower, cor King Wm and Walnut
Cooper Matthew C, glassblower, 125 King Wm
Cooper R C, grocer, 31 Macnab n, h 112 Catharine s
Cooper R T, salesman, 112 Catharine s
Cooper Thos, fruiterer, 30 King Wm
Cooper Wesley, engineer, 136 Barton e
Cooper Wm, laborer, 51 Stuart e
Cooper Wm H (H G Cooper & Co) 6 Park s
Copeland Geo, harness maker, bds 89 John s

Copeland Geo S, rope manfr, 204 Wellington n
Copeland John, carpenter, 6 Davenport
Copeland Thos, carpenter, 38 Markland
Copham Wm, moulder, 227 John n
Copley Geo C., clerk, h 89½ Hess n
Copley James, carder, 93 Murray e
Copp Alfred E, clerk, concession hd Caroline s
Copp Anthony, (Copp Bros) "West Lawn" n w cor York and Queen
Copp Bros (Anthony & Wm J) iron founders, n w cor York and Bay
Copp Harold E, cashier Copp Bros, Concession hd Caroline s
Copp Samuel E "West Lawn" n w cor York and Queen
Copp Wm J (Copp Bros) h Concession hd Caroline s
Coppins John, laborer, 3 Harriet
Corbett Thos, fireman, bds 144 Cannon e
Corbett Timothy, Oxford w s nr Barton
Corby Patrick, hostler, Flamboro House hotel
Corcoran Miss Catharine, 59 Peter
Corcoran Dennis, carpenter 51 Young
Corey Elijah W, mariner, 280 Hughson n
Corey Mrs Catharine, (wid John) 43 Vine
Corke Frederick, steam fitter, 54 Wilson
Cormack Mrs Kate (wid John) 20 Ray s
Cornell George, bartender Victoria Hotel King e

Cornell Nelson, salesman, 43 Hunter e
Cornell ——, laborer, 257 John n
Cornell Richard J, carpenter, Robinson s s nr Locke
Cornell S W, merchant, 86 James s
Cornell Mrs Susan (wid Thos) Robinson s s nr Locke
Cornell Wm, carpenter, 99 Ferrie e
Corner R, boots and shoes, 222 King e
Cornish Morris G, flour and feed 127 James n
Cornwall Wm, lumber measurer, 97½ Hunter e
Corporation Weigh Houses 366 John n, Macnab cor Stuart and Market Square
Corridi Peter, bookkeeper, 8 Peter
Corrigan John, laborer, 255 Macnab n
Corrigan John, carpenter, 175 Cannon e
Corrigan Thos, bricklayer, 236 Catharine n
Corry Hugh W, laborer, 44 Florence
Cory Mrs Fanny, 18 Herkimer
Cosgrove Patrick, laborer, 85 Simcoe e
Cosgrove Rev Philp (Roman Catholic) 244 King e
Cosgrove Wm, agent New Home sewing machine, 50 Hunter e
Cosmopolitan Hotel, John G Geiger, prop, 214-16 King w
Costello Ed, laborer, 67 Cherry
Costello Ed jr, laborer, 67 Cherry
Costello Patrick, baker, 56 Queen s
Costello Thos, printer, 26 Tisdale
Costie Hugh, tinsmith, 3 Liberty
Costie Mrs Jas (wid Wm) 3 Liberty

Costie Wm, carpenter, 3 Liberty
Cotter Daniel, tinsmith, 8 Head
Cotter Jas, tailor, 145 Park n
Cotter John, carter, 8 Head
Cotton Herbert, bricklayer, 43 Caroline n
Cotton John, builder, 2 West ave n
Cottrell Samuel, bricklayer, 41 Hannah w
Coughlan Michael, laborer, foot Victoria ave n
Coughlan Patrick, laborer, 239 Catharine n
Coulter Mrs Bella **(wid** Andrew) 151 Mary
Coulter David, **policeman, 151** Mary
Coulter John, shoemaker, **51** James n
Coulter Robt, gardener, **bds 103** King w
Coulter **Robt,** shoemaker, **87** King e
Coulter Samuel J, shoemaker, **99½** York, bds 109 Bold
Coulson Geo S, flour and feed, **46** Catharine n
Coulson Wm **H (Hord & Co)** bds 11 Mill
Coulston Samuel, blacksmith, **90** Maria
Counihan Gerald W, barber, **111** Cherry, 4½ King Wm
Counsell C M, private banker, **14** James **s, h** 1 Herkimer
Counsell G S, county clerk, Court House, 89 Jackson w
County Jail, James Ogilvie, governor, Barton e
Courteau Mrs Louisa, 31 Catharine s
Court House, Main cor John
Court Honse Hotel, (Wm Gowland propr), 57-9 John s
Cousins John, carpenter, 2 St Mary's Lane
Cousins John, messenger Bank of Commerce, 56 Walnut s

Cousins Mrs Mary, (wid **George)** No 1, r 185 Bay n
Cousins Michael, laborer, **107** Ferguson ave
Coutts Archibald, cabdriver, **15** Mulberry
Coutts John, **pattern maker, 39** Stuart e
Coutts Wm, teamster, 10 Mill
Couture John, shoemaker, **33** Mulberry
Coventry Mrs Jane, **15** Barton w
Covener Louis, pedler, 51 Little Wm
Cowan Andrew, clerk G T R, **54** Smith ave
Cowan John, 34 Ferrie w
Cowan Mrs Lucy, **(wid Peter),** 278 King **w**
Cowan Robert **D, 50½ Hunter** e
Cowan Samuel, painter, bds **165** Macnab n
Cowan Samuel, **34 Ferrie w**
Cowan Wm, platelayer, 234 Bay n
Cowell Wm, laborer, 158 **Catharine** n
Cowie James, wagonmaker, **35** Macauley e
Cowie Robert S, carpenter, **275** Macnab u
Cowie Wm, laborer, 185 **Catharine** n
Cowing **Henry,** machinist, **121** Rebecca
Cowley **Wm, laborer, bds n w cor** Dundurn **and Florence**
Cox Alfred sr, **manufacturer, 157** Wellington n
Cox Alfred J, cork factory, h 103 Murray e, 157 Wellington n
Cox Andrew J, 78 Caroline s
Cox Mrs Ann, (wid James), **147** King Wm
Cox Miss Annie **L, 78 Caroline s**
Cox Bernard, shoemaker, **240** Cannon e
Cox David, 50 **Kelly**
Cox James, laborer, **57 Young**

Cox James A, cutter, 34 Peter
Cox John, carpenter, 168 Wilson
Cox John, coffee and spice manf 25 Pearl s
Cox Thomas, furcutter, 147 King Wm
Cox William, engineer, 203 Main w
Cox Willam, laborer, bds 89 Hess n
Cox Wm, pork butcher, 139 King w
Cox Mrs Wm, 55 Young
Cox ———, carpenter, 4 Greig
Coxwill Mrs, 34 Queen s
Coy Chas, harness maker 52 Sutart e
Coyne John, laborer, 17 Sheaffe
Cracknell Thos, machinist, 119 King e
Craft Henry W, butcher, 126 Jackson w
Craft Wm, pork butcher, 50 York
Craig Alex, caretaker cemetary, hd York s s
Craig David, machinist, 18 Sophia n
Craig David, laborer, 8 Kinnell
Craig Jas, photographer, 132 Cannon e
Craig Jas, laborer, bds 209 Bay n
Craig John, carpenter, 108 Florence
Craig John, painter 65 Caroline s
Craig Joseph H, veterinary surgeon, 20 Market. h 34 Market
Crana Patrick, trackman G T R, hd York w Canal
Crankshaw Wm J, bookkeeper, 129 Rebecca
Cranston Mrs Jane, 228 John n
Craven Rev John (Roman Catholic) 244 King e
Crawford Albert, confectioner, 38 King w
Crawford Mrs Elizabeth J (wid W F) 20 Catharine s

Crawford Geo, confectioner, 38 King w
Crawford Hy, confectioner, 38 King w
Crawford Hy, carpenter, 27 Elgin
Crawford Hy, machinist, 148 Wellington n
Crawford Jas, confectioner 38 King w
Crawford John, moulder, 43 Pearl n
Crawford Mrs Mary (wid Wm G) 79 Robinson
Crawford Mrs Patrick, 27 Elgin
Crawford Rich, coachman, 24 Young
Crawford Samuel, grocer, 132 King w, h 42 Pearl n
Crawford Thos, 155 Main e
Crawford Wm, bridge inspector, 92 Park n
Crawford William, laborer, 131 Napier
Crawford Wm P, inland revenue, 93 Wellington n
Crawley Wm O, salesman, 66 Robinson
Crear Donald, tailor, 179 John n
Creel Henry, 169 Macnab n
Creighton Mrs Margaret (wid David) 255 Hughson n
Crerar John (Crerar, Muir & Crerar) county attorney, h Merksworth, n e cor Macnab and Herkimer
Crerar, Muir & Crerar John Crerar, John Muir, M A, P D Crerar, M A) barristers, Hamilton Provident Chambers, 1 Hughson s
Crerar Peter, carpenter, South w, n s
Crerar P D, M A, (Crerar, Muir & Crerar) h 149 James s
Cresswell Mrs Eliza, 29 Simcoe e
Creswell Miss Rebecca, 164 Jackson w

Crier Philip, shoemaker, 22 Mulberry
Crilly Patrick, merchant tailor, 17 Market Square
Cripps Charles, builder, 52 Steven
Cripps Daniel, bricklayer, 215 Cannon e
Cripps Joseph, laborer, 65 Steven
Crisp Alfred C, clerk P O, 27 Erie ave
Crisp Mrs Elizabeth, 25 Erie ave
Crisp Mrs Elizabeth (wid Thos) 159 Hunter w
Crisp James, locksmith, 95 King w
Crist Alfred, glassblower, 243 Catharine n
Crist Samuel, glassblower, 19 Stuart e
Critchley William, teamster, 99 Mary
Crites Geo A, contractor, 44 Erie ave
Croal George, blacksmith, 67 Emerald n
Crockett Mrs Emma (wid John M) toll gate keeper, Main, e of Wentworth
Crockett, Muirhead & Co (Wilson Crockett and Walter Muirhead) Wentworth Canning House, s e cor Queen and Peter
Crockett Wm, bookbinder, 105 West ave n
Crockett Wilson, (Crockett Muirhead & Co) h Mountain brow
Croft John, driver, 91½ Locke n
Crofton Edward, grocer, 265 John n
Crofton E J, painter, 62 Bay n, h 24 Elgin
Crofton Mrs Honora (wid Martin) Barton w, s s, nr Locke
Crofton Walter, moulder, Barton w s s nr Locke

Crombie Mrs Elspeth (wid Francis) 74 Cannon w
Cron John, stableman, 102 Jackson e
Croyne Daniel, carter, 249 James n
Croyne Dennis, hackman, 249 James n
Crooks Alex, dairyman, 60 Hannah w
Crooks James, prop The Brunswick, 7-9 King Wm
Crooks John, laborer, 106 Queen n
Crooks Mrs Margaret (wid Frank) 35 Hughson n
Crooks Mrs Mary Ann (wid Richard) Barton w s s nr Crooks
Crooks Richard, bartender, 9 King Wm
Crooks Thos, 32 Queen n
Cross Albert, basketmaker, 97 East ave n
Cross Arthur, tea merchant, 175 John n
Cross Mrs Eliza, 27 Simcoe w
Cross Miss Hattie, dressmaker, 34 Hunter e
Cross & McConnell Misses, dressmakers, 34 Hunter e
Cross Moses, carter, 105½ Jackson e
Cross Robt, moulder, 58 Lower Cathcart
Cross Thos, laborer, 16 Guise
Cross Wm, toll gate keeper, hd York
Cross Wm sr, trackman G T R hd York w canal
Crossland Walter, cigar maker, 132 Bay n
Crossley Irving, dry goods, James cor King Wm, h 4 Nelson ave
Crossley John, merchant, 73 Herkimer
Crossley Wm, dry goods, 73 Herkimer

Croslin John, laborer, 297 John n
Crossman Adam, laborer, r 77 Cannon w
Crossman Wm M, painter, 117 Hess n
Crotty Mrs Bridget, 249 Mary n
Crotty Patrick, carpenter, 247 Mary n
Crowe Alfred, machinist, 161 Mary
Crowe Robt, machinist, Robinson s s nr Garth
Crowe Wm, cigarmaker, 161 Mary
Crowley Wm J, potatoe merchant, 114 York
Crowther W T M, music teacher, 172 McNab n
Cropper John, stovemounter, Wentworth n
Croxford David H, coachman Rennoch Lodge, hd of John s
Croy Wm B, com traveler, 109 Bay n
Crozier Rich, laborer, 108 Jackson e
Cruikshank Alex S, teacher, 18 Vine
Cruickshank John, policeman, 150 Wellington n
Cruickshanks John, stonemason, 167 Hunter w
Cruickshank Robert, builder and contractor, h 47 Maria, 55 Jackson e
Crystal Palace, Locke n, opp Peter
Cuckow Edwine, shipper, 77 Stinson
Cuff Robert C, butcher, 309 York
Cuff Thos, engineer, 65 Napier
Culham Joseph A, (Bruce, Burton & Culham), "West Lawn," n w cor York and Queen
Culhane Patrick J, billposter, 42 Cannon e
Culhane Stephen, billposter, 42 Cannon e
Culican John, laborer, 16 Picton w
Culican Matthew, painter, 20 **Picton** w
Culican Peter, carpenter, 20 Picton w
Cullen Michael, laborer, 82 Macauley e
Cullinan Mrs Sarah, 101 Caroline n
Cullon Arthur, laborer, 69 Simcoe e
Cullum **David**, carpenter, 2 Ferguson ave
Cullum Miss Mary, dressmaker, 2 Ferguson ave
Culm Wm, laborer, 126 Picton e
Culp Isaac H, machinist, 185 King e, h 139 Main e
Culp Jacob, wheel maker, 162 Catharine n
Culp Matthew, laborer, bds 202 James n
Culp Sylvester, laborer, bds 202 James n
Cumbers Wm, bookkeeper, 168 Macnab n
Cummer J H, (Grant & Son), h 89 Wellington n
Cummer W L, (Grant & Son), h 123 Bay n
Cumming Bros, grocers, 112 James n
Cumming John, cutter, 131 King w
Cumming Wm, (Cumming Bros) h 110 James n
Cummings, Mrs Catharine, grocer, 245-247 King e
Cummings Cornelius, laborer, 186 Emerald n
Cummings James, tax collector, 158 Main e
Cummings John, malster, 117 Macnab n
Cummings Maurice, engineer, 244 Bay n

Cummings Thomas, porter, 247 King e
Cunard Steamship Line, W J Grant, agent, 33 James n
Cunningham Mrs Alice, (wid Michael), 75 Young
Cunningham Arthur, watchman, 42 Cannon w
Cunningham Geo, broom sorter, bds 55 York
Cunningham John, bread peddler, 52 Robert
Cunningham Samuel, teamster, 87 Cannon e
Cunningham Samuel, conductor, 136 Wellington n
Cunningham, W H, marine engineer, bds 76 John n
Cunningham Wm, teamster, foot of Macnab n
Cunningham Wm J, clerk, bds 76 John n
Curell Archibald, blacksmith, bds 215 James n
Currell Crawford, stovemounter, 60 Lower Cathcart
Curell J G, barrister, 34 James n, h 140 Cannon e
Curran John, printer, Dundurn e s nr York
Curran Mrs Margaret, (wid Jacob) 83 Main e
Curran Patrick, laborer, 33 Wood e
Curran Richard, laborer, King e of Wentworth
Curran Rev Cannon Wm, rector St Thomas Church, 240 King e
Currie Robert, carpenter, r 39 Ray n
Curry Edward, porter, 25 Cannon e
Curry George, checker G T R, 106 Bold
Curry Robert, dyer, 54 Robert
Curry Wm D, engineer G T R, 10 Greig
Curtin Mrs Ellen, 289 James n

Curtis Thomas, tailor, 93 Maria
Curtis Wm, cigar maker, 50 Cannon w
Cuscak Mrs Elizabeth, (wid P R) 79 Elgin
Cusack Mrs Mary J, (wid Wm), 11 Mulberry
Cuseck Wm, laborer, Robinson s s nr Garth
Cusha Mrs Mary, 71 Hannah e
Cushen Geo, butcher, 62 James s
Cusheon Henry, cutter, bds Victoria Hotel, King e
Cushing William, moulder, 130 East ave n
Custom House, 2 John s
Custom House Hotel, (G Goering propr), 17 John s
Cutbrush Mrs Annie, dressmaker 292 Macnab n
Cutler Archibald, polisher, 188 Robert
Cutler Charles, woodworker, 277 King e
Cuthberton Alex, grocer, 210 King w
Cutt James, cutter, 86 Hunter w
Cuttriss Edward W, carpenter, Wentworth n
Cuttriss Engraving Co., (Geo H Cuttriss, mangr), 28 John n
Cuttriss Fredrick W, upholsterer, 138 Main e
Cuttris Geo H, mangr Cuttriss Engraving Co, 63 Wellington n
Cuttris, Mrs Mary A, (wid Wm) 138 Main e
Cuzner John, hide and wool dealer, 15 York
Cuzner Luke, tinsmith, 13 Lower Cathcart
Dabb Mrs Christina, (wid Louis) 26 Peter
Dack Samuel, laborer, bds 65 Park n
Daily Wm, tailor, 35 Park n
Dake M J, hotel, 228 James n
Daley Ed, laborer, 13 Macauley w

Daley Michael, laborer, 36 Macaulay e
Daley Mrs Olivia (wid John) 125 Market
Daley Timothy, shedman G T R 32 Inchbury n
Dallas Donald, rubber 172 York
Dallas Mrs Eliza, 5a West ave s
Dallas Hy, com traveller, 25 Wellington s
Dalley E A (F F Dalley & Co) h 34 Elgin
Dalley Fenner F (F F Dalley & Co) 41 Jackson w
Dalley F F & Co, Hamilton Chemical Works, 99 James n
Dalley Mrs Maria (wid Edmund) 132 John s
Dallyn Mrs Ann, 170 James n
Dallyn Charles hairdresser, 33 James n, h 166 West ave n
Dallyn Frederick E, bookkeeper, 90 Stinson
Dalton Albert, flagman, 104 West ave n
Dalton Andrew, moulder, 15 Hess s
Dalton Jas, laborer, 199 Mary n
Dalton Patrick, laborer, 261 Hughson n
Dalton Thos S, ship builder, 59 Robert
Daly Hugh, Eagle House hotel, 30 and 32 Cannon w
Daly Jas, 87 Murray e
Daly John, railroader, 101 Locke n
Daly John, yardsman G T R, 18 Locomotive
Daly Wm, tailor, 50 Wood e
Dance Hy St John, laborer, 125 Queen n
Danforth **Benj** M, nailer, 51 Caroline n
Danger John, hostler, 67 John s
Daniel Jas, 46 Markland
Daniels Bernard, 1 Young
Daniels Edward, cutter, 44 Locomotive

Daniels Geo, fireman G T R, 124 Napier
Daniels Geo, tailor, 44 **Locomotive**
Daniels Mrs Jane (wid Thos) 61 Mary
Daniels Wesley, millwright, 56 Pearl s
Darby Alfred W, laborer, 39 Little Wm
Darby Richard G, machinist, 123 Caroline n
Darche Robt, conductor, 145 Robert
Darc Wm, file cutter, bds 54 Gore
Darling J B, clerk, Cherry
Danbreville Frederick, scalemaker, 14 Mill
Davey Mrs Ann (wid Wm) 38 West ave n
Davey Geo H, asst manager News Co, G T R, s w cor Sophia and York
Davey Wm, carpenter, 6 Bruce
Davey Mrs Wm, 36 West ave n
Davidson Alex, accountant, 2½ James s, h 3a West ave s
Davdison Duncan, laborer, 127 Locke n
Davidson Edward, jeweler, bds 48 James n
Davidson Mrs E H, 60 James s
Davidson Geo, laborer, r 61 Jackson e
Davidson Mrs Isabella (wid John F) 66 Caroline s
Davidson Jas, goldsmith and manufacturing jeweler, 78 King e, h 62 Herkimer
Davidson Jas H, com traveller, 46 Main w
Davidson John, collector, 166 Bay n
Davidson John, salesman, 8 Hess n
Davidson Mrs Margaret (wid Robt) teacher Collegiate Instiaute, 66 Duke

Davidson Thos, cashier Canada Life Assurance Co, 3a West ave s
Davidson Thos, laborer, 328 James n
Davidson Thos, machinist, bds 17 Caonon w
Davies E R, grocer, cor Hughson and Barton
Davies Harry, salesman, 129 John s
Davies Jas, blacksmith, r 42 Hughson n
Davies Jas M, foreman E & C Gurney Co, 19 West ave n
Davies Mrs John, 44 Main w
Davis Allan, clerk, 124 Main e
Davis Mrs Ann (wid Wm) 7 Canada
Davis Archibald, 124 Main e
Davis & Burt, dentists, 68 King e
Davis C A, Davis & Burt, h 44 Emerald s
Davis Calvin, reporter *Spectator*, 124 Main e
Davis Chas A, com traveller, 25 Young
Davis Ebenezer, asst supt Ontario Rolling Mills Co, bds 26 Ray n
Davis Ed, porter, 183 Main e
Davis Mrs Eleanor (wid Thos) 266 Mary n
Davis Frank, fish dealer, Aikman ave
Davis Fred, com traveller, Main e
Davis Geo, canfectioner, 77 Cannon w
Davis George fitter, Dundurn s s nr York
Davis Mrs Hannah (wid Warren) 127 Wellington n
Davis Mrs H C, 20 Maria
Davis Henry, tailor, 129 John s
Davis Henry jr, porter, 129 John s
Davis H H, com traveller, Wentworth s

Davis H N C, market clerk, 44 East ave s
Davis Isaac, blacksmith, 74 East ave n
Davis James F, nickelplater, 160 Catharine n
Davis James G, market clerk, 44 East ave s
Davis James G, 239 Maine e
Davies J M, foreman, E & C Gurney Co
Davis Jonathan, 194 Main e
Davis John, brickmaker, 193 Main w
Davis John, Aikman ave
Davis John, 129 John s
Davis John, bds 55 York
Davis John E, machinist, 102 Barton e
Davis John H, Wentworth s
Davis John N, crockery, 51 Macnab and 62 York n
Davis Joseph, butcher, 104 James n
Davis Joseph, butcher, 41 Stuart e
Davis Mrs J R, 25 Young
Davis Loyal, carpenter, 129 Locke n
Davis & McCullough, (W R Davis, J D McCullough) watchmakers & jewellers, 12 King w
Davis N H, issuer of marriage license, 6 James s, h 64 Jackson w
Davis Nicholas, bellman, 85 Rebecca
Davis Peter, 41 Macaulay n
Davis Robert, car checker, 217 Victoria ave n
Davis Samuel, market clerk, 60 Catharine s
Davis Samuel, 44 East ave s
Davis Thomas, com traveler, 8 Grove
Davis Thos E, clerk, Wentworth s
Davis Walter, laborer, Aikman ave

CITY OF HAMILTON.

Davis Walter L, market clerk, 44 East ave s
Davis Wm, photographer, bds 45 Wilson
Davis Wm J, blacksmith, 72 East ave n
Davis W R, (Davis & McCullough), h 37 Hannah w
Davis W, head master Victoria st school, 68 Bay s
Davison Alfred, cigarmaker, 6 Evans
Davis Mrs Clara, (wid Thomas), 151 John s
Davison Samuel, moulder, bds 37 Catharine n
Davison Wm, tailor, 24 Locke s
Dawe George, blacksmith, 35 Magill
Dawe James, polisher, 35 Magill
Dawe Wm, letter carrier, 35 Magill
Dawes Thomas, mechanic, 13 Oxford
Dawson Donald, tax collector, 144 Hunter e
Dawson John, laborer, 257 York
Dawson Meredith, letter carrier, 8 Concession
Dawson Robt, baker, 217 James n
Day Edward, laborer, ft Ferguson ave
Day Frank T, com traveller, 51 Wellington s
Day John, shoemaker 280 James n
Day Joseph, porter, 6 Tisdale
Dayfoot P W, 219 Main e
Deacon G, law student, bds 190 Macnab n
Dean Anson, machinist, Shaw
Dean Francis, sr, brick manfr, Robinson s s nr Garth
Dean Francis, jr, brick maker Robinson s s nr Garth
Dean Harry, machinist, bds 122 Cannon e
Dean Henry, laborer, 280 Macnab n

Dean Mrs Joanna, 78 Bold
Dean Jonn, laborer, 7 Little Wellington
Dean Levi, com traveller, 58 Vine
Dean Wm, shoemaker, 58 Peter
Dean Wm H, com traveller, 3 Caroline s
Dearden Richard, shipper, bds Bold s s opp Ray
Deary Robt, mechanic, 203 James n
Death Henry, laborer, 69 Main w
Debus Mrs Annie, (wid Wm J), 183 Napier
DeCew Egerton, Sec Ontario Canning Co, 44 Victoria ave s
Deegan Edward, burnisher, bds 142 Cannon e
Deeley Frank, huckster, 62 Oak ave
Defour Alfred, wiremaker, 139 Jackson w
Degarmo Mrs Martha, 128 Cannon e
Deleaney James, laborer, 7 Strachan w
Deleany Wm, moulder, 7 Strachan w
Delanty Mrs Ellen, 165 Macnab n
Delmonico Hotel, And Dillon, propr, 21 John n
Delorme Cyprian, carriagemaker, 130 Macnab n
Dempsey George, ins agent, 112 Main w
Dempsey Joseph H C, clerk P O 112 Main w
Dempster Charles H, (Brayley & Dempster), 13 Young
Demun Mrs Elida, broker, 42 King Wm
Demun Hiram, whitewasher, 42 King Wm
Denbury Thomas, laborer, 230 Barton e
Dench George, freight agent, N & N W, 112 Mary

Denew John, engineer, 75 James s
Denison Geo, moulder, 204 Cannon e
Denison Geo H, agent, 77 Hughson n
Dennis George, carter, 72 Jackson e
Dennis Mrs George H, Dundurn, w s nr York
Dennis James, shoemaker, h 15 Lower Cathcart, 54a Wellington n
Dennis John B, painter, 52 Canada
Dent John, driver, 54 Pearl s
Derby William, buffer, 60 East ave n
Dermody Mrs Ann (wid Patrick) baker, 151 Main e
Dermody Frank, **bread** pedler, 151 Main e
Dermody John, baker, 151 Main e
Dermody Wm, porter, 300 John n
Deronde Emile, laster, 128 Young
Derrick Townsend J, tobacco roller, 8 Napier
Derrington Mrs Emeretta (wid Thos) 3 Walnut s
Desmond **John, gas** stoker, 181 Bay n
Deutscher Paul, file **cutter, 81** Bold
Devine Mrs Jane (wid Edward) 182 Catharine n
Devine John, moulder, 102 Victoria ave n
Devine John, shoemaker, 152 **York**
Devine Maurice, moulder, 106 Hess n
Dew John, **laborer,** 37 Caroline n
Dewar Mrs Emily (wid Plummer) 31 Jackson w
Dewar Ernest, coachman A G Ramsey
Dewar Henry, laborer, bds 74 John s

Dewart Wm, laborer, 30 Wellington n
Dewey Daniel (D Dewey & Son) 11 Caroline s
Dewey D R (D R Dewey & Co) h Caroline cor George
Dewey D R & Co, coal dealers, 12 James s, yard Wellington and GTR track
Dewey D R & Co, publishers of first sides for Canadian weekly newspapers, 3 Hughson n
Dewey **D &** Son (Daniel & John W) ice dealers, 15 George
Dewey John W (D Dewey & Son) bds Franklin house
De Witt Edwin A, grocer, 87½-89 Victoria ave n
De Witt Hiram, porter, 79 Ray s
Dexter David, managing director Federal Life Assurance Co, h 31 East ave e
De Zocher Rev Gustave, Lutheran pastor, 74 Hughson n
Diack Wm, miller, 91 Main w
Diamond Andrew J, machinist, 103 Elgin
Dick David, fireman, 132 Victoria ave n
Dick Mrs Elizabeth (wid Peter) 48 Locomotive
Dick George, laborer, 356 John n
Dickenson Mrs **Mary** [wid **Chas]** 48½ Augusta
Dickenson Robert **T, engineer,** 174 Victoria ave **n**
Dickenson Thomas, 252 James n
Dicker Mrs Francis, 59 Young
Dicker Wm, shoemaker, 81½ King **e,** bds 43 Jackson e
Dickinson Benjamin, laborer, 89 Hunter w
Dickinson Robt T, engineer, 150 Duke
Dickman Mrs Eliza [wid Alexander] 78 Hughson s
Dickson Magnus, **machinist,** Hopkin

Dickson M C, 143 James n
Dickson John M, manfr chemist, 76 Hannah w
Dickson William, **carpenter**, 62 Duke
Dickson W, salesman, 28 Peter
Didman James, butcher, 56-58 Hunter e
Dill Mrs Julia [wid Wm] hd Queen s, e s
Dillabough Edmund H, M D, 18 Gore
Dillon Andrew, prop Delmonico hotel, 21 John n, h 215 Bay n
Dillon Benjamin, moulder, 21 John n
Dillon James, grocer, 159 Bay n
Dillon James M, Nautilus hotel, 262 Macnab n
Dillon James S, hotel, 261 John n
Dillon John, grocer, 159 Bay n
Dillon John, machinist, 23 Ferrie e
Dillon John, moulder, 21 John n
Dillon Joseph, clerk, 13 Cannon w
Dillon Joseph, laborer, 117 Maria
Dillon Patrick, laborer, 93 Hannah e
Dillon Patrick, laborer, 17 Murray e
Dillon Wm, coachman, 40 Markland
Dillon Wm, Eclipse hotel, 209 Bay n
Dillon Wm, glassblower, 261 John n
Dillon William, laborer, 165½ Bay n
Dilworth James, laborer, 39 Wood w
Dingle Wm, potter, bds West
Dingle Wm B, machinist, 88 Wellington n
Dingmon Henry, clerk, 71 Locke n
Dingmon Peter, shoemaker, 71 Locke n

Dingman John, carpenter, 40 Mulberry
Dingwall Alexander, stonecutter, r 57½ York
Dingwall Alexander, jr, machinist 160 Hughson n
Dingwall Mrs Alexander, 162 Hughson n
Dingwall James M, machinist, 93 Napier
Dinsse H, clerk P O
Disher Mrs Amy [wid John] 24 Hunter e
Dittrick Fred, bender, 167 East ave n
Ditty James, tinsmith, 60 Steven
Dixon Bros [Wm and James] wholesale and retail fruiterers, wholesale 33 King e, retail 6 King w
Dixon Charles J, clerk, 100 Jackson w
Dixon Daniel, teamster, 95 Bay n
Dixon Herbert A L, chief landing waiter customs, 4 **Hess** s
Dixon James [Dixon Bros] 37 East ave s
Dixon John, knitter, 115 York
Dixon John, pattern maker, 176 King w
Dixon Mrs Lucy, grocer, 176 King w
Dixon Mrs Millie [wid Henry] 29 Mary
Dixon Thomas I, mechanic, 59 Napier
Dixon William [Dixon Bros] 35 East ave s
Dixon Mrs Wm, 47 Wellington n
Doak Simeral, blacksmith, 32½ Hunter e, h 26 Augusta
Dobbie Oliver, watchman, 334 Macnab n
Dobson John, stovemounter, 213 Bay n
Dobson William, 35½ Catharine n
Dodd George, piano finisher, 294 York

Dodd Henry, laborer, 32 Little Wm
Dodds Miss Isabell, fancy goods, 110 James n
Dodds Robert, stonecutter, 23 Elgin
Dodge Wm, laborer, 32 Little Wm
Dodman Frederick J, grocer, 58 Caroline s
Dodman James, agent, 38 Caroline s
Dodson Bros [John R and James] brass founders, 92 Macnab n
Dodson Hector, whip lash maker, 183 Bay n
Dodson James [Dodson Bros] h 16 Barton e
Dodson John R [Dodson Bros] h 161 West ave n
Dodson Joseph, printer, 118 Catharine n
Dodson Wm, paper hanger, 29 John n, h 65 Victoria ave n
Doherty Arthur, grocer, chemist and druggist, 245 King w
Doherty Mrs Hester, 2 Park s
Doherty Hugh, engineer, 296 Macnab n
Doherty John, stonemason, 60 Locke s
Doherty Patrick, moulder, 119 Victoria ave n
Doherty Peter, laborer, 108½ Simcoe e
Doherty Thomas, tea and coffee dealer, 63 Cannon e
Doherty Thos, jr, tea and coffee dealer, 63 Cannon e
Doherty ——, laborer, 133½ Ferrie e
Dolan Mrs Hannah [wid Michael] 133 John n
Dolan Jas, teamster, 133 John n
Dolan John, teamster, 109 Ferrie e
Doll Clemence, laborer, 108 Caroline s

Dolman David, sen, driver, Herkimer n s, nr Garth
Dolman David jr, driver, Herkimer n s, w Locke
Dolman Samuel, laborer, 48 Burlington w
Domville C K, chief mechanical engineer GTR, 27 Main w
Domville Fred J, supt GTR, 114 Rebecca
Domville Herbert T, mechanical engineer GTR, 27 Main w
Dominion Furniture Co, 122 King e
Dominion Hat Co, Jas Walker prop, John Tunstead mangr, 260-4 King e
Dominion Hotel, Caughell & Weaver, props, 80-82 King w
Dominion Plate Glass Insurance Office, David McLellan, agent, 84 James n
Dominion Shirt Factory, S G Treble, prop, 2 King e
Dominion Steamship Line, David McLellan, agent, 84 James n
Donald Alexander, bottler, 53 Sheaffe
Donald James, engineer, bds 228 York
Donald Mrs Jane [wid Wm] 4 Burlington n
Donald John, laborer, 186 Jackson w
Donald Mrs, 4 Burlington n
Donald Wm, laborer, 188 Main w
Donaldson David, laborer, bds 166 Bay n
Donaldson Hugh, builder, 93 Bay s
Donaldson John, carpenter, 236 King w
Donaldson John, engineer, 15 Caroline s
Donaldson John, engineer, 105 Cherry
Donaldson & Paterson, builders, n w cor Hannah and Bay

Donlay Luke, cabinetmaker, 32 Colborne
Donnelly Patrick, laborer, 245 John n
Donnelly Patrick, 277 Hughson n
Donnell ——, painter, bds 103 King w
Donnovan John, blacksmith, 44 Pearl s
Donohoe Mrs Agnes [wid Francis] Wentworth n
Donohoe Alexander, shoemaker, Wentworth n
Donohue Dennis, laborer, 298 Macnab n
Donohoe Ebenezer, butcher, Wentworth n
Donohoe Michael, tinsmith, 116 West ave n
Donohue Patrick, blacksmith, 11 Ferrie e
Donohoe Stephen, laborer, r 61 Jackson e
Donohoe Thomas, shoemaker, 24 Tisdale
Donohoe Wm, machinist, Wentworth n
Donovan Cornelius, inspector separate schools, 74 Maria
Donovan Cornelius, moulder, 135 York
Donovan Jeremiah, laborer, 190 King Wm
Donovan Jeremiah, tailor, 71 Cherry
Donovan Mrs Mary [wid Wm] 34 Caroline n
Donovan Michael, hackman, 13 Hunter w
Donovan Randolph, 63 Burlington w
Dooley James, tuner, bds 84 King w
Doolittle Chas E, president Ontario Rolling Mill Co, 46 Bay s
Door Ernest, coachman, 2 Markland

Doran Bros (Michael and Wm) vinegar manfrs, 31 Stuart
Dordy Mrs Mary (wid Patrick) 271 Macnab n
Doran Mrs Mary (wid Peter) 11 Hess n
Doran Michael (Doran Bros) bds cor James and Stuart
Doran Wm (Doran Bros) h 189 Macnab n
Doran Wm, carter, 154 Napier
Doran & Wright Co, C F Abraham, correspondent, 18 James s
Dore James, laborer, 20 Little Market
Dorman George, laborer, 74 Locke n
Doston Mrs Mary J, dressmaker, 111 Herkimer
Dougall Andrew, machinist, 95 Elgin
Dougherty Michael, laborer, 81 Emerald s
Douglas Robert, glassblower, 326 Macnab n
Douglas Robert, moulder, 15 Devonport
Douglas Summerfield (Imperial Straw Works) 18 Augusta
Douse Mrs Deborah (wid Henry) 172 Jackson w
Douse Patrick, laborer, 172 Jackson w
Dow David, contractor, 31 Bold
Dow Henry (H and J Dow) 18 Canada
Dow H & J, (Henry & John) wood and coal dealers, 45 Main w
Dow John, buffer, 149 Wellington n
Dow John [H & J Dow] 41 Hess s
Dow Moses, plasterer, 18 Canada
Dowe Richard, cooper, bds 65 Stuart w
Dow Robert, plasterer, 36 Ray s

Dow Robert H M, steam fitter, 31 Bold
Dow Wm, bookbinder, 18 Canada
Dow Wm Y, moulder, hd Garth w s
Dowd Patrick, laborer, 86 Simcoe e
Dowd Wm, laborer, 145 Bay n
Dowden James, whitewasher, 30a Catharine s
Dowe John, cooper, 70 Hess n
Dowle Richard, clerk GTR, 230 Macnab n
Dowling Albert, scalemaker, 151 Wellington n
Dowling Edward, boilermaker, 5 Sophia s, nr King
Dowling Mrs Mary [wid Peter] dry goods, 85 John s
Dowling Peter, jr, tobacco roller, 85 John s
Downing Edward, carpenter, 176 Jackson w
Downing James O, whitewasher, 152 John n
Downs Daniel, blacksmith, 17 Kelly
Downs Mrs Lina, 17 Kelly
Downs Wm, photographer, 94 Emerald n
Dowrie David, carpenter, 61 Queen s
Dowrie David C, letter carrier, Bruce e s nr Markland
Dowrie John, carpenter, 47 Caroline s
Dowrie Wm, carpenter, 59 Queen s
Dowsan George, mechanic, 153 Bay n
Dowswell George, mechanic, 153 Bay n
Doxey Cornelius, mechanic, r 241 Bay n
Doyle Anthony, laborer, 111 Maria
Doyle Brian, detective, 208 King William

Doyle Cornelius, moulder, 102 Wellington
Doyle Daniel, wagon maker, 89 Macnab n
Doyle Daniel, sr, wagon maker, 89 Macnab n
Doyle Edward, laborer, r 79 Cannon w
Doyle Mrs Ellen [wid John] 23 Wood w
Doyle James, mariner, Brock
Doyle Mrs Jane [wid John] r 194 King Wm
Doyle John, packer, 385 John n
Doyle J E, grocer, 220 James n, h 165 Hughson n
Doyle Luke, Commercial hotel, s w cor York and Park
Doyle M, baggage master, 163 Bay n
oyle Mallack, baggagemaster G TR, 36 Stuart e
Doyle Mrs Margaret [wid John] 29 Railway
Doyle Patrick, moulder, 97 Young
Doyle Patrick, tailor, 24 Little Market
Doyle Philip, laborer, 17 Burlington w
Doyle Thomas, laborer, 369 Hughson n
Doyle Thomas, laborer, 15 Wood e
Drake Amos E, foreman Cotton mills, 190 Macnab n
Drake Robert F, packer, 50 Tisdale
Draper Mrs Sarah [wid John] Nightingale
Dreaver Wm, carpenter, 349 John n
Dreaver Thos, laborer, 7 Macauley w
Dresch Frederick, tinsmith, bds 35 Hughson n
Dressel J A, hotel, 41 Macnab n
Drever Thomas, carpenter, 299 John n

Drew Alfred F, carpenter, 18 Herkimer n s w Locke
Drew Chas, tinsmith, 28 York, h 30 Napier
Drew Louis, tinsmith, bds 55 York
Drew Mrs Lydia, 30 Napier
Drewett Geo, butcher, 44 Ray s, h Maple
Drinnon Mrs Ahn (wid Wm) 42 Hughson n
Driscoll John, laborer, 46 Robinson
Drope Henry T, printer, 129 Market
Dryden James, driver, 7 George
Dryden Wm, ale bottler, r 100 James n, h 355 John n
Dryland Edward, painter, 69 Napier
Dryland Mrs Margaret [wid John] 15 Mill
Drysdale Alexander, passenger agent C & A R R, 181 Main e
Drysdale John, government engineer, 77 Catharine s
Drsdale Mrs Sarah, ironer, 182 Napier
Dublin Joshua, whitewasher, 28 Augusta
Duff Chas [John Duff & Son] h 142 York
Duff George H, saleman, 144 York
Duff J B, clerk, 49 Caroline n
Duff John [John Duff & Son] 144 York
Duff John L, organist Congregational Church, 142 York
Duff John & Son [John & Chas Duff] grocers and butchers, 144-6 York and s w cor Bay and Duke
Duff W A H, barristers, Victoria Chambers, 31 James s, h Mountain top, hd James s *see card*
Duffield Edward, bookkeeper, 141 York

Duffield Harry, clerk, 141 York
Duffield Mrs Jane C [wid Sam'l] 92 Bay s
Duffield Mrs Mary [wid Wm H] 141 York
Duffield W S, bookkeeper, 38 Herkimer
Duffy Mrs Ann, 187 Hughson
Duffy Mrs Bridget [wid Thomas] 29 Park n
Duffy Mrs E, fancy goods, 53 Macnab n
Duffy F J, mangr Royal Roller Rink, 70 Ray n
Duffy James, machinist, 50 Lower Cathcart
Duffy Mrs Jane [wid John] 83 Peter
Duffy John, gardener, Wentworth n
Duffy John, clerk St Nicholas hotel, 150 Bay n
Duffy John, com traveler, 68 Ray n
Duffy Michael, moulder, 252 Hughson n
Duffy Patrick, blacksmith, 70 Ray n
Duffy Patrick, farmer, 150 Bay n
Duffy Peter, hotel, 55 Macnab n
Duffy Thomas, carpenter, 48 Stuart e
Dufton James, bricklayer, 138 Barton e
Duggan Arthur, brickmaker, King w nr limits
Duggan Fred, shoemaker, 118 Cannon e
Duggan Jas C. tailor, 26 Ferrie e
Duggan Mrs Libby (wid John) 29 Bay n
Duggan Mrs Lucy (wid James) 107 Cannon w
Duggan Mrs Margaret (wid John) laundress, 81 Hunter w
Duggan Mrs Mary (wid Martin) 181 King Wm
Duggan Thomas A, clerk, 135½ Park n

Duley Frank, laborer, 5 Garth
Dummer Henry F, fireman, 18 Simcoe e
Dummer Wm, glassblower, 182 Macnab n
Dummer Wm, glassblower, 28 Strachan w
Dunbar Alexander, moulder, bds 57 John s
Dunbar Charles, laborer, 73 Bay n
Dunbar Michael, carpenter, 3 Oak ave
Dunbar Patrick, **carpenter**, 3 Oak ave
Duncan Alex, clerk, 54 Hunter w
Duncan Mrs Alice (wid Chas) 39 Charles
Duncan Bros (Chas and Henry) wholesale teas and coffees, 71 King e
Duncan Charles (Duncan Bros) h 16 Wilson
Duncan David, machinist, Maple s s nr Locke
Duncan Edward, laborer, Dundurn w s nr King
Duncan George, **laborer**, 5 Nightingale
Duncan George, 8 Pearl s
Duncan Henry [Duncan Bros] 59 George
Duncan Lithographing Co, R Duncan, prop, James cor Market square
Duncan R, (R Duncan & Co) h Charles cor Jackson
Duncan Robert & Co, booksellers and stationers, James cor Market Square
Duncan Thos, laborer, 73 Peter
Duncan Mrs Thos, 76 Jackson w
Duncan William, gardener, 147 Duke
Duncan Wm E, manager Hamilton Coffee and Spice Mills, bds 8 Hess n
Dundon John, carpenter, 125 Catharine n

Dundon Wm, laborer, 229 Mary n
Dundurn Hotel, Jas Little prop, cor York and Locke
Dunford Thos, laborer, Maple s s nr Locke
Dunkerley Mrs Elizabeth (wid **John**) 101 Caroline s
Dunlop David, harness maker, 78-80 John s, h 68 Walnut s
Dunlop Hy, clerk, 78 Walnut s
Dunlop James, flour and feed, 107-9 John s, h 69 Hunter e
Dunlop Robt, ins agent, 36 Catharine n
Dunn Alexander, prop St Nicholas hotel, 35-41 James n
Dunn Bros (John and William) **butchers**, 227 **James n**
Dunn **Chas** M, stableman, 20 Market
Dunn Mrs Ellen (wid John) Barton w ss nr Locomotive
Dunn Geo P, spice miller, Caroline s e s nr Markland
Dunn James H, mechanic, 8 Nightingale
Dunn John, butcher, 227 Jas n
Dunn John, laborer, 37 Wood e
Dunn John (Russell & Dunn) 190 Hughson n
Dunn John, 190 Hughson n
Dunn Lawrence laborer, 52 Wood e
Dunn Mrs Margaret, dressmaker, 111 Park n
Dunn **Mrs** Mary, 86 Macnab n
Dunn Stephen, foreman McKay's wharf, 25 Guise
Dunn Thos, **laborer**, 13 Burlington e
Dunn W G & Co, Canada Coffee and Spice Mills, 57 Main w
Dunn W G (W G Dunn & Co) n w cor Queen and Main
Dunn Wm, butcher, 227 James n
Dunnett Ed H, clerk P O, 6 Kelly

Dunnett Mrs Eliza, 34 East ave n
Dunnett Geo, moulder, 124 Wilson
Dunnett Hy B, carpenter, 3 Ferguson ave
Dunning Thos, teamster, 60 Young
Dunphy Jas, 87 York
Dunsford W H, receiving teller, Bank of Commerce, bds 14 Caroline s
Dunsmore Jas, driver, 151 Duke
Dunsmore Wm S, porter 140 Duke
Dunstan Kenneth J, city agent Bell Telephone Co, 1 Hughson s, h 159 James s
Dunstan R J, com traveller, 165 James n
Dunn Wiman & Co, G J Williams, manager, 3 Hughson s
Dunard Alex, carpenter, 122 Wellington n
Dunard Geo, machinist, bds 56 King Wm
Dunard Jas, presser, bds 56 King Wm
Dunard John, telegraph messenger, bds 56 King Wm
Dundan Wm, engineer, 171 John n
Durfey John A, carpenter, 50 Emerald n
Durham Daniel, axe maker, 1 Mill
Durling Albert G, brickmaker, Herkimer s s w Locke
Durling Wm, laborer, Duke s s w Locke
Durphy Geo, carpenter, bds 27 Lower Cathcart
Durphy John, carpenter, 76 Locke n
Durphy Mrs Mary (wid Augustus) 76 Locke n
Duston Wm, cotton weaver, 36 Picton e
Duval H C, barber, 16 Hughson n, h 7 Cherry

Dwyer Jas, undertaker, 124 James n
Dwyer John, agent, bds 153 King e
Dwyer Michael, moulder, 248½ Barton e
Dwyer Michael, shoemaker, 130 Young
Dwyer Michael, 63 Hannah e
Dwyer Michael F, collector *Palladium* 98 Elgin
Dwyer M H, travelling agent, 210 John n
Divine Jas, foot Victoria ave n
Dyer Ed L, drug clerk, n w cor King and Wellington
Dyer Wm J, bookkeeper, 62 Canada
Dyer Wm R, laborer, 7½ Florence
Dyke John laborer, 7 Little Peel
Dynes J V, salesman, 208 Cannon e
Dynes Mrs Margaret, rear 207 Hughson n
Dynes Richard, moulder, 97 Robert
Eadie **Miss Ann**, 3 Wilson
Eager Hy A, clerk P O, 80 Jackson w
Eager H T, salesman, 80 Jackson w
Eager Mrs Sarah (wid Benjamin) 25 Hunter w
Eaglesham Mrs Agnes (wid John) Wentworth n
Eaglesham Jas, porter, 19 Cannon w
Eaglesham Wm H, gardener, Wentworth n
Earle John, shoemaker, 242 Barton e
Earl Patrick, 44 Guise
Earle Wm, teamster, 57 Canada
Earley Ed, gardener, Aikman ave
Early John, teamster, 148 Bay n
Early Thos H, salesman, 111 Park n

East End Coffee Room, Hamilton Coffee Tavern Co, props, N & N W Railway Station
East Hamilton, that part of the township situated between Wentworth st and the Delta
East Henry, bricklayer, end Wilson
Easter Frederick (Easter & Purrott) Mountain top
Easter & Purrott, painters (F **Easter,** G Purrott) 81 James s
Easter Samuel, saloon, 23 James **n**
Easterbrook E, steward City Hospital
Easterby Miss Sarah, 67 John **n**
Eastman Mrs Catharine, **138** John **n**
Eastman Mrs Catharine (wid Wm O) 138 John n
Easton Thos R, agent, hd Garth w s
Eastwood John (John Eastwood & Co) h Main, e Hamilton
Eastwood John & Co, booksellers and stationers, 16 King e
Eastwood J M, Main, East Hamilton
Eaves William, laborer, 30 **Oak ave**
Ecclestone Eugene A, **grocer,** 167-9 Wellington n
Ecclestone James, tailor, 80 Victoria ave n
Ecclestone W R, gents' furnisher, 138 King e
Ecclestone Walter **V,** salesman, 82 Bay s
Echart J H, collector and ins agent, 73 Cannon w
Eckbrusch Shann, weaver, **174** Napier
Eckerson Luther, photographer, 70 Stinson
Eckerson N G, photographer, 68 King e, h 70 Stinson

Economical Mutual Fire Ins Co, Wm Strong, agent, 15 Arcade
Ede Wm, salesman, 9 Mill
Ede W H, clerk, 4 Main e
Eden John, laborer, Wentworth n
Edgar David, clerk G T R, 43 Victoria ave **s**
Edgar David, **lumber merchant,** 8 Locomotive
Edgar Frank, carpenter, 129 Macnab n
Edgar Robert, laborer, 8 Little Peel
Edgar William, carpenter, 63 Park n
Edgar Wm, lumber merchant, 43 Victoria ave s
Edgar Wm, polisher, 8 Little Peel
Edgecombe Mrs Ann (wid Orlando) 139 East ave n
Edgecombe Wm, carpenter, **93** Young
Edick Louis A, cotton spinner, 232 James n
Edison Lamp Co (C F Stilwell, mangr) 26 King Wm
Edmonds John, laborer, 32 Murray w
Edmondson Thos, laborer, bds 17 Sheaffe
Edmonson George, butcher, 161 **York**
Edmonstone John, conductor G T R, 58 Napier
Edmunds John, stableman, 32 Murray w
Edson Albert E, **151** James n
Edson Mrs L N, 151 James n
Edward A, clerk, 17 Park s
Edwards Benj, confectioner, 100-**102** King w
Edwards Chas, machinist, 265 Barton e
Edwards C P, boots and shoes, 104 King w and 24 James n
Edwards Miss Esther, milliner, **122 James n**

Edwards George, salesman, 102 King w
Edwards Robert, butcher, 90 East ave n
Edwards Robert (Ham&Edwards) h 18 Napier
Edwards Thos, huckster, 91-3 King Wm
Edwards Vincent, baker, 52 Pearl s
Edwards William, laborer, 73 Robert
Edwards W A, architect, 9 James n, h 104 Main e
Edworthy Frederick, butcher, 83 Bay n
Edworthy Lewis, patternmaker, 13 Park s
Egan Edward, machinist, 34 Locomotive
Egan James F, com traveler, 171 Park n
Egan Thomas, fitter, 120 Cannon w
Egan Thos, jr, fitter, 120 Cannon w
Egener Adolph, excise officer, 70 Herkimer
Egener Charles, clerk, 45 Cannon e
Eickoff Chas, cigarmaker, 119 Napier
Eisenberg Ignatius, presser, 49 Catharine s
Eland Henry, rag dealer, Macklin
Elder Alex, machinist, 19 Crooks
Elleber James, moulder, Burton
Ellen Harry, machinist, bds 23 Wilson
Elley Mrs Eliza (wid Frederick) 179 Napier
Ellicott John M, com traveler, 17 Walnut s
Ellicott Richard, assessor, 17 Walnut s
Elliott Mrs Annie, 189 York
Elliott George, expressman, 106 Elgin

Elliott George, hotelkeeper, 71 John s
Elliott Henry E, cutter, Burlington s
Elliott's Hotel (George Elliott, prop) 71 John s
Elliott John, 80 Bay s
Elliott John, hair dresser, 65 King w
Elliott John, laborer, 13 Mill
Elliott Simon, watchman, 96 Victoria ave n
Elliott Thos, s s engineer, 257 Macnab n
Elliott William, driver, 139 King w
Elliott Wm, packer, 156 Victoria ave n
Elliott Wm, shoemaker, 145 Main e
Ellis David G, broker, 8-10 Hughson s, h 64 Wellington s
Ellis George, machinist, 263 York
Ellis George, grocer, 126 James n, h 263 York
Ellis James, laborer, 304 Hughson n
Ellis John, laborer, 55 Little William
Ellis Mrs Rachel (wid John) 4 Mill
Ellis Thomas, laborer, 184 Jackson w
Ellison Wm, machinist, bds 208 Macnab n
Ellsworth James, carpenter, 59 Lower Cathcart
Elmer Lucias, clerk, 32 Tisdale
Elrington Mrs Catharine (wid John) 44 Hughson n
Elrington Wm, printer, 44 Hughson n
Elsaesser Henry, baker, bds 101a John s
Elvin Wm, com traveler, 33 Wilson
Elwell John, moulder, 16 Locke s

Elwell Thos, laborer, 14 Railway
Elz John, cutter, 106 Walnut s
Elz Louis, machinist, 106 Walnut s
Elz Mrs Magdalene (wid Philip) 106 Walnut s
Emerson Alfred, coal oil dealer, 192 King Wm
Embling Joseph, laborer, 136 Jackson w
Emerald Street Methodist Church, Rev J H White, pastor, Emerald n
Emory C Van Norman, M D, 18 Main w
Emory John W, carpenter, 261 Cannon e
Emory Rev V H, pastor Simcoe Street Methodist Church, 232 Macnab n
Emory Wm A, Imperial Straw Work, 22 Locomotive
Emory W H, agent, bds Victoria Hotel, King e
Engel Nicholas, tinsmith, 99 Young
England Frank, hair dresser, 45 James n, h 55 East ave n
England Richard, fruit dealer, 63 Stuart w
England Robert W, boarding house keeper, 56 Locomotive
England Walter, hair dresser, 5 Cherry
English John, horse dealer, bds 57 John s
English Richard, nailer, bds 198 Macnab n
Ennis Charles L, piano maker, 59 Walnut s
Ennis & Cook (James Ennis, Adam Cook) printers, 24 Main e
Ennis James (Ennis & Cook) h 134 Mary
Ennis James, cabinetmaker, r 51 Young
Ennis ———, carpenter, 24 Canada
Ennis ———, tailor, 134 Mary
Enniskillen Hotel (Edw'd Nixon, prop) 20 King Wm
Enright Mrs Bridget (wid Cornelius) Dundurn w s nr Jones
Enright George, laborer, 33 Crooks
Enright James, clerk G T R, 75 Locomotive
Enright Mrs Mary (wid Maurice) 130 Bay n
Enright Thos, gas stoker, 64 Mulberry
Epps Mrs Mary, r Baptist church
Eppstein Archibald, rag dealer, h 15 Wellington n
Eppstein & Zidersky, rag merchants, 31 John n
Eppstein Robt, rag gather, 101 Picton e
Eppstein Simon, pedler, 331 Catharine n
Erdman Chas, grocer, 147 Wellington n
Erkert Mrs Ellen, 107 Strachan e
Erskine H, mechanic, 34 Bay n
Erskine Presbyte'n Church, Rev Thos Scoular, pastor, Pearl cor Little Market
Erwood Joseph, carter, 2 South e
Escritt Robert, shoemaker, bds 24 Hunter e
Essex Mrs A M, 38 West ave n
Etherington Walter, carpenter, 79 Canada
Eustace John, laborer, 98 Ferguson ave
Eustice John, laborer, 24 Simcoe e
Evans Mrs Ann (wid Evan) 103 West ave n
Evans Charles, lamplighter, r 51 Young
Evans & Co, merchant tailors, 6 Market square
Evans Danford, com traveler, 84 Hess n
Evans Edward, laborer, 17 Main w

Evans Francis, blacksmith, 112 Locke n
Evans James, carpenter, 131 York
Evans James, hostler, bds 57 John s
Evans John D (Grant & Sons) h 121 Bay n
Evans Rev J S, governor Childrens' Home, Main e of Wentworth
Evans Mrs P T, prop Evans' Dining Rooms, 11 John n
Evans Rees, printer, 28 Caroline n
Evans Robert (Evans & Co) h 10 Main e
Evans Robert (Robert Evans & Co) 50 Charles
Evans Robert & Co (Robert Evans, Andrew Angus) seedsmen, York cor Market
Evans Mrs Sarah Jane (wid Robert) 139 Macnab n
Evans Thos, com traveler, 52 Hughson s
Evans Thomas, crockery, 91 King e
Evans Thos, naval pensioner. 100 Park n
Evans Thos, pedler, 79 Merrick
Evans Wesley, huxter, Princess
Evans Wm, planing mill, 72 Caroline n, h 131 York
Evans Wm, [O'Connell & Evans] 26 York
Evans Wm, foreman Bell Telephone Co, 29 Park s
Evans Wm jr, carpenter, 131 York
Evans Wm J, driver C Brennan, Hughson s
Evans ——, painter, r 275 Hughson n
Evel Jas J [Semmens Bros & Co] 100 Cannon w
Eveleigh E S, 147 Main w
Evenden Jas W, bricklayer, 85 Bold
Everett Jas, trackman G T R, hd York w canal
Ewing Mrs Jane R (wid Alex) 60 Bay s
Exley Thos, printer, 171 Hunter w
Eydt Adam, driver, 295 King w
Eydt John, teamster, 295 King w
Eyres Ed (J Eyres & Son) 71 James n
Eyres J & Son, dyers, 71 James n
Fagan Alfred, painter, hd York w toll gate
Fagan Francis, rope maker, 134 Ferrie e
Fagan Wm H, teamster, 44 Smith ave
Fahey John, shoemaker 47 Hess
Fahey John, bartender, 57 John s
Fahey Patrick, laborer, r 13 Barton w
Fair John, laborer, Maple n s nr Garth
Fair Thos, machinist, 153 Wellington n
Fairburn ——, moulder, bds 55 Catharine n
Fairbank Edwin, finisher, hd York
Fairbank Mrs Henry, hd York
Fairchild's Hotel, T B Fairchild, prop, 128-130 King w
Fairchild Theodore B, hotel keeper, 128-130 King w
Fairclough D J, printer, 158 Market
Fairclough Jas, carpenter, 158 Market
Fairgrieve J C, clerk, 23 Victoria ave n
Fairgrieve Hugh, consulting engineer, bds 40 Market
Fairgrieve J B, coal dealer and ship owner, 6 James s, h 61 Macnab s
Fairhurst Richard, wire weaver, 138 Hunter w

CITY OF HAMILTON.   73

Fairley Joseph, carpenter, 210 Mary n
Fairley & Stewart, plumbers, steam and hot water heaters, (Wm Fairley, Jas Stewart) 18 John n
Fairley Wm (Fairley & Stewart) h 132 King Wm
Fairweather Wm G, grocer, 263½ Macnab n
Falconer Jas, carpenter South w n s nr Locke
Fall John, carpenter, 109 Cannon w
Fallahee Jas, laborer, 21 Steven
Fallahee Jas, laborer, 60 Strachan e
Falahee Michael, grocer, 301 John n
Falahee Thos, car checker, 303 John n
Fallan John, laborer, r 32 Walnut s
Fallis Hy, brakesman bds 107 Hunter e
Fallis Wm, watchman bds 107 Hunter e
Fallis Jas, switchman G T R, 89 Hess n
Fanning Michael, **68 Locke s**
Fanning Thos, grocer, n w cor Locke and Robinson
Fanson Jas, barber, bds 47 Cannon e
Fardy Wm, printer, 30 Murray w
Farish Frank, whip maker, 38 Augusta
Farish Mrs Mary (wid John) 38 Augusta
Farley Patrick, laborer, 368 John n
Farmer Bros, photographers, 8-10 King w
Farmer F N, carter, 374 Hughson n
Farmer Jas, 118 Victoria ave n
Farmer Jas S, blacksmith 125 John s

Farmer J H, (Farmer Bros) hd Queen s
Farmer Mrs Maria, hair works, 56 York
Farmer Mrs Mary (wid John) dress maker, 112 Rebecca
Farmer Thomas, photographer, 8½ King e, h 27 Florence
Farmer T D J, B C L, (Smith & Farmer) barrister, h 159 Park n
Farmer Wm, photographer, 35 King w, h 124 Victoria ave n
Farmer Wm, plumber and gas fitter, 110 James n
Farmer Wm F, watchmaker, 56 York
Farmers' Dairy Co, W G Walton, manager, 70 Vine
Farr Chas E, plasterer, 45 Steven
Farr David, constable G T R, 11 Simcoe e
Farr Jas, bricklayer, 75 Robert
Farr John, carter, 165 Mary
Farr John jr, laborer, 165 Mary
Farrant John, hostler, bds 11 Rebecca
Farrar Wm, manager Oak Hall, 41 Victoria ave n
Farrell Chas, salesman, 140 Rebecca
Farrell Mrs Elizabeth [wid Dennis] 274a King e
Farrell Jas, laborer, 20 Locke s
Farrow E H, clerk, 112½ East ave n
Farrow **Thomas**, carpenter, 112½ East ave n
Farthing Jno, machinist, 15 Grove
Faulkner Alexander, shipper, 7 South w
Faulkner Chris P, cotton carder, bds 188 Macnab n
Faulkner Geo C, builder, **157** Napier
Faulknor John B, bricklayer, 8 Canada
Faulknor Joseph, builder, 157 Napier

10

Faulknor Robt J, bricklayer, 57 Queen s
Faulknor Thomas, bricklayer, 77 Pearl n
Faulks Robt, carpenter, 190 East ave n
Faustman Ernest, cooper, 45 **John n**
Faustman John, cooper, 58 Hughson n
Fawcett **David**, cabinetmaker, 227 Victoria ave n
Fawcett James, fireman N N W, bds 175 Mary
Fawcett Mrs Mary (wid Thos E) 168 Hughson n
Fawcett Thomas, laborer, 217 Barton e
Fearman Edward, plasterer, 172 Mary
Fearman F C, pork packer, 72 East ave s
Fearman Frank D, bookkeeper, Ivy Lodge, 58 Stinson
Fearman F W, pork packer, 17 Macnab n, factory Rebecca, h 58 **Stinson**
Fearman Henry O, salesman, Ivy Lodge, 58 Stinson
Fearman H H, clerk, bds 58 Stinson
Fearman R C, pork packer, 75 East ave s
Fearman Wm J, bookkeeper, Ivy Lodge, 58 Stinson
Fearnside Edward C, florist, 302 King Wm
Fearnside John H, asst supt letter carriers P O, 48 Main w
Fearnside Thomas, 302 King William
Fearnside Wm, laborer, 302 King Wm
Feasel George, gardener, 95 Hunter w
Feast Mrs Edwin B, grocer, n w cor Napier and Hess
Feast Mrs Mary (wid Alfred) 97 **Wilson**

Feast Mrs Mary (wid Samuel) 73 Main w
Feast Miss Sarah A, dressmaker, 73 Main w
Featherston Robert L, salesman, 172 King w
Feaver Miss, prop Star Hotel, 68-70 Elgin
Feaver Thos, butcher, 31 Little Wm
Federal Life Assurance Co, David Dexter, managing director, 97 James n
Fee Thomas, hackman, 9 Margaret
Feelay Marshall, com traveler, 167 Main e
Feeley Michael, laborer, 95 Young
Feist Henry, gardener, 51 **Robinson**
Fell Arthur, machinist, 104 Hunter w
Fell Henry, fireman, 149 King e
Fell John, mechanic, 47 Macauley w
Fell Wm, sealmaker, 4 Market square
Fell William T, porter, 46 Pearl s
Fenton David J, nickle plater, 121 Market
Fenton James, Patrick
Fenton Jeremiah, policeman, 152 Wellington n
Fenton Philip K, salesman, 52 Young
Fenton Robt, laborer, 51 Locomotive
Fenwick E J, com traveler, bds Royal Hotel
Ferguson Alex, messenger customs, Main e
Ferguson James, machinist, 273 Mary n
Ferguson James, cigarmaker, 42 Guise
Ferguson J D, bookkeeper, Gore
Ferguson John, shoemaker, 55 Erie ave

Ferguson John M, laborer, 273 Mary n
Ferguson Mrs Margaret (wid James) 92 Bay s
Ferguson Robert, printer, 158 Napier
Ferguson Thomas, shoemaker, 1a Walnut s
Ferguson Wm, cigarmaker, bds 46 Cannon w
Ferguson William, tailor, 77 Walnut s
Ferguson William, fitter, 123 Picton e
Fernihough Henry, laborer, 127 Macnab n
Ferres & Co, hardware, paints and window glass, etc, 38 James n
Ferres James (Ferres & Co) h 90 James s
Ferrie A E, clerk, 12 Queen s
Ferrie Campbell, accountant Ham Prov & Loan Society, 12 Queen s
Ferrie Mrs Emily (wid John) 12 Queen s
Ferrie Mrs Harriet (wid Robert) 14 Ray s
Ferrie R B, clerk, 14 Ray s
Ferrie R R, clerk Bank of Montreal, George cor Queen
Ferrie Walter B, clerk, 12 Queen
Ferris ——, 172 Emerald n
Ferris Peter, policeman, 55 Wellington s
Ferris Simon, mechanic, 324 Macnab n
Fickle Gustave, packer, 60 Wood e
Fickley Gottlieb, shoemaker, 35 Cherry
Fickley Wm, moulder, 36 Canada
Fiddler Samuel, sailor, 33 Tom
Field John, glassware, 174-6 James n
Field Mrs Mary J, (wid Richard) 23 Main w

Field Wm J, 9 Caroline s
Fielding Chas W W, letter carrier, n w cor Garth and Concession
Fielding Geo, cotton warper, 133 Wood e
Fielding Jas, engineer, 94 Picton e
Fielding John, fireman, bds 93 Murray e
Fielding John S, civil engineer, n w cor Garth and Concession
Fielding Jos M, moulder, n w cor Garth and Concession
Fielding Mrs Mary J (wid Jos) n w cor Garth and Concession
Fielding Wm M, com traveller, n w cor Garth and Concession
Fields Mrs (wid Charles) 59 Catharine n
Fields David, laborer, 59 Catharine n
Fields Stephen, laborer, 59 Catharine n
Filgiano Augustus T, bookkeeper, 143 Victoria ave n
Filgiano Frederick, clerk G T R, 115 Bay n
Filgiano H E J, clerk P O
Filgiano The Le P, dentist, 4 James n, h 286 James n
Filitrault Trovite, tobacco roller, r 81 Caroline n
Filkin Robt, laborer, 273 Mary n
Filman Geo A, salesman, 21 Young
Filman Peter, 298 Barton e
Finch Bros (W H & T S) staple dry goods, 18 King w
Finch Frank, salesman, 225 Victoria ave n
Finch Robt, bricklayer, 302 Hughson n
Finch T S (Finch Bros) h 225 Victoria ave n
Finch Wm H (Finch Bros) h 34 George
Finch Wm, foreman Copp's foundry) 225 Victoria ave n

Finchamp Wm, moulder, 10 Locke s
Findlay Mrs Ann (wid Wm) 66 Victoria ave n
Findlay David, moulder, 173 Hughson n
Findlay Geo S, com traveller, 23 Oxford
Findlay **Henry H, com** traveller, 158 York
Findlay Jas, laborer, 59 Jackson
Findlay James, compositor, 59 Jackson e
Findlay Jas jr, slate roofer, concession s s opp Locke
Findlay Jas sr, slate roofer, Concession s s opp Locke
Findlay John [Smith & Findlay] 53 James n
Findlay Wm, slate roofer, Concession s s opp Locke
Findlay Mrs Robt, 173 Hughson n
Findlay W F, accountant and insurance agent, Wentworth Chambers, 25 James s, h 71 George *See card*
Fink Wm, teamster, 11 Dundurn
Finlayson Alex, salesman, 117 Young
Finlayson Geo, clerk, bds 51 Park n
Finlayson John, **harness maker,** 37 Wilson
Finlayson ——, com traveller, 50 Ferguson ave
Finn Thos, laborer, 134 Picton e
Finsterbeck Chas, bds 35 Catharine n
Finucane A E, clerk Bank of Montreal, 3 Nelson ave
Fire Insurance Association, J T Routh, agent, 16 James s
First Methodist Church, Rev John Kay, pastor, King cor Wellington s
First Ward Hotel [Thos Bain, prop] 60 Cherry

Firman John, laborer, 47 Queen
Firth James, blacksmith, 172 Emerald n
Fischer Henry, manufacturer, 93 Hunter e
Fischer John jr, laborer, Aikman ave
Fischer Mrs Margaret [wid John] Aikman ave
Fiset Miss M B, milliner, 163 James n
Fish Arthur, painter, 84 Stinson
Fish W R, tobacconist, 72 King w, h Stinson cor Erie ave
Fisher Geo, porter, 207 King e
Fisher Horace, **burr** maker, 71 Napier
Fisher Mrs Isabella (wid Robt) Park s w s nr Robinson
Fisher Jas, stovemounter, 57 Oak ave
Fisher John, **cigar maker,** 51 Hannah e
Fisher Mrs Julia (wid Jas) 11 Bold
Fisher Samuel laborer, Sherman
Fisher Walter, moulder, 143 Ferrie e
Fisher Wm H, laborer, 30 Queen s
Fitch Bros (John & Wm) fish dealers, 100 James n
Fitt Hy, cabinetmaker, 10 Tom
Fitzgerald Chas, laborer, 43½ Young
Fitzgerald Duncan, collector, *Times,* 138 Main w
Fitzgerald Mrs Ellen [wid John] 105 Walnut s
Fitzgerald Francis, barrister, 10 King w, h 1 Caroline s
Fitzgerald Geo, lamplighter, Hunter w s s nr Poulette
Fitzgerald Jas, 179 Bay n
Fitzgerald Jas, laborer, 95 Mary
Fitzgerald Mrs John, 105 Walnut s
Fitzgerald, Mrs Col Maria, 4 Canada

Fitzgerald Michael J, laborer, 45 York
Fitzgerald Lawrence, boiler maker, 14 Picton w
Fitzgerald Patrick, moulder, 34 Hess n
Fitzgerald Patrick, laborer, 72 Tisdale
Fitzgerald Robt M, clerk P O, 1 Caroline s
Fitzgerald Thos, laborer, King e of Wentworth
Fitzgerald Wm, 1 Caroline s
Fitzgerald Wm, car builder, 45 Young.
Fitzgerald Wm E, 1 Caroline s
Fitzmaurice Robert, moulder, 35 Alanson
Fitzmorris Mrs Julia (wid Patrick) 19 Aurora
Fitzpatrick Mrs Catharine (wid Martin) 77 Park n
Fitzpatrick E W, clerk, 21 Hunter w
Fitzpatrick Miss Jane, 11 Victoria ave n
Fitzpatrick John, clerk, 128 York
Fitzpatrick John J, painter, Markland n s w Locke
Fitzpatrick Miss Mary, 11 Victoria ave n
Fitzpatrick P E, bookkeeper, 57 Wilson
Fitzpatrick Peter, carpenter, 121 Mary
Fitzpatrick W P, clerk, 77 Park n
Fitzsimmons Henry, coachman, Inglewood, Concession
Flack Mrs Lucy (wid Thomas) 63 Caroline s
Flahaven John, japanner, 220 Catharine n
Flaherty Francis, laborer, 80 Canada
Flaherty James, laborer, 84 Walnut s
Flanders Chas, brakemen, 139 Ferguson ave

Flanigan Michael, laborer, 208 Victoria ave n
Flannery Edward, moulder, 3½ Oak ave
Flatt & Bradley (J I Flatt, John Bradley) timber merch's, Barton cor Wellington
Flatt J I (Flatt & Bradley) res Millgrove
Fleck Alex, sign painter, 106½ James n, h 6 O'Reilly
Fleck George, laborer, 64 Pearl s
Fletcher Mrs Catherine [wid Joseph] 112 Napier
Fletcher Rev Donald H, pastor Macnab St Presbyterian Church, 58 Macnab s
Fletcher Geo, 14 Main w
Fletcher Joseph, cigarmaker, 215 John n
Fletcher Joseph, jr, carpenter, 53 Ray n
Fletcher Joseph, sr, shoemaker, 53 Ray n
Fletcher Peter, laborer, s w cor Dufferin and West
Fletcher William, laborer, 76 Canada
Flett James, bricklayer, 102 Market
Flett John, carpenter, 102 Market
Flett Mrs Margaret (wid James) 102 Market
Fleming John, laborer, Burlington n
Fleming John, grocer, 246 Barton e
Fleming John, laborer, 110 Young
Fleming J R, broker, 7 Hughson s, h 6 Park s
Fleming Mrs Rachael, 25 Stuart e
Fleming Mrs Susan [wid Wm] 10 Greig
Flight James, stonecutter, 80 Emerald n
Flitcroff Wm, blacksmith, 62 Bay n, h 117 Hess s

Flock Mrs Catharine [wid Wm], 24 Magill
Flockton John, fireman, 270 Macnab n
Flood Valentine, trackman G T R, hd York
Flooks Wm, letter carrier, r 58 Emerald s
Florida Hotel, James H Smith, prop, 39 Mary
Flowers Albert, moulder, bds 57 John s
Flowers Henry, laborer, bds 74 John s
Flowers Henry, sr, hostler, bds 74 John s
Flukes Hugh, salesman, 57 Walnut s
Flynn Daniel, **laborer**, **338** John n
Flynn Daniel, **stovemounter**, **23** Stuart e
Flynn Edward, **laborer**, 16 Greig
Flynn James, **laborer**, 32 Magill
Flynn Mrs Jane [wid James] 40 Charles
Flynn John, **laborer**, **53** Walnut s
Flynn John, moulder, 16 Barton w
Flynn John, moulder, 16 Greig
Flynn Matthew, engineer GTR, 260 York
Flynn Michael, clerk, 53 Walnut
Flynn Michael, 50 Walnut s
Flynn Thos, laborer, 112 Cannon w
Flynn William, clerk P O, **29** Liberty
Fogwell Mrs Mary [wid Wm] 45½ Cannon w
Foley Daniel, jr, porter, 114 **Cherry**
Foley Frank, whipmaker, 46 Cannon e
Foley Mrs Julia [wid Daniel] 114 Cherry
Foley Maurice, **moulder**, **107** Walnut s
Foley Michael, polisher, 114 Cherry

Foley Timothy, laborer, 119 Hannah e
Forger Caleb, laborer, 23 **Napier**
Fonger Charles, laborer, 23 Napier
Fonger Mrs Ellen (wid Caleb) 23 Napier
Fonger Hiram, teamster, 30 Catharine s
Fonger Wm H, laborer, 23 Napier
Foote Charles, supt Meriden Britannia Co, 10 Victoria ave n
Foote Henry, laborer, 187 Wellington n
Foote John, 67 Main w
Forbes A, hatter, bds Walker House
Forbes Alex, 181 Wellington n
Forbes A F, stockbroker, 7 Hughson s
Forbes David, laborer, 5 Evans
Forbes George, fireman, 92 Wilson
Forbes Geo, stableman, 87 King William
Forbes Geo, scalemaker, 177 Wellington n
Forbes John, 177 Wellington n
Forbes John jr, 177 Wellington n
Forbes Robt, hd Queen s w s
Ford Alfred, stovemounter, 8 Napier
Ford Grafton, whitewasher, 32½ Cannon w, h Burlington n
Forde Mrs Henriette, (wid Jos) 133 Main e
Ford Jas, health inspector, 269 John n
Ford John, laborer, 37 Strachan e
Ford John, weaver, 206 Macnab n
Ford John sr, painter, 37 Strachan e
Ford Thos, baker, 42 Peter
Ford Thos, biscuit maker, r 79 Pearl n

CITY OF HAMILTON. 79

Ford Wm, salesman, 141 Jackson w
Ford Wm, moulder, 8 Augusta
Foreman Geo, moulder, 49 John
Forman Jas, brakman, 136 West ave n
Forman John, expressman, 59 Tom
Foreman John, com traveller, 197 Cannon e
Foreman Mrs May (wid Wm) 16 Liberty
Foreman Peter, shoemaker, 197 Cannon e
Forester Jas, freight checker, 243 Bay n
Foresters' Hall, 108 James n
Forneret, Rev George A, M A, rector All Saints' Church, 250 King w
Forest Mrs Armanda (wid Wm) 54 John s
Forsyth B, clerk Bank of Hamilton, 17 King w
Forster A M (A M Forster & Co) h 91 Murray
Forster A M & Co (A M Foster & T J Carroll) brass finishers, 173-175 James n
Forster Arden, wood turner, 13 Colborne
Forster Mrs Ellen (wid Jas) 73 Lower Cathcart
Forster Geo, fireman, 73 Lower Cathcart
Forster John H, 43 Wellington n
Forster Matthew, woodworker, 14 West ave n
Forster Samuel, pattern maker, 73 Lower Cathcart
Forster Thos Wm, machinist, 73 Lower Cathcart
Forster Wm, wood turner, 13 Colborne
Forster Wm C, artist, 41 Jackson w
Forsyth Wm, 39 Murray e
Fortier C J, collector Inland Revenue, 237 King w

Fortier H D, clerk, 237 King w
Foster Chas, food inspector, 38 George
Foster Elias I, laborer, 127 Napier
Foster Frank, barber, bds 122 King e
Foster Frederick, tobacco roller, 39 Peter
Foster Frederick G, florist, 53 Charles
Foster Geo, glassblower, 42 Macaulay w
Foster James, cutter, 7 Caroline n
Foster Jas, plater, 6 Wellington n
Foster J F, plumber, 61 Strachan e
Foster Jos, engineer G T R, 118 Locke n
Foster Leonard, flower pot manfr Main w s s w Garth
Foster Mrs Martha (wid Jas R) 46 Hess n
Foster Matthew J, bridge builder, 111 Walnut s
Foster Sydney, brushmaker, 40 Smith ave
Foster Thos, laborer, r 185 Bay n
Foster Thos K, 145 John n
Foster Wm, foreman Young & Bro, 214 King Wm
Foster Wm W, foreman Young & Bro, 71 Carharine n
Fotheringham John, wagonmaker, 14 Erie ave
Foule Henry, teamster, 23 Guise
Foulis Wm B, engineer, 152 Duke
Foulton Thos, laborer, 19 Greig
Fowkes Thos, dry goods, 11 King Wm
Fowler Benjamin, scale maker, 8 Ontario
Fowler Geo, salesman, bds 45 Hess n
Fowler Hy, shoemaker, 182 King Wm

Fowler John, tailor, e of Wentworth
Fowler Walter, moulder, 243 Cannon e
Fowler Wm, laborer, 225 Hughson n
Fowler Wm, laborer, bds 65 Stuart w
Fox Andrew M C, carpenter, Oxford w s nr end
Fox Mrs Ann (wid George) 26 West ave s
Fox Chas, foreman Allardyce's, bds 42 Vine
Fox George, manager W Webster's 26 West ave s
Fox James (Fox & Work) 8 Spring
Fox John, 19 Florence
Fox John W, gardener, 58 Hannah e
Fox Mrs Leonord (wid Geo) 18 Ray n
Fox & Work (J Fox, W Work) confectioners, 187½ King e
Fralick J, salesman, 46 Catharine n
Francis Wm, pedlar, 139½ John s
Franey Bros, (M M Franey, M T Franey) gardeners, Main e of Wentworth
Franey Frank, gardener, 82 John
Franey Thos, laborer, Duke n s nr Locke
Frank Alfred, compositor, 328 Catharine n
Frank Charles, manufacturer, 328 Catharine n
Frank E, letter carrier, 328 Catharine n
Frank George, machinist, 126 West ave n
Frank Geo, machinist, 202 East ave n
Frank James G, bookkeeper, 8 East ave n
Frank Solomon, laborer, 12 Mill
Franklin House, Daniel Poole propr, 94 King w

Franklin Thomas, messenger Bank of Commerce, 14 Caroline s
Franks C B, civil engineer, GTR bds 36 Bay s
Franks James, (Stamp & Franks) h 137 West ave s
Fraser Abner, bookkeeper, 80 Merrick
Fraser Alex (Fraser, Johnson & Co), Wentworth s
Fraser Alexander, jr, bookkeeper, Wentworth s
Fraser Alex, salesman, 76 Murray e
Fraser Mrs Ann, [wid John] 22 Stinson
Fraser Donald, tailor, 9 Little Peel
Fraser Duncan, laborer, bds 26 Ray n
Fraser George, 24 Strachan w
Fraser George, driver, 308 King w
Fraser Geo J, bookkeeper, 22 Stinson
Fraser & Inches, [Wm Fraser, Jas Inches] grocers, 18 John s
Fraser James, moulder, 6 Hess s
Fraser, Johnson & Co, saddlery hardware etc, 9 John n
Fraser Louis, com traveller, 76 Murray e
Fraser Mrs Maggie, 12 Charles
Fraser Rev Mungo, pastor Knox Church, 147 Park n
Fraser O S McN, clerk Bank of Hamilton, 63 Macnab s
Fraser Robert S, cutter 16 Emerald n
Fraser Simon W, watchman Asylum, 99 Robinson
Fraser William, porter, 143 John s
Fraser Wm, butcher, 67 Napier
Fraser Wm, (Fraser & Inches) 211 King Wm
Frawley Michael, laborer, 139 Locke n

Frazier Wm, moulder, bds 144 Cannon e
Free Henry, engineer, 326 James n
Freeborn George, laborer, 370 Catharine n
Freeborn John, laborer, 8 Clarke ave
Freeborn Thomas, fireman, 13 Clark ave
Freeborn Thomas, laborer, 79 Young
Freed A T, editor *Spectator*, 57 Jackson w
Freed James, gardener, Aikman ave
Freed John B, boiler compound manfr, 68 Mary, h 164 West ave n
Freel Jerome, bds 105 King w
Freel Thomas, cotton dyer, 126 Ferrie e
Freely Nicholas, bricklayer, 77 Bold
Freeman Mrs Catharine, (wid S B), 161 James s
Freeman Chas, rag dealer, 77 Macnab n, h 79 Macnab n
Freeman Clarkson, bookkeeper, 70 East ave n
Freeman Elijah, (E Freeman & Son) h 7 Caroline s
Freeman E & Son, (Elijah and Ranson) real estate agents, 9 King w
Freeman Mrs Grace, (wid Chas), 96 Bay s
Freeman Mrs Isabel, (wid Peter W) 13 Grove
Freeman Mrs Isabella, (wid Peter), wood dealer, 1 Ferguson ave, h 13 Grove
Freeman Ranson, (E Freeman & Son), h 7 Caroline s
Freeman Stephen, laborer, 53 Oak ave
Freeman W A, wood and coal dealer, 169 James n, h 80 Elgin

Freeth John, teamster, 99 Catharine n
French George, gardener, 23 Maria
French Geo S, bookbinder, 23 Maria
French Francis, grainbuyer, 1 Wentworth n
French Mrs Florence P (wid James) 128 West ave n
Frew Arch, freight agent C P R, 26 East ave n
Frewing Frederick, plasterer, 176 Wilson
Fricker Walter, stove **driller, 137** West ave n
Frid Alfred, brickmaker, 250 Main w
Frid Geo, brick manfr, Main s s w Garth, h 221 Main w
Frid Geo W, brick manfr, 221 Main w
Frid John W, **brick maker,** 11 Nelson
Frid Mrs Sarah (wid Wm) 70 Locke s
Friday Geo, laborer, 40 Sheaffe
Frier Wm, **dry** Goods, 61 Catharine n
Fitzman Jos, **glass blower,** 311 Macnab n
Froude Philip W, shipper, 137 Main e
Frowde Francis, polisher, bds 87 John s
Frowley Thos, laborer, **197 Main** w
Fry Mrs H M (wid Chas) 58 Ferguson ave
Fryburger, Mrs, 49 George
Fuerd Richard, laborer, 41 Wood
Fuerd Thos, laborer, 27 Strachan w
Fuller **Mrs Cynthia,** 75 **Jackson** w
Puller Edward, **lamplighter, 137** Wood e
Fuller Henry, tailor, **Dundurn** w s nr Florence

Fuller John, gardener, 62 Locke s

Fuller, Nesbitt & Bicknell, (V E Fuller, J W Nesbitt, Jas Bicknell) barristers, 20 James s

Fuller S B, policeman, 120 Wilson

Fuller Richard, contractor, 73 Emerald s

Fuller Vallency E, (Fuller, Nesbitt & Bicknell) h 34 Queen s

Fulton James, teamster, 110 Market

Fulton William, laborer, 103 York

Furber George, painter, bds 43 Vine

Furber Jabez, painter, bds 43 Vine

Furlong & Beasley, (E Furlong, L L B, A C Beasley), barristers, 2½ James s *See card*

Furlong Edward (Furlong & Beasley) h hd Hess s

Furlong Moses, cab driver, 295 Macnab n

Furlong James, laborer, bds 32 Magill

Furlong Thomas, laborer, r 124 Queen n

Furlong Thomas, laborer, 6 Locke n

Furmidge Peter, laborer, 81 Catharine n

Furmidge Samuel, laborer, 81 Catharine n

Furmidge Samuel, jr, blacksmith, 81 Catharine n

Furminger David H, blacksmith, 6 Burlington s

Furniss Edmund N (**Furniss & Son**) h 51 York

Furniss & Son (Edmund M & Spencer) marble cutters) 51 York

Furniss Spencer (Furniss & Son) h 82 Stinson

Furniss Wm, marble cutter, 39 Tom

Furneaux Edwin, carpenter, 23 Emerald n

Furnivall E J, tailor, 11 Macnab n, h 25 Pearl n

Fursdon Thomas, laborer, 109 Simcoe e

Gadsby Mrs Francis E (wid Jas) Caroline s, w s nr Markland

Gadsby James, bookbinder, Caroline s, w s, nr Markland

Gagan Henry, laborer, 40 Guise

Gage A W (A W Gage & Co) h 38 East ave s

Gage A W & Co, wholesale jewelers, 57 King e

Gage Mrs Catharine, 2½ Oak ave

Gage Mrs Eliza (wid Wm) 79 Herkimer

Gage Emerson, 74 Wellington n

Gage George, boots and shoes, 58 King e

Gage George, farmer, King, e of toll gate

Gage Mrs Henrietta [wid Peter] 78 Main w

Gage James, farmer, King, east of toll gate

Gage & Jelfs [R R Gage, G F Jelfs] barristers, 8 Hughson s

Gage M D, laborer, 45 Burlington w

Gage R R [Gage & Jelfs] h Main e of Hamilton

Gage Rufus R, com traveler, 78 Main w

Gage Samuel, laborer, 18 Crooks

Gage Walter, farmer, King e of toll gate

Gage Wm [Jones & Gage] 91 Barton e

Gage Wm, hackman, 78 East ave s

Gage ——, gardener, 121 Cannon w

Gagnier Mrs Oliver, 250 James n

Gainey Mrs Ann [wid Dennis] 19 Steven

Gain Thos, com traveler, Mountain ave
Gair Matthew, finisher, 114 Caroline s
Galbraith Miss Elizabeth, 58 Hess n
Galbreaith D B, C H O, 116 Main e
Galbreaith N D, grocer, 104 King e, h Main cor East ave
Galbreaith Walter, drug clerk, bds 37 Robert
Gallagher Charles F, com traveler, 74 Mary
Gallagher Geo, boilermaker, 37 Inchbury n
Gallagher James, watchman, 113 Walnut s
Gallagher Michael, shoemaker, 109 Walnut s
Gallagher Patrick, employe railroad, bds 62 Mulberry
Gallagher R E, principal Canada Business College, h 120 Market
Gallagher Robt, tailor, 128 John s
Gallivin Mrs Annorah, 33 Margaret
Gallivan Michael, laborer, 27 Margaret
Galtrey John, laborer, 39½ Stuart e
Galvin Daniel, tanner, 126 Main e
Galvin Edward, salesman, 282½ King e
Galvin Mrs Ellen [wid Patrick] 282½ King e
Galvin John, machinist, 282½ King e
Galvin Patrick, salesman, 282½ King e
Gant J, barber, 186 James n
Gardner Alex, carter, Caroline s e s nr Concession
Gardner Chas, engineer, bds 11 Rebecca
Gardner C W (Gardner & Thomson) 290 King Wm

Gardiner Mrs Euphemia (wid Andrew) Bold n s nr Pearl
Gardner George, sewing machine maker, bds 11 Rebecca
Gardner Geo, brakeman, 135 Park n
Gardiner Herbert F, editor *Times*, 4 Bold
Gardner James, com traveler, Wood & Leggat
Gardiner John, letter carrier, 290 King Wm
Gardner John P, cutter, 17 Steven
Gardiner Robert, blind maker, 56 Robert e
Gardiner Samuel, telephone lineman, 56 Robert
Gardner & Thomson [C W Gardner, Thos Thomson] gents' furnishers, 92 James n
Gardiner Wm R, potter, Bold n s nr Pearl
Garity David, hammerman, bds 161 Queen n
Garity Samuel, examiner customs, 58 Ray n
Garity Samuel, baker, 16 Ray n
Garity ——, laborer, 18½ Mulberry
Garland James, painter, 29½ Park n
Garland Louis [Garland & Rutherford] 14 Park s
Garland & Rutherford [Louis Garland, Andrew Rutherford] druggists, 6 King e
Garner Jas, provision dealer, 178 Jackson w
Garner Mrs Mary (wid John) dressmaker, 112 Rebecca
Garner Thomas H, cooper, 85 Locke n
Garner W, blacksmith, 7 Macnab
Garner Wm B, blacksmith, 57 Merrick, h 62 Catharine s
Garrett Arthur, clerk, 1 Bold
Garrett James, moulder, 22 Devonport

Garrett Mrs Jessie [wid John] 1 Bold
Garrett Thomas, moulder, 102 Simcoe e
Garrick Arthur, laborer, 96 Simcoe e
Garrick David J, merchant, 75 East ave n
Garrick James, stonemason, 189 King e
Garrity James, tinsmith, end Ferrie e
Garrison John, engineer, 114 Cannon e
Garrow Thos, 60 Ray n
Garry John, weaver, 157 Park n
Garson David, brushmaker, 63 Canada
Garson Geo, wood dealer, bds 134 King Wm, cor King Wm and Mary
Garson James, carpenter, 126 John s
Gartland James, laborer, 23 Railway
Gartshore Alex, Canada Pipe Foundry, Stuart cor Caroline, h 43 Charles
Garvin Wm, machinist, ; Little Wm
Gas Inspector's Office, 2 John s
Gas Works Office, 91 Park n
Gaskell Henry, patternmaker, 256 Barton e
Gaskin Arthur, 5 Jones
Gaskin Jas, engine turner G T R, 5 Jones
Gaston Thos G, wireweaver, 16 Inchbury s
Gatenby William, tailor, 128 Bay s
Gates Arthur R, accountant, 121 Bay s
Gates Frederick W, sr, pres Hamilton Gas Co, 7 Herkimer
Gates F W, jr, [Willson & Gates] 148 Bay s
Gates Geo E, clerk, 7 Herkimer

Gates H E, accountant Canada Life Assurance Co, 7 Herkimer
Gates H G, clerk Bank of Montreal, 7 Herkimer
Gates Joseph, detective, 30 Elgin
Gathercole William, bds 84 Hughson n
Gauld C M, 64 Duke
Gauld Rev John, Presbyterian, 64 Duke
Gausby J D, [Mackelcan, Gibson & Gausby] h 23 Main w
Gavey James, jr, scalemaker, 47 Florence
Gavey James, sr, watchmaker, 47 Florence
Gaviller Alex, 21 Herkimer
Gaviller Edwin A, M D, n e cor Main and Park
Gay James, 66 Hughson s
Gay John B, bookseller, 78 King e
Gay Mrs Helen [wid Walter] 98 Cannon w
Gay Wm, cabinetmaker, bds 285 York
Gayfer Henry, manager A Murray & Co, 79 Wellington s
Geary Wm, moulder, 253 Catharine n
Gebhard Jacob, shoemaker, 59 Robinson
Geddes James, checker, 67 Ferrie e
Geddes Mrs J T, 205 Main e
Geddes Mrs Mary, 290 John n
Gee James, fitter, 15 Sophia n
Gee John, piler, 33½ Tisdale
Gee Philip, scrap piler, 51 Victoria ave n
Geiger Albert, baker, 218 King w
Geiger E A [Rattray & Geiger] h 214 King w
Geiger H J, watchmaker, 70 King w, h 214 King w
Geiger John H, prop Cosmopolitan hotel, 214-6 King w

CITY OF HAMILTON. 85

Geiger Wm, 11 Grove
Geisel Louis, tailor, 112 John s
Geiss Chris, printer, 4 Elgin
Geiss Ernest, machinist, 98 Bay n
Geiss Henry, wood turner, 4 Elgin
Geiss William, machinist, 98 Bay n
Geldart Geo H, picture framer, 131 King w, h 42 Barton w
Geldart Wm, machinist, 42 Barton w
Gell John, tinsmith, 52 Gore
Gell Wm, broker, 17 King Wm, h 52 Gore
Gentle John, 20 Margaret
Gentle Thos, manager Hamilton Dry Plate Co, h 2 Margaret
George Mrs Eliza (wid Wm) Duke n s w Locke
George Richard, shoemaker, Ashley
George Robt, driver, bds 39 Macnab n
George Robt, tailor, 100 John s, h 102 John s
George Mrs Robt, variety store, 102 John s
Georgian Bay Transportation Co, W J Grant, agent, 33 James n
Gerbrand Frederick, tailor, 57 Mary
Germania Hall, 33 John s
Germania Hotel (Robt Jahn, prop) 20-22 John s
Gerrard Andrew, dairyman, King w s s nr limits
Gerrie Edward, gardener, King e of toll gate
Gerrie Edward, blacksmith, bds 5 John n
Gerrie John, 58 Young
Gerrie J W, druggist, 30 James n h 5 Caroline s
Gerrie Michael, laborer, Wentworth n
Ghent Fred, clerk, 89 Main e

Ghent Harry A (Ghent & Staunton) 89 Main e
Ghent S H, clerk County Court, deputy clerk of the Crown, Court House, h 89 Main e
Ghent & Staunton (Harry A Ghent, C F Lynch Staunton, real estate agents, 17-19 Arcade
Gibb Albert, paper box manfr, 120 King Wm, h 122 King Wm
Gibb Robt, 122 King Wm
Gibb Wm A, clerk, 122 King Wm
Gibbon Chas, laborer, bds 26 Ray n
Gibbons Jas, laborer, 235 James n
Gibbons Jas, gardener, 90 Robert
Gibbons John, meahanic, 24 Jones
Gibbs Chas, hatter, 39 Lower Cathcart
Gibson David R, bricklayer, 64 Victoria ave n
Gibson J M, M A, LL B, (Mackelcan, Gibson & Gausby) h 102 Main w
Gibson Joseph, driver, 142 Market
Gibson P F, bds 18½ Walnut s
Gidley Mrs Sarah [wid John] 41 Cherry
Gilbert David, baker, 145 Mary
Gilbert Edward S, collector, 20 Cherry
Gilbert Mrs Harriet A [wid Roswell] 87½ Jackson w
Gilbert H J, clerk, 31 Gore
Gilbert John, machinist, 15 Gore
Gilbert Mortimer E, com traveler, 99 Hannah w
Gilchrist Mrs Agnes [wid Jas] 84 Market
Gilchrist Jas, carpenter, 78 Elgin
Gildon Mrs Janet, grocer, 51 Wellington n

Giles Wm, moulder, 44 Tisdale
Giles W P & Co, clothiers, 26 James n
Giles W P [W P Giles & Co, h 16 Market
Gill Mrs Elizabeth [wid Jos] 13 Cannon e
Gill John, farmer, 13 Cannon e
Gill Matthew, boilermaker, 102 Ferrie e
Gill Robt, machinist, 128 Macaulay e
Gillaland Wm, moulder, hd Garth w s nr Concession
Gillard John [W H Gillard & Co] 26 George
Gillard Mrs Maria, 12 Liberty
Gillard W H [W H Gillard & Co] Concession n s nr Bay
Gillard W H & Co [W H & John Gillard, Hy N Kittson] wholesale grocers, 11 Main w
Gilles George, compositor, 71 Vine
Gillesby & Barnes [W F Gillesby & E P Barnes] flour and feed, 4 John s
Gillesby Samuel, carpenter, 6 Upper Cathcart
Gillesby Thos, printer, 139 York
Gillesby Wm, grain and wool merchant, 6 John s, h 62 Wentworth s
Gillesby Wm F [Gillesby & Barnes] 62 Wentworth s
Gillespie Alex, clerk, 9 Emerald s
Gillespie Mrs Christina [wid Wm] 24 Margaret
Gillespie Geo H [Gillespie & Powis] h 9 Emerald s
Gillespie Geo H jr, clerk, 9 Emerald s
Gillespie Hugh, grocer, 263 Macnab n
Gillespie J C, salesman, 9 Emerald s
Gillespie John, machinist, 195 Hughson n

Gillespie & Powis [Geo H Gillespie, Alfred Powis] brokers, commission merchants and insurance agents, 31 King e
Gillespie Thos, laborer, 136 Victoria ave n
Gillespie Wm, pattern maker, 192 Hughson n
Gillett Edward, cor Stinson and Wellington
Gillett Thos, cor Stinson and Wellington
Gilliard Mrs Lucinda, laundress, 117 Market
Gillies Alex, com traveler, 40 Hunter w
Gillies Mrs Catharine [wid Geo] 66 Charles
Gillies David, 66 Charles
Gillies Wm sr, com traveler, 159 York
Gillies Wm jr, grocer, 159 York
Gillies Wm, watchman, 71 Vine
Gilligan Jos, glassblower, 64 Wood e
Gillim Henry, laborer, 367 Hughson n
Gilmore John, agent, bds 79 Cannon w
Gilmore John, jr, piano maker, 90 Hunter w
Gilmore Mrs Rosa (wid Daniel) 123 Park n
Gilmore Mrs Sarah, 216 James n
Gilmore Thos, cabinetmaker, 54 Queen s
Gilmore Wm, shoemaker, 92 Rebecca
Gilmore Wm, butcher, cor Main and Spring
Gillmore Wm, asst undertaker, bds 47 King w
Gilmore Wm J, shoemaker, 65 Wellington n
Gilmore Wm J furniture dealer, 34 Merrick, h 90 Hunter w
Gilpin Thomas W, lumber measurer, 128 Jackson e

Godfrey Wm, baggageman, 131 Rebecca
Goff Edward, com traveler, 254 Barton e
Goff Mrs Emma (wid Geo) 164 Ferguson ave
Goff F G, engine driver, 164 Ferguson ave
Godwin Everard, 126½ Emerald n
Godwin Herbert, 126½ Emerald n
Godwin Walter, 126½ Emerald n
Gold F M, clerk G T R, 124 Hughson n
Goldberg Wm, second hand dealer, 244 York
Goldblat Powell, rag pedler, 142 Jackson w
Golden Mrs Mary, 22 Wilson
Golden J B, teamster, South
Goldsmith Rev Thomas, Presbyterian, 19 West ave s
Gompf John, Ontario brewery, 360 John n
Gompf Wm, teamster, 262 Catharine n
Goodale Emerson, driver, bds 66 Market
Goodale George, laborer, 72 Market
Goodale James, laborer, 17 Nightingale
Goodall Andrew, gardener, 100 Bay s
Goodenough John C, clerk, 195 Macnab n
Goodfellow John, painter, 116 Cherry
Goodfellow Walter, finisher, 179 Cannon e
Goodfellow Wm, finisher, 181 Cannon e
Goodhart Julius J, clothes cleaner, 29 York, bds 71 John s
Goodman Abraham, laborer Wentworth n
Goodman Mrs Charlotte (wid John) Wentworth n

Goodman Frank, stovemounter, 117 Cannon w
Goodram Wm, puddler, 12 **Little** Market
Goodson John W, shoemaker, 32 Wilson
Goodwin Alfred J, laborer, 58 Catharine s
Goodwin Mandwell, machinist, 276 Bay n
Goodwin Wm D, moulder, 1 Clark ave
Goodwin Wright M, telegraph inspector, 72 Herkimer
Goodyer William, malster, 103 Mulberry
Gordon Edwin, prop John St House, 74 John s
Gordon Mrs Emma (wid David W) 124 Cannon w
Gordon Geo, bricklayer, bds 11 Canada
Gordon James, bds 45 Hess n
Gordon Jas, clerk, 240 Mary n
Gordon Mrs Jane (wid John) 90 Locke n
Gordon Jos, gardener, Fairleigh Park, Main e of Wentworth
Gordon Mrs, nurse, 207 Main w
Gordon Robt, mounted policeman, bds 60 Hess n
Gordon Robt, blacksmith, 124 Cannon w
Gordon Robt, bookkeeper, 97 Wellington n
Gordon Robt jr, carpenter, 72 Wellington s
Gordon Robt sr, builder, 72 Wellington s
Gordon Thos, distiller, 87 Locke
Gordon Walter, moulder, 282 John n
Gordon W J F, coal and builders' supplies, 108 James n, h 108a Mary
Gordon Wm, cooper, 82 Rebecca, h 32 Catharine n
Gore John, letter carrier, 122 Cannon w

Gilroy Mrs Deborah, captain Salvation Army, 5 Hunter e
Gibson John G, conductor, 48 Ferguson ave
Gimblett Robert, shoemaker, 107 Jackson e
Ginnis Wm, glassblower, **bds** 194 James n
Girls' Home, **Mrs M A** Scott, matron, 77 George
Girouard Mrs Margaret (wid Candid) Barton w s nr Locomotive
Givey John, blacksmith, 33 Kelly
Givey Michael, shoemaker, 33 Kelly
Givin William, accountant, 35 Robert
Glass James, shoemaker, 136 Hunter w
Glass Mrs Sarah (wid George) 164 Rebecca
Glass Thomas, fancy goods, 126½ Cannon e
Glassco C S, commission merchant, 102 Hughson s
Glassco F S, 102 Hughson s
Glassco Geo F (G F Glassco & Co) h Park cor Robinson
Glassco G F & Co, wh furriers, 7 James s
Glassco Henry W, 109 Bay s
Glassco John T, [Macpherson, Glassco & Co] h Macnab cor Markland
Glassco W H, 102 Hughson s
Glassford John, fireman N N W, 155 West ave n
Glassford John, laborer, 174 West ave n
Glasgow John, 65 **Vine**
Glazier W N, porter Bank of Montreal
Gleason Dennis, agent, 80 Market
Gleason Mrs Kate, r 104½ Bay **n**
Gleason Mrs Mary (wid James) 69 Bay **n**

Gleason Michael, boilermaker, 26 Inchbury
Gleason Wm, 139 Ferrie e
Glebe Henry, tailor, 48 Victoria ave n
Glennie Wm E, com traveler, 54 Victoria ave s
Globe Newspaper, J H Mattice, correspondent and agent, Arcade, 33 James n
Glover Alexander, dairyman, King e of Wentworth
Glover Daniel M, carpenter, 84 Queen s
Glover Thos, moulder, bds 35 Hughson n
Glover Wm, marble cutter, bds 71 Caroline n
Glyndon Wm, **bookkeeper**, 8 Young
Goddard Mrs Andrew, 60 Hughson n
Goddard Mrs Emma, 9 Crooks
Goddard George A, pressman, 9 Crooks
Goddard John, laborer, 33 Crooks
Goddard Nathaniel, fish and fruit dealer, 178 King w
Goddard Wm, com traveler, 84 East ave n
Godden Mrs Elizabeth (wid John) 87 Hughson n
Godsall Thomas, waiter, bds 261 Bay n
Goedde **John, jeweler**, 8 Henry
Goering Mrs Anna, 54 West ave s
Goering Geo, Custom House Hotel, 17 **John** s
Goering Henry, hotel, 61-63 York
Goering H P, clerk, 54 West ave s
Goering Wm (W Goering & Co) h cor West ave and Stinson
Goering W & Co, wh wine and spirit merchants, 16-18 Merrick

Gore Coffee Tavern, Hamilton Coffee Tavern Co, props, 13 Hughson n
Gore District Mutual Fire Insurance Co, Elford G Payne, agent, 97 James n
Gore St Methodist Church Rev C O Johnson, pastor, John cor Gore
Goring Chas, carpenter, 141 Wellington n
Goring Mrs **Mary (wid** Arthur) 19 Gore
Gorman Anthony, rougher, 153 Locke n
Gorman Edward, barber, 5 York 6 Market
Gorman Hugh, porter G T **R,** 80 Hannah w
Gorman John, laborer, 370 James n
Gormley Jos, glassblower, 280 John n
Gorman Miss Mary A, 7 Robert
Gorman Michael tailor, 131 Hunter e
Gorman Mrs Patrick, 131 Hunter
Gorman Peter, blacksmith, **244** Mary
Gorman Peter, blacksmith, 162 King w, h 164 Market
Gorvin John, shoemaker, 99 James n
Gosnay Herbert (Gosnay & Walker) King e of Wentworth
Gosnay Jas, filesmith, King e of Wentworth
Gosnay & Walker, mattrass manufacturers, Main e of Wentworth
G sell **Thos S, inland revenue,** 41 Bay **s**
Gosney Wm, baker, bds 55 York
Gospel Hall, 36 Merrick
Gotte John, jeweler, 8 Henry
Gottorff Frederick, **marble** works, 118 York
Gould D H (D H Gould & Son) 162 James n

Gould D H & Son (D H Gould, Thos Gould) boot and shoe dealers, 160½ James n
Gould Jacob, carpenter, 19 Grove
Gould Jas, marble **cutter, 41½** Pearl n
Gould John laborer, 44 Canada
Gould Thos (D H Gould & Son) 162 James n
Goulding Arthur, caretaker Hess street school, 83 Hess n
Gourlay Miss Eleanor, 156 Napier
Govier Hy, butcher, 16 West ave **n**
Govier Mrs Sarah J (wid Jas) 16 West **ave n**
Gow Andrew, carpenter, **134** Hunter e
Gow Jas, boots and shoes, 184 King e, h 134 Hunter e
Gow J M, cutter, bds 21 West ave n
Gow James **N,** com traveller, bds 97 James s
Gow Mrs Wilhalmina (wid Wm) **134** Hunter e
Gowanlock Robt, engineer G T R 47 Magill
Gowland Wm, prop Court House Hotel, 57 John s
Goyott Jos, cooper, 65 Cherry
Grace Jos, shoemaker, 179½ Wellington n
Grace Mrs Mary, **203** Mary
Grace Pierce, laborer, 156 Bay n
Grace Thos, **wood** dealer, 256-256½ Hughson n
Gracey Chas, laborer, 108 Young
Graham Daniel, carpenter, 64 Colborne
Graham David, laborer, 32 Ferrie e
Graham David, gents' furnisher, 3 James n, h 53 Hunter w
Graham Donald, fireman, 26 East **ave n**

Graham Duncan, soapmaker, 270 Cannon e
Graham Mrs Ellen (wid Robt) 44 Burlington w
Graham Mrs Elmira (wid Wm) 13 **Baillie**
Graham Mrs Emeline (wid Sam'l) 105 Jackson e
Graham George, laborer, bds cor Barton and Wentworth n
Graham George, tailor, 101 Hess s
Graham Geo, salesman, 245 King w
Graham Harry, clerk American hotel
Graham John, machinist, 13 Little Wm
Graham George, grocer, 317 **Barton e**
Graham Misses, hair workers, 42 James n
Graham Mrs, 63 Lower Cathcart
Graham Richard, dye works, n e cor Herkimer and Queen, h 50 Markland
Graham W, clerk Bank B N A, Burlington
Grainger Frederick, expressman, 130½ **King Wm**
Grames Robert, machinist, 162 Macnab n
Grand Opera House, James cor Gore
Grand Trunk Offices, Stuart w
Grand Trunk Railway, city passenger agency, Charles E Morgan, agent, 11 James n
Grand Trunk Station, Stuart w
Granger Harry, agent, 71 **Caroline n**
Grant Alexander, brakeman, 23 Locomotive
Grant Alexander, inspector waterworks, **42 Alanson**
Grant Mrs Augusta (wid Wm W) 284 Bay n

Grant Col C C, hd John s
Grant Mrs Peter, 297 King e
Grant Mrs Margaret (wid John) 235 Cannon e
Grant P **H**, salesman, King cor Wentworth
Grant P & Sons, brewers and malsters, **spring** brewery, cor **Bay and Mulberry**
Grant Mrs Robert, 33 Emerald n
Grant Sydney, bookkeeper, 284 Bay n
Grant Thomas, carpenter, 10 Magill
Grant Thos W, bookkeeper, 297 King e
Grant William, reporter, 286 **John n**
Grant W J, city agent N & N W R, M C & C P R, Arcade, 33 **James n**, h Stinson cor East ave s
Grassie Jas M, yardsman G T R, 32 Locomotive
Gray And, checker G T R, 86 Caro**line** n
Gray Charles, laborer, Beulah
Grey Mrs Eliza (wid Daniel) Hannah w s nr Locke
Gray Henry, locker customs, 37 Strachan w
Gray James, helper, 185 Hughson n
Grey James F, gardener, Blake
Gray John, machinist, bds 198 Macnab n
Gray John, laborer, 71 Strachan
Gray John, laborer, 10 Stuart e
Gray Joseph, clerk, 19 Sheaffe
Gray Luke, mechanic, 106 Barton e
Gray Patrick, laborer, 226 John n
Grey Ralph, carpenter, 35 Cath**arine n**
Gray Richard, 102 Florence
Gray Robert, conductor, 105 Bay n
Gray Robt, glassblower, 249 Catharine n

Gray Robert, laborer, 288 Hughson n
Grey Mrs Sarah F (wid James) 7 Cannon w
Grey Walter, com traveler, 44 Cannon e
Grey W, for man, 134 Cannon w
Gray William, laborer, 70 Locke n
Gray Wm, cigarmaker, bds 162 Rebecca
Gray Wm, weaver, 272 Mary
Gray Wm, 143 Bay n
Gray Wm, 214 Hughson n
Gray William H, mason, 19 Sheaffe
Graysley Thomas, gardener, 36 Smith ave
Grayson **Geo**, springmaker, 26 Caroline n
Great Northwestern Telegraph Co, Geo Black, agent, 18 James s
Gregg Miss Catharine, 13 East ave n
Gregg Miss Mary, 13 East ave n
Gregory S E, 57 Catharine s
Greene Mrs A [wid Richard] 66 East ave s
Green Alfred, laborer, s e cor Robinson and Garth
Green Edwin, furniture dealer, 86 King w, h 124 York
Green Mrs Eliza [wid James] 107 Rebecca
Green Frederick, tea dealer, 77 Mary
Green Frederick A, merchant, 77 Mary
Green George, laborer, 2 Oak
Green Geo, foreman Lawry & Son, 13 Charles
Green George, laborer, 123 Hess n
Green Harry, stoves and tins, 29 Macnab n
Green Horace, millwright, 163 Wellington n
Green Jas, laborer, 123 Hess n

Green James, laborer, 178 Victoria ave n
Green James, laborer, 20 Picton e
Greene J J, bookkeeper, bds 94 James s
Green John, com traveller, 73 Vine
Greene R H, John McPherson & Co, h 89 Hughson s
Green Richard, 30 Guise
Green Samuel, clerk bds 54 Park n
Green Samuel, laborer, Grant
Green Thos A, master mariner, 168 Ferguson ave
Green Wm, laborer, **108 Strachan** e
Green **W J**, compositor, 107 Rebecca
Greenan Thos, moulder, 89 Hughson n
Greenaway Job, foreman Charlton's, end Wilson
Greenaway John, moulder, 132 Catharine n
Greenaway Robt, moulder, 132 Catharine n
Greenaway Thos, moulder, 62 John n
Greenaway Thos, timekeeper, 170 Ferguson **ave**
Greenfield Jos, bailiff and auctioneer, **12** King Wm, h 77 Elgin
Greenhill Walter **W**, harness maker, 90 Queen **s**
Greening B & Co, Victoria Wire Mills, 41 Queen n
Greening Samuel O (B Greening & Co) 63 Queen n
Greening T B (T B Greening & Co) 63 George
Greening T B & Co, wholesale teas, 23 King **w**
Greenlees Jas, moulder, 17 Murray e
Greenly James, carpenter, 66 Pearl n

Greenley John, lithographic artist, 66 Pearl n
Greenman Wm, machinist, 269 York
Greenway Jos F, ornamental painter, 54 Pearl n
Greenway Wm, **laborer**, 136 Wood e
Greenwood Jas, bds 161 East ave
Greenwood Mrs J R, school of dressmaking, 8½ King e
Greer D G, real estate, 20 James s, h 13 Duke
Greer James, shoemaker, 141 James n
Greer, Mrs John H, teacher, 9 Murray w
Greer Wm, carpet weaver, bds 168 Mary
Greig Geo B, carpenter, 8 Burlington n
Greig Geo C, salesman, 149 John s
Greig Hy G, bookkeeper, 149 John s
Greig Jeremiah, stonemason, 191 Wilson
Greig John jr, salesman, 119 Queen n
Greig John sr, bookseller, 2 York h 119 Queen n
Gribben Thos, carpenter, 143 Hughson n
Grice James, 116 Napier
Griffin A, letter **carrier**, P O
Griffin Mrs Catharine (wid Thos) 28 West ave n
Griffin Mrs Harriet (wid Absolum) 7 Caroline s
Griffin Henry, 38 Jackson e
Griffin H S M D, 15 Walnut s
Griffin Justus A (Griffin & Kidner) 190 King w
Griffin & Kidner (Justus A Griffin, Frank Kidner) general printers, 47 King Wm
Griffin Lawrence, 48 Jackson e
Griffin Miss Maggie, dressmaker, 48 Jackson e

Grffin John, laborer, 263 James n
Griffin Wm, sailor, 55 Burlington w
Griffith Mrs Elizabeth, 228 Hughson n
Griffith Mrs Ellen (widow Thos) 34 Wilson
Griffith Hy J, shoemaker, 3 East ave n
Griffith James jeweler, 87 Cherry
Griffith Robt, engine driver, bds 208 Macnab n
Griffith Robt, com traveller, 143 John s
Griffith Samuel, porter, 74 Tisdale
Griffith Thos, laborer, 12 Tiffany
Griffith Wm (Wm Griffith & Co) h 139 James s
Griffith Wm & Co, wholesale boots and shoes, 57 King w
Griffith Wm H, printer, 34 Wilson
Griffiths Miss, 12 Upper Cathcart
Griffiths Tunis B, ticket agent G T R, 6 Ray s
Grigg Alfred, clerk, Concession n s nr Locke
Grigg Mrs Janet, confectioner, 216 King e
Grigg R A, clerk, Concession
Griggs Christopher S, policeman, 37 Locomotive
Grills Geo, shoemaker, bds Franklin House
Grill Joseph, hooker, Eliza
Grill Mrs Mary, Eliza
Grimer Joseph, laborer, Athol
Griner W D, glassblower, 161 James n
Griswold Thaddeus M, whip maker, 19 Elgin
Grossman Augustus, music dealer, 24 West ave s
Grossman Hall, 47½ James
Grossman Julius, music dealer, 22 West ave s

Grossman P, music dealer, 47 James n, h 168 Main e
Grotz Adam J, nailer, 66 Locomotive
Grove Samuel, laborer, 16 Stuart e
Grover G A, supt American Express Co, 18 James s
Grover Jos, gardener, 66 Robinson
Groves Jas, blacksmith, 138 West ave n
Groves Samuel, blacksmith, 37 York, h 125 East ave n
Grundy Claude, gardener, 5 Clark ave
Guardian Fire and Life Assurance Co of London, Gillespie & Powis, agents, 31 King e
Guarantee Co of North America, Seneca Jones agent, 6 James s
Guest Samuel, laborer, 165 Catharine n
Gugel Wm, boot and shoemaker 122 Rebecca
Guggisberg John [Scharlach & Co] 39 Main w
Guillett Napoleon, tobacco roller, 74 Market
Gully John, shoemaker, Wentworth n
Gully Mrs Mary Ann [wid Wm] 41 Sheaffe
Gully Mrs Sophia [wid Joshua] 46 Cannon w
Gully Thos, 162 Mary
Gully Wm, soda water manfr, 41 Sheaffe
Gummore Henry C, mason, 46 Markland
Gummo John B, harness maker, 109 Herkimer
Gunn Edward, bookkeeper, Bay s
Gunn R L, clerk 9th Division Court, Court House, h 28 Hannah e

Gunner William, tea dealer, 37 Ray n
Gunther Geo, tailor, bds 134 King Wm
Gurney Charles [E & C Gurney Co] hd John s
Gurney Charles, jr, manager retail dept E & C Gurney Co, 51 Walnut s
Gurney E & C Co, [limited] (J H Tilden managing director) founders, 36-42 John n
Gurney Mrs Edward, hd of John s
Gurney George, hd of John s
Gurneys & Ware, manfrs of platform and counter scales, James cor Colborne
Guth Martin, cabinetmaker, 163a John n
Guthrie Thomas, poultry dealer, 125 Rebecca
Guttridge Charles, 306 James n
Guy Hugh, 376 James n
Guy John, barber, bds 205 Wellington n
Guy Robert, stovemounter, bds 205 Wellington n
Gwin William, bookkeeper, 35 Robert
Gwyder Richard, whitewasher, 84 Macnab n
Haas Gottlieb, nurseryman, 47 Wellington s
Hacker G G, gents' furnishings, 6 James n, h 30 George
Hackett John, machinist, 23 Barton e
Hackett Michael, steel polisher, 115 Cherry
Hadden Geo, laborer, Ashley
Hafner John, glassblower, 270 James n
Hager Thomas, stovemounter, 4 Grove
Hagerty Mrs Johanna [wid John] 33 Napier
Hahnan John, bricklayer, Markland s s w Locke

Haigh Richard, bookbinder and paper box manfr, 60 King w, h 134 West ave n

Haines Mrs John, laundress, 284 King w

Haines Samuel, potter, 31 Margaret

Haines Thomas P, machinist, 64 Steven

Haines Wm, loom fitter, bds 27 Simcoe w

Haining Wm, packer, ft Sherman Barton e

Halcrow James, locker customs, 230 James n

Halcrow Wm, stonemason, 230 James n

Hale Henry, laborer, 34 Picton w

Hales Mrs Eliza [wid Richard J] 135 West ave n

Halford Harry J, barber, 55 John

Haliot Eugene, foreman cotton mills, 209 Mary

Hall Alfred, 66½ King Wm

Hall Chas A, brickmaker, 12 Locke n

Hall David, blacksmith, 3 Locke s

Hall Edward, laborer, 16 Henry

Hall Mrs Edward, music teacher, 16 Henry

Hall George, mechanic, 173 Macnab n

Hall Mrs Harriet [wid George] 91 Locke n

Hall Henry, com traveler, Main e of Wentworth

Hall Henry, laborer, Robinson s s nr Locke

Hall Herbert R, fireman G T R, 63 Locomotive

Hall Jacob M, engineer, 48 Cannon w

Hall James, moulder, 51 John n

Hall John, cabinetmaker, 93 James n

Hall John, foreman G T R, 7 Peter

Hall John, laborer, 17 Napier

Hall John, patternmaker, 167 John n

Hall John, 209 Mary

Hall John H, confectioner, 100½ James n

Hall John T, [McCallum & Hall] 91 Locke n

Hall Mrs Mary [wid Robt G] 66½ King Wm

Hall R, valuator, Wentworth s

Hall Thos, engine driver HNW, 173 West ave n

Hall Thomas, fitter, 13 Inchbury n

Hall Thos K, blacksmith, 93 Locke n

Hall Wm, milk pedler, 71 Colborne

Hall Wm, wood turner, Beulah

Hall Wm J, porter, 21 West ave n

Hall ——, carpenter, 16 Henry

Haller Harvey, laborer, 53 Mary

Halliday Christopher, laborer, 134 Macnab n

Halliday Frank B, com traveler, 108 Catharine s

Halliday John, laborer, 82 Walnut s

Halliday R J, salesman, 108 Catharine s

Halliday Wm (Reid & Halliday) 131½ Main e

Hallisey Wm, policeman, 82 Maria

Halloran Bros (John & Edward) carriage supplies, 53 King w

Halloran Mrs Catharine, 217 Catharine n

Halloran Ed (Halloran Bros) 177 Wellington n

Halloran James, baker, 119 Cherry

Halloran James W, grocer, 48 Peter

Halloran Jas, moulder, 49 Elgin

Halloran Jas E, livery stable, h 68 John n, 22 Hugeson n

Hamilton Geo, mason, 30 Tisdale

Hamilton Geo E, com traveller, 101 King w

Hamilton Glass Co, 309 Hughson n

Hamilton Gun Works, J Holman, prop, 79 James n

Hamilton Homestead Loan and Savings Society, I A Studdard, sec, Court House

Hamilton House Building Co, R L Gunn, sec, Court House

Hamilton House Furnishing Co, Henry H Laing, prop, 88½-90 King w

Hamilton Industrial Works Co, manfrs of Clothes Wringers, Mangles and Washing Machines, cor Bay and Murray

Hamilton Iron Forging Co, Thos D Beddoe, manager, Sa J Whitehead, supt, n e cor Queen and Barton

Hamilton Jas, druggist, 104 Main w

Hamilton Jas, clerk, 104 Main w

Hamilton James, agent Shedding Co, 64 Ferguson ave

Hamilton James, carpenter, 98 East ave n

Hamilton James, laborer, 28 Jones

Hamilton James, tobacco roller, 7 Hess n

Hamilton James H, builder, 81 East ave n

Hamilton John H, com traveller, 10 King w

Hamiton Michael, laborer, 8 Wood w

Hamilton Mrs Marian (wid John M) 109 Jackson w

Hamilton Mineral Water Co, Pilgrim Bros, props, 1 Spring

Hamilton Newspaper and Bill Distributing Co, David Bewick, manager, 22 Macnab s

Hamilton & North-Western Railway, Maitland Young, sec, 33 Main e

Hamilton Orphan Asylum, Miss Jane McFarlane, matron, 115 Wellington s

Hamilton Packing House, Thos Lawry & Son, props, 16-20 Macnab s

Hamilton Piano Stool Co, John W Smoke, proprietor, 145 King w

Hamilton Powder Co, James Watson, resident director, 69 James n

Hamilton Provident and Loan Society, H D Cameron, treasurer, King cor Hughson s

Hamilton Right Rev Charles, D D, D C L, Bishop of Niagara, 121 John n

Hamilton Robert, 258 Bay n

Hamilton Robt J, 101 King w

Hamilton Sewer Pipe Co, (Picton C Brown, mangr), Wentworth n

Hamilton Stained Glass Works (H Longhurst & Co) 16 John n

Hamilton Straw Works (John McArthur) Ferguson ave, h 138 Hughson n

Hamilton Street Railway, Stuart w

Hamilton Turkish Baths, O H Hudson, James n

Hamilton Vinegar Works Co [limited] (B E Charlton, pres) 3-9 Wellington n and 85 James s

Hamilton Wheel Works (F H Hore & Son) Elgin n

Hamilton Whip Co (T D Murphy, mangr, 81 Mary

Hamilton Wrought Iron Works, Brayley & Dempster, props, 47-49 King Wm

Hamilton William, laborer, 8 Wood w

Halloran John (Halloran Bros) h 181 Mary
Halloran Patrick, glassblower, 219 Catharine n
Halloran Patrick, grocer, **cor** Barton and Catharine
Halloran Timothy, laborer, end Mary e s
Halloran William, moulder, -49 Elgin
Halloran Mrs Alice [wid Martin] 68 Walnut s
Halm Rev Michael S, Roman Catholic, 25 Sheaffe
Halter **Jos**, butcher, 21 Little Wm
Ham Thos (Ham & Edwards) h 64 Lower Cathcart
Hamberg Francis E, loom fixer, 223 Catharine n
Hamberg Wm E, student, bds 99 York
Hamberg Mrs Emily, **290** James n
Hamberg Lawson, **laborer, 30** Simcoe e
Ham & Edwards (Thos Ham, Robt Edwards) tinsmiths, 17 York
Hamill Hy, gardener, 69 Duke
Hamill Wm **J**, laborer, 138 Locke n
Hamilton A & **Co**, druggists, 2 King w
Hamilton **Mrs A** E (wid Alex) **37** Rebecca
Ham'n Agricultural Works L D Sawyer & Co, proprietors, ft Wellington n
Hamilton Alex (A Hamilton & Co) 104 Main w
Hamilton Alex, clerk, 112 Queen n
Hamilton Alex, com traveller, 56 Catharine n
Hamilton Mrs **Alice** (wid Martin) 69 Walnut **s**
Hamilton Mrs Ann (wid Francis) **s w** cor Barton and Magill

Hamilton Bottling Co, Masonic Hall Building, James n
Hamilton Bridge and Tool Co, Wm Hendrie, Pres, C Teiper, Manager, John Stewart, Sec-Treas ft Caroline n
Hamilton Brush Co, Jas O'Brien, Manager, Wanzer building, King e
Hamilton Business College, Rattray & Geiger, props, 2½ James s
Hamilton Charles, bookkeeper, 8 Aurora
Hamilton Cigar Co, Reid, Birely & **Co**, props, 102 King e
Hamiton Club, J B Young, sec, 2 Main e
Hamilton Coffee and Spice **Co,** W E Duncan, manager, r **33** Main e
Hamilton Cotton Co (J M Young, R A Lucas) 184 Mary
Hamilton Coffee Tavern Co, **13** Hughson n, Alexandra Arcade, and N & N W R station, King e
Hamilton Dry Plate **Co**, Thos Gentle, manager, Concession
Hamilton and Dundas Express Office (B Hunt & Co) 105 John s .
Hamilton and Dundas St Railway, John Weatherstone, lessee and **manager,** 16 Main e
Hamilton **East,** that part of the township **situated** between Wentworth **street** and the Delta
Hamilton Electric Light Co, W Boisfenillet, manager, 1 Catharine s
Hamilton Mrs Emily (wid Jos) 105 James s
Hamilton Mrs Francis (wid Wm) 66 Ray n
Hamilton Gas Light Co, 9 Park n

Hamilton Wm, blacksmith, bds 72 Cannon w
Hammill Henry, laborer, 94a Hunter e
Hammill Samuel R, teamster, 94a Hunter e
Hammond Mrs B, 43 Stuart e
Hammond James, city coal weigher, 353 John n
Hammond Mrs Matilda (wid Wm H) 51 Park n
Hammond Richard, whitewasher, 51 Oak ave
Hammond Samuel R, coachman, 75 Jackson w
Hampson Henry, shoemaker, 79 Emerald n
Hampson James, laborer, 79 Emerald n
Hampson John, shoemaker, 161 King Wm
Hampson J Edward, com traveler 112 Jackson w
Hampson Miss Mary, 21 Lower Cathcart
Hampson Willis, turner, 102 East ave n
Hampton Harry J, machinist, 56 Hughson s
Hanrahan James, moulder, 170 Park n
Hancock Chas, bricklayer, 140 Hunter w
Hancock Edward, carpenter, 273 Macnab n
Hancock James, whipmaker, r 50½ Young
Hancock John, builder, 24 Wellington n
Hancock J, saw grinder, 301 York
Hancock Joseph, 20 Hannah e
Hancock Oliver, tobacconist, 110 King w
Hancock Wm, builder, 27 Locomotive
Hand Prof Wm, firework manfr, 310 King w, h Head
Handcock Samuel R, laborer, 107 Florence

Hanes James B, signalman, 103 East ave n
Hanes John A, laborer, 68 Peter
Haney Robt, commission dealer, bds 95 Macnab n
Hanham A W, teller Bank BNA, Markland
Hanlan Mrs Margaret (wid Edward) 108 Bay n
Hanley Henry, laborer, **36 Simcoe** e
Hanley Martin, blacksmith, 37 Hannah e
Hanley Patrick, bricklayer, 233 John n
Hanley Patrick, laborer, 34 Simcoe e
Hanley Timothy, laborer, 101 Simcoe e
Hanley Wm, blacksmith, 32 **Bay** s
Hanley William, laborer, 275 John n
Hanlon Mrs Ann (wid Daniel) 81 Hunter w
Hanlon Patrick, grocer, 13 Hess n
Hanna Mrs Ann (wid Wm) 46 Wellington n
Hannaford Alfred (Hannaford Bros) 100 Robinson
Hannaford Bros (Robert and Alfred) plain and ornamental plasterers, 76 Merrick
Hannaford Robert, (Hannaford Bros) h 102 Robinson
Hannah Alex, bricklayer, r 57 **York**
Hannah George, driver, bds 56 Locomotive
Hannah James, stonemason, 135 James n
Hannah John, r 57 York
Hannah Street Methodist Church, Rev Joseph Odery, pastor, Hannah cor Queen
Hannah Thomas, teamster, 309 Barton e
Hannah Wm, stonecutter, 185 Wilson

Hanning Mrs Jennie (wid Robt) 15 Murray w
Hannon Mrs Barbara [wid John] 231 Hughson n
Hannon Emerson, **grocer**, 11 Lower Cathcart
Hannon Joseph, 245 Hain e
Hannon ——, laborer, 178 Hughson n
Hanton Alexander, machinist, 5 Ferguson ave
Harcourt W L, MD, 10 Emerald s
Hardiker Frank H, clerk G T R 74 Napier
Hardiker Mrs Jane (wid John) 74 Napier
Hardiker Mrs Mary [wid John] 2 Tiffany
Hardiker Thos, confectioner, 77 Hunter w
Harding Henry, plumber, 119 James n
Hardstaff Mrs Annie (wid Wm) 161 Victoria ave n
Hardy Capt Chas, Woodland, Wentworth n
Hardy Daniel, moulder, 22 Simcoe e
Hardy Edward, bookkeeper, 171 Macnab n
Hardy Joseph, carpenter, 111 Wood e
Hargrove Henry, machine operator, 206 Cannon e
Hargrove Joseph, manager Singer Manf Co, h 107 Emerald n
Harlow Geo, 69 Young
Harlow Thos, grocer, 69 Young
Harmon James, laborer, 165 Jackson w
Harold John, Glassblower, 348 James n
Harper Andrew, butcher, Main e of Wentworth
Harper Drury, polisher, 1.7 Simcoe e
Harper Mrs Elizabeth (wid Richard) 16 O'Reilly

Harper Geo, prrinter, 20½ Ray n
Harper Geo, 1 Hess s
Harper John, butcher, Main e of Wentworth
Harper Mrs Margaret (wid Andrew) Main e of Wentworth
Harper Mrs Mary (wid Richard) 113 Caroline
Harper Mrs, 16 O'Reilly
Harper Robt, carpenter, 66 Colborne s
Harper Robert, florist, cor King Wm and Wellington h 18 Wellington n
Harper Thos sr, Ida
Harper Geo G, electro plater, Herkimer n s w Locke
Harper Thos, gardener, Burlington s
Harper Wm, railroader, 70½ Lower Cathcart
Harper Wm, shoemaker, 113 King Wm
Harper Wm, printer, 128 Market
Harper Wm, street car driver, 225 Catharine n
Harrigan John, glassblower, 378 James n
Harris Mrs Ann, 97 Hunter e
Harris Bros (F J & W J) bakers, 14 Market Sq
Harris Edwin, boarding, 140 Bay s
Harris Mrs Eliza, 187 Wilson
Harris F J (Harris Bros) h 14 Market Sq
Harris Duncan, salesman, 182 King e
Harris Geo, porter, 16 Upper Cathcart
Harris Geo, 22 Strachan w
Harris Geo E, pressman, 71 Queen s
Harris James, engineer G T R, 7 Oxford
Harris James, gardener L Springer, Maple ave, East Hamilton
Harris Jas, bds 30 Hughson s

Harris James, policeman, 39 Locomotive
Harris John, drain contractor, 227 McNab n
Harris John, plasterer, 69 John n
Harris John jr, laborer, 69 John
Harris John C, teacher, 55 Ferguson ave
Harris John M, bookkeeper, 11 Cannon w
Harris Louis, organist, St Paul's Church, 28 Main w
Harris Mrs Lucy (wid William) 77 Hunter e
Harris Mrs Margaret E (wid Thos B) 40 Jackson w
Harris Mrs Mary (wid James) 85 John n
Harris Samuel, teamster, 93 John n
Harris Wm, printer, 49 Maria
Harris Wm, laborer, bds 19 Hughson n
Harris Mrs Wm, 49 Maria
Harris Wm, 55 Park n
Harris Wm Henry, painter, 36 Cannon w
Harris W J (Harris Bros) h 14 Market Sq
Harris Wm J, carter, 3 Inchbury s
Harris Mrs Amelia (wid Frank R) dressmaker, 71 Hunter w
Harrison Mrs Arabella (wid Hy Ed) 84 Rebecca
Harrison Bros [J & F S] druggists, 274 James n
Harrison Edward, wood and coal dealer, and hackman, n e cor Main and Locke, h 181 Main w
Harrison Geo, machinist, 13 New
Harrison G P, com traveller, 17 West ave s
Harrison Hy, furnace fitter, 178 Cannon e
Harrison Henry, butcher, 51 James s

Harrison James [Harrison Bros] h 159 Park s
Harrison James, hackman, 40 Pearl s
Harrison John, machinist, 8 Oak
Harrison John [Osler, Teetzel & Harrison] h 2 Nelson ave
Harrison John, 37 Steven
Harrison J G, clerk, Steven cor Wilson
Harrison Luke, butcher, 48 Wellington s
Harrison Misses L & C, milliners, 178 King e
Harrison Thos, stonecutter, 79 Macauley e
Harrison Wm H C, herbalist, 71 York
Harron Andrew, cab driver, 205 James n
Harron R J, clerk P O
Harron Wm, salesman, 205 James n
Harron Wm, laborer, 205 James n
Harett A W, clerk Molson's Bank, 34 Bay s
Hart Emery Wheel Company, limited, James T Barnard, sec-treas, Samuel Briggs, superintendent, emery wheels and machines, 19 Hunter w
Hart Herbert, dairyman, 292 Cannon w
Hart Mrs John, toll gate keeper, King e
Hart Richard R, clerk American Express Co, bds 7 Bold
Hart Robert J, teamster, 46 Kelly
Hart Mrs Rose [wid John] 132 Park n
Hart Mrs Sarah [wid James] 28a Catharine s
Hart Thos, laborer, 14 Lower Cathcart
Harte Patrick, clerk, 248 Hughson n
Harte R R, clerk, 7 Bold

Harter Jos, moulder, 181 East ave n
Hartford Fire Insurance Co, Geo McKeand, agent, 57 James n
Hartley Jos, laborer, 33 Simcoe e
Hartley Mrs Mary A [wid Samuel] 17 Pearl s
Hartley Mrs Sarah, fancy goods, 131 James n
Hartley Mrs Sarah (wid Thomas) r 64 Hughson n
Hartnett Mrs Elizabeth (wid John) 148 King Wm
Hartness Mrs Janet (wid Adam) 83 East ave n
Harvey Alex, (Alex Harvey & Co) 226 King w
Harvey Alex & Co, wholesale grocers 21 King e
Harvey Mrs Alex, 226 King w
Harvey Miss Annie, 43 Jackson e
Harvey Chas A, porter, 169 East ave n
Harvey Mrs Ellen, nurse, 93a Murray e
Harvey Henry, plumber, 17 Queen n
Harvey Horace, cabinetmaker, 101 Emerald s
Harvey James, farmer, 63 East ave s
Harvey James A, printer, 26 Merrick, h 25½ Spring
Harper James F, mail clerk GTR, 127 Market
Harvey James S, clerk, 226 King w
Harvey John (John Harvey & Co) h Robinson cor Macnab
Harvey John & Co, wool merchants, 69 James n, warehouse 8-10 Rebecca
Harvey Joseph P, hotel, 350 James n
Harvey J S, clerk, 226 King w
Harvey Mrs Margaret (wid Wm) 34 Bay s

Harvey Samuel, auctioneer, 7 Baillie
Harvey Walter G, ledger keeper, 34 Bay s
Harper Wm, engineer G T R, 156 Market
Harvey Wm, grocer, 108½ King w, h Herkimer
Harvey Wm, stonecutter, Nelson
Harvey W C (Orr, Harvey & Co) 7 Main w
Harvey Wm J, roller, Dundurn w s opp Tom
Harvey Wm M, salesman, bds 30 Hughson s
Haskins Gerald M, com traveler, 226 King e
Haskins R L (Barnes & Haskins) h 226 King e
Haskins Wm, city engineer, 226 King e
Haslett Thomas C [Haslett & Washington] h 27 Hannah w
Haslett & Washington [Thos C Haslett, S F Washington] barristers, 20 James s
Hastie Mrs Isabella [wid John] 41 East ave n
Hastings Mrs Ann E [wid Jas] 56 West ave n
Hastings James, laborer, 55 Emerald n
Hastings James, trunk maker, 55 Emerald n
Hastings Philip, carpenter, 45 West ave n
Hatchard Wm, cabinetmaker, bds 98 Hess n
Hathaway Alfred, laborer, 37 Caroline n
Hatt Mrs Lucy E [wid John O] 63 Macnab s
Hattersly Walter, machinist, bds 215 James n
Hatton Amos, toolmaker, 131 Emerald n
Hatzfeld Louis E, bookkeeper, bds 15 Main w

Havers James, glassblower, 328 Macnab n
Haverscroft Wm, messenger Molson's Bank, 36 King e
Hawkes Edward, collector *Spectator*, 154½ John n
Hawkes Frederick C, bartender Commercial hotel
Hawkins David, 6 Bay s
Hawkins Geo D (Geo D Hawkins & Co) 2 Bay s
Hawkins Geo D & Co, Shirt & Suspender manfrs, 2 George
Hawkins Henry, plasterer, 10 Cherry
Hawkins James, turnkey jail
Hawkins Robert J, carpenter, 283 King Wm
Hawkins Wm, machinist, 11 Inchbury n
Hawkins Wm, policeman, 195 Cannon e
Hawthorn Hugh, laborer, 110 Strachan e
Hawthorne John, moulder, bds 35 Hughson n
Hay Alex, carpenter, 82 Canada
Hay A L, salesman, 77 Main e
Hay Andrew, carpenter, 275 Hughson n
Hay Wm, scalemaker, 168 Victoria ave n
Hayden John L, brakeman G T R, Barton w s s nr Crooks
Haydon Jas, tinsmith, 226 York
Haydon Jas W, tinsmith, 226 York
Hayes Alexander, grocer, 44 Victoria ave n
Hayes Edward, hackman, 15 Sophia s nr Head
Hayes George, grocer, cor East ave and Barton e
Hayes John, laborer, 166 Catharine n
Hayes John, laborer, bds 82 Hughson n
Hayes John, stovemounter, 167 Mary

Hayes Matthew, hackman, 15 Sophia s nr Head
Hayes Michael, 15 Sophia s nr Head
Hayes Patrick, laborer, 112 Maria
Hayes Thomas, laborer, 44 Peter
Hayes Thomas, shoemaker, 38 Macauley e
Haygarth Jacob, machinist, 102 Emerald n
Haygarth John J, stovemounter, 38 Tisdale
Haygarth Mrs Mary, 102 Emerald n
Haygarth Robert, stovemounter, 102 Emerald n
Hayhoe C, fruiterer, 258 King e
Hayman Albert, laborer, 42 Wellington n
Haynes Jacob P [S A Pocock & Co] 45 Caroline n
Haynes Price, saw maker, 45 Caroline n
Hazell Horace, **carter**, 50 Victoria ave n
Hazell Tom, salesman, 50 Victoria ave n
Hazell Wm, porter, 50 Victoria ave n
Hazell Wm, baker, 80 Mary
Hazell Wm S C, (Hazell & Dawson), 6 Hilton
Hazen George, tailor, 98 Wilson
Headland Henry, laborer, 2 Little Wm
Healey Egerton, **com** traveller, 28 Nelson ave
Healey F B, clerk, 274 King e
Healey Henry J, collector, 26 Nelson ave
Healey John W, 274 King e
Healey M D, dry goods, 18-19 Market sq, h 111 Bay n
Healey Mrs S M, 274 King e
Healey Thomas, 86½ Hunter e
Heard Samuel, 26 Victoria ave n
Hearne Matthew, manager A C Quimby & Co, 72 Ferguson ave

Hearne Richard G, salesman, 72 Ferguson ave
Hearne William, watchman, 12½ Margaret
Heath Adlie J, dairman, 293 King e
Heath Grove, machinist, 91 Cannon e
Heath James, blacksmith, 51 Pearl n
Heath Milo, machinist, 91 Cannon e
Heath Saml, blacksmith, 36 Ray n
Heath Mrs Sarah, (wid Louis), 295 King e
Hebner Fredk, laborer, 128 Jackson w
Heddle David, mason, 98 Wellington s
Heddle Mrs David, grocer, 98 Wellington s
Heddon Thos, blacksmith, 48 Pearl s
Hedeberg, J V, engineer, 295 King e
Hedge Harry, shoemaker, 64 Ray s
Hedley Thomas, upholsterer, 19 Macnab s, h 110 Herkimer
Heenan Very Rev E I, Vicar General Diocese of Hamilton, the Palace, 25 Sheaffe
Heenan Mrs Mary, 192 Robert
Heeney Wm, bookkeeper, 17 Victoria ave n
Heilig George, contractor, 95 John n
Heilig Geo W, salesman, 240 King e
Hembecker Henry, photographer 56 Emerald s
Heins Mrs Catharine, children's clothing, 138½ Main e
Heintsman Joseph, cigarmaker, 18 Sheaffe
Heisrodt Cornelius N, auctioneer 47 East ave n
Held Fred, teamster, 268 Macnab n

Helmsley Geo, bookkeeper, bds 40 Market
Heming G E: clerk, mountain top
Heming H P, clerk, mountain tp
Heming P G, clerk Merchant's Bank, mountain top
Hempill W S, clerk, 101 Market
Hempill Z, manger A & S Nordheimer, h 101 Market
Hempstock Geo, butcher, 199 Main w
Hempstock Mrs Jane, (wid Thos) Main w, s s w Garth
Hempstock, Mrs May A, (wid Joseph) 156 Jackson w
Hempstock Wm, laborer, 61 Canada
Hempstock Wm, laborer, Robinson n s w Locke
Henderson Alex, carpenter, bds 30 Hughson s
Henderson Andrew, clerk, Main w
Henderson Mrs Annie, (wid Gilbert), 180 Napier
Henderson Mrs Annie, 14 Main w
Henderson Dugald, clerk, 59 Herkimer
Henderson George, gardener, E Rutherford, Main e of Wentworth
Henderson Geo, 84 Merrick
Henderson James, salesman, 131½ Emerald n
Henderson James, machinist, 131½ Emerald n
Henderson James, teamster, 353 Hughson n
Henderson James, 33 Emerald n
Henderson Mrs Janet, (wid Andrew), 68 Bay s
Henderson John, blacksmith, 17 Harriet
Henderson John, laborer, n w cor Hunter & Macklin
Henderson John, teamster, 80 Catharine s

Henderson John, teamster, bds 102 Jackson e
Henderson J E, clerk, 190 Macnab
Henderson J M (J M Henderson & Co) h Robinson between Macnab **and Park**
Henderson J M & Co, tailors, 20 King w
Henderson Miss Lizzie, dress maker, bds 113 Cannon w
Henderson Mrs Margaret, [wid David] 58 Napier
Henderson Mrs Mary [wid Geo N] 117 King Wm
Henderson Robt, carpenter, 50 Steven
Henderson Wm, laborer, 159 Catharine n
Henderson Wm, tinsmith, bds 33 Inchbury n
Henderson Wm S, bookkeeper, 68 Bay s
Hendershot Oscar, driver, Robinson n s nr Garth
Hendershot Morris, driver, 127 Hannah w
Hendrie Alex, ward foreman, 67 Perl n
Hendrie & Co [Wm & George] cartage agents, 33 King w
Hendrie Geo M, clerk, 23 Bold
Hendrie Jas W, contractor, 23 Bold
Hendrie John S, contractor, 93 James s
Hendrie Wm (Hendrie & Co) h 23 Bold
Hendrie Wm jr, clerk, 23 Bold
Hendry A F, clerk, 19 Mulberry
Hendry Mrs Helen, 45 Magill
Hendry John, patent solicitor and pattern maker, 1 Rebecca, h 100 Concession
Henery Mrs Mary (wid Capt John) 8 Ferguson ave
Henigan Jas, gents' furnisher, 108 King e
Henkel Mrs Mary [wid Hy] 145 Hunter w

Hennerberry Andrew, 72 Locke n
Hennerbery James, moulder, 72 Locke n
Hennerbery Thos, moulder, 72 Locke n
Hennessy Cornelius, tinsmith, bds 20 King Wm
Hennessey Hugh, blacksmith, 63 Mary, h 19 Wilson
Hennessey James, carpenter, 54 Ray n
Hennessey John, com traveller, Concession n s nr Garth
Hennessey Patrick B, locksmith, 17 Oxford
Hennings Lamatine, cabinet maker, 182 James n
Henry A H, parcel and baggage express, Arcade, h 85-7 Macnab n
Henry Daniel, grocer, 54 Hannah w
Henry David, carpenter, 131 West ave n
Henry James, boot and shoe dealer, 22 York
Henry James, moulder, 131 West ave n
Henry John, boiler cleaner G T R, 17 Florence
Henry John, carpenter, 49 West ave n
Henry John, 235 King w
Henry John C, teamster, 78 Mary
Henry Mrs Leah A [wid Walter] 144 Main w
Henry Mrs Margaret, bds 178 York
Henry Patrick, 131 West ave n
Henry R, butcher, 117 James n
Henstridge W H, painter, Main e
Henwood Thos, ropemaker, 111 East ave n
Herald Chas A, manager B Greening & Co, 59 Queen n
Herald Mrs E Anna, [wid Wm] 61 Queen n

McKAY BROTHERS,

—IMPORTERS OF—

STAPLE AND FANCY DRY GOODS,

Carpets and House Furnishings.

NOTED HOUSE FOR

Carpets, Oil Cloths, Lace Curtains

AND GENERAL HOUSE FURNISHINGS.

48 King Street East, HAMILTON.

ANDERSON & BATES,

Eye and Ear Surgeons

34 JAMES STREET NORTH,

HAMILTON,   -   -   ONTARIO.

CROSS EYES STRAIGHTENED.

Exclusive attention given to the treatment of Eye and Ear Diseases.

OFFICE HOURS—9 A. M. to 4 P. M.

JOSEPH HERRON,

MERCHANT TAILOR,

Opposite the Wesleyan Ladies' College,

82 King Street East, Hamilton, Ont.

Herald Jos, piano manfr, 11 Peter
Herbert John W, messenger loco dept GTR, 53 Locomotive
Herbert Thos H, stonecutter, 192 Wilson
Herbert Wm, tinsmith, 120 Florence
Heriot ——, laborer, 93 King Wm
Heritage John, tailor, 12 King Wm, h Markland w of Queen
Herman Wm, notary public, accountant and steamship **agent**, 16 James s, h 68 Main w
Hermann D, laborer, 168 East ave n
Hermann John, laborer, South
Herne Geo S, farmer, Main e of Wentworth
Herod Richard, bricklayer, 140 **Hunter** w
Herriman Jeptha, mail **contract**or, 8 Bay s
Herring J H, com traveller, 28 George
Herring Robt, polisher, 33 **Tis**dale
Herron Jas, moulder, 101a Elgin
Herron Joseph, merchant tailor, 82 King e, h 67 Welling ton s *See card*
Hesse Furniture Co, J R Hesse, prop, 76 James n
Hess Jacob, Hannah e, hd of Aurora
Hess J R, prop **Hesse Furniture Co**, h 4 Liberty
Hetherington Wm, bds 70½ Ferguson ave
Hewitt Alfred, **driver**, r 79 Caroline n
Hewitt Chas J, engineer, Wentworth n
Hewitt Hugh, salesman, bds 76 John n
Hewitt John, railroader, bds 176 Bay n

Hewitt Mrs Sarah A (wid Hy) 150 Rebecca
Hewson Geo W, cabinetmaker, 55¾ Walnut s
Heyburn Geo, lithographer, 44 East ave n
Hydemann Robt, bolt maker, 17 Locke s
Heyes Jas, 3 Emerald s
Hibbard Mrs Ann, (wid Orvill), 125 Dundurn
Hickey John, **brakeman**, 293 John n
Hickey Wm, 293 John n
Hickok H C, St Charles Restaurant, 64 James n
Hicks Richard, carpenter, 166 James n
Hicks W S, carver, 34 James s, h 79 Stinson
Higby Mrs Julia, (wid Edwin), 59 John n
Higgins Andrew, confectioner, **83** G orge
Higgins Edward, M D, 54 Catharine n
Higgins Moore A, 28 Victoria ave s
High Matthew, hotelkeeper, 65-7 John s
Higham Thos, blacksmith, 131 Queen n
Hignell Albert, **printer**, 62 Lower Cathcart
Hilderbrand Gotliep, laborer, 117 **Napier**
Hilder Mrs Jane, (wid Edward), 39 Inchbury n
Hildreth Alfred, laborer, 105 Maria
Hiles Jacob, ins agent, 5 Pearl n
Hiles W C, clerk, 5 Peal n
Hill Mrs Ann (wid Henry) 180 Hughson n
Hill Baldwin, baker, 102 James n
Hill Charles, carpenter, 15 **Hun**ter e
Hill Edment, grocer, 282 King e

Hill E, laborer, 185 Victoria ave n
Hill George H, butcher, 192 King w
Hill G H H, stenographer, 54 Emerald s
Hill Harvey, laborer, 12 Jones
Hill Henry, butcher, 98 Rebecca
Hill Henry F, clerk P O, 38 Emerald n
Hill James, grocer, 300 Macnab n
Hill James, laborer, 118 Caroline s.
Hill Mrs Jane, 28 Emerald n
Hill Jasper, grocer, 113 Cannon e, h 86 Ferguson ave
Hill Miss Jennie, 126 York
Hill John, cigarmaker, 183 East ave n
Hill John, laborer, Breadalbane w s nr Jones
Hill Jonathan A, teacher, 113 Cherry
Hill Mark, baker, 102 James n
Hill Reginald, baker, 102 James n
Hill Robert, cabinetmaker, r 3 Queen s
Hills Rolland, sec Canada Life Ins Co, 30 Jackson w
Hill Rowland, provision dealer, 50 Hess n
Hill Mrs Sophia (wid John) 34 Vine
Hill Thomas, cabinetmaker, 91 John n
Hill Thomas S, jeweler, 90 John s
Hill Walter, baker, 102 James n
Hill William, butcher, 252 King e
Hill Wm A, 15 Hunter e
Hilliard Mrs Mary (wid John) 44 Sheaffe
Hilliard Thos, 2 O'Reilly
Hillier Robert, salesman, Caroline s w s nr Concession
Hilman O S, accountant, 57 James n, h 36 Hunter w

Hillman Peter, carpenter, Marklaud n s nr Garth
Hillman Mrs Sophia, 164½ James n
Hills A S (prop Anchor Hotel) cor Hughson and King Wm
Hills C H, grocer, 14 Macnab n, bds Dominion hotel
Hills Lucian, architect, 10 King Wm, h 278 King w
Hilton J, agent, Cannon e
Hilton Thos, 39 Caroline n
Hilton Wm, laborer, 47 Ferrie w
Hillyard Mrs Mary Ann [wid Thos] 80 Hunter e
Hillyard Wm, shoemaker, 80 Hunter e
Hinchey Edward, moulder, 163 Catharine n
Hinchey Michael, laborer, 161 Catharine n
Hinchliffe Miss Ada, mangr Parker's Dye Works, 10 Inchbury s
Hinchliffe James, grocer, 297-9 York
Hinchcliffe James D, machinist, 75 Pearl n
Hincks Henry, machinist, 217 Victoria ave n
Hinds Rudolphus, printer, 289 King Wm
Hines Charles H, butcher, 50 Ray n
Hines Otis, butcher, 230 York, h 98 George
Hines Richard, laborer, 16 Steven
Hinman Charles, 8 James n
Hinman Mrs M C A, milliner, 8 James n
Hipkins Alfred, printer, 120 Napier
Hipkins Edward, printer, 120 Napier
Hipkins Lewis, blacksmith, 85 Bay n
Hirst Frederick, carpenter, 62½ Young

Hirst James, manfr pain exterminetor, 35 Park s
Hiscox James, chimney sweep, 2 Main w
Hislop Francis, **laborer, 30** Strachan w
Hislop John, blacksmith, 34 Park n, h 127 Hess s
Histead John, laborer, 128 Picton e
Hitzroth **Chas, shoemaker,** 101a John s
Hoag Mrs Isabella [wid Thos] 238 King **Wm**
Hobbs David, loborer, Maple **s s** nr Garth
Hobbs George N, clerk inland revenue, 7 Nelson ave
Hobbs James, carpenter, **170** Emerald n
Hobbs Mrs Jenny [wid **Albert**] 115½ Rebecca
Hobbs Wm, carpenter, **185** Emerald n
Hobden Wm H, tailor, 16 Pearl n
Hobson Abraham, porter, 61 Lower Cathcart
Hobson John, carpenter, 126 **Napier**
Hobson John, civil engineer G T R, n w cor Concession and Bay
Hobson Mrs Julia, 14 Sophia n
Hobson Mrs Mary (wid James) **126** Napier
Hobson Robert, clerk GTR, n w cor Concession and Bay
Hobson Robert, engineer, 126 Napier
Hobson Wm J, clerk, 61 Lower Cathcart
Hockaday Jos, cabinetmaker, 40 Maria
Hockaday Mrs **Louisa** (wid Thos) 40 Maria
Hockbrish John, **laborer, 76** Locke s
Hodd Mrs Elizabeth, 55 Tisdale

Hodd Geo, salesman, 55 Tisdale
Hodd Wm, 25 Tisdale
Hodge F H, salesman, 17 Charles
Hodges Humphrey, r 184 Macnab n
Hodges Miss Susan, 98 Emerald n
Hodgins **Isaac,** engineer, 59 Pearl **n**
Hodgins Mrs Myra (wid Alex) 50 Hughson s
Hodgkiss Ed, piano and organ tuner, 49 Wilson
Hodgson Thos, laborer, **Wentworth n**
Hodson Jeremiah, laborer, 331 Hughson n
Hodson Thos, laborer, Bay n
Hodson Wm, butcher, 327 Barton e
Hoe John, tinsmith, bds 55 York
Hoey Wm C, machinist, 46 Ray **n**
Hoffer Frederick, **com traveler,** 13 Murray w
Hogan J H, **47** Park n
Hogarth Geo, carpenter, 128½ John **n**
Hogg David, weaver, bds 264 Macnab n
Holcomb Mrs Harriet **(wid** Wm H) 65 Caroline **s**
Holden **Geo C, 241 King Wm**
Holden James B, machinist, 55 **Mary**
Holden John P, bookkeeper, **Asylum for the** Insane, bds 21 **Hunter w**
Holden **Walter,** engine driver, 140 Victoria ave n
Holden Wm W, clerk, 55 Mary
Holding Wm, railroader, bds 206 Macnab n
Holdsworth Chas H, **warehouse**man, 102 Hannah w
Holdsworth Jos, second hand store, 87 York
Holland Chas, detective G T R, 126 Mary

Holland Chas, freight agent, 126 Mary
Holland Chas, machinist, 276 Macnab n
Holland G A, teller Bank of Commerce, 61 George
Holland James, 82 Peter
Holland James F, boiler maker, 140 Market
Holland James H, gun and locksmith, Dundurn w s nr York
Holland Robert, salesman, 114 Catharine n
Holland Thos J, hay and straw dealer, 47 Mary
Holland Timothy, laborer, Brock
Hollingrake Wm, engineer GTR 80 Locke n
Hollywell Dewitt Clinton, stove-mounter, bds 100 Park n
Holman J, gunsmith, 79 James n
Holmes Alex, shoemaker, 140½ Main e
Holmes Alex B, shoemaker, 34½ Emerald n
Holmes Alonzo, com traveler, 200 East ave n
Holmes Asher, insurance agent, 10 West ave n
Holmes Harvey A, painter, 4 Poulette
Holmes James sr, shoemaker, 140½ Main e
Holmes James jr, shoemaker, 140½ Main e
Holmes John, carter, 37 Wood w
Holmes John, painter, 132 Jackson w
Holmes Mrs Rebecca (wid Burrell) 16 Napier
Holmes Robt, laborer, 198 Cannon e
Holmes Robt, machinist, 16 Napier
Holmes Wm, brushmaker, 171 Wilson
Holmes Wm, wireworker, 198 Cannon e

Holmes Wm H, tinsmith, 320 King w
Holt John, engine driver, 272 James n
Holt John, carder, 208 Mary n
Holt Samuel, carder, 243 Mary n
Holton Warren, nursery man, Main e of Wentworth
Holton Wm, nursery man, Main e of Wentworth
Home John, tinsmith, 160 Mary
Home of the Friendless, Mrs Helen Mair, matron, 72 Caroline s
Homer Frank, bds 83 Main e
Homer Wm H, confectioner, 122 John s
Homer, Wm J, blacksmith, bds 214 King w
Homer John, gardener, 318 King Wm
Homewood John, carriage trimmer, 106 Bay n
Honeyborne Geo, carpenter, 36 O'Reilly
Honeyborne Geo jr, 36 O'Reilly
Honeycomb Thos R, bricklayer, 24 Locomotive
Honeyford James, fitter, 41 Inchbury n
Honeysett Thos, laborer, 101 Caroline n
Hood & Bro (Thos & John) props Royal Hotel
Hoodless John (J Hoodless & Son) h 43 Jackson w
Hoodless Joseph (J Hoodless & Son) h Catharine cor Jackson
Hoodless J & Son [Joseph & John] furniture manufacturers, warerooms 51 King w, factory Catharine cor Main
Hooker Jos, gardener, Wentworth s
Hooper Chas, tinsmith, 34 Colborne
Hooper Frederick L, insurance agent 144 Main w

Hooper George, blacksmith, 198 King Wm
Hooper H S, confectioner, 200 King e
Hooper James, com traveler, 69 Victoria ave n
Hooper John, com traveler, 35 Victoria ave n
Hooper Herman, gardener Judge O'Reilley's
Hooper Mrs Martha (wid Alonzo) 9 Macnab s
Hooper Wm C, compositor, 16 East ave n
Hope Adam & Co, (C J & R K Hope) iron and hardware merchants, 102 King e
Hope Adam H (L D Sawyer & Co) h 93 Macnab s
Hope Charles James (Adam Hope & Co) h 15 Duke
Hope George, com traveler, 3 Charles
Hope George, hardware merchant, h 15 Duke
Hope Mrs Hannah (wid Hon Adam) 95 Macnab s
Hope John, tanner, 182 East ave n
Hope **John H, clerk**, 95 Macnab s
Hope John O, agent, 24 Macnab n, h 101 York
Hope Mrs Margaret (wid John) 35 Ray n
Hope Robert J, printer, 35 Ray n
Hope Robert Knight (Adam Hope & Co) h 15 Duke
Hopgood Edward H, **butcher**, 69 to 73 Barton w
Hopkins George, **boot and shoe** dealer, bds 202 Victoria ave n
H opkin Geo, tinner, 134 Macauley e
Hopkin Geo H, boots and shoes, 10 King Wm, **h 202** Victoria ave n
Hopkin Mrs Janet I. (wid Jas) carpet weaver, 213 King e

Hopkin John, blacksmith, 213 King e
Hopkin Robert, carpet weaver, 213 King e
Hopkin Robert, King e of Wentworth
Hopkins **Chas A**, hooker, 50 Magill
Hopkins Mrs Christina (wid Jas) 89 Cannon e
Hopkins Daniel **W**, 48 Emerald s
Hopkins Joseph, carpet weaver, 166 Mary
Hopkins Silas D, 104 Cannon w
Hopkins S F, pickle factory, 185 189 **King** Wm, h 281 King Wm
Hopper Herbert, cabinetmaker, 134 Jackson w
Horan Miss Margaret, 80 Caroline **n**
Hord & Co, druggists, 116 James n
Hord Joseph (Hord & Co) 116 James n
Horan Mrs **Mary Ann** (wid Jas) laundress, 77 Napier
Hore Mrs Catharine **(wid F W)** 147 Victoria ave n
Hore F W (F W Hore **& Son)** h 155 Victoria ave n
Hore F W & Son, hubs & spokes, ft **Elgin**
Hore John **R**, painter, 144 Victoria ave n
Horn George, carpenter, **241** Hughson n
Horn **Thos**, carpenter, **239** Hughson n
Horn Thos E, spice miller, 11 Nelson ave
Horn Wm, letter carrier, **168 Bay** n
Hornby Wm, engineer, 25 Magill
Horning Mrs Charity **(wid Jere**miah) 13 Queen **n**
Horning John W, finisher, 19 Locomotive

Horsburg Mrs Helen [wid James] 124 Market
Horsfield Wm, laborer, 27a Wellington n
Horspoole Wm, clerk, 45 Hess s
Horton Henry, laborer, 9 Stuart w
Horton Joseph, rag merchant, 95 King Wm, h 128 King Wm
Hoskins Frederick, laborer, 277 John n
Hossack James S, builder, 43 Hannah w
Hoth Frat, jr, laborer, 2 Poulette
Aoth Frat H, sr, laborer, 2 Poulette
Hoath William, laborer, 2 Poulette
Hotrum Cyrus, railroader, 147 Ferguson ave
Hotrum John, carpenter, 292 John n
Houghey William, machinist, 46 Ray n
Houghton John, carpenter, 83 Locke n
Houlden James, builder, cor John and Barton, h 156 John n
Housago Henry, laborer, 8 Devonport
Housden Charles, laborer, r 205 Catharine n
House Alexander, gardener, King e of tollgate
House Jarvis, laborer, bds 68 Peter
House J B, agent, 166 Main e
House of Refuge, Frank Sturdy steward, ft John n
Housego Edward, fireman GTR, 118 Florence
Hover & Hoyle [Wm Hover, Jas Hoyle] tailors, 12 Hughson n
Hover John, boilermaker, 29 Pearl s
Hover Wm [Hover & Hoyle] 92 Jackson e

Howard Chas, laborer, bds 33 Ray n
Howard Chas, carpenter, 49 Victoria ave n
Howard Chas, huckster, 129 Queen s
Howard Fredk B, butcher, 35-7 Queen n
Howard John, bricklayer, 32 Emerald n
Howard John, stonemason, 33 Ray n
Howard Mrs Mary, 80 James s
Howard R J, blacksmith, 16 Jackson e, h 99 Hunter e
Howard Samuel, contractor, Oak
Howard Samuel, carpenter, 57 Merrick, h 15 Nightingale
Howard Thos, bricklayer, Oak
Howard Thos, laborer, King e of Wentworth
Howard Wm, builder, 80 Tisdale
Howard Wm H, tailor, 17 Rebecca
Howard ———, Markland w Locke n s
Howat Robt, butcher, 311 York
Howat Wm, packer, 311 York
Howe Frank, cigar maker, 52 Cannon w
Howell F J [Howell Lithograph Co] 65 Victoria ave s
Howell Lithographic Co, F J Howell, manager, 18 James s
Howell Wm A, chemist and druggist, 1 Hunter w, h 62 Macnab s
Howells Mrs Victoria [wid Thos D] 152 Macnab n
Howes Thos, coachman, 2 Tisdale
Howick Geo S, salesman, 306 King w
Howick Wm, grocer, 285-287 King w
Howith John, blacksmith, 85 Ferrie e
Houson Chas, engine driver, 12 Sophia n

Hoyle James [Hoover & Hoyle] 45 Catharine s
Hoyle James jr, painter, 45 Catharine s
Hubbard Mrs Amelia [wid John] 142 King Wm
Hubbard Mrs E, milliner, 56 James n
Hubbard Richard, packer, 142 King Wm
Hubbard Wm, marble cutter, 56 James n
Hudson Chas, stovemounter, bds 55 York
Hudson Edmund, clerk, 87 Jackson w
Hudson Geo, marble polisher, cor South and Garth
Hudson Ormsby, cabinetmaker, 161 Main w
Hudson Wm, joiner, 134 King w
Hudson Mrs Wm, fancy goods, 134 King w
Hudson ——, pork packer, bds 71 John s
Huebner August, 115 Jackson w
Hugel Jonathan, carpenter, r 81 Merrick
Hughes Chas, carpenter, 89 Lower Cathcart
Hughes Edward, grocer, 94 and 96 Bay n
Hughes Frank, silver plater, 61 Colborne
Hughes Geo, laborer, 31 Park s
Hughes James, mariner, 175 Emerald n
Hughes John, gardener, 230 King w
Hughes John, laborer, Caroline s e s nr Concession
Hughes John, laborer, r 110 Young
Hughes Thos J, fitter, 5 Inchbury n
Hughes Wm, carpenter, 93 Ferrie e
Hughes Wm, grocer, 94 and 96 Bay n

Hughson Geo N, carpenter, 34 Hunter e
Hugill James, 142 Rebecca
Hull Chas, shoemaker, 6 Ferguson ave
Hull Chas, laborer, 35 Burlington w
Hull Wm, bookkeeper, 20 Pearl s
Hull Wm, trimmer, 57 Tom
Hull Wm A, 186 Macnab n
Hume Mrs Isabella, 207 Main w
Hummel Gellert, bricklayer, 53 Hess n
Hummel John, contractor, contractor, Robinson s s w Locke
Humphrey Geo, moulder, 145 Ferguson ave
Humphrey Nelson (Humphrey & Newbery) 184 John n
Humphrey & Newbery (Nelson Humphrey, Chas E Newbery) tanners, Arcade and 125 Jackson e
Humphreys Jos, laborer, 138 Picton e
Hunt B & Co, Queen's Livery, 105 John s
Hunt Benjamin, carriagemaker, 20 Young
Hunt Chas, tinsmith, 101 Elgin
Hunt Chas F, salesman, 101 Elgin
Hunt Daniel, 120 Main e
Hunt David, shoe cutter, bds 55 York
Hunt Edward, blacksmith, end Wilson
Hunt Francis, wire weaver, bds 55 York
Hunt Frederick, stovemounter, 58 Oak ave
Hunt Frederick, foreman B J & Co, 126½ Emerald n
Hunt Geo, grocer, s w cor Caroline and Herkimer
Hunt Geo M, insurance agent, 69 George
Hunt Hy J, engineer, 39 Hannah e

Hunt James, brakeman, 99 Elgin
Hunt Mrs Mary (wid Lawrence) caretaker German Catholic Church, 46 Charles
Hunt Richard, moulder, 147 Robert
Hunter Robt, watchman, 65 Maria
Hunt Wm, laborer, 14½ Young
Hunt Wm, gardener, Concession s s nr Bay
Hunt Wm, butcher, 126 Macnab n
Hunt Wm H, wood turner, 69 East ave n
Hunter Adam, bookseller and srationer, and lending library, 52 James n, h 130 Park
Hunter Alfred, mechanic, 6 Greig
Hunter Alex, laborer, 252 Mary
Hunter Mrs Catharine [wid Wm] 66 Ray s
Hunter F Wm, bookkeeper, 292 York
Hunter George, moulder, bds 41 John n
Hunter George, tailor, 64 Tisdale
Hunter Geo, bailiff and collector, 11 Canada
Hunter Geo E, tinsmith, 93 John s
Hunter Hugh, fitter, 40 Ray s
Hunter James, porter, 75 Mary
Hunter John [Hunter & Ross] h 64 Tisdale
Hunter John, laborer, 4 Albert Road
Hunter John, laborer, 135 Picton e
Hunter John, laborer, 4 Albert road
Hunter John, tailor, 64 Tisdale
Hunter John & Son (John and John, jr) grocers, 192 James n
Hunter Joseph, driver, 73 Caroline n

Hunter Mrs Margaret (wid Joseph) 14 Steven
Hunter Mrs Matilda (wid Joseph) 6 Greig
Hunter Matthew, carpenter, 1 Tom
Hunter Mrs Olivia (wid John) 64 Hannah w
Hunter Robert, auctioneer, 24 Merrick, h Ida
Hunter & Ross, tailors, 128½ King e
Hunter Samuel, 162 King Wm
Hunter Rev S J, D D, pastor Centenary Methodist Church, 107 James s
Hunter Wm, bailiff first division court, 24 Merrick, h 27 Magill
Hunter Wm, brassfounder, 38 Wellington n, h 19 Wellington s
Hunter Wm, laborer, 56½ Lower Cathcart
Hunter Wm, policeman, bds 37 Wilson
Hunter W E L, law student, 99 Market
Hunter Rev W J, D D, pastor Wesley Church, 69 Catharine n
Hunting Henry, city fireman, 37 Kelly
Huntoon Josiah, Main e of Wentworth
Hurd Mrs Alice (wid Wilkins) 113 Catharine n
Hurd Hiram H, (Hurd & Roberts) h 10 Bay n
Hurd John, laborer, 12 Cherry
Hurd Nathaniel, laborer, 230 King Wm
Hurd & Roberts (Hiram H Hurd, David E Roberts) marble and granite dealers, 98 Merrick
Hurd Stephen, laborer, 185 Napier
Hurley David, engineer, 109 Macnab n

Hurley James, moulder, 158 Emerald n
Hurley James, moulder, 272 Hughson n
Hurrel Jasper, compositor, bds 100 Park n
Hurrell John, **carpenter**, 269 **King** w
Hurst William, carpenter, 20 Henry
Hurton Chas, caretaker collegiate institute, 69 Main w
Husband George, agent, 38 Augusta
Huusband George E, M D, 75 Main w
Husband R J (Drs R J & T H Husband) h 62 East ave s
Husband T H (Drs R J & T H Husband) 9½ West ave s
Hussell Mrs Mary, fancy goods, 128 James n
Husted Daniel, glassblower, 261 Macnab n
Husted James, **moulder**, 55 Steven
Huston John, fruit dealer, 35 Ray n
Hutcheson J Happle, merchant tailor, 126 King e
Hutchings John, **bookkeeper,** 21 Victoria ave n
Hutchinson George, 44 West ave s
Hutchinson **Mrs** Mary E, 98 Bay s
Hutchinson Thomas, painter, 37 Alananson
Hutchinson Thos L, driver, 13 Queen n
Hutchinson ——, shoemaker, hd **York** w toll gate
Hutchison Alex, gardener, 17 Cannon w
Hutchison **Daniel, laborer,** 144 King Wm
Hutchison James, 129 Bay s
Hutchison R A, manager Wm Bell & Co, 129 Bay s

Hutchison Thos, engineer, 196 Hughson n
Huton Chas, merchant tailor, 80 King e, h 103 Market
Hutt Mrs Mary (wid John) Concession s s, opp Caroline
Hutton David, wood worker, 138 Macauley e
Hutton Francis **R,** builder, 5 Augusta
Hutton Gilbert, machinist, 90 Locke n
Hutton Henry, bookkeeper, 24 Liberty
Hutton Henry, **machinist,** 131 Emerald n
Hutton James, pedler, 261 James n
Hutton **William,** laborer, 33
Hutton Wm, teamster, 341 Queen John n
Hutty Frederick, laborer, 49 Hannah w
Huxtable John, shoemaker, 200 James n
Hyatt Henry, shoelaster, 159 Wellington n
Hyde Edward W, com agent, 38 Lower Cathcart
Hyde Frank, laborer, 41 Alanson
Hyde James, loom fixer, 356 James n
Hyde Mrs Mary Ann (wid Thos) 40 Wellington n
Hyland Thomas, laborer, Main e of Wentworth
Hymes Mrs, dressmaker, 152 Rebecca
Hyndman Wm, blacksmith, 10 Kinnell
Hyndman Wm, blacksmith, 173 Park n
Hynds R W, bookkeeper, **67** Hunter e
Hysert Frank, bds 70 Barton e
Hyslop D A & Co, carpets and housefurnishings, 1 King e
Hyslop Robt, com traveler, 92½ Emerald n

Hyslop Wm, merchant, 27 Wellington s
Ibbetson Wm, painter, 21 Railway
Ibbetson Wm sr, tailor, 19 Railway
Ike Frank, moulder, 49 Robert
Iles Jesse, carriagemaker, 34 Ferguson ave
Imboden Chas, foreman Tuckett & Son, 75 Robinson
Immigration Office, John Smith, agent, 85 Stuart w
Imperial Mineral Water Co, Jas S Pearson, manager, 9 Jackson e
Imperial Straw Works, S Douglas, A T Collyer, W A Emory, straw hat manfrs, 26-28 Market
Inch Alfred, carriage blacksmith, 235 Macnab n
Inch James, machinist, 235 Macnab n
Inch Wm, moulder, 27 Simcoe e
Inches James [Fraser & Inches] 141 John s
Ing Henry, watchmaker and jeweler, 106 James n *See card*
Inglehart Hiram F, 60 Vine
Inglis Wm, laborer, 90 Simcoe e
Ingram Geo, watchman, bds 222 Macnab n
Inkson Wm, Com traveler, Dundurn
Inland Revenue Office 2 John s
Inman Steamship Line, Geo McKeand, agent, 57 James n
Insole James G, com traveler, 114 Catharine s
Inspector of Weights and Measures, Thos H McKenzie, inspector, 2 John s
Insurance Co of North America The, marine, Gillespie and Powis, agents, 31 King e
I O G T Hall, Stinson' Chambers, 1 King Wm

I O O F Hall, 24 John n
Iredale Miss Grace, 13 Bold
Iredale James, blacksmith, Main e of Wentworth
Iredale Wm, broom maker, 13 Bold
Ireland Frank, engraver, 24 Hughson n
Ireland Hy, fruiterer, 91 Rebecca
Ireland Samuel J, principal art school, 33 Bay n
Ireland Thos com traveler, 131 John n
Irish Chas, shemaker, 209 King e
Irons Robt, bricklayer, 121 Caroline n
Ironside Geo, coachman John Eastwood, Main e of Wentworth
Irvine Mrs Agnes, 14 Markland
Irvine Archibald, sailor, 293 Macnab n
Irvine Mrs Helen (wid Alex) 66 Duke
Irvine John, fireman, James n
Irvine Lendrum, dry goods, 79 John s
Irvine Thos, 14 Markland
Irvine Wm, carpenter, s w cor Hess and Markland
Irving Adam, picture dealer, 6 Mulberry
Irving Æmelius Q C, court house h 137 James s
Irving Frank, machinist, 4 Barton terrace, Wellington n
Irving John, laborer, 243 King e
Irving Wm, machinist, 252 Bay n
Irwin John T [Thos Irwin & Son] 50 Hannah w
Irwin Richard, prop Victoria Hotel, 79 King e
Irwin Robert [Ralston & Irwin] bds Temperance Dining Rooms, 48 James n
Irwin Thomas [Thos Irwin & Son] 53 Herkimer
Irwin Thos, laborer, 64 Oak ave

Irwin Thomas & Son [Thos & John T] galvanized iron, felt roofing, tinware, etc, 12 Macnab s
Irwin Wm H, tinsmith bds 100 Caroline s
Irwin W H [W H Irwin & Co] h 53 Herkimer
Irwin W H & Co, directory publishers and publishers agents, 14 Merrick, and 12 Macnab s   *See card*
Isard Edward, laborer, 274 Cannon e
Isard Frederick J, 237 King e
Isbister John, builder, 81 Wellington s
Israel Chas, confectioner, 64 King e
Israel Mrs Chas, confectioner, 194 King e
Issell Geo, shoemaker, 134 York
Ives Geo, porter Bank B N A, 47 Cherry
Ivory Mrs Nora (wid James) 101 Park n
Izzard G B, traveler, 80 Queen s
Jacobs Mrs Flora [wid Bernard] 40 Hunter e
Jacobs Louis, cigarmaker, 40 Hunter e
Jacobson J, butcher, 109 John s
Jack Daniel, engineer, 19 Magill
Jackman Thos, fitter, 112 Florence
Jackson Mrs Ann (wid Thos) 207 Main e
Jackson Mrs Catharine (wid Sydney) 2 Wellington terrace, Wellington n
Jackson David, retinner, 8 Wood Market
Jackson David, laborer, 15 Simcoe w
Jackson Geo, laborer, Robinson n s w Locke
Jackson Geo, shipper, 66 Hunter
Jackson Geo K, laborer, bds 137 Wood e
Jackson Henry, laborer, Duke s s nr Locke
Jackson Henry, laborer, 67 Ferguson ave
Jackson James, sailmaker, 91 Hughson n
Jackson James H, laborer, 24 South
Jackson James R, carpenter, 72 Victoria ave n
Jackson Mrs Jane (wid Wm) 58 Catharine n
Jackson John, heater, 93 Picton e
Jackson John, laborer, 73 Emerald n
Jackson John, carpenter, 304 James n
Jackson John, shipper, 140 Locke n
Jackson Joseph, glassblower, 96 Picton e
Jackson Joseph, blacksmith, 219 Main w
Jackson Joshua, fireman G T R, Barton w s s nr Magill
Jackson Mrs Mary, laundress, 64 Peter
Jackson R, plasterer, 139 James n
Jackson Robert, weaver, 25 Murray e
Jackson Robert, wire weaver, 64 Peter
Jackson Street Planing Mill, Robt Cruickshank, mgr, 55-7 Jackson e
Jackson Thos C, laborer, 101 George
Jackson Thos C, butcher, 75 York
Jackson Walter, mechanic, bds 55 Ferguson ave
Jackson Wm, com traveler, 34 Emerald n
Jackson Wm, Robinson n s w Locke
Jacques Robert, laborer, 89 Canada s s

Jaeger Henry, bricklayer, 82 Wellington n
Jaggar Albert, gardener, 34 Tisdale
Jaggard Chas, polisher, Grant
Jaggard Walter, laborer, Sherman
Jagoe H B, traveling agt N Y C and HRR, 20 Stinson
Jagoe John F, custom broker, 28 John, h 20 Stinson
Jahn Robert, prop Germania hotel, 20-22 John s
James Alfred T, shipper, 58 Kelly
James Alonzo T, 28 King Wm
James Mrs Annie, 24 Ferguson ave
James C, bookkeeper, Delta
James Chas, machinist, r 57 King Wm, h 37 Walnut s
James Mrs Catharine (wid Stephen) 7 West ave n
James Edwin, printer, 54 Ferguson ave
James Mrs Eliza (wid Joseph) 259 Macnab n
James George, dry goods, 70 King e, h 53 East ave s
James' Hotel [W T James prop] 28 King Wm
James W, bookkeeper, 95 Macnab n
James Mrs Sarah [wid Wm] 54 Ferguson ave
James Simon, tavernkeeper, Delta Main e
James Thos, roller, 111 Locke n
James Wallace T, prop James' Hotel, 28 King Wm
James Wm, bricklayer, 180 Emerald n
James Wm H, letter carrier, 116½ East ave n
Jamieson Chas, telegraph repairer, 152 Park n
Jamieson James [Bowes & Jamieson] h 12 Emerald s
Jamison John, painter, 55 Locomotive

Jamieson Mrs John, 243 Barton e
Jamieson Patrick, bds 4 Jones
Jamieson Wm, watchman, 162 East ave n
Jamieson Wm, moulder, 242 Hughson n
Jamieson Wm, hatter, 243 Barton e
Jaquith O S, salesman, 32 Liberty
Jardine Jas, clerk, bds 98 Cannon w
Jarrett Robt, engineer, 108 Queen n
Jarritt Wm, hd York s s nr Dundurn
Jarvis Æmilus, mangr Traders Bank of Canada, 58½ Herkimer
Jarvis Mrs Ann [wid John] 236 King e
Jarvis Bold, huckster, Grant
Jarvis Mrs Emma [wid Samuel] 45 Queen n
Jarvis Frederick, 71 Jackson e
Jarvis George, hackman, 13 Spring
Jarvis James, engineer, 6 Jones
Jarvis Mrs Jane [wid Chas] 70 Canada
Jarvis John H, laborer, 48 Ray n
Jarvis Miss N A, fancy goods, 236-8 King e
Jarvis Robt H, inspector Federal Life, 60 East ave s
Jarvis Samuel, laborer, 70 Canada
Jarvis Thos, upholsterer, 31 Caroline n
Jarvis William, jr, hackman, 13 Spring
Jarvis Wm, 13 Spring
Jarvis Wm, confectioner, 262 King e
Jeffery Mrs A [wid Wm] 57 Park
Jeffrey Andrew, auctioneer, 98 James n, h 229 Hughson n
Jeffery Ephraim, plasterer, 26 Smith ave

Jeffrey John, bookbinder, 59 Young
Jeffrey John, carpenter, 39 Cherry
Jeffery Joseph, city steam laundry, 60 Main w, h n w cor Hannah and Macnab
Jeffs Job B, machinist, 115 Hunter e
Jeffs John, shipper, 99 East ave n
Jeffs Wm, machinist, 115 Hunter e
Jelfs George F (Cage & Jelfs) h 60 Herkimer
Jenkins Alfred, machinist, 20 Wilson
Jenkins Chas, engineer, 151 Macnab n
Jenkins Geo, cabinet maker, end Main w
Jenkins John, laborer, 175 Catharine n
Jenkins **John**, carpenter, 133 Ferrie e
Jenkins John C N, machinist, 118 Wilson
Jenkins Stephen, machinist, 134 Queen n
Jenkins Wm, laborer, 54 Locomotive
Jennings David J, wood carver, 293 King w
Jennings John, moulder, 236 Cannon e
Jermyn Mrs Annie [wid Wm D] 57 Robinson
Jermyn T H, bookkeeper, 57 Robinson
Jessop Wm, shipper, 45 Strachan e
Jewel Wm, laborer, 207 James n
Jewish Synagogue, Rev Dr H Birkenthal, Rabbi, Hughson s
Jinks Mrs Leah [wid Thos] 126½ Queen n
Jinks John, mechanic, 126½ Queen n
Jinks John, heater, 126½ Queen n

Jinks Thos, heater, 98 Queen n
Jimmie's Restaurant, James McKeown, prop, 5-7 John n
Job Wm R, shoemaker, 33 Markland
Jobborn C, second hand dealer, 315 James n
Jobborn Ed, market gardener, 274½ Hughson n
Johborn Moses, locksmith, 23½ York
Jobson James, pork curer, 97 Caroline s
Jocelyn Jos, plasterer, 37 Florence
Johns Thos, carpenter, 330 King Wm
Johnston Alex, machinist, 123½ Queen n
Johnson Allen, bds 48 Hunter w
Johnson Amos, huxter, 49 Mary
Johnson A W, bookkeeper, Canada Life Building
Johnson Brent, carpenter, 128 Wellington n
Johnson Mrs Catharine, 145 Wellington n
Johnson Chas, tailor, 146 **Cannon** e
Johnson Rev Chas A, 54 **Herkimer**
Johnson Mrs Charlotte] wid Wm] 125 Mary
Johnson Christopher, laborer, bds 74 John s
Johnson Rev C O, pastor Gore St Methodist Church, 33 Gore
Johnstone Miss Emma, milliner, 128 King w
Johnson Mrs Fanny [wid Caleb] 103a John s
Johnson Frank, barber, 68 Hughson n
Johnson Frederick (Fraser, Johnson & Co) 52 Emerald s
Johnston Frederick, moulder, 18 Henry

Johnson Fred G, wheel maker, 245 Mary n
Johnson Freeman, pipe maker, 152 Hughson n
Johnson Geo jr, carpenter, 238 Hughson n
Johnson Geo sr, carpenter, 238 Hughson n
Johnson G W, B A, teacher, 167 John s
Johnson Mrs Hannah, 76 Napier
Johnson Henry, tender fitter, 87 Victoria ave n
Johnson Henry, 37 Smith ave
Johnson Rev J A, African Methodist Episcopal, 82 John s
Johnston Jacob, tailor, 121 Hunter w
Johnson Jas, music teacher, 14 Liberty
Johnson James, laborer, 20 O' Reilly
Johnston Jas, laborer, 394 James n
Johnston Jas, auctioneer, 22 Merrick, h 31 Victoria ave n
Johnston James, messenger Merchants' Bank, 83 Victoria ave n
Johnston James, machinist, 267 King w
Johnston James W, mariner, 201½ John n
Johnston J H, manfr of upholstered goods, 128 King e, h 276 King e
Johnston John, helper, 313 Barton e
Johnston John, crockery store, 182 King w
Johnston John, carter, 187 Emerald n
Johnson John, machinist, 45 Ferguson ave
Johnson John, engine driver, 19 Tiffany
Johnson J P, agent American Express Co, h 62 Hannah w
Johnson John T, mechanic, 106 Queen n

Johnson Joseph F, laborer, 14 Cherry
Johnson Louis, contractor, 63 Steven
Johnston Louis, blacksmith, 180 Catharine n
Johnston Mrs Maria (wid Wm) 117 Catharine n
Johnston Mrs, 185 James n
Johnston Mrs, 174 John n
Johnston Mrs, 29 Queen n
Johnson Neil, laborer, 90 Market
Johnson Octavius M, com traveler, 49 Park n
Johnston Peter, cigar maker, 11 Barton e
Johnston Robt, mariner, 37 Ferrie w
Johnston Robt, carpenter, 160 Victoria ave n
Johnson Thos, stove mounter, 51 Robert
Johnston Thos, boiler maker, 26 Jones
Johnston Thos, carpenter, 1 Main w
Johnston Thos, blacksmith, 74 Macnab n, h 166 Victoria ave n
Johnston Thos, marblecutter, 29 Queen n
Johnston Thos J, policeman, 56 Barton e
Johnston Wesley, teacher, bds 17 Vine
Johnson Wm, laborer, bds 74 John s
Johnston Wm, stovemounter, 26 Strachan e
Johnston Wm, carpenter, 238 Hughson n
Johnston Wm, painter, 117 Catharine n
Johnston Wm, laborer, 203 Emerald n
Johnston Wm, blacksmith, Burlington s, h Aikman ave
Johnston Wm, carpenter, 1 Main w

Johnson Wm, brushmaker, 85 Main e
Johnson Wm, painter, 35 Inchbury n
Johnston Wm L, blacksmith, 124 Bold
Joice Felix, engineer, 10 Little Market
Joice George, 20 Strachan w
Jolley Chas J, (Jas Jolley & Son) 17 Hunter e
Jolley Chas O, **supt nail works,** 56 George
Jolley James (James Jolley & Sons) 17 Hunter e
Jolley James & Sons (Jas, C J, W D Jolley) saddlers etc, 45-7 John s
Jolley W D (James Jolley & Sons) 17 **Hunter e**
Jones Albert, 174 East ave n
Jones Albert, laborer, 58 Duke
Jones Miss Alice E, caligraphist, 8½ King e
Jones Mrs Alice, 275 Mary
Jones Mrs Catharine, 190 John n
Jones Chas K, roof painter, 60 Smith ave
Jones C J, agt Canadian Pacific Railway Telegraph, h 144 Bay s
Jones C T, 80 Ferguson ave
Jones E C, patent iron and wire fencing, 47 King Wm, **h 79** Catharine s
Jones & Gage (M Jones, Wm Gage) wood and coal dealers, 150 John n
Jones George, carpenter, 47 Markland
Jones George, patternmaker, bds 40 Mulberry
Jones G orge, salesman, 61 Herkimer
Jones George M, laborer, 41 John
Jones Mrs Harriet (wid Wm) 275 Mary
Jones Hiram, bricklayer, 81 Macauley e

Jones James, moulder, 77 Catharine n
Jones John, laborer, bds 74 John s
Jones John, mechanic, 103 Hess n
Jones John, moulder, 57 Steven
Jones John, bricklayer, 75 Macauley e
Jones John W, LL B, barrister, Victoria Chambers, 31 James s, h 19 Maria *See card*
Jones Mrs Martha (wid John) 63 Ferguson **ave**
Jones Mrs Mary **(wid Thos)** 45 Robinson
Jones Mrs Mary A (wid **Samuel]** 105 Catharine n
Jones Miss Minerva, dressmaker, 65 Hunter e
Jones Nathanial (Jones & Gage) h 150 John n
Jones Patrick, quarryman, 20a Liberty
Jones Robert, plasterer, 183 Main w
Jones Seneca, ins agent, 6 James s, h 116 Main e *See card*
Jones Stephen, laborer, 27 Blyth
Jones Sylvester, farmer, 41 John n
Jones Thomas, quarryman, r 126 Hannah e
Jones Thos, tailor, **75 John n**
Jones Thos, moulder, 15 Little Wm
Jones Thos, glassblower, 303 Macnab n
Jones Walter, moulder, bds 103 James n
Jones Wm, street car driver, 226 Hughson n
Jones Wm, polisher, South w s s nr Garth
Jones William, laborer, 11 Stuart w
Jones Wm, moulder, 105 Catharine n

Jones W H, bookkeeper, 24 Victoria ave n
Jones Wm J, tollgate keeper, Barton e
Jones W J, inspector Bell Telephone Co, 45 Robinson
Jones W McLean, clerk, h 11 Stuart w
Jordan Mrs Ellen, 87 Macauley e
Jost Henry, hatter, 3 Rebecca
Jost Mrs M, hair works, 94 James n
Jowett John, laborer, end Ferguson ave
Joy Edward, laborer, 157 Macnab n
Joy Wm, shoemaker, 177 Rebecca
Joy Wm, jr, tobbacconist, 117 Rebecca
Joyce Edward, painter, 57 Barton e
Judd Chas, clerk P O, 99 Market
Judd H W, fruit canner, 47 King Wm, h 4 Pine
Judd James P (Judd Bros) 95 Florence
Judd Wm H, soap manfr, 72 Bay n
Judd Wm H & Bro, soap works, 71 Bay n
Judge Mrs Robert, 76 Young
Julian Wm, laborer, r 26 East ave n
Junginger Geo, butcher, 40 East ave n
Jutton Thos, boat builder, 95 Picton e
Kahn Ferdinand, salesman, 8 Young
Kail Richard, farmer, 68 Steven e
Kaiser Frank, machinist, 44 Vine
Kaiser James, cooper, 3 Cherry
Kale Geo, moulder. bds 46 Cannon w
Kane John, carpenter, ft Ferguson ave
Kane Wm, laborer, Aikman ave

Kappele David, tailor, 54 West ave n
Kappele Geo W, bookkeeper, 51 Wilson
Karsten Albert, presser, 164 Wilson
Karsten Chas, cigar maker, 259 King Wm
Karsten Hy (Blumensteil & Karsten) 39 Tisdale
Karsten John, laborer, 31 Florence
Karsten Mrs Sophia (wid Martin) 39 Tisdale
Kartzmark Harman, machinist, 36 Robinson
Kartzmark Martin, blacksmith, 40 Robinson
Kartzmark Martin jr, machinist, 13 Canada
Kavanagh Dennis, laborer, 16 Wood w
Kavanagh Edward, core maker, 41 Mulberry
Kavanagh Frank, 17 Mulberry
Kavanagh John, blacksmith, 13 Railway
Kavanagh John, laborer, 116 Queen n
Kavanagh John F, grocer, 39 York, h 64 Bay s
Kavanagh Jos, 64 Bay s
Kavanagh Matthew, boiler maker 329 Catharine n
Kavanagh Terrance, moulder, 100 Barton e
Kavanagh Thos, laborer, 15 Burlington e
Kavanagh Wm, 233 King w
Kay Rev John, pastor First Methodist Church, 179a Main e
Kay Alex K, electrician, 28 Bay n, h 132 York
Kay Robt, 164 Macnab n
Kaye Wm, laborer, 62 Hannah w
Keagan Mrs Ann, 162 Jackson w
Kean Mrs, hd York w Canal

Keane Mark, laborer, 97 John n
Keane Thos, 19 Caroline s
Kearman Mrs Ann (wid Jas) 71 Young
Kearman Thos, moulder, 71 Young
Keating James, machinist, 26 O'Reilly
Keating John, laborer, 102 Picton e
Keating Wm, confectioner, 59 Ferrie e
Keats Mrs Mary (wid James E) 103 Hunter e
Keays R F, real estate agent, 57 James n h 61 Napier
Keeble Arthur, teamster, 22 Kelly
Keefer Nelson, grocer, 45 Walnut s
Keefer Robt, com traverer, 30 Liberty
Keegan Wm, glass blower, 94 Macauley e
Keele Mrs Hy, 47 Walnut s
Keenan Andrew, laborer, 139 Napier
Keenan James, section foreman N & N W, 100 Victoria ave s
Kehoe Lawrence, hackman, 176 John n
Keil L W, grocer, cor Tisdale and Wilson
Keirmer Geo, agent, Mary n
Keith Mrs Mary [wid James] 304 King w
Keith Wm, **cabinet maker, 304** King w
Kelher Rev Robt, 24 Magill
Kelk, Francis, tailor, 23 York
Kelk Jas, tinsmith, 207 John n
Kelk John G, paper bag manfr, 72 Queen s
Kelk Wm, musician, 70 Maria
Kell Wm, 57 Maria
Kell Wm C, hackman, 57 Maria
Keller Thos, agent, 6 Margaret
Kellar Wesley, foreman Hendrie & Co, 208 King w

Kellner Ed, tailor, 167 Robert
Kellner John, tailor, 167 Robert
Kellogg L M [Kellogg & McKenzie] 21 James n
Kellogg & McKenzie (L M Kellogg, Alex McKenzie) hotel 21 James n
Kellond Frederick, bookbinder, 101 Wellington s
Kellond Geo, shoemaker, 134 York
Kellond John, ruler, 134 York
Kells Wm, laborer, bds 41 John n
Kelley Mrs Bridget, 323 James n
Kelly Daniel, 198 Main e
Kelly Dennis, laborer, 293 King Wm
Kelly Dennis, machinist, 68 Markland s s w Locke
Kelly Dennis jr, bricklayer, Ashley
Kelly D J, wood and coal dealer, 135 James n, h 161 Hughson n
Kelly Edward, laborer, 28 Macaulay e
Kelly Francis, laborer, 42 Locke n
Kelly Hugh, laborer, 208 John n
Kelly Jas, grocer, 44 Gore
Kelly James, hotel, 198 James n
Kelly Miss Jennie (Kelly & Lockwood) h 2 Mill
Kelly John, boilermaker, 78 Caroline n
Kelly John, laborer, 334 John n
Kelly John, shoemaker, 30 Railway
Kelly John **F,** cigarmaker, 2 East ave n
Kelly J **P,** custom boots and shoes, 13 Macnab n, h 30 Railway
Kelly Lawrence, 299 Macnab n
Kelly & Lockwood (Miss Jennie Kelly, Miss Eliza Lockwood) British American laundry, 162 York

Kelly Mrs Maria (wid Barnard) 58½ Robert
Kelly Mrs Mary (wid Thomas) 83 Hunter w
Kelly Michael, laborer, 32 O'Reilly
Kelly Patrick, laborer, 31 Macauley e
Kelly Patrick, laborer, 51 Sheaffe
Kelly Patrick J, tailor, 138 Catharine n
Kelly Thos, laborer, Garth ws nr King
Kelly Thos, shoemaker, 247 Mary
Kelly T M, grocer, 50 John s, h 48 West ave s
Kelly Timothy, stovemounter, King e of Wentworth
Kelly Wm, cabinetmaker, bds 181 John n
Kelly Mrs, r 1 Evans
Kemp Chas J, fireman, 17 Margaret
Kemp David, painter, 59 Barton e
Kemp Geo W, tinsmith, 104 Queen n
Kemp John, laborer, r 142 King Wm
Kemp Mrs Mary (wid Alex F) 113 Jackson w
Kemp Samuel, com traveler, 19½ Elgin
Kemp Wm, laborer, 39 Robinson
Kemp Wm, stovemounter, bds 43 John n
Kench Wm, fruiterer, 253 York
Kendle Jas H, gardener, Highfield, Concession
Kennard Edward O, cabinetma'r, 8 Albert Road
Kennard G H, laborer, 27 Simcoe e
Kennedy Andrew, stonemason, 155 Wellington n
Kennedy Mrs Catharine (wid Hugh) 85 Main w
Kennedy Mrs Catharine (wid Owen) 76 Hughson s

Kennedy & Co, merchant tailors, 49 James n
Kennedy Edward, cabinetmaker, Sherman
Kennedy Francis, carpenter, 116 Maria
Kennedy George, carpenter, 179 Main w
Kennedy James, blacksmith, Bowen, h 7 Canada
Kennedy James, roller coverer, 81 Picton e
Kennedy James F, cutter, 61 Wellington s
Kennedy Mrs Jane [wid John] 72 Lower Cathcart
Kennedy Mrs Jessie [wid Donald] 65 Hunter w
Kennedy John, boilermaker, 132 Picton e
Kennedy John, carpenter, 31 Queen n
Kennedy John, machinist, 91 Mary
Kennedy John, moulder, 94 Barton e
Kennedy John A [Kennedy & Co] h 61 Wellington s
Kennedy John H, buyer, 38 Market
Kennedy Joseph, cutter, 116 Maria
Kennedy Mrs Margaret [wid Benjamin] Sherman
Kennedy Martin, glassblower, 25 Simcoe e
Kennedy Matthew, cooper, 138 Ferrie e
Kennedy Michael, 91 Mary
Kennedy Patrick, moulder, 116 Maria
Kennedy Patrick, 91 Mary
Kennedy Patrick, jr, moulder, 91 Mary
Kennedy Reginald Æ, *Times* Printing Co, 8 Ray s
Kennedy R D, provincial land surveyor and civil engineer, 42 James n, h 85 Main w

Kennedy Thos, cotton operator, 201 Wellington n
Kennedy Thomas, machinist, 40 Pearl n
Kennedy Wm, clerk Bank BNA, 56 Jackson w
Kennedy Wm, machinist, 116 Maria
Kennedy Wm, tender, 121 Queen n
Kennedy Wm, bricklayer, 221 Barton e
Kennedy Wm, 38 George
Kenney A E, mechanic, 60 Barton w
Kenney E A, salesman, 81 Catharine s
Kenny James, carpenter, 53 Steven
Kenny Jeremiah, laborer, r 61 Jackson e
Kenny S M, ins inspector, 9½ West ave s
Kenney Thos, glassblower, 327 James n
Kenny Wm, bds 5 John n
Kenrick John, grocer, 67 West ave n
Kent Mrs E [wid George] 51 Elgin
Kent George, packer, 51 Elgin
Kent Geo T, ward foreman, 51 Pearl s
Kent Henry, salesman, s w cor Bay and Duke
Kent Joseph (Cathro, Kent & Rogers) h 25 Nelson ave
Kent Joseph, bds 61 George
Kent Samuel H, assistant city clerk, 76 Bay s
Keppell Mrs Hattie, seamstress, 64 Hess n
Kerley Henry, **weaver, 81** John n
Kern M Didacus, draughtsman, 9 James n
Kern Mrs Sarah A (wid David W) grocer, 29-31 Canada
Kernahan Wm, tinsmith, bds 103 York

Kerner Christian, hotel, **7 York** and 8 Market
Kerner John, 48 Hunter w
Kerner Joseph, laborer, tt Ferguson ave
Kerner W **H,** confectioner, **14** John n
Kerney James, tobacco **roller,** Robinson s s w Locke
Kerr Albert, polisher, 89 Cannon e
Kerr Alexander, 81 Wellington n
Kerr Alfred, salesman, 81 Wellington n
Kerr A R (A R Kerr & Co) h 41 Charles
Kerr A R & Co, dry goods, millinery, mantles, etc, 34 King w
Kerr Mrs Caroline (wid Chas H) 89 Cannon e
Kerr Chas J, machinist, **264** Mary
Kerr George, caretaker Crystal Palace grounds, Locke n opp Peter
Kerr George, gate keeper GTR, 45 Florence
Kerr George, laborer, 276a King e
Kerr John, moulder, **265** Macnab n
Kerr Mrs Martha A (wid Wm G) 76 Jackson w
Kerr Michael, laborer, **55** Strachan e
Kerr Murray A, 76 Jackson w
Kerr R H, salesman, 8 Hess n
Kerr Mrs Susan (wid David) 228 Macnab n
Kerr Thomas, moulder, Nightingale
Kerr Wm, clerk, 81 Wellington n
Kerr Wm H, moulder, 127 Caroline n
Kerr Wm J, moulder, **125** Caroline n
Kerran John, carpenter, r 62 Locke n

Kerrigan Dennis, merchant tailor, 170 King e
Kerrigan John, merchant tailor, 24 York
Kerruish Mrs Ellen (wid Thos) 119 Maria
Kerslake Joseph, cabinetmaker, 227 Hughson n
Ketcheson Byron, moulder, 131 Wellington n
Keyes Robert, laborer, 34 Ferguson ave
Keymer Harry, boilermaker, 206 Macnab n
Kiah Captain David, mariner, 46 Cannon w
Kidby Richard G, porter, Shaw
Kidd David, agent Canada Life, 57 Bold
Kidd Samuel, confectioner, 65 Rebecca
Kidner Edward, printer, 53 James s
Kidner Frank (Griffin & Kidner) 99 Cherry
Kidney Miss Mary, r 51 Young
Kiedby Richard, laborer, Shaw
Kieley Michael, 42 Hughson n
Kievell John F, carpenter, 8 West ave n
Kilgour Mrs Elizabeth (wid Robt) 81 Catharine s
Kilgour James (J & R Kilgour) 83 Catharine s
Kilgour J & R, pianos, organ manfr, etc, 64 John s
Killey Joseph H (Osborne & Killey manfr Co) 5 Hess s
Kilroy John, machinist, 21 King Wm
Kilroy Mrs Margaret, broker, 21 King Wm
Kilvert & Biggar (F E Kilvert & S D Biggar) barristers, Canada Life Chambers, James s
Kilvert F E, M P (Kilvert & Biggar) 10 West ave s
Kilvington Thos, sr, gardener, King e of Wentworth

Kilvington Thos, jr, florist, 254 King e
Kime Wm Henry, laborer, GTR e of Wentworth
Kindergarten School, Miss F Davis, teacher, 53 Macnab s
King Alfred, painter, 28 South
King Cyrus, grocer, 10 Market sq, h 78 Main w
King Elias, porter, 16 Catharine n
King Mrs Ellen, laundress, 87 King w
King Mrs Elsie, 74 Vine
King Francis, mechanic, 22 Little Wm
King Francis, rope maker, 245½ Mary
King Frederick W, com traveler, 21 Wilson
King George, laborer, 150 Emerald n
King George, painter, 143 Picton e
King George, saw filer, 179 Rebecca
King Geo T, drill master's asst, 175 Mary
King Henry, painter, 179 Rebecca
King Henry, hostler Dominion hotel, 32 Main w
King Hiram, 156 King Wm
King Jeremiah, potter, 12 Margaret
King John, porter, Maapherson, Glassco & Co
King Joseph, boot finisher, 98 Hunter w
King Mrs Mary (wid Francis) 143 Mary
King Robert, laborer, 34 Lower Cathcart
King Rufus, 78 Main w
King Samuel S, building mover, Dundurn w s nr York, h 2 Jones
King Simeon V, moulder, 14 Elgin

King Thos, fireman, r 143 Locke n
King Thos, laborer, Herkimer n s nr Garth
King Thos, machinist, 47a East ave n
King Wm, fireman, 167 Jackson w
King Wm, laborer, 34 Lower Cathcart
King Wm, merchant tailor, 30 Main w
King ——, carpenter, 22 Little Wm
Kingdom Mrs Elizabeth, (wid Abraham), 177 King e
Kingdom Charles, silver plater, 93 Robert
Kingdon James, blacksmith, 216 King Wm
Kingdon James, tailor, 128 Mary
Kingdon Wm J, printer, 46½ Hannah w
Kingston Geo, laborer, 37 Picton w
Kinleyside John, manager Hamilton Industrial Works, 3 Hess s
Kinney Jas, gardener, Concession n s nr Bay
Kinrade Geo N, blacksmith, Barton e
Kinrade Hiram N, moulder, Barton e
Kinrade Thos L, teacher, Barton e
Kinrade Thos P, Barton e
Kinsella Edward, engineer, 31 Napier
Kinsella John, laborer, 89 Simcoe e
Kinsella Wm, moulder, 135 Ferrie e
Kinsella Miss Eliza, 348½ James n
Kirby P J, grocer, 244 James n
Kirby Thomas, painter, 52 Main w

Kirk Jas, barber, 31 York
Kirk Wm, baker, 72 Vine
Kirkendale Mrs Lyall, (wid Norris), 44 Hunter e
Kirkendall Marshall, painter, 18 Pearl s
Kirkendall Miss Martha, 18 Pearl s
Kirkendall Wesley, painter, 18 Pearl s
Kirkham Mrs Mary A, (wid John), 62 Robert
Kirkness John, cooper 237 Barton e
Kirkonell Thos, bds 17 Kelly
Kirkpatrick Henry, 256 James n
Kirkpatrick J, grocer, 167 Wellington n
Kirkpatrick Neil, engineer, 346 James n
Kirkpatrick Robt, saddler, 256 James n
Kirkpatrick Thos, laborer, 34 O'Reilly
Kirkpatrick Wm, carpenter, 19 Simcoe w
Kirwin John B, shipper, 314 King Wm
Kirkwood John, laborer, 97 Picton e
Kitchen John, pedlar, 321 King w
Kitchen J B, photographer, 76 King w, h 82 Hannah w
Kite Harry, com traveller, 26 Emerald n
Kittson E E, (Martin, Kittson & Martin), h 4 Nelson ave
Kittson Mrs Harriet, (wid Wm H), 4 Nelson ave
Kittson Henry N, (W H Gillard & Co), 29 Wellington s
Kittyle Francis, sailor, 169 Hunter w
Kivell John, stonemason, 178 Rebecca
Klayer Michael, bricklayer, 54 Jackson w
Kleinsteiber, Hugo, piano maker, 103 Robinson

Klingbeil Christian, laborer, 58 Steven
Klingbeil Wm, butcher, 22 Oak ave
Kilngbeil Wm, laborer, 36 Emerald n
Klingler Herman, machinist, 18 Cherry
Klock John D, cigarmaker, 53 Emerald n
Klock Russell, cigar maker, Mountain ave, east Hamilton
Klotz Emil W, buyer, 38 George
Knaggs William, music teacher, 8 Elgin
Knapman Mrs Agnes, (wid Jno), 14 Emerald n
Knapman John, laborer, 100 Locke s
Knapman J S, clerk, 14 Emerald n
Knapman Wm, laborer, 146 Jackson w
Knapp Ethelbert, shoemaker, 14 Henry
Kneeshaw Joseph, clerk, 46 Lower Cathcart
Knetsch Augustus, tailor, 174 Cannon e
Knight Mrs Ellen, (wid Patrick), 60 Tisdale
Knight Henry, laborer, 45 Peter
Knight Joseph, base ball player, 92 Peter
Knight Peter, broom maker, 42 Hess s
Knight, Samuel, laborer, 124 West ave n
Knott Charles, cashier, Bay n
Knott Charles, manufacturer, 49 Walnut s
Knott George, laborer, 10 Tiffany
Knott Mrs Sarah, 18 Barton e
Knowles Henry, salesman, 6 Peter
Knowles John, salesman, 84 Wilson
Knowles Mrs, 33 Macaulay e

Knox Church, Rev Mungo Fraser, pastor, James cor Cannon
Knox Geo, engineer G T R, 93 Hess n
Knox John, (Knox, Morgan & Co), 54 Hunter w
Knox John, policeman, 351 James n
Knox, Morgan & Co, (John Knox, Alfred Morgan), wholesale drygoods, 7 King e
Korn John W, furrier, 88 Markland nr Garth
Korn Mrs Pauline (wid John W) 88 Markland nr Garth
Kouber Mathew, hatter and furrier, 114 King w
Kraft E L & Son (Elizabeth L Adolph A) harness, saddles and trunks, etc, 8-10 York
Kraft Mrs Elizabeth L (E L Kraft & Son) h 63 Wentworth s
Kraft Ernest L, merchant, Wentworth s
Kramer Mrs Barbara, Black Elephant Saloon, 157 James n
Kramer Geo, Eureka Saloon, 36 38 York
Kramer Jesse L, cigarmaker, 73 West ave n
Kreiger Carl, laborer, 196 Main
Kretschmann Louis, brushmaker, 6 Steven
Kretschman R H, prop Walker House, n e cor King and Ferguson ave
Kronsbein Hy, tailor, 7 Jackson
Krug John B, tobacconist, 115 Cannon w
Krum Franklin, 167 York
Kuhn John, basket maker, bds 26 Peter
Kuntz Hy, brewer, 15 Bay n
Kurpinsh Mrs Agatha (wid Jos) laundress, 42 Canada
Labatt John, J H Linfoot, agent, 4 Hughson s

Labatt R H, clerk, h 80 James s
Labelle Frederick, shoemaker, bds 66 West ave n
Lacely Robt, moulder, 3 Kelly
Lacey James, laborer, Hopkin
La Chance Wm E, com traveler, 79 Main w
Lackie Thos, laborer, 112 Bold
Lackie Wm, piler, 267 York
Lackner Wm, salesman, s w cor Locke and Main
Lafferty Jas, M D, 122 James n
Lagarie Octave, wagon maker, Wellington n, h 180 Emerald n
Lahey Michael, bricklayer, 128 Hannah e
Lahey Thos, express messenger, 41 Catharine n
Lahiff John, laborer, 144 Bay n
Laidlaw Adam, manager Laidlaw Mfg Co, h 17 Wilson
Laidlaw James, carpenter, Ashley
Laidlaw James A (Laidlaw Mfg Co) h 72 Mary
Laidlaw John D, clerk, 17 Wilson
Laidlaw Manufacturing Co, limited, founders. Adam Laidlaw, manager, 84-90 Mary
Laidlaw Rev R J, pastor St. Paul's **Presbyterian** Church, 85 Hughson s
Laidlaw Robert sr, photographer, 147 Main w
Laidlaw Robert jr, photographer, 147 Main w
Laidlaw Thos, **carpenter, bds 173 East ave n**
Laidlaw Thos, clerk, 89 Mary
Laidman Richard, carpenter, 130 **Emerald n**
Laing Mrs Elizabeth (wid **James** S) 159 Park n
Laing Hy H, prop **Hamilton House Furnishing Co**, h 70 Cannon w
Laing John **T**, bricklayer, 60 Robinson
Laing John T, machinist, Maple n s nr Garth

Laing Wm, conductor, 19 Mill
Laird Harry G (Orr & Laird) 26 John n
Laird Mrs Isabella (wid Jos) 67 Hunter e
Laird Thos W, machinist **245** • Hughson n
Lake Albert, **broom maker, 22 Barton w**
Lakeland James, artist, 65 Colborne
Lalor Simon, **hotel, 10-12-14** Market
Lamb Frederick H, assignee and accountant, 7 Hughson s, h 58 Jackson w
Lambe Harold, broker, 6 Hughson s, h 87 Hughson s
Lambert Chas, manager Gore **Coffee Tavern**, 13 Hughson n
Lambert Geo W, teamster, 62 Robinson
Lambert John, teamster, 62 Robinson
Lambert Jos, teamster, 62 Robinson
Lambert Wm, mechanic, 8 Kinnell
Lambert Wm, rubber, 15 Locomotive
Lambrock Mrs, 68 Oak ave
Lamond Mrs Isabella, dressmaker, 141 Main e
Lamond James, laborer, **141 Main** e
Lamont John, gardener, Main e Wentworth
Lamplough Geo, **blacksmith, 8** Inchbury **n**
Lamplough Jeremiah, watchman, 8 Inchbury n
Lampman John, mechanic, bds 4 **Mill**
Lampman Wm, mechanic, bds 4 Mill
Lampman Wm H, teamster, **88** Ferguson ave
Lampshire Mark, South
Lamrock Mrs Mary A, 68 Oak

Lancashire Fire and Life Insurance Co, Geo A Young, agent, 5 King w
Lancefield Chas J, carriage trimmer, 105 York
Lanceley Wm, engineer, 155 Hunter w
Land Allen, clerk, 136 Hughson n
Land Mrs Eliza, 159 Main w
Land Miss Elizabeth, 16 John s
Land Col John, Woodland, Wentworth n
Land John H, Dominion Sec Royal Templars, 296 Barton e
Land Miss M M, music teacher, 159 Main w
Land Peter M, brick manfr, Wentworth n
Land Stephen, machinist, 50 Smith ave
Landan Frederick, pedler, 121 John s
Landed Banking & Loan Co, Samuel Slater, treasurer, 3 James s
Landers John, laborer, Nightingale
Landor Lorandor, agent, 121 John s
Lane Edmund, carpenter, 62 Mulberry
Lane Wm, bricklayer, Hess s w s nr Markland
Lang A B, agent, bds 35 Hughson n
Lang Mrs Grace [wid Wm] 126 Catharine n
Lang Miss Jessie, 7 Walnut s
Lang Thos, laborer, 4 Oak
Langberg Frederick, cabinetmkr, 83-5 King e
Langdon Joseph, engineer, 74 Canada
Langdon Mrs Sarah, 18 Stuart e
Langford John, carpenter, 74 Queen s
Langhorn John, 56 Ferrie w

Langley Philip, watchman, Shaw
Langlois Mrs Margaret [wid Thos] 59 Hunter w
Langton Rev Henry, 22 Sheaffe
Langton James, machinist, 134 Jackson e
Langton John, painter, 134 Jackson e
Langton Mrs Julia [wid Robt] 134 Jackson e
Lannin Thos W, moulder, 25 Oxford
Lansdowne Park, ft Wentworth n
Lappin Joseph, brakeman, 32 Stuart e
Larabee Hinckley S, shoemaker, 25 Walnut s
Larey Mrs Louisa [wid Wm] 134 Cannon e
Larkin Andrew, machinist, 100 Simcoe e
Larkin Fred, weaver, 240 James n
Larkin Hall, 8 John n
Larkin Wm, moulder, 9 Elgin
Larmer George, tinsmith, 137 Napier
Larmer John, laborer, 3 Sophia s
Lanigan Geo H, bookbinder, 68 Ferguson ave
Larvey John, salesman, bds 175 Mary
Laskie Mrs Janet [wid Wm] 62 Ray n
Latham John, laborer, 137 Ferguson ave
Latham Shepherd, machinist, 11 Crooks
Latimer James M, machinist, 72 Locomotive
Latremouille J P, confectioner, 33 Sheaffe
Lauder Mrs Elizabeth [wid John] 146 Bay s
Laurence Thos, druggist, 81 James n
Laurie James, crockery, 106 King w
Laurie Jno, carpenter, Macauley e

Laut John W, manager Laut Tea Co, h 42 Vine
Laut Tea Co, John W Laut manager, 3 Market sq
LaVallee Mrs Martha, 297 James n
Lavell John, cigarmaker, 65a East ave n
Lavelle Mrs Ann [wid Owen] 63 Maria
Lavelle Anthony, 1 Bold
Lavelle Geo, broommaker, 67 Main w
Lavelle John, laborer, 123 Hunter w
Lavelle Patrick, baker, 63 Maria
Lavelle Robt, stoves and tins, 19 John n, h 63 Maria
Lavers Mrs Jane [wid James] Maple n s nr Locke
Lavers Wm, carpenter, Maple
Lavery Henry, bookkeeper, 95 Walnut s
Lavery James, carpenter, 31 East ave n
Lavery W J, solicitor, 4 Main e, h Main, East Hamilton
Lavin Mrs Ellen [wid Thomas] 146 Catharine n
Lavis Albert, laborer, 204 King Wm
Lavis David, shoemaker, 204 King Wm
Lavis Edward, carpenter, 105 Rebecca
Lavis Edward, pork buyer, 204 King Wm
Lavis Mrs Fanny [wid Wm] 37 Ferguson ave
Lawless Thomas, journalist, 31 Wellington n
Lawley Thos, 270 Hughson n
Lawlor John, cabinetmaker, 69 Strachan e
Lawlor Mrs Mary, 20 Wood w
Lawlor Patrick, teamster, 16 Railway
Lawlor Thomas, machinist, 42 Wilson

Lawrason Mrs Hannah [wid Douglas] 162 Napier
Lawrence Frank W, builder, 61 Wellington n
Lawrence John, painter, 9 Wood e
Lawrence John A R, salesman, 21 Tom
Lawrence Thomas, carpenter, end Wilson
Lawrence Walter A, com traveler, 12 Erie ave
Lawrence Wm, florist, bds 60 James s
Lawrence Wm, letter carrier, 39 Emerald n
Lawrie John, bookkeeper, bds 46 Duke
Lawrie Robert, laborer, 99 Hunter w
Lawrie Simon, collector, 161 Wellington n
Lawry Chas, hide and skin dealer, 26 Merrick res Dundas
Lawry Henry, pork packer, 35 Bay n
Lawry John, carpenter, 143 Macauley e
Lawry Thomas [Thos Lawry & Son,] 136 James s
Lawry Thomas H (Thomas Lawry & Son) 35 Bay n
Lawry Thos & Son (Thos & Thos H) pork packers and provision dealers, 16-20 Macnab s
Laws James, billposter, 241 King e
Lawson A & Co, printers, 10 York
Lawson Miss Hannah, 154 James n
Lawson Mrs Isabella (wid Alex) 55 Macnab s
Lawson John, laborer, 55 Magill
Lawson John, salesman, 78 John n
Lawson Mrs Mary (wid Abraham) 55 Magill

17

Lawson Thomas, laborer, 18 Guise
Lawson Wm, traveler, bds 37 Robert
Lay Andrew, White Elephant Saloon, 21 James n
Lay George, gardener J Huntoon, Main e of Wentworth
Laycock Miss Martha A, tailoress, 46 Magill
Layland Edwin, driver, 93 Robinson
Lazarus George J, turner, 14 Magill
Lazier & Monck, [S F Lazier, M A, LL B, J F Monck] barristers, 42 James n *See card*
Lazier S F, M A, LL B, [Lazier & Monck] h 67 Charles
Leanea Wm, baggageman, 149 Ferguson ave
Leask A R, clerk, 324 York
Leask R P, hats, caps and gents' furnishings, 24 King e, h 324 York
Leather Matthew, laborer, 55 Little Wm
Leather Thos E, com traveler, 97 Market
Leatherdale Thos J, photograph toucher, bds 100 Park n
Leaver Uriah, laborer, 52 Strachan e
Leavers George, painter, 147½ Jackson w
LeBlanc Isaac, laborer, 32 Macauley w
Leckenby Francis, com traveler, 9½ Park s
Leckie Wm R, bookkeeper, 172 West ave n
Leckie W R, bookkeeper, 172 West ave n
Ledgerwood Mrs Mira, 45 Robert
Ledgerwood Wm J, mechanic, 45 Robert
Lee Arthur G, salesman, 69 Duke
Lee Christopher, salesman, 78 Jackson e

Lee Rev C R, M A, incumbent Holy Trinity, Mountain top, bds 80 James s
Lee George, accountant, 4 Bay s
Lee Harry, mangr Burlington Glass Works, 11 Brock
Lee James, cotton weaver, 238 Catharine n
Lee Joseph, contractor, Burlington s
Lee Lyman, B A, barrister, 14 Hughson s, bds 190 Macnab n
Lee Mrs Martha (wid Chas) 373 Hughson n
Lee Robert, fireman GTR, 12 Crooks
Lee Thomas, baker, bds 56 Park n
Lee Thomas, glassblower, 50 Ferrie e
Lee Wesley, ship builder, 380 Hughson n
Lee Wm, blacksmith, 253 York
Lee William, builder, 191 Wellington n
Lee Wm, pedler, 28 Elgin
Lee Wm G, 4 Bay s
Leegrice Jeremiah, bracket mkr, r 75 Jackson e
Leehine John, laborer, 35 Napier
Leeming Ralph, accountant, 28 Hannah e
Lees G H (G H Lees & Co) h 78 Napier
Lees G H & Co (G H and Wm) manfr jewelers, 29 Main e
Lees Mrs Jane (wid George) 74 James s
Lees Thomas, watchmaker, jeweler and optican, 5 James n, h 145 Main w
Lees Wm, employee Express Co, bds Victoria Hotel
Lees Wm, (Walker, Scott & Lees) h 31 Main e
Lees Wm & Son, (Wm and A A) bakers, 31 Main e
Lefevre Robt H, carpet weaver, 13 Rebecca

Legarie John, blacksmith, 223 John n
Legault Felix, shoemaker, 28 Smith ave
Legault Jacques, shoemaker, 30 Smith ave
Leggat John, salesman, 5 Duke
Leggat Matthew (Wood & Leggat) h 5 Duke
Leggitt John, chair maker, bds 31 Gore
Lehann Daniel, laborer, r 258 King w
Leighton Augustus, laundry, 12 Hunter e
Leishman James Fred, bookkeeper, 72 Catharine n
Leishman Mrs Malcolm, 32½ Emerald n
Leitch Alex W, com merchant, 14 Hannah w
Leitch Andrew (Leitch & Turnbull) 18 Barton w
Leitch Mrs Ann (wid Wm) 14 Hannah w
Leitch John, (J Leitch & Son) h 50 Hughson n
Leitch John, mechanic, 215 King e
Leitch Robert, blacksmith, 207 Mary
Leitch J & Son, Central Iron Works, 27-29 Rebecca
Leitch & Turnbull (Andrew Leitch, Michael Turnbull) Canada Elevator Works, s e cor Queen and Peter
Leitch Wm G, manfr, 36 Hughson s
Leith Alex, teller Stinson's Bank, 71 Main w
Leith Mrs Ann (wid Wm) 71 Main w
Leith George, 56 John n
Leith J A, clerk, 173 Mary
Leith Wm, clerk, 71 Main w
Lemberg M. tinsmith, 34 Canada
Le Messurier Daniel, painter, 17 Charles, h 59 Hunter w

Lemmond James, laborer, Robinson n s w Locke
Lemon Charles, barrister, 14 Hughson s, h 42 Geo *See card*
Lemon Mrs Margaret (wid Wilson) 30 Wilson
Lendon Hy J, machinist, 29 Crooks
Lennox John (Wm Griffith & Co) h 164 Main w
Lennox William, laborer, s e cor Markland & Hess
Lenz August, laborer, 47 Tisdale
Lenz Frederick, laborer, 47 Steven
Leonard E R, porter, Stuart w
Leonard James, laborer, Patrick
Leonard Mrs Louisa, 30 Stuart e
Leonard Patrick, laborer, Eliza
LePage Pierre, shoemaker, 25 Liberty
LePatourel Elias, engineer, 117 Main e
Lepstritz Lew, rag dealer, 142 Jackson w
Lepstritz Moses, rag dealer, 142 Jackson w
LeRiche George (J Winer & Co) h 102 Catharine s
Leslie Geo, laborer, bds King e of Wentworth
Leslie James, M D, 37 Main w
Leslie J W, com traveler, Main cor Park
Leslie Robt, clerk G T R, 44 Macaulay w
Leslie Robt, shoemaker, 35 Florence
Leslie Robert, wholesale and retail fruiterer, 270 King e
Leslie Robt P, clerk G T R, 44 Macaulay w
Lessard Irene, brush maker, Wentworth n
Lest Chas, laborer, Garth w s nr King
Lester John M, 32 Victoria ave s
Lester Thos sr, 80 Emerald s

Lester T W [Rutherford & Lester] 80 Emerald s
Lever ——, gardener, T H Pratt, Strachan e
Levi Isaac, tailor, 99 Jackson e
Levis John, laborer, 145 Catharine n
Levis Samuel J, polisher, 145 Catharine n
Levy Abraham (Levy Bros) h 89 James s
Levy Adolph, clerk, 89 James s
Levy A, rag dealer, 79 Macnab n
Levy Brothers (Herman & Abraham Levy) wholesale jewelers, 27 King e
Levy Herman (Levy Bros) h 89 James s
Levy Jacob, clerk, 89 James s
Levy John, pedler, 44 Locke s
Lewin Geo, grocer, 209 John n
Lewington Thos, laborer 209 Main w
Lewis Ambrose, whitewasher, 32 Oak ave
Lewis Andrew, teamster, 135 Barton e
Lewis Benjamin, laborer, 79 Lower Cathcart
Lewis Benjamin, wool sorter, 59 Gore
Lewis Mrs Clarissa (wid Jas) 14 Charles
Lewis Edward, plasterer, 38 Charles
Lewis Mrs Elizabeth, 129 Simcoe
Lewis Frank, moulder, 43 Steven
Lewis Hy, sewing machine agent bds 153 King e
Lewis Jacob, blind maker, 37 Spring
Lewis Jacob, second hand dealer 85 James n
Lewis James, carpenter, 255 Cannon e
Lewis James, finisher, 57 Young
Lewis John, grocer, 148 York
Lewis John, shoemaker, 89 King Wm

Lewis John B, painter, 80 Maria
Lewis J L, city editor *Spectator*, 103 James s
Lewis Louis, laborer, bds 209 Bay n
Lewis Marvin, machinist, 39 Kelly
Lewis Ralph, carpenter, 304 Macnab n
Lewis Mrs Susan (wid Daniel) 83 Peter
Lewis Thos, carter, 118 West ave n
Lewis Thos, cigar manfr, 27 Spring
Lewis Thos, laborer, 141 Locke n
Lewis Mrs Virginia [wid Adolphus] 32 Oak ave
Lewis Wm, plasterer, 66 Oak ave
Lewis Wm J, carpenter, 120 East ave n
Lewis W H, agent, bds Simcoe Ho el
Leyden Chas, manager Duncan Lithograph Co, 20 Barton e
Libke Chas, brushmaker, 59 Steven
License Commissioners' Office, John I Mackenzie, inspector, 4 James s
Lightfoot Frederick, shoemaker, 159 James n
Lightfoot J L, shoemaker, 159 James n
Lillis John S, cigar manfr, 3 Centre, h 9 Cannon w
Lilly Jonathan, express messenger, 171 Wellington n
Limage Wm, cutter, 43 Mary
Limin Chas, butcher, 26 Jackson w
Limin W, salesman, 26 Jackson w
Linas Frederick, laborer, 189 Main w
Lindsay Thos, laborer, end Ferguson ave
Lindsay Thos, laborer, end Ferguson ave

CITY OF HAMILTON.   133

Lindsay Walter J, paying teller Bank of Hamilton, 114 Main w
Lindsay Wm, fitter, end Ferguson ave
Lindsay Wm, laborer, ft Ferguson ave
Linebald Henry, tailor, 47 Jackson e
Linfoot John, livery, cor Cannon and Wellington
Linfoot J H, agent John Labatt, 6 Hughson s, h Robert cor Victoria ave
Linfoot Leonidas, salesman, 118 East ave n
Ling John, carpenter, 72 Cannon w
Ling Peter, salesman, 72 Cannon w
Linger Jesse, caretaker Christ Church Cath, James n
Lingwood ———, bds 40 Mulberry
Linklater Andrew, porter, 206 King Wm
Linstead Mrs Caroline, [wid Fredk), r 206 Catharine n
Linsted William, laborer, 205 John n
Linsted Mrs, r 206 Catharine n
Linton Henry, shoemaker, 18 Lower Cathcart
Linton Herbert, laborer, 109 West ave n
Lipkie Frank, laborer, 46 Hess s
Lipkie John, laborer, 46 Hess s
Lister Harry M, student 'Woodlawn,' Victoria ave s
Lister James, 195 John n
Lister J E & Co, clothiers, hatters and gents' furnishers, 58-60 James n cor Rebecca
Lister Joseph, 42 James n, h 'Woodlawn' Victoria ave s
Lister J Edmund, (J E Lister & Co), h 'Woodlawn' Victoria ave s
Lister Mrs J M, dressmaker, 292 Macnab n

Lister W L B, lawstudent, 'Woodlawn' Victoria ave s
Lithgow Jas, laborer, 210 King w
Little Mrs Catharine, (wid Wm), 104 Hughson n
Little David, barber, 7 Grove
Little Hector, grocer, cor Mary and Barton
Little James, contractor, 104 East ave n
Little James, propr Dundurn Hotel, 287-289 York
Little John, carpenter, King e of Wentworth
Little John, livery, bds Franklin House
Little John M, (Walter Woods & Co,) h 5 Victoria ave n
Little J R, clerk Merchants' Bank 104 King e
Little & Linfoot, livery, 6 Park n
Little Matthew H, shipper, 238 Cannon e
Little Wm, pot maker, 13 Burlington w
Littlehales John, detective, 234 Cannon e
Littlehales Thomas, manager Hamilton Gas Light Co, h 99 Park n
Littlejohn Charles, wood inspector, G T R, 130 Queen n
Littlejohns Wm, bricklayer, 121 Emerald n
Littlewood Thomas, brakeman, 9 Murray e
Livernois Joseph, merchant, 24 Spring
Livingston Earnest N, law student, 100 Main w
Livingston Stuart, law student 100 Main w
Livingston Thos C, Dominion land surveyor; 100 Main w
Livingston W Churchill, Victoria Chambers 31 James s, h 100 Main w
Lloyd Griffith R, bookkeeper, 108 Cannon w

Lloyd H H, shipper, bds 44 Murray w
Lloyd James, laborer, 104 Hess n
Lloyd Joseph, storekeeper, 108 Cannon w
Locke Andrew, moulder, 47 Oak ave
Locke Anthony, painter, 123 Rebecca
Locke Chas, stovemounter, 84 Hannah e
Locke Fredk C, mechanic, 97 Mary
Locke Mrs Margaret G R, (wid Chas F A) 109 Jackson w
Locke Mrs Mary E (wid Joseph) 109 Jackson w
Lock Wm J, ins agent, 123 Rebecca
Locke, Wm J, salesman, s w cor Markland and Caroline
Locke Mrs Walter, 15 Spring
Lockhart James, manfr, 51 Hannah w
Lockhart James, 45 Hannah w, s s nr Caroline
Lockhead James, laborer, bds 66 Catharine n
Lochead J A, bookkeeper, bds 6 Park s
Lockie Alex, pressman *Times*, 67 Hunter w
Lockman Willam, carpenter,, 36 Florence
Lockman Wm H, bridge builder 40 Florence
Lockwood Miss Eliza, (Kelly & Lockwood) h 2 Mill
Loemans Mme Alexandra Francis, 151 King w
Loemas Joseph W, (Loemas Juvenile Band, 167 James n
Loewy Siegmund, confectioner, 42 Market
Loftus James, laborer, 119 Caroline n
Logan Hugh, salesman, 91 Victoria ave n

Logan James, laborer, bds 43 John n
Logan John, coachman, 32 Poulette
Logan John, excise officer, 198 Bay n
Logan Mrs Maggie, (wid Adam), 8 Margaret
Logie James, 17 Hess s
Logie Mrs Mary R, (wid Alex), Markland s s nr Park
Lomes Joseph, laborer, 8 Tiffany
London China House, C M Bradfield, manager, 7 Market Square
London Guarantee and Accident Insurance Co, Geo A Young, agent, 5 King w
London & Lancashire Fire Insurance Co, W F Findlay, agent, Wentworth Chambers, 25 James s
London & Lancashire Life Co, J T Routh, agent, 16 James s
London Mutual Fire Insurance Co, Walter Ambrose, agent, 14 Hughson s
Loney Alfred, shoemaker, r 111 John s
Loney Christopher, shoemaker, 84 John s
Loney Thos, shoemaker, 37 Young
Long & Bisby (W D Long, G H Bisby) wool merchants, 58 Macnab n
Long David H, hotel keeper, 14 John s
Long Geo, wood and coal yard, Hunter cor Cherry
Long Horace, bookkeeper, h 94 James s
Long Mrs Helen (wid Wm) 80 Caroline n
Long John, laborer, Sherman
Long Jos, laborer, 148 Jackson w
Long Mrs Mary A, 2 Oak ave

Long Mrs Matilda (wid James) 148 Jackson w
Long Philip, 174 John n
Long Robt J, blacksmith, 92 Caroline n
Long Thos, laborer, 255 King Wm
Long Walter, painter, 189 Hughson n
Long Wm, laborer, 2 Oak ave
Long W D (Long & Bisby) h 54 John n
Longhurst Edwin, moulder, 309 King w
Longhurst Henry (H Longhurst & Co) h 11 Nightingale
Longhurst H & Co, stained glass works, 16 John n
Lonsdale Frank, sec Young Mens' Christian Association, Beulah
Loosley Ed W, cutter, 20 Liberty
Lord Robt, tailor, 53 Gore
Lord Wm, dairyman, Queen s s nr Herkimer
Loretto Convent, Mount St Mary, King cor Ray
Lorimer James, laborer, 224 Ferguson ave
Lorme Thos, machinist, 50 Wilson
Lot John, tea dealer, bds 42 Vine
Lottridge J M (Grant & Sons) h cor Bay and Herkimer
Lottridge Robt, 126 Bay s
Loucks Hilton, harness maker, 186 Main w
Loughrea Samuel B, com traveler 94 Victoria ave n
Louis Jacob, carpenter, 138 Hunter e
Lounsbury Rev Edward, Methodist, 15 Victoria ave n
Love David, carpenter, 285 King Wm
Love Mrs Mary, 93 King w
Lover Thos, shipper, r 166 Mary
Lovejoy Chas, plasterer, 157 Hunter w

Lovejoy Thos, bricklayer, 57 Emerald n
Lovell A R, clerk, 172 King e
Lovell John B, tobacconist, 172 King e
Lovell Hy T, fireman G T R, 186 Napier
Lovell Thos P, marbleizer, 95 Napier
Lovering W J, Club Chambers, 16 Hughson s
Lowe David, wireworker, 122 Napier
Lowe Harry, salesman, 69 Queen s
Lowe Wm, carpenter, 23 Caroline n
Lowe Wm, machinist, 208 Macnab n
Loves John, com traveler, 272 King e
Lowry Chas T, machinist, 94 Market
Lowery David, cigarmaker, bds 103 James n
Lowrey Jacob, 94 Market
Lowrey James A, moulder, 32 Caroline n
Lowrey John, policeman, 138 Wellington n
Lowrey John B, moulder, 32 Caroline n
Lowrie Marthew, carpenter, 22 Smith ave
Lowry Philip, laborer, 22 Pearl n
Lucas Chas H, bookkeeper, 10 Crooks
Lucas Edgar V, shoe laster, 174½ Victoria ave n
Lucas James, lunch room, 11 Market square
Lucas Luke, moulder, 85 Catharine n
Lucas, Park & Co (R A Lucas, J H Park, G E Bristol, R T Steele) wholesale grocers, 59 Macnab n
Lucas Robt, foreman E & C Gurney Co, 117 Bay n

Lucas Robt, moulder, 48 Tisdale
Lucas Robt, teamster, 146 Picton e
Lucas Robt N, moulder, 31 Market
Lucas R A (Lucas, Park & Co) 23 Duke
Lucas Samuel, carpenter, 6 Henry
Lucas Thos, blacksmith, 130 Picton e
Lucas Thos, laborer, 94 Ferrie e
Lucas Thos O, butcher, 40 Catharine n
Luetzenger, August, hatter, 68 Lower Cathcart
Lumgair Wm S, agent, 175 Main w
Lumsden Bros, wholesale grocers 64 Macnab n.
Lumsden Mrs Frances (wid Wm) 43½ Cannon w
Lumsden Fred H, salesman, h 43½ Cannon w
Lumsden Paul E, salesman, h 11 Bailey
Lumsden Wm, bookkeeper, h 104 Queen n
Lumsden W G (Lumsden Bros) h 43 Cannon w
Lumsted ——, coal weigher, 104 Queen n
Lund Mrs Ada, 16 Ray s
Luscombe Samuel, butcher, 68 Emerald n
Lutes Alonzo, salesman, 24 Queen s
Lutz John, teamster, 55 Pearl s
Luxton George, grain and wood dealer, 12 York
Lyle John, plumber, 82 West ave n
Lyle Mrs Martha (wid Andrew) 80 West ave n
Lyle Rev Samuel B D, pastor Central Presbyterian Church, 20 Jackson w
Lyle Wm J, machinist, 80 West ave n

Lynch Francis, teamster, 113 Barton e
Lynch James, switchman, 214 John n
Lynch James, printer, 132 Ferrie e
Lynch John, laborer, 254 Mary n
Lynch Mrs Mary (wid Andrew) 167 Wilson
Lynch Mrs Mary (wid Patrick) 132 Ferrie e
Lynch Mrs Mary (wid Thomas) Aikman ave
Lynch Patrick, laborer, 167 Wilson
Lynch Peter, mason, 169 John n
Lynch Wm, engineer N & N W, 169 John n
Lynd Mrs Helen (wid Wm) laundress, 79 Pearl n
Lyne John, shoemaker, 59 Little Wm
Lyng James, carpenter, 33 Oak ave
Lyon Anthony, foreman Matthew Wilson & Co, 165 Queen n
Lyon Thos, mariner, 31 Railway
Lyons Calvin, agent, 81 Lower Cathcart
Lyons John, shipper, 9 Head
Lyons Thos, laborer, 189 Victoria ave n
Lyons Townsend, laborer, 60 Oak ave
Lyons Wm, laborer, Concession s s nr Queen
McAdam Low, stonemason, 98 Queen s
Macadams A H [Parkes & Macadams] h 130 Hughson n
Macadams Alexander, lumber dealer, 130 Hughson n
McAdams Minian, broommaker, 50 Young
McAlden Mrs Harriet (wid Geo) 73 Wellington s
McAllister Harmon, grocer, 123 York

McAllister John, grocer, 121-3 York, h 128 Macnab n
McAllister John, laborer, 50 Hannah w
McAllister John J, builder, 128 Macnab n
McAllister L D, sewing machine agt, n w cor Pearl and Bold
McAllister Wm J, lumber merchant, 34 East ave s
McAndrew Patrick, laborer, 50 Stuart e
McAndrew William, manager A Lawson & Co, 116 Mary
McArthur Alex C, laborer, 90 Peter
McArthur James, manager Smart's Tea Co, bds Victoria hotel
Macarthur John W, manfr, 138 Hughson n
McArthur Mrs Mary [wid Peter] 90 Peter
McAulay John, millwright, 30½ Magill
Macaulay John, huckster, 195 King e
Macaulay Wm, buyer, Blake, e Hamilton
McAuliffe Daniel J, clerk, 105 Market
McAuliffe Daniel laborer, 17 Wood w
McAuliffe Jeremiah, machinist, 105 Market
McAuliffe Jeremiah, prop Mansion Saloon, 6 Hughson n
McAuliffe Mrs Julia [wid Patrick] 105 Market
McAvay Patrick, gilder, 143 Ferguson ave
McBean John, pattern maker, 14 Kinnell
McBeth Peter, contractor, 80 Napier
McBeth Sinclair, 118 Napier
McBeth Wm, machinist, 47 Hannah w
McBrayne Walter Scott, law student, John cor Robert

McBriar Mrs Alice (wid Alex) nurse, 68 Duke
McBride Mrs Ann, 181 Catharine n
McBride Daniel, coal oil dealer, 227 Catharine n
McBride Dennis, moulder, 218 John n
McBride J F, grocer, 218-220 John n
McBride John, policeman, 11 Oxford
McBride Patrick, 100 Murray e
McBride Richard, packer, 94 George
McBride Thos, superintendent Hendrie & Co, 34 Hunter w
McBride William, laborer, r 14 Hess s
McBrien Henry, plumber, 58 Wellington s
McBrien Henry D, plumber, 58 Wellington s
McBrien David, painter, 25 Cherry
McBrier Mrs Elizabeth (wid Jas) 79 Caroline n
McCabe Mrs Agnes (wid James) 32 Crooks
McCabe Chas J, teacher, bds 125 Market
McCabe John, laborer, 114 Queen n
McCabe Patrick, laborer, 108 Queen n
McCabe Thos, engineer, 25 Aikman ave
McCall Thos, driver, 66 Market
McCallum Alex, moulder, 42 Picton w
McCallum Caroline (wid Daniel) 46 Duke
Macallum Mrs D, 50 James s
McCallum Edward, 152 Mary
McCallum & Hall [Thos McCallum, jr, John T Hall] furniture dealers and manfrs, 16-18 Macnab n, factory 158 Main w

18

McCallum James, laborer, 121 Simcoe e
McCallum John, moulder, 16 Ferrie w
McCallum John J B, laborer, 58 Locomotive
McCallum Mary [wid Daniel] 152 Mary
McCallum Mary B [wid Arch] 61 Bold
McCallum Thomas [McCallum & Hall] h 111 Wellington n
McCamis Arthur, laborer, 236 Macnab n
McCamis Henry, brakeman, bds 236 Macnab n
McCandlish Alfred, hat maker, 105 Wellington s
McCandlish Peter, shipper, 105 Wellington s
McCandlish Peter, jr, brushmkr, 105 Wellington s
McCandlish Stewart, salesman, 105 Wellington s
McCann Ann [wid Henry] 9 Ferrie e
McCann Henry, confectioner, 62 West ave n
McCann John, boots and shoes, 101 James n
McCann Joseph, plater, 101 James n
McCann Rev P, Roman Catholic, 25 Sheaffe
McCardle M [wid Patrick] 130 John n
McCardle Robert, plumber, 19 Lower Cathcart
McCargow Wm, M D, 16 Gore
McCarter Mrs Mary (wid Arthur) 3 Bold
McCarthy Callan, hackman, 20 Harriet
McCarthy Catharine [wid Chas] 19 Locke n
McCarthy Chas, Dundurn
McCarthy Daniel, railroader, 220 Catharine n

McCarthy Daniel, rougher, 119 Locke n
McCarthy Daniel, steward asylum, 9 Nelson ave
McDarthy Elizabeth [wid Julius C] 113 Hunter e
McCarthy James, nurseryman, 77 Hannah e
McCarthy John, stovemounter, 200 Barton e
McCarthy John, express messenger, 96 Wilson
McCarthy John, laborer, 202 Hughson n
McCarthy Patrick, driver, 26 Hess n
McCarthy Patrick, laborer, 1 Harriet
McCarthy Richard, hack driver, 16 Harriet
McCarthy Robert, brakeman, bds 165 Bay n
McCarthy Thos, teamster, 32 Burlington e
McCarthy Wm, dresser, 295 John
McCarthy Wm, laborer, 41 Oak ave
McCarthy David, fruiterer, 158 James n
McCartney Eliza [wid Wm] 92 Hess n
Macartney Eliza [wid Wm] 92½ Hess n
McCartney John, plasterer, 158 James n
McCartney Patrick, carter, end Victoria ave n
Macartney W C, ins agent, 77 Victoria ave n
MeCarty Daniel, yardsman, 230 Catharine n
McCarthy John, hackman, 57 Wood e
McCarty Michael, moulder, 98 Barton e
McCarty Richard, laborer, 150½ Duke
McCarty ——, carpenter, 41 Oak ave

McCauley John, lithographer, 9 Spring
McCawley Ellen [wid Hugh] 86 Wilson
McCawley Robt J, shipper, 86 Wilson
McCawley Wm P, clerk P O, 86 Wilson
McCleave Richard R, shoe trimmer, 53 Macnab s
McClellan Andrew, laborer, 132 Young
McClellan George, laborer, 191 Bay n
McClellan Robert, 132 Young
McClelland Andrew, laborer, 167 Queen n
McClelland Peter, compositor, bds 31 Lower Cathcart
McClelland Thos J, engineer, 91 Elgin
McClelland Wm, coffee roaster, 26 Spring
McClenahan Robert, porter, 226 King w
McCloy Mrs Agnes, 54 Emerald n
McClure Mrs James F, 46 Jackson w
McClure Wm, car foreman, 250 Bay n
McCoey Alexander, grainer, 48 East ave n
McColl Hugh, employee Express Co
McColl Jessie [wid Hugh] 17 Crooks
McColl John, tailor, bds 19 Hughson n
McColl John, fireman GTR, 17 Crooks
McComas Wm, laborer, 111 Catharine n
McComb Eliza [wid Thomas] 126 Hess n
McComb John, tailor, 56 West ave n
McComb Wm, moulder, 7 Oak ave

McComb Wm H, machinist, 126 Hess n
McConachie David [S Thorne & Co] h 153 York
McConnel Henry, engineer G T R, Barton w, s s nr Magill
McConnell Wm, overseer cotton mills, bds 100 Park n
McConochie Samuel W, M D, cor Hannah and Hess
McCormack Lawrence, conductor, 2 Harriet
McCormick Ralph, teamster, 55 Hannah e
McCowan Ann, (wid John), 63 Ray n
McCowan Bernard, baggage master G T R, 63 Ray n
McCowell Bernard, laborer, 21 Dundurn
McCowel John, wireworker, 17 Dundurn
McCowell Miss Mary, seamstress 35 Sheaffe
McCoy Archd, mariner, 24 Guise
McCoy J C, salesman, 77 Wellington n
McCoy Jeremiah, carpenter, 218 James n
McCoy John, asst inspector Ham Prov & Loan Society, 36 Victoria ave n
McCoy John A, general dry goods, 40 James n, h 77 Wellington n
McCracken John, tailor, 224 John n
McCracken John, moulder, bds 19 Hughson n
McCready John, moulder, bds 121 Rebecca
McCreath James, blacksmith, 135 Jackson e
McCue James, engineer G T R, 110 Locke n
McCulloch David W, clerk, 64 Main w
McCulloch Harriet, (wid Robt), 147 Hughson n

McCulloch James, engine driver G T R, 30 Tom
McCulloch J O, clerk P O
McCulloch, Margaret, (wid David), 52 Jackson w
McCulloch Matthew, clerk G T R, 52 Jackson w
McCulloch Peter, laborer, s e cor Florence and Dundurn
McCullough George, blacksmith, 123 King Wm, h 120 Bold
McCullough Miss Harriet, dressmaker, 25 Lower Cathcart
McCullough J D, (Davis & McCullough) h 70 Jackson w
McCullough John, clerk, 70 Jackson w
McCullough John, builder, 70 Jackson w
McCullough Peter T, com traveller, 70 Jackson w
McCully Alex, shoemaker, 146 Hughson n
McCully Bernard, machinist, 15 Steven
McCully G A, custom boots and shoes, 73 James n
McCully Misses, tailoresses, 144 Hughson n
McCurdy Wm, carpenter, 12 Wellington n
McCusker Eliza, (wid Thos) 132 Cannon w
McCusker Francis, provision dealer, 2 Nelson
McCusker Wm, produce dealer, 132 Cannon w
McCutchen Miss Fanny, 124 Jackson e
McCutcheon G E, bookkeeper, bds 122 Cannon e
McDaid Wm, laborer, 132 Locke n
McDermid Isabella, (wid Arch), 61 George
McDermid Miss Nancy, 32 Wellington n
McDermott Daniel, painter, 1 Pine

McDermott James, moulder, 236 Barton e
McDermott James, laborer, 125 Napier
McDermott John, cabinetmaker, bds 8 Bay s
McDermott Michael, laborer, bds 8 Bay s
McDermott, Neil, lumber miller, bds 174 Bay n
McDonagh Anthony, gardener Main e of Wentworth
McDonagh John, gardener, Main e of Wentworth
McDonagh John, milk peddlar, 48 Augusta
McDonagh Mrs Mary, Main e of Wentworth
McDonald Mrs Alex, 4 Wellington n
McDonald Alex, com traveller, 5 Erie ave
McDonald Alex A, com traveller 101 Rebecca
McDonald Archibald, (prop Rob Roy Hotel), 87 John s
McDonald Arthur, cigarmaker, 209 Hughson n
McDonald David, grocer, 77 York
McDonald D B, com traveller, bds 48 James n
McDonald Duncan, stonemason, 139 Hunter w
Macdonald Elizabeth, (wid Hugh), 101 Caroline s
McDonald Mrs Ellen, 46 Burlington w
McDonald Mrs Grace, (wid Duncan), 6 Florence
McDonald James, carpenter, 290 Mary
McDonald James, 209 Hughson n
McDonald James, foreman J McPherson & Co, 79 Wellington s
Macdonald J D, M D, 10 Duke

Macdonald John, **laborer,** 58 Maria
McDonald John, custom shoemaker, 107½ John s, h 87 Wellington n
McDonald John, moulder, r Lower Cathcart
McDonald John, laborer, **r** 64 Hughson n
McDonald John, inspector Weights and Measures, 9 Simcoe e
McDonald John R, ticket clerk, 39 **East** ave n
Macdonald John W, lumberman, 146 Queen n
McDonald Lewis, machinist, 30 **Hess n**
Macdonald Mrs Marian (wid Alex) 53 **Hess n**
McDonald **Owen, laborer,** 28 Bay s
McDonald Robt, laborer, 6 Concession
McDonald Roderick, **salesman,** 21 Walnut s
McDonald Mrs Sarah, 89 **Strachan e**
McDonald Mrs Sarah (wid Wm) boarding house keeper, 20 **Main w**
Macdonald Thos, teamster, 71 **John n**
McDonald Wm, moulder, 88 **Hess n**
McDonald Wm, time-keeper, **h** 180 Mary
Macdonald **Wm, packer,** 189 York
Macdonald Wm, scalemaker, 115 Victoria ave n
Macdonald W J, carpenter, etc., r 116 King Wm, h 8 Emerald s
Macdonald W R, barrister, 33 James s, h 12 Herkimer
McDonnell Chas, basketmaker, 271 **King w**
Macdonnell Mrs Esther (wid Patrick) 26 Aurora

Madonnell John, broommaker, 26 **Aurora**
McDonnell John, flour and feed, 156 Main w
Macdonnell Thos, laborer, **26** Aurora
McDonnell Wm J, asst inspector weights and measures
McDonough Michael, rougher, 60 **Locomotive**
McDougall **Albert D,** brakeman G T R, 30 Inchbury n
McDougal **Andrew,** machinist, **95** Elgin
Mc**Dougall** Daniel, **blacksmith,** 40 Ray n
McDougall Duncan, railway contractor, 29 Locomotive
McDougall Hugh, stonemason, hd **Garth** w s nr Concession
McDougall J, coal oil and lamps, 10 Macnab n
McDougall John, car checker, 185 Macnab n
Macdougall John, brewer, bds 97 Cannon w
McDougall Joseph R, clerk N & N W R, 133 Locke n
McDougall Wm, machinist, 133 Locke n
McDougall Wm, salesman, 10 Macnab n
McDowell Alex, **laborer,** 134 Park n
McEachern A, teller Ham Prov & Loan Society, 131 Macnab n
McEachren Malcolm A, boilermaker, 59 Locomotive
McEachren Mrs Margaret C [wid Roderick] 59 Locomotive
McElcheran W H, 56 Barton e
McEntee James, laborer, 321 James n
McEvoy Henry N, artist, **Y M** C A rooms
McEwen John, laborer, **Concess**cession s s nr Locke
McEwan P C, clerk, 11 Hess s
McFadden John, **329** John n

McFadden Wm, grocer, 28 Wood e
McFadden W J, grocer, 342 Hughson n
McFaddin Rev T J, Reformed Episcopal, 10 Young
McFarlane Alex, flour and feed, 246-248 King e, h 154 Hunter
McFarlane James, mechanical engineer, Beach
McFarlane Miss Jane, matron Orphan Asylum, 115 Wellington s
McFarlane John, teamster, Aikman ave
McFarlane Miss Margaret, matron Aged Woman's Home, 115 Wellington s
McFarlane Mark, machinist, 31 West ave n
Macfarlane William, machinist, 56 Maria
McFarlane Wm, laborer, hd Queen w s
McFarland Arhur, laborer, Hunter w n s w Poulette
MacFarland James, coachman, Highfield, Concession
McFedries Wm, salesman, 151 Hunter w
McFee Malcolm, trackman G T R, hd York w canal
McFerran Mrs Martha, 137 Emerald n
McGahey Wm, loom fixer, 358 James n
McGainey James, hostler, 55 Macnab n
McGallagher John, laborer, 91 Lower Cathcart
McGann John, moulder, 126 Jackson e
McGargle Mrs Susanna (wid Francis) 70 Oak ave
McGarth Mrs Ann (wid Peter) 32 Ferguson ave
McGaw W H, salesman, 9 Grove
McGee James, teamster, 25 Burlington w

McGibbon Wm, baker, 24 Barton e
McGill Samuel, carpenter, 137 York
McGillicuddy Mrs E A, 169 Main e
McGillivray Kenneth, carpenter, cor Wood and Wellington n
McGilvary A E, salesman, 75 Elgin
McGilvary Donald, packer, 75 Elgin
McGilvary Sarah (wid Donald) 75 Elgin
McGilvary Geo, conductor N & N W, 36½ Ferguson ave
McGinn John, blacksmith, bds 83 Main e
McGinnis John, stovemounter, 12 Jackson e
McGiverin Mrs Emma, 100 Queen n
McGiverin W F, sec Ham Ind Works Co, h 115 Macnab s
McGiverin Thomes, bds 10 Main e
McGoff John, machinist, 152 King Wm
McGolrick Henry, laborer, 204 Catharine n
McGorman David, fireman Bay st fire station, bds 25 Stuart w
McGovern John, pensioner, 68 Ferrie e
McGovern Patrick, carriagemkr, 269 Cannon e
McGowan Arch, machinist, 77 Hess n
McGowan Daniel, mechanic, 2 Mill
McGowan Francis M, artist, 22 Macnab s
McGowan Hugh, butcher, 33 Elgin
McGowan James, laborer, 286 Macnab n
McGowan J P, clerk GTR, 120 Macnab n

McGowan Manus, butcher, 23 Dundurn
McGowan Mrs Mary Ann, 49 Strachan e
McGrath ——, trackman G T R, hd York w canal
McGrath Edward, blacksmith, h 23 Cherry, 41 James s
McGrath Henry, laborer, 66 Cherry
McGrath Joanna, (wid Michael), 72 Canada
McGrath John, clerk, 86 East ave n
McGrath Patrick, potter, 72 Canada
McGrath Patrick, laborer, 15 Burlington w
McGrath Patrick, laborer, 42 Robinson
McGrath Thos, porter, 86 East ave n
McGregor Alexander, tailor, 12 Henry
Macgregor D G, manager Bank of British North America 5 King e
McGregor Duncan, carriage builder, 215 King w
McGregor G K C, druggist, 142 King e
Macgregor Miss Jane, 111 Cannon w
McGregor & Parke, (Chas K McGregor, Walder Parke), druggists, 1 Market Square
McGregor Mrs Phoebe, 48 Victoria ave s
McGregor Thomas, moulder, 87 Catharine n
McGrogan Mrs, 284 Hughson n
McGrogan Hugh, mechanic, 284 Hughson n
McGuigan Catharine, (wid Felix) 74 Caroline n
McGuigan Wm, laborer, 87 Hess n
McGuire Frank, plumber, 34 Jackson e

McGuire Frank, shoemaker, 95 King w
McGuire Mrs Frank, second hand 95 King w
McGuire John, bookbinder, ft Ferguson ave
McGurk John, carpenter, 54 Young
McHaffie John, (J Winer & Co), h 141 Main w
McHaffie Robt, com traveller, 115 Rebecca
McHarg James, agent, 285 York
McHattie Geo, engine cleaner G T R, 117 Locke n
McHendrie J, carpenter, 7 Stuart w
McHendrie John, hotel, 239 James n
McHenry Mrs Mary, (wid Peter S), 21 Hunter w
McIlroy David, machinist, 17 Simcoe w
McIlroy James, watchman G T R, s w cor Barton and Magill
McIlroy Miss Lizzie, tailoress, 4 Jones
McIlroy Mrs Sarah, (wid Wm), s w cor Barton and Magill
McIlroy Samuel R, bookkeeper, 30 Victoria ave n
McIlroy Wm, laborer, 15 Vine
McIlroy Wm, 58 Bay n
McIllroy W H, com traveller, res Bartonville
McIlwraith Elizabeth, (wid Alex), 48 Lower Cathcart
McIlwraith J G, (McIlwraith & McMaster), h 57 Herkimer
McIlwraith & McMaster, (J G McIlwraith. John McMaster), staple and fancy dry goods, 12 James n, *see advt page 2*
McIlwraith Thomas, coal dealer, 54 Main e, h Cairnbrae ft Macnab n
McIlwraith Thomas F, coal merchant, 36 Jackson w

McIlwraith's Wharf, foot Macnab n
McIndoe John, machine hand, 17 Pearl n
McInerney James, cigarmaker, 29 Devonport
McInerney John, laborer, 29 Devenport
McInerney John, moulder, 133 Catharine n
McInerney Jos, stovemounter, 133 Catharine n
McInerney Michael, moulder, 133 Catharine n
McInerney Patrick, watchman, 85 Strachan e
McInnes Alex, 173 John s
McInnes D H, clerk Bank of Hamilton, 37 Jackson w
McInnes Margaret E (wid Hugh) 37 Jackson w
McIntosh Angus, blacksmith, 174 Bay n
McIntosh Mrs Edward, 265 James n
McIntosh Hugh, porter, bds 166 Bay n
McIntosh James, conductor G T R, 95 Hess n
McIntosh John, cutter, 23 Erie ave
McIntosh John, machinist, South w n s nr Locke
McIntyre Alex, laborer, 156 Emerald n
McIntyre E, clerk, 59 Charles
McIntyre Ellen (wid Peter) 59 Charles
McIntyre J G, foreman boiler maker GTR, 46 Murray w
McIntyre John, carpenter, 59 Charles
McIntyre John, cutter, 111 Cherry
McIsaac Alex, teamster, 133 Jackson e
McIver Wm, prop Columbia Hotel, King cor Park
Mackay A B, clerk, h 381 James n

Mackay Mrs Æ D, 381 James n
Mackay Alex, 136 Mary
Mackay Alex, machinist, 132 York
McKay Alex, 24 Grove
McKay Angus, machinist, 169½ John n
McKay Bros (Robt & Jas D) dry goods and carpets, 48 King e *See advt*
McKay Donald R, laborer, 260 Hughson n
Mackay G W, excise officer, 174 Macnab n
McKay James, grocer, 118 Main e
McKay James, porter GTR, 109 Jackson w
McKay James D, (McKay Bros) h 8 Maria
MacKay Janet (wid Geo) 136 Mary
MacKay John, 232 Bay n
McKay J E B, clerk P O
McKay John, conductor G T R, 119 Cannon w
McKay John, street inspector, 68a Hunter e
McKay John, conductor, 81½ Bay n
McKay Neil, vintner, 84 Hunter
McKay Nellie (wid Alex) 98 Market
McKay Margaret, 8 Maria
McKay Peter, builder, 92 Victoria ave n
McKay Peter, packer, 86 Jackson e
Mackay Richard, real estate agt, 100 James s
Mackay R O, manager Mackay's wharf, h 381 James n
McKay Robert, coal merchant, 17 Wood e
McKay Robt, plasterer, 26 Augusta, h 82 Caroline s
McKay Samuel, livery stable keeper, 73 Main e

Mackay Thos, grocer, 48 King w, h 29 Victoria ave s
McKay Thos L, electrician, 132 York
Mackay's Wharves, ft James n
McKay Wm, conductor G T R, 151 York
Mackay William H, laborer, 12 **Grove**
McKean David, 109 Hughson n
McKean Jane (wid David) 8 Young
McKean John, law student, 8 Young
McKeand George, ins and steamship ticket agt, 57 James n, h 72 Hannah w *See card*
McKeand J C, accountant, Concession
McKee Eliza (wid Wm F) 73 Pearl n
McKee Henry, bridge builder, 51 Catharine n
McKee Mary (wid Wm) 73 Hunter e
McKee W H, grocer, 11 East ave
McKee Wm W, nailer, 73 Pearl n
McKeegan Nicholas, plasterer, 8 Hess n
McKeever Eliza [wid P] 148 Wood e
McKeever James, laborer, 266 Bay n
McKeever **Robt,** wood and coal merchant, **15 Vine**
McKeever Wm, livery, 15 Vine
McKeever Wm, baker, 138 James n
Mackelcan Frank, Q C [Mackelcan, Gibson & Gausby] h 52 Catharine n
Mackelcan G L, M D, 14 Gore
Mackelcan, Gibson & Gausby, [F Mackelcan, Q C, J M Gibson, M A, LL B, J D Gausby, George E Martin] barristers, etc, 16 James s *See card*
19

Mackelcan H A, barrister, 20 Main e, h 177 Main e *See card*
Mackelcan John, 9 Park s
Mackelcan Mrs [wid John] 38 Catharine n
McKellar Arch, sheriff, Court House, h 18 Hannah w
McKellar Hugh [Mills & McKellar] h 9 Ontario
McKellar Lachlan, **com traveler,** 32 Victoria ave n
McKelvy Samuel, laborer, 95 Bold
McKelvey Thos, paper bag mkr, 151 Duke
McKenna Mary Ann [wid Robt] 43 Florence
McKenna **Chas,** shoemaker, bds 66 King w
McKenna James, tailor, bds 29 Railway
McKenna Jas, engineer GTR, 79 Peter
McKenna John, broommaker, 8 Baillie
McKenna John, fitter, 203 Catharine n
McKenna John, printer, 8 Baillie
McKenna Maurice, laborer, 148a Mary
McKenna Thos, laborer, 256½ Macnab n
Mackenzie A I, acting collector customs, Main cor Emerald
McKenzie Alex [Kellogg & McKenzie] 21 James **n**
McKenzie Alexander, mechanic, b's 206 Macnab n
McKenzie Alex S, custom shoemaker, 94 King e
McKenzie Andrew, painter, 153 Macnab n
McKenzie Archibald, laborer, 49 Little Wm
McKenzie Archibald, **carpenter,** 112 Emerald n
Mackenzie Donald, **150** Napier
McKenzie Donald employee Express Co

Mackenzie Dougald, engineer, 43 George
McKenzie Duncan, wood and coal dealer, 209 Wellington n
McKenzie Mrs Ellen, 122 Market
McKenzie Esther [wid John] 136 Hunter e
McKenzie Evan, carpenter, 23 Spring
Mackenzie Geo, stonemason, bds 30 Florence
McKenzie Ian, detective, 21 Elgin
McKenzie James, machinist, 46 Augusta
McKenzie John, lumber, wood and coal dealer, 149 Macnab n, h 1 Sheaffe
McKenzie John, carpenter, 7 Inchbury n
McKenzie John I, license inspector, 4 James s, bds 61 George
McKenzie Kenneth, checker, 89 Robert
McKenzie Kenneth, porter G T R, 11 Locomotive
McKenzie Kenneth, painter, 153 Macnab n
McKenzie Malcolm, laborer, 108 Emerald n
McKenzie Robt, 139 Wood e
McKenzie T H, general ins agent, 3 Market
McKenzie Thomas H, inspector weights and measures, res Dundas
McKenzie Wm, driver, 41 Bay n
McKenzie Wm J, melter, 186 Victoria ave n
Mackenzie Wm J, car cleaner G T R, 43 George
McKeown Arthur H (Reddall & McKeown) h 47 Robinson
McKeown Eliza (wid John) 246 York
McKeown Hugh, harnessmaker, 72 John s, and 29 Market Sq

McKeown Mrs Hugh, grocer, 72½ John s
McKeown James, prop Jimmie' Restaurant, 5-7 John n
McKeown James A, carriage builder, 61 Robinson
McKeown John, carpenter, 12 Peter
McKeown John, moulder, 7 Ontario
McKeown John, moulder, 136 Park n
McKeown Peter, clerk, bds 42 Vine
McKerlie Alex, com traveler, 81 Peter
McKerlie Francis B, 200 Main e
McKerlie Loretta (wid David) 200 Main e
McKichan J R, paper bag manfr 8-10 John s, h 53 West ave n
Mackie James, carpenter, 17 Hughson n
McKillop Archibald, health inspector, 278a King e
McKillop David, mechanic, 8 Upper Cathcart
McKinley John, laborer, 286 Hughson n
McKinney Thos, 232 Catharine n
McKinnon Donald, chief police, 61 Hannah w
McKinty John, landing waiter customs, 21 Barton e
McKinty Thos, laborer, 129 Park n
McKittrich Wm, moulder, 146 Victoria ave n
McKnight John, engineer, 155 Wilson
McLagan Alexander, 182 Main e
McLardy James A, train dispatcher, 100½ Queen n
McLaren A D, law student, 58 East ave s
McLaren Henry, Balquidder, 153 James s
McLaren James A, com traveler, 35 East ave n

McLaren Mrs W P, Oak Bank, 155 James s
McLaren John, sewing machine agent, 231 Macnab n
McLaren John, com traveler, 35 East ave n
McLaren John I, com traveler, 35 East ave n
McLaren Mrs Margaret, 237 John n
McLaren Mrs Marjory, 35 East ave n
McLaren Wm, fancy goods, 226 James n
McLaren Wm, 99 West ave n
McLaren W H, grocer, 6 King Wm, h 35 East ave n
McLaughlan Alex, laborer, 68 Locomotive
McLaughlan Hugh, horse trainer, 160 Market
McLaughlan Alex, com traveler, 140 Hunter e
McLaughlan David, laborer, 163 Wilson
McLaughlin Ed, civil engineer, 38 Hunter w
McLaughlan Garrett, laborer, 163 Wilson
McLaughlan Geo, moulder, 177 Mary
McLaughlin James, moulder, 149 Bay n
McLaughlan John, book ruler, bds 41 John n
McLaughlan John, moulder, bds 21 John n
McLaughlan Matthew, blacksmith, 61 Ray n
McLaughlan Morgan, moulder, 163 Wilson
McLaughlin Neil, miller, 83 John n
McLaughlan Wm, laborer, 47 Robert
McLean Mrs Alice, 179 Mary
McLean Alex, clerk GTR, 324 King e
Maclean Arch, 61 Hunter w

McLean David, carpenter, 45 Hannah e
McLean Donald, shipper, 81 Caroline n
Maclean Mrs F, fancy goods, 4 King e, h 61 Hunter w
McLean George, shoemaker, 11 Bold
McLean Hugh, barber, 76 Queen s
McLean James B, cabinetmaker, 70 Queen s
McLean John, tailor, 13 Head
McLean John, boilermaker, Robinson s s nr Garth
McLean John D, hoetl keeper, 141 King w
McLean N A, restaurant, 14 King w
McLean Patrick, tobacco roller, bds 125 Market
McLean Mrs Sarah, 39 Simcoe e
Maclean T A, 61 Hunter w
McLellan David, agent Royal Insurance Co, 84 James n, h 55 Herkimer *See advt back cover*
McLelland Wm, collarmaker, 34 Mary
McLennan Alex, caretaker, Dundurn Castle
MacLennan Kenneth, 165 Locke s
McLeod Alex, laborer, bds 109 King Wm
McLeod Mrs Ann, 76 Wilson
McLeod Campbell, 9 Napier
McLeod Chas, dyer, 123 James n
McLeod Colin, cutter, bds 151 Hunter w
McLeod Colin, porter, bds 100 Cherry
McLeod David, moulder, 3 Sheaffe
McLeod Mrs Dora [wid Angus] 7 Cannon e
McLeod Elizabeth, dye works, 123 James n

McLeod John, agent, 36 Bay s
McLeod John, bar tender, s e cor Locke and Peter
McLeod John P, printer, 20 York, h 9 Napier
McLeod Oliver, blacksmith, 26 Crooks
McLeod Robt, clerk, 70 Duke
McLeod Wm, boilermaker, bds Street Car Inn, King e
McLeod William, printer, 76 Wilson
McLerie Chas, bookkeeper, bds Commercial hotel
McLerie James, freight agent, 39 Strachan w
McMaguire Mary (wid Bernard) 80 Caroline n
McMahon Bernard, asst sergeant police, 73 Strachan e
McMahon, Broadfield & Co [J S McMahon, George E Broadfield] wh crockery, **china**, glassware and plate glass, 104 King e
McMahon Donald, laborer, 54 Robinson
McMahon Edward, laborer, n w cor Caroline and Herkimer
McMahon Elijah, loom fixer, 245 Catharine n
McMahon Geo H, builder, 30 Spring
McMahon James, laborer, 28 Strachan e
McMahon Jeremiah, moulder, 53 Cherry
McMahon John, baker, 20 Cannon w
McMahon John, laborer, 63 Wood e
McMahon John, dairyman, 27 Wilson
McMahon J S [McMahon, Broadfield & Co] h 57 Emerald s
McMahon Patrick, 200 King w
McMahon Thomas, clerk, 93 Cherry

McMahon John, shearsman, 109 Florence
McMann Wm, melter, Barton w s s nr Locomotive
McManus James, shoemaker, 82½ Wellington n
McManus John, finisher, 82½ Wellington n
McManus John, corn traveler, 87 John n
McManus John, grain dealer, bds 97 Cannon w
McManus Robert, laborer, 10 Wood w
McMaster Archibald, painter, 35 Wellington n
McMaster Donald, mason, Burlington n
McMaster J K, clerk, 90 Bay s
McMaster John, carpenter, Burlington n
McMaster John [McIlwraith & McMaster] 90 Bay s
McMaster Walter, painter, 35 Wellington n
McMeekin John, ins agt, 2½ James s, h 141 Robert e
McMeekin William, carpenter, 54 Gore
McMenemy Ann J [wid James] 132 West ave n
McMenemy Hannah [wid Alex] 69 Main w
McMenemy Wm, baggage master 237 Wellington n
McMenemy Wm, policeman, 39 Crooks
McMichael Mrs Calista, 55 Catharine n
McMichael Chas P, dairyman, 72 Duke
McMichael Franklin J, milk dealer, 81 Jackson e
McMichael Isaac, whiplash manfr 54 Napier
McMichael Lovina (wid Joseph) 24 Queen s
McMichael Luther, moulder, 55 Catharine n

McMicking Mrs Thomas, 189 Cannon e
McMillan **Bessie** (wid John) 111 Market
McMillan **Chas**, hatter, 6 Elgin
McMillan Elizabeth (wid James) 39 Catharine s
McMillan **James**, fireman, 42 Catharine s
McMillan James, laborer, **bds** 65 Stuart w
McMillan John, shoemaker, 26½ Catharine s
McMillan John, grocer, 272 King e
McMillan **Roderick**, carpenter, 27 Oak ave
McMullen D, cooper, Catharine n
McMullen **John**, 142 John n
McMurray **James**, agent, 10 Inchbury s
McMurray John, driver, 28 Hess n
McMutrie David, com traveler, 67 Victoria ave n
McNab Alexander, stonecutter, 249 John **n**
Macnab **Chas**, mechanic, bds 206 Macnab **n**
McNab Duncan, dairyman, Concession s s w Garth
McNabb Duncan A, 67 Elgin
McNabb Jas, jeweler, 50 Roert **e**
McNab Miss H, 14 Barton w
McNabb Peter McK, 67 Elgin
Macnab Street Presbyterian **Church**, Rev Donald H Fletcher, pastor, Hunter cor Macnab
McNabb R, bds Noble's Hotel
McNab **Wm**, mariner, 42 Burlington w
McNair Albert, clerk, Main e **of** Wentworth
McNair Albert E, clerk, h Main East Hamilton
McNair Samuel, provincial constable, Stinson's Chambers, **1** King Wm, 89 West ave n

McNamara Luke, laborer, 316 John n
McMamee Peter, laborer, **125** Ferguson ave
McNichol Charles, glassblower, 320 John n
McNichol David, carpenter, **31** Barton e
McNichol **John**, laborer, 314½ John n
McNichol **John**, glassblower, 10 Wood **e**
McNichol Nichol, machinist, **51** Canada
McNider **S** (R Spence & Co) h 80 James s
McNeaney Owen, laborer, **Robinson** n s w Locke
McNeill Angus, moulder, bds 49 Park n
McNeil Charlotte (wid Robt) 98 Hess n
McNeill James, cabinetmaker, bds 60 James s
McNeil John, laborer, 247 King Wm
McNeil Mrs John, r 126 **Catharine** n
McNeil Smith, laborer, 19 Tisdale
McNeil W C, clerk, **bds** 25 Wood e
McNeilly Geo, mechanic, 119 Barton **e**
McNeilly **Henry**, salesman, 142 Hunter e
McNeilly James, salesman, **142** Hunter e
McNeilly Mary (wid Henry) 142 Hunter e
McNoah Thos, laborer, 195 **Bay** n
McPhail Hugh, agent, 294 **King** Wm
McPhail James, com traveler, bds 106 Hunter w
McPherson Mrs A, fancy goods, 125 James n
McPherson Alex, teamster, 160 King Wm

McPherson **Alex**, book and job printer, 51 James n, h 140½ John n

Macpherson, Glassco & Co (T H Macpherson, John T Glassco) wholesale grocers, 67-9 King e ,

McPherson Lachlan, plasterer, bds 166 Bay n

Macpherson James A, 195 Main e

McPherson John & Co, manfr boots and shoes, 53-55 King e

Macpherson T H (Macpherson, Glassco & Co) h 11 Duke

McPhie Alexander, biscuit pedler, 49a Wellington n

McPhie Donald, plumber, 93 King e, h 57 East ave s

McQuesten & Chisholm (I B McQuesten, M A, Jas Chisholm, B A) barristers, Victoria Chambers, 31 James s *See card*

McQuesten I B. (McQuesten and Chisholm) h Jackson cor Macnab

McQuillan Robt, carter, 110 West ave n

McQuillan Robert, jr, carter, 110 West ave n

McQuinn Wm, moulder, 71 Simcoe e

McRae Colin, wh boots and shoes, 15 King w, h 80½ Main

McRae Colin, bookkeeper, 15 Cannon w

McRae Ronald, salesman, 104 Barton e

McRoberts John, moulder, bds 36 Market

McSherry Margaret (wid Thos) 108½ Jackson e

McStravick Grace (wid Henry) 99 John n

McStravick Henry, shipper, 62 Wellington n

McTague Michael, laborer, 253 Cannon e

McVeigh Mrs, 28 Guise

McVicar Jane (wid Angus) 23 Wilson

McVinnie Robt, shipper, 21 South

McVittie George, coachman, 32 Queen s

McVittie James, 157 East ave n

McVittie John, laborer, 157 East ave n

McVittie John, cooper, 130 Rebecca

McVittie Robert, shoemaker, 7 Park s

McVittie Wm, driver, bds 119 Market

McWaters W H (W H McWaters & Co, bds Franklin House

McWaters W H & Co. tea merchants, 56 Macnab n

McWinney James, machinist, bds 21 Gore

McWilliam Robt, machinist, 29 Macauley w

Mack Ann (wid Patrick) 27 Burlington w

Mack George, teamster, bds 27 Burlington w

Mack John S, druggist, Merrick

Mackie Andrew, moulder, 47 John n

Mackie Robert, mechanic, r 173 Bay n

Macklem Miss Margaret, 84 Locke s

Madden Elizabeth (wid Patrick F) 124 Maria

Madden James, weaver, bds 63 Colborne

Madden —, laborer, 35 Margaret

Maddox George, blacksmith, 25 Tom

Maddocks Samuel, shoemaker, 144 Rebecca

Maddocks Wm, blacksmith, 1 Jones

Maden John, cotton spinner, 193 Mary n

Madgett Caroline (wid Thomas) 122 Catharine n
Madgett Clarke, machinist, 122 Catharine n
Madgett Geo, wood turner, 128 Catharine n
Madgett John, machinist, 126 Macauley e
Madigan James, laborer, 91 Strachan e
Madigan John, bridge builder, 18 Mulberry
Magee Bros, grain warehousemen, ft Bay n
Magee Frank (Magee Bros) h 206 James n
Magee Henry, saddler, 4 York, h 110 Mary
Magee Wm, flour and feed deal'r 206 James n
Magee Wm, jr, ice and coal dealer, 206 James n, h 40 Barton w
Magen Christopher, butcher, Main e of Wentworth
Magen Richard, butcher, 19 John s
Magill Mrs A E, 12 Main w
Magill Lieut Col Chas, 5 Jackson w
Magill Geo, moulder, 51 West ave n
Magill Geo, bds 9 King Wm
Magill Geo, 94 Hunter e
Magill Mrs Henry, 50 John n
Magnus Matthias, dairyman, 206 Catharine n
Magnus Robt, cutter, 5 O'Reilly
Maguir John, painter, 40 Cannon
Mahaffy James, machinist, 4 Wilson
Mahon John, laborer, 25 Ferrie e
Mahony Andrew, stovemounter, 114 Catharine n
Mahony Daniel, laborer, 38 Aurora
Mahony Daniel, 58 Cherry
Mahony Daniel, stovemounter, 86 Hannah e

Mahony Daniel, teamster, 366 James n
Mahoney Dennis, shoemaker, cor York and Locke, h 5 Tom
Mahoney James, laborer, 17 Macauley w
Mahoney James, operator, bds 61 Colborne
Mahoney John, teamster, 13 Macauley w
Mahoney Martin, sailor, 12 Wood w
Mahoney William, laborer, 51 Maria
Mail Newspaper, (Toronto) Julian R F Boyd, agent, 16 James s
Main Alex, rope maker, 238 Mary
Main Alex & Son, (Alex & Wm), ropemakers, 238 Mary
Main James, grocer, 167 John n cor John & Barton
Main Wm W, (A Main & Son) h 238 Mary
Mair Miss Helen, matron Home of the **Friendless**, 72 Caroline s
Maitland Margaret, (wid James), 200 King Wm
Maitland Stewart, painter, 31 Spring
Makins Ed, boilermaker, 49 Locomotive
Makins Ed, machinist, 22 Little Market
Makins John, (Ross & Makins), h 47 Locomotive
Makinson Chas, salesman, 7 Macnab s
Makinson George, laborer, Sherman
Malamphy Michael, 82 Hess n
Malamphy Susan, (wid Thos) 82 Hess n
Malcolm James, bookkeeper, 38 Robinson
Malcolm James A, (Malloy & Malcolm), 246 York

RALSTON & IRWIN,
REAL ESTATE AGENTS

....

Properties For Sale or to Rent.

FIRE AND LIFE ASSURANCE.
CUSTOM HOUSE BROKERS.

Rents Collected.   *Money to Loan.*

REAL ESTATE EXCHANGE,

31 JOHN ST. SOUTH, HAMILTON, ONT.

106 James St. N. HAMILTON.   Brant Street, BURLINGTON.

Watchmaker and Jeweller, Gold and Silver Plater.

The only store where you can buy Alligator Teeth Jewellery.

Special attention paid to repairing. All work warranted if taken in to be thoroughly repaired. A post card sent will be promptly attended to.

PETER BRASS, ARCHITECT

Furnishes Plans and Specifications for every description of buildings, and having been a Mechanic and Contractor for a number of years, all work will be superintended in a practical and proper manner. Also Measurement and Valuation of every description of buildings, either new or old, or of any works connected with buildings, made up in a correct and reliable manner.

OFFICE, 52 HUNTER ST. WEST, OPP. CENTRAL SCHOOL.

Residence, 49 Bay St. South, HAMILTON, ONT.

Malcolm & Souter, (Wm Malcolm, A M Souter), furniture manufacturers, carpet merchants, 67-69 King w, *See aavt*
Malcolm Wm, (Malcolm & Souter), h 78 George
Malcolmson Agnes, (wid Geo), 266 Macnab n
Malcolmson Allan T, clerk, 26 Ferrie w
Malcolmson Mrs Elizabeth, 26 Ferrie w
Malcalmson Geo, clerk, J S S & Co
Malcolmson Hy, carpenter, 13 Ferrie e
Malcolmson Herbert, clerk, 26 Ferrie w
Malcolmson Hugh, carpenter, 10 Queen n, h 27 Queen n
Malcolmson James, 140 Macnab n
Malcolmson James F, 311 John n
Malcolmson J C, foreman Glass Works, 21 Picton e
Malcolmson James W, wire weaver, 27 Queen n
Malcolmson John carpenter, 27 Queen n
Malcolmson Samuel, mariner, 288 James n
Malcolmson Saml C, mariner, 17 Barton e
Male Charles, laborer, 49 Hess s
Male John, laborer, 124 Hunter w
Male William, laborer, 141 Hunter w
Malins William, carter, 18 Tisdale
Mallin John, moulder, s w cor Ashley & King Wm
Malloch Archibald E, M D, 70 James s
Malloch Mrs Elizabeth, 68 James s
Malloch F S, 72 James n

Malloch Margaret, (wid John), 57 Jackson w
Mallory Eli H, 161 East ave n
Mallory William, broker, 107 John s
Malloy John, (Malloy & Malcolm) 39 Bold
Malloy John, glassblower, 314 John n
Malloy & Malcolm, carriage builders, 9 Park n
Malloy Patrick, laborer, 283 John n
Malone Michael, porter customs, 124 Catharine n
Malone Martin, barrister, 2½ James s, h 188 John n
Malone Thos, confectioner, 53 Catharine n
Maloney Ed, stableman, 15 Macauley w
Maloney Thomas, laborer, 106 Simcoe e
Maloney Wm P, lineman, 120 Catharine s
Maltman Chas, box maker, 96 Catharine s
Mandelbaum Mrs F, fancy goods 72 King e, h 70 Hughson s
Mandelbaum Julius L, salesman, 121 King e
Manders Geo, heater, 142 Hess
Mann Aaron, expressman, 31 Gore
Mann Chas, stonemason, 181 Main w
Mann Henry, laborer, 20 Pearl n
Mann Samuel, grocer, etc, 256-60 King e
Mann Wm F, carpenter, 166 Main w
Manning Catharine (wid John) 5 Devonport
Manning Fred, moulder, 29 Lower Cathcart
Manning Wm, hackman, 5 Devonport
Mannocks James, carpenter, 178 Catharine n

Mansergh Henry, clerk, 67 Queen s
Manson Donald (W H Ryckman & Co) 24 Hannah e
Manson Joshua, gas meter mkr, 81 Cannon w
Manser Wm T, brickmaker, 4 Margaret
Mansfield Alex, cabinetmaker, bds 39 Mulberry
Mansfield George, engineer, 39 Mulberry
Mantle Richard, laborer, r 6 Steven
Mapplebeck Wm, shearsman, 15 Oxford
Marcham John, moulder, 123 Mary
Marchan Wm, engineer, 144 Catharine n
Marck Joseph, barber, 214 James n
Margetts Wm H, lithographer, 21 Mulberry
Marie James, whip lash maker, r 146 Jackson w
Marigold Harriet (wid Adolphus) 205 Wellington n
Markle Hiram, carpenter, 16 Cannon w
Marks Chas, shipper, 183 John n
Marks Edward, moulder, 183 John n
Marks Miss Mary, dressmaker, 144 King w
Marlatt Rebecca (wid Geo) 51 Hunter w
Marr Mrs, nurse, 103 John n
Marriott Henry, laborer, 70 Lower Cathcart
Marriott John, packer, 75 Market
Marris Henry, shoe cutter, 12 Queen n
Mars Alexander, bookbinder, 14 Hughson n
Mars William, laborer, 64 Locke s
Marsden Samuel, fitter, 15 Tom

Marsden & Son (Thos and Wm) manfrs of mouldings and picture frames, agents Domestic fashions, 46 James n
Marsden Thomas, (Marsden & Son) h 92 Jackson w
Marsden Wm, (Marsden & Son) 122 Jackson w
Marsh H, employee GTR, 218 Macnab n
Marsh Wm, blacksmith, Markland s s nr Garth
Marshall Mrs Agnes [wid Wm] 55 Canada
Marshall Allan, engineer, Asylum pumping house
Marshall Benjamin, laborer, 152 Catharine n
Marshall Bros [Miss A E Thomas clerk] Arcade
Marshall Christian [wid Butler] 72 Locke s
Marshall David G, law student, bds 8 Hess n
Marshall D G, law student, 7 Caroline s
Marshall Mrs Geo, 98 James s
Marshall Henry, gardener, Wentworth s
Marshall J A, salesman, 9 Grove
Marshall John, polisher, 75 Locke
Marshall John, moulder, bds 51 Park n
Marshall John, foreman Oil Co, Wentworth n
Marshall John, wire rope maker, 15 Florence
Marshall John, flax dresser, 205 Mary n
Marshall Joseph, carpenter, 44 Queen s
Marshall Leonard, laborer, 33 Strachan e
Marshall Mrs, 55 Locke s
Marshall Mrs, 137 James n
Marshall Thos, tailor, 2 King Wm, h 95 Concession
Marshall Thos, moulder, bds 51 Park n

Marshall Thos, laborer, Main e of Wentworth
Marshall Thos, student, bds 104 Hunter w
Marshall Mrs Thomas, 68 East ave n
Marshall Wm, salesman, 22 Victoria ave n
Marshall William, sec treas Ham Vinegar Works Co [limited] 10 Erie ave
Marshall Wm, fitter, s w cor Barton and Crooks
Marter Mary [wid Louis] 42 Kelly
Martin Adam, presser, bds 68 Hughson s
Martin Albert, tinsmith, 176 West ave n
Martin Alex, laborer, 84 Peter
Martin Andrew, butcher, 66 John s, h 43 Young
Martin Archibald, moulder, 176 Robert
Martin Benjamin, jr, upholsterer, 82 Main w
Martin Benj, sr, cabinetmaker, 82 Main w
Martin Bernard, cabinetmaker, 114½ King w
Martin Chas, bricklayer, 77 Emerald n
Martin Chas H, laborer, 56 Hannah e
Martin Edward, Q C, [Martin, Kittson & Martin] h Ballynahinch, James s
Martin George, student, bds 99 York
Martin George E [Mackelcan, Gibson & Gausby] h 58 Hunter w
Martin James, laborer, 160 Hughson n
Martin Jas, baker, 96 Robinson
Martin James, shoemaker, 92 Bay n
Martin James, laborer, 176 West ave n

Martin J E, prop Martin Manufacturing Co, h 114 James n
Martin John, laborer, 58 Ray n
Martin John, contractor, 77 Emerald n
Martin John, com traveler, 23½ Emerald n
Martin Jos, salesman, bds 114 James n
Martin Kirwan, B A (Martin, Kittson & Martin) h Ballynahinch, James s
Martin, Kittson & Martin (Edward Martin, Q C, E E Kittson, Kirwan Martin, B A) barristers, etc, Wentworth Chambers, 25 James s *See card*
Martin Manufacturing Co, general house furnishings, J E Martin, prop, 114 James n
Martin Hector H, 8 Wellington n
Martin Hy, hotel, 196 King e
Martin Hy, artist, 7 Rebecca, h 10 Hannah w
Martin Hy L, foreman Orr, Harver & Co, 15 Locke s
Martin Herbert A, printer, 13 John n
Martin Hubert, wholesale shoe findings, 5 King Wm, h 134 James s
Martin Philip, 94 Catharine n
Martin Mrs Richard, Derryclare, hd of John s
Martin Richard jr, clerk, Derryclare, hd of John s
Martin Robt, engineer GTR, 15 Magill
Martin Thos, mail clerk N & N W, 45 Wellington n
Martin Thos A, laborer, 32 Ray n
Martin Wm, blacksmith, 23 South
Martin Wm, laborer, 189 Bay n
Martin Wm, bookkeeper, bds 55 Ferguson ave
Martin Wm, accountant, 134 James s

Martin Wm H, machinist, 46 Tisdale
Maslem Alice (wid S) 84 Stinson
Maslem Geo, laborer, 29 Steven
Maslin Arthur, tinsmith, bds 74 Cannon w
Maslin Wilby, teamster, bds 74 Cannon w
Mason Chas, florist, 166 Rebecca
Mason Christopher, engineer, 35 Emerald n
Mason Geo, accountant GTR, n e cor Concession and Queen
Mason Hedley V, salesman, 57 East ave n
Mason James, fruiterer, 133 Queen n
Mason Jas, confectioner, 160 York
Mason J J, accountant, 86 James n, h 63 Hunter w
Mason Jos, caretaker Masonic Hall, Markland n s w Queen
Mason Thos, hats and caps, 13 James n, h 23 East ave n
Massie Alex, boat builder, 209 Macnab n
Massey Arch, timekeeper GTR, Barton w, opp Magill
Massey James, boat builder, 209 Macnab n
Massey Thos, laborer, bds 7 Ferguson ave
Massie Wm, machinist, 209 Macnab n
Massie W & A G, props Globe Hotel, 84 King e
Massie Rev Wm, M A, rector St Luke's Church, 45 Macaulay w
Masters Albert, stableman, n e cor Jackson and Macnab
Mat High's Hotel, Matthew High, prop, 65-7 John s
Matches Mrs Janet (wid John) 87 Park n
Mathers Samuel, rag merchant, 102 York, h 82 Hannah w
Mathesins Rudolph, artist, 5 West ave s

Matheson Alex, moulder, bds 21 Florence
Mathison Alex, moulder, 8 Locke s
Mathieson Donald, laborer, 64 Locomotive
Mathieson Geo, wool buyer, 28 Rilway
Mathieson John, porter, 75 Vine
Mathieson Wm, moulder, 244 Hughson n
Mathews Augustus (Matthews Bros) 107 Ferrie e
Matthews Bros (Oscar & Augustus) grocers, 107 Ferrie e
Matthews Frederick C, caretaker cricket grounds, Bold s s opp Ray
Mathews Geo, mail clerk GTR, 74 Hunter e
Mathews Geo H, livery stable prop, 37 Market
Mathews Henry, moulder, 149 Mary
Mathews James (Jas Mathews & Son) 37 Victoria Ave s
Mathews James jr, painter, 95 Victoria ave n
Mathews Jas E (Jas Mathews & Son) 93 Victoria ave n
Mathews James & Son (James, James E Mathews) 15 Hughson n
Mathews John, clerk, 18 Elgin
Mathews J S, clerk P O
Mathews Miss Minnie, 35 Market
Mathews Oscar, carpenter, 117 Picton e
Mathews Robt V, city assessment collector, 37 Victoria ave n
Matthews Walter, tailor, bds 134 King Wm
Maxsted Geo, machinist, 102 Murray e
Maxwell David, bds 67 Stuart w
Maxwell Fred, boilermaker, 124 Picton e
Maxwell Geo, laborer, 91 Macaulay e

Maxwell James, fireman, 122 Macaulay e
Maxwell John, machinist, Duke s s nr Locke
Maxwell John, painter, 163 Main w
Maxwell Thos G, policeman, 94 East ave n
Mattice J H, correspondent and business agent *Globe*, 33 James n, h 70 Catharine n
Mattice Wm H, 98 Locke s
Maver Alex, asst supt GTR, 186 John n
May Efner, carpenter, 53 Hannah e
May Mrs M, 10 Main e
May Richard, laborer, 219 York
May Thos, laborer, 48 Ray s
Mayhew John, knitter, 142 King w
Mayhew W E [Mayhew & Co] bds American Hotel
Mayhew W E & Co, staple and fancy dry goods and millinery, 8 King e
Mayo Wm T, fireman GTR, 122½ Queen n
Mayo Alfred, laborer, 237½ John n
Maynard James, painter, 153 Wilson
Meade Miss Annie A, 45 Charles
Mead John, machinist, 29 Peter
Mead J R, mangr Ont Shirt Co, 18 Nelson ave
Meade Thomas, builder, 12 Young
Mearce Joseph, carter, 50 West ave n
Meakin C [wid James] gents' furnishings, 190 James n
Meakins Charles, laborer, 6 Tiffany
Meakins Chas W [Meakins & Sons] cor Main and Victoria ave
Meakins Geo H, machinist, 11 Erie ave

Meakins & Sons, brush manfrs, [C W Meakins, C W Meakins jr] 225-9 King e
Meaney John, laborer, bds 33 Inchbury n
Meaney Thos, bookkeeper, cor James and Vine
Mechanics' Hotel [Wm Cameron prop] 153 Catharine n
Medley Samuel, druggist, bds 49 Caroline n
Medley Samuel, stonecutter, 58 Victoria ave n
Meegan Patrick, tanner, 119 Jackson e
Meegan Patrick jr, moulder, 119 Jackson
Meegan Peter, prop Central Hotel, 135 King e
Meegan Thos, moulder, 29 Mulberry
Meek Matthew G, bookkeeper, 88 Macnab n
Meienn Geo, marblecutter, Main e of Wentworth
Meienn John, laborer, Main e of Wentworth
Meikle Mrs Anna [wid James] 25 Maria
Meiler Geo, tailor, bds 214 King w
Meiler John, tailor, 87 Florence
Meinke Frederick, stovemounter 110 John s
Meitzmer Chas, laborer, 3 Poulette
Mellis David, tinsmith, bds 13 Gore
Mellon Elizabeth [wid John] 19 Liberty
Mellon Geo, 98 Catharine s
Mellon John, builder, 6 Nightingale
Mellon John, brushmaker, 6 Nightingale
Mellon Robt, bricklayer, 56 Steven
Mellon Stephen, plumber, 11 Wilson

Melody James, gas stoker, 38 Sheaffe
Melody William, carter, 58 Canada
Membery Geo D, feather renovator, 155 James n
Memory John, machinist, 164 Napier
Menary Robert, dairyman, 29 Oak ave
Menorgan Margaret (wid John) 130 Cannon e
Mepham Joseph, laborer, 63 Ray
Mepham Mrs, 67 Ray s
Mepham Thomas, plasterer, 211 Main w
Mepham Wm, plasterer, 103 Caroline n
Mercer James, builder, 40 Ferguson ave
Merchants' Bank of Canada J S Meredith, mangr, King cor John s
Meredith Miss E, music teacher, 28 Catharine s
Meredith J S, mangr Merchants' Bank, res Ham Prov and L S Chambers
Meriden Britannia Co, (John E Parker, mangr) Wellington cor Cannon
Merin Mary F (wid Patrick) 143 Park n
Merrick Miss Catharine, 94a Victoria ave n
Merrick Mrs Helen, 84 Market
Merrillees Robt, carpenter, bds Victoria hotel, King e
Merriman Miss Ann, 83 Young
Merriman James, checker GTR, 124 Locke n
Mesle Frank, brushmaker, 74 Victoria ave n
Messmore Daniel, tailor, Maple s s nr Garth
Meston Thomas, bookkeeper, 58 Herkimer
Metcalfe George, painter, 71 Locke s

Metcalfe Mary (wid Christopher) grocer, 26 Ray n
Metman Henry S, laundry, 26 Mulberry
Metman S H, Chicago laundry, 124 Macnab n
Metz Peter, shoemaker, 106 Young
Mewburn L T, mangr Jas Turner & Co, 60 Macnab s
Mewburn Sydney C, (Patten & Mewburn) h 148 Main w
Mewburn Thos C, insp of customs ports, 148 Main w
Meyers William, grocer, 48 Young
Michigan Central Railroad, W J Grant agent, 33 James n
Michael George, brushmaker, H B Co
Michael William, laborer, 114 Queen n
Michael Wm, laborer, 191 Victoria ave n
Middlemiss Eli A, checker GTR, 116 Queen n
Middleton J T, wholesale marble 140 John n, h Main e, East Hamilton
Middleton John M, moulder, 131 James n
Midgeley Chas, salesman, 172½ James n
Midgley Geo, shoemaker, 172½ James n
Midgley Geo, jr, bookseller, 172 James n
Midgley Peter, laborer, Chestnut ave
Midgley Wm H, japanner, 172 James n
Midwinter Job, carpenter, 153 Park n
Midwinter John, machinist, Duke s s nr Garth
Midwinter Joseph, machinist, 95 Ferrie e
Milburn John H, scalemaker, 117 Barton e

Miles Alex G, plumber, 72 Merrick, h 54 Park n
Miles John, carpenter, 30 Wellington s
Millard C J, druggist, 42 Vine
Millard James W, accountant, 80 East ave s
Miller Adam, stovemounter, 63 Ray s
Miller A J, stewart Hamilton Club
Miller Alex, car cleaner, Wentworth n
Miller Mrs Alex, 266 James n
Miler Alfred, shoemaker, 20 Devonport
Miller Andrew, laborer, 201 Main w
Miller Rev Andrew E, church of England, 66 Bay s
Miller Arthur, fireman, 8 Wood e
Miller Arthur J, carpenter, 71 Peter
Miller August, weaver, 194 East ave n
Miller Chas, carter, 282a King e
Miller Mrs Eliza, 66 Bay s
Miller Mrs Emily A, 58 Locke s
Miller Francis H, wood and coal dealer, 95 Caroline s
Miller Frank, carpenter, 81 James s. h 94 Victoria ave s
Miller Fredk, butcher, 117 John s
Miller Geo, policeman, 30 East ave n
Miller George, mechanic, bds 55 Ferguson ave
Miller Miss Henrietta, 94 Catharine s
Miller James, porter, 31 Steven
Miller James, grocer, **69-71** Elgin
Miller James, butcher, 41 Wellington n
Miller Mrs Jane, 30 Macauley e
Miller John, moulder, bds 84 John n

Miller John, laborer, 246 Catharine n
Miller John, tinsmith, 30 Ferguson ave
Miller John A, cigarmaker, bds 56 Park n
Miller John E, moulder, 105 Wood e
Miller Joseph, artist, 6 Macnab s
Miller Mrs L, 8 Main w
Miller Miss Mary B, dressmaker, 52 Markland
Miller Nicholas, cigarmaker, 63 Ray s
Miller Peter, tinsmith, 97 Cherry
Miller & Pitcher, (F Miller, C Pitcher), manfrs Gum Door Check, 81 James s
Miller Rev Robt, British Meth Episcopal, Wentworth n of Barton
Miller Robt, 56 Park n
Miller Robt S, clerk P O, 81 Victoria ave
Miller Thomas, M D, 181 King w
Miller Wm, cigarmaker, 106 John n
Miller Wm, painter, 266 James n
Miller Wm, hostler, Flamboro House Hotel
Miller Wm, shoemaker, 3 Hilton
Miller Wm, boilermaker, bds 9 Hess n
Miller Wm, laborer, 245 Cannon e
Miller Wm, foreman J M Williams & Co, 212 King Wm
Miller ———, 69 Hannah w
Milligan Mrs Agnes (wid Samuel) 178 Hunter w
Milligan Edward, engineer, 22½ Little Market
Milligan John, stovemounter, **Garth** e s nr Duke
Milligan John, laborer, 276 Hughson n
Milligan Thos, packer, 85 Hunter w

Milligan Thos W, provision dealer, 122 Locke n
Milligan Wm, laborer, Hunter w n s nr Locke
Milligan Wm J, baker, 9 Florence
Millman James, **carpenter, 31 Oak ave**
Millns Geo R, packer, 62 Peter
Mills Alice, (wid Geo) 151 Main w
Mills Mrs Ann H, 22 Queen s
Mills Arthur J, cabinetmaker, 57 Emerald n
Mills Aurora (wid Samuel) 20 Charles
Mills Chas, grocer, 142-144 Main
Mills Chas, 106 Jackson w
Mills Chas D, cab prop, 9 Queen n
Mills Chas D, 42 Queen s
Mills Edwin J, law student, 286 King e
Mills Francis H, s e cor Robinson and Park
Mills Frederick, collector, 286 King e
Mills Geo, 290 King e
Mills Geo, grocer, 24-26 Stuart e
Mills Geo, bricklayer, 8 Kelly
Mills George H, barrister, Wentworth Chambers, **25** James s, h 73 George
Mills Isaac, electrician specialist, 320 York
Mills James, fireman, 98 Strachan e
Mills James E, laborer, 42 Ray n
Mills James H, 115 Main w
Mills J Bidwell, land and loan agent, 32 Elgin
Mills J D & Co, steam paper box factory, Wanzer building, King
Mills Jane (wid Anson) 12 O'Reilly
Mills Joseph & Son, hatters and furriers, 7 James n
Mills & McKellar (John Mills, Hugh McKeller) builders and contractors, 2 Caroline n

Mills John (Mills & McKellar) h 40 Markland
Mills John D (J D Mills & Co) bds Victoria Hotel, King e
Mills Wm, carpenter, 286 King e
Mills Wm, 62 Maria
Mills Wm H, 151 Main w
Mills Wm R (Jos Mills & Son) h 135 James s
Millward Geo, engineer, 31a Wellington n
Millward Geo, stationer, 95 York
Milne Adam, shoemaker, 99 Hannah e
Milne Alex, builder, 38 Hughson s
Milne Geo H, builder, 45 Mary
Milne James, gardener, n w cor Caroline and Markland
Milne John (Burrow, Stewart & Milne) h **45 Elgin**
Milne John, 90 James s
Milne Robt A, builder, 38 Hughson s
Milne Thos, laborer, 121 Locke n
Milne Wm, 86 Bay n
Milne Wm, Wentworth n
Milne Wm, shipper, 123 Locke n
Miner Cyrus E, cabinetmaker, 61 Victoria ave n
Mines Edward, traveler, 185 Mary
Mines James, moulder, 187 Mary
Mines Samuel, moulder, 280 Mary n
Minnes James, blacksmith, 132 Bold
Minnes John R, blacksmith, 126 Lock n
Minty Hy, clerk, bds 14 Caroline s
Mitchell Alfred, harnessmaker, 41 Catharine s
Mitchell Bradferd, engineer, 23 Liberty
Mitchell Catharine (wid Joseph) Shaw

Montgomery Mary (wid Wm) 116 Young
Montgomery Mary (wid Wm) 244 Macnab n
Montgomery Robert, laborer, 87 York
Moodie C W, salesman, 56 Bay s
Moodie John (J Moodie & Sons) h 56 Bay s
Moodie John jr, (J Moodie & Sons) 56 Bay s
Moodie J & Sons (John and John, jr) fancy goods and silverware, 16 King w
Moodie Matilda (wid James) 149 Catharine n
Moody Chas, carpetweaver, 25 Wood w
Moody Christopher, watchmaker, 27 York
Moody Miss F E, Hamilton Bassinette, 162 King e
Moody Robt, salesman, 83 Hunter
Mooney Albert, glassblower, 43 Burlington w
Mooney Chas, beer pedler, 126 Emerald n
Mooney Ellen (wid Patrick) 15 Railway
Moore Major Alex H, mangr Stinson's Bank, Kildallan, hd Hess s
Moore Alfred A, policeman, 56 East ave n
Moore Arthur, watchman, 48 Wellington n
Moore Caleb, pedler, Nelson
Moore Calvin P, 241 Main e
Moore Mrs Caroline, 95 King e
Moore Chas, accountant Bank B N A, 43 Bay s
Moore Chas P, file cutter, 190 Victoria ave n
Moore C P, 241 Main e
Moore & Davis (W P, W G Moore) real estate and ins agts, 2 King Wm

Moore D & Co, iron founders, manfrs and importers, 98-100 King e, foundry Catharine cor Robert
Moore Dennis (D Moore & Co) h 12 Hannah e
Moore Edward, salesman, 5 Ontario
Moore E E W, salesman, 69 Herkimer
Moore E J, bookkeeper, 13 West ave n
Moore Elizabeth (wid Wm) 21 Augusta
Moore Mrs Elizabeth, 46½ York
Moore Miss Emma, 92 Emerald n
Moore Mrs Emma, dressmaker, 20 Barton w
Moore Frederick, builder, 179 West ave n
Moore George, laborer, 14 Jackson e
Moore George, G T R dining rooms, 41 Murray w
Moore George, 123 Macnab n
Moore George, tinsmith, bds 50 Wilson
Moore George, clerk, 197 John n
Moore George, laborer, 117 Ferrie e
Moore George, speculator, 30 Emerald n
Moore George D, brushmaker, 74 Locke s
Moore H S, bookkeeper, 241 Main e
Moore Jane (wid John) 124 Jackson e
Moore Mrs John, 69 Herkimer
Moore John, laborer, 63 Locke s
Moore John, laborer, Dundurn w s nr Jones
Moore John D, brickmaker, 74 Locke s
Moore John H (Bowman & Moore) 54 King e
Moore Lawrence, laborer, Dundurn Castle

Mitchell Chas, blacksmith, 56 Catharine s
Mitchell Chas, broommaker, 25 Inchbury n
Mitchell Chas, lamp lighter, 130 **Bold**
Mitchell David, shoemaker, 8 Baillie
Mitchell David, shoemaker, 20 Hughson n, h 57 Wellington n
Mitchell D H, bookkeeper, 61 Napier
Mitchell Edward, manager Canadian Bank of Commerce, h Main E Hamilton
Mitchell Ellen (wid Thos) 71 Hughson n
Mitchell Emily (wid Joseph) 56 Catharine s
Mitchell Geo, machinist, 175 Napier
Mitchell John, stonemason, 72½ Bay s
Mitchell John, laborer, n w cor Ray and Bold
Mitchell Mrs Isabella, 270 King e
Mitchell James, porter, 176 Hughson n
Mitchell James, stovemounter, 225 Barton e
Mitchell James, mariner, 40 **Ferrie w**
Mitchell James, laborer, 99 Caroline s
Mitchell John, shoemaker, 82 Bold
Mitchell Mrs **Sarah A**, nurse, 34 Hughson s
Mitchell Thos, 37 Queen s
Mitchell William, machinist, 265 York
Mitchell **Wm**, stonemason, 30 Florence
Mitchell Wm B, tailor, 64 John s, h 84 Hunter e
Mitchell ———, bailiff, 93 James n
Mitchell ———, carriagemaker, South n s nr Garth

Mockridge Rev Charles H, D D, rector Christ Church Cathedral, 156 Macnab n
Modlin John, commission agent, 26 Margaret
Moffatt Robt, **shoemaker,** 38 Cannon w
Moffatt Robert, **mechanic,** 118 Bay n
Moffatt **Thomas,** teamster, 77 Market
Moffatt Wm, driver, 7 Florence
Moir Wm, ornamenter, 47 Catharine s
Molson's Bank, J M Burns manager, 2 James s
Monagan Mrs Margaret, 250 Hughson n
Monck J F, (Lazier & Monck), h 25½ East ave n
Monger David, 58 Oak ave
Monk Bros, (W E & H W Monk), grocers, 65 Pearl n
Monk Henry W, (Monk Bros), 89 Locke n
Monk Joseph, finisher, 89 Locke n
Monck Wm, chief clerk water works department, 89 Locke n
Monk Wm E, (Monk Bros) 89 Locke n
Monkman Mrs Martha, 8 Main w
Monroe Hugh, grocer, 267-269 James n
Monteith John, moulder, 79 John n
Montgomery Edgar, **blacksmith,** 140 West ave n
Montgomery James, **car** driver, 244 Macnab n
Montgomery John, grocer, 170 Main w, h 35 Pearl s
Montgomery John, porter, 116 Young
Montgomery J W, M D, assistant supt Asylum for the Insane
Montgomery Maria (wid Gabriel) 72 Ray n

21

Moore Lewis, gardener, Barton e
Moore Lyman, 33 Jackson w
Moore Margaret [wid Owen] 63 Locke s
Moore Peter, **shipper**, **26** Hunter e
Moore Robert, tailor, 129 Hunter e
Moore Robert, machinist, **bds 142** Hunter w
Moore Samuel A, clerk GTR, 46 Young
Moore Samuel J, tinsmith's tools, 44-46 Victoria ave s
Moore Sarah [wid Charles] Nelson
Moore S G, bookkeeper, **26** Hunter e
Moore Thos, Wentworth s
Moore Thos, engineer, 14 Barton e
Moore **Thomas, laborer,** 126 **Wood e**
Moore Traiton, clerk, 123 Macnab n
Moore Wm, stovemounter, 102 Young
Moore Wm, bookkeeper, **21** Augusta
Moore W G [Moore & Davis] h 174 Main **e**
Moore William, painter, 1 Oak
Moore W P [Moore & Davis] h 241 Main e
Moore W S, salesman, **42 East ave s**
Moore ——, laborer, Grant
Moran Antoine, saloon, 134 James n
Moran Miss Catharine, 146 Catharine n
Moran Edward, japanner, 230 Bay n
Moran Michael, laborer, 103 Picton e
Moran Patrick, laborer, **12 Napier**
Morden **Chas**, teamster, bds **21** Sheaffe

Morden Jacob, laborer, 21 Sheaffe
Morden Jackson, brakesman G T R, bds 33 Crooks
Morden John, watchman, bds **21** Sheaffe
Morden John D, 17 **Magill**
Morden J W (W & J Morden) h 27 West **ave** s
Morden J R, clerk P O, **bds 93** Market
Morden W & J, commission merchants, 7 Market sq
Morden W J (W & J Morden) h 8 Crooks
Morgan Alfred (Knox, Morgan & Co) 49 Victoria ave s
Morgan B J [Morgan Bros] h 51 East ave s
Morgan Bros [W S, R R, B J Morgan] roller mills, whip **manfrs and saddlery hardware,** 25-7-9 John s
Morgan Chas, carriage trimmer, 13 Park n
Morgan Chas E, exchange and general railway and steamship ticket agency, 11 James n h 191 Macnab n
Morgan Richard, carriage trimmer, 29 Market
Morgan Mrs [wid Richard] 58 Emerald s
Morgan R R, [Morgan Bros] h 77 Emerald s
Morgan Thomas, **tanner.** 14 Victoria ave s
Morgan Wm, machinist, 44 Barton w
Morgan W S [Morgan Bros] h **227** Main **e**
Moriarty Bartholomew, laborer, 250 Barton e
Moriarty John, laborer, 9 Mulberry
Moriarty John, laborer, 7 Mulberry
Moriarty Michael, laborer, 31 Sheaffe
Moriarty Patrick, 78 Bold

/

Moriarity Wm, restaurant, 69 Stuart w
Moriarty Wm, eating house keeper, 175 Bay n
Morin Mrs Catharine, 274 James n
Morin Joseph, boot and shoe dealer, 224 James n
Morin Napoleon, shoemaker, 35 Smith ave
Morison Fredk S, bookkeeper, Hannah w s s nr Locke
Morison John, woodworker, Shaw
Morley John, blacksmith, 19 Margaret
Morley John, carpenter, bds 133 Wood e
Morley Thomas, moulder, 16 Crooks
Morphy John, bartender, 15 James n
Morrell Edward, fireman, bds 208 Macnab n
Morris Alfred [Philip Morris & Sons] 129 John n
Morris C, tailor, 133 James n
Morris Chas, locksmith, 18 O'Reilly
Morris Chas, machinist, 27 Inchbury n
Morris Frank, laborer, bds 49 Hughson n
Morris George, grocer, 271-3 York
Morris Geo butcher, 18 Locke s
Morris James, grocer, 225 Macnab n
Morris James, tailor, 137 James n
Morris John, fruiterer, 25 James n
Morris John, boat builder, foot of Wentworth n
Morris John, 11 Park s
Morris John M, engineer, 92 Duke
Morris Joseph [Philip Morris & Sons] 129 John n
Morris Lewis, butcher, King e of Wentworth

Morris Moses, laborer, 124 Macauley e
Morris Philip [Philip Morris & Sons] 129 John n
Morris Philip & Sons [Philip, Joseph and Alfred Morris] grocers, 129 John n
Morris Thomas, laborer, 178 James n
Morris Thomas, flour and feed, 21 Wellington n, h 26 Wellington n
Morris Mrs Thos, fancy goods, 178 James n
Morris Thos jr, salesman, 26 Wellington n
Morris Wm, grocer, s w cor Cherry and Maria
Morris Wm, brass founder, 64 Ray n
Morris Wm, expressman, 11 Park s
Morris ——, 18 O'Reilly
Morrisey James, clerk, 12 Victoria ave s
Morrisey John, grocer, 248 King w
Morrisey Margaret (wid Michael) 12 Victoria ave s
Morrisey Thomas, laborer, 253a Catharine n
Morrison Alexander, laborer, 43 West ave n
Morrison Alexander, grocer, 105 John s
Morrison Alexander R, broker, 132 Hughson n
Morrison Andrew, clerk, 123 John s
Morrison Frederick, Temperance hotel, hd York s s
Morrison Edward, stenographer, 132 Hughson n
Morrison George C, engine and boiler works, ft Caroline n, h 163 Park n
Morrison John, grocer, 66 Main w
Morrison John, laborer, 93 Mary

Morrison John, wood worker, Shaw
Morrison Samuel, agent, 99 Locke n
Morrison Thomas, 98 John s
Morrison Rebecca (wid Wm) 123 John s
Morrison Wm J, machinist, hd York s s
Morrow & Co, stock brokers, 6 John n
Morison Alfred E, bookkeeper, 92 Bay s
Mortimer Edgar, teamster, 45 Alanson
Mortimer James, moulder, 167 King Wm
Mortimer Joseph, stovefitter, 120 Maria
Morton Mrs Addie, fruiterer, 254 King e
Morton Andrew, laborer, 35 Spring
Morton Ann (wid Andrew) 37 Lower Cathcart
Morton Bros (John and Thomas) wholesale grocers, 1 Charles
Morton David, manfr, 186 Main e
Morton David jr, bookkeeper, 36 Markland
Morton David jr, com traveler, 186 Main e
Morton David sr, 36 Markland
Morton Edward, painter, 70 Jackson e
Morton Edward clerk, 37 Lower Cathcart
Morton Ezekiel, laborer, Maple s s nr Garth
Morton George, barber, 87 John s
Morton George, 52 Herkimer
Morton George, grocer, 27 Lower Cathcart
Morton Geo jr, grocer, 37 Lower Cathcart
Morton H M, salesman, bds 34 Bay s
Morton James, salesman, 52 King w

Morton John, laborer, 35 Railway
Morton Rev John, minister Congregational Church, 41 Hannah w
Morton John, salesman, 52 King w
Morton John (Morton Bros) 254 King e
Morton John, manfr, 53 Emerald s
Morton John G, machinist, 42 Magill
Morton Mrs Mary, 52 King w
Morton Robert, manfr, 51 Emerald s
Morton **Stephen**, tinsmith, bds 35 Hughson n
Morton Thos (Morton **Bros**) 37 Lower Cathcart
Morton Valley, polisher, bds 89 Cannon e
Morton William, fruiterer, 52 King w
Morton Rev William, 50 Emerald s
Morton W C, teacher, 50 Emerald s
Morty John, laborer, 119 Market
Morrow Charles, mason, 58 Wilson
Morrow Chas jr, bricklayer, 58 Wilson
Morrow John, policeman, 121 James n
Morrow **Mrs** M, confectioner, 168 James n
Morrow Wm, laborer, 17 Lower Cathcart
Moses **Hannah** (wid Meier) clothing, 51 John s
Mosher Edward, finisher, 107 Hunter e
Mosher Wm, com traveler, 107 Hunter e
Moss Chas, shoemaker, hd York s s nr Dundurn
Mossman Mark, shoemaker, 23 Gore

Mostyn John, tinsmith, 150 Hunter w
Mosure F B, law student, 34 Bay
Mott Daniel V, canvasser, 42 Main w
Mott Thos, laborer, nr toll gate, King e
Mottashed Chas, builder, 17 West ave n
Mottashed Mrs Lezetta, 18 East ave n
Mount Jacob, carpenter, bds 11 Mill
Mount Mary (wid John) 11 Mill
Mount Wm, clerk, bds 11 Mill
Mowat Andrew, mason, 56 Erie ave
Mowat Elizabeth (wid Andrew) 94a Victoria ave n
Mowat George, bricklayer, 87 Young
Mowat James, tailor, 56 Erie ave
Mowat Mary (wid William) 85 Mary
Moyer L A, bookkeeper, 45 East ave n
Moyer J G, com traveler, bds 48 James n
Moyes Miss Isabella, 33 Walnut s
Moyes George, moulder, 33 Walnut s
Moylan Thos, shoemaker, 37 Napier
Muckersie James, fitter, n w cor Concession and Caroline
Muckersie James, fitter, 107 Herkimer
Mugford Richard, painter, 108 Ferguson ave
Muir Annie (wid Andrew) 211½ Main w
Muir Andrew, bookkeeper, 211½ Main w
Muir Arch A, clerk, 45 Wellington s
Muir David, pile driver, 42 Barton e
Muir Henry B, carpenter, 8 Emerald n

Muir James, baggageman GTR, 141 Emerald n
Muir John, M A, (Crerar, Muir & Crear) h 37 Duke
Muir John G, bricklayer, 170 West ave n
Muirhead Stephen, butcher, 66 Catharine s
Muirhead Walter (Crockett, Muirhead & Co) h cor Liberty and Main
Mulcahey Dennis, stovemounter, 57½ Wood e
Mulanay John, file cutter, 93 West ave n
Mulanay Mary (wid John) 93 West ave n
Mulanay Thomsa, file cutter, 93 West ave n
Mulhern Thos, moulder, 91 West ave n
Mulholland Mrs H, 63 Colborne
Mulholland James, laborer, 121 Walnut s
Mulholland John, wood dealer, 169½ Wilson
Mulholland Mrs Margaret (wid John), 126 West ave
Mulholland Peter, laborer, r 126 Hannah e
Mulholland Samuel, laborer, 65 Barton w
Mulholland Thos (Wm and Thos Mulholland) h 52 Catharine n
Mulholland Wm (Wm and Thos Mulholland) h 52 Catharine n
Mulholland Wm & Thos, wood dealers, 30 Lower Cathcart
Mullens Thos, carpenter, 21 Oak ave
Mullett —, telephone agent, bds 44 Main w
Mulligan C W, architect, court house, h 43 Hannah w
Mullin David F, 123 Main e
Mullin, George, glassblower, 315 Macnab n
Mullen Henry, carpenter, 3 Picton w

Mullin John A, M D, 124 James n
Mullin Mrs Mary, 123 Main e
Mullin Mrs Peter, 382 James n
Mullings Mrs, Emily, grocer, 122 Macnab n
Mullins Thos, laborer, 278 Mary
Mulliss Wm, laborer, 65 Park n
Mulquinn, Mathew, shoemaker, bds 170 Jackson w
Mulroy Michael, laborer, 128 Bay n
Mulvale Wm, laborer, 15 Clark ave
Mummery Albert, boilermaker, bds 59 Locomotive
Mundell Ebenezer, com traveler, 15½ Elgin
Mundie Margaret (wid Wm) 1 Robinson
Mundt Chas, laborer, Robinson s s w Locke
Mundt Robt, laborer, 44½ Robinson
Mundy Angus, grocer, 125 Park n
Mundy Mark, druggist, 164 King e
Mundy Wm A, letter carrier, 96 Park n
Mungold Conrad, cigarmaker, bds 42 Kelly
Munn Charlotte (wid Wm) 79 Maria
Munn James, farmer, 53 Robert
Munn James, laborer, 101 John n
Munro Alex, com traveler, n e cor Concession and Bruce
Munro Colin, traveler, 177 John n
Munro Emma (wid Malcolm) 78 Merrick
Munro James, laborer, Bay s w s nr Hunter
Munro James, cutter, 33 East ave n
Munroe John, printer, bds 31 Gore
Munro Mrs, 88 Robinson

Munro Mrs Mary, 26 Guise
Munson Guy, fireman, 179 Wellington n
Munson Patrick, painter, bds 122 Cannon e
Munson Sarah (wid Ephram) 134 King Wm
Munsie Herbert, accountant, 210½ Victoria ave n
Muntz Adolphus, laborer, 61 Locke s
Munzinger John M, bookbinder, 23 York
Murden John H, express driver, 109 Rebecca
Murdie Janet (wid Alex) 38 East ave n
Murdoch Andrew, com traveler, 37 Hannah w
Murdoch James, policeman GTR, 152 Napier
Murdoff Michael, 8 Hannah w
Murdoff M W (Barnard, Murdoff & Co) h 8 Hannah w
Murison Geo, health inspector, 113 Herkimer
Murphy Mrs Ann, 26 Picton w
Murphy Ann (wid Martin) 9 Macnab s
Murphy Catharine (wid John) 53 Young
Murphy Cornelius, catcher, 2 Greig
Murphy Edward, laborer, 5 Macauley w
Murphy Edmund, tailor, 32 Aurora
Murphy Edward, sign painter, 91 James n
Murphy Ed, laborer, 291 John n
Murphy James J, cigarmaker, 10 O'Reilly
Murphy John, laborer, 3 Greig
Murphy John, supt letter carriers, 37 Jackson e
Murphy Kate (wid Michael) 122 Emerald n
Murphy Lawrence, laborer, 164 Park n

Murphy Matthew, marble polisher, 233 Main w
Murphy Matthew, laborer, 120 Emerald n
Murphy Michael, saloon, cor Jackson and Catharine
Murphy Michael, tobacco roller, bds 50 Napier
Murphy & Murray, grocers, 66 King e
Murphy Mrs Patrick, grocer, 313½ Macnab n
Murphy Mrs Sarah, fancy goods, 74 King w
Murphy Sarah (wid Jos) 3 Young
Murphy Timothy, laborer, 131 Macaulay e
Murphy T D, mangr Ham Whip Co, 31 Wellington s
Murphy Thomas, machinist, 37 Jackson e
Murphy Wm, carpenter, 142 Duke
Murphy Wm, stonemason, 24 Catharine n
Murphy Wm (Murphy & Murray) 53 Ferguson ave
Murray A & Co, importers of staple and fancy dry goods, manfrs of millinery, mantles and dresses, 18-20 King e
Murray Alex (A Murray & Co) Arlo House, Main w
Murray Alex jr, clerk, Queen cor Herkimer
Murray Anthony, 188 King Wm
Murray Mrs Catharine, 63 Merrick
Murray David, blacksmith, 139 West ave n
Murray David, gardener, 76 Tisdale
Murray David, clerk, 76 Tisdale
Murray Duncan, flour and feed, 16-18 York
Murray Eliza (wid Richard) 92 Maria
Murray Chas S, cashier Hendrie, Symmes & Co) bds 48 Hunter w

Murray Geo, clerk GTR, 76 Tisdale
Murray Hugh, clerk customs, 88 Main e
Murray James, cabinet finisher, 137 Robert
Murray James, clerk, Main cor Hess
Murray James, tailor, 121 Ferguson ave
Murray James H, bartender, 103 Main e
Murray John, salesman, Arlo House, Main w
Murray John, rag carpet mfr, 148 King w
Murray Robt, shoemaker, 41 Robinson
Murray Robt B, whip ferule manfr and plater, 49 King Wm, h 167 Hughson n
Murray Thos, carpenter, 23 O'Reilly
Murray Thos, porter, 79 West ave n
Murray Walter, saddler, 121½ Queen n
Murray William, accountant, Athol Bank, Queen cor Herkimer
Murray Wm, gardener, 76 Tisdale
Murray Wm, 229 John n
Murton Chas, clerk, Main e of Wentworth
Murton Chas A, bookkeeper, bds Royal hotel
Murton E C, bookkeeper, 25 West ave s
Murton Edward, merchant, Main e of Wentworth
Murton John W [Murton & Reid] Main, e Hamilton
Murton Miss, private school, 182 John n
Murton Percy, student, Main e of Wentworth
Murton & Reid, coal merchants, 44 John n

Murton Wm, clerk, 282 John n
Musgrove Caroline (wid James) 76 John n
Muskoka Lake Steamboat Line, W J Grant, agent, 33 James n
Mutter Anthony, gardener, 4 Erie ave
Mutter Philip, pattern letter mfr, 46 York
Mutter Wm, laborer, 46 York
Mutual Accident Association of England, Walter Ambrose, agent, 14 Hughson s
Mutual Plate Glass Association, Walter Ambrose, agt, 14 Hughson s
Myers Adolph, cabinetmaker, 68 Hess n
Myers Benjamin, engineer, 52 Napier
Myers Catharine [wid George] 18 Devonport
Myers Edgar, cooper, 66 Hughson n
Myers Henry, engineer, 11 Oak ave
Myers **Herbert,** laborer, bds 109 King Wm
Myers John, laborer, 56 Young
Myers Joseph, laborer, 306 King e
Myers Mrs, 12 Main e
Myers Rose A [wid Jacob] 33 Queen s
Myers Theodore, laborer, 281 King w
Myers Wm, fireman, 306 King e
Myers Wm, coachman, 31 Queen s
Myers Wm, tinsmith, 84½ West ave n
Myers Rev Wm, pastor St Stephen's Church, Canada cor Pearl
Myers Wm J, painter, 46 Hunter e
Myles Alfred H, coal merchant, 146 John n

Myles Annie [wid Joseph J] **56** Gore
Myles **C J** [Thomas Myles & Son] h 7 Elgin
Myles James, teamster, bds 57 John s
Myles Thomas [Thos Myles & Son] h Victoria ave cor Hunter
Myles Thos & Son [Thos & C J] coal merchants, Hughson cor Main
Myles William, **laborer, 96** Walnut s
Myles Wm, laborer, 7 Wood e
Mylne Herbert, brakeman, bds 51 Park n
Myrick James H, picture framer, 132 John n
Nadin Edgar, carpenter, **129** Cannon w
Nadin Samuel, bookkeeper, **129** Cannon w
Nagle Edward, railroader, 176 Catharine n
Naismith D, clerk **Alex** Turner & Co
Nallon Thos, tinsmith, bds **57** Robert
Nangle Edward, 170 Catharine n
Napier James, driller, Robinson n s w Locke
Nash Alfred, express messenger, 260 James n
Nash David, laborer, **105** King Wm
Nash Elvin, **engineer,** 162 Ferguson **ave**
Nash George, carpenter, **151** Wilson
Nash Wm, fireman, 54 Barton e
Naylor James, fancy dry goods, 147 York
Neal **Edward,** brickmaker, **151** Jackson w
Neal Mrs Eliza, laundry, 151 Jackson w
Nealin Mary A [wid Thomas] 100 Bold

22

Nealin Patrick, lather, 100 Bold
Neelon Ellen [wid John] 172 Bay n
Neelon Wm, tinsmith, bds 76 John n
Neff Edmund, stove polisher, 294 John n
Neff Mrs Eleanor, 126 Wellington n
Neff Wm, com traveler, 306 Macnab n
Neigle George, scalemaker, bds 174 Bay n
Neill Andrew T, city asst collector, Canada Life Chambers
Neil Jas, stonemason, 98 Ferrie
Neil Robt, laborer, 15 New
Nelligan Bartholomew [G & B Nelligan] 232 James n
Nelligan Mrs C, fancy goods, 180 James n
Nelligan G & B, gents' furnishers, 232 James n
Nelligan George [G & B Nelligan] 232 James n
Nelligan George, tinsmith, 180 James n
Nelligan John B, bookkeeper, 234 Macnab n
Nelligan M D, wagon maker. James n, h 263 Hughson n
Nelligan Mrs Margaret, 265 Hughson n
Nelligan Thomas, laborer, 8 Jones
Nellis W P, com traveler, bds 98 James s
Nelson Alfred, glassblower, 83 Lower Cathcart
Nelson Daniel, laborer, 55 Stuart e
Nelson Edward, com traveler, 64 Cannon w
Nelson Frank J, correspondent *Globe*, 68 Wellington n
Nelson Ira, dairyman, n w cor Concession and Locke
Nelson Mrs Jane E [wid Robt] 223 King e

Nelson J D, teamster, 53 Barton e
Nelson John, hackman, 105 Florence
Nelson Michael, fireman, bds 65 Stuart w
Nelson Patrick, 195 Victoria ave n
Nelson Thos, oil refiner, Wentworth n
Nelson Sylvester, brakeman, 69 Robert
Nelson Wm, laborer, Wentworth n
Nelson Wm, yardsman, 219 Victoria ave n
Nelson Wm T, foreman Bridge Works, 64 Cannon w
Nesbitt J W (Fuller, Nesbitt & Bicknell) h 16 Hughson s
Nevills Emerson, laborer, bds Union Hotel
Nevills James, teamster, 178 King Wm
Neville Joseph, machinist, 24 Inchbury n
Neville Robt, engineer, Barton
Nevills Thos, laborer, 33 Wellington n
Nevills Wm, mechanic, 101 Lower Cathcart
New Edward, brick manfr, 307 King w
New Mrs Eliza [wid Daniel] 228 Main w
New David, potter, 138 Jackson w
New Hy, sec-treas Campbell Sewer Pipe Co, h 154 Main w
New Mrs James, 231 Main w
New Samuel, carriagemkerr, 250 Main w
News, (Toronto), Daily and Weekly, Macnab cor Main
Newberry Chas E, (Humphrey & Newberry), 80 Robert
Newberry Frank, salesman, 80 Robert
Newbiggins Robt, cabinetmaker, 104 Cherry

Newbigging Wm, 104 Cherry
Newcomb Mrs L, supt Kindergarten, 46 Duke
Newcomb Wm, engineer G T R, 51 Magill
Newcomb Wm, laborer, 151 John s
Newcomb William, laborer, 116 Bold
Newington Daniel, gunsmith, 166 Hughson n
Newlands James, machinist, Robinson s s nr Locke
Newman Albert, mechanic, 22 Railway
Newman Albert, heater, 27 Oxford
Newman Chas J, L A M, music teacher, Victoria ave n
Newman Edward, moulder, 94 Simcoe e
Newman Ed, jobber, 133 Macauley e
Newman John, cigarmaker, 70 Ray s
Newman Maitland, com traveler, 55 Hunter w
Newman Mrs Margaret, 34 Bay n
Newmarch James, machinist, bds 24 Caroline n
Newman P E, clerk, bds 77 James n
Newport E, carterer, 186 King e
Newport Wm, confectioner, 180 King e
Newson Wm, trunk maker, 14 Pearl n
Newton David, agent, 6 Main e h 64 Macnab s
New York Central and Hudson River Railroad, W J Grant, agent, 33 James n
New York Hair Works, Miss E Pargeter, proprietress, 83 King w
Newyear Postal, 60 Hess n
Nex Charles R, piler, 242 York

Nex Wm, carpenter, 46 Florence
Nex Wm J, laborer, 99 Hunter w
Niblock George, teamster, 98 Murray e
Niblock Mrs **Mary Ann**, 63 Jackson e
Niblock Moses, laborer, King e of Wentworth
Nichol Mrs Cynthia J, 90 Catharine s
Nichol George, laborer, 54 Erie ave
Nichol James, teamster, 67-69 Jackson e
Nichol James, planer, King e of Wentworth
Nichol **Wm**, plumber, bds 83 Main e
Nicholls John R, yard clerk GTR 78 Hannah w
Nichols Thomas E, Hamilton Iron Fencing & Wire Works, 158 King w
Nicholls Wm, brickmaker, West e s
Nichols W H, butcher, King cor East ave s
Nicholson Andrew, laborer, 163 Macnab n
Nicholson Mrs Catharine, (wid James), 111 King w
Nicholson Mrs Elizabeth, (wid John), 73 Locke n
Nicholson Geo, (J & G Nicholson), s e cor Herkimer & Kent
Nicholson Geo, teamster, 36 Ferguson ave
Nicholson Mrs Helen, (wid Donald,) 15 Markland
Nicholson Henry, porter, r 98 Cannon w
Nicholson J & G, (John & Geo), wood and coal dealers, 110 York
Nicholson John, (J & G Nicholson), n e cor Markland and Kent
Nicholson John, cutter, 89 Rebecca

Nicholson Mrs Mary E, (wid Edward), 89 Rebecca
Nicholson Richard, laborer, 205 Catharine n
Nicholson Robt, cutter, 89 Rebecca
Nicholson Thos, 111 King w
Nicholson Wm, wood and coal dealer, 111 King w, h 72 George
Nickling James, laborer, 13 Magill
Nicol Geo, stableman, 20 Market
Nicol James, laborer, 129 King Wm
Nicol Peter, machinist, 70 Hunter e
Nicolls Wm B, contractor, hd Garth w s
Nicoll Capt Willoughby H, farmer, hd Garth w s
Nie A J, machinist, 176 Victoria ave n
Nieghorn Albert, com traveler, 96 Florence
Nieghon Chas, marble cutter 96 Florence
Nieghorn Wm, 3 O'Reilly
Nielson Mrs Eliza, (wid James), 83 Main w
Nielson Geo, bookkeeper, 83 Main w
Nielson Peter, engineer, 123 Hunter e
Nielson Wm, baker, 83 Main w
Nimmo Mrs S E, 103 James s
Nisbet Matthew, hats, caps and gents' furnishings, 168 King e
Nisbet Walter, carpenter, 21 Inchbury s
Nixon Ed, propr Enniskillen Hotel, 20 King Wm
Nixon Henry, quarryman, 122 Wellington s
Nixon Hugh, coachman, 149 King w
Nixon John, laborer, 187 James n
Nixon Thos, policeman, 345 James n
Nixon Wm, laborer, 83 Bold
Nixon W S, printer, 72 Wellington n
Noble Albert W, chair caner, 8 Main w
Noble C J, ledger keeper, Bank of Commerce, 14 Caroline s
Noble James, laborer, 60 Bay n
Noble John, bricklayer, 86 Stinson
Noble John W, express messenger, 87 Mary
Noble Wm, hotel keeper, 121 James n
Noblett Robert, foreman cotton mills, 45 East ave s
Noel Mrs Susan (wid Thomas) 20 Catharine s
Nolan James, laborer, 132 Wood e
Nolan John, laborer, 140 Rebecca
Nolan Joseph, laborer, 216 Hughson n
Nolan Martin, glassblower, 16 Simcoe e
Nolan Michael, 3 Little Wellington
Nolan Owen, 35 Rebecca
Nolan Sylvester, laborer, 14 Stuart w
Nolan William, cutter, 32 East ave s
Nordheimer A & S, 2 Hemphill, mangr, 80 James n
Noonan John, sailor, 243 Hughson n
Noonan Patrick, machinist, 245 Wellington n
Norman Henry, shipper, 150 East ave n
Norman John W, laborer, 1 Florence
North British and Mercantile Fire and Life Insurance Co, J T Routh agent, 16 James s

North Chas W, bricklayer, 4 Elizabeth
North John W, letter carrier, 34 Ray s
Northern Fire Assurance Co, Seneca Jones agent, 6 James s
Northern & Northwestern Railway, W J Grant ticket agent, 33 James n
N & N W R R Offices and Cartage Agency, 33 Main e
Northern & Northwestern Railway Passenger Station, King cor Cherry
Norris Mrs Margaret (wid Patrick) 39 Catharine n
Norris Nathaniel, hay and straw, 30 Catharine s, h 7 Wood Market
Northey Diggory, engineer, 120 Hannah e
Northey Francis, engineer, 18 Wellington n
Northey Henry, horse dealer, 45 Hannah w
Norwich Union Fire Insurance Society (Eng) Walter Ambrose, agent, 14 Hughson s
Norwood George, laborer, Duke s s w Locke
Norwood George A, brickmaker, Duke s s w Locke
Nott George, butcher, 127 King Wm
Nott Wm J, butcher, Wentworth
Nottle J T, Wentworth s
Nottle Thomas T, Wentworth s
Notz Augustus, blacksmith's helper, Herkimer s s w Locke
Notz Fredk, carriage painter, Herkimer s s w Locke
Notz Mrs Sophia (wid Augustus) Herkimer s s w Locke
Noyes E F, bookkeeper, 12 Hannah w
Noyes F, salesman, 18 Wilson
Noyes James, laborer, bds 82 Hughson n

Noyes James, 88 James s
Noyes Joseph, scalemaker, 91 Robert
Nugent Arthur, dairyman, Main e of Wentworth
Nugent William, laborer, 101 Hannah e
Nunn James, teamster, 26 Elgin
Nunn Wm, blacksmith, 12 West ave n
Nurden J H, driver Express Co, 109 Rebecca
Nutley David, laborer, 37 Sheaffe
Nuttell Robt, roller cover, 90 Macauley e
O'Brien Andrew, laborer, 38 Simcoe e
O'Brien Andrew, laborer, 241 John n
O'Brien Andrew, salesman, 168 John n
O'Brien David, cigarmaker, 4 Stuart e
O'Brien D J, prof of music, 28 Sheaffe
O'Brien Mrs E, 4 Stuart e
O'Brien Edward, laborer, Burlington n
O'Brien Hy, gunsmith, 55 Gore
O'Brien James, conductor, 4 Stuart e
O'Brien James, moulder, 43 East ave n
O'Brien James, mangr Ham Brush Co, 159 John n
O'Brien James, laborer, 50½ Young
O'Brien James jr, lithographer, 50½ Young
O'Brien J F, excise officer, 21 Evans
O'Brien John, railroader, 137 Park n
O'Brien John jr, cigarmaker, 55 Walnut s
O'Brien Mrs Margaret (wid John) 55 Walnut s
O'Brien Martin, track foreman, 52 Ferrie e

O'Brien Michael, laborer, 97 Strachan e

O'Brien Patrick, insp waterworks 159 John n

O'Brien Patrick, laborer, 182 Robert

O'Brien Patrick, laborer, 73 Young

O'Brien Robt, caretaker Loretto convent, n w cor King and Ray

O'Brien Samuel, printer, 55 Gore

O'Brien Thomas, machinist, 4 Stuart e

O'Brien Thos, hairdresser, 202 King e

O'Brien Wm, shoemaker, 6 Pearl s

O'Brien William, moulder, 21 Evans

O'Brien W J, grocer, 88 James n, h 168 John n

O'Brien Mrs, nurse, 20 Napier

O'Callaghan Frank, inspector of buildings, 179 Park n

O'Callaghan John, cigarmaker, 12 Stuart e

O'Connell Daniel, laborer, 9 Locomotive

O'Connell Daniel, gardener Mrs E Gurney, hd of John s

O'Connell & Evans, (John C O'Connell, Wm Evans), marble and marbleized slate mantel dealers, 26 York

O'Connell James, milkdlr, 134 Catharine n

O'Connell John C, (O'Connell & Evans) 26 York

O'Connell Patrick, laborer, 106 Maria

O'Connell Daniel, laborer, 104 Maria

O'Connor Ed, conductor, 4 Tiffany

O'Connor James, dairyman, 149 Locke n

O'Connor Jeremiah, laborer, Eliza

O'Connor John, laborer, 17 Devonport

O'Connor John, 278 Hughson n

O'Connor Patrick, laborer, Eliza

O'Connor Thos, carriage painter, 160 King w

O'Connor Thos, laborer, 36 Barton e

O'Connor Thos, laborer, r 24 Aurora

O'Connor Thos, laborer, Robinson w s nr Locke

O'Connor Thos, glassblower, 61 Wood e

O'Dea Mrs Bridget, (wid Patrick) Burlington n

O'Dell Edmund W, bread pedlar 138 Jackson e

O'Donell James, glassblower, 16 Stuart w

O'Donnell P, clerk P O, Maple ave

O'Donnell Patrick J railroader, bds 7 Ferguson ave

O'Donnell Steven, glassblower, 21 Simcoe w

O'Dowd, John, laborer, 87 Simcoe e

O'Driscoll Martin, finisher, 61 Caroline s

O'Dyer Frank, painter, bds 37 Robert

O'Grady James, moulder, 178 Robert

O'Grady John, moulder, 139 Robert

O'Grady Martin, laborer, 140 Picton e

O'Grady Martin, marble works, cor Hess and York

O'Grady Thos, moulder, 165 Wellington n

O'Hara John, laborer, 180 Wilson

O'Heir Arthur, (Staunton & O'Heir), barrister, h 54 Wellington s

O'Heir James, machinist, 124 Catharine s

O'Heir Peter, landing waiter, 54 Wellington s
O'Heron Mrs Arabella, (wid Morris) boarding, 36 Market
O'Keefe D C, land surveyor, 117 Maria
O'Kelly Charles, laborer, 52 Maria
O'Kelly John, moulder, 52 Maria
O'Kelly Miss Minne, 52 Maria
O'Laughlin James, baker, 30 Peter
O'Leary Mrs Elizabeth, (wid James) 136 Locke n
O'Leary James, upholsterer, 136 Locke n
O'Malley Miss Annie, 124 Hughson n
O'Mara Martin, laborer, 23 Burlington w
O'Neil Mrs Ann, r 61 Jackson e
O'Neil Arthur, 95 Hannah e
O'Neil Mrs Bridget, 283 John n
O'Neil Daniel, tobacconist, 152 James n
O'Neil Mrs Ellen, grocer, 194 James n
O'Neil Felix, hackman, 54 Hunter e
O'Neil James, woodworker, s w cor Wellington & Rebecca
O'Neill James, carriage painter, n e cor Dundurn and Tom
O'Neill John, laborer, 27 Walnut
O'Neill John, tailor, 138 Victoria ave n
O'Neill John, laborer, 122 Young
O'Neill John, foreman Spectator, 122 Jackson e
O'Neil John, laborer, 106 Strachan e
O'Neil John, tinner, Macauley e
O'Neil Martin, moulder, 1 Evans
O'Neil Mrs Mary, 35 Wood e
O'Neill Matthew, scalemaker, bds 56 Park e
O'Neil Michael, glassblower, 32 Picton w

O'Neill Michael, gardener, head York w canal
O'Neill Michael, laborer, 289 John n
O'Neil Patrick, bricklayer, 14 Clarke ave
O'Neil Patrick, teamster, 327 Catharine
O'Neill Patrick, laborer, 199 Bay n
O'Neill Patrick, 150 Market
O'Neil Robt, laborer, 55 Wood e
O'Neill Thomas, laborer, 335 Hughson n
O'Neill Thomas, blacksmith, n e cor Dundurn and Tom
O'Neil Thos, laborer, 210 Hughson n
O'Neil Thomas, baker, 153 Main e
O'Neil William, laborer, 190 Robert
O'Neil ——, laborer, 25 Macauley
O'Reilly Mrs Catharine (wid James) Concession n s nr Garth
O'Reilly Daniel, laborer, 4 Locomotive
O'Reilly Edward B, M D, 37 James s
O'Reilly Frank, plumber, 152 King w
O'Reilly James, laborer, 92 Walnut s
O'Reilly James, dyer, r 205 Catharine n
O'Reilly J E, master Supreme Court, Court House, h 53 Catharine s
O'Reilly Miles, Q C, master Supreme Court, Court House, h Catharine s
O'Reilly Patrick, laborer, 4 Locomotive
O'Reilly Peter J, brush maker, 179 Macnab n
O'Reilly Robt, brush maker, 179 Macnab n

O'Reegan John, yard foreman Bridge and Tool works, 188 Emerald n
O'Sullivan Frank, gardener, Burlington s
O'Sullivan Henry, gardener, Burlington s
O'Sullivan Maurice, moulder, Burlington s
O'Toole John, scalemaker, 103 Strachan e
O'Toole Stephen, 13 Simcoe w
O'Toole Wm, cigarmaker, 207 Hughson n
Oakes Edward, tailor, 120 Catharine n
Oakes Edward, tobacco roller, 35 Peter
Oakes Frederick, butcher, 42 Ferguson ave
Oak Hall, Wm Farrar, mangr, 10 James n
Oaklands Jersey Dairy, 20 James s
Oaten Walter, salesman, 9 Victoria ave n
Oaten Walter, salesman, 9 Victoria ave n
Obermeyer Henry M, printer, 106 Market
Obermeyer Matern, piano maker, 106 Market
Obermeyer Philip J, printer, 106 Market
Oddfellow's Hall, 24 John n
Oddy Joseph, carpenter, 413 Wood e
Oder Charles, laborer, 101 Hunter e
Oder Gustave, laborer, 88 John n
Oder Hugo, 88 John n
Odery Rev Joseph, pastor Hannah St Methodist Church, 77 Herkimer
Ogg Alexander, grocer, 177 Mary
Ogilvie James, governor county jail, Barton e
Ogilvie John, porter, bds 168 Mary

Old John, laborer, 37 Little William
Old Thomas, laborer, 132 Hunter
Old Wm, laborer, 6 Aurora
Oliver Mrs Ann, candy store, 80 Jackson e
Oliver Cyrus, trimmer, Markland s s w Queen
Oliver Mrs David, 95 Hughson n
Oliver Capt D M, 95 Hughson n
Oliver Frank, bartender, bds 74 John s
Oliver Hamilton, collector, 142 Rebecca
Oliver James, moulder, Burton
Oliver James M, com traveler, 20 Erie ave
Oliver Mrs Matilda (wid Thos) 25 Inchbury s
Oliver Thos, mangr W E Sanford & Co, 79 Emerald s
Oliver Thomas, shoemaker, 158 Bay n
Oliver Thos, 122 Bold
Ollman John, brickmaker, West nr King
Ollman Henry, brick manfr, n e cor Dufferin and Macklin
Olmstead Chas W, laborer, 154 Rebecca
Olmstead Hiram, laborer, 85 Robert e
Olmsted Russell G, 41 Bay s
Olmsted Mrs Sarah (wid Samuel) 11 Hess s
Olmsted W H, grocer, 76 John s, h 39 Hunter e
Olsen Chas, laborer, Augusta, East Hamilton
Omand Gilbert, carpenter, 142 Hughson n
Omand James, engineer, 34 Barton e
Omand Joseph, watchman, 11 Wood e
Omand Wm, machinist, 28 Murray w
Omand Wm jr, machinist, 31 Murray e

Omeyer H F, photo operator, bds Blaases hotel
Ontario Brewery, J Gomph proprietor, 360 John n
Ontario Canning Co (Egeton De Cew Sec, A E Carpenter Pres) cor Young and Liberty
Ontario Cotton Mills Co, Macnab n
Ontario Pharmacy, John W Yeomans, prop, King cor Ferguson ave
Ontario Rolling Mill Co (Chas E Doolittle pres) ft of Queen n
Ontario Sewing Machine Co (F M Willson pres, James Lockhart sec-treas) 22 James s
Ontario Shirt Co, J R Mead mangr, 10½ Market sq
Orange James, 210 Catharine n
Orme E V G, clerk, 52 Hunter w
Orr, Harvey & Co (John A Orr, W C Harvey) wh boots and shoes, 21 King w
Orr John, laborer, 47 **Ray** n
Orr John A (Orr, Harvey & Co) h 82 James s
Orr & Laird (W C Orr, H G Laird) wh perfume and extracts 26 John n
Orr Richard, bartender, 10 Main e
Orr Watson C (Orr & Laird) 26 John n
Orr Wm, carpenter, 102 Main e
Orth Charles, bds 10 Main e
Orton Mrs Ann (wid Henry) Beulah
Orton Thomas H, M D, 170 King w
Orttobin Mrs Elizabeth, 65 Jackson e
Ortwiner Chas, tinsmith, 56 Catharine s
Osborne A B, M D, City Hospital
Osborne Alex G, bookkeeper, 10 Herkimer

Osborne Mrs Eliza (wid James) 10 Herkimer
Osborne Francis, cooper, 3 South
Osborne Francis, laborer, 7 New
Osborne James, engineer, 29 Tisdale
Osborne James & Son, grocers, 4 James s
Osborne John Y (James Osborne & Son) h 10 Herkimer
Osborne, Killey Mfg Co (Wm Osborne, R B Osborne, J H Killey) mfrs engines, boilers, steam fire engines, scales, Barton e
Osborne R Bryson (Osborne, Killey & Co) 159 King w
Osborne Wm [Osborne, Killey & Co] s e cor Robinson and Macnab
Osborne W W, **law student,** 79 Robinson
Osier Tanse, **foreman Bell Telephone Co,** 40 Wilson
Osler Frank, file cutter, 117 Jackson e
Osler H S, solicitor, 16 Hughson s
Osler, Teezel & Harrison [B B Osler Q C, J V Teetzel, John Harrison] barristers, etc, Canada Life Chambers, James s
Otto Albert, carver, 49 Augusta
Otto Mrs N [wid George] 151 John n
Ouimet Felix, **shoemaker,** 24 Mulberry
Ouimet Francis, shoemaker, r 79 Caroline n
Overell Edward [E Overell & Co] h 15 West ave s
Overell E & Co, booksellers, 24½ King w
Overend George, laborer, 36 Charles
Overend Miles, deputy registrar, 57 Jackson w
Overholt John, laborer, bds 202 James n

Overholt Moses, tailor, 60 Victoria ave n
Owen James, laborer, 49 Ray n
Owens Henry, melter, 222 Hughson n
Owens James, stovemounter, 39 Bay n
Owens Wm, laborer, 126 Bay n
Oxley Mrs Elizabeth [wid Philip] 137 Rebecca
Oxley Frederick, grocer, 69 York
Packham Richard, cigarmaker, 109 George
Packham Thos, laborer, 7 Garth
Padden Patrick, laborer, 86 Maria
Padden Robt, bds Victoria hotel King e
Page James, 36 Steven
Page Mrs Sarah Ann [wid Isaac] 192 Main w
Page Mrs Sophia, 20 Catharine n
Pain Albert (Bowering & Pain) h 21 Main w
Paine George, salesman, 112 Wellington s
Paine Thomas B, bookkeeper, 166 James n
Painter James E, fireman G T R, 12½ Crooks
Painter John, bread pedler, 43 Hannah e
Palace Roller Rink, J M Webber, mangr, 4 Jackson w
Palladium of Labor, W H Rowe prop, Wanzer building, King e
Palm Wm, 94 Bay s
Palmer Benjamin, moulder, 31 Crooks
Palmer John C, engineer, 14 Colborne
Palmer Wm B, com traveler, 157 Main w
Paltridge Joseph, clerk, 28 Gore
Papps C S, clerk GTR, 45 Duke
Papps G S, barrister, 33 James s, h 3 Robinson
Papps Mrs Laura (wid Henry S) 45 Duke

Paquin Joseph, grocer, 287 Macnab n
Paradine Thomas, sexton Ascension Church, 128 John s
Parady Wm, carpenter, 42 James n
Pargeter Miss Emma, New York hair works, 83 King w
Parish Samuel, book dealer, 39 Robert
Park Mrs Elizabeth (wid Robt H) Markland hd Park
Park Henry G, teacher, n e cor Pearl and Canada
Park James D, asst insp weights and measures, 62 Locke n
Park John H (Lucas, Park & Co) Markland hd Park
Park & Lee, custom brokrs, 31 King e
Park Mrs Margaret [wid Wm] 38 Ferguson ave
Park Robt H, 35 Hannah w
Parke Walder [McGregor & Parke] 40 Victoria ave
Park Wm O, clerk, 38 Ferguson ave
Parker Mrs Charlotte, 9 Cherry
Parker David W, carpenter, 106 Emerald n
Parker Edward, harnessmaker, 29 Macnab s
Parker John E, mangr Meriden Britannia Co, h 11 Herkimer
Parker Robt & Co, steam dyers, 4 John n
Parker Mrs Sarah (wid James) Eliza
Parker Wm, blacksmith, 116 Wood e
Parker Wm, tinsmith, 100 Strachan e
Parkes James (Parkes & Macadams) h 63 Charles
Parkes & Macadams (Jas Parkes, A H Macadams) barristers, Hamilton Provident Chambers, 1 Hughson s *See card*

Parkhill A, salesman, 84 West ave n
Parkhill Mrs Mary A (wid Hamilton) 84 West ave n
Parkins Mrs Emma (wid John) 138 Mary
Parkinson Mrs E J, 28 Ray n
Parkinson Mrs I, 30 Ray n
Parkinson James, moulder, 119 Cannon w
Parkinson John, brushmaker, 103 Ferrie e
Parks David, shoemaker, 146 King Wm
Parks Samuel, machinist, 127 Ferguson ave
Parmenter A W, 116 Catharine s
Parmenter Chas, baker, 93 Elgin
Parnell Geo, shoemaker, bds 54 Park n
Parnell Samuel painter, 120 Hughson n
Parrett Benjamin, carter, 24 Steven
Parrett Wm, carter, 24 Steven
Parry John, laborer, s e cor Barton and Locomotive
Parry Thos, carpenter, 70 Park n
Partridge John, machinist, 148 Emerald n
Partridge Richard, engineer, 83 Simcoe e
Partridge Thos, engineer, 147 Ferrie e
Partridge Thos, wood turner, 134 Emerald n
Pascoe Wm, ropemaker, 7 Clark ave
Paslow Chas, painter, 149 Main e
Pass —— E K, watchmaker, bds 109 King Wm
Passmore Ed, blacksmith 215 John n
Passmore Frank, painter, bds 34 Barton e
Passmore Frank W, painter, 105 Catharine s
Passmore Mrs Jane (wid C W) 105 Catharine s

Pastine August, fruiterer, 150 King w
Patterson Abraham B, teller Merchants' Bank, 2 Hess s
Patterson Mrs Agnes (wid Peter) 75 Locke n
Paterson Andrew, teacher, 266 King e
Paterson Andrew, 78 Bay s
Patterson Bros (John & Thos Patterson) planing mills, builders, etc, foot of Lower Cathcart
Patterson Mrs Charlotte C (wid Alex) 137 York
Patterson Donald, laborer, 46 Caroline s
Patterson ——, laborer, Brock c
Patterson Harry C, clerk, bds 44 Main w
Patterson H M, teller Landed Banking Co, 2 Hess s
Patterson James, wool grader, 100 Cherry
Patterson James sr, carpenter, 100 Stinson
Patterson James jr, carpenter, 44 Alanson
Patterson James McC, com traveler, 68 Queen s
Paterson James S, bookkeepeer, 78 Bay s
Paterson John, machinist, 60 Ray s
Patterson John, 2 Hess s
Patterson John, cutter, 29 Inchbury n
Patterson John (Patterson Bros) bds St Nicholas hotel
Patterson John, carpenter, bds 60 James s
Patterson John sr (John Patterson & Co) 105 Cherry
Patterson John jr (John Patterson & Co) 101 Cherry
Patterson John B, manager Hyslop, Cornell & Co, s e cor Duke and Hess
Paterson John M, salesman, 4 Kelly

Patterson John & Co, tailors, 41 John s
Patterson Lauchlan, brakesman, 1 West ave s
Paterson Mark J, custom officer, 4 Kelly
Paterson Miss M M, dressmaker, 78 Bay s
Patterson Peter, carpenter, 44 Alanson
Patterson Robt, laborer, 374 Catharine n
Patterson Robt, patternmaker, South w n s nr Locke
Paterson G Stirling, stenographer, 78 Bay s
Patterson Thos, 119 East ave n
Patterson Thos, salesman, bds 48 James n
Patterson Thos, laborer, 213 Victoria ave n
Patterson Thos, moulder, 105 Cherry
Patterson Thomas jr (Patterson Bros) h 112 East ave n
Patterson Wm, teamster, 49 Sheaffe
Patterson Wm J, tailor, 105 Cherry
Paton James, polisher, r 103 Hunter w
Paton John, 22 Barton e
Paton Robt, laborer, 103 Hunter w
Patrick Nathaniel, packing case maker, bds Bruce e s nr Markland
Patrick Robt, laborer, Robinson s s nr Locke
Patten L H (Patten & Mewburn) h 194 King w
Patten & Mewburn (L H Patten, Sydney C Mewburn) barristers, Chancery Chambers 18-20 Hughson s
Patten Rowland, build'r, 23 Pearl s
Pattison Zaccheus, confectioner and cigar manfr, 71-73 King w, 69-71 Cannon w, h 65 Cannon w

Patton Andrew J, mail clerk CPR, hd Queen s e s
Patton Mrs Geo, 23 West ave s
Patton James, carpenter, 215 York
Patton Lorenzo, dyer, 61 Stuart w
Patton Robt, laborer, 46 Strachan e
Pauley Joseph, carpenter, 328 Hughson n
Pausell John, laborer, 190 Main w
Pawser William, laborer, 68 Bold
Paxton F H, clerk, 45 Wellington s
Payne Elford G, ins agent, 97 James n, h 3 West ave s *See card*
Payne John, janitor Ham Prov Loan Society
Payne Wm, coal and wood dealer, Cannon cor Cathcart, h 98 Ferguson ave
Payne Wm, engineer, 23 Pearl n
Payne Wm, nailer, 113 Napier
Payton Joseph, machinist, Grant
Pazius Alexander, upholsterer, 141 Catharine n
Peace D J, tobacconist, 88 King e, h 67 Vine
Peace John W, iron worker, 143 Locke n
Peace Wm, carpenter, 101 East ave n
Peace Wm, watchman, 39 Ferrie w
Peacock Arthur, butcher, 304 King e
Peacock Mrs Eliza, dry goods, 75 John s
Peacock John, health inspector, 95 West ave n
Pearce Alfred, telegraph operator 95 Wellington n
Pierce George, laborer, 77 Caroline n
Pearce George, baker, 142 Mary
Pearce Henry W, painter, 17 Park n
Pierce James, polisher, 78 Young

Pearce John, laborer, 44 Wellington n
Pearce Joseph, Queen s e s nr Concession
Peirce Mrs Julia P (wid George) 27 Jackson w
Pearce Lewis, laborer, 120 **Ferguson ave**
Pearce Richard, grocer, 142 Mary
Pearce Wm, engineer G T R, 86 George
Peard Edwin, caretaker Canada **Life Ins Co** building, South w n s nr Locke
Pearson Frederick, tobaccoroller, 13 Greig
Pearson George, carter, 10 Victoria ave s
Pearson Henry, hotel, 113 York
Pearson Henry, **shoecutter,** 7 Spring
Pearson James S, mangr Imperial Mineral Water Co, 21 Jackson w
Pearson John, accountant, real estate, rent, ins and commission agent, New Raymond sewing machine, chancery chambers, 18-20 Hughson s, h **Concession cor** Queen *See card*
Pearson John, **cab driver, 264** Hughson n
Pearson Joseph, laborer, ft Ferguson ave
Pearson **Thos,** glassblower, 100 Wood e
Pease Mrs Eliza, second hand **dealer,** 34 John n
Pease Williamson, barber, 4 Hughson n, h 34 John n
Peart Albert, machinist, 11 Vine
Peart Joseph, agt Eagle Steam washers and wringers, 13 Arcade, h 11 Pine
Peat Thos G, 127 John n
Peatro Zaisi, image maker, bds **Robt**

Pecover Fred C, salesman, 136 King e
Pecover Joseph, furniture manfr, 136 King e, **factory** 16 Upper Catchcart
Peden John, **provision dealer,** 107 Hess n
Peden Joseph, moulder, bds 119 Cannon w
Peden Mrs Mary [wid James] 35 Pearl s
Peden Thos, baggageman, 211 Bay n
Peebles C H, prop Wentworth warehouse, grocer, 39 Macnab n
Peebles & Hamilton, **builders,** 226 King Wm
Peebles John, watchmaker, jeweler and optican, 190 King e, h 28 Wellington s
Peebles Robert, **carpenter,** 28 Wellington s
Peebles Robert, **salesman,** 28 Wellington n
Peebles Wm, carpenter, 85 **East ave n**
Peel Wm, machinist, **88 Locke n**
Peene Alfred S, contractor, 24 Sheaffe
Peene G E, agent *World,* 24 Sheaffe
Peer James, cutter, 137 Hunter e
Peer Philip, carpenter, 45 Murray w
Pegler Mrs Emma **(wid Thomas)** 18 George
Pegler Wm, shirt ironer, 18 George
Pemberton James, laborer, 118 Queen n
Pender Michael, laborer, hd York **w canal**
Pennel Wm, soap maker, **Bruce**
Pennell **Wm** jr, laborer, **124** Hess n
Penney George, mechanic, **bds** 206 Macnab n
Penney Wm, machinist, Maple n s

Pennington & Baker (John D Pennington, Edward Baker) school furniture makers, r 79 James s
Penniugton John D, school furniture maker, h 11 Upper Cathcart
Pennington M A, ins agent, 51 James n, h 68 Jackson w
Pennington Printing Co, 51 James n
Penny Alexander, 97 Jackson e
Penny Alexander jr, saddler, 97 Jackson e
Penny Wm, joiner, 97 Jackson e
Pentecost Albert L, (Campbell & Pentecost), h 84 Cannon e
Pentecost Richard, 296 York
Pentecost Robt W, com traveler, 9 Bold
Pepper J Tolbert, manfg chemist 4 Crooks
Perior Joseph, laborer, 164 Catharine n
Perior Joseph, grocer, 40 Picton e
Perkins John, laborer, bds Locke s w·s nr Robinson
Perkins Mrs Sarah, (wid Wm), 133 West ave n
Perkins Wm, engine cleaner, 133 West ave n
Perrie Wm, shipper, bds 95 Jackson e
Perrin James, laborer, 1 Margaret
Perriton Walter H, upholsterer, 69 Hughson s
Perry Arthur, solderer, 145 West ave n
Perry Geo B, com traveler, 132 Main e
Perry George W, 132 Main e
Perry Mrs Julia, (wid Samuel) 145 West ave n
Perry Wm, solderer, 63 Emerald n

Perth Mutual Fire Insurance Co, Elford G Payne, agent, 97 James n
Pessell Wm J, laborer, 26 Ferguson ave
Peter R, machinist, 76 Macnab n
Peters Andrew S, laborer, Maple n s nr Garth
Pe ers Charles, teamster, 221 King e
Peters George, salesman, 5 Upper Cathcart
Peters Rudolph, machinst, 24 Vine
Peterson Geo E, wood sawyer, 44 Kelly
Petsley Henry, carpenter, bds 62 Cannon e
Pett James, mat manfr, 94 Murray e, h 65 Lower Cathcart
Pettigrew Mrs Anna, (wid Hy), 172 Rebecca
Pettigrew John, wood buyer, 71 West ave n
Pettigrew Robert C, wood and coal yard, cor Wilson and West ave n
Pettinger George, 97 Bay n
Pettitt John, dairyman, 228 Main w
Pfann George, cabinetmaker, 96 Caroline s
Pfeifer Frederick, laborer, 9 Harriet
Pfeifer John, laborer, Duke n s nr Garth
Phelan James, steward Royal Hotel, 66 Catharine n
Phelan John, scalemaker, 5 Cannon e
Phibbs Geo D, wheelwright, 40 Barton e
Philip David, machinist, 49 Markland
Philips Alexander L, blacksmith, 9 Wilson
Phillips Charles, carpenter, 164 King Wm

Phillips David, carpenter, 22 Ferguson ave
Phillips Edward, heater, 171 Garth e s nr Maple
Phillips Mrs Ellen, (wid Joseph), 54 Ferrie e
Phillips George, merchant tailor, 242 King e, h 157 West ave n
Phillips Henry, machinist, 108 Market
Phillips James, (Phillips & Mottashed,) 11 West ave n
Phillips James, machinist, 33 West ave n
Phillips John, blacksmith helper, 171 Garth e s nr Maple
Phillips John, sailmaker, 33 Macauley w
Phillips John, stovemounter, 110 Wood e
Phillips Joseph, glassblower, 54 Ferrie e
Phillips Joseph, locksmith, bds 208 Macnab n
Phillips Joshua A, carpenter, 7 Upper Cathcart
Phillips Markham, laborer, 231 Wellington n
Phillips & Mottashed, (James Phillips, Chas Mottashed) builders, 184 King Wm
Philips William, butcher, 256 York
Phillips V O, barber, 38 Merrick
Philp Frank, (Philp & Son), h 40 Young
Philp H W, bookkeeper, 15 Barton e
Philp James, (Philp & Son) h 40 Young
Philp Joseph, salesman, 15 Barton e
Philp & Son, (James & Frank,) harness and saddlery, 3 York and 4 Market
Philp T Frank, salesman 15 Barton e
Philp Wm, M D, cor York and Hess

Philps Wm, laborer, 136 Picton e
Philps Wm jr, laborer, 136 Picton e
Phœnix Albert H, carpenter, 309 John n
Phœnix Fire Insurance Co, Gillespie & Powis, agents, 31 King e
Phœnix Insurance Co, (Marine), J B Fairgrieve, agent, 6 James s
Phœnix Wm, patternmaker, 120 Ferrie e
Photoglyptic Co, R Laidlaw, E S Eveleigh, props, 77 King w
Pickard John, miller, 26 Tom
Pickard Wm, bds 172 York
Pickering Thos, laborer, Sherman
Piercy Chas, printer, 35 Steven
Piercy James W, clerk, 92 Wellington s
Pierson Hugh, tailor, 16 John s
Pigott M A, contractor, 83 Park n
Pilgrim Bros, Hamilton Mineral Water Co, (F M, S F, E F Pilgrim) r Spring
Pilgrim Edward, manufacturer, 1 Spring
Pilgrim Fredk M, manufacturer, 1 Spring
Pilgrim Robt, 9 Young
Pilgrim Sydney F, manufacturer, Hughson d
Pilkey Alfred, agent, 37 East ave
Pilkey Joseph B, agent, 127 Bay s
Pillman Thos K, butcher, 208 King w
Pilton Wm, laborer, 1 241 Bay n
Pim Mrs Hannah (wid Wm) 70 Hannah w
Pinch Edmund, machinist, 23 Wellington s
Pinch James C, policeman, 85 West ave n

Pinch John, fitter, 224 Hughson n
Pingle Mrs Henrietta (wid Jacob) 98 Market
Pinkett James, laborer, 159 Hunter w
Pipon J H, accountant Bank of Montreal, 44 Hannah w
Pitcher Chas (Miller & Pitcher) bds 60 James s
Pitt Mrs Theresa (wid Wm) 132½ Macnab n
Place John, laborer, 144 Picton e
Plank John, grocer, 107 Hunter w
Plant John, wood dealer, 15 Cherry
Plant Richard, manfr, 118 Wellington s
Plastow Chas A, carpenter, 205 Main w
Plastow Jos, caretaker Court House, 34 Hughson s
Plater Chas, shoemaker, 49 Florence
Plater Chas, salesman, 49 Florence
Platt Mrs Hannah (wid Thos) fancy goods, 73 York
Pietz Michael, tailor, 7 Kelly
Poag Mrs Janet (wid James) 183 Mary
Poag John, carpenter, 183 Mary n
Pocock John G, butcher, 15 Augusta
Pocock Stephen H (S H Pocock & Co) h 19 Bay n
Pocock S H & Co (S H Pocock, J P Haynes) Beaver Saw Works, 22-24 Market
Pointer James E, traveler 42 West ave s
Pointer John, laborer, 47 Little Wm
Points Geo, moulder, 27 Wood e
Poland Wm, mechanical engineer GTR, hd Hess s e s

Police Court, James Cahill, police magistrate, Thos Beasley, clerk, King Wm cor Mary
Police Stations, No 1 (Headquarters) City Hall; No 2, James cor Stuart; No. 3, King Wm, cor Mary; No 4 11 Napier
Polkingham Miss Carrie, 31 Catharine n
Polkingham Wm, plumber, 79a John n
Pollard Lawrence, laborer, 129 Queen n
Pollard Robt, carpenter, 43 Florence
Pollington Chas, brickmaker, 150 Jackson w
Pollington Noah, laborer, 154 Jackson w
Pollitt Mrs Mary (wid John) 154 Park n
Pollitt Stephen, plumber, 234½ James n
Pollock John, tinsmith, bds 13 Gore
Polucco Antoine, cabinetmaker, 14 Pearl s
Pomford John, loom fixer, 259 Mary
Poole A L, clerk, Franklin House
Poole Daniel, prop Franklin House, 94 King w
Pope Ed, cabinetmaker, 160 James n
Pope Wm H, laborer, Wentworth
Porteous David, 50 Murray
Porteous James, machinist, 228 York
Porteous Thos, butcher, 40-42 Bay n
Porteous Thomas jr, butcher, 40 Bay n
Porter Edward, collarmaker, 241 Catharine n
Porter George, machinist, Robinson n s w Locke
Porter Samuel, baker, 83 Cherry

Porter Wm, machinist, 95 Robinson
Porter W H, painter, end Ferrie e
Post Andrew F, livery stable, 12 Rebecca
Post Chas, livery, 26 Rebecca
Post Justice, engineer, 72 Elgin
Post Office, King cor John s
Pothica Wm, burnisher, 63a East ave n
Potter Alvin, ins agent, **bds** 43 John n
Potter Mrs Bessie (wid Wm) tailoress, 54 Florence
Potter Geo, carpenter, 150 King Wm
Potter George C, **painter,** 97 York
Potter Henry, laborer, 232 Barton e
Potter James, brickmaker, 1 Little Wellington
Potter James, laborer, 35 Kelly
Potter John, gardener, 208 Main e
Potter Samuel, laborer, bds **172** Bay n
Potter Walter, laborer, 168 King Wm
Potter Wm, machinist, 26 Locke n
Potter Wm, rope maker, 10 Murray e
Pottinger John, laborer, 5 Smith ave
Pottruff Jonathan, salesman, 97½ Hunter e
Pottruff Levi, clerk, 42 Hunter e
Pottruff Mrs Rath (wid Levi) 44 Hunter e
Poulter Alfred, bookkeeper, 55½ Lower Cathcart
Pounden Mrs Harriet A (wid John W) 24 Main w
Povey Wm H, painter, 33 Barton e
Powel Mrs Ann (wid Thomas) 107 Hunter e
Powell Chas, machinist, 39 John n

Powell G W, **blind** manfr, **220** King e
Powell Robert, butcher, **Main** e of Wentworth
Powell R T S, florist, cor Hunter and Hughson s, h Mountain tp
Powell Thomas, laborer, 37 Burlington w
Powell Wm R, 70 Wellington n
Power Nicholas, Markland n s w Locke
Powers John, shoemaker, **bds** 220 Macnab n
Powis Alfred, (Gillespie & Powis) h Concession cor Hess
Powis Charles, clerk, 118 Catharine s
Powis Frederick, accountant, 118 Catharine s
Powncely Frederick, cutter, 121 York
Poynton John, laborer, 47 Little Wm·
Poynton Joseph, butcher, Burlington n
Pratt Bros, boots and shoes, 60-62 King e
Pratt Joseph, laborer, end Ferrie e
Pratt T H (Pratt & Watkins) h 6 East ave n
Pratt & Watkins (T H Pratt, F W Watkins) dry goods and clothing, 16-18 James n
Pratt Wm, barber, 3 John n, h 4 Pine
Pray R & Son, undertakers, 29 King w *See adv't*
Pray Richard, 80 Hughson s
Pray W R (R Pray & Son) h 29 King w
Precore Joseph, grocer, 240 King e
Prentice J A, bookkeeper, 18 James s
Prentice Joseph, sergeant police, 81 George
Presby'n Mission Church, end Herkimer and Wentworth n

Prescott Thos, cotton operative, bds 62 Robert
Press Richard H, contractor, 76 Ferguson ave
Preston Joseph, watchman, 97 Cannon w
Preston William, laborer, 41 Park s
Price John, dyer, 97 Elgin
Price John, carpenter, Hess s w s nr Concession
Price Wm, bricklayer, 228 Barton e
Priddis Mrs M A (wid John) 122 East ave n
Priestland Harry, laborer, 38 Ferrie w
Priestland Thos G, mechanic, 139 Park n
Priestman James, butcher, Wood market John s, h Mountain top
Prillipp Herman, laborer, 33 Locomotive
Prindiville John, carpenter, 69 Cherry
Pringle Mrs P E, 4 Hannah e
Pringle R A, barrister, Victoria Chambers, 31 James s, h 4 Hannah e
Pringle Robt, bookkeeper, 158 Rebecca
Pringle Mrs Sarah H (wid John) 157 John n
Proctor Henry, 47 West ave n
Proctor James, boilermaker, 138 Robert
Proctor John [John Proctor & Co] h Cedar Grove, King e of Wentworth
Proctor John & Co, Railway supplies, 2½ James s
Proctor John jr, brakeman, 29 Catharine n
Proctor Mrs Margaret [wid John] 29 Catharine n
Proctor Robert, sawyer, 47 West ave n
Proctor William, 29 Catharine n

Proctor W G (Laidlaw Mnfg Co) 179 Main e
Pronguey J C, coachmaker, 96 James n
Proper Wm, Continental Hotel, 162-4 Bay n
Providence, Washington Insurance Co, David McLellan, agent, 84 James n
Provost Andrew, barber, 56 Robinson
Prowse Henry J, patternmaker, 42 Emerald n
Pryke John, 124 Wellington s
Pugh Thos, carter, 90 Bold
Pugh Wm, shoemaker, 130-2 Barton e
Pulkingham Mrs A (wid James) 79a John n
Pulkingham Wm, plumber, 79a John n
Pulling Mark, foreman Robert Thomson's, 21 Napier
Pumfrey Thomas, moulder, 12 New
Punshon P H, salesman, 73 East ave s
Purnell Samuel, painter, 120 Hughson n
Purrott George (Easter & Purrott) h 148 Duke
Purvis James, carpenter, 229 Victoria ave n
Purvis Samuel, bds 215 James n
Pyle David, salesman, 44 Market
Pyle George, machinist, 44 Market
Pyle George, bartender, 44 Market
Qua Jas, sawyer, 37 West ave n
Quarry Joseph, com traveler, 39 Market
Quarrier John, miller's agent, 29 Main e, h 35 Wilson
Quebec Fire Assurance Co, J T Routh agent, 16 James s
Quebec Fire Assurance Co, M A Pennington agent, 51 James n

CITY OF HAMILTON.

Queen Fire & Life Ins Co, George A Young agent, 5 King w

Queen Fire & Life Ins Co, R Benner agent, 6 Main e

Quigley Matthew, laborer, ft of Wellington n

Quigley Michael, moulder, 139 Wellington n

Quilter Thomas, laborer, r 185 Bay n

Quimby A C & Co, tobacconist, 27 James n

Quimby Rebecca (wid A C) 16 Vine

Quinlan Miss Ann, 87 York

Quinlan C, laborer, 204 Hughson n

Quinlan Michael, laborer, 113 Simcoe e

Quinlan Wm, boilermaker, 213 Mary n

Quinn Alex, moulder 63 West ave n

Quinn Frank, patternmaker, 274 King e

Quinn John, patternmaker, 77 Victoria ave n

Quinn Mrs Maria, Main e of Wentworth

Quinn Richard, hotel, 307-309 James n

Quinn Richard, machinist, 5 Ferrie e

Quinn Wm, fitter, 315 York

Quirk James, brakeman, bds 153 King e

Quirk John, finisher, 105 Locke n

Rabitoy James, barber, 21 O'Reilly

Racey J Hamiton, machinist, bds 285 York

Rackley John, laborer, 64 Hannah w

Radford Wm, baker, 117 York

Raidigan John, tinsmith, 68 Mary, h 44 Wilson

Rae W C, turnkey jail

Rake James, shoemaker, 7 Simcoe e

Ralph Frank, teamster, 154 Bay n

Ralph Wm, glass stainer, 9 Nightingale

Ralston Ed, laborer, bds 28 Emerald n

Ralston Henry (Ralston & Co) h 114 John s

Ralston & Irwin [J S Ralston, Robt Irwin] real estate agents, 31 John s *See advt*

Ralston Joseph S (Ralston & Irwin) h 63 Hunter e

Ralston R & Co (Robert & Hy Ralston) stove polish and blacking manfrs, 114 John s

Ralston Robt (Ralston & Co) 114 John s

Ralston Thos, caretaker Central School, 40 Bold

Ram Alfred, carpenter, 50 Robinson

Ram Alfred G, printer, 164 Hunter w

Ram Ed J, carpenter, 162 Hunter w

Ram Henry, carpenter, 50 Robinson

Ramsay A G, F I A, president and managing director Canada Life Assurance Co, h Dunedin, 157 James s

Ramsay Alex, supt Canada Life Assurance Co, h 134 Bay s

Randall David, nailer, 9 Inchbury n

Randall Jacob H, 45 Wellington s

Randall James, com traveler, 49 Wellington n

Randall Mrs Margaret (wid Chas) 190 Hunter w

Randall Nicholas F, feeder, 28 Locomotive

Randall Ralph W, carpenter, 42 Tisdale

Randall Wm, laborer, 280 King w
Randall Wm, laborer, 190 Hunter w
Ranger Chas, carpenter, 141 Park n
Rankin Douglas, moulder, bds 21 John n
Rankin J J, assistant accountant, Bank of Montreal, 61 George
Rankin John, laborer, West
Rankine J, teller Bank of Montreal, 19 Nelson ave
Raphael Isaac, tailor, 96 John s
Rastrick Francis R, 22 Maria
Rastrick F J, architect, 22 Maria
Ratcliffe James, laborer, 115 Bold s s
Rattenbury J W, wagonmaker, 22 Hunter e
Rattray & Geiger (M L Rattray, E A Geiger) prop Hamilton Business College, 2½ James s
Rattray M L (Rattray & Geiger) h 2½ James s
Raw Robt & Co, book and job printers, 28-30 John n
Raw Robt sr, bookkeeper, 23 Bay s
Raw Robt jr (Robt Raw & Co) h 94 Park n
Raw Robt M, printer, 94 Park n
Ray Arthur, salesman, bds 138 Jackson e
Ray Henry A, buffer, 22 Emerald n
Ray Joseph, huckster, 128 Emerald n
Ray Joseph, laborer, 132 Emerald n
Ray Peter, fireman, 47½ Catharine s
Raycroft Richard, grocer, 65 Herkimer
Raycroft Thos J, machinist, 65 Herkimer
Raymond James, gardener, cor Caroline and Markland

Raymond Montague, piano tuner, 53 Wellington s
Rayner Geo J, grocer, cor Steven and King Wm
Rayner Jos W, com traveler, 9 Steven
Read Geo, carpenter, 115 King w
Read Geo, hackman, 10 Main w
Read Mrs Mary (wid Robt) 115 King w
Read S jr, accountant Bank of Commerce
Reardon Mrs Catharine (wid Cornelius) 29 Sheaffe
Reardon Mrs Helen (wid Dennis) 82 Peter
Reardon John, moulder, 49 Cannon w
Reardon John, boilermaker, 356 Hughson n
Reardon Michael, driver, 51 Inchbury n
Reardon Michael, 360 Hughson n
Reardon Morris, hotel, 390 James n
Reader Robert, moulder, 202 Wellington n
Reardon Terrance, sailor, 48 Guise
Reasnor, W R, 196 Main e
Reuburn John, coachman, 181 King w
Regan Miss C R, 170 Bay n
Registry Office, Court House
Rehder Christopher, mechanic, 34 Little Wm
Reche Mrs Catharine, (wid Anthony), 119 Mary
Reche John A, (R M Taylor & Co), 119 Mary
Reche Thos, mangr Grand Opera House, h 119 Mary
Reckhow Isaac, preserver, 77 Jackson e
Reddall & McKeown, (Thos Reddall, Arthur H McKeown) stove dealers and tinsmiths, 112 King w

CITY OF HAMILTON. 189

Reddall Thos, (Reddall & McKeown), h 51 Hunter e
Redden Daniel, glassblower, Bay n
Redden Timothy, laborer, 1 Devonport
Redding J, gardener, 17 Grove
Reddy James, (Sullivan & Reddy) 142 John n
Redfield James, burnisher, 84 Wellington n
Red Star Steamship Line, W J Gran , agent, 33 James n
Reed John propr Reed's Hotel, 56 King Wm
Reed Joseph D, conductor GTR 10 Locomotive
Rees Evans, printer, 28 Caroline n
Reeves Arthur L, baker, 190 King w
Reeves Arthur L, jr, 41 Young
Reeves Benjamin, laborer, bds 142 Cannon e
Reeves Charles, teamster, 142 Cannon e
Reeves Richard, **baker,** 190 King w
Reeves Samuel, baker, 15 Little Peel
Reeves Wm, baker, 1 Hess
Reformed Episcopal Mission and Sunday School, 119 Hunter w
Reid Alex, bookkeeper, 45 Hess n
Reid **Alexander,** cutter, 146½ **York**
Reid **Alex, market gardener,** hd **York** s s nr cemetery
Reid **C,** M D, 55 Hughson n
Reid **Angus,** gardener, Barton **e**
Reid Angus, teamster, 58 Hughson s
Reid Mrs Ann, 320 Hughson n
Reid, Birely & Co, (W G Reid, G F Birely), tobaccos and tobacconists sundries, wine and spirit manfrs, 104 King **e**

Reid Charles, foreman, 61 Robert
Reid **David, pork** packer, bds 121 Rebecca
Reid Donald, gardener, hd **York** s s nr cemetery
Reid Mrs Elsie, (wid W W), 25 Wellington n
Reid Fletcher, laborer, **73** Cherry
Reid Frederick, pedlar, 218 King w
Reid George, carriage maker, **77** Merrick s s nr Park
Reid George, gardener, hd **York** s s nr cemetery
Reid **George,** printer, Ennis & Cook
Reid Geo **Jas,** express messenger 66 Vine
Reid & Halliday, carpenters, etc, (W J Reid, W Halliday), 1 1½ Main e
Reid Henry, machinist, 149 King Wm
Reid Mrs Isabella, (wid Alex), 72 Elgin
Reid Mrs Isabella, (wid Peter), 10 Liberty
Reid James, carpenter, 100 Caroline s
Reid James, fireman N & N W, 143 Robert
Reid Mrs Jane, (wid Robt), 143 Robert
Reid John, glassfinisher, **44** Picton w
Reid John, **moulder,** bds **19** Hughson n
Reid John, railroader, bds 61 Caroline
Reid John B, burnisher, 13 Steven
Reid John S, com traveler, **188** King w
Reid Joseph W, carpenter, 116 Locke n
Reid Peter, carpenter, 10 Liberty
Reid Mrs Peter, 8 Liberty

Reid Robt, butcher, Sherman
Reid Robt, carpenter, 140 King Wm
Reid Thos, machinst, 111 James
Reid Thos W, carpenter, 8 Cherry
Reid William H, compositor, 45 Hess n
Reid Wm, carpenter, 51 Macauley w
Reid William, foreman Victor Engine Works, 75 Cannon e
Reid Wm, teamster, 60 Hughson s
Reid Wm, 206 East ave n
Reid Wm G, detective, 44 Emerald n
Reid W G, (Reid, Birely & Co) 31 Victoria Ave s
Reid W J (Reid & Halliday), 131 Main e
Reid W J, printer, 107 Rebecca
Reid Mrs, 295 King Wm
Reiger Edward, driver, 39 Florence
Reinholt Mrs Christina, (wid Henry), Markland n s nr Garth
Reinholt Henry, shoemaker, Markland n s nr Garth
Reinholt Hermann, carpenter, Markland n s nr Garth
Reinholt Robt, presser, 62 Ray s
Reliance Hall, 1 Rebecca
Relph Mrs Margaret (wid Walter) 192 Hunter w
Rendell Wm H, blacksmith, 8 Locke n
Renner Chas, teamster, 17 Tisdale
Renner Mrs Philipina, 282a King e
Rennie Wm, letter carrier, 247 Bay n
Renton Thos, carpenter, 239 Bay n
Renwick Alex K, checker N & N W R, 255 York
Renwick Mrs Elizabeth, grocer, 255 York

Renwick Thos, engineer, 133 Wellington n
Renwick Wm A, porter, 147 Hunter w
Repp Geo, merchant tailor, 113 James n
Resnor W R, salesman, Main cor Erie ave
Reubin L, dealer, 45 Cherry
Rewbury Wm H, checker GTR, 118 Emerald n
Reynolds Mrs Ellen (wid John) 36 Bay s
Reynolds Geo, butcher, Robinson n s nr Locke
Reynolds James, laborer, 79 Caroline s
Reynolds James T, painter, 175 Hunter w
Reynolds Robt, baker, 31 Tisdale
Reynolds Mrs Sophia (wid Isaac) 12 Charles
Reynolds Thos W, M D. asst physician, Asylum for the Insane
Rheader Chris, nickelplater, 14 Little Wm
Rhodes Geo, painter, bds 134 King Wm
Rhynd James G H, fireman GTR, St Mary's Lane
Riach Geo, salesman, 61 Park n
Riach John, general dealer, 8 Macnab n and 188 King e, h 14 Augusta
Riach Wm, 61 Park n
Rice Frederick, laborer, 82 Caroline n
Rice James, janitor, 97 James n
Richards Ed T, packer, 156 Mary
Richards Frederick, woodworker, Garth e s nr Markland
Richards G H, moulder, 160 Macnab n
Richards Wm, laborer, 4 Aurora
Richardson Andrew, checker, 37 Picton e

Richardson Chas E, tobacconist, 258 King w
Richardson Geo, stoves, etc, 36-40 King Wm
Richardson Geo, watchmaker, 156 James n, h 26 Strachan e
Richardson Geo H, miller, 226 Main w
Richardson Mrs Isabella (wid Thos) 47 Catharine n
Richardson James, gardener, bds Concession s s nr Bay
Richardson Mrs Jessie (wid Wm 58 George
Richardson John, machinist, 47 Catharine n
Richardson Mrs **Mary (wid Wm)** 26 Hess n
Richardson Matthew, **shoemaker** 260 King w
Richardson Wm, hackman, 29 Hess n
Richardson Wm, patent medicines, 2 Catharine s
Richardson Wm, bricklayer, 329 Hughson n
Richardson Wm, laborer, 13 Macnab s
Riche C, harnessmaker, 337 John n
Richelieu and Ontario Navigation Co, Geo McKeand, agent, 57 James n
Richmond Alfred, grocer, 247 James n
Richmond **Arthur**, butcher, 276 York
Richmond Geo sr, moulder, 177 Cannon e
Richmond Geo jr, printer, 91½ Victoria ave n
Richmond John, butcher, 121 Hunter e
Richmond Thos, grocer, 369-371 James n
Richter Gottlieb, shoemaker, 49 Catharine n
Richter T, saloonkeeper, James cor Vine

Rickards Jos, com traveler, 82 Tisdale
Rickerson Ed, machine operator, 16 Sheaffe
Ricketts Frederick J, painter, 11 Rebecca
Rickett ———, **laborer**, 107 Strachan e
Riddell Mrs Ann (wid John) 160 Hunter w
Riddell James, laborer, 312 King Wm
Riddell J E, stoves and tins, 214 King e, h 24 East ave n
Riddell John, stock broker, 4 Main e, h 141 James s
Riddell John, traveler, Wood & Leggat
Riddell Jos, tinsmith, 28½ **East ave n**
Riddell Thos, moulder, 67a **East ave n**
Riddell Wm, moulder, 110 Victoria ave n
Riddell ———, carpenter, 292 Mary n
Ridler Wm, shoemaker, 156 Jackson w
Ridley Hy T, M D, 31 Main w
Riddle Mrs Ann (wid John) 1 51 Young
Riddle Mrs, 168 Park n
Ridout H, clerk Bank of Hamilton, Bay cor Jackson
Rieger Alfred, blacksmith, 32 Hess n
Ried Alfred, machinist, 19 O f rd
Rieger Chas, bartender, 26 Peter
Rieger Christopher, laborer, 19 Napier
Riehl Jacob, laborer, 21 Burlington w
Rigg Isaac, moulder, 60 Florence
Rigg Wm, car inspector, 180 John n
Rigsby John, builder, **133 King** Wm
Riley Mrs Sarah (wid Thos) 221½ Main w

Ringer E, melter, 12 Barton e
Ringrose Horace, stovemounter, 34 Mulberry
Rinner Chas, 282a King e
Rioch George D, printer, 115 Maria
Ripley Abraham, moulder, 158 Victoria ave n
Ripley James W, moulder, 135 Emerald n
Ripley John, carpenter, 228 Main w
Rissman Rudolph, asst emigration agent, 86 Hunter e
Ritchie Cameron, moulder, 44 Magill
Ritchie Mrs Jessie (wid James) 26 Charles
Ritchie Mrs Mary (wid Thos) 44 Magill
Ritchie Michael, machinist, 120 Queen n
Ritch Robert, carpenter, bds 102 Market
Riviere John, laborer, 67 Hannah w
Roach Andrew P, hotel, 67 Stuart
Roach Bernard, moulder, bds 82 Hughson n
Roach David J, livery keeper, 42 Hughson s
Roach George, 43 Barton w
Roach John, laborer, 40 Burlington w
Roach John, laborer, 312 Hughson n
Roach Michael, laborer, 104 Picton e
Roach Patrick, laborer, 11 Wood w
Roach Patrick, laborer, 2 Brock
Roantree Charles, brushmaker, 29 Queen s
Rob Roy Hotel (A McDonald prop) 89 John s
Robb Andrew, engineer, s w cor Hess and Robinson
Robb Wm, foreman *Spectator* office, 7 East ave s

Robbins Alford, engineer, 123 Wellington n
Robins Frank, shipper, 24 Wilson
Robbins Henry, finisher, 187 King e
Robins James, butcher, 110 George
Robins John, tinsmith, 63 East ave n
Robbins Joseph sr, shoemaker, 13 Florence
Robbins Joseph jr, compositor, 13 Florence
Robbins N B, 38 Wellington s
Robins Samuel, tinsmith, 24 Wilson
Robbins Mrs Sarah, laundry, 187 King e
Robins Thomas, tinsmith, 95 Robert
Robins Wm, tailor, 95 Robert
Robins William, carpenter, 28 Wilson
Robertson Alexander, carpenter, 10 Augusta
Roberts Albert, United States Consul, GTR station, h 128 Hughson n
Roberts Daniel H C, clerk, 78 Tisdale
Roberts David E, (Hurd & Roberts) h 46 Emerald s
Roberts Mrs Dora, 78 Tisdale
Roberts Mrs Ester (wid Wm) 7 Wilson
Roberts Captain John, 63 Hannah w
Roberts Paul, clerk GTR, 128 Hughson n
Roberts William, laborer, 239 Cannon e
Robarts Wm P, clerk, 80 Main w
Robertson Mrs Agnes (wid Jas) 69 Wellington n
Robertson Alexander, stonecutter 28 Tisdale
Robertson Archibald, ship build'r, 23 Brock

Robertson A W, bookkeeper, 19 Walnut s
Robertson Chas, lumber dealer, 79 Bay n
Robertson Charles, teacher, 126 Hughson n
Robertson Duncan, machinist, 19 Pearl s
Robertson Duncan, carpenter, 171 East ave n
Robertson Edward, **carpenter**, 137 Wellington n
Robertson Mrs **George**, 127 King e
Robertson H H (Robertson & Robertson) barrister, Rannoch Lodge, hd John s
Robertson James (A R Kerr & Co) h 35 Main w
Robertson Mrs James, **69 Wellington** n
Robertson James, patternmaker, 25 O'Reilly
Robertson James, moulder, 124 Rebecca
Robertson John, engineer, 86 **Peter**
Robertson John, bricklayer, bds 49 Hughson n
Robertson Malcolm, grain pedler, 45 Sheaffe
Robertson Mrs Margaret (wid James) 25 O'Reilly
Robertson P T, grocer, 212 King w
Robertson **R A**, clerk, 127 King e
Robertson Robert, **watchmaker**, 69 Wellington n
Robertson Robert, **stonemason**, 28 Tom
Robertson & Robertson, (Thomas, Q C, and H H) barristers, Court House
Robertson Thomas, Q C, (Robertson & Robertson) Rannoch Lodge, hd John s
Robertson Wm, birch beer manf, 90 Ferguson ave

Robertson **Wm**, bookkeeper, 109 Victoria ave n
Robertson Wm, tailor, r 87 Hughson n
Robertson Wm, ship carpenter, 50 Burlington w
Robertson Wm, salesman, 96 Queen s
Robertson Wm **L**, salesman, 96 Queen s
Robinson Annie, matron county jail
Robinson Mrs Catharine (wid James) 39 Picton w
Robinson Chas, laborer, 298 John n
Robinson Ed, shipper, 20 Victoria ave n
Robinson **E F**, druggist, 36 James n
Robinson Geo, bandmaster, 19 Barton e
Robinson Geo J, wood turner, 19 Barton e
Robinson Hy, bricklayer, 148½ John n
Robinson Herbert, com traveler, 39 East ave s
Robinson Hugh, plasterer, 33 Little Wm
Robinson James, moulder, 100 West ave n
Robinson James, moulder, 84 Jackson e
Robinson Miss Jane, 54 Emerald n
Robinson **John**, tinsmith, bds 89 Cannon e
Robinson **John**, tinsmith, **64** Main w
Robinson John, 20 Victoria ave n
Robinson John H, Flamboro Hotel, 53 Merrick
Robinson Jonathan E, 36 George
Robinson Miss Mary, 36 George
Robinson Mrs Mary (wid Chas) 3 Pine
Robinson Robert, stonemason, 151 Victoria ave n

25

Robinson Robt G, cutter, 212½ King Wm
Robbins Mrs S C, tobacconist, 210 King e
Robinson Thos, Robinson House hotel, 47-49 Merrick
Robinson Wm, 72 Catharine s
Robinson Wm, acting sergeant police, 116 Emerald n
Robinson Wm, brakeman, 197 Wellington n
Robinson Wm, carpenter, 242 Barton e
Robinson Wm, foreman N & N W, 85 Wellington n
Robinson Wm, laborer, 197 Wellington
Robinson Wm, clerk, 282 Macnab n
Robinson Wm A, 6 Hannah e
Robinson Wm D, 65 Bold
Robinson W H, clerk, 19 Barton e
Robinson W W, (D Moore & Co), h 39 East ave s
Robinson Hy J, waiter, bds 261 Bay n
Robinson James, brickmaker, 20 Inchbury s
Robitaille A, laborer, 350 Hughson n
Robson David, laborer, 174 Hughson n
Robson George, laborer, 74 Cherry
Robson John, hostler, bds Union Hotel
Robson Robert, driver, 83 Market
Robson Thomas, carpenter, Grant
Robson W B, clerk, bds 66 King w
Robson W E, clerk, bds Russel House, King w
Robson Wm, patternfitter, 65 East ave n
Robson W B, miller, 278 York, h 71 Pearl n

Rock Michael, harness maker, 87 Bay n
Rock Thos, druggist, 64 Emerald n
Rodger Robt, blacksmith, 67 Barton w
Rodger, John, blacksmith, 52-54 Market, h 48 Market
Roderick Edward, laborer, bds 109 King Wm
Roderick Francis E, lather, 90 Hess n
Roderick John, tailor, 136 John n
Rodgers Alex, machinst, Robinson n s nr Garth
Rodgers Chas, laborer, bds 67 Stuart w
Rogers Miss G, fancy goods, 115 James n
Rodgers James, plasterer, 128½ Emerald n
Rodgers James, teamster, bds 29 Railway
Rodgers James H, baker, 154 York
Rodgers Patrick, laborer, 168 Catharine n
Rodgers Mrs Sarah, (wid Wm,) 92 West ave n
Rodgers ——, laborer, 145 Macauley e
Rodwell Wm, painter, 147 Main e
Roe Mrs Caroline A, (wid John A), 91 Caroline s
Roe Mrs Eliza, fancy goods, 216 King
Roe George, tailor and renovator, 218 King e
Roe Wm, moulder, 237 Hughson n
Roehm Lawrence, tailor, 171 Hughson n
Roehmer Mrs Amelia, (wid Louis) 70 Cherry
Roehmer, Herman, bartender, 70 Cherry
Rhoemer Louis, carpenter, 70 Cherry

Rogers Henry, gardener, end Wilson
Rogers Judson, porter, bds 57 John s
Rogers Mrs Martha, (wid Geo,) 48 Hannah w
Rogers Robt, 44 West ave n
Rogers Samuel C, manager Hart Emery Wheel Co, 75 Herkimer
Rohr Mrs Fredk, 28 Canada
Rohr Henry, blacksmith, 28 Canada
Roland J, basket maker, 282 James n
Rolls Samuel S, carriagetrimmer, 130 Hunter e
Rolstin John A, E I Thompson, Gore cor Hughson
Rolston Robert, upholsterer, 48 Florence
Roman Mrs Ann, 61 Merrick
Roman Catholic Bishop's Palace, 25 Sheaffe
Roman Jno W, mechanic, bds 61 Merrick
Rome George, carpenter, bds 57 John s
Ronald James, grocer, 37 Bay n
Ronald John W, 69 Locomotive
Ronald Wm, engineer, 127 Cannon e
Ronald Wm, general dealer, 20 York, h 37 Bay n
Ronan John, grocer, 152 Cannon e
Ronan Miss Nora, 103 Wellington n
Ronan P, flour and feed, 2 Market sq, h 136 Cannon e
Roney Albert, tailor, 52 Walnut s
Rooks David, mechanic, 55 Lower Cathcart
Rooney George Sidney, salesman, 34 Bay n
Rooney John, hostler, 55 Macnab n
Rooney Michael, moulder, bds 19 Hughson n

Roos S B, watchmaker, 224 King e, h 21 Bay n
Roos Solomon, com traveler, 30 East ave s
Rosbrook George, laborer, 103 George
Rose Charles, policeman, 47 Caroline n
Rose John, brakeman, 168 West ave n
Rose Richard H, barber, bds 99 York
Rosebrugh J W, M D, 52 James s
Rosenberger Mrs Harriet (wid Walter) 1 Queen s
Rosenberger Joseph, sawyer, bds 1 Queen s
Rosenstadt Edward, com travel'r bds 53 John s
Rosenstadt Mrs Edward, clothing, 32 King Wm
Rosenzweig Max, rag pedler, Burlington n
Ross Adam H, painter, 104 Ferguson ave
Ross Alex M, (Ross Bros) h 68 Colborne
Ross Andrew, carriagemaker, 167 King e, h 39 Victoria ave n
Ross Andrew, commission merchant, 124 Wellington n
Ross Bros [Alex M, James W and Joseph T] painters and decorators, 1 Main w
Ross C H, clerk, 16 Ray s
Ross David, bricklayer, 42 West ave n
Ross David, teamster, 78 Lower Cathcart
Ross David, 67 Queen n
Ross Edwin D, salesman, 83 Wellington n
Ross Mrs Elizabeth [wid Geo] 9 Cannon e
Ross Fredk B, 16 Ray s
Ross Fred H, bookkeeper, 21 Erie ave

Ross Frederick L, shoemaker, 48 Steven
Ross George, superintending clerk P O, 24 Emerald n
Ross George, law student, 42 West ave n
Ross George H, George n s nr Locke
Ross James W [Ross Bros] res Bartonville
Ross John, blacksmith, 14 Inchbury s
Ross John, foreman M Brennen & Sons, 39 Victoria ave n
Ross John, tailor, bds 58 Vine
Ross John, teacher, 83 Wellington n
Ross John, tinsmith, 39 Victoria ave n
Ross Joseph, carriagemaker, 173 King e
Ross Joseph T [Ross Bros] King e Wentworth
Ross Leon, agent, 21 Bay n
Ross Mrs Nancy, boarding, 79 Cannon w
Ross Mrs Nancy, 181 Napier
Ross Robert, painter, 66 Wellington n
Ross Robt A, cigarmaker, George n s nr Locke
Ross Sam B, watchmaker, 21 Bay n
Ross S F, deputy collector inland rev, 16 Ray s
Ross Thomas [Hunter & Ross] 49 Victoria ave n
Ross William, finisher, 66 Wellington n
Ross Wm L, law student, 16 Ray s
Ross Miss, 38 Wilson
Ross ——, detective GTR, hd York w canal
Ross ——, rag dealer, Macklin
Rossell Victor, carpenter, 17 Caroline s
Rossell William, machinist, 92 John s
Rossell ——, ins agent, 75 Hunter w
Roth George, dairyman, 153 Wellington n
Rothwell Benjamin, dry goods, 112 Victoria ave n
Rotterdam Steamship Line, Wm Herman agent, 16 James s
Rourke John J, bricklayer, 7 Greig
Rouse Alfred, fireman, 37½ Steven
Rouse Benj, fruiterer, 107 James n
Rouse Frank, fruiterer, 107 James n
Rouse James, boilermaker, 82 Elgin
Rouse John, porter, 37 Steven
Rousseaux J M [J M Rousseaux & Co] h 101 James s
Rousseaux J M & Co, grocers, 76 King e
Rousseaux John B, detective, 7 Victoria ave n
Rousseaux Jos B, bartender, bds 261 Bay n
Rousseaux Jos B, watchman, 42 Vine
Rousseaux Wm M, carpenter, 3 Wentworth n
Routh Ed, cigarmaker, 100 Catharine n
Routh Geo, carpenter, 89 East ave n
Routh John, packer, Wood & Leggat
Routh John T, ins agent, 16 James s, h 194 Macnab n
Routh Mrs Rosanna, 368 James n
Routh Thos, laborer, 202 Catharine
Routh Thos, teamster, 339 John n
Rowan Anthony, laborer, 64 Young
Rowan John, barber, 6 Merrick, h 25 Catharine n

Rowan John G, driver, 28 Charles
Rowan Martin, carter, 101 Maria
Rowan Robt, teamster, 76 Maria
Rowe Jas, gardener, Herkimer n s w Queen
Rowe Jeremiah, mason, Ashley
Rowe John N, stonecutter, 71 Locke s
Rowe Miss L, milliner, 90 King e
Rowe Mrs Mary A (wid Richard) florist, 65 Hannah w
Rowe Richard, grocer, 114 Ferguson ave
Rowe Mrs Sarah (wid Wm) 52 Wilson
Rowe W H, prop *Palladium of Labor*, 90 Main e
Rowland Wm, lumber measurer, 121 Wellington n
Rowley John, mechanic, bds 143 Bay n
Rowley Martin, moulder, 228 Cannon e
Rowlin & Co (G H Rowlin, E Rowlin) fertilizing, nr GTR, e of Wentworth
Rowlin Frank, manager Fertilizing Co, 261 Barton e
Rowlson Wm, telephone clerk, bds 37 Robert
Roy Alex W, accountant, 7 Duke
Roy Mrs Anna (wid Robt) 7 Duke
Roy O G, asst accountant, Bank of Commerce, 80 James s
Royal Canadian Fire Insurance Co, Seneca Jones, agent 6 James s
Royal Canadian Marine Insurance Co, J B Fairgrieve, agent, 6 James s
Royal Hotel, Hood & Bro, props, 59, 61, 63 James n
Royal Insurance Co, David McLellan, agent, 84 James n
Royal Mrs Jane (wid Ed) 71 Ray n

Royal Jos, laborer, 90 Jackson e
Royal Laundry, Mrs S Robbins, prop, 187 King e
Royal Roller Rink, F J Duffy, manager, cor Main and Catharine
Royal Wm, carriagemaker, 71 Ray n
Ruach Mrs Margaret (wid James) 68 Jackson e
Rubin Louis, button hole maker, 86 Rebecca
Rudell Mrs Margaret, 45 Jackson e
Ruland Geo, butcher, 24 Caroline n
Rule John R, cutter, 109 Main e
Rumple Ernest G, cabinetmaker, 16½ Sophia n
Rumple Wm, laborer, bds 166 Bay n
Rumsey Thos, polisher, 71 Victoria ave n
Runstatler Alex, cigarmaker, bds 42 Kelly
Rupay Wm, tanner, 4 Walnut n, 1st flat
Ruppell Lawrence, driver, 227 Main w
Rush Mrs Elizabeth (wid John) 38 Pearl n
Rush Thos, laborer, n w cor Dundurn and Florence
Rushbrook Wm, cabinetmaker, bds 88 Ferguson ave
Rushton James W, boilermaker, 52 Pearl n
Russell Alex, salesman, 45 Hess n
Russell Alex G, jeweler, 94 Wilson
Russell Christopher, laborer, Robinson s s nr Garth
Russell & Dunn (Wm Russell, John Dunn) agricultural implements, 9 Market
Russell Felix, laborer, 31 Peter
Russell Geo, soap maker, 97 Wellington n

Russell Geo E, harnessmaker, Markland s s w Locke
Russell House, Thos Armstrong, prop, 66-68 King w
Russell James, laborer, 86 Macaulay e
Russell James W, bookkeeper, 79 Wellington n
Russell John, laborer, 79 Hunter w
Russell John, pensioner, 31 Peter
Russell Mrs Mary (wid Moses) Maple n s nr Garth
Russell Richard, manufacturing jeweler, 5 King w, h hd James s
Russell Richard, com traveler, 9 Market
Russell Stephen M, foreman Meriden Works, 101 Victoria ave n
Russell Wm, laborer, 16 George
Russell Wm (Russell & Dunn) 188 Hughson n
Russell Wm S, driver, Robinson n s nr Garth
Rutherford Adam (Rutherford & Lester) 80 Emerald s
Rutherford Adam, laborer, hd York nr cemetary
Rutherford Mrs Alex, 12a Grove
Rutherford Andrew (Garland & Rutherford) h 96 Bay s
Rutherford George (J Winer & Co) Main, east Hamilton
Rutherford James, moulder, 54 Hess n
Rutherford James, barber, 281 James n
Rutherford J R, clerk G T R, King e Hamilton
Rutherford & Lister (Adam Rutherford, T W Lester) ins agents, 6½ James s
Ruthven A, prop Atlantic House, 29 Macnab n
Ruthven Peter, 117 Hughson n

Rutley George, machinist, 43 Macauley w
Rutley George, machinist, 27 Steven
Rutter Theodore, stovemounter, 89 Main w
Ruttley John, mechanic, cor Burlington and Wellington n
Ryall Isaac, M D, 71 Main e
Ryan Albert, shoemaker, 77 Maria
Ryan Dennis, laborer, Burlington n
Ryan James, laborer, 277 Mary
Ryan James, tailor, 107 Caroline n
Ryan James C, com merchant, 1 Cherry
Ryan Mrs Mary Ann (wid John) 55 Barton e
Ryan Michael, 16 Blyth
Ryan Michael, bricklayer, 127 Young
Ryan Michael, laborer, 75 Steven
Ryan Philip, shoemaker, 32 Simcoe e
Ryan William F, shoemaker, 71 Peter
Ryckman Edward, laborer, 10 Devonport
Ryckman Freeman S, contractor, 35 Walnut s
Ryckman George B, jeweler, 79½ John s
Ryckman Mrs Margaret A (wid John) 115 Locke n
Ryckman Samuel, conductor G T R, 115 Locke n
Ryckman Samuel S, grocer, 71 Hughson s
Ryckman Wm H (W H Ryckman & Co) 20 Hess s
Ryckman W H & Co (W H Ryckman, D Manson) grocers, 62 John s
Ryerson George M, mangr Metropolitan Mfg Co, 43 John s

Ryerson James, carpenter, 20 Jones
Rymal Eli, hotel, 13 Market Square
Rymal Jacob S, 73 Napier
Rymal Miss Margaret, 51 Hess n
Rymal M B, local mangr Trade Association, wh and retail mercantile agency, 14 Merrick, h 6 Crooks
Rymal Oliver, brakeman, 196 Bay n
Rymal William, teamster, 170 Mary
St George's Hall, 2 King Wm
St James Reformed Episcopal Church, Rev T J McFadden rector, Hunter cor Park
St James Saloon, W J Brush prop, 19 Hughson n
St John's Presbyt'n Church Rev Thos Goldsmith pastor, Emerald cor King
St Joseph's Catholic Church Jackson cor Charles
St Joseph's Convent, Rev Mother M Vincent superioress, 138 Park n
St Luke's Church, Rev Wm Massey curate, John cor Macauley
St Mark's Church, Rev R G Sutherland rector, Bay cor Hunter
St Mark's Mission Church, Herkimer s s w Locke
St Mary's Roman Catholic Cathedral, Park cor Sheaffe
St Nicholas Hotel, Alex Dunn prop, 35-41 James n
St Patrick's Church (Roman Catholic) King cor Victoria ave s
St Paul's Evangelican Lutheran Church, Rev Christopher De Zocher pastor, Gore cor Hughson

St Paul's Presby'n Church, Rev R J Laidlaw pastor, James cor Jackson
St Stephen's Reformed Episcopal Church, Rev Wm Myers pastor, Canada cor Pearl
St Thomas' Church, Rev Canon W B Curran, rector, Main cor West ave
Sachs Adam, grocer, 55 Locke s
Sadleir C A, barrister, 8 Main e
Sænger Eli, laborer, 102 Catharine n
Sage James, builder, 18 Blyth
Sala Claude S, draughtsman, 155 Locke n
Salisbury Benjamin, saddler, 267 Cannon e
Salisbury Benj, saddler, 61 Locomotive
Salisbury Wm, wire worker, 61 Locomotive
Sallaway Mrs Mary (wid Wm) 39 Ray n
Salmon Geo, messenger Canada Life Assurance Co
Salovie Francis, 229-231 James n
Salter George, salesman, 4' Jackson e
Salvation Army Barracks, 3-7 Hunter e
Sammons Miss Hester, wax flower artist, 74 Hannah w
Sammons Martin, 74 Hannah w
Sandburg Chas A, brass finisher, 147 John n
Sandercock John, stamper, 21 Locomotive
Sandercock Thomas G, fitter, 8 Magill
Sandercock Wm, boilermaker, 28 Inchbury n
Sanders Aaron, barber, 130-2 James n
Sanders Brownlow, 286 Bay n
Sanders James W, ornamenter, 47 Elgin

Sanders Wm A, baker, 32 Augusta
Sanderson R J, laborer, 105 Ferguson ave
Sandford Chas H, sausage mak'r, 51 Hess s
Sandyford Place, s s Duke between Macnab and Park
Sanford W E, (W E Sanford & Co) h Jackson cor Caroline
Sanford W E & Co, wh clothing manfr, 45 9 King e
Sangster John W, 94 Merrick
Sangster Mrs Mary (wid Wm) 48 York
Santee Ephriam B, stamper, r Robinson n s nr Garth
Sabli Geo, street car driver, 239 Barton e
Sarge R W, clerk, bds 16 Augusta
Sarginson, Mrs Elizabeth (wid John) 66 Walnut s
Saunders Jabez, carpenter, 144 Rebecca
Saunders James, moulder, 151 Bay n
Saunders John, painter, 151 Bay n
Saunders Philip, driver, 217 Main w
Saunders Wm, teamster, bds 66 John n
Savage Edmund, bookkeeper, 95 Bay s
Savage John, laborer, 130 Wellington n
Sawyer Mrs Jane (wid Samuel F) 30 Jackson w
Sawyer Luther D (L D Sawyer & Co) h 114 Macnab s
Sawyer L D & Co (L D Sawyer, Jonathan Ames, H P Coburn, A H Hope) Hamilton Agricultural Works, ft Wellington n
Saxby Steven, carpenter, 118 Wood e
Sayer Chas, shpper, 53 Hannah w

Sayers Mrs Addie (wid Jos) 68 Hunter e
Sayers H R, bookkeeper, 68 Hunter e
Sayers Mrs Isabella (wid Chas) 41 Bay n
Sayers James, laborer, hd York w toll gate
Sayers Wm, laborer, 130 Locke n
Sayman Aaron, cutler, 147 James n
Scarlett David, tobacconist, 86 Market
Schabel Geo, brewer, 63 Market
Schadel Frederick, blacksmith, 183 Main w
Schadel Hy, Market View Hotel, 28 Merrick
Scharlach & Co (Hy Scharlach, John Guggisberg) cigar box manfrs, 2 Caroline s
Scharlach Henry (Scharlach & Co) 1 Queen s
Scharp John F, laborer, 88 Florence
Scharp Kristan, laborer, 106 Florence
Schau Andreas, laborer, 43 Tisdale
Scheck August, piano maker, 26 Devenport
Scheck Louis, foreman Semmens Bros, 26 Devenport
Scheller Harry, moulder, bds 43 Vine
Schelling Bernard, machinist, 35 Canada
Schierstein Mrs Catharine M (wid John) 124 Jackson w
Schleissing Chas, machinist, 80 Bold
Schrader Frederick J, tobacconist 91 Bay n
Schram J W, boots and shoes, 43-45 Macnab n
Schroer Henry, shoemaker, 46 Mary
Schuhl Hy, bookseller, 124 King e

Schuhl Niphtalie, music teacher 124 King e
Schultz Ernest, **tinsmith**, 16 Lower Catharth
Schultz Max, laborer, Sherman
Schumacher Geo, cabinetmaker, 78 Macnab n
Schumacher Geo, compositor, 218 King Wm
Schwab Jacob, coachman Arkelden, hd of John s
Schwab Peter, glassblower, 10 Ferguson ave
Schwarz C W G, **bookkeeper**, 136 **John s**
Schwarz Ed, shoemaker, 36 Walnut s
Schwarz Ed jr, cutler, **36** Walnut
Schwarz E L (E L Schwarz & Co) h 82 Market
Schwarz E L & Co, tobacconists, 4 James n
Schwartz F, cigar manfr, 3 Bay n
Schwarz Louis, tobacconist, 48 James n, h 50 Catharine n
Schwarz Wm, machinist, 36 Walnut s
Schwindau A J, clerk, 14 East ave n
Schwindau Alphonso, cutter, 14 East ave n
Schwindau Eugene, painter, 14 East ave n
Schwindau Mrs Magdalene (wid John) 14 East ave n
Schwing Chas, bartender White Elephant
Schwinger John gardener E Martin
Schwinger John, laborer, 12 Jackson w
Scollard John, butcher, 20 West ave n
Scott Mrs Agnes (wid Robert) 73 Hunter w
Scott Mrs Ann (wid James) 294 York
Scott Chas D, **law student, 85** Jackson w

26

Scott Chas E, waiter, 41 Park s
Scott Charles L, (John Stuart, & Co) h 104 Park s
Scott Mrs Christina (wid John) 75 Market
Scott George, **driver**, bds 49 Caroline n
Scott George, wood and coal dealer, 176 York, bds 172 York
Scott George, engineer, 23 Bay n
Scott Gideon, billiardist, St Charles restaurant
Scott James, fancy **goods**, 152-4 King e, h 27 East ave n
Scott James, ornamenter, 129 Emerald n
Scott John, laborer, 33 Peter
Scott John, patternmaker, bds 174 Bay n
Scott John J, (Walker, **Scott** & Lees) h 35 Jackson w
Scott Jonathan, clerk, bds **70** Duke
Scott Mrs Mary Ann, matron Girls' Home, 77 George
Scott Richard, teamster, 31 Guise
Scott Robt, iron planer, Robinson n s nr Garth
Scott Thomas, tailor, 118 Hunter w
Scott T L, salesman, 73 Hunter w
Scott T W, hotel, 16 Market **Square**
Scott Samuel, grocer, cor Victoria ave and Robert
Scott ——, agent, bds 55 York
Scott W, boots and shoes, 32 James s
Scott Walter, steamboat engineer, 261 Bay n
Scott Wm, laundry and shirt manfr, 34 York, h n e cor Ray and Bold
Scott Wm, cutter, 41 Aurora
Scott William, shoemaker, 26 Blyth

Scott Wm, laborer, 118 Hunter w
Scott Wm, packer, 44 Hess s
Scott Wm G, com traveler, 196 King w
Scott Wm J, heater, bds 241 York
Scott Wm S, porter, 89 Hannah w
Scragg George, moulder, 22 Inchbury s
Scragg John, moulder, 7 Inchbury s
Screeton Arthur, shoemaker, 125 Picton e
Scriven P I., engraver, 2½ James s, h 101 Jackson w
Scriver Mrs Mary J (wid Benj H) nurse 117 Market
Scriver Robert J, boilermaker, 23 Queen n
Scouler Rev Thos, pastor Erskine Presbyterian church, 160 Main w
Scudamore John, law clerk, bds 56 Park n
Scully Kenneth J, painter, 33 York, h 81 Park n
Scully Mrs Mary (wid Richard) 81 Park n
Scully Richard, painter, 81 Park n
Seal Thos, brickmaker, Wentworth n
Seal William, laborer, 20 Oak ave
Sealey Wm, laborer, n e cor Maple and Garth
Sealey Wm E, ward foreman, 25 Barton w
Seaman Mrs Annie, 41 Inchbury n
Seaman Shadrach L, 29 West ave n
Searle Henry, machinist, 219 John n
Searle Stephen, 159 Mary
Searle Walter, tinsmith, bds 83 Main e
Searles George, teamster, 18 Clark ave

Searles Henry, laborer, end Ferrie e
Searl Thos C, wood turner, 127 Queen s
Searls ——, 142 Barton e
Seaton Robert, moulder, 89 Elgin
Seaton Wm, machinist, 95 Murray e
Seaton Wm, blacksmith, bds 19 Hughson n
Seaver Murray, carpenter, 203 Wellington n
Seaver Nelson, laborer, 203 Wellington n
Seaver Wm (Cook & Seaver) h 203 Wellington n
Secord Geo, bookkeeper, bds cor Barton and Wentworth
Seddon James, dyer, 102-104 Bay n
Seelbach Mrs Bena (wid Wm) 82 Murray e
Sequin Joseph A, 111 Catharine s
Seitz John, telegraph operator, 148 John n
Selbeck Louis, biscuit maker, 174 Catharine n
Seldon Richard W, grocer, 86 Cannon e, h 111 Mary
Selig George, moulder, bds 37 Catharine n
Sellar James, laborer, 20 Hunter e
Sellars James, porter, 20 Hunter e
Sellens, Geo, law student, bds 135 Main e
Sellens Geo T, stenographer, 16 James s
Semmens Arthur W (Semmens Bros & Co) 44 Markland
Semmens Bros & Co (Arthur W Semmens, James J Evel) coffin manfrs, cor Florence and Inchbury
Semmens James, 3 Tom
Semmens John, carpenter, 3 Little Peel

Semmens Thos H, painter, 279 King w
Sendall Wm S, carpenter, 15 Charles
Senn Geo, carpenter, 5 Wellington Terrace, Wellington n
Sentry John F, laborer, 12 Aurora
Setzkorn Frederick, engineer, 116 Caroline s
Service Miss Helen, 92 Robert
Servos Mrs Sarah, 20 Hess n
Servos Jos, fireman city, Shaw
Servos Wm, clerk, 126 Cannon e
Servos Wm J, yardsman, 138 East ave n
Sevier Ed, letter carrier, 93 Jackson e
Sewart John, bricklayer, bds 103 Main w
Sewell Bros (H W & J E) grocers 32 James n, h 47 Bay s
Sexton Chas E, patternmaker, 9 Robert
Sexton Francis, laborer, 119 Simcoe e
Sexton Matthew, burnisher, 225 Hughson n
Seymour Alex, bottled milk, 30 James s
Seymour Mrs R (wid Robt) 12 Colborne
Shackell Thos, conductor, 277 Bay n
Shackelton Freeman, laborer, Breadalbane
Shadbolt John, cabinetmaker, 48 Queen s
Shadbolt Thos, 48 Queen n
Shaddock John, moulder, 59 Victoria ave n
Shaffer Adolph, pedler, bds 44 Locke s
Shaffer, Mrs Louise, 83 Rebecca
Shaftesbury Boys' Home, Rev R Ward, M A, supt, King e of Wentworth
Shambrooke Geo, bookkeeper, 9 Erie ave

Shannon Frederick, laborer, bds 35 Hughson n
Shannon John, laborer, 184 Victoria ave n
Shannon Miss Margaret, dressmaker, 116 Cannon w
Sharkey Geo, caretaker R C cemetery, Head s s w Dundurn
Sharkey George P, bookkeeper Brayley & Dempster, 49 King Wm
Sharpe Frederick H, barber, 4 Walnut n, h 22 Erie ave
Sharpe Geo, laborer, 71 Catharine n
Sharp Geo, 70 Main w
Sharp Geo, carpenter, 49½ Hunter e
Sharp Harry, carpenter, 44 Cherry
Sharp Ichabod, agent, 44 Stuart e
Sharp John, laborer, 144½ Bay n
Sharpe Mrs Martha (wid Wm) 71 Catharine n
Sharp Thos H, bookkeeper, 93 Victoria ave n
Sharp Wm, baker, 106 John s
Sharp Wm, assessor, 5 Queen s
Sharples James, collector, 134 Robert e
Shaughnessy Martin, laborer, 101 Strachan e
Shaughnessy Wm, laborer, 177 Wilson
Shaw Arthur, farmer, 14 Tiffany
Shaw Mrs Elizabeth (wid Thos) 110 Queen n
Shaw Mrs E B, 18 Grove
Shaw Geo, gardener, 68 John s
Shaw Mrs Geo, candies, etc, 68 John s
Shaw G M, M D, 122 James n
Shaw Mrs Harriet (wid Jos) 28 Margaret
Shaw Henry, laborer, 296 John n
Shaw James, boilermaker, 184 Emerald n

Shaw John, telegraph operator, bds 201 John n
Shaw John, clerk, 13 Gore
Shaw Mrs Kate (wid John) 13 Gore
Shaw Mrs M, matron Boys' Home, Stinson
Shaw Mrs Marion [wid Hugh] 202 Victoria ave n
Shaw Wm, packer, 14 Clarke ave
Shawcross Wm, com traveler, hd Garth e s
Shaylor Douglas, laborer, 6 Spring
Shea Daniel, laborer, 75 Young
Shea James, leather cutter, 47 Hannah e
Shea James, dry goods, 42 King e, h 47 Charles
Shea Jeremiah, machinist, 254 James n
Shea John, machinist, 72 Maria
Shea Mrs John, 36 Strachan e
Shea John, machinist, 77 Robert
Shea John F, boots and shoes, 40 King e, h 47 Charles
Shea Mrs Mary, 74 West ave n
Shea Patrick, machinist, 48½ Emerald n
Shea Patrick, laborer, 258 York
Shea Thos, laborer, 95 George
Shearer James, carpenter, 117 Rebecca
Shearman Carey, 33 Catharine s
Shearsmith Frederick G, carpenter, 77 Wilson
Shedden Co The (limited) cartage agents G T R, James Hamilton agent, 6-8 Catharine n
Sheed George, moulder, 74 Emerald n
Sheehan Mrs Bridget (wid John) 124 Young
Sheehan Daniel, baker, 85 Hess n
Sheehan John, agent, 5 Little Peel

Sheehan John, shoemaker, 113 Caroline n
Sheehan John, bread pedler, 124 Young
Shehan Miss Mary, 115 Caroline n
Sheehan Patrick, laborer, 5 Little Peel
Sheehan Richard, cigar manfr, 78½ King e, h 124 Young
Sheehan Timothy, laborer, 96 Maria
Sheehan Wm, cutter, 124 Young
Sheen John, laborer, 306 John n
Sheen Miss Mary, 113 Caroline n
Sheerin D P, book agent, bds 153 King e
Sheffield S J, pawnbroker, 77 James n
Shields John, laborer, 9 Hunter w
Sheill Wm T, shoemaker, 125 Wellington n
Sheldrick Richard, carter, 114 Simcoe e
Shepard Edward, carpenter, 137 Catharine n
Shepard Mrs Harriet E (wid Gideon R) boarding-house keeper, 49 Caroline n
Shepherd Benjamin, teacher, bds 15 Gore
Shepherd David, law student, bds 15 Gore
Shepherd Francis, customs officer 133 Park n
Shepherd George, law student, bds 15 Gore
Sheppard Mrs Jennie, Barton w
Sheppard Thomas, laborer, Burlington n
Shepherd Wm, teacher, bds 15 Gore
Shepherd Mrs, 24 Macnab s
Shenton Wm, carpenter, Sherman
Sherdon John, laborer, 53 Stuart e
Sheridan Mrs Ann [wid Patrick] 185 Bay n

Sheridan Walter B, blacksmith, 18 Margaret
Sheriff Wm, grocer, cor Barton and Victoria ave n
Sherk Levi, machinist, 79 Bold
Sherman James, 160 Rebecca
Sherring John G, plasterer, 97 Caroline n
Shield Chas, bread pedler, 11 George
Shields John, laborer, 104 Emerald n
Shields John, laborer, 144 Market
Shields Joseph, laborer, 43 Robinson
Shields Thomas, blacksmith, 14 Ray n
Shields Thomas, blacksmith, 164 Market
Shields Wm, laborer, 44 Jackson e
Shieler Henry, laborer, 77 Cherry
Shieler Peter, laborer, 72 Cherry
Shine Melbert, barber, 7 Macnab n
Shipley Vincent, laborer, Duke n s nr Garth
Shipley Joseph, potter, 3 Margaret
Shipman Wm, laborer, bds 55 Hess n
Shoots George (G & J Shoots) h 278 Cannon e
Shoots G & J (George & James) carriagemakers, 67 Merrick
Shoots James (G & J Shoots) h 172 Victoria ave n
Shouldice George, goldbeater, 81 **Elgin**
Shouldice James H, ins agent, 41 Hunter e
Shutes Wm, file cutter, bds 54 **Gore**
Shuttle James, machinst, 132 Macauley e
Shuttleworth Wm, salesman, 16 Grove
Siddall Hiram, carter, 99 Simcoe e

Sievert Augustus W, **cabinet**maker, 58 Pearl n
Silk James, teamster, 101 **West** ave n
Sillett George, cooper, 70 Rebecca
Sillett Jasper, tailor, 70 Rebecca
Silver Charles J, com traveler, 124 John n
Silver Creek Brewery, C A **Bur**don agent, 11 Jackson e
Silver Wm, jr, boot and shoe manfr, 83 Macnab n, h 27 Murray e
Silverman G**e**orge, **butcher, bds** 44 Locke s
Sim David, porter, 253 **Hughson** n
Sim James, silverplater, 167 West ave n
Simms James, moulder, 173 Mary
Simcoe Hotel (A W Burke prop) 153 King e
Simcoe Street Methodist Church. Rev V H Emory pastor, John cor Simcoe
Simkins George, painter, South w s s
Simon A, confectioner, **208-210** James n
Simon Henry, cigar manfr, 36 Merrick, h 12 Augusta
Simons Chas, packer, 12 Clark ave
Simons John, laborer, 97 Ferrie e
Simons Mrs Maria (wid Solomon) 138 King Wm
Simons Oliver, laborer, 10 Oak ave
Simons Peter, brushmaker, 138 King Wm
Simons Richard, laborer, 92 Simcoe e
Simple Wm, laborer, 32 **Macau**lay e
Simpson Chas W, carpenter, 8 O'Reilly
Simpson Mrs Francis, [wid Maltward] 29 Jackson w

Simpson James sr, h 62 Merrick
Simpson James, laborer, 1 East ave n
Simpson James & Son, brokers, 22 Main e
Simpson James F, ticket agent GTR, 27 Crooks
Simpson James W, wholesale Canadian knitted goods, 64 Hughson n, h 55 Hughson n
Simpson Mrs Jeannette (wid Wm) end Canada n s
Simpson John, cigarmaker, 84 Cherry
Simpson Joseph B, conductor GTR, 2 Canada
Simpson P H, barrister, 4 Main e, h 29 Jackson w
Simpson Robt, salesman, 43 Jackson e
Simpson Robt, clerk, 62 Merrick
Simpson Robt, laborer, 355 James n
Simpson Samuel, engineer, bds 94½ Catharine n
Simpson Mrs Sarah (wid Thos) 2 Canada
Simpson Thos, moulder, Duke s s nr Locke
Simpson Wm, railroader, 48 Hess n
Simpson Wm, moulder, Duke s s nr Locke
Simpson W G, boots and shoes, 28 King w, h 82 Main w
Sinclair Alex, painter, 126 East ave n
Sinclair David, laborer, 66 Steven
Sinclair Ed L, brakesman GTR, s e cor Barton and Crooks
Sinclair Geo, carpenter, r 51 Hunter e
Sinclair J G, D D S, dentist, 22 King e, h 18 Main w
Sinclair James S, county judge, Court House, h 23 Herkimer
Sinclair James W, finisher, 59 Canada
Sinclair John W, 32 Little Wm
Sinclair John W, painter, 124 East ave n
Sinclair Mrs Mary (wid Geo) r 51 Hunter e
Sinclair Mrs Peter, 11 Walnut s
Sinclair Peter, laborer, 14 Grove
Sinclair Peter G, gardener, 55 Charles
Sinclair Wm P, laborer, Barton w s s nr Crooks
Singer Manufacturing Co, Jos Hargrove, manager, college building, 65 King e
Sinker John, laborer, 127 Queen
Sinnett Mrs Mary (wid Peter) 81 Main e
Sintzel Mrs A B, (wid Thos) 49½ Augusta
Sintzel John, tailor, 78½ King e, h 18 Liberty
Sirois Elgear, shoemaker, 38 Smith ave
Sisman Thos, shoemaker, 175 Wellington n
Skelly Dennis, machinist, 59 Ferguson ave
Skelly Ed J, mail clerk, 61 Ferguson ave
Skelly John, laborer, bds 95 York
Skelly Martin, moulder, bds 56 King Wm
Skerritt Fred, clerk, 149 Main w
Skerrett John, warehouseman, 140 Main w
Skerrow Fred, laborer, 35 Strachan e
Skill Richard, clerk GTR, 75 Duke
Skilling Wm, carpenter, bds 114 Queen n
Skimin James, iron founder, n e cor Peter and Queen, h 57 Queen n
Skimin Geo H, dental student, 57 Queen n
Skinner Mrs Andrew, Fairleigh Park, Main e of toll gate
Skinner Fergus, Fairleigh Park, Main e

Skinner Hugh, clerk, Fairleigh Park, Main e Hamilton
Skinner James A & Co, wholesale crockery, 9 King e
Skinner John, watchmaker, 79 King w
Skinner R B (James A Skinner & Co) h Fairleigh Park, Main e Hamilton
Skinner R H, clerk, Fairleigh Park, Main e Hamilton
Skinner Seymour, laborer, 57 Little Wm
Skinner Thos, laborer, 112 Cherry
Skory Mrs Frances, (wid Anth'y) 151 Catharine n
Skuse Geo, laborer 28 Locke n
Slaght Freeman, porter, 136 Main e
Slaght Jefferson, polisher, 136 Main e
Slater Frank H, machinist bds 92 Hess n
Slater James, merchant tailor, 54 King w, h 147½ Main w
Slater John, carter, 320 Macnab n
Slater John, stonemason, 85 Lower Cathcart
Slater Mrs Mary, (wid R H), 52 Victoria ave s
Slater Samuel, treasurer Landed Banking & Loan Co, h 25 Jackson w
Slattery James D, machinist, bds 109 Bold
Slaughter John, 38 Mulberry
Slaughter Leander, tobacco roller, 101 Dundurn
Slee Wm, carpenter, 136 Ferguson ave
Slidders Geo, porter, 47 Caroline n
Sloan James, 28 Magill
Sloan J H, clerk, 36 Elgin
Sloan Thos, 36 Elgin
Sloggat Rev Richard L, curate Church of Ascension, 3 Bold

Smale John, laborer, 166 Ferguson ave
Smale Wm, 86 Elgin
Smale Wm jr, 86 Elgin
Small Alex, ins Bell Telephone Co, Mountain top
Small A W, shipper, 180 Victoria ave n
Small Mrs Eliza (wid James) 178 Napier
Small George, potter, 178 Napier
Smallwood George, tobacconist, 31 James n
Small James D, carpenter, Clarke ave
Small Thomas, butcher, King e of Wentworth
Small Wm, laborer, Dufferin
Smart's Tea Co (Jas McArthur, mangr) 120 King e
Smart Wm L, barrister, 114 Park s
Smee Edmund, shoemaker, 44 Young
Smellie John, bookkeeper, bds American hotel
Smilea John, bookkeeper, 22 Hess s
Smiley John, teamster, 101 Murray e
Smiley James, 101 Murray e
Smith Mrs Addie, 196 Robert
Smith Albert, polisher, 54 Steven
Smith Alexander, salesman, 73 John s
Smith Alex, sergt police, No 2 station
Smith Alex K, teamster, 314 King w
Smith Alfred, painter, bds 19 Hughson n
Smith Alfred E, bricklayer, 16 Margaret
Smith Alonzo, blacksmith, 132 East ave n
Smith Mrs Ann, 336 Hughson n
Smith Mrs Annie (wid Charles) 176 East ave n
Smith Arthur, laborer, 68 Tisdale

Smith Mrs Annie, candy store, 204 King w
Smith A W, fancy goods, 274 King e, h 15 East ave n
Smith Byron, vice-principal Canada Business College, 163 John n
Smith Mrs Catharine (wid John) 102 Young
Smith Chas, lithographer, Breadalbane e s nr Florence
Smith Chas, coachman E Martin, Ballynahinch, James s
Smith Chas, city messenger, 2 Wellington n
Smith Chas, flint glassblower, 336 Hughson n
Smith Chas, cigarmaker, 176 East ave n
Smith Charles, tailor, 33 Catharine n
Smith Chas, laborer, 66 Ray n
Smith Chas jr, paper boxes and printing, 5 King w, h 43 Wilson
Smith Chas J, laborer, 100 Jackson e
Smith Charles L, builder, 177 West ave n
Smith C R, commission, John n, h 11 West ave s
Smith Charles W, 30 Magill
Smith Daniel, carpenter, bds Eagle House
Smith Daniel Day, M D, druggist, n w cor King and Wellington
Smith Mrs D I McGee, 107 Victoria ave n
Smith D B, cutter, 116 Rebecca
Smith Donald, merchant tailor, 14½ James n, h Avon cottage, Main e Hamilton
Smith Edward, mechanic, 52 Ray n
Smith Edward, whipmaker, 103 John n
Smith Ed F, clerk, 97 West ave n
Smith Elijah B, com traveler, 14 Emerald s
Smith Mrs Elizabeth, grocer, 103 John n
Smith Mrs Elizabeth (wid James) 133 Market
Smith Mrs Elizabeth (wid W B) 130½ Emerald n
Smith Mrs Ellen (wid Connell) 81 Maria
Smith Mrs Emily (wid Robert) 84 Locke n
Smith Ernest, baker, 74 Markland s s w Locke
Smith Erskine, bricklayer, 5 Oak ave
Smith Mrs Esther, 138½ Hunter e
Smith & Farmer, (L C Smith, B A, T D J Farmer, B C L) barristers, etc, 9 James n
Smith & Findlay (W G Smith, John Findlay) saloon keepers, 53 James n
Smith Francis, moulder, 18 Simcoe e
Smith Mrs Francis, 7 Burlington e
Smith Frank, driver, 42 Ray s
Smith Frank, glassblower, 308 John n
Smith Frank, laborer, Burlington n
Smith Frederick C, nickelplater, 89 Bay n
Smith George, gardener, 69 York
Smith G, clerk P O
Smith George, painter, 251 King Wm
Smith George, carpenter, 11 Colborne
Smith George, painter, bds 68 Colborne
Smith George, laborer, 92 East ave n
Smith George, watchman, 186 Catharine n
Smith George, laborer, Little Wellington
Smith George, cigar manfr, 15 East ave n

Smith Geo A, bricklayer, 56 Lower Cathcart
Smith G B, wood and coal dealer, 8 Mary, h 297 Barton e
Smith Geo H, shoemaker, 155 Cannon e
Smith Geo J, grocer, 307 York
Smith George W, tinsmith, 49 Cherry
Smith Mrs H, crockery, Arcade
Smith Hampden, King e Hamilton
Smith Hanson E, hatter, 196 Robert e
Smith Henry, gardener, 297 King e
Smith Henry, shipper, 57 Robert
Smith Henry, locksmith, 22 O'Reilly
Smith Henry, laborer, bds 74 John s
Smith Henry, laborer, 59 Stuart w
Smith Henry, shoemaker, Wentworth n
Smith Jacob W, shoemaker, 202½ King w
Smith James, laborer, 5 Oak ave
Smith Jas, gardener Woodlawn, Victoria ave s
Smith James, carpenter, bds Eagle House
Smith James, moulder, 143 James n
Smith James, shoemaker, bds 150 Rebecca
Smith James, rougher, 181 **Na**pier
Smith James, 307 York
Smith James, carpenter, Beulah
Smith James, gilder, 66 Hannah w
Smith James, blacksmith, 281 John n
Smith James B, laborer, 326 York
Smith Jas Blois, day and evening school teacher, 1 Rebecca
Smith James H, florist, 168 Mary

Smith Jas H, prop Florida hotel, 39 Mary
Smith J J, cigar manfr, 117 Wilson, bds 34 East ave n
Smith James O, blacksmith, 65 Emerald n
Smith Mrs Jane (wid Samuel) 40 Market
Smith John, tinsmith, 166 King Wm
Smith John, tailor, Concession n s nr Locke
Smith John, emigration agent, Stuart w, h 131 Bay s
Smith John, laborer, Herkimer s s nr Garth
Smith John, laborer, 39 Wood e
Smith John, laborer, 144 Duke
Smith John, machinist, 5½ Oak ave
Smith John, 22 Catharine s
Smith John, baker, 99 Wilson
Smith John, saloon, 43 James n
Smith John, bricklayer, 14 Oak ave
Smith John H, clerk, 13 Nightingale
Smith John W, foreman Imp Min Water Co, 101 West ave n
Smith John W, laborer, 144 Duke
Smith Joseph, biscuit pedler, 23 Oak ave
Smith Joseph, carpenter, 176 East ave n
Smith Joseph, cabinetmaker, 30 Charles
Smith Joseph, shipper, bds 37 Catharine n
Smith L C, B A (Smith & Farmer) barrister, 8 Nelson ave
Smith Mrs Louisa, 204 Barton e
Smith Miss Maggie, 30 Catharine n
Smith Mrs Margaret, grocer, 223 James n
Smith Mrs Margaret (wid **Erskine**) 5 Oak ave

Smith Martin, tinsmith, 61 Emerald n
Smith Miss Mary, 33 Spring
Smith Mrs Mary, 191 James n
Smith Mrs Mary (wid James) 16 Wellington n
Smith Mrs Mary (wid Geo) 25 Cannon w
Smith Mrs Mary D (wid John S) 94 Hunter w
Smith Mrs Mary R (wid Alex) 18½ Walnut s
Smith Michael, porter, 16 Wellington n
Smith Miss Mima, artist, 2½ James s
Smith P, cigarmaker, bds 103 James n
Smith Peter, carpenter, 3 Oxford
Smith Richard, laborer, 84 Locke n
Smith Richard T, baggageman G T R, 168 Mary
Smith Robert, laborer, 25 Tisdale
Smith Robert, laborer, 312 Macnab n
Smith Robert, confectioner, 60 John s
Smith Robert J, 27 Tisdale
Smith Samuel, laborer, Wentworth n
Smith Samuel, glassblower, 310 John n
Smith Mrs Sarah [wid Wm] 230 King w
Smith Silas C, teamster, Locke s w s nr Robinson
Smith Theodore, fireman Bay st fire station, 30 Bay n
Smith Theophilus, 18½ Walnut s
Smith Thomas, butcher, r 164 Wilson
Smith Thos, contractor, 74 Catharine n
Smith Thomas, grocer, 319 James n
Smith Thos, general dealer, 278 Macnab n
Smith Thomas, stableman, 5 Charles
Smith Thos E, machinist, Barton w s s nr Locomotive
Smith Thomas F, artist, 333 York
Smith Thomas T, laborer, 45 Little Wm
Smith Walter, glasscutter bds 109 King Wm
Smith William, stonemason, 54 Lower Cathcart
Smith William, machinist, 21 Tisdale
Smith Wm, 25 Margaret
Smith William, laborer, 34 Stuart e
Smith Wm, dyer, Robinson s s nr Locke
Smith Wm, ropemaker, 148 Victoria ave n
Smith Wm, gardener, Main e of Wentworth
Smith Wm, 103 John n
Smith Wm, packer, 133 Market
Smith Wm, painter, 30 Bay s
Smith William, moulder, 19 Sophia n
Smith Wm, accountant, 42 Emerald s
Smith Wm, traveller, 173 King Wm
Smith Wm A, 10 Little Peel
Smith Wm B, sawyer, 130½ Emerald n
Smith W G, (Smith & Findlay), 53 James n
Smith William G, laborer, 49 Young
Smith ——, laborer, Burlington n
Smith Mrs, 172 Hughson n
Smith ——, teamster, 133 Barton e
Smith ——, janitor, Wentworth Chambers, 25 James s
Smoke John W, propr Hamilton Piano Stool Co, res East Flamboro

Smuck Ithamar, 46 West ave n
Smye Frederick T, clerk, 38 Mary
Smye Joseph, **wagonmaker**, 50 Hess s
Smye William, collarmaker, 38 Mary
Smye William jr, salesman, 38 Mary
Smyth Geo, tinsmith, 22 King Wm
Smyth John C, manager Canada Glass House, h 22 Liberty
Smyth John S, polisher, 39 Steven
Smith Robt, tinsmith, 22-24 King Wm
Snaith Wm, butcher, 32 West ave n
Snaudee James, printer, 20½ Locke s
Snaudee Mrs Jane, (wid James), 20 ½ Locke s
Snelson John, **machinist,** 135 Ferguson ave
Snider Bros, (Geo H, James A), flour and feed, 215 York
Snider Rev D W, pastor Zion Tabernacle, 126 Market
Snider Fredk G, 103 Main w
Snider Geo H, (Snider Bros), 9 Kinnell
Snider **George R, grocer,** 270 York
Snider James A, (Snider Bros), 22 Magill
Snider, Lake & Barley, flour merchants, Market cor Park
Snider Peter, driver, 14 George
Snider Thos, baker, 99 James s 16½ Augusta
Snoddy David, **plumber, Main e** of Wentworth
Snodgrass Mrs Janet, (wid Wm), 72 Peter
Snodgrass Peter, laborer, 72 Peter
Snodgrass Robt, 99 York

Snow Chas B, manager O C C, h 17 Robert
Snow David, **burnisher,** bds 56 King Wm
Snowden Henry, bartender, 42 Cannon w
Snowden Samuel, cabinetmaker 74 Elgin
Snowden Thos, blacksmith, 19 Burlington w
Snowden Wm, blacksmith, 375 John n
Soby **George,** com traveller, 11 Magill
Solbesburg John, laborer, Aikman ave
Somerville **Francis,** laborer, 163 Queen n
Somerville James, signpainter, 99½ James n, h 44 Mulberry
Somerville Jas, carpenter, Nelson
Somerville James, clerk, 158 Main w
Somerville James H, **com travel**ler, 61 Bay s
Somerville Robt, carpenter, 48 Smith ave
Somerville Wm, jr, commission merchant, 79 George
Somerville Wm, sr, commission merchant, 158 Main w
Somerville W & Co, commission merchants, 8 Hughson n
Somerset George, shoemaker, 67 Duke
Sommers, Wm, packer, 194 King Wm
Sonntag H **O,** tobacconist, 10 King w, h 17 Elgin
Soper I. N, piano tuner, 273 King e
Soper Robt, sail maker, etc, 259 Bay n
Soughton Alfred, machinist, 276 Cannon e
Souter A M, (Malcolm & Souter), h 123 Market
Souter David, carpenter, 123 Market

Souter David A, clerk, 123 Market
Souter James, cabinetmaker, 123 Market
Souter Wm M, cabinetmaker, 123 Market
Southam Wm, (Southam & Carey), 33½ Bold
Southwell Wm C, machinist, 154 West ave n
Southworth, George, laborer, 53 Pearl n
Sowerby James, tailor, bds 35 Hughson n
Sowerby Wm, tailor, bds 35 Hughson n
Spackman G W, assistant druggist J A Barr, York cor Macnab
Spanton Mrs Mary, (wid John), 34 Sheaffe
Spears Hamilton, laborer, 220 Ferguson ave
Spears Wm, agent, 87 York
Spectator [Daily and Weekly] Southam & Carey managing directors, 18 James s
Speight Chas, carpenter, 90 Robinson
Speight James, laborer, 90 Robinson
Spellacy Thomas, broker, 212 King e
Spence Mrs Elizabeth [wid Peter] 79 Jackson e
Spence George, carpenter, 44 Walnut s
Spence Geo, shoemaker, 79 Walnut s
Spence James, carpenter, 158 King Wm
Spence James, actg sergeant police 85 West ave n
Spence John, clerk, bds 29 Gore
Spence John, carpenter, 19 O'Reilly
Spence Joseph, mariner, 143 East ave n
Spence Matthew, stonecutter, 79 Ferrie e

Spence R & Co, Beech File Works, 222 King e
Spence Thomas B, watchman, 20 Sheaffe
Spence William, laborer, 20 Tisdale
Spencer James, tinsmith, 72 Ray s
Spencer Robert, driver, 71 Market
Spencer Samuel, laborer, 36 Sheaffe
Spencer Walter, organ builder, 15 Bay n, h 87 Main w
Spencer William, plumber, 36 Sheaffe
Spera R B, fancy goods, 198 King e
Spera Wm A, fruiterer, 280 King e
Spera Wm A, grain buyer, 7 Pearl n
Spies Rev August, pastor German Methodist Church, 98 Market
Spiers John, teamster, 82 Jackson e
Spohn Warren, photographer, 11 Cherry
Sphon Charles, engineer, bds 35 Hughson n
Spriggs John, shoemaker, 67 York
Springate, George, letter carrier, 61 Ray s
Springate John, boilermaker, 61 Ray s
Springer Mrs Emeline (wid Oliver) 52 John n
Springer Lewis, hd Springer ave Main e
Springstead James, laborer, 198a West ave n
Springstead Mrs James, grocer, 98a West ave n
Springstead Wm, laborer, 226 Barton e
Squibb Frank, plumber, 39 John s, h Main e, e Hamilton

Stacey George, laborer, 103 Maria
Stacey John, sawyer, 88 Rebecca
Stacey James B P, mattrass mfr, 82 Hunter w
Stacy John C, mattrass mfr, 99 Hess s
Stafford Mrs Elmira (wid Theodore) 32 Jackson e
Stafford James, mechanic, 57 Cherry
Stainton G W, ins agent, 78½ King e, h 34 Erie ave
Stalker Mrs Margaret (wid David) 4 O'Reilly
Stamp & Franks (W H Stamp, James Franks) painters, 114 King Wm
Stamp Wm H (Stamp & Franks) 116 King Wm
Standard Life Assurance Co, David McLellan agent, 84 James n
Stanley Walter, porter, 47a Wellington n
Stannard G C, 193 Hughson n
Stannard J H, carpenter, 193 Hughson n
Stanton Green, tobacco roller, Wentworth n
Stanton Thomas, painter, 43 Cherry
Stapleton George, rougher, 124 Queen n
Stapleton Joseph, laborer, bds 124 Queen n
Star Life Assurance Society E Freeman & Son agent, 9 King w
Stark Charles, salesman, 5 Bold
Stark John, stovemounter, 210 Victoria ave n
Stark Wm G, M D, 149 King w
Staunton C F Lynch (Ghent & Staunton) h Burlington s
Staunton F H Lynch, P L surveyor, 17 Arcade, h Burlington s

Staunton George Lynch, (Staunton & O'Heir) Burlington s
Staunton John, Revere house, 106 King e
Staunton & O'Heir, (George Lynch Staunton, Arth'r O'Heir) barristers, 18 James s
Stead John W, printer, bds Robinson n s w Locke
Steadford John, laborer, 196 East ave n
Steane Frederick, laborer, bds 125 Hunter w
Steanger James, hotel, 79 Stuart w
Stebbins John, gardener, Barton e
Steed Wm, carpenter, 190 Emerald n
Steedman James, machinist, 47 Napier
Steedman J P, bookkeeper, 78 West ave n
Steedman Wm, carpenter, bds 215 James n
Steele Mrs David, bds 80 James s
Steele George, musician, 26 Sheaffe
Steele George, grocer, 291-293 York
Steele James, helper, 96 Strachan e
Steele John T, 80 Hughson n
Steele R T, (Lucas, Park & Co) h 51 Jackson w
Steele R Thomas, teacher of vocal music, 105 Main w
Steele Wm, accountant, 4 Main e
Steer Edward, painter, 35 Tisdale
Stein Charles, butcher, 196 James n
Stein James, laborer, Wentworth n
Stein Mrs Mary, confectioner, 81 John s
Stein Samuel, com **traveler,** 81 **John** s

Steinberg Maximilian, rag merchant, 19 Wellington n, h 77 West ave n
Steinhoff Geo F, tinsmith, 11 Cannon e
Steinmetz Valentine, tailor, 25 Emerald n
Stender Wm, moulder, 46 East ave n
Stephany Herman, hairdresser, 192 King e
Sterling Daniel, 7 Bold
Sterling Geo A, bookkeeper, 7 Bold
Sterling Geo N, ledgerkeeper, Ham Prov & Loan Society, 7 Bold
Sterling Robt, 34 Jackson w
Sterling Thos H, 135 Main e
Stern Wm, com traveler, 31 Walnut s
Sterrett Wm, policeman GTR, 6 Mill
Steven Robt, boots and shoes, 64 King w
Steven H S, asst cashier Bank of Hamilton, 28 West ave
Stevens Mrs Ann (wid Wm) 126 Young
Stevens Chas, carpenter, 41 Steven
Stevens Mrs Eliza (wid John W) 2 Margaret
Stevens Geo, laborer, 83 Ferrie e
Stephens H, accountant, Court House
Stevens James, 135 Macaulay e
Stevens Isaac, fancy goods, 120 James n
Stevens Isaac, fishmonger, r 104½ Macnab n
Stephens James, moulder, 131 Ferguson ave
Stevens James, 124 Wood e
Stevens Jefferson, carpenter, 267 King w
Stephens John, machinist, 110 Bold
Stevens John, baker, 148 Mary
Stevens John, painter, 13 Sophia n
Stevens Louis, 124 Wood e
Stevens Nelson, tobacco roller, 7 Park n
Stevens Philip, machinist, 32 Charles
Stephens Samuel, 88 Elgin
Stephens Mrs Sarah (wid Jefferson) 94 Elgin
Stevens Stiles, moulder, 153 John n
Stevens Thos, porter, 7 Evans
Stephens Thos, machinist, 105 Hunter w
Stephens Thos I, picture dealer, 132 King e
Stevens Wm, engineer, bds 120 James n
Stephenson Alex, plumber, bds 60 James s
Stevenson Arthur, 107 Wood e
Stephenson Chas D, lather, 2 Centre
Stephenson Chas H, inspector block pavement, 46 Wellington s
Stephenson Edward, laborer, Maple n s
Stevenson Geo, baker, etc, 4 Hunter e
Stevenson Geo, steam, water and ventilating engineer, 77 King e h 60 James s
Stevenson Hugh, salesman, C Bremner
Stevenson Isaac, polisher, 31 Mary
Stevenson James, salesman, 73 Wellington s
Stevenson James, hay and straw dealer, Duke n s w Locke
Stevenson James, 241 York
Stephenson John, grocer, 53 Hunter e
Stephenson Mrs Mary (wid John) 94 Robert e
Stevenson Mrs Mary (wid Andrew) 73 Wellington s

Stevenson Robt C, bookkeeper, 131 East ave n
Stevenson Robt M, umbrella vendor, 122 Ferguson ave
Stevenson Thos, carpenter, 86 Duke
Stevenson Thos, cabinetmaker, 27 Mary
Stevenson Wm, carpenter, 59 Hunter e
Stevenson Wm, stovemounter, 88 Bay n
Steward, Edgar, porter, 122 Hess n
Steward Mrs Jane (wid Peter) n e cor Pine and Locke
Steward Thos, cellarman, 122 Hess n
Steward Thos J, ornamenter, 211 King e
Stewart A A, law student, bds 44 Hess n
Stewart Adam A, bookkeeper, 221 Main e
Stewart Alex, cutter, 17 Spring
Stewart Mrs Almira, 35 Lower Cathcart
Stewart Archibald D, moulder, bds 21 John n
Stewart Charles (Burrow Stewart & Mine) h 122 John n
Stewart Chas, carpenter, 142 Cannon e
Stewart Chas, printer, 154 Catharine n
Stewart Chas E, shipper 25 Hunter w
Stewart Chas J, stableman, 5 Charles
Stewart Daniel, laborer, 131 Jackson w
Stewart Mrs E, milliner, 156 King e
Stewart Ed, hatter, 60 Walnut s
Stewart Frank, machinist, 21 East ave n
Stewart Gavin, tinsmith, 122 John n
Stewart Geo, driver, 12 George

Stewart Jas (Jas Stewart & Co) bds Royal Hotel
Stewart James (Fairley & Stewart) h 130 Market
Stewart James, com traveler, bds 81 Catharine s
Stewart James & Co (Jas Stewart, John F Stewart, Wm C Stewart, Thomas Cook) stove founders, 75 Macnab n
Stewart James W, carpenter, 45 Tisdale
Stewart John, sec-treas Hamilton Bridge & Tool Co, 47 Duke
Stewart John, clerk, 88 Victoria ave s
Stewart John, mangr Hendrie & Co, 47 Duke
Stewart John, laborer, Concession s s w Garth
Stewart John, 70 Bay s
Stewart John, bookkeeper, 132 Market
Stewart John, clerk, 289 Macnab n
Stewart John, builder, 97 Hughson n
Stewart John F, (Jas Stewart & Co) h 55 Victoria ave s
Stewart J M, salesman, 88 Victoria ave s
Stewart John Y, machinist, 57 Pearl n
Stewart L, clerk, 55 Victoria ave s
Stewart Levi, com traveler, 71 Hunter e
Stewart Mrs Margaret (wid Geo) hd Queen s w s
Stewart Mrs Mary (wid Hugh) grocer, 16-18 Ferguson ave
Stewart Mrs Mary, 126 Napier
Stewart Norman, porter, 31 Liberty
Stewart N L, com traveler, h 55 Victoria ave s
Stewart Peter, varnisher, 1 Grove
Stewart Robert, sheriff's bailiff, 10a Grove

Stewart Robert (Robert Stewart & Co) 186 King e
Stewart Robert, civil engineer G T R, 27 Jackson w
Stewart Robert, bottler, 27 West ave n
Stewart Robert, soapmaker, bds 7 Ferguson ave
Stewart Mrs Robert, grocer, 27 West ave n
Stewart Robert & Co, grocers, 186 King e
Stewart Thos C, com traveler, 7 West ave s
Stewart Wm, architect, supt, building surveyor and valuator, Wentworth Chambers, 25 James s, h 165 Main e *See advt on front cover*
Stewart William, carpenter, 51 Steven
Stewart Wm, watchman, bds 142 Cannon e
Stewart William, laborer, 57 Pearl
Stewart William, carpenter, 28 Queen s
Stewart William, brushmaker, 1 Grove
Stewart Wm C, (Jas Stewart & Co) h 25 Hunter w
Stewart W H, salesman, 33 East ave s
Stibbs Jesse, glassblower, 59 Wood e
Stickle Chas H, letter carrier, 59 West ave n
Stiff Charles, supt GTR, 140 James s
Stiff George H, clerk, 155 Park n
Stillaway Thos, painter, Concession n s w Garth
Stillman Chas W, mechanic, 52 Wellington n
Stilwell Chas F, mangr Edison Lamp Co, 295 King e
Stinson's Bank, Alex H Moore mangr, 10 Hughson n
Stinson Frank, shipper, 86 Victoria ave n

Stinson James, proprietor Stinson's Bank, 92 Queen n
Stinson Thos H, solicitor, etc, Stinson's Chambers, 1 King Wm, h 5 Herkimer
Stirton John, printer, 221 John n
Stirton Thos, stonecutter, 221 John n
Stock David, foreman city yards, 17 Barton w
Stock John T, county treasurer, Court House
Stockdale Arthur, laborer, 198 East ave n
Stockwell Ed, dyer, 81 King w
Stokes Hy, 55 Pearl n
Stoker James, tailor, 158 Rebecca
Stokes Thos, wood worker, 33 Inchbury n
Stokes Wm, laborer, r 110 Young
Stokes Wm, mail clerk, 3 Barton Terrace, Wellington n
Stone Chas, laborer, 20 South
Stone Capt John H, 8 Victoria ave n
Stone Mrs Mary (wid Jacob) Duke n s w Locke
Stone Roland, tinsmith, 47 Cannon e
Stone Thos, baker, 83 Jackson e
Stonehane Wm, plasterer, 78 Hunter e
Stonehouse Geo, painter, 60 Hunter e
Stonehouse John (G W Blasdell & Co) s w cor Locke and Robinson
Stonehouse Michael, shoemaker, 25 Ferguson ave
Stonehouse Michael, shoemaker, 60 Hunter e
Stoneman Chas, compositor, 59 Young
Stoneman Chas, stonecutter, 35 Queen s
Stoneman John, com traveler, 43 Victoria ave n
Stoneham Jos, machinist, 241 Cannon e

Stoneman Robt, moulder, Albert Road
Stoney John L, general agent Ontario Mutual Life Assurance Co, 57 James n, h 44 Herkimer
Storm Albert Ed, tea merchant, 47 Wilson
Storm Bros, tea merchants, 128½ King e
Storm ——, painter, bds 55 Hess n
Storms Douglas G, M D, 92 Merrick
Storror Mrs Anne (wid Wm) 21 Macnab s
Stot Peter, engineer, 184 Catharine n
Stout Thomas, engineer, 7½ Cherry
Stow Mrs Alfred, 114 Main w
Stow Robert, laborer, Dundurn w s nr York
Stow Thos, carpenter, Dundurn w s nr York
Stow Wm, laborer, Dundurn w s nr York
Stow Wm M, laborer, Dundurn w s nr York
Strachan Alexander, bookkeeper, 57 Kelly
Strachan Mrs Harriet (wid Alex) 2 Jackson e
Strahler Jacob, com traveler, 96a Victoria ave n
Strain George, boilermaker, 36 Colborne
Strampel George, laborer, 332 Hughson n
Strange Thos, pedler, Burlington n
Strathdee John, salesman, 69 King Wm
Strathdee Wm G, engineer, 25 Hannah e
Stratton Robert, letter carrier, 52 Ferguson ave
Stratton S J, clerk, 70 Ferguson ave

Strauss Henry, grocer, 101½a John s
Strauss James, messenger P O, 68a Hunter e
Street John, bricklayer, end Wilson
Strickland Arthur, carriagemak'r, Concession n s nr Garth
Strickland Wm P, machinist, 31 Emerald n
Stringer Geo, laborer, bds 54 Gore
Strohm W B, salesman, bds 18 Wilson
Strong William, insurance, land and financial agent, 15 Arcade, h 149 John n
Strongman James, salesman, 76 Hunter e
Strongman Wm, policeman, 76 Hunter e
Strongman W, letter carrier P O
Strongman Wm, carpenter, s w cor Dundurn and Tom
Stroud Alfred, tanner, h 7 **Macnab** n
Stroud Alfred & Son, tanners and hide dealers, Ferrie e
Stroud George, tanner, 214 Victoria ave n
Stroud John, hotel, 37 Macnab n
Stroud Mrs Mary A, 288 York
Stroud Wm, hide merchant, 62 Vine
Strumble **Jacob**, teamster, 351 John n
Struthers James, **student**, bds 99 York
Stry George, laborer, 6 Stuart e
Stuart Alexander, city treas, 56 Victoria ave s
Stuart Alexander jr, asst city treas, 33 Alanson
Stuart Andrew, ornamental designer, 230½ Bay n
Stuart Mrs Andrew, 96 James s
Stuart Bros (John & W R) wh grocers, 23 Macnab n
Stuart Mrs Catharine (wid Wm) 92 Wellington s

Stuart Mrs Donald, 88 Hunter e
Stuart Mrs Isabella (wid James) 23 Nelson ave
Stuart James [John Stuart, Son & Co] h 9 West ave s
Stuart James jr, 9 West ave s
Stuart J J, [John Stuart, Son & Co] h 8 Hannah e
Stuart John [John Stuart, Son Co] Inglewood, Concession
Stuart John [Stuart Bros] 156 Main w
Stuart John, Son & Co, [limited] wholesale grocers, 37 John s
Stuart Lewis, bookkeeper, 56 Victoria ave s
Stuart Paul, wood market clerk, 120 Hunter e
Stuart P H, teller Molson's Bank 96 James s
Stuart R C, civil engineer, Jackson w
Stuart Robert, 128 West ave n
Stuart Wm R [Stuart Bros] 62 Main w
Studdart I A, sec H H L & Homestead Society, Court House, hd Queen s
Studdart John A, hd Queen s w s
Studholme Allan, stovefitter, 25 Elgin
Stull Mrs Jane [wid George] 68 Park n
Sturdy Frank, supt House of Refuge, 215 James n
Sturdy James, foreman William Magee, 154 Mary
Sturdy Thomas, manfr, 26 Catharine s
Sturt W P, com traveler, 64 Stinson
Sullivan Mrs Catharine [wid John] 117 Hunter e
Sullivan Mrs Catharine [wid Patrick] 11 Caroline n
Sullivan Daniel, cotton grinder, 252 Hughson n
Sullivan Daniel, grocer, 71 Walnut s
Sullivan Daniel, laborer, 170 Jackson w
Sullivan Daniel, livery, 5 Charles h 47 Queen s
Sullivan Daniel, moulder, 106 Wellington s
Sullivan Dennis, trackman GTR, hd York w toll gate
Sullivan Mrs Ellen [wid John] 81 Cherry
Sullivan Mrs Ellen [wid Michael] 25 Aurora
Sullivan Mrs Hannah (wid John) 129 Catharine n
Sullivan James, laborer, 55 Cherry
Sullivan James, laborer, 279 John n
Sullivan John, brakeman, 172 Ferguson ave
Sullivan John, carter, Burlington e
Sullivan John, laborer, r 206 Catharine n
Sullivan John, laborer, 6 Locke n
Sullivan John, laborer, 114 Emerald n
Sullivan John, shirt ironer, King e of Wentworth
Sullivan John (Sullivan & Reddy) 11 Caroline n
Sullivan Jos, blacksmith, 129 Catharine n
Sullivan Mrs Maria [wid James] King e of Wentworth
Sullivan Mrs Margaret, 284 John n
Sullivan Mrs Mary (wid Thos) 132 Queen n
Sullivan Mrs Mary (wid John) 110 Cherry
Sullivan Michael, hotel, 232 King e
Sullivan Michael, laborer, 117 Hunter e
Sullivan Michael, laborer, 29 O'Reilly
Sullivan Patrick, laborer, 5 Greig

Sullivan & Reddy (John Sullivan, James Reddy) livery, 52 Main e
Sullivan Mrs Sarah (wid Michael) 99 Maria
Sullivan Thos, laborer, 106 Wellington s
Sullivan Timothy, laborer, 232 King Wm
Sullivan Timothy, laborer, 17 Tisdale
Sullivan Timothy, laborer, 99 Maria
Sullivan Timothy, laborer, 20 Elgin
Sullivan Timothy, laborer, 219 Cannon e
Sullivan Timothy, machinist, bds 67 Stuart w
Sullivan Timothy, cooper, 18 Railway
Sullivan Timothy, 11 Caroline n
Sullivan Wm, laborer, 108 Cherry
Sullivan Wm, shoemaker, 60½ Oak ave
Sully Robt, stableman, n e cor Jackson and Macnab
Summerfield John, laborer, bds 204 East ave n
Sumn(ers Stephen, shoemaker, Herkimer s s nr Garth
Summers Stephen, porter, Herkimer
Summers Wm W, 50 Main w
Sun Accident Insurance Co, David McLellan, agent, 84 James n
Sunderland Michael, laborer, 99 Strachan e
Suter R W, ins agent, 12 James s
Sutherland A F, inspector Ham Prov and Loan Society, 37 Wellington s
Sutherland Alex, turnkey jail
Sutherland Alex, carpenter, 60 Hannah e
Sutherland Angus, 81 Jackson w
Sutherland Chas H, draughtsman GTR, 168 Main w

Sutherland **Donald**, grocer, 100 Rebecca
Sutherland **James B**, purser, 81 Jackson w
Sutherland Mrs Janet (wid D G) 45 Catharine n
Sutherland John W, lumber merchant, 113 Hughson n
Sutherland J W, druggist, 206 King w
Sutherland Miss Mary, 90 Bay n
Sutherland Rev Robert G, M A, rector S Mark's Church, 49 Hunter w
Sutherland Wm, gardener, Wentworth n
Sutherland Wm, freightman, 233 Macnab n
Sutton Benjamin, manfr, 72½ Elgin
Sutton John, huckster, 129 Queen s
Sutton Peter, tobacco roller, 213 York
Sutton Philip, 213 York
Sutton Wm, box maker, bds 129 Queen s
Sutton Wm, harnesmaker, 71 Emerald n
Swackham Wm, laborer, bds 58 Ray n
Swain Mrs Mary (wid John) 16 Angusta
Swales Michael, **carpenter**, 116 East ave n
Swallow Geo, mason, 235 King e
Swallow Isaac, mason, 105 Simcoe e
Swallow Wm, carpenter, 157 King Wm
Swann Ed, stovemounter, bds hd York n s e toll gate
Swanton Geo, broommaker, 105 Hannah w
Swartz Frederick, **cigar manfr**, 82 Market
Swartz John, com tsaveler, 30 Caroline n

Swartzenburg, Geo, shoemaker, 3 Elgin
Swazie A flour and feed, 228 King e
Swayzie Albert, grocer, Grant
Swayzie Andrew, laborer, 85 Young
Swayzie Mrs Eliza (wid Abraham) Grant
Sweeney Hugh, moulder, 37 Catharine n
Sweeney James, stoves, tins, etc, cor King Wm and Hughson
Sweeney Michael, com traveler, 113 Bay n
Sweeney Mrs Susan (wid Hugh) 59 Mary
Sweeney Thos, moulder, 59 Mary
Sweeney Wm, moulder, bds 39 Mary
Sweetlove Geo, watchman, 56 Tisdale
Sweetlove James, carpenter, 137 Macaulay e
Sweet Ephraim B, teamster, 20 Walnut s
Sweet Geo, manager W E Sanford & Co, Mountain ave
Sweet Walter, warehouseman, 49 East ave n
Sweetman Harry, prop The Hub 6½ James n
Sweezey Stephen, laborer, Robinson n s nr Locke
Swenerton Benjamin, com traveler, 171 Main w
Swinton Chas, laborer, 34 Ray n
Swinton Wm, mechanic, 56 Ray n
Swinton Wm J, carpenter, 56 Ray n
Swinyard M H, clerk, 8 Young
Sylvester Charles, tailor, 2 King Wm
Sylvester Thos, tinsmith, 82 Hunter e
Syme Gibson, laborer, end Ferrie e

Symington Wm, clerk, 46 Catharine n
Symmers James, clerk, 41 Florence
Symmington John J, laborer, 34 Poulette
Symonds Thos J, laborer, 115 Wellington n
Symons Samuel, 153 Mary
Symons Wm, 129 Simcoe e
Synet John boilermaker, 202 Barton e
Taafe Francis, butcher, 40 Catharine s
Taafe Joseph, moulder, 114½ Locke n
Taafe Mrs Madeline [wid Richard] 30 Young
Taafe Patrick, butcher, 117 King e
Tabb N H, com traveler, 3 Spring
Tabb Silas W, carpenter, 171 Emerald n
Taft John W, fireman GTR, 131 Market
Tait William, packer, 22 Inchbury n
Taggert Alexander, carpenter, 157 Bay n
Taggert Frederick, wireweaver, 157 Bay n
Tait W R, salesman, 80 Robert
Talbert Arthur, teamster, 274 Macnab n
Talbot Jas, laborer, 103 Simcoe e
Tallman Edward, porter, 131 Ferrie e
Tallman Ernest, stovemounter, 74 Lower Cathcart
Tallman Nelson, moulder, 54 Wellington n
Tallman Walter, moulder, 56 Wellington n
Tallman Wm, 90 John n
Tallman W H & Co, wood and coal, 43 Cannon e
Tallman Wm H, wood dealer, 98 John n

Talty Michael, laborer, Ferrie e
Tanner Wm, cigarmaker, 59 Emerald n
Tansley Henry, woodworker, 169 Wilson
Tansley John, gardener, Wentworth n
Tansley Mrs Minnie (wid Robt) 169 Wilson
Tarbox Edward B, solderer, 212 Victoria ave n
Tarrant Thos, Hamilton Club
Tate Frederick, hatter, 145 East ave n
Taufkirch Augustus, teamster, 79 Park n
Taverner Joseph, tinsmith, 5 George
Taylor Alfred, teamster, 70 Barton e
Taylor Alfred H, painter, 26 Queen s
Taylor Alfred J, gents' furnisher, 40 King w, h 185 King w
Taylor Eby, laborer, 313 Macnab n
Taylor Edward A, laborer, 111 King Wm
Taylor Edward E, clerk, 37 Markland
Taylor Mrs Eliza, Burlington n
Taylor Mrs Elizabeth (wid John) 84 Market
Taylor Enoch, file grinder, 127 Picton e
Taylor Ephraim, pressman, 122 Hughson n
Taylor Francis H, foreman Ont Rolling Mills, 69 Pearl n
Taylor Fred, carpenter, 87 Stuart w
Taylor Frederick G, polisher, 46 Ferguson ave
Taylor George, sec-treas Laidlaw Mfg Co, 92 James s
Taylor George, laborer, 31 Locomotive
Taylor Geo, checker, 106 Ferguson ave

Taylor Henry, grocer, 284a King e
Taylor James, stovemounter, bds 43 John n
Taylor James, bricklayer, 35 Caroline n
Taylor James, polisher, 129 Picton e
Taylor Mrs Jane (wid Joseph) 46 Hughson n
Taylor J C, lamp goods and glassware, 27 King w, h 36 Markland
Taylor John, laborer, 322 King w
Taylor John, malster, 76 Bay n
Taylor John, 121 Hess n
Taylor John, flour and feed, 40 York
Taylor John, laborer, 133 Picton e
Taylor John E, confectioner, 129 James n
Taylor John O, blacksmith, 107 Emerald n
Taylor Joseph, bartender, 46 Jackson e
Taylor Joseph, iron turner 3 Jones
Taylor Mrs Joseph, watchmaker, 42 King w
Taylor Josiah, laborer, 4 Nelson
Taylor Lachlan, dairyman, Beulah
Taylor Louis E, carpenter, 84 Bold
Taylor Mrs, 27 Ferrie e
Taylor Mrs Maria (wid Thos) r 1 Queen s
Taylor Mrs Mary, 84 Macauley e
Taylor Mrs Mary J, 300 King w
Taylor Nelson, harnessmaker, 87 Lower Cathcart
Taylor Peter, grocer, Wentworth n
Taylor Mrs R N, 26 Hannah e
Taylor R N & Co, druggists, etc (P C Blaicher, J Reche) 35 & 97 John s
Taylor Robt, shoemaker, 32 Walnut s

Taylor Robt J, cabinetmaker, 122 Wilson
Taylor Samuel Taylor's hotel, 21 23 and 25 Stuart w
Taylor Sellar, laborer, 98 Caroline s
Taylor Mrs Susanna (wid John) 122 Hughson n
Taylor Thos baker, 56 Cherry
Taylor Thos, carpenter, 223-5 Cannon e
Taylor Thos H, bookkeeper, 6 Nelson
Taylor Thos J, machinist, Herkimer s s nr Garth
Taylor Wm P, laborer, 322 King w
Taylor Wm, tinsmith, bds 65 Park n
Taylor Wm, patternmaker, bds 16 Market Sq
Taylor Mrs W J, 37 Mulberry
Taylor Wm H, laborer, 111 King Wm
Taylor ——, laborer, 215 Main w
Teehan Mrs Johanna, 91 Young
Teenan Mrs (wid Campbell) 192 Robert e
Teeter Edgar, butcher, 126 Wilson
Teeter John M, fireman, 202 James n
Teetzel J V (Osler, Teetzel & Harrison) h Park cor Herkimer
Teiper Casper, manager Hamilton Bridge and Tool Co, 197 Macnab n
Temperance Dining Rooms, Mrs Wm Tocher, prop, 48 James n
Temperance and General Life Assurance Co, M A Pennington, agent, 51 James n
Temple Benjamin, machinist, 70 Victoria ave n
Temple Findly, bookkeeper, 60 Gore

Temple John, livery, etc, 20 Catharine n, h 60 Gore
Temple Thos, teamster, bds 79 Robert
Templeman Peter, warehouseman, 126 John n
Ten Eyck Arthur, fireman, 196 King Wm
Ten Eyck John, salesman, 64 Catharine s
Ten Eyck Martin, 64 Catharine s
Ten Eyck M, veterinary surgeon, 24 Jackson e, h 64 Catharine s
Terryberry Mrs A, (wid Wm) 68 Catharine s
Terryberry David, butcher, 5 Simcoe e
Terryberry Wellington, 68 Catharine s
Terryberry Wm, clerk P O, 229 King w
Tew Mark L, 104 Robinson
Tew Richard, merchant, Woodmount, hd John s
Thatcher Mrs Ann, 8 Macnab s
Thatcher Ezekiel, wagonmaker, bds 180 Hunter w
Thatcher Geo, laborer, 48 Napier
Thatcher Rudolph, laborer, 180 Hunter w
Theale A M, organist, 87 King w, h Queen s
The Hub, Harry Sweetman, prop 6½ James n
Thom John, 74 Jackson w
Thomas Arthur, moulder, bds 150 Rebecca
Thomas C F, clerk, 29 Tom
Thomas C L, piano maufr, 92 King w, h 203 King w
Thomas E W, clerk, 95 Jackson e
Thomas Geo H, manager Bank of Montreal, 95 Jackson e
Thomas Harry N, marblecutter, Breadalbane e s nr Jones
Thomas Henry N, Cemetary Marble Works, cor York and Dundurn, h 29 Tom

Thomas Herbert N, marblecutter 57 Ray n
Thomas James, shoemaker, 99½ James s, h 88 Catharine s
Thomas James, stonecutter, 45 Ray n
Thomas Jeremiah, fireman, 62 Emerald n
Thomas John J, piano manfr, 243 King w
Thomas Patrick, laborer, Aikman ave
Thomas Philip J, contractor, 46 Markland
Thomas Wm J, 120 Cannon e
Thompkins Ed, laborer, 289 King w
Thompkins Thos, cigarmaker, 93 Lower Cathcart
Thoms Mrs Elizabeth, bds 11 Catharine s
Thomsett Chas, driver, 88 Bold
Thomson Alex, patternmaker, hd Garth w s nr Concession
Thomson Alex, proof reader, Times Office, h 148 Wilson
Thomson Alex, cabinetmaker, 29 Gore
Thomson Alfred H, clerk, 7 Bay
Thomson Miss Ann, 28 Young
Thomson Arch J, finisher, Concession n s nr Garth
Thomson Chas, carpenter, 18 Magill
Thompson Chas H, engineer, 56 Jackson e
Thompson David S, 123 Bay s
Thompson E B, draughtsman, 123 Bay s
Thomson Ed W, carpenter, Con n s nr Garth
Thompson E J (E J Thompson & Co) h Barton cor Mary
Thompson E J & Co, wholesale jewelers, 55 King e
Thomson Mrs Ellen (wid Alex) 7 Bay s
Thompson Frank, butcher, bds Street Car Inn, King e

Thomson Geo, cigarmaker, bds 39 Mary
Thomson G C (Bell & Thomson) h 16 Herkimer
Thompson George S, laborer, 98 Florence
Thompson Gregor, shoemaker, 53 Duke
Thompson Henry, cigarmaker, bds 39 Mary
Thompson Mrs Isabella (wid Wm) 254 Bay n
Thompson James, shoemaker, 106 Hunter w
Thomson James, laborer, 53½ Steven
Thomson James (Thomson & Wright) h 70 George
Thompson James, railroader, 82 Lower Cathcart
Thomson James, moulder, 82 Napier
Thompson James R, wood carver, 95 Jackson w
Thomson Mrs Jane (wid Robt) 21 Napier
Thomson John [Thomson & Wright] h 10 Peter
Thomson John, appraiser of customs, 94 Cannon e
Thompson John, laborer, bds 43 John n
Thompson John, grocer, 370 Hughson n
Thomson John, 70 George
Thompson John H, boat builder, 368 Hughson n
Thompson John R, carver, 4 Market sq
Thomson John W, com traveler, 53 Hess n
Thompson Joseph, laborer, 12 Guise
Thompson Joseph, laborer, 193 Emerald n
Thompson Joseph, ropemaker, bds 89 James n
Thomson Mrs Kate, 16 Herkimer

Thompson Mark, carpenter, 154 Victoria ave n
Thompson Peter, 104 Victoria ave n
Thomson R A, B A, mathematical master Collegiate Institute, 68 Bay s
Thompson Robert, laborer, n w cor York and Queen
Thomson Robert, lumber dealer, 89 Stuart w, res Burlington village
Thompson Robert, builder, 171 York
Thompson Thomas, laborer, 256 Macnab n
Thomson Thomas (Gardner & Thomson) h 290 King Wm
Thomson Thomas, shoemaker, 143 Hunter w
Thompson Wm, blacksmith, 246 Mary n
Thompson Wm, conductor, bds 17 Vine
Thompson Wm, machinist, 119 Hess n
Thompson Wm H, nailer, 91½ Hess n
Thompson Wm H, com traveler, 40 Peter
Thomson & Wright, James & John Thomson, Robert Wright) lumber dealers, 107 York
Thorley Cattle Food Co (T H Butler mangr) 48 John s
Thorne Frederick, moulder, Main e of Wentworth
Thorne Michael, laborer, 61 Young
Thorne S (S Thorne & Co) h 133 York
Thorne S & Co, importers of staple and fancy dry goods, 14 James n and 160 King e
Thornton James, laborer, 113 Cannon w
Thornton James, musical instrument dealer, 123 King w

Thornton John, mechanic, 35 Macauley w
Thornton Thomas F, mariner, 123 King w
Thorpe John, laborer, 235 John n
Thresher Wm, baker, 73 East ave n
Thresher Wm, baker, 73 East ave n
Thresher Wm J, baker, cor East ave and Cannon
Thurling James, laborer, 161 Queen n
Thurston James, saw maker, bds 49 Park n
Tice Wellington, teamster, 73 Walnut s
Tice Wesley, salesman, 209 King Wm
Tickle James, engineer, 59 Ray n
Tiderington Ralph S, bolt maker, 5 Oxford
Tidswell W O, civil engineer G T R, 10 Main e
Tilden John H, manager E & C Gurney Co (ltd) h 60 Catharine n
Tilley Chas, laborer, 131 Catharine n
Tilley David, bookkeeper, 12 East ave n
Tilley Edgar, painter, bds 23 Napier
Tilley Jesse, bookkeeper, 131 Catharine n
Tilley John H, salesman, 56 Wellington s
Tilley Joyce, patternmaker, 25 Railway
Times Printing Co, 1-3 Hughson n
Timson John, policeman, 48 Robinson
Tindill Mrs Elizabeth, prop Street Car Inn, King e of Wentworth
Tindell Thos, baker, 154 York
Tinling C W (Archdale Wilson & Co) h 19 Macnab n

Tinling Henry J (Culp & Tinling) h 75 Stinson
Tinsley Ed, engineer, 15 Colborne
Tinsley Geo, shipper, 15 Colborne
Tinsley Jos, compositor, 62 Walnut
Tinsley Robt, clerk, 15 Colborne
Timson John, policeman, 84 Robinson
Tisdale Mrs Mary (wid John) 190 King w
Titer Henry, laborer, bds 139 Locke n
Tocher's Temperance Hotel and Dining Rooms, 48 James n
Tocher Mrs Wm, prop Temperance Hotel and Dining Rooms, 48 James n
Tocher Wm, clerk, 48 James n
Todd Israel, whitewasher, 90 Rebecca
Tolmie Chas E, station agent, Harrisburg, 54 George
Tomes Mrs Annie (wid Wm) 4 Florence
Tomkins Geo, **cigarmaker**, 199 East ave n
Tompkins George, plumber, 199 East ave n
Tomkins Joseph, shoemaker, 134 Hunter w
Tomlinson Chas T, harnessmak'r 89 King e
Tomlinson Harry, fireman GTR, 46 Locomotive
Tomlinson Richard, warehouseman, 88 Queen s
Toner Hugh, laborer, 1 Poulette
Toner John, teamster, 80 Duke
Tope Richard, bricklayer, 73 Robinson
Topp Samuel, laborer, 142 Picton e
Topping Robert S, engineer, 39 Hannah w
Torbut Robert, gardener, King e of Wentworth

Torrance C E, farmer, 58 Catharine n
Torrance **David**, tailor, 2 Simcoe e
Torrance Hugh, 2 Simcoe e
Torrance Thomas, saddler, 58 Wellington n
Torrance Wm, moulder, 12 Ferrie w
Tory Alfred, clerk G T R, 115 West ave n
Tout William J, fitter, Wentworth
Tovel John E, **gardener**, Burlington n
Tovel Samuel A, gardener, Burlington n
Tovell Wm, **saw** maker, bds 49 Park n
Towers David, carpenter, 170 East ave n
Towers George, laborer, 175 East ave n
Towers George, laborer, 206 Hughson n
Towers Mrs Jane, 173 East ave n
Towers John J, foreman E Gurney & Co, 2 Evans
Towers Thomas, carpenter, Markland n s w Locke
Towersey Joseph, watchman, 120 King e
Towersey **Mrs Joseph, milliner**, 120 King e
Towler David, 62 **Hannah** e
Towler Michael J, **laborer**, 62 Hannah e
Towler Wm, broommaker, 20 Crooks
Townsend **Emond** J, florist, 64 Park n
Townsend **George F**, printer, 65 Young
Townsend John, elocutionist, 130 West ave n
Townsend Samuel W, custom officer, 27 Bay n
Townsend Sherman E, accountant, 6½ James s, h n w cor James and Duke *See card*

29

Townsend W G, custom house broker, 21 John s, h 31 Bay n
Toye Walter C, porter, 135 Robert
Tracey Daniel, teamster, 334 Hughson n
Tracie James, brakeman GTR, 64 Locke n
Tracey Thomas, brakeman 266½ Bay n
Trade Association, wh and retail mercantile agency, M B Rymal, local manager, 14 Merrick
Traders' Bank of Canada, Æmilius Jarvis manager, 36 King e
Trafford John T, laborer, 61 Jackson e
Trafford Thomas, driver, 61 Jackson e
Traill Allan, porter, 65 West ave n
Traill Alexander, salesman, 65 West ave n
Traill Andrew, clerk, Wood & Leggat
Traill Mrs Carrie (wid James) 15 Cherry
Traill Mrs Johanna (wid Wm) 79 Hunter e
Trainor James, laborer, 41 Simcoe e
Trainor John, tailor, 135 Catharine n
Trampkowski Mrs Laura (wid John) 127 Rebecca
Travelers' Life & Accident Co, J T Routh agent, 16 James s
Travers J N, manager Bank of Montreal, James cor Main
Treavar Thos, laborer, 7 Macauley w
Trebilcock John, carpenter, 249 King Wm
Treble S G, hats, caps, furs and gents' furnishings, King cor James, h 1 West ave s

Tregenza Charles, salesman, 69 East ave n
Treganza Edward, grocer, 162 Park n
Treiter Benjamin, cigarmaker, 36 Jackson e
Tremlett Mrs Elizabeth, boots and shoes, 122 King e
Tremlett John, shoemaker, 219 James n
Trenwith Geo, blacksmith, 2 Locke s
Trevaskis George, wagonmaker, Breadalbane w s nr Jones
Trevaskis John, blacksmith, 286 King w
Trevaskis Mrs Martha (wid Richard) Breadalbane w s nr Jones
Trevaskis Thomas, railroader, bds 162 Park n
Trevaskis Wm, blacksmith, King w s s nr Locke, h 319 King w
Tribbeck Wm, packer, 102 Queen
Tribbeck W R, nail feeder, 102 Queen n
Tribute Frederick W, cutter, 152 Main w
Tribute Thomas, machinist, 300 York
Tribute Wm H, machinist, 57 Locomotive
Trimble John, carpenter, 149 West ave n
Tristram Mrs Annie (wid Geo A) 70 Herkimer
Tristram George, bookkeeper G T R, 41 Pearl n
Trotman John, polisher, 3 Florence
Troup Mrs Elizabeth (wid Wm) 46 Hunter w
Trudgen Daniel, coachman Chas Gurney, hd John s
Truesdale Geo, teamster, 68 Steven
Trusdale John, laborer, 129 Jackson w
Truesdale Watson, com traveler, Mountain ave

Trumnan Arthur, hairdresser, 224 King e
Truman Chas, collector, 60½ Hunter e
Truman Frank, barber, 226 King e
Truman Fred W, bookseller and stationer, 230 King e
Truman Geo A, plumber, 191 King e
Truman Samuel, printer, 60½ **Hunter e**
Truman Wm, bookkeeper, 60½ **Hunter e**
Trumbull Mrs Eliza (wid Geo) 57 **John n**
Truscott Chas, carpenter, 84 Tisdale
Truscott Edwin, carpenter, 109 Wellington n
Truscott James, machinist, 66 **Lower** Cathcart
Truscott Mrs Jane (wid Wm) 109 Wellington n
Truscott John, carpenter, 78 East ave n
Truscott John, painter, 199 Wellington n
Truscott Mrs Mary Ann (wid James) 35½ Lower Cathcart
Truss Augustus, clerk, bds 87 Park n
Tshann **Antoney, butcher, 204** King w
Tshann **Jos, butcher, 204 King w**
Tuck Henry, policeman, 90½ **Hess n**
Tucker Geo, shoemaker, **43 Aurora**
Tucker Hy, laborer, r 166 John n
Tuckett Geo E (Geo E Tuckett & Son) 217 King w
Tuckett Geo E & Son (Geo E, Geo T, & John E) tobacco manfrs, 118-122 King w
Tuckett Geo T (Geo E Tuckett **& Son) 207** King w

Tuckett John E (Geo E Tuckett & Son) h 61 Hunter e
Tufford Alonzo, carriagemaker, 16 Sophia n
Tufford Isaac, carter, 2 Crooks
Tufford Lemuel, tobacconist, **53** York
Tufford Robt, clerk, Franklin House
Tufford Washington, driver, 62 Market
Tulk Alfred, moulder, 234 King Wm
Tulk Mrs Elizabeth (wid John) 234 King Wm
Tulk John J, emery **wheel** moulder, 5 Hunter w
Tunis Jacob M, grocer, **73 John s**
Tunstead John, manager Dominion Hat Co, 242 King e
Turk Wm, laborer, 310 Macnab n
Turnbull A C, bookkeeper, 24 Erie ave
Turnbull Adam, **laborer, 56** Pearl n
Turnbull Mrs Bella (wid W C) 2 Wilson
Turnbull Hy, caretaker Central Presbyterian Church, 78 Hunter w
Turnbull James, cabinetmaker, **53 Robinson**
Turnbull **James,** laborer, 36 Peter
Turnbull James, clerk Spectator, **2 Wilson**
Turnbull J D, 10 Wilson
Turnbull Michael (Leitch & Turnbull) 158 Mary
Turnbull Walter, painter, 39 Park s
Turnbull Walter, wire weaver, 36 Peter
Turnbull Wm, assessor, 10 Wilson
Turnbull W R, salesman, 10 Wilson

Turner Alex (James Turner & Co) h 83 Hughson s
Turner Duke, salesman, 46 Wellington s
Turner Geo T, carpenter, 40 Lower Cathcart
Turner Hy, gardener, 15 Macnab s
Turner James & Co, wholesale grocers, 11-13 Main e
Turner Hon James (James Turner & Co) h Highfield, Concession
Turner James, machinist, 108 Wood e
Turner John B, teacher, 264 King e
Turner Jos, boilermaker, bds 43 Vine
Turner Richard, 91 Simcoe e
Turner Thos Wm, engineer, 183 Victoria ave n
Turner Wm, 172 Main e
Turner Wm, Highfield, Concession
Turner Wm, bookkeeper, bds 192 Macnab n
Turner Wm jr, shoe manfr, 12 Macnab n, h 172 Main e
Turney Philip, laborer, bds 222 Macnab n
Turpin James, com traveler, 38 Jackson w
Turpit Mrs Susan (wid John) 22 Devenport
Tutty Mrs Wealthy, 47a Wellington n
Twhy Hy, collector Water Works, 150 Macnab n
Twomey Mrs Mary (wid James) 119 Hunter e
Tyson Adam, feather renovator, 111 John s
Tyson John, builder, 131 Cannon w
Tyson Thos, builder, 131 Cannon w
Tyson Wm, bricklayer, 5 Little Wellington

Underhill John, teamster, 162 Wilson
Underwood Chas, engraver, 114½ East ave n
Union Hotel, James Burgess, prop, cor Hughson and Hay Market
United States Consulate, Albert Roberts, Consul, GTR Station
United Workman Hall, 14 Macnab s
Unsworth Geo, painter, Markland s s w Queen
Unsworth James, dyer, 305 John n
Unsworth John, painter, Markland s s w Queen
Union Thomas, huckster, Hopkins
Upfield Jessie J, com traveller, 46 West ave s
Urry Walter, hair dresser, 67 James n, 11 Murray w
Ussher E S, clerk Bank of Hamilton, 17 King w
Vail A S, (A S Vail & Co), h 88 Hughson n
Vail A S & Co, wh manfrs ready made clothing, 16-18 James n
Vale Frank, collector, bds 49 Park n
Vale Lemuel N, carpenter, 9 Greig
Vale William J, printer, 1 Elgin
Valentine Chas, laborer, 121 Ferrie e
Vallance Geo, cashier, 50 Hunter w
Vallance James, carpenter, 14 Picton e
Vallance James jr, salesman, 14 Picton e
Vallance Wm, (Wood & Leggat), h 46 Hannah w
VanAllen E, contractor, 2 Bay s
VanAllen Edwin, bookkeeper, 91 Jackson w

Vannatter James, acting sergeant police, 45 Hunter e
Vance John, weaver, 251 John n
Vanderbilt Henry, moulder, 50 Wellington n
Vanderbilt Walter, baggage master, 126 Queen n
Vandusen Joseph, carpenter, 172 Wilson
Vandusen Peter, carpenter, 172 Wilson
Vane Thomas, cellarman bds 97 Cannon w
VanEvery Charles, painter, 33½ Spring
Vannorman Mrs E C, 67 Cannon e
VanNorman Mrs Elizabeth, 9 Victoria ave n
VanNorman W P, (W P Van Norman & Co), h 67 Cannon e
VanNorman W P & Co, agents Wanzer S M Co, 75 King e
VanOrder Geo R, conductor, 5 Barton Terrance, Wellington n
VanWyck Gilbert, tailor 87 Elgin
Varey Mrs Eliza, (wid Eli) bds 60 Vine
Vaugham Albert, clerk, 68 West ave n
Vaughan Cornelius, driver, Robinson s s nr Garth
Veale Thos O, gardener, 33 Steven
Veasey Henry, 34 Bay s
Veidenheimer Phillip, baker, 125 Hannah w
Vellee Francois, broommaker, 22 Upper Cathcarth
Venard Wm, policeman, Park n
Venator Edward, Wm A Venator & Sons), 54 Main w
Venator Fred, woodturner, 69 Coborne
Venator Jacob, (Wm A Venator & Sons), 54 Main w
Venator Wm A, (Wm A Venator & Sons) 54 Main w

Venator Wm A Sons, (Wm A, Jacob & Edward) wood and ivory turners, and manfrs of cotton mill work, 56-58 Main w
Venator Wm L, wood turner, 127 Cannon w
Venn Walter, machinist, 10 Devonport
Vent David, laborer, 1 Oxford
Verner Andrew, moulder, bds 21 Florence
Vernon Elias, M D, 78 James s
Vernon Henry, manager W H Irwin & Co, 145 John s
Vernon W E, com traveller 78 James s
Verral Wm, butcher, 144 John n
Veth Chas, laborer, 168 East ave n
Victor Engine **Works,** 66 and 68 Rebecca
Victor Soap Works (David Morton, prop) 43 9 Emerald s
Victoria Chambers, 31 James s
Victoria Hotel, Richard Irwin, prop, 79 King e
Victoria Mutual Fire Insurance Co, W D Booker, sec-treas, Wentworth Chambers, 25 James s
Vila Mrs Ann, (wid Augustine) grocer, 253 Bay n
Vila Augustine jr, **chandler, 255** Bay n
Villiers Frederick H, clerk **GTR,** 64 Catharine n
Vincent A & Co, druggists, 230 James n
Vincent Arthur, druggist, 230 James n
Viner Thos, salesman, 149 York
Vint Charles, shoe cutter, bds 9 Hess n
Vint James, carpenter, 184 Hunter w
Vint Samuel J, marble cutter, 33 Park s

Vint Mrs Sarah (wid James) 33 Park s
Vint Thos, shoe cutter, bds 9 Hess n
Vint Wm, tobacco roller, 9 Hess n
Vipond Eli, carpenter, 201 East ave
Virgint John D, tanner, 146 Hunter w
Voelker Chas shipper, 120 Mary
Voelker Guenther, laborer, 120 Mary
Voelker Jacob, tailor, 64 Hunter e
Voelker Wm, shipper, 120 Mary
Vogel Charles, hatmaker, 177 Emerald n
Voght Louis, presser, bds 63 Market
Voik Jos, moulder, 27 Macauley e
Voll John, glassblower, 85 Macauley e
Volland August, moulder, 233 King e
Volland Frank, machinist, 233 King e
Vollick John, woodturner, 99 Catharine s
Vollick Wesley, cabinetmaker, n e cor Locke and Herkimer
Von Hoxer Alex, compositor, 10 Jones
Von Hoxer, Mrs Hy G, 10 Jones
Vulcan Iron Works (Chas James, prop, r 57 King Wm
Waddell Frank R (Waddell & Waddell) 31 Hunter w
Waddell Geo C, law clerk, 94 James s
Waddell James N (Waddell & Waddell) 31 Hunter w
Waddell Mrs Mary, 31 Hunter w
Waddell R R, 31 Hunter w
Waddell & Waddell (J N & F R) barristers, Court House
Waddell Mrs W W, 94 James s
Waddell Wm F, salesman, 67 Bold
Waddelton Philip, **tailor**, 2 King Wm, h 39 Markland
Wade Hy, laborer, 272 Cannon e
Wade Robt, laborer, 23 Margaret
Wade Robt, baker, 78 Queen s
Wade Robt, Hamilton Club
Wadland Thos H, supt of construction, Bell Telephone Co, 35 Bold
Wagner Chas, shoemaker, 46 Mary
Wagner Mrs E, (wid Benjamin) 73 John n
Wagner Frederick, butcher, bds 175 Hughson n
Wagner Geo, salesman, 114 Mary
Wagner James, tailor, 128½ King e, h 73 John n
Wagner Mrs S A, (wid Wm) 114 Mary
Wagstaff Walter, tinsmith, 23 Magill
Wagner W H, salesman, 114 Mary
Wah Lee, laundry, 87 James n
Wah Sing, laundry 87. King e
Wainwright J R, clerk Molson's Bank, 6 Bay s
Waite Geo, grainer, bds 84 John n
Waite Ed, laborer, bds 21 Florence
Wakeham Alfred E, engineer, 86 Caroline n
Wakeham John, **ship** carpenter, 52 Burlington w
Wakeham Thos H, tinsmith, 106 Jackson e
Wakley Richard, carter, 31 Lower Cathcart
Wakelin Frederick, 38 Walnut s
Waldhof Chas, whipmaker, 28 Rebecca
Waldhof Wm, hay and straw dealer, 28 Rebecca, h 23 Charles
Waldren Mrs Harriet (wid Thos) 58 Barton e

Waldren Wm, foreman Hendrie & Co, Robinson s s nr Locke
Walford John, packer, 30 Markland
Wales James, miller, 9 Sophia s
Walker Alexander, carpenter, 16 Young
Walker Mrs Alice (wid James) 92½ Jackson e
Walker Alfred E, 68 Cannon w
Walker Chas, confectioner, 75 Wellington n
Walker C G, ticket clerk, 58 Hunter w
Walker Frank E (Frank E Walker & Co) h 63 Wellington s
Walker Frank E & Co, carpets and housefurnishings, King cor Walnut
Walker Geo, grocer, 75 King w
Walker George, machinist, 240 **King** Wm
Walker, Geo, painter, 58 Ferrie w
Walker George, shoemaker, 92½ Jackson e
Walker H H, wood worker, 294 Hughson n
Walker House, R H Kretschman, prop, n e cor King and Ferguson ave
Walker Hugh, planer, 6 Locomotive
Walker James, ins agent, 20 Main e, h 58 Hunter w
Walker James, soap manfr, 21 Bay s, h 19 Bay s
Walker Mrs Jane (wid James) 103 Rebecca
Walker John, moulder, 70 Tisdale
Walker **John**, blacksmith, 65 John n
Walker John, moulder, Wentworth n
Walker Joseph, **dairyman**, 70 Garth
Walker Miss Margaret, 36 Wilson

Walker **Mrs** Mary (wid **Albert**) millinery, 11 York
Walker Raymoud, merchant, 65 Wellington s
Walker Robt, car driver, 7 Murray e
Walker **Robt**, grocer, **205-7 York**
Walker **Mrs** Sophia, **5** Walnut s
Walker Mrs T F, saloon, 15 James n
Walker **Thos**, salesman, **205-7** York
Walker Thos D, **tie** inspector GTR, 62 Jackson w
Walker Wm, **brakesman GTR**, 53 Magill
Walker William, huckster, 55½ Catharine n
Walker W F, M A, LLB, (Walker, Scott & **Lees**) h 140 Bay s
Walker, Scott & Lees (W F Walker, M A, LLB, John J Scott, Wm Lees, Thos Hobson) barristers, 10 James s *See card*
Walker ——, machinist, 171½ East ave n
Walkinshaw **J**ohn, moulder, **bds** 173 East ave n
Wall James, blacksmith, 136 Jackson e
Wall James, hatter, **126 Park** n
Wall James jr, blacksmith, 136 Jackson e
Wall M **J, nail cutter,** 10 Ferrie w
Wall **Robert**, cab driver, 136 Jackson e
Wallace Francis, canvasser, 95 Caroline n
Wallace Hugh S (J Wallace & Son) 4 Wellington Terrace, Wellington n
Wallace James, moulder, **49** Cannon e
Wallace John (J Wallace & Son) **82** George

Wallace Joseph T, clerk, 66 Jackson w
Wallace J McL, medical supt Asylum for the Insane
Wallace J & Son, (J, & Hugh S Wallace) stoves, house furnishings etc, 15 John n
Wallace Robert S, clerk, 102 Park s
Wallace Roscoe, carpenter, 155 John n
Wallace R R, M D, 82 Cannon e
Wallace Wm, Markland n s nr Bay
Wallace Wm, machinist, South w n s nr Locke
Walling Jas, laborer, 51 Brock e
Wallington Robert, painter, 211 Wellington n
Wallington Thomas, painter, 211 Wellington n
Walls John, cotton weaver, 293 James n
Wallscraft George, laborer, 130 Ferguson ave
Walsh David, messenger P O, 29 Barton e
Walsh Edward E, bookkeeper, 15 Margaret
Walsh Hiram H, policeman, 304 John n
Walsh James, machinist, 98 Jackson e
Walsh John, shoemaker, 43½ York
Walsh John, shoemaker, 136 Young
Walsh John, 198 King w
Walsh Mrs Martha (wid James) 15 Margaret
Walsh Mrs Mary (wid John) 98 Jackson e
Walsh Mrs Mary (wid Michael) 150½ Duke
Walsh Patrick, 255 James n
Walsh Samuel, tobacco roller, 18 Mill
Walsh Thomas, machinist, 189 James n

Walsh Thomas, salesman, 15 Margaret
Walsh Thomas, tinsmith, bds 150 Rebecca
Walsh Thomas, grocer, 217 York
Walsh William, fitter, 45 Florence
Walsh W J, plumber, 96 King e
Walter Augusta, laborer, Robert w
Walter Chris, laborer, Duke s s nr Garth
Walter Ernest, laborer, 49 Steven
Walter Frank, laborer, Duke s s nr Garth
Walterhouse James A, millwright, 39 Wilson
Walters Edward, potter, Maple n s nr Locke
Walters Frederick, moulder, 6 Albert road
Walton Mrs Elizabeth (wid Jos) 83 Caroline n
Walton Frederick, clerk, bds 17 Vine
Walton Mrs Hannah (wid John) 48 Charles
Walton Ice Co, W G Walton, mgr, 70 Vine
Walton Joseph, salesman, 52 Lower Cathcart
Walton Nelson, butcher, 43 Walnut s, h 68 Maria
Walton Wallace, laborer, 83 Caroline n
Walton Watson G (Walton Ice Co) h 54 Napier
Walton Wm, mechanic, bds 206 Macnab n
Walton William, laborer, 128 Wood e
Walwork John, 359 James n
Walwork John, 33 Picton e
Walwork Thomas, clerk, 359 James n
Wands Ebenezer H, carpenter, 184 Main w

Wanzer Frank L, (R M Wanzer & Co) h 82 Victoria ave s
Wanzer R M, (R M Wanzer & Co) h 47 West ave s
Wanzer Sewing Machine Co (R M Wanzer & Co) Barton cor Elgin
Wanzer Thomas D, (R M Wanzer & Co) h 73 Victoria ave s
Ward Mrs Ann (wid Joseph) 17 Hunter w
Ward Mrs Ellen (wid Patrick) Herkimer n s nr Kent
Ward George, machinist, 17 Hunter w
Ward Henry, laborer, bds 11 Rebecca
Ward John A, asst paymaster G T R, 196 Macnab n
Ward John M, brakeman, 95 Lower Cathcart
Ward Mrs Margaret [wid Chas] 176 Rebecca
Ward Mrs Marion [wid Wm] 12 Ray n
Ward Richard, railroader, 84 Lower Cathcart
Ward Rev Robt, supt Shaftesbury Boys' Home, King e of Wentworth
Ward Thomas, laborer, 107½ Wood e
Ward ——, agent, 1 Bold
Warden Benj, 107 James n
Wardlaw Mrs Amelia [wid John] dressmaker, 6 Ontario
Ware E W, [Gurney & Ware] h 9 Vine
Wark David, policeman, 87 Emerald n
Wark John, clerk, 183 Macnab n
Warmington H G, carpenter, 73 Elgin
Warnick Wm, 104 Young
Warnke Peter, tailor, 25 Canada
Warner John, mechanic, 160 John n

Warner Mrs Mary Jane [wid Francis] 40 Jackson e
Warner Mrs Thomas, 22 Young
Warren Donald, sexton Knox's Church, 147 Mary
Warren Edward, 51 Catharine s
Warren Mrs Ellen [wid Edward] 52 Cherry
Warren George A, laborer, 212 Hughson n
Warren Mrs Mary, 68 Strachan e
Warren Miss Mary, dressmaker, 51 Catharine s
Warren Patrick, laborer, 83 Strachan e
Warren Robert, butcher, cor Tisdale and King Wm
Warren Wm, machinist, 170 Macnab n
Warren W E, clerk Wood & Leggat
Warring Mrs M G [wid Wm] 154 Rebecca
Warwick Mrs Ellen [wid Alex] 101 Catharine s
Warwick John, cabinetmaker, 101 Catharine s
Warwick Wm, carpenter, 51 Hunter e
Washaline Co (Geo Dempey prop) 47 King Wm
Washington S F [Haslett & Washington] 27 Jackson w
Wass Mrs Mary Ann, 53 Little Wm
Waters Alfred M, marblecutter, 39 West ave n
Watters Francis, driver, 10 Macnab s
Waters Mrs Harriet, dressmaker, 7 Walnut s
Waterloo Mutual Fire Insurance Co, Seneca Jones agent, 6 James s
Waterman Clifton R, painter, bds Bold s s opp Ray
Waterman W L, clerk P O, 196 John n

Watkins Edgar H, merchant, 64 East ave s
Watkins F W [Pratt & Watkins] h King e nr Burlington
Watkins Thomas C, dry goods, carpets, etc, 30-32 King e, h King cor Emerald
Watkins Wm T, merchant, 71 Emerald s
Watson Mrs Anne [wid Wm] 42a West ave n
Watson Andrew, tailor, 68 King Wm
Watson Chas, laborer, 62 Young
Watson David, cigarmaker, 42½ West ave n
Watson Edward, horse and cattle doctor, 25 Mary
Watson Geo, cabinetmaker, 110 Emerald n
Watson George, machinist, 10 Picton w
Watson Geo, shoemaker, 83 West ave n
Watson James, moulder, 50 Florence
Watson James, carpenter, 22 Locke s
Watson James, pres Strathroy Knitting Co, Sandyford place, 9 Duke
Watson J W G, ledger keeper Bank of Montreal, 9 Duke
Watson John, horse and cattle surgeon, 25 Mary
Watson John W, checker, 268 James n
Watson Joseph, shipper, 55 York
Watson Mrs Mary [wid David] 126 Bay s
Watson Rupert M, secretary Strathroy Knitting Co, Sandyford place, 9 Duke
Watson Thomas, tinsmith, 136 Catharine n
Watson T H, clerk, 83 West ave
Watson Thos J, policeman, 29 Maria

W. G. TOWNSEND,
CUSTOM HOUSE BROKER,

IMPORTERS', MANUFACTURERS' AND SHIPPERS' AGENT,

FORWARDER AND SHIPPER.

OFFICE:

No. 21 JOHN STREET SOUTH,

(Opposite the Custom House)

HAMILTON, - - ONTARIO.

P. O. Box 285.

Watson William, 42a West ave n
Watson William, machinist, bds 172 Bay n
Watt George, teamster, 70 Hughson n
Watt George, laborer, 82 Macnab n
Watt James, gardener, 146 King w
Watt J J [J M Rousseaux & Co] 76 King e
Watt John & Son [John & Alex] merchant tailors, 15 Macnab n, h 112 West ave n
Watt Mrs Sarah, confectionery, 146 King w
Watt Samuel, machinist, 21 Oxford
Watt Robert, shipper, 67 Duke
Watts Mrs Elizabeth [wid Thos] 134 Locke n
Watts Henry, laborer, bds 11 Rebecca
Watts James, spinner, 100 Ferrie e
Watts John, laborer, bds 243 Mary n
Watts Mrs Sarah [wid Thos] Markland s s w Locke
Waud B W, com traveler, 34 James n
Waugh John, 78 Bay n
Waugh W J, hats, caps and gents' furnishings, 68 King e, h 144 James s
Way Bidwell, bursar Asylum for the Insane
Way George, tailor, 171 King e
Way James, carpenter, 280 Cannon e
Way James, painter, 26 Mary
Way John E, blacksmith, 15 Crooks
Way Joseph, gardener, 151½ John s
Waybrant Henry, machinst, 82 Malberry
Weakley Jacob, tinsmith, bds 121 Rebecca

Weatherspoon Alex, carpenter, 234 Catharine n
Weatherston James, carpenter, Devonport
Weatherston James P, clerk, 6 Kinnell
Weatherstone John, lessee and mangr Hamilton & Dundas Street Railway, h 33 Victoria ave n
Weaver Charles, [Caughell & Weaver] h 176 Macnab n
Weaver Cyrus, laborer, 11 Picton w
Weaver Mrs Elizabeth [wid John] 92 Elgin
Weaver Frederick, switchman G T R, 21 Crooks
Weaver Miss Hattie, cadet Salvation Army, 5 Hunter e
Weaver Henry, teamster, 32 Locke n
Weaver Herbert, piano maker, bds 50 Wilson
Webb Anthony, gardener, King e of tollgate
Webb George, builder, 99 Murray
Webb Geo N, shoemaker, 185 Main w
Webb Mrs Hannah (wid Geo) 150 Catharine n
Webb Isaac, laborer, 78 Canada
Webb James W, shoemaker, 145 Jackson w
Webb John, carpenter, 101 Jackson w
Webb John, builder, 99 Murray e
Webb John jr, bricklayer, 1 South e
Webb Wm R, bookkeeper, 101 Jackson w
Webber Alfred F, builder, 64 Maria
Webber B H (Winslow & Webber) h 89 Caroline n
Webber Chas, builder, 42 Maria
Webber Chas H, 134 John s
Webber Emmerson P, salesman 104 Bold

Webber Frederick C, 97 Catharine s
Webber Geo H, builder, 103 Catharine s
Webber Mrs Isabella [wid Esau] 42 Maria
Webber John A, clerk P O, 44 Maria
Webber J M, prop Palace Rink, 66 James s
Webber Mrs Maria A (wid Tilman C) dressmaker, 63 Napier
Webber Orin H, bookkeeper, 121 East ave n
Webber P E, salesman, 104 Bold
Webber Walter B, prop Palace Roller Rink, 13 Hess s
Webster A, machinist, 103 Ferguson ave
Webster Edmund, machinist, 142 Victoria ave n
Webster George, merchant tailor, 118 King e
Webster Geo, machinist, 128½ King e
Webster James, florist, Wentworth n
Webster James, mason, 17 O'Reilly
Webster John, turner, 270 Bay n
Webster Mrs Mary (wid John) 134 Bay n
Webster Robt, cabinetmaker, 140 Barton e
Webster W F, flour and feed, 8 Market, h 53 Park n
Wedge Chas, tobacco roller, 104 Florence
Wedge James, carter, 200 Robert
Wedge Richard, 104 Florence
Weights and Measures Office, 2 John s
Weimar Ferdinand, japanner, 82 Mary
Weir Arthur, machinist, 114 Locke n
Weir Arthur, prop Weir's hotel, 101 King Wm

Weir James, baker, 79 Napier
Weir James, boat builder, ft of Wentworth n
Weir James G, grain buyer, 23 Steven
Weir John, clerk, 48 Strachan e
Welby Geo, patternmaker, 231 Victoria ave n
Welch Mrs Helen (wid John) 80 Caroline n
Welch Mrs Louisa, 24 Catharine s
Wellington Geo, laborer, 65 Ferguson ave
Wellington House, Thos Wilson, prop, 101 Wellington n
Wellington St Swimming Baths, 11 Wellington n
Weller James, laborer, 21 Little market
Wellar Wm J, potter, 8 Little Market
Wells Alfred, porter, 15 South w
Wells Mrs Jane (wid Frederick) 94 Jackson e
Welsh Hy, **machinist**, 19 Barton w
Welsh Thos, railroader, bds 62 Mulberry
Welsher Harvey, carpenter, 173 Napier
Wennesheimer Philip, 292 James n
Wentworth Canning House Crockett, Muirhead & Co, props, Queen cor Peter
Wentworth Chambers, 25 James s
Wesley Church, Rev W J Hunter, pastor, John cor Rebecca
Wesleyan Ladies' College, Rev A Burns, D D, LL B, governor, 57 King e
West Benjamin, baker, bds 83 Main e
West Chas, biscuit baker, 254 Cannon e
West David, laborer, 130 John s
West Mrs Eliza [wid Wm] 90 Victoria ave ave n

West Geo, baker, 75 Jackson e
West Mrs Janet [wid John] 75 Jackson e
West John, baker, 75 Jackson e
West Mrs Mary A, Markland n s nr Queen
West Thos, laborer, 199 Catharine n
Westbrook Mrs Nora, 102 John n
Westaway John, packer, 72 **Barton** e
Western Assurance Co, Geo A Young, agent, 5 King w
Western Assurance Co [marine] J B Fairgreive, agent, 6 James s
Western Assurance Co, (ocean and inland marine, Toronto) W F Findlay, agent, 25 James s
Western H B W, **clerk,** 67 Hughson s
Western John, **bootmaker,** 23 Lower Cathcar.
Westmore Albert, grocer, ft Mary n
Westfall Mrs Hannah (wid Hy) 14 Florence
Westfall John, laborer, 33 Florence
Westfall **Wm,** laborer, **29** Florence
Weston Mrs Elizabeth, 73 Locke n
Weston George, watchman, 29 Little Wm
Weston Robert, shoemaker, 81 Merrick
Weston Wm H, Hamilton Spice Mills Co, 33 Hughson n
Wetherall Alex, dry goods, 134 King e, h 141 Victoria ave n
Wetherall Harry, 354 Hughson n
Wetherall Joseph, 354 Hughson n
Weybrant Wm, machinist, 124 Bay n
Whalen Jas, laborer, 217 John n

Whalen John, laborer, 367 John n
Whalen John, 376 Catharine n
Whalen Sylvester, silversmith, 183 Emerald n
Whalen Thomas, shoemaker, bds 111 Park n
Wharry Wm, blacksmith, Oxford w s nr Barton
Whately Mrs Harriet [wid Henry] 35 Hannah e
Whatley Fred L, clerk, 3 Nelson ave
Wheaton Wm, mechanic, 3 Mill
Wheaton Wm, laborer, 9 New
Wheeler Mrs **Ann** [wid H] 89 Macauley e
Wheeler George, engine driver, 228 Catharine n
Wheeler Henry, cabinetmaker, 89 Macauley e
Wheeler Jacob **S,** carpenter, **84** Elgin
Wheeler Mrs Jane [wid Roland P] tailoress, 32 Peter
Wheeler Mrs Nancy M, temperance hotel, hd York n s **nr** toll gate
Wheeler R N, wood and coal, cor Cannon and Tisdale, h 233 Cannon e
Whelan James, shoemaker, 129 Main e
Whelan Mrs Mary [wid John] 129 Main e
Whelan Michael, laborer, 59 **Maria**
Whipple E S, land agent and issuer of marriage licenses, 78½ King e, **h** 80 Cannon e
Whipple Herbert B, real estate agent, 55 Wellington n
Whipple Vernon B, book and job printer, 128 ½ King e, h 10 Bay s
Whitby Albert W, shoemaker, Albert road
Whitby John, engine fitter, 245 Bay **n**

White Abraham, machinist, 93 Hannah w
Whyte Alexander R, bookkeeper, 18 Erie ave
White Alfred E, shipper, 3 Erie ave
White Andrew, 240 Bay n
Whyte Archibald, foreman, 73 Market
Whyte Charles, cigarmaker, 131 King e
Whyte Charles B, com traveler, 22 Hess s
White David, 109 Robert
White Mrs Elizabeth, 3 Erie ave
White Frank, stovemounter, Patrick
White Frederick E, carpenter, Burlington n
Whyte George, carpenter, 131 King e
White Geo A, bricklayer, 311 King w
White Mrs Henrietta (wid John) 98 Bay s
White Henry A, electric instrument maker, 44 Murray w
White James, laborer, 37 Macauley w
White James, moulder, 10 Henry
White Rev James H, pastor Emerald st Methodist Church, 45 Emerald n
White James, M D, coroner, 8 Cannon w
White Jas P, moulder, 6 Pearl s
White Mrs Jane (wid John) 6 Pearl s
White Mrs Jane, matron House of Refuge
White J C, fancy goods, 86 King e
White John, laborer, 40 West ave n
White John, collector, bds 89 Market
White Mrs John, 10 Henry
White John E, flour and feed, 220 King w

White Joseph, carpenter, Strachan e of Ferguson ave
White Joshua J, evangelist, 25 Steven
White J R, clerk, 86 King e
White J T, clerk, 109 Robert
White Mrs Nancy, bds 11 Catharine s
White Nicholas, laborer, bds 220 Macnab n
Whyte R L, chief clerk customs, 12 West ave s
White Samuel, bus driver American hotel, 34 Charles
White Samuel, news agent etc, 9 Walnut s
White Samuel, shoemaker, 94 John s
White Thomas W, bds 83 Hess n
White Wm, clerk, bds 42 Vine
White William, laborer, 122 Simcoe e
White Wm, engraver, 9 James n
White Wm, blacksmith, 7 Nightingale
White Wm C, 10 Burlington n
Whitehead Buckley, Albion hotel, 211 James n
Whitehead E S, watchmaker, 161 John n
Whitehead Charles, gardener, Wentworth n
Whitehead S J, supt Hamilton Iron Forging Co, 108 Hess n
Whitelock Mrs Alice (wid John) 142 West ave n
Whitelock Frank C, shipper, 98 West ave n
Whitelock Wm J, bricklayer, 147 East ave n
Whitely James, laborer, 96 Ferrie e
Whiteside Wm, machinist, cor Elgin and Barton
Whiteside Wm J, grocer, 105 Elgin
Whiting Lewis, com traveler, 61 Barton e

Whitley C, helper, 282 Hughson n
Whitling Benjamin, gardener, 47½ Voung
Whitmore Albert, laborer, 3 Evans
Whitmore Daniel S, driver, 72 Bay s
Whitmore Mrs Maria, 3 Evans
Whitney John, laborer, 7 Harriet
Whitney Matthew, mail driver, 68 Market
Whittaker Elijah, machinist, Wentworth n
Whittaker Thomas, clerk, Wood & Leggat
Whittier A M, bds 48 James n
Whitwam Christopher A, com traveler, 25 East ave n
Wholton Wm, lunch rooms, 22 Macnab n, h 158 West ave n
Wickham James, stove fitter, 43 Wood e
Wickham John, laborer, 96 Macauley e
Wickham Michael, laborer, 113 Hannah e
Wickham Patrick, stovemounter, 84½ Macauley e
Wickham Wm, stovemounter, 284 Mary
Widger Mrs Elizabeth, 43 East ave s
Wiers Robt, teamster, 62 Cannon e
Wigmore Edward B A, law student, bds 100 Park n
Wigmore Mrs M H (R A M) Organist Gore Street Church, 100 Park n
Wilbee Frederick, laborer, 313 James n
Wilcox Charles A, agent, 96 Catharine n
Wilcox Charles S, treas Ontario Rolling Mill Co, Canada Life Buildings
Wilcox Mrs Jane (wid John) r 61 Jackson e

Wilcox Mrs **Mary (wid Wm L.)** 96 Catharine n
Wilcox Oscar, carpenter, **25 Little Wm**
Wilcox Richard, laborer, **129 Ferrie e**
Wild Mrs Electa, r **64 Hannah e**
Wild Ed, laborer, **end Hunter w n s**
Wild John, dyer, 274 Hughson n
Wild M B, clerk GTR
Wilde Wm C, printer, 108 Maria
Wilds **James**, teamster, Wentworth s
Wilds James, gardener, **Barton e**
Wilds **Mrs** Elizabeth (wid **Geo**) Wentworth s
Wilds Geo, gardener, Barton e
Wilds Mrs Sarah (wid **Stephen)** 129 Ferguson ave
Wilkes Chas, **carpenter, 191** Main e
Wilks Chas R, carpenter, **Wentworth s**
Wilkes ———, carpenter, bds **83 Main e**
Wilkin Chas, laborer, **180 King Wm**
Wilkins Miss Harriet A, music teacher, 64 Main w
Wilkinson Mrs Barbara (wid Wm) 202 King Wm
Wilkinson Frank, grain buyer, 98 Concession
Wilkinson Mrs **Mary J, (wid Richard S) 9 Park s**
Wilkinson Samuel, manager China and Japan Tea Warehouse, **4 King Wm, h 133 Ferguson ave**
Will Andrew, shoemaker, **55** Victoria ave n
Will Mrs Eliza (wid **Geo) 122** Cannon e
Will Ramsey, machinist, **62** Pearl s
Will Smith, teamster, 81 Hunter e
Willard Abner (Willard Bros) bds American House

Willard Bros (A & G W) harnessmakers, 21 Macnab n
Willard G W, electrician, bds 66 King w
Willard Henry H, sec Ontario Rolling Mill Co, 87½ Jackson w
Willcock Geo, farmer, Main e of Wentworth
Willcock Stephen, watchmaker, 126 James n
Willer Samuel, pork butcher, 127 John s
Williams Mrs Alice, laundress, 29 Peter
Williams Mrs Ann, bds 11 Catharine s
Williams Arscott, gardener, Barton e
Williams, Mrs Celia (wid Henry) 36 York
Williams Chas, carriage trimmer, 61 Maria
Williams C J, prop Canadian Oil Co, h 42 Catharine n
Williams Ed, engineer, 53 Wilson
Williams Enoch R, laborer, 2 Little Margaret
Williams Geo, builder, 16 Baillie
Williams Geo, plasterer, 28 Margaret
Williams Geo, plasterer, 39 Canada
Williams Geo, stovemounter, 66 Robert
Williams Geo J, manager Dunn, Wiman & Co, Markland n s w Queen
Williams Hy, teamster, 129 West ave n
Williams Henry R, hd Queen s e s
Williams H R (J M Williams & Co) hd Queen s
Williams H S, bookseller, 144 King e, h 13 Victoria ave
Williams Jacob, laborer, 48 Inchbury n
Williams James, teamster, 20 Kelly
Williams James, clerk, 111 Rebecca
Williams James H, 49 Hughson n
Williams J M, registrar, Court House, h hd Queen s
Williams J M & Co, stove founders and stamping works, 59-61 Hughson n
Williams James M jr, (J M Williams & Co) hd Hess s
Williams John, fishmonger, 23 Ferguson ave
Williams John, pedler, bds 286 King w
Williams John, laborer, 79 Cherry
Williams John, laborer, 59 Hannah e
Williams John, stovefitter, 81a John n
Williams John, machinist, 111 Rebecca
Williams John, carpenter, 26 West ave n
Williams John, brakeman G T R, bds 46 Cannon w
Williams John C, gardener, 40 Walnut s
Williams Joseph, machinist, 98 Picton e
Williams Julius M, druggist, 115 Hess n
Williams Lenton, millwright, 52 Park n
Williams Mrs Mary (wid Patrick) 1 Greig
Williams Matthew, harnessmak'r, 111 Rebecca
Williams Mrs, 50 Caroline s
Williams Patrick, boilermaker, 1 Greig
Williams Percy, stableman, 9 Margaret
Williams R Edward, nail plate roller, 100 Hess n
Williams Robert, pork packer, bds 131 Rebecca

Williams Wm, mechanic, bds 4 Mill
Williams ——, gardener, West
Williamson A P, stationery, 204 James n
Williamson Mrs Eliza (wid Peter) 38 Cherry
Williamson James, teamster, 268 Catharine n
Williamson R, wood and coal merchant, 296 James n
Williamson Richard, tinsmith, 314 James n
Williamson Robert, sailor, 268 Hughson n
Williamson Robert, laborer, 25 Ferrie w
Williamson Robert, laborer, 13 Picton w
Williamson Thos, laborer, 266 Hughson n
Williamson T M, grocer, 176 Cannon e
Williamson T & R, wood and coal, cor Stuart and Macnab n
Williamson W B, ice dealer, 312 James n
Williamson Wm, teamster, 16 Mill
Williamson Wm, carpenter, 23 Strachan w
Williman Daniel, moulder, 113 Wood e
Willis Albert E, laborer, bds Dundurn e s nr York
Willis Frederick, moulder, 25 Simcoe w
Wills Charles, machinist, bds 124 Rebecca
Wills James, shoemaker, 1½7 John s
Wills Wm W, draughtsman, 71 Locomotive
Willman Mrs Joanna (wid Frederick) 112 Caroline s
Willmore Alfred, machinist, 12 Elgin
Wilmit John, scalemaker, 88 Market

Wilson Andrew F, law student, 45 Duke
Wilson Mrs Ann (wid Frederick) r 61 Jackson e
Wilson Mrs Ann (wid Peter) 121 Hannah e
Wilson A McD, clerk, 44 Main w
Wilson Arch, hotelkeeper, 288 King w
Wilson Arch (Archdale Wilson & Co) h 132 Bay s
Wilson Archdale & Co (Archdale Wilson, C W Tinling) wh druggists, 19 Macnab n
Wilson Archibald, moulder, 35 West ave n
Wilson Chas, laborer, 217 Bay n
Wilson Chas, laborer, 39 Sheaffe
Wilson Chas sr, 165 John n
Wilson Chas jr, finisher, 165 John n
Wilson Mrs Charlotte, 54 Strachan e
Wilson Ed C, manufacturer, 153 Cannon e
Wilson Mrs Elizabeth (wid Wm H) dressmaker, 81 Main w
Wilson Mrs Emma (wid Geo) 87 Hughson n
Wilson Frederick, carpenter, 110 Wellington s
Willson F J (Willson & Gates) 45 Bay s
Willson F M, accountant, 22 James s, h 5 Young
Willson & Gates (F J Willson, & F W Gates jr, mnfrs brooms, wh wooden ware, 31 King w
Willson & Gates, stock brokers, room 3 Larkin Hall, 8 John n
Wilson Geo, file cutter, r 58 Wilson
Wilson Geo, tinsmith, 37 Catharine s
Wilson Geo E, provision merchant, 75 Ray n
Wilson James, hotelkeeper, 250 York

Wilson James, laborer, 29 Strachan w
Wilson James, clerk, 63 Hughson s
Wilson James, dyer, 77 John n
Wilson James, second hand store 47 York
Wilson James D (Wm Wilson & Son) h 9 Hess s
Wilson James G, moulder, 183 York
Wilson Mrs Jane (wid Andrew) 27½ Tisdale
Wilson John, painter, 44 Wellington s
Wilson John, stoves and tins, 35 York h 49 Ray s
Wilson John, dyer, 101 Ferguson ave n
Wilson John, laborer, 3 Devenport
Wilson John, engineer, 182 Victoria ave n
Wilson John, salesman, 18 King e
Wilson John, engineer, city Hospital
Wilson John, carpenter, 11 Bay s
Wilson Jos, watchman, Wentworth n
Wilson Jos, letter carrier, 56 Wilson
Wilson Jos, grocer, 33 West ave n
Wilson Jos. pork curer, 122 Queen n
Wilson J, painter, 1 Walnut n, h44 Wellington s
Wilson Jos H, pork butcher, 111 Hess n
Wilson Lowell. Concession s s w Garth
Wilson Matthew (Matthew Wilson & Co) h 187 Macnab n
Wilson Matthew & Co, manfrs hay tools, s w cor Caroline and Barton
Wilson Miss Mary, 65 Hughson s
Wilson Robt, city fireman, 103 Napier
Wilson Robt, laborer, 46 Brock
Wilson Robt, boots and shoes, 56 King e, h 118 Rebecca
Wilson Robt, clerk, bds 51 Park n
Wilson Robt, laborer, 281 Hughson n
Wilson Robt G jr, clerk, 118 Rebecca
Wilson Robt, com traveler, 45 Park n
Wilson Ross R, com traveler, 184 King w
Wilson Stephen, laborer, 247 John n
Wilson Thos, foreman fire dept, 42 Market
Wilson Thos, carpenter, hd Queen s w s
Wilson Thos, messenger Bank B N A, 5 King e
Wilson Thos, blacksmith, bds 57 John s
Wilson Thos, laborer, 109 Wood e
Wilson Thos, 24 Walnut s
Wilson Thos, laborer, Robinson n s w Locke
Wilson Thos, Wellington House, 101 Wellington n
Wilson Thos, salesman, r Canada Life Building
Wilson Thos, clerk, 45 Wellington s
Wilson Thomas H, M D, 154 Main e
Wilson Wm A, tinsmith, 100 Emerald n
Wilson Wm, spinner, 259 John n
Wilson Wm, 193½ Wellington n
Wilson Wm, 29 Victoria ave n
Wilson Wm, laborer, 315 King Wm
Wilson Wm, laborer, 178 Wilson
Wilson Wm K, carpenter, 7 Augusta
Wilson Wm L, boarding, 103 King w
Wilson Wm & Son, merchant tailors, 44 King w

Wilson Wilmot, switchman GTR 140 Hess n
Wlson ——, laborer, 188 Main w
Winkler Adolph, cooper, 120 Rebecca
Winkler Chas H, cutler, 97 King w
Winckler Julius, machinist, 15 Main w
Winer J & Co, (Geo Rutherford, Geo LeRiche, John McHaffie) wholesale druggists, 23-25 King e
Winer John, 96 Main e
Wing George, loom fixer, 32 Picton e
Wing John E, machinist, 128 Hunter w
Wing Michael, laborer, 244 Catharine n
Wingfield Alex H, landing waiter customs, 8 Queen n
Winfield Thomas, grocer, 142 Hunter w
Winfield Thos, foreman Cruickshanks, 94 Caroline n
Winn George, shoemaker, 257 Cannon e
Winn Wm, shoemaker, 20 Emerald n
Winnifreth Bernard, grocer, 246 King e
Winslow & Webber, carriage furnishings, 140 King w
Winter Edward, blacksmith, cor York and Dundurn
Winter Timothy, fireman GTR, 9 Inchbury s
Wise John, laborer, 154 Emerald n
Wise John, machinist, 76 Victoria ave n
Wishart George W, bds 14 Colborne
Wishart James, blacksmith, r 57 King Wm, h Beulah
Witherby Harland F, watchmak'r, 60 Jackson w

Witherspoon Mrs E (wid **Henry**) 63 Robert
Witherspoon Jacob F, bookkeeper, 63 Robert
Witherspoon R W (Cameron & Witherspoon) h 192 John n
Witton H B, law student, 12 Murray w
Witton H B, canal inspector, 12 Murray w
Wodehouse Arthur, Wentworth s
Wodell Mrs **Ann** (wid Richard) 283½ King Wm
Wodell Miss F, stenographer, 283½ King Wm
Wodell F W, night editor *Spectator*, 136 York
Wodell Frank, blacksmith, 283½ King Wm
Wolf Joseph R, pawnbroker, 53 John s
Wolfe M J, hotel, 65 Stuart w
Wolfe N, varieties, 78 King **w**
Wolfinden Thos, cotton spinner, bds 93 Murray e
Wonham P C B, clerk Bank **of** Montreal, Bay cor Jackson
Wood A T (Wood & Leggat) h Elmwood, James s
Wood Cornelius, carter, 46 Canada
Wood D P, 19 Stuart w
Wood Fred L, 5 West ave s
Wood George, blacksmith, 11 Elgin
Wood H E, baker, 19 Stuart w
Wood James, clerk, 181 Macnab n
Woods John, miller, 105 East ave n
Wood Joseph, carpenter, bds 57 John s
Wood & Leggat, (A T Wood, Matthew Leggat, Wm Vallance, W A Wood) wholesale and retail hardware) 44 King e
Wood Mrs Margaret, 112 Macnab n
Wood Mrs Martha, 11 Elgin

Wood W A (Wood & Leggat) h Linwood, James s
Wood Walter F, boots and shoes, 22 King h 21 Hunter w
Woodcock Henry, laborer, 60½ Tisdale
Woodcock John W, laborer, 120 Simcoe e
Woodcock Thomas, laborer, 60½ Tisdale
Woodcroft Levi, laborer, 96 Hannah w
Woodhall Mrs Ann (wid Wm) 4 Nightingale
Woodhall Wm, bricklayer, 12 Oak ave
Woodhams Joseph, laborer, r 132 Catharine n
Woodhouse Wm H, timekeeper, 85 George
Woodley Samuel, boots and shoes, 22 James n, h 49 Jackson w
Woodman Frank, machinist, bds 98 Hess n
Woodman John, baggageman, 80 Lower Cathcart
Woodman John, machinist, 70 Emerald n
Woodman Thos, checker N & N W, 82 East ave n
Woodruff Edgar, piano tuner, 10 Margaret
Woods George, laborer, r 104 Bay n
Woods George, laborer, 122 Wood e
Woods Henry, laborer, 107 Bay n
Woods John, laborer, Aikman ave
Woods Robert, cabinetmaker, 45 Napier
Woods Walter (Walter Woods & Co) h 154 Macnab n
Woods Walter & Co (Walter Woods, John M Little, Wm Woods) manfrs and dealers in woodenware, grocers' sundries, etc, 60-62 Macnab n

Woods Wm, (Walter Woods & Co) h 175 Main e
Woodward A, clerk, 173 Main e
Woodward Frederick, upholsterer, 61 Main e
Woodward Henry W, accountant C H, 173 Main e
Woodward Henry W jr, 173 Main e
Woodward Percival, shipper, 173 Main e
Woodward Stewart, shipper, 173 Main e
Woolcott Chas J, engineer GTR, 45 Queen s
Wooldridge Henry, coachman, 60 Maria
Woolley Robert, spinner, 130 Macauley e
Woolley Wm, stave manfr, 1 South
Woolley Major Wm, Salvation Army, 15 Elgin
Wolliung Emile, pork butcher, cor Barton and Hughson n
Woolverton Algernon M D, 153 James n
Woolverton Mrs E W, Homœathic Pharmacy, 85 King w
Woolverton F E, M D, 119 King e
Word Wm, mariner, 181 Macnab n
Work Donald, quarryman, 31 Liberty
Work John, laborer, 21 Magill
Work Thos, porter, 35 Barton e
Work Wm (Fox & Work) h 31 Liberty
World Toronto, news paper, G E Peene, agent, 5 Arcade
Worrall Walter, cabinetmaker, 77 James s
Worrall Wm, cabinetmaker, 77 James s
Wragg Alfred, plasterer, ft Wellington n
Wren John, laborer, 118 Cherry
Wren Maurice, tinsmith, 98 Cherry

Wright Alfred, **keysmith**, **42** Cherry
Wright Alfred J, clerk, 79 Robert
Wright Alfred W, locksmith, 18 King Wm, h 79 Robert
Wright Mrs Clara (wid Chas) 108 Hess n
Wright Elijah, 21 Locke s
Wright Mrs Eliza (wid Thos W) 37 Emerald n
Wright Emerson, supt Bridge Works, 16 Mulberry
Wright Ed T (E T Wright & Co) 92 Catharine s
Wright E T & Co (E T, **H G** Wright) 26 Catharine n
Wright Geo, stonemason, **bds** 103 King w
Wright Hy G (E T **Wright & Co**) h 37 Emerald **n**
Wright Mrs Eughine, 29 Wood e
Wright James, mariner, 84 Mulberry
Wright Mrs Jane (wid James) 91 Wilson
Wright Mrs **J H** (wid James) 279 King Wm
Wright John, stoves, etc, 16 **King** Wm, h 48 King Wm
Wright John, butcher, 286 York
Wright John, agent, 281 Mary
Wright Jos E, laborer, Aikman
Wright Leslie, baggagemaster N & N W, 10 Grove
Wright Lewis, salesman, 21 Locke n
Wright Mrs Margaret (wid **Alex**) tailoress, 55 Main w
Wright Matthew, cotton **broker**, 8 Park s
Wright Peter, laborer, **52** Florence
Wright Robert [Thomson & Wright] h 32 George
Wright Robt, driver, 16 Pearl s
Wright Mrs Sarah McB, 19 Augusta
Wright Wm, machinist, 4 Concession

Wright Wm, machinist, 67 **Locke** s
Wright Wm, machinist, **49 Ferguson** ave
Wright Wm, laborer, 36 Crooks
Wright Wm, huckster, 51 James n
Wright Wm G, machinist, **5** West ave n
Wright Wm jr, moulder, **111** Macnab n
Wright W S, whipmaker, **82** East ave **n**
Wrigley Daniel, machinist, 105 Napier
Wrigley John T, machinist, 105 Napier
Wurst Frederick, carpenter, 145 King Wm
Wurst John, **bricklayer**, **151 King** Wm
Wurster C H, salesman, bds 48 James n
Wurzel Mrs Sophia, 43 Main w
Wyatt Mrs Lillies, Robinson n **s** nr Garth
Wyles Wm, laborer, 108 Maria
Wyllie Allison A, overseer cotton mills, 193 Macnab n
Wyllie Andrew A, appraiser customs, 158 Macnab n
Wylie Mrs Maria [wid James] 31 Hannah e
Wyllie Mrs Marion [wid **Wm**] dressmaker, 62 Hess n
Wyman **Alonzo P, carpenter, 43** Peter
Wynkham Wm, **packer**, King e of Wentworth
Wynn Dominick, cotton dryer, 288½ James **n**
Wynn **Geo, shoe** manfr, **124** King **Wm**
Wynn Hugh, bds 165 Macnab **n**
Wynn John, laborer, 54 Canada
Wynn John, teamster, bds 66 John n
Wynn Mrs Mary [wid Thos] 61 Maria

Wynn Percy A, shoemaker, 262-4 York
Wynn ——, dyer, 36 Ferrie w
Wyth Eleazar, carpenter, 261 York
Yaldon John, clerk, 198 Macnab n
Yaldon R W, hotel, 103-105 James n
Yaldon Wm, hotelkeeper, 198 Macnab n
Yates Geo H, watchman, 193 Bay n
Yates Wm, riveter, 216 John n
Yates Wm, bricklayer, hd of Evans
Yeager John W, carpenter, 90 West ave n
Yeager Willis, carpenter, 87 Wellington n
Yearsley Samuel, painter, bds 293 King w
Yeoman John W, prop Ontario Pharmacy, King cor Ferguson ave
Young Miss Agnes, dressmaker, 184 Macnab n
Young Albert, bookkeeper, 241 Bay n
Young Alex, ironorker, w 52 Locomotive
Young Alfred C, arpenter, bds 175 Mary
Young Miss Ann, dressmaker, 84 Bay n
Young & Bro, (Wm and Robert Young) plumbers' supplies and chandeliers manfrs, 17 John n and 135 King Wm
Young Charles, agent, 116 Cannon e
Young Daniel, gardener, hd York w canal
Young D H, salesman, 31 Gore
Young David, 4 Oak
Young Edward, plasterer, 86 Ferrie e
Young Edward, piano maker, 116 Cannon e
Young Edward, salesman, 19 John n
Young Frank, bartender, 64 John
Young Frank R, bartender, 7 Gore
Young George A, ins agent, 5 King w, h 11 Young
Young George A, salesman, 169 York
Young Hamilton, Hamilton Cotton Co, 41 Duke
Young Henry, carpenter, Henry
Young J M, manager Hamilton Cotton Co, 98 Macnab n
Young Jacob, wheelwright, 233 Hughson n
Young James, bookkeeper, 88 Napier
Young James, carriagemakrr, 272 James n
Young James, laborer, 34 Aurora
Young James, tea merchant, 13 Barton e
Young James M, foreman cotton mill, 188 Macnab n
Young John B, accountant, 33 Hannah w
Young John B, accountant, 20 Charles
Young John H, architect, 117 King w
Young John, stovemounter, 102 Ferguson ave
Young John, engineer, 6 Oak
Young Lewis J, cotton carder, 188 Macnab n
Young M jr, clerk Bank of Hamilton, Burlington
Young Maitland, sec Hamilton & Northwestern Railway, 33 Main e, res Burlington
Young Mrs Margaret (wid Hugh) 16 Locomotive
Young Mrs Matilda (wid Henry) 107 Catharine n
Young Men's Christian Association, 38 King e
Young Robert (Young & Bro) h 3 East ave s

Young Robert, yardmaster N &
 N W, 52 Evans
Young Robt, patternmaker, 13
 Barton e
Young Samuel, timekeeper, 204
 Macnab n
Young Thomas, heater, 335 York
Young Thos, Unique saloon, 7
 Gore
Young Thomas, porter, 137 Hunter w
Young Thomas, saloonkeeper,
 64 John n
Young Wallace, foreman
 Young & Bros, h 55 East ave n
Young Wm, bookkeeper, 33
 Hannah w
Young William [Young &
 Bro] h 45 Jackson w
Young ——, 7 Bay n
Young Mrs, 102 Ferguson ave
Yuker Clark, com traveler, 40
 Erie ave
Yule James, clerk Domion hotel
Zealand Mrs Edward, 16 Murray
 w
Zealand E G, deputy sheriff,
 16 Murray w
Zealand Henry W, clerk, 257
 Bay n

Zealand's Wharf, Brock
Zealand Wm, master mariner,
 257 Bay n
Zidersky Hugo, rag dealer, 31
 John n, h 15 Wellington n
Ziecs Henry, laborer, bds 62
 Cannon e
Ziecs Theodore, laborer, bds 62
 nan e
Zimmerman A, merchant
 tailor, 50 James n, h 65 George
Zimmerman J, dentist, 38 King
 e, h Blake
Zimmerman J A, druggist, 114
 King e
Zimmerman S, M D, D D S,
 King cor Macnab n
Zimmerman W E, salesman, 134
 Hughson n
Zingsheim Jacob, furniture mfr,
 225 Mary, h 173 John n
Zion Tabernacle, Pearl cor
 Napier
Zoeller John, tailor, 109 James n
Zoeller Mrs John, Queen's laundry, 109 James n
Zwick Chas A, chief attendant
 asylum, 84 Hannah w
Zwick W H, real estate agent,
 2½ James s

CITY AND COUNTY DIRECTORIES

The following are now ready, and will be sent on receipt of price:

City of Hamilton $2 50
City of Kingston, including Frontenac County 2 00
City of St. Catharines, including Lincoln and Welland 2 00
City of Brantford, including Brant County 2 00
County of Simcoe 2 00
County of Wentworth 2 00
County of Waterloo 2 00

WE ARE ALSO AGENTS FOR THE

City of Guelph $2 00
County of Wellington 3 00
City of Quebec 2 50
City of Ottawa 2 50
City of Montreal 3 00

All books are recent editions.

W. H. IRWIN & CO.,

12 MACNAB ST. SOUTH,   HAMILTON, ONTARIO.

HAMILTON STREET DIRECTORY.

Aikman's Ave, from Wentworth south, runs east
James Freed, gardener
Mrs Mary Lynch
Thos Collins, coachman
Ira Blain, laborer
Joseph E Wright
Thos Birbeck, laborer
Wm Kane, laborer
John Davis, fishmonger
John Woods, laborer
Walter Davis, laborer
Mrs Margaret Fisher
John McFarlane, teamster
John Solbisburg, laborer
Wm Johnston, blacksmith

Burlington-st intersects

John Early, gardener
Thos McCabe, engineer
David Bruce

Alanson-st from west of Erie ave east to Wentworth
Blythe-st intersects
30 Jeremiah O'Connors, laborer
Erie-ave intersects
29 J J Armstrong, quarryman
31 Chas Anstey, clerk
33 Alex Stuart, clerk
35 Robt Fitzmaurice, moulder
37 Thos Hutchinson, painter
39 G W Cooper, blacksmith
41 Frank Hyde, laborer
43 Jas Bartle, laborer
44 Peter Patterson, carpenter
45 Edgar Mortimer, teamster

42 Alex R Grant, inspector

Albert Road, from 229 Victoria ave n
4 John Hunter, laborer
6 Fred Walters, moulder
8 Ed O'Kennard, cabinetmak'r
Edmund Callaghan, laborer
Robt Stoneman, moulder
Wm J Caldwell, moulder
Albert W Whitby, shoemak'r

Ardvolich-st, from Dundurn west
No houses

Ashley-st, from end King east north to Barton
Dennis Kelly, bricklayer
John Mallin, moulder
James Laidlaw, carpenter
Jeremiah Rowe, mason
George Hadden, laborer
Richard George, shoemaker

Athol-st runs from King w near Limits
Joseph Grimes, laborer

Augusta-st, north side, from 85 James south to Catharine
5 F R Hutton, builder
7 Wm K Wilson, carpenter
9 Vacant

15 J G Pocock, mason

Hughson-st intersects.

19 Mrs Sarah Wright
21 Wm Moore, bookkeeper
23 Mrs John Bowes
25 James Cooper, barber

John-st intersects.

39-41 Ballentine Bros, grocers
47 Wm G Buchanan, packer
49 Albert Otto, carver
49½ Mrs Thomas Sintzel

Catharine-st intersects.

Augusta-st. south side

2 Wm J Ballentine, grocer
6 John Beal, grocer
8 Wm H Ford, moulder
10 Alex Robertson, carpenter
12 Henry Simon, manfr
14 John Riach, merchant
16 Mrs Mary Swain
16½ Thos Snider, baker
18 D Summerfield, manfr
20 R S Ambrose, music teacher

Hughson-st intersects.

22 Simeral Doak, blacksmith
26 Robert McKay, plasterer
28 J Dublin, whitewasher
30 Mrs Jane Butler
32 Wm A Sanders, baker
34 Thomas Bryce, baker

John-st intersects.

28 Mrs John Farrish
46 James McKenzie, machinist
48 John McDonough, dairyman
48½ Mrs Chas Dickenson

Catharine-st intersects.

Aurora-st. east side, from Grove to Hannah

2 Vacant
4 Wm Richards, laborer
6 Wm Old, laborer
8 Chas Hamilton, clerk

32

12 John Santry, laborer

Young-st intersects.

22 Vacant
24 Vacant
24½ Thos O'Connor, laborer
26 Mrs Patrick McDonald

Maria-st intersects.

32 Edmund Murphy, tailor
34 James Young, laborer
38 Thos Mahoney, laborer

Hannah-st intersects.

Aurora-st, west side

19 Mrs Julia Fitzmaurice
25 Mrs Michael Sullivan

Maria-st intersects.

41 Wm Scott, cutler
43 George Tucker, shoemaker

Hannah-st intersects.

Baillie-st, from 72 Hunter East

5 Elijah Burkholder
7 Samuel Harvey, auctioneer
4½-6 Vacant
8 David Mitchell, shoemaker
10 John P Cline, marble cutter
11 P E Lumsden, merchant
13 Mrs Wm Graham
16 Geo Williams, builder

Barton-st east, north side from 196 James north to City Limits.

11 Peter Johnston, cigarmaker
13 Robt Young, patternmaker
15 Joseph Philip, salesman
17 S C Malcolmson, mariner
19 Geo Robinson, band master
21 John McKinty, customs
23 John Hackett, machinist

Hughson-st intersects

25 Mrs Thos Callon

29 David Walsh, messenger P O
31 Donald McNichol, carpenter
33 Wm H Povey, painter
35 Thos Work, porter
39 Robt Bennett, moulder
   James Main, grocer

John-st intersects

   Mrs H Broderick, grocer
53 John D Nelson, teamster
55 Mrs John Ryan
57 Ed Joyce, painter
59 David Kemp, painter
61 Lewis Whiting, traveler
63 Patrick Halloran, grocer

Catharine-st intersects

91 Wm Gage, wood dealer

Mary-st intersects

91 Wanzer Sewing Machine Co

Elgin-st intersects

   County jail

Ferguson-ave intersects

113 Francis Lynch, teamster
117 John H Milburn, scalemak'r
119 George McNeilly, mechanic
131 Osborne, Killey Mfr Co
133 — Smith, teamster
135 Andrew Lewis, teamster

Wellington-st intersects

   Flatt & Bradley, lumber
   City hospital

Victoria-ave intersects

215 Wm Sheriff, grocer
217 Thos Fawcett, laborer
219 Mrs Carlisle Bradley
221 Wm Kennedy, bricklayer
223 Mrs Mary Burt
225 Jas Mitchell, stovemounter
233 George Hayes, grocer

East-ave intersects

237 John Kirkness, cooper
239 George Sahli, car driver
243 Mrs Elizabeth Jamieson

Emerald-st and Oak-ave intersect

   Vacant lots
261 Frank Rowlin, laborer
265 Chas Edwards, machinist
267 John Anderson, bricklayer
297 G B Smith, wood dealer
309 Thos Hannah, teamster
311 Joseph Bissell, carpenter
313 John Johnston, helper

Little William-st intersects

319 John Graham, grocer
327 Wm Hodson, butcher
329 David Buick, laborer

Wentworth-st intersects

   Wm J Jones, tollkeeper
   Wm Arscot, gardener
   Lewis Moore, gardener
   Albert Swayzie, grocer
   Peter Belleville, tobaccorollr

Barton-st e, south side

10 John Cahill, blacksmith
12 E Ringer, melter
14 Thos Moore, engineer
16 James Dodson, moulder
18 Mrs Sarah Knott
20 Chas Leyden, lithographer
22 John Paton
24 Wm McGibbon, baker
26 E R Davis, grocer

Hughson-st intersects

34 James Omand, engineer
36 Thos O'Connor, laborer
38 Isaiah Audett, blacksmith
40 Geo D Phibbs, wheelmaker
42 David Muir, pile driver

John-st intersects

54 Wm Nash, engineer
56 W H McElcheran
58 Mrs Thos Waldron

Catharine-st intersects

70 Alfred Taylor, teamster
72 John Westway, packer

74 Vacant
80 H Little, grocer

Mary-st intersects

Private grounds

92 Wm C Barnfather, engineer
94 John Kennedy, moulder
96 Wm Whiteside, machinist

Elgin-st intersects

98 Michael McCarty, moulder
100 T Kavanagh, moulder
102 John E Davis, machinst
104 Mrs Geo Allan
106 Luke Gray, mechanic

Ferguson-ave intersects

Round house
128-130 Vacant
132 Wm Pugh, shoemaker
134 Vacant
136 Wesley Cooper, engineer
138 James Dufton, bricklayer
140 Robt Webster, cabinetmaker
142 John Earle, shoemaker

Wellington-st intersects

Vacant lots
Public school

West-ave intersects

198 Edward Campbell, moulder
200 John McCarthy, stovemt'r
202 John Synet, boilermaker
204 Mrs Louisa Smith

Victoria-ave intersects.

226 Wm Springstead, laborer
228 Wm Price, bricklayer
230 Thos Denbury, laborer
232 Henry Potter, laborer
234 John Beveridge, shoemaker
236 James McDermott, moulder

East-ave intersects

240 Wm Robinson, carpenter
246 John Fleming, grocer

Emerald st intersects

248 Mrs Mary Jane Batty

248½ Michael Dwyer, moulder
250 Bartholemew Moriaty, laborer

Oak-ave intersects

254 Ed Goff, traveler
Hy Gaskell, patternmaker

Smith-ave intersects

296 John H Land
298 Peter Filman

Wentworth-st intersects

John Stebbins, gardener
James Wilds, gardener
Angus Reid, gardener
Thos L Kinrade, teacher
Geo N Kinrade, blacksmith
Thos P Kinrade

Barton-st west, north side, from 125 James north to Locke

12 Miss Hannah Macnab
14 Wm Allan, contractor
16 John Flynn, moulder
18 Andrew Leitch, machinist
20 Mrs Hugh Moore
22 Albert Lake, broommaker

Macnab-st intersects

40 Wm Magee jr, ice dealer
42 Wm Geldhart, machinist
44 Wm Morgan, machinist
52 Ed Treganza, butcher

Park-st intersects

58 James Binney, mason
60 A E Kenney, mechanic

Bay-st intersects

Vacant lots to Locomotive street
A Massie, time-keeper
Vacant lots to end

Barton-st west, south side

13 Mrs Bridget Blake
113 Patrick Fahey, laborer
15 Mrs Edwin M Coventry

17 David Stock, city foreman
19 Henry Welsh, machinist
25 W A Sealey, carpenter

Macnab-st intersects

35 Harris Brown, teamster
43 George Roach

Park-st intersects

65 Samuel Mulholland, laborer
67 Robt Rodger, blacksmith
69 E H Hopgood, butcher

Bay-st intersects
Caroline-st intersects

Mrs Jennie Sheppard
Vacant lots

Greig-st intersects

John Borland, laborer
Mrs Margaret Girouard
Mrs John Dunn
John Parry, laborer

Locomotive-st intersects

Wm McMann, melter

Magill-st intersects

James McIlroy, watchman
Joshua Jackson, fireman
Henry McConnel, engineer
Mrs Richard Crooks
Ed L Sinclair, brakeman

Crook-st intersects

Wm Marshall, fitter
John L Hayden, brakeman
Wm P Sinclair, laborer
Thos Crofton, moulder
Valentine Burn, laborer

Locke-st intersects

Bay-st north, e side, from 128 King w to Brock

8 R Buskard, carriagemaker
10 Hiram Hurd, marble dealer

Market-st intersects

26 John Rodgers, blacksmith
28 Alex L Kay, machinist
30 Geo W Alderson, plasterer
34 Mrs Margaret Newman
36 John Armstrong
38 Vacant
40-4 Thos Porteous, butcher
50 David McDonald, grocer

York-st intersects and Merrick-st ends

58 Wm McIlroy
60 James Noble, laborer
62 Wm Flitcroft, blacksmith
62 E J Crofton, painter

Vine-st ends

72 Wm H Judd, soap manfr
76 John Taylor, malster
78 Mrs John Waugh
80 James Ailes, mechanic
82 Robt Alingham, mechanic
84 Miss A Young, dressmaker
86 Wm Milne
88 Wm Stevenson, stovemounter
90 Miss Mary Sutherland
92 James Martin, shoemaker

Cannon-st intersects

94-6 Edward Hughes
98-100 Wm Geiss, machinist
102-4 James Seddon, dyer
r 104 Geo Woods, laborer
106 John Homewood, mechanic
r 106 Mrs Kate Gleason
108 Mrs Edward Hanlan
110 Wm Ashby, laborer
112 Henry Boothby, draughtsm'n
114-6 Gas works

Mulberry-st intersects

118 Robert Moffatt, mechanic
124 Wm Weybrant, machinist
126 Wm Owens, laborer
128 Michael Mulroy, laborer
130 Mrs Mary Enright
132 Walter Crossland, cigarmaker
134 Mrs Mary Webster
136 Mrs Bleckart

Sheaffe-st intersects

142-2 Edwin Harris, boarding
144 John Lahiff, laborer
144½ John W Sharp, laborer
146 John Black, butcher
148 John Early, teamster
150 John Duffy, farmer

Colborne-st intersects

152 Samson Beavis, gas stoker
154 Frank Ralph, teamster
156 Pierce Grace, laborer
158 Thos Oliver, shoemaker
160 Vacant

Barton-st intersects

162 Wm Proper, hotel keeper
166 John Davidson, collector
168 Wm Horn, letter carrier
170 Miss C R Regan
172 Mrs John Neelon, boarding
174 Angus McIntosh
176 Wm Brown, brakeman

Murray-st intersects

Hamilton Industrial Wks Co
196 Oliver Rymal, brakeman
198 John Logan, inland revenue

Stuart and Strachan-sts intersect

Vacant lots

Simcoe-st intersects

230 Ed Moran, japanner
230½ Andrew Stuart, designer
232 John Mackay
234 Wm Cowan, platelayer
238 Thos Hodson, laborer
238½ Wm Campaign, policeman
240 Andrew White, laborer
244 Morris Cummings, engineer

Ferrie-st intersects

250 Wm McClure, carpenter
252 Wm Irving, machinist
254 Mrs Wm C Thomson
256 Wm Campbell, checker
258 Robt Hamilton
260 Capt John C Burrows

Picton-st intersects

266 James McKeever, laborer
266½ Thos Tracy, brakeman
268 Samuel Bennett, brassfinisher
270 John Webster, turner
274 Jos Charlton, glassblower
276 Maydwell Goodwin, mach't

Macaulay st intersects

284 Mrs Augusta Grant
286 Mrs Brownlow Sanders

Burlington & Brock-sts intersect

Bay-st north, west side

1 T B Fairchilds, hotel
3 F Schwartz, cigarmaker
5-7 Vacant
9 T G Archer, tuner
11 Vacant
13 Walter Spencer, organs
15 Hy Kuntz, brewer
17 John Baxter, teamster
19 Stephen Pocock, saw manfr
21 L Rose, agent
23 Geo Scott, engineer

Market st-intersects

25 James Anderson, M D
27 Sam W Townsend, customs
29 Mrs John Duggan
31 W G Townsend, customs broker
33 Samuel J Ireland, artist
35 Hy Lawry, porkpacker
37 Wm Ronald, grocer
39 James Owens, stove moulder
41 Mrs Isabella Sayers
43 Fred Call, moulder

Napier-st commences

51 Vacant

York-st intersects

Copp Bros, foundry
71 W H Judd & Bro, soap mfrs
73 Chas Dunbar, laborer
75 David Cook, bartender
77 Matthew Burns, teamster
79 Chas Robertson

81 Mrs Mary Byrne
81½ John McKay, conductor
83 Fred Edworthy, butcher
85 Lewis Hipkins, blacksmith
87 Michael Rock, harnessmkr
89 F C Smith, plater

Cannon-st intersects

91 F J Schrader, tobacconist
93 Wm Aitchison, hotel
95 Daniel Dixon, teamster
97 Geo Pettinger
101 Mrs Jane Budge
103 Albert E Blake, fireman
105 Robt Gray, conductor
107 Hy Woods, laborer
109 Wm B Croy, com traveler
111 M D Healey, drygoods merch
113 Michael Sweeney, traveler
115 Fred Filgiano, clerk
117 Robt Lucas, moulder
119 Michael Arland, laborer
121 John D Evans, brewer
123 Wm L Cummer, brewer

Mulberry-st intersects

Spring brewery

Sheaffe-st intersects

143 Wm Gray
145 Wm Dowd, laborer
147 Albert Berryman, telegraphist
149 James McLaughlin, moulder
151 John Saunders, painter
153 George Dowswell, mechanic
155 Robert Amos, salesman
157 Alex Taggert, carpenter
159-161 John Dillon, grocer

Barton-st intersects

163 M Doyle, baggageman
165 Brock Burtch, mason
167 Wm Dillon
169 Mrs James Gleason
173 Mrs Elizabeth Chambers
r 173 Robt Mackie, engineer
175 Wm Moriaty, restaurant
177 Mrs Timothy Boyle
r 177 Henry Burrows, laborer
179 James Fitzgerald, laborer

181 John Desmond, laborer
183 Hector Dodson, whipmaker
185 Mrs M Sheridan
r 185 Mrs George Cousins
" Mrs Kate Callan
" Thos Quilter, laborer
" Thos Foster, laborer
187 John Cahill, blacksmith
189 Wm Martin, laborer
191 George McLennan, laborer
193 George H Yates, watchman
195 Thos McNash, laborer
197 Thos Chadwick, railroader
199 Patrick O'Neill, laborer
Allison House

Stuart-st intersects

207 G T R engineer's office
Gillesby's grain warehouse

Strachan-st intersects

209 Wm Dillon, hotel
211 Thos Peden, baggageman
213 John Dobson, stovemounter
215 Andrew Dillon, hotelkeeper
217 Charles Watson, laborer

Simcoe-st intersects

239 Thos Renton, carpenter
241 Albert Young, bookkeeper
r241 C Doxey, mechanic
r241 Wm Pilton, laborer
243 James Forester, checker
245 John Whitby, fitter
247 Wm Rennie, letter carrier

Ferrie-st intersects

J Massie's boat house
253 Mrs Ann Vila, grocer
255 Austin Vila, chandler
257 Capt Wm Zealand
259 Robert Soper, sailmaker
261 Walter Scott, engineer

Picton-st intersects

265 H L Bastien, boatbuilder
269 L H Bastien, boat builder

Macauley-st intersects

277 Thos Shackell, conductor

84 Vacant
86 Vacant
88 Vacant

Robinson-st intersects

90 John McMaster, merchant
92 Walter Ambrose, ins agent
94 Wm Palm
96 Mrs Chas Freeman
98 Mrs John White
100 Andrew Goodall, gardener

Hannah-st intersects

124 James M Lottridge, brewer

Herkimer-st intersects

126 Robt Lottridge
128 Wm Gatenby, tailor
130 James Balfour, architect
132 Archdale Wilson, merchant
134 Wm Carey, publisher

Markland-st intersects

134 Alex Ramsay
140 W F Walker, barrister
144 C J Jones, Telegraph Co
146 Mrs Elizabeth Lauder
148 F Wm Gates

Blythe-st, from 72 Stinson south to Alanson

14 Josiah Baker, carpenter
16 John Butterworth, carpenter
18 James Sage, carpenter
26 Wm Scott, shoemaker
   Stephen Jones, laborer

Bold-st, north side, from 80 James south to Pearl

4 H F Gardiner, journalist

Macnab-st intersects

Private grounds

Charles & Park-sts intersect

Central school grounds
40 Thos Ralston, janitor

Bay-st intersects

66 Mrs Samuel Blair
68 Wm Pawser, laborer

Caroline-st intersects

76 James M Carroll, bricklayer
78 Mrs Joanna Dean
80 Chas Schleissing, machinist
82 John Mitchell, shoemaker
84 Louis E Taylor, carpenter
88 Chas Thomsett, driver
90 Thos Pugh, carter
92 Vacant
96 James Baxter, coal dealer
98 Mrs Collins, laundress
100 Mrs Mary Ann Nealin
102 Mrs James Carroll

Hess-st intersects

104 E P Webber, salesman
106 George Curry, checker
110 John Stephens, machinist
112 Thos Lackie, laborer
114 Kenneth Campbell, laborer
116 Wm Newcomb, laborer
118 Vacant
120 G McCullough, blacksmith
122 Thos Oliver
124 Wm L Johnstone, blacksmith

Queen-st intersects

128 Matt J Carroll, bricklayer
130 Chas Mitchell, lamplighter
132 James Minnes, blacksmith

Ray & Pearl-sts intersect

Wm Gardiner, potter

Bold-st, south side

1 Mrs John Garrett
3 Mrs Arthur McCarter
5 Vacant
7 Daniel Sterling
9 Robt W Pentecost, traveler
11 Mrs James Fisher
13 Miss Gracie Iredale

Macnab-st intersects

53 Wm Hendrie, contractor

285 Robert Soper, sail loft
287 Vacant
Wood-st intersects
Sweet's warehouse
Brock-st intersects

Bay-st south, east side, from 101 King west to the mountain
1 G C Briggs, drugs etc
3 Wm Atkinson
5 Vacant
7 Mrs Ellen Thomson
7½ Wm Birkett, manfr
9 David Aitchison, manfr
11 John Wilson, cabinetmaker
Main-st intersects
19-21 J Walker, soap manfr
23 R N Raw, bookkeeper
25 Fire station
Jackson-st intersects
39 C H Bamfylde, clerk
41 R G Olmstead
43 Chas Moore, accountant
45 F J Willson, merchant
47 H W Sewell, grocer
49 Peter Brass, architect
51 Geo E Bristol, merchant
Hunter-st intersects
Central school grounds
Bold-st intersects
61 J H Somerville, com trav
69 C S Chittenden, dentist
Duke-st intersects
Vacant lots
Robinson-st intersects
93 Hugh Donaldson, builder
95 Edmund Savage, bookkper
Hannah-st intersects
109 Hy W Glassco, hatter
121 A R Gates, bookkeeper

Herkimer-st intersects
123 David S Thompson
127 J B Pilkey, agent
129 Robt A Huchison, mrcht
131 John Smith, emigration agt
Markland-st intersects
Thos Cassels, gardener
Concession-st intersects

Bay-st south, west side
2 G D Hawkins, shirt manfrs
4 Geo Lee, accountant
6 David Hawkins
George-st commences
8 J Herriman, stage driver
10 Vernon B Whipple, printer
Main-st intersects
24 Walker's soap factory
28 Owen McDonald, laborer
30 Wm Smith, painter
32 Wm Hanley) blacksmith
Jackson-st intersects
34 Mrs Wm Harvey
36 John McLeod, agent
46 Chas E Doolittle, manfr
Hunter-st intersects
St Marks, Church of England
Bold-st intersects
56 John Moodie, merchant
60 Mrs Alex Ewing
64 Jos Kavanagh
66 Rev A E Miller
68 Mrs Janet **Henderson**
70 John Stewart
72 Daniel S Whitmore, porter
Duke-st intersects
John Duff & Son, grocers
72½ John Mitchell, mason
74 John Karnahan, brushmaker
76 S H Kent, clerk
78 James S Paterson, bookkper
80 John Elliott
82 Walt V Ecelestone, salesman

Park-st intersects

31 David Dow, contractor
33 St Clair Balfour, merchant
33½ Wm Southam, publisher
35 Thos H Wadland, supt Bell Telephone Co
37 John W Bickle, broker
39 John Malloy, carriagemaker

Bay-st intersects

57 D Kidd, agent Can Life
61 Mrs A Macallum
65 Wm D Robinson
67 Wm F Waddell, salesman

Caroline-st intersects

77 N Freeley, bricklayer
78 Levi Sherk, machinist
81 Paul Deutscher, filecutter
83 Wm Nixon, laborer
85 James W Evenden, brickly'r
87 Vacant
91 Jas Baxter & Son wood deal's
95 Samuel McKelvy, laborer

Hess-st intersects

101 Samuel Coulter, shoemaker

Queen-st intersects

111 G McLean, shoemaker
115 James Ratcliffe, laborer
 F C Matthews, caretaker

Bowen-st from 48 Main east to Jackson

James Kennedy, blacksmith
Jolley & Sons, harness
Joseph Hoodless & Son, warehouse

Breadalbane, from Head to Jones

Freeman Shackelton, laborer
Chas Smith, lithographer
H N Thomas, marblecutter
John Hill, laborer

Geo Trevaskis, wagonmaker

Brock-st west, north side, from foot of Bay to Macnab

Magee's warehouse
Sweet's warehouse
Robertson's shipyard
Zealand's wharf
James Doyle, sailor
Browne's wharf
2 Patrick Roach, laborer

Brock-st, south side

23 Arch Robertson, shipbuilder
11 Harry Lee, bookkeeper

Brock-st east, from Hughson to Mary

46 Robt Wilson, laborer
51 James Walling, laborer
 Timothy Halleran, laborer
 George Patterson, laborer

Bruce-st, from Markland between Bay and Caroline, south to Concession

1 D C Dowrie, letter carrier
3 Mrs Carroll
6 Wm Davey, carpenter
 Wm Pennell, laborer

Concession-st intersects

Burlington-st north, Tp of Barton, east side

John S Beer, butcher
Grant Ford, plasterer
Mrs Jane Donald
D O Furminger, blacksmith
Geo B Greig, carpenter
W C White, builder

Wilson-st intersects

John Fleming, laborer

Nelson-st intersects

33

Harry Atwell, porter
Donald McMaster, mason
John McMaster, carpenter
Mrs Patrick O'Dea
Frank Smith, laborer
Thos Sheppard, laborer
Thos Strange, pedler
Max Rosenzweig, rag pedler
Joseph Poynton, butcher
Edward O'Brien, laborer
Dennis Ryan, laborer
— Smith
Mrs Eliza Taylor

Burlington-st, west side

Samuel A Tovel, gardener
John E Tovel, gardener

Burlington-st south, Tp of Barton, east side

Henry E Elliott, cutter
Thos Harper, gardener

Ida-st intersects

M. O'Sullivan, moulder
Joseph Lee, contractor

Burlington-south, west side

Wm Johnston, blacksmith

Ida-st intersects

F H Lynch-Staunton, P L S

Burlington-st east, north side from 368 James n to John

7 Mrs Francis Smith
13 Vacant
15 Thos Kavanagh, laborer

Hughson-st intersects

Vacant lots to end

Burlington-st east, south side

Hughson-st intersects

32 Thos McCarthy, carter

John-st intersects

John Sullivan, carter

Burlington-st west, north side from 347 James n to Bay

Private grounds

Macnab-st intersects

Burlington Glass Works
40 John Roach, sailor
42 Wm McNab, sailor
44 Mrs Robt Graham
46 Mrs Ellen Macdonald
48 Samuel Dolman, laborer
50 Wm Roberson, shipbuilder

Wood-st intersects

52 John Wakeham, carpenter
54 Hy Bosselman, laborer
56 Alvin Clark, engineer
58 Ed Burniston, carpenter

Bay-st intersects

Burlington-st w, south side

13 Wm Little, pot maker
15 P McGrath, laborer
17 Philip Doyle, laborer
19 Thos Snowdon, blacksmith
21 Jacob Riehl, laborer
23 Martin O'Mara, laborer
25 James McGee, carter
27 Mrs A Mack

Macnab-st intersects

33 Vacant
35 Chas Hull, laborer
37 Thos Powell, laborer
39 Lawrence Connoly, laborer
43 Albert Mooney, glassblower
45 M D Gage, laborer

Wood-st intersects

53 Wm Griffin, sailor
57 D Barker, carpenter
63 Randall Donovan

Bay-st intersects

Burton-st commences on the east side of Victoria ave, between South and Ferrie

James Oliver, moulder

John Christian, porter
Robt Neville, engineer
James Ellaber, moulder

Clarke-ave intersects

Canada-st, north side, from 42 Queen south to western limits

2 J B Simpson, conductor
4 Mrs Col Maria Fitzgerald
8 John B Faulknor, bricklayer

Ray-st intersects

18 Moses Dow, plasterer
20 John D Campbell, enameler
24 — Ennis, carpenter
26 Thos Cockburn, wireworker
28 Mrs Fred Rohr

Pearl-st intersects

34 Maer Lemberg, tinsmith
36 Wm Fickley, moulder
42 Mrs Joseph Kurpinsk, laund's
44 John Gould, laborer
46 Cornelius Wood, carter

Locke-st intersects

52 John B Dennis, painter
54 John Wynn, laborer
56 John Brass, tinsmith
62 Wm Melody, carter
62 Wm J Dyer, bookkeeper

Poulette-st intersects

64 John Bawden, brickmaker
68 Thos Collins, potter
70 Mrs Chas Jarvis
72 Mrs Michael McGrath
74 Joseph Langdon, engineer
76 Wm Fletcher, laborer
78 Isaac Webb, laborer
80 Francis Flaherty, laborer
82 Alex Hay, carpenter
86 Aaron Bawden, brickmaker

Garth-st intersects

Canada-st, south side

3 Vacant

5 Henry Carpenter
6 James Kennedy, blacksmith
11 George Hunter, bailiff

Ray-st intersects

13 Martin Kartzmark, machinist
25 Peter Warnke, tailor
29-31 Mrs David W Kern, grocer

Pearl-st intersects

35 Bernard Schelling, machinist
37 St Stephen's Church
37½ Rev Wm Myers
39 George Williams, plasterer
43 John Blain, painter

Locke-st intersects

49 Mrs Emily A Miller
51 Nichol McNichol, machinist
57 Wm Earle, teamster
59 Jas W Sinclair, painter
61 Wm Hempstock, laborer
63 David Garson, brushmaker
65 Thos Brown, teamster

Poulette-st interects

75 Joseph Clarke, laborer
79 Walter Etherington, carpenter
83 Robt Budge, laborer
89 Robt Jacques, machinist

Garth-st intersects

Cannon-st east, north side, from 126 James north to Wentworth

Knox Church
Cannon street school

Hughson-st intersects.

Vacant
Malleable Iron Works

John-st intersects.

42 P J Culhane, bill poster
44 Walter Grey, traveler
46 Frank Foley, whipmaker
48 H J Black

Catharine-st intersects.

62 Robert Wiers, teamster
80 E S Whipple, land agent
82 R R Wallace, M D
84 A L Pentecost, merchant
86 R W Seldon, grocer

Mary-st intersects.

94 John Thompson, customs

Elgin-st intersects

N & N W Railway offices

Ferguson-ave intersects

112 Jasper Hill, grocer
114 John Garrison, engineer
116 Chas Young, agent
118 Fred Duggan, shoemaker
120 Wm J Thomas
122 Mrs George Wills
124 Vacant
126 Wm Servos, clerk
126½ Thos Glass, fancy goods
128 Mrs Martha Degarmo
130 Mrs John Menorgan
132 James Craig, photographer
134 Mrs Wm Larey

Cathcart-st intersects

136 P Ronan, flour dealer
138 Geo Allan, telegraphist
140 J G Curell, barrister
142 Chas Stewart, carpenter
144 E H Brooks, brakeman
144 R White, carpenter
144 C Reeves, teamster
144a John Brenton, stoveplater
146 Chas Johnson, tailor
148 W Arnold, polisher
152 John Ronan, grocer

Wellington-st intersects

158 Walter Bastedo, gardener

West-ave intersects

174 Augustus Knetsch, tailor
176 Thos M Williamson, grocer

Victoria-ave intersects.

178 Henry Harrison, fitter
199 Robt Holmes, laborer

East-ave intersects

200 John Almas, agent
202 Wm Cole, traveller
204 Geo Denison, moulder
206 Henry Hargrove
208 John V Dynes, salesman
210 Vacant

Emerald st intersects

220 Thomas Armitage, machinist
226 J Burton, cabinetmaker
228 Martin Rowley, moulder

Oak-ave commences

Wm Blair, grocer
234 John Littlehales, detective
236 John Jennings, moulder
238 M H Little, packer
240 Bernard Cox, shoemaker

Smith-ave intersects

254 Chas West, buscuit maker

Henry-st intersects

270 Duncan Graham, soapmkr
272 Henry Wade, laborer
274 Edward Isard, laborer
276 Alfred Soughton, machinist
278 Geo Shoots, carriagepainter
280 James Way, carpenter

Leeming-st intersects

282 Chas Bush, grocer
284 Vacant
286 Vacant
288 Vacant
Herbert Hart, dairyman

Wentworth-st intersects

Cannon-st east, south side

5 John Phelan, scalemaker
7 Mrs Angus McLeod
9 Mrs E Ross, dressmaker
11 Geo F Steinhoff, tinsmith
13 Mrs Elizabeth Gill

Hughson-st intersects

Congregational Church
25 Edward Curry, porter
27 John Caffrey, furnaceman

John-st intersects

43 W H Tallman & Co, wood
45 Charles Egener, clerk
47 Ronald Stone, tinsmith
49 James Wallace, moulder

Catharine-st intersects.

57-63 Thos Doherty, coffee mills
65 Vacant
67 W P VanNorman, agent
75 Wm Reid, machinist

Mary-st intersects

87 Sam'l Cunningham, teamster
89 Mrs J Hopkins
91 Grove Heath, machinist

Elgin-st intersects

N N W premises

Ferguson-ave intersects

119 Thos Chub, railroader
119 Chas Boquet, teamster
119 Wm Payne, wood dealer

Cathcart-st intersects

127 Wm Ronald, engineer
131 Wm Chappell
137 Thos Wilson, hotel

Wellington-st intersects

153 E C Wilson, manfr
r 153 Michael Connolly, laborer
155 Geo H Smith, shoemaker

West-ave intersects

175 John Corrigan, carpenter
177 Geo Richmond, moulder
179 W Goodfellow, patternfitter
181 Wm Goodfellow, finisher
183 E A DeWitt, butcher

Victoria-ave intersects

189 Mrs M McMicking
191 Geo Broadbent, engineer
193 Richard Clark, moulder
195 Wm Hawkins, policeman
197 Peter Foreman, shoemaker
199 W J Thresher, baker

215 Danl Cripps, bricklayer

East-ave and Emerald-st intersect

215 Vacant
217 Timothy Sullivan, laborer
223-5 Thos Taylor, carpenter
227 Wm Arde, shoemaker
227 James Cameron, laborer
229 R N Wheeler, wood dealer

Tisdale-st intersects

235 Mrs John Grant
237 Ed Broadley, lumber insp'r
239 Wm Roberts, laborer
241 Jos Stoneham, machinist
243 Walter Fowler, moulder
245 Wm Miller, laborer
247-49-51 Vacant

Steven-st intersects.

253 Michael McTague, laborer
255 James Lewis, carpenter
227 Geo Winn, shoemaker
259 Wm Bevis, machinist
261 John W Emory, carpenter
267 Benj Salisbury, saddler
269 P McGovern, mechanic

Ashley & Wentworth-sts intersect

Cannon-st west, north side, from 119 James n to Hess

8 James White, M D
16 Hiram Markle, carpenter
20 John McMahon, baker
22 A Bell, tailor

Macnab-st intersects

3 - Eagle House hotel
32½ Granson Ford, plasterer
36 Wm H Harris, painter
38 Robt Moffat, shoemaker
40 John Maguire, painter
42 A Cunningham, watchman
44 Geo Bessey, egg dealer
46 Mrs Joshua Gully
48 Jacob M Hall, engineer
50 Wm Curtis, cigarmaker
52 Frank Howe, cigarmaker

Park-st intersects

64 Ed Nelson, traveler
68 A E Walker
70 Hy H Laing, merchant
72 John Ling, carpenter
74 Mrs Francis Crombie
80 Wm Carter, plasterer

Bay-st intersects

90 J C Schrader, tobacconist
98 Mrs Helen Gay
98 Hy Nicholson, porter
100 James J Evel, manfr
102 R J Bampfylde, traveler

Railway-st intersects

104 S D Hopkins
Vacant lots

Caroline-st intersects

108 Jos Lloyd, grocer
110 J McKay, conductor GTR
112 John Flynn, laborer
114 James Belling, jeweler
116 Miss M Shannon, dressmkr
120 Thos Egan, fitter
122 John Gore, letter carrier
124 Mrs David W Gordon
126 Richard Berryman, machinist
132 Mrs Thos McCusker
134 Wm Grey, foreman GTR

Cannon-st west, south side

1 Wm Noble, hotel
7 Mrs Sarah F Grey
9 J S Lillis, cigar manfr
11 John M Harris, clerk
13 Jos Dillon, clerk
15 Colin McRae, bookkeeper
17 Alex Hutchison, gardener
19 Jas Eaglesham, porter
25 Mrs Geo Smith

Macnab-st intersects

41 J M Byrens, builder
43 W G Lumsden, grocer
43½ Mrs Francis Lumsden
45 Capt David Kiah
45½ Mrs Wm Fogwell
47 Thos Barrett, baker

49 John Reardon, moulder

Park-st intersects

63-71 Z Pat ison, confectioner
73 Jos Clark, clerk
75 — Childs, moulder
77 Geo Davis, cofectioner
177 Adam Croasman, laborer
79 Mrs Margaret Angus
179 Ed Doyle, laborer
81 Jos Mawson, gas meter mkr

Bay-st intersects

95 F J Schrader, cigar manfr
97 Jos Preston, watchman

Caroline-st intersects

107 Mrs James Duggan
109 John Fall, carpenter
111 Mrs Jane Macgregor
113 James Thornton, laborer
115 John B Krug, tobacconist
117 F Goodman, stovemounter
119 Jas Parkinson, moulder
121 — Gage, gardener
123 Yacant
125 Wm Clucas, builder
127 Wm L Venator, wood turner
129 Samuel Nadin, bookkeeper
131 John Tyson, builder

Hess-st intersects

Caroline-st north, east side, from 168 King west to Stuart

2 Mills & McKellar, builders

Market-st intersects

24 George Ruland, butcher
26 Geo Grayson, spring maker
28 Rees Evans, printer
30 John Swartz, traveler
32 John B Lourey, moulder
34 Mrs Wm Donovan

Napier-st intersects

46 George Carlisle, carpenter

York-st intersects

Fred Gottoroff, marble cut'r
68 John Browne, blacksmith
r 68 Vacant
70-2 Wm Evans, planing mill
74 Mrs C McGuigan
76 Vacant
78 John Kelly, boilermaker
80 Miss Margaret Horan
82 Fred Rice, laborer
84 Henry P Breay, expressman
86 Andrew Gray, checker

Cannon-st intersects

90 Thos Winfield, carpenter
92 Robert Long, blacksmith
94 Thos Winfield, foreman

Barton-st intersects

Vacant lots
G C Morrison, engine works
Hamilton Bridge & Tool Co

Stuart-st intersects

Caroline-st north, west side

7 James Foster, cutter
9 John K Binkley, farmer
11 Mrs P Sullivan

Market-st intersects

23 Wm Low, carpenter
31 Thomas Jarvis, upholsterer
33 Wm Aitchison, manfr

Napier-st intersects

35 James Taylor, bricklayer
37 Alfred Hathway, laborer
39 Thos Hilton
41 — Callagen, laborer
43 Herbert Cotton, mason
45 Price Haynes, sawmaker
47 John Campbell, collector
47 Chas Rose, policeman
49 Mrs A F Sheppard
51 B M Danforth, nailor

York-st intersects

71 Harry Granger, agent
73 Joseph Hunter, driver
77 George Pierce, laborer

79 Mrs Jas McBrier
r 79 Francis Ouimet, shoemaker
r 79 Alfred Hewitt, driver
81 Donald McLean, shipper
r 81 Wm Bunt, laborer
r 81 Zovite Filitrault, tobacco rol'r
r 81 H M Arthur
83 Wallace Walton, laborer

Cannon-st intersects

87 Mrs James Duggan
89 B H Webber, merchant
93 Vacant
95 Francis Wallace, agent
97 John G Sherring, plasterer

Mill-st intersects

101 Mrs Sarah Cullinan
103 Wm Mepham, plasterer
105 Vacant
105 Vacant
107 James Ryan, tailor
109 Richard Bolton, laborer
111 Vacant
113 Miss Mary Sheen
115 Miss Mary Shehan

Harriet-st intersects

119 James Loftus, laborer
121 Robert Irons, bricklayer
123 Richard G Darby, machinist
125 Wm J Kerr, foreman
127 Wm H Kerr, moulder

Ellen-st intersects

M Wilson & Co, manfrs

Barton-st intersects

Eliza-st intersects.

Canada Pipe Foundry

Caroline-st south, east side, from 139 King west to Concession

1 Wm Fitzgerald, miller
3 W H Dean, com traveler
5 J W Gerrie, druggist
7 E Freeman, ins agent
9 W J Field
11 D R Dewey, coal dealer

11 D Dewey, ice dealer
George-st intersects
Collegiate Institute
Main-st intersects
15 John Donaldson, engineer
17 Victor Roswell, carpenter
19 Thos Keane
Jackson-st intersects
W E Sanford, merchant
Hunter-st intersects
47 John Dowrie, carpenter
51 Mrs P Butler
Bold-st intersects
61 Martin O'Driscoll, finisher
63 Mrs Thos Flack
65 Mrs Wm H Holcomb
Duke-st intersects
77 Samuel Aylett, gardener
79 James Reynolds, laborer
81 Anthony Belau, tailor
Robinson-st intersects
91 Mrs John A Roe
93 Vacant
95 F H Miller, wood dealer
97 James Jobson, pork curer
99 James Mitchell, laborer
    Mrs Hugh Macdonald
Hannah-st intersects.
113 Mrs Richard Harper
Herkimer and Markland-sts intersect
    Geo J Dunn, manfr
    John Hughes, laborer
    Alex Gardner, carter
Concession-st intersects

Caroline-st south, west side

2 Scharlach & Co, cigar box manfrs
George & Main-sts intersect

14 Thos Franklin, bank messenger
Jackson-st intersects
Private grounds
Hunter-st intersects
38 James Dodman, agent
46 Donald Paterson, laborer
48 Wm R Allan, blacksmith
50 Mrs Williams
52 Wm Ballantine, laborer
46 A B Baxter, butcher
Bold-st intersects
58 F J Dodman, grocer
66 Mrs J F Davidson
72 Home of the friendless
Duke-st intersects
78 Miss Annie L Cox
80 Mrs Wm Chisholm
82 Robt McKay, plasterer
Robinson-st intersects
96 Geo Pfann, cabinetmaker
98 Sellar Taylor, laborer
100 Jas Reid, carpenter
Hunter-st intersects
108 Clemence Doll, laborer
110 Vacant
112 Mrs Fred Willman
114 Mathew Gair, pianomaker
116 Fred Setzkorn, engineer
118 James Hill, laborer
120 Edward McMahon, laborer
Herkimer-st intersects
George Hunt, grocer
James Milne, gardener
Markland-st intersects
James Rayment, gardener
Mrs F E Gadsby
Robert Hillier, salesman
Concession-st intersects

Catharina-st, see Young

Catharine-st n, east side, from 102 King east to the Bay

6-8 The Shedden Co

King William-st intersects

16 Elias King, porter
20 John Temple, livery
22 Peter Armstrong, carriage maker
24 Wm Murphy, mason
26-28 E T Wright & Co, manfrs tinware

Rebecca-st intersects

Miss Maggie Smith
32 Wm Gordon, cooper
34 Mrs Geo Barr
36 Robert Dunlop, ins agent
38 Mrs John MacKelcan
40 T O Lucas, butcher
42 C J Williams, oil manfr
44 Miss Mary E Clement
46 Geo S Coulson, grain dealer
48 James S Amos
50 Louis Schwarz, tobacconist
52 Frank MacKelcan, barrister
54 Edward Higgins, M D
56 Alex Hamilton, traveler
58 C E Torrence
58½ Vacant
60 John H Tilden, manfr
62 John Bradley, lumber merchant
64 F H Villiers, clerk
66 James Phelan, steward
70 J H Mattice, agent *Globe*
72 Fred Leishman, bookkeeper
74 Thos Smith, carpenter

Cannon-st intersects

94 Philip Martin
94½ T E Brown, checker
96 Chas A Wilcox, agent
100 Edward Routh, carpenter
102 Eli Saenger, laborer
110 D Moore & Co, founders

Robert-st intersects

114 And'w Mahony, stovemounter
34

116 John Brooks, wood turner
118 Joseph Dodson, printer
120 Edward Oakes, tailor
122 Clark Madget, machinist
124 Michael Malone, clerk
126 Mrs Wm Lang
r " Mrs John McNeil
128 Geo Madgett, wood turner
130 Henry Baker, manfr
132 Robert Greenaway, moulder
134 James Connell, dairyman
136 Thos Watson, tinsmith
138 Patrick J Kelly, tailor
144 Wm Marchman, engineer
146 Mrs Ellen Lavin
150 Mrs Geo Webb
152 Benjamin Marshall, laborer
154 Chas Stewart, printer
160 James F Davis, pedler

Barton-st intersects

162 Jacob Culp, wheelmaker
164 Joseph Perior, laborer
166 John Hayes, laborer
168 Patrick Rodgers, laborer
170 Edward Nangle
172 James Bunting, painter
174 Louis Selbeck, biscuit baker
176 Edward Nagle, railroader
178 Jas Mannocks, cabinetmaker
180 Lewis Johnston, blacksmith
182 Mrs Edward Devine
184 Peter Slott, engineer
186 Geo Smith, watchman

Murray-st intersects

202 Thos Routh, laborer
204 Henry McGoldrick, laborer
206 M Magerus, dairyman
r " Mrs Fred Linsted
r " John Sullivan, laborer

G T R Track intersects

210 James Orange

Strachan-st intersects

220 John Flahaven, ornamenter

Simcoe-st intersects

228 Geo Wheeler, engineer

230 Daniel McCarty, yardsman
232 Thos Kenny, car examiner
 Ferrie-st intersects
234 Alex Weatherspoon, carpen'r
236 Thos Corrigan, bricklayer
238 James Lee, cotton weavear
 Picton-st intersects
244 Michael Wing, laborer
246 John Miller, laborer
 Macaulay st intersects
252 Wm Gomph, teamster
268 James Williamson, teamster
 Wood-st intersects
328 Chas Frank, manfr
 Brock-st ends
370 Geo Freeborn, teamster
372 Robt Patterson, laborer
374 Robt Patterson, laborer
376 John Whalen, laborer
 Vacant lots to end

Catharine-st n, west side

15 Adam Hope & Co, hardware
 King Wm-st intersects
19 Gurneys' warehouse
 Rebecca-st intersects
25 John Rowan, barber
27 David Boyd, cooper
29 Mrs Margaret Proctor
31 Miss Carrie Polkingham
33 Chas Smith, tailor
35 Ralph Gray, carpenter
35½ Wm Dobson
37 Hugh Sweeney, moulder
39 Mrs Patrick Norris
41 Thos Lahey, messenger
43 Hilda Boyle
45 Mrs David Sutherland
47 Mrs Thos Richardson
49 Gottlieb Richter, shoemaker
 Gore-st intersects
51 Hy McKee, ironworker

53 Thos Malone, confectioner
55 Mrs C McMichael
55½ Wm Walker, huckster
57 Albert Almas, barber
59 Mrs Chas Fields
61 Wm Frier, dry goods
63 Ed Bethune, bookkeeper
65 Mrs James Aikins
69 Rev W J Hunter, D D, Methodist
71 Mrs Wm Sharpe
75 Patrick Allen
77 James Jones, moulder
 Cannon-st intersects
79 James M Byrens, builder
81 Samuel Furmidge, moulder
85 Luke Lucas, moulder
87 Thos McGregor, moulder
89 Nicholas Buck, tailor
95 Wm Bowstead, machinist
99 John Freeth, teamster
103 Wm Clinton, patternfitter
r 103 Mrs Thos Appleyard
105 Wm Jones, moulder
107 Mrs M Young
109 Vacant
111 Jos Seguin
113 Mrs W Hurd
115 Mrs Jos Sinclair
117 Mrs Wm Johnston
 Robert-st intersects
109 Vacant
123 Robt Baker, engineer
129 John Dundon, carpenter
129 Jos Sullivan, blacksmith
129 Mrs John Sullivan
131 Chas Tilley, laborer
133 Michael McInerney, moulder
135 John Tranior, tailor
137 Ed Sheppard, carpenter
141 Alex Pazius, upholsterer
143 Patrick Barrett, tinsmith
145 John Levis, laborer
147 Vacant
149 Mrs James Moodie
151 Mrs Francis Skory
153 Wm Cameron, hotel

Barton-st intersects

155 P Halloran, grocer
159 Wm Henderson, laborer
161 Michael Hinchey, laborer
163 Ed Hinchey, moulder
165 Samuel Guest laborer
167 John Beaufort, carpenter
175 John Jenkins, laborer
181 Mrs Ann McBride
185 Wm Courie, laborer

Murray-st intersects

199 Wm Bolton, carpenter

Stuart-st ends

201 John Barry, laborer
203 John McKeand, fitter
205 Richard Nicholson
r 205 Chas Housden, laborer
r 205 James O'Reilly, dyer
G T Railway Bridge

Strachan-st intersects

219 Mrs Kate Halloran
221 Wm Bragg, yardsman
223 Francis E Hamburg, loomfixr
225 Wm Harper, cardriver
227 Daniel McBride, coal oil dlr

Simcoe-st intersects

223 John Callaghan, watchman
225 John Christie, blacksmith

Ferrie-st intersects.

235 Daniel Mullen, cooper
239 Patrick Coughlin, laborer

Picton-st intersects

241 Edward Porter, collarmaker
243 Alfred Crist, glassblower
245 Eljah McMahon, loomfixer
247 — Allan, laborer
249 Robt Gray, glassblower
251 Mrs Kenneth Cook
253 Thomas Morrisey, laborer
255 Vacant

Macauley-st intersects

253 Wm Geary, moulder
257 Vacant

Wood-st intersects

327 Patrick O'Neil, teamster
329 M Kavanagh, boilermaker
331 Samuel Epstein, pedler

Burlington and Brock-sts intersect

367 J H Ainsborough, moulder

Guise-st intersects

Catharine-st s, east side, from 73 King e to the Mountain

1 Hamilton Electric Light Co
11 Fred Woodward, upholsterer

Main-st intersects

Joseph Hoodless' factory
Lumber yard

Jackson-st intersects

27 J Hoodless, cabinetmaker
31 Mrs Louise Courteau
33 Mrs Carey Shearman
35 **Douglas** Campbell, moulder
37 Geo Wilson, tinsmith
39 Mrs J McMillan
41 A Mitchell, harnessmaker
45 Jas Hoyle, tailor

Hunter-st intersects

47 Wm Moir, broommaker
47½ **Peter** Ray, fireman
49 Isaac Eisenberg, tailor
51 Edward Warren
53 J E O'Reilly,
65 S E Gregory
73 Miles O'Reilly, Q C
77 John Drysdale, **engineer**
79 E C **Jones**, manft
81 Mrs Robert Kilgour
83 **James Kilgour**, music. dealer

Young-st intersects

97 F C Webber, builder
99 John Vollick, wood turner
101 John Warnick cabinetmaker
103 Geo H Webber, builder
105 F W Passmore, painter
107 Mrs Edward Burns
109 Geo W Browne, exciseofficer

111 Joseph A Sequin, druggist
113 Vacant
115 W A Bellhouse, clerk
Maria-st intersects.
117 H C Bliss, patent medicines
Hannah-st intersects.

Catharine-st s, west side

2 W Richardson
Main-st intersects
McIlwraith's coal yard
20 Mrs Susan Koll
22 John Smith
24 Mrs Louisa Welch
26 Thos Sturdy, tinsmith
26½ John McMillan, shoemaker
28 Miss E Meredith, teacher
30 Hiram Fonger, teamster
30 Michael Murphy, saloon
Jackson-st intersects
28 Mrs James Hart
30 James Dowden, whitewasher
30 N Norris, hay and straw
40 Francis Taffe, butcher
42 James McMillan, fireman
44 John Anderson, machinist
Hunter-st intersects
52 Wm Mulholland, wood deal'r
54 Vacant
56 Chas Mitchell, blacksmith
58 Alfred J Goodwin, laborer
60 S Davis jr, clerk
62 Wm Garner, blacksmith
64 Martin TenEyck
66 Stephen Muirhead, butcher
68 Wellington Terreberry
70 David Baird, laborer
72 Wm Robinson
Augusta-st intersects
76 Chas Barlow, carpenter
80 Frank Allan, fireman
82 Jacob Burgess, fish dealer
88 James Thomas, shoemaker
90 Mrs C J Nichol
92 Ed T Wright, manfr

Young-st intersects.
94 Miss Hy Miller
96 Chas Maltman, boxmaker
98 Geo Mellon
102 Geo LeRiche, druggist
104 Jos Cable, policeman
106 Vacant
108 F B Halliday, traveler
110 H Barnard, manfr
112 Richard C Cooper, merchant
114 James G Insole, com travel'r
116 A W Parmenter
Maria-st intersects
118 Chas Powis, clerk
120 Wm P Maloney, lineman
122 Robt Berryman, wood deal'r
124 James O'Heir, machinist

Cathcart-st, Lower, east side, from 166 Rebecca to Barton

Wilson-st intersects
12 Roscoe Wallace, carpenter
14 Thos Hart, laborer
16 Ernest Schultz, tinsmith
18 Hy Linton, shoemaker
20 Jos Aitchison, polisher
Vacant
Kelly-st intersects
30 Wm & Thos Mulholland, wood dealers
32 J Buckingham, laborer
34 Robt King, laborer
36 Vacant
38 E W Hyde, com agent
40 G T Turner, carpenter
46 Jos Kneeshaw, clerk
48 Mrs E McIlwraith
Cannon-st intersects
50 James Duffy, machinist
52 Jos Walton, clerk
54 Wm Smith, stonemason
56 G A Smith, bricklayer
56½ Wm Hunter, laborer
58 Robt Cross, moulder
60 Crawford Curell, stovemtr
62 A Hignell, printer

64 Thos Ham, tinsmith
66 James Truscott, machinist
68 August Lutzenger, hatter
70 Hy Marriott, laborer
70½ Wm Harper, laborer
72 Mrs John Kennedy
74 Ernest Tallman, stovemtr
76 Alex Church, blacksmith
78 David Ross, teamster
80 John Woodman, baggageman
82 James Thompson, railroader
84 Richard Ward, railroader
   Patterson Bros, lumber

Cathcart-st, Lower, west side.

1 John Macdonald, moulder

Wilson-st intersects

11 Emerson Hannon, grocer
13 Luke Cuzner, tinsmith
15 James Dennis, shoemaker
17 Wm Morrow, laborer
19 Robt McArdle, plumber
21 Miss Mary Hampson
23 John Western, shoemaker
25 Miss Harriet McCullough
27 Geo Morton, grocer

Kelly-st intersects

29 Fred Manning, moulder
32 Richard Wakely, teamster
33 Thos Anderson, machinist
35 Mrs Almira Stewart
35½ Mrs James Truscott
37 Mrs Ann Morton
39 Chas Gibbs, hatter
43 Vacant

Cannon-st intersects

53 James Carter
55 David Rooks, mechanic
r 55 Alfred Poulter, bookkeeper
57 David Congo, porter
59 Jas Ellsworth, carpenter
61 Abe Hobson, porter
69 Mrs Graham
71 Jas Pett, tanner
73 Mrs Jas Forster
79 Benj Lewis, laborer
81 Calvin Lyons, agent

83 Alfred Nelson, glassblower
85 John Slater, mason
87 Nelson Taylor, harnessmaker
89 Chas Hughes, carpenter

Robert-st intersects

91 John McGarigle, laborer
93 Thos Thompkins, cigarmaker
95 John M Ward, brakeman
97 Mrs Thos Bogges
99 Edwin Burton, brakeman
101 Wm Nevills, mechanic

Cathcart, Upper, east side, from 198 King e to King William

2-4 Vacant
6 Samuel Gillesby, carpenter
8 David McKillop, machinist
10 James Campbell, lather
12 Miss Griffiths
16 George Harris, porter
20 Lawrence Beltz, tailor
22 F X Valle, broommaker
   Brennan's lumber yard

King William-st intersects

Cathcart, Upper, west side

1 Miss N A Jarvis
5 Geo Peters, clerk
3 Joshua A Phillips, carpenter
9 Bryan Carpenter, carpenter
11 J D Pennington, manfr
15 Ed Beatty, laborer

King Wm-st intersects

Centre-st, from 11 Colborne-st

2 Chas D Stephenson, lather
  J S Lillis, cigarmaker

Charles-st, east side, from 57 King-st w, south to Bold

1 Morton Bros, grocers
3 George Hope, traveler
5 Daniel Sullivan, livery

7-9 Thos Lawrey's warehouse
11 Mrs Annie Brown
13 Geo Green, pork curer
15 Wm M S Sendall, carpenter
17 Dan LeMessurier, painter
23 Wm Waldoff, hay dealer

Main-st intersects

Vacant grounds

Jackson-st intersects

39 Robert Duncan, merchant
41 A R Kerr, merchant
43 Alex Gartshore, manfr
45 Miss Anna A Meade
47 James Shea, merchant
53 Fred G Foster, florist
55 Peter G Sinclair, gardener

Hunter-st intersects

57 Lewis D Birely
59 Mrs Peter McIntyre
63 James Parkes, barrister
67 S F Lazier, barrister

Bold-st intersects

Charles-st, west side

American Hotel
12 Mrs Isaac Reynolds
14 Mrs James Lewis

Main-st intersects

20 John B Young, accountant
26 Mrs James Ritchie
28 John Ronan, driver
30 Joseph Smith, cabinetmaker
32 Philip Stephens, laborer
34 David White, bus driver
36 Geo Overend, laborer
38 Ed Lewis, plasterer
40 Mrs James Flynn

Jackson-st intersects

46 Mrs Mary Hunt
48 Mrs John Walton
50 Robt Evans, seedsman
54 Nursery

Hunter-st intersects

66 David Gillies, merchant

Bold-st intersects

Cherry-st, east side, from 116 Main east to Mountain

1 James C Ryan, agent
3 James Kaiser, cooper
5 Walter England, barber
7 Hy Duval, barber
7½ Thos Stout, engineer
9 Mrs Charlotte Parker
11 Warren Spohn, photographer

Jackson-st intersects

15 John Plant, wood dealer
23 Ed McGrath, wagonmaker
25 David McBrien, painter

Hunter-st intersects

35 G Fickley, shoemaker
39 John Jeffrey, carpenter
41 Mrs John Gidley
43 Thos Stanton, painter
45 L Reuben, dealer
47 Geo Ives, porter
49 Geo W Smith, tinsmith
51 James Stafford, mechanic
53 J McMahon, moulder
55 James Sullivan, laborer

O'Reilly-st intersects

65 Jos Goyott, packer
67 Ed Costello, laborer
69 John Prindiville, carpenter
r 69 James Canary, laborer
71 Jeremiah Donovan, tailor
73 Fletcher Reid, laborer

Young-st intersects

77 Hy Shieler, laborer
79 Thos Burns, laborer
81 Mrs E Sullivan
83 Samuel Porter, baker
85 Vacant
93 Thos McMahon, clerk

Maria-st intersects

97 Peter Miller, tinsmith
99 Chas Kidner, printer
101 John Patterson, tailor

103 Dennis Connell, gardener
105 John Patterson, tailor
111 John McIntyre, cutter
113 A Jonathan teacher
115 Michael Hackett, polisher
117 Vacant
119 James Halloran, baker

Hannah-st intersects

High level pumping station

Cherry-st west side

N & N W Station

Main-st intersects

8 Thos W Reid, carpenter
10 Hy Hawkins, plasterer
12 John Hurd, laborer
14 Jos F Johnson, laborer
16 John P Cline, marble cutter

Jackson-st intersects

18 Herman Klinger, machinist
20 Ed S Gilbert, collector
22 Thos Brick, carter
24 Jesse Iles, blacksmith

Hunter-st intersects

30 Geo Long, wood dealer
32 Vacant
38 Mrs Peter Williamson
42 Alfred Wright, keysmith
44 Hy Sharpe, carpenter
46 Vacant
48 Hy Alderholy, laborer
52 Mrs Ed Warren
54 Miss B Burke
56 Thos Taylor, baker
58 Dan Mahoney
60 T H Baine, grocer

O'Reilly-st intersects.

66 Hy McGrath, laborer
68 Chas Bolingbroke, upholste'r
70 Louis Roehmer, carpenter
72 Peter Shieler, laborer
74 George Robson, laborer

Young-st intersects

84 John Simpson, cigarmaker

Maria-st intersects

Wm Morris, grocer
98 Maurice Wren, tinsmith
100 James Patterson, wool grader
104 Wm Newbigging
108 Wm Sullivan, laborer
110 Mrs Mary Sullivan
112 Thos Skinner, laborer
114 Mrs Daniel Foley
116 John Goodfellow, painter
118 John Wren, laborer

Hannah-st intersects.

Chisholm-st, see Oak Avenue

Clark ave, east side, between Wellington-st and Victoria ave

2 John J Connell, bricklayer
8 John Freeborn, laborer
12 Chas Simons, packer
14 Patrick O'Neil, bricklayer
16 J D Small, carpenter
18 Geo Searls, laborer

Clarke-ave, west side

1 Wm D Goodman, moulder
5 Claude Grundy, gardener
7 Wm Pascoe, rope maker
9 Wm Barclay, carpenter

Ferrie-st intersects

13 Thos Freeborn, fireman
15 Wm Mullvale, laborer

Colborne-st, north side, from 185 James n, west to Bay

2 Gurneys & Ware, scale mfs
12 Mrs R Seymour
14 John C Palmer, engineer
16 Walter Applegarth, merchant

Macnab-st intersects

3. James Cochrane, laborer
32 Luke Donlay, cabinetmaker

34 Mrs Rosa A Canute
36 Geo Strain, boilermaker

Park-st intersects

64 Daniel Graham, carpenter
66 Robt Harper, carpenter
68 Alex M Ross, painter

Bay-st intersects

Colborne-st, south side

11 Geo Smith, carpenter

Center-st intersects

13 Wm Foster, wood turner
15 Edwin Tinsley, engineer
17 C M Belknap, lumber dealer

Macnab & Park-sts intersect

61 Frank Hughes, silver plater
63 Mrs H Mulholland
65 James Lakeland, artist
67 Mrs Mary A Bell
69 Fred R Venator, turner
71 Wm Hall, milk pedler
73 Frank Barling, machinist

Bay-st intersects

Concession-st north side, from James to city limits

4 Wm Wright, machinist
6 Robert McDonald, laborer
8 M Dawson, letter carrier
10 Wm Cook, coachman
12 Chas S Carleton
   W H Gillard, merchant

Bay-st intersects

Joseph Hobson, C E
John Alexander, merchant

Hilton and Caroline-sts intersect

James Muckersie, fitter
Alex Munro, traveler

Bruce & Hess-sts intersect

98 F Wilkinson, grain dealer
100 John Hendry, patternmaker
   Geo Mason, accountant

Queen-st intersects

John Pearson, accountant

Kent & Locke-sts intersect

Ira Nelson, dairyman
John Smith, tailor
Alfred Grigg, clerk
E W Thomson, carpenter
A J Thomson, finisher
A Strickland, carriagemaker

Garth-st intersects

Thos Stillway, painter

Concession-st, south side

John Stuart, merchant
Wm Hunt, gardener
James Turner, merchant
YMCA Recreation Ground
Wm J Copp, manfr
Thos Marshall, tailor

Hess-st intersects

A Powis, merchant

Queen-st intersects

Wm Lyons, laborer
John McEwen, hammerman
James Findlay, roofer

Mountain-ave intersects

Jas C McKeand

Locke & Garth-sts intersect

Capt Nichol's farm
Lowell Wilson, weaver
John Stewart, laborer
Duncan McNab, dairyman

Crooks-st east side, from York to Barton

2 Isaac Tufford, carter
4 J T Pepper, chemist
6 Marshall B Rymal
8 W J Morden, com agent
10 Chas H Lucas, bookkeeper
12 Robt Lee, fireman
12½ James E Painter, fireman
14 John Brace, mechanic
16 Thos Morley, moulder

18 Samuel Gage, laborer
20 Wm Towler, broommaker
22 Geo Cook, watchman
26 Oliver McLeod, blacksmith
32 Mrs Agnes McCabe
36 Wm Wright, laborer
Barton-st intersects

Crooks-st, west side

9 Mrs Emma Goddard
11 Shephard Latham, machinist
15 John E Way, blacksmith
17 Mrs J McColl
19 Alex Elder, fitter
21 Fred Weaver, switchman
23 John Clayton, painter
27 James F Simpson, ticket agt
29 Hy J Lendon, machinist
31 Benj Palmer, moulder
33 John Goodard, laborer
35 James S Black, baggageman
37 James Badger, shoemaker
39 Wm McMenemy, policeman
Barton-st intersects

Devenport-st, east side, from 337 York to Tom

6 John Copeland, carpenter
8 Hy Housago, laborer
10 Ed Ryckman, laborer
18 Mrs Geo Myers
20 Alfred Miller, shoemaker
22 James Garrett, moulder
26 Louis Scheck, cabinetmaker
Tom-st intersects

Devonport-st, west side

1 Timothy Redden, laborer
3 John Wilson, laborer
5 Wm Manning, hackman
7 Frank Baker, fitter
9 Geo Carson, laborer
15 Robt Douglas, moulder
17 John O'Connor, laborer
19 Walter Venn, machinist
21 Jas Weatherston, carpenter
29 John McInerney, laborer
Tom-st intersects

Dufferin-st runs from Macklin to Limits.

Wm Small, laborer
Peter Fletcher, laborer

Duke-st, north side, from 100 James s to western limits

2 Vacant
4 Vacant
10 Dr J D Macdonald
Macnub and Park-st intersect
36 Alex Bruce, barrister
40 Vacant
42 James Angus, sr
44 James Angus jr, hatter
46 Mrs C McCallum
Bay-st intersects
58 Albert Jones, laborer
62 Wm Dickson, carpenter
64 Rev John Gauld
66 Mrs M Davidson
68 Mrs Alice McBriar
70 Robert McLeod, clerk
72 C P McMichael, dairyman
Caroline-st intersects
80 John Joner, teamster
86 Thos Stevenson, carpenter
Hess-st intersects
92 John M Morris, engineer
Queen-st intersects
140 Alfred Best, gardener
142 Wm Murphy, carpenter
144 John Smith, laborer
146 Frank Connor, carriagemaker
148 Geo Purrott, painter
150 R T Dickinson, engineer
150½ Richard McCarty, laborer
152 Wm B Foulis, engineer
154 Henry Blankstein, carpenter
Ray-st intersects
Cricket grounds
Locke-st intersects

Daniel Buckley, laborer
Thos Franey, laborer
Chas Burgess, laborer
Mrs Elizabeth McGeorge
James Stevenson, hay dealer
Vincent Shipley, laborer
John Pfeiffer, laborer
Jesse Coombes, laborer

Garth-st intersects

Duke-st, south side

5 Matthew Leggat, merchant
7 Alex W Roy, accountant

Macnab-st intersects

6 James Wason, Pres knitting company
11 T H Macpherson, merchant
13 Adam Brown, merchant
15 Charles J Hope, merchant } Sandyford Place

23 R A Lucas, merchant

Park-st intersects

37 John Muir, barrister
41 Hamilton Young, manfr
43 Vacant
45 Mrs Laura Papps
47 John Stewart, accountant

Bay-st intersects

53 Gregor Thompson, shoema'r
67 Robt Watt, shipper
69 Henry Hamill, gardener
73 James Castell, sergt police

Caroline-st intersects

75 Richard Skill, clerk
79 John B Pattison

Hess and Queen-sts intersect

143 Vacant
145 Louis Banks, laborer
147 Wm Duncan, gardener
149 Wm S Dunsmore, porter
151 James Dunsmore, driver

Ray and Locke-sts intersect

James Cook, painter

Arthur C Burns, laborer
Henry Jackson, laborer
John Maxwell, machinst
Thos Simpson, moulder
Wm Simpson, moulder
Vacant
Geo A Norwood, brickmaker
Geo Norwood, laborer
John Midwinter, machinist
Christopher Walter, laborer
Frank Walter, laborer

Garth-st intersects

Dundurn-st, east side, from end of King west to York

Tom-st intersects

Thos O'Neill, blacksmith
Geo Davis, fitter
John Curran, compositor

Dundurn-st, west side

2 Edward Duncan, laborer

Head-st intersects

10 Wm Fink, teamster
John McCowell, wireworker
Bernard McCowell, laborer

Ardavolich-st intersects

22 M McGowan, butcher

Florence-st intersects

Thos Rush, laborer
Henry Fuller, tailor
Mrs Ann Hibbard
Wm Strongman, carpenter

Tom-st intersects

Leander Slaughter, tobacco roller
Wm J Harvey, roller
John Moore, laborer
John Harvey
Chas McCarthy, laborer

Jones-st intersects

S King, building remover
Wm M Stow, laborer
James Holland, locksmith

York-st intersects

East-ave n, east side, from 258 King east to South

John F Kelly, cigarmaker
6 Thos H Pratt, merchant

King William-st intersects

8 James Frank, bookkeeper
10 Vacant
12 David Tilley, bookkeeper
14 Mrs John Schwindau
16 W C Hooper, compositor
18 Mrs Joseph Mottashed
20 Vacant
22 Gustave Brizzie, moulder
24 J E Riddell, tinsmith
26 D Graham, fireman
r " Wm Julian, fireman
28 Vacant
28½ J Riddell, tinsmith
30 Geo Miller, policeman
34 Mrs Benj Dunnett

Wilson-st intersects

36 Samuel Bowes, machinist
38 Mrs Janet Murdie
40 Geo Junginger, butcher
42 John W Blakeley, policeman
44 Geo Heyburn, lithographer
46 Wm Stender, moulder
48 Alex McCoey, grainer
50 Victor Rossell, carpenter
54 Robt Christie, supt
56 Alfred A Moore, policeman
58 Mrs Samuel Anderson
60 Wm Derby, buffer
66 Henry Angold, machinist
66½ Albert Baker, jeweler
68 Mrs Thos Marshall
70 Clarkson Freeman, bookkeepr

Evans-st intersects

70a Mrs John Burke
76 Vacant
72a Wm J Davis, blacksmith
74 Isaac Davis, blacksmith

Cannon-st intersects

78 John Truscott, carpenter
82 Thos Woodman, checker
84 Wm Godard, traveler
86 John McGrath, clerk
88 Jeremiah Amiss, gardener
90 Robert Edwards, butcher
92 Geo Smith, laborer
94 Thos G Maxwell, policeman
96 Wm Blackburn, carpenter
98 James Hamilton, carpenter
100 H Norman, clerk
102 Willis Hampson, turner
104 Jas Little, contractor
108 Wm Burgess, machinist

Robert-st intersects

112 Thos Patterson, manf
112½ Thos Farrow, carpenter
114 Arthur Catchpole, laborer
114½ C Underwood, engraver
116 Michal Swales, carpenter
116½ Wm H James, letter carrier
118 L L Linfoot, clerk
120 W J Lewis, carpenter
122 Mrs John Priddis
124 John W Sinclair, painter
126 Geo Coleman, painter
128 Martin Allen, laborer
130 Wm Cushing, moulder
132 Alonzo Smith, blacksmith

Barton st-intersects

162 Wm Jamieson, watchman
168 Chas Veth, laborer
170 David Towers, carpenter
172 D Hermann, laborer
174 Albert Jones
176 Mrs Chas Smith
182 John Hope, tanner
190 Robt Falks, carpenter
194 August Miller, weaver
196 John Steadford, laborer
198 Arthur Stockdale, laborer
200 I. Holmes, clerk
202 Geo Frank, machinist
204 Chas Brydges, laborer
206 Wm Reid

South-st intersects

East-ave north, west side

1 James Simpson, laborer
3 Hy J Griffiths, shoemaker
9 John E Brown, tanner

King Wm-st intersects

11 Wm H McKee, grocer
13 Miss Mary Gregg
15 Geo Smith, cigarmaker
17 Mrs Jane Burns
21 Frank Stewart, machinist
23 Thos Mason, hatter
25 C A Whitman, traveler
25½ J F Monck, barrister
27 James Scott, fancy goods
29 Samuel Bell, constable
31 James Lavery, carpenter
33 James Munro
35 Mrs Peter McLaren
37 Alfred Pilkey, agent
39 J R McDonald, ticket agent
43 James O'Brien, moulder

Wilson-st intersects

45 L A Moyer, bookkeeper
47 C N Heisrodt, auctioneer
41 Mrs I Aastie
43 Frank England, barber
47a Thos King, machinist
49 Walter Sweet, grain dealer
55 Wallace Young, bookkeeper
57 Hedley V Mason, salesman
63 John Robins, tinsmith
55 Wm Robson, patternmaker
67 Vacant
69 Chas Tregenza, salesman

Evans-st intersects

73a Wm Pothiea, burnisher
65a John Lavell, cigarmaker
67a Thos Riddell, moulder
69a Wm H Hunt, turner
73 Wm Thresher, confectioner

Cannon-st intersects

75 David J Garrick
77 Thos Bradley, butcher
79 Geo Charles, moulder
81 J H Hamilton, builder
83 Andrew Begg, laborer

85 Wm Peebles, carpenter
89 Geo Routh, carpenter
91 Vacant
97 Albert Cross, basketmaker
99 John Jeffs, shipper
101 Wm Peace, carpenter
103 James B Hanes, signalman
105 John Woodmiller
107 Geo A Iams, stovefitter
111 Thos Henwood, ropemaker

Robert-st intersects

117 Central Wood Yard
119 Thos Patterson, blacksmith
121 O H Webber, bookkeeper
123 Vacant
125 Samuel Groves, blacksmith
131 R C Stevenson, bookkeeper
137 James Franks, painter
139 Mrs O Edgecombe
143 Jos Spencer, sailor
145 Fred Tate, hatter
147 Wm J Whitelock, mason

Barton-st intersects

155 Geo N Camon, plater
157 Geo McVittie, laborer
161 Eli H Mallory
167 Fred Dittrick, bender
169 Chas Harvey, porter
171 D Robertson, carpenter
171½ — Walker, machinist
173 Mrs Wm Towers, boarding
175 Geo Towers, laborer
179 Robt Booth, wheelwright
181 Jos Harter, moulder
183 John Hill, cigarmaker
195 Wm Albins, machinist
197 Gustave Ante, moulder
199 Geo D Tompkins, plumber
201 Eli Vipond, carpenter

South-st intersects

East-ave s, east side, from end of King e to Stinson

1 Wm A Nichols, butcher
3 Robt Young, manf
7 Wm Robb, printer

Main-st intersects

31 David Dexter
33 J D Climie, merchant
35 Wm Dixon, fruiterer
37 **James Dixon, fruit dealer**
39 W W Robinson, manager D Moore & Co
41 Geo Black, Northwestern Tel Co
43 Mrs James Widger
45 Robt Noblett, foreman
51 B J Morgan, flour dealer

Hunter-st intersects

53 Geo James, merchant
55 Vacant
57 Donald McPhie, plumber
61 A W Brown, forwarder
63 James Harvey, farmer
73 Percy Punshon
75 Robt C Fearman, bookkeepr
77 David Blackley, accountant
79 W J Grant, ticket agent

Stinson-st intersects

East-ave s, west side

St Patrick's Church

Main-st intersects

30 S Rose, traveler
32 Wm Nolan, cutter
34 Wm J McAllister, lumber dealer
38 Andrew W Gage, merchant
40 John G Bowes, manfr
42 W S Moore, merchant
44 **Samuel Davis sr**

Hunter-st intersects

58 A D Cameron, barrister
60 R H Jarvis, ins inspector
62 R J Husband, dentist
64 Edgar H Watkins, merchant
66 Mrs Richard Greene
68 **Vacant**
76 F C Fearman, merchant
78 **Wm** Gage, hackman
80 W J Millard, accountant

Elgin-st, east side, from 16 Wilson n to Barton

1 Alex Boyd, varnisher
4 H Geiss, turner
6 Chas McMillan, hatter
8 Wm Knaggs, music teacher
10 Crosier Brown
12 Alfred Wilmore, machinist
14 S V King, moulder

Kelly-st intersects

16 **Samuel** Arthur, builder
18 J Matthews, clerk P O
18½ James Boyd, tobaccopresser
20 Timothy Sullivan, laborer
22 — Barnes, laborer
24 Ed Crofton, painter
26 James Nunn, teamster
28 Wm Lee, pedler
30 Jos Gates, detective
32 J Bidwell Mills, land agent
34 E A Dalley, druggist
36 Thos Sloan

Cannon-st intersects

Vacant grounds

Robert-st inssersects

68 Miss Feaver, hotel
72 Justice Post, engineer
72½ Benj Sutton, manfr
74 Lemuel Snowden, cabinet-maker
76 Thos Beasley, conductor
78 James Gilchrist, carpenter
80 W A Freeman, coal dealer
82 James Rouse, boilermaker
84 Jacob Wheeler, carpenter
86 Wm Smale
88 **Samuel Stephens**
90 **Thos** Amey, laborer
92 Mrs John Weaver
94 **Mrs** Jeff Stevens
96 John Burns, printer
98 M F Dwyer, collector
106 George Elliot, expressman

Barton-st intersects

County jail
Hamilton **Wheel Works**

Elgin-st, west side

1 Wm J Vale, printer
3 G Swartzenburg, shoemaker
7 Chas J Myles, coal dealer
9 Wm Larkin, moulder
11 Geo Wood, blacksmith
13 Jas Connolly, grocer

Kelly-st intersects

15 Major Wm Woolley, Salvation army
15½ E Mundell, traveler
Henry O Sontag, tobacconist
19 T M Griswold, whipmaker
19½ Samuel Kemp, traveler
21 Lin McKenzie, detective
23 Robt Dodds, stonecutter
25 Allen S udholme, stovefitter
27 Mrs Elizabeth Crawford
29 Vacant
31 James Bennett, carpenter
33 Hugh McGowan, butcher

Cannon-st intersects

45 John Milne, manf
47 J W Sanders, japanner
49 James Holleran, moulder
51 Mrs G Kent
63 D A MacNabb

Robert-st intersects

69-71 James Miller, grocer
73 H G Warnington, carpenter
75 Mrs Donald McGillivray
77 Joseph Greenfield, bailiff
79 Mrs Patrick R Cusack
81 Geo Shouldice, goldbeater
83 Richard Brockelsby, moulder
87 Gilbert VanWyck, tailor
89 Robt Seaton, moulder
91 Thos J McLelland, engineer
93 Chas Parmenter, baker
95 Andrew Dougall, machinist
97 John Price, dyer
99 James Hunt, brakeman
101 Chas Hunt, tinsmith
101½ James Herron, moulder
103 And J Diamond, machinist
105 Wm J Whiteside, grocer

Barton-st intersects

R M Wanzer & Co's factory

Elizabeth-st, from New to Garth

4 Chas W North, mason

Eliza-st, commencing on the west side of Caroline north of Stuart

Patrick Leonard, laborer
Mrs James Parker
Patrick O'Connor, laborer
Mrs Mary Grill
Jeremiah O'Connor, laborer

Ellen-st, from 133 Caroline n, west to Hess

Not built upon

Emerald-st n, west side, from 258 King e to South st

Vacant lots

King William-st intersects

23 E Furneaux, carpenter
23½ John Martin, traveler
25 V Steinmetz, tailor
31 Wm P Strickland, machinist
33 James Henderson
35 Christopher Mason, engineer
37 Mrs. Thos Wright
39 Wm Lawrence, letter carrier
41 Emerald Street Methodist Church
45 Rev J H White, Methodist

Wilson-st intersects

53 J D Klock, cigarmaker
55 James Hastings, laborer
57 Arthur J Mills, traveler
59 Wm Tanner, carriagemaker

61 Martin Smith, tinsmith
63 W P Perry, solderer
65 James O Smith, blacksmith
67 Geo Croal, blacksmith
71 Wm Sutton, collar maker
73 John Jackson, laborer
75 Thos Lovejoy, bricklayer

Evans-st intersects

77 John Martin, contractor
79 Henry Hampson, shoemaker
81 Wm A Arland, mail clerk
83 Thos Bale, traveler

Cannon-st intersects

87 David Wark, constable
97 Vacant
99 Thos Cline
101 John J Cline
103 Vacant
105 James Campbell, contractor
107 John O Taylor, blacksmith
119 Jos Hargrove, agent

Robert-st intersects

121 Wm Littlejohns, builder
123-7 Wm Chriswell, moulder
129 James Scott, painter
131 Amos Hutton, machinist
131½ Jas Henderson, machinist
133 Vacant
135 James W Ripley, moulder
137 Mrs Martha McFerran
141 James Muir, baggageman

Barton-st intersects

171 Silas W Tabb, carpenter
175 James Hughes, mariner
177 Chas Vogel, hatmaker
179 Wm Ayers, carpenter
183 Sylvester Whalen, silversmith
185 Wm Hobbs, carpenter
187 John Johnston, carter
193 Joseph Thompson, laborer
203 W Johnston, laborer

South-st intersects

Emerald-st n, east side
St John's Church
2 John Brennan, laborer

4 James Anderson, stonecutter
8 Henry B Muir, carpenter

King Wm-st intersects

14 Mrs John Knapman
16 Robt S Fraser, cutter
18 Robt Clohecy, architect
20 Wm Winn, shoemaker
22 Henry A Ray, buffer
24 Geo Ross, clerk P O
26 H Kite, traveler
28 Mrs Wm Hill
30 Geo Moore
32 John Howard, bricklayer
32½ Mrs Malcolm Leishman
34 Wm Jackson, traveler
34½ A B Holmes, shoemaker
36 Wm Kleinbeil, laborer
38 Henry Hill, clerk P O
40 Joseph Brown, laborer
42 H J Prowse, patternmaker
44 Wm Geo Reid, detective

Wilson-st intersects

48 Geo Barlow
48½ Patrick Shea, machinist
50 John A Durfey, carpenter
52 Thos Canary, fireman
54 Mrs Agnes McCloy
58 Vacant
60 Vacant
62 Jeremiah Thomas, fireman
64 Thos Rock, druggist
66 Morris Cohen, pedler
68 Samuel Luscombe, butcher
70 John Woodman, machinist
74 Geo Sheed, moulder

Evans-st intersects

78 Alex Clark, stonecutter
80 James Flight, mason
84 Thos B S Austin, letter, ca'r
90 Geo Bailey, laborer
92 Miss Emma Moore

Cannon-st intersects

92½ Robt Hyslop, traveler
94 Wm Downs, photograper
96 H Baird, shoemaker
98 Miss Susan Hodges
100 Wm A Wilson, tinsmith

102 Mrs Wm Haygarth
104 John Shields, laborer
106 D W Parker, carpenter
108 Malcolm McKenzie, laborer
110 Geo Watson, cabinetmaker
112 Arch McKenzie, carpenter
114 John Sullivan, laborer
116 Wm Robinson, constable
118 W H Rewbury, checker GTR
120 Matthew Murphy, laborer
122 Mrs Michael Murphy
126 Chas Mooney, teamster
126½ Herbert Goodwin
128 Vacant
128½ James Rodgers, **plasterer**
130 Richard Laidman, carpenter
130½ W B Smith, sawyer
132 Jos Ray, huckster
136 Thos Partridge, turner
138 Thos Cain, shoemaker
142 Geo Bradt, lather
154 Alex Baker, painter
146 James Anderson, patternmkr
148 John Partridge, machinist
150 Geo King, laborer
152 John Wise, laborer
156 Alex McIntyre, laborer
158 James Hurley, moulder

Barton-st intersects

168 James Bews, shipper
170 James Hobbs, carpenter
172 James Firth, blacksmith
174 Simon Buchanan, carpenter
180 Wm James, bricklayer
182 James Aiken, carpenter
180 G Lagarie, blacksmith
182 Mrs Allison
184 James Shaw, boilermaker
186 Cornelius Cimmings, laborer
188 John O'Regan, bridgebuild'r
190 Wm Steed, carpenter
192 E H Austin, painter

South-st intersects

Emerald-st s, east side, from King e to Stinson

3 James Heyes
9 Geo H Gillespie, merchant

Main-st intersects

43 David Morton, soap factory
53 John Morton, manfr
55 A N Barber
57 John S McMahon, merchant
71 Wm T Watkins, merchant
73 R Fuller, contractor
75 Vacant
77 R R Morgan, flour and feed
79 Thos Oliver, manager

Stinson-st intersects

81 Michael Doherty, laborer
91 John Black, brushmaker
93 Geo Britton, painter

Alanson-st intersects

101 Horace Harvey, cabinetmakr

Emerald-st s, west side

Vacant grounds
8 W J McDonald, builder
10 W L Harcourt, M D
12 Jas Jamieson, manfr
14 E B Smith, traveler

Main-st intersects

40 P S Campbell, teacher
42 Wm Smith, accountant
44 C A Davis, dentist
46 D C Roberts, marble dealer
48 Daniel W Hopkins
50 Rev Wm Morton
52 Fred Johnson, merchant
54 G H H Hills, stenographer
56 Hy Heimbecker, photogra'r
58 Mrs C Morgan
r 58 Wm G Flooks, letter carrier

Hunter-st intersects

60 Geo E Broadfield, merchant
74 H D Cameron, Ham Prov and Loan Society
80 Adam Rutherford

Stinson-st intersects

Erie-ave, east side, from end of Main south to Alliston

2 Arthur Bond, file cutter

4 Anthony Mutter, gardener
10 Wm Marshall, manf
12 Walter A Lawrence, traveler
14 John Fotheringham, carriage maker
18 A R Whyte, bookkeeper
20 James M Oliver, traveler
22 F H Sharpe, barber
24 Alex C Turnbull, bookkeepr
34 James W Stanton, ins agent
40 Chas Yuker, traveler
   Geo A Crites, contractor

Stinson-st intersects

54 John Connors, laborer
56 Andrew Mowat, mason

Alanson-st intersects

Erie-ave, west side

Vacant lots
3 Mrs S J White
5 A McDonald, traveler
9 Geo Shambrook, bookkeeper
11 Geo H Meakins, machinist
21 Fred H Ross, bookkeeper
23 John McIntosh, cutter
25 Mrs Alfred Crisp
27 A C Crisp, clerk P O

Stinson-st intersects

54 Geo Nichol, laborer
58 Jno Ferguson, shoemaker

Alanson-st intersects

Evans-st, north side, from 87 Wellington north, east to Emerald

1 Martin O'Neil, moulder

West-ave intersects

3 Albert Whitmore, laborer
5 David Forbes, laborer
7 Thos Stevens, porter

Victoria-ave intersects

21 Wm O'Brien, moulder

East-ave intersects

Vacant

Emerald st intersects

Wm Yates, bricklayer

Evans-st, south side

2 J J Towers, fitter

West-ave intersect

6 Alfred Davison, cigarmaker

Victoria-ave intersects.

Mission Sabbath School

East-ave & Emerald-sts intersect

52 Robt Young, yardmaster

Ferguson-ave, east side, from 164 King e to the Bay

2 David Cullum, carpenter
4 Thos Cathcart, baker
6 Chas Hull, shoemaker
8 Mrs Mary Henery
10 Peter Schwab, glassblower

King Wm-st intersects

15 Mrs Hugh Stewart, grocer
22 David Phillips, carpenter
24 Mrs Annie James
26 Wm John Pessell, laborer
28 Nicholas Carroll, teamster
30 John Miller, tinsmith
32 Mrs A McGarth
34 Robt Keyes, laborer
36 Geo Nicholson, teamster

Rebecca-st intersects

36½ Geo McGilvray, conductor
38 Mrs Wm Park
40 James Mercer, builder
42 Fred Oakes, butcher

Wilson-st intersects

44 R Blair, grocer
46 F G Taylor, polisher
48 J G Gibson, conductor
50 — Finlayson, traveler
52 Robt Stratton, letter carrier
54 Mrs Sarah James

58 Mrs Chas Fry
Kelly-st intersects
65 James Hamilton, agent
68 Geo H Lanigan, bookbinder
70 S J Stratton, stenographer
70½ Mrs Arthur Armstrong
70 Richard Hearne, tobacconist
76 Richard H Press, builder
78 Vacant
80 Chas T Jones
Cannon-st intersects
86 Jasper Hill, grocer
88 Wm H Lampman, teamster
90 Wm Robertson
98 Wm Payne, coal dealer
N & N W R shops and stores
Barton-st intersects
162 Elvin Nash, fireman
164 Mrs Geo Goff
166 John Smale, laborer
168 Thos A Green, mariner
170 Thos Greenaway, timekeepr
172 John Sullivan, brakeman
Railway Crossing
Hamilton Straw Hat Works
Strachan-st intersects
222 Hamilton Spears, laborer
224 James Lorimer, laborer
Simcoe-st intersects
98 John Eustace, laborer
100 Thos Allison, machinist
102 John Young, stovemounter
104 Adam H Ross, painter
106 Geo Taylor, checker
108 Richard Mugford, painter
114 Richard Rowe, grocer
Ferrie-st intersects
120 Mrs Lewis Pearce
122 R M Stevenson, tinsmith
Picton-st intersects
Ed Day, laborer
Jos Kerner, laborer

Geo Wallscraft, laborer
Macaulay st intersects
Jos Pearson, laborer
Wood-st intersects
Wm Lindsay, fitter
Burlington-st intersects

Ferguson-ave, west side

1 Mrs P W Freeman, coal dlr
3 H B Dunnett, carpenter
5 Alex Hanton, machinist
7 James Aldridge, shoemaker
King Wm-st intersects.
23 John Williams, fishmonger
25 Michael Stonehouse
Rebecca-st intersects
37 Mrs Wm Lavis
Wilson-st intersects
45 John Johnson, machinist
47 Fred Aldridge, printer
49 Wm Wright, machinist
51 Mrs Mary Byrne
53 Wm Murphy, grocer
55 John C Harris, teacher
59 Dennis B Skelly
61 E J Skelly, clerk
63 Mrs Martha Jones
Kelly-st intersects
65 Geo Wellington, laborer
67 Hy Jackson, laborer
Cannon-st intersects
N & N W freight sheds
Robert-st intersects
121 James Murray, tailor
123 Walter Catton, car inspector
125 Peter McNamee, sectionman
127 Samuel Parks, machinist
129 Mrs Stephen Wilds
131 James Stephens, moulder
133 Mrs Peter Barr
135 John Snelson, machinist
137 John Latham, wagonmaker
139 Chas Flanders, brakeman

141 Wm Beattie, engineer
143 Patrick McAvay, gilder
145 Geo Humphrey, moulder
147 Cyrus Hotrum, railroader
149 Wm Leanea, baggageman

Barton-st intersects

G T Railway

Strachan-st intersects

John Jowett, laborer
Stephen Bonny, laborer

Simcoe-st intersects

101 John Wilson, dyer
103 A Webster, machinist
105 R J Sanderson, laborer
107 Michael Cousins, laborer

Ferrie & Picton-sts intersect

Wm Shee, carpenter
John McGuire, bookbinder
John Kane, carpenter

Macauley and Wood sts intersect

Ferrie-st e, north side, from 298 James north to Victoria avenue

5 David Audette, clerk
7 Oliver Beatty jr, clerk
9 Mrs Henry McCann
11 Patrick Donohue, blacksmith
13 Henry Malcolmson, carpenter

Hughson-st intersects

23 John Dillon, machinist
25 John Mahon, laborer
27 Mrs Taylor

John-st intersects

51 Patrick Burns, glassblower
55 Richard Quinn, machinist

Catharine-st intersects

59 Wm Keating, confectioner
67 James Geddes, clerk GTR

Mary-st intersects.

79 Matthew Spencer, stonecut'r
83 Geo Stevens, laborer
85 John Howith, blacksmith
89 Thos Briggs, watchman
91 Robert Birdie, car driver
93 Wm Hughes, carpenter
95 Joseph Midwinter, machinist
97 John Simons, laborer
99 Wm Cornell, carpenter
101 John Badeau, shoemaker
103 John Parkinson, brushmaker
105 J Buskard, blacksmith
107 Mathews Bros, grocers
109 John Dolan, carter

Ferguson-ave intersects

117 Geo Moore, laborer
121 Chas Valentine, laborer
125 Michael Cahill
129 Richard Wilcox, laborer
131 Edward Tallman, porter
133 John Jenkins, carpenter
133½ — Doherty, laborer
135 Wm Kinsella, moulder
139 Wm Gleason, laborer
143 Walter Fisher, moulder
147 Thos Partridge, engineer

Wellington-st intersects

Stroud's tannery

Victoria-ave intersects

Gibson Syme, laborer
Joseph Pratt, laborer
W H Porter, painter
Thos Carter, laborer
Henry Searles, laborer
James Garriety, tinsmith

Clarke-ave intersects

Ferrie-st e, south side

12 Vacant

Hughson-st intersects.

26 James C Duggan, tailor
28 Vacant
32 David Graham, laborer

John-st intersects.

46 Wm Blain, laborer
48 J Atkins, spinner
50 Thos Lee, glassblower
52 Martin O'Brien, sectionman
54 Mrs Joseph Philips

Catharine-st intersects.

60 Michael Taulty, laborer
68 John McGovern, laborer

Mary-st intersects

86 Ed Young, plasterer
94 Thos Lucas, helper
96 James Whitley, laborer
98 James Neil mason
100 James Watts, spinner
102 Matthew Gill, boilermaker
104 Vacant

Ferguson-ave intersects

120 Wm Phœnix, patternmkr
126 Thos Freel, dyer
132 Mrs Patrick Lynch
134 Francis Fagan, ropemkr
138 Matthew Kennedy, cooper

Wellington-st intersects

Robt Bernard, laborer
231 Isaac Bernard, tanner

Victoria-ave intersects

Ferrie-st w, north side, from 281 James north to the Bay

10 Mark J Wall, laborer
12 Wm Torrance, moulder
16 John McCallum, moulder
26 Mrs Elizabeth Malcolmson

Macnab-st intersects

34 John Cowan
36 — Wynn, dyer
38 Hy Priestland, helper
40 Capt James Mitchell
42 A Anderson, boilermaker
44 Vacant
46 Vacant

Bay-st intersects

56 John Langhorn

58 Geo Walker, painter
  Burlingt Yacht Club
  Massie's boat house

Ferrie-st w, south side

Ontario Cotton Mills Co
25 Robt Williamson, fitter

Macnab-st intersects

31 Hugh Gillespie, grocer
37 Robt Johnson, mariner
39 Wm Peace, watchman
41 Vacant

Bay-st intersects

47 Wm Hilton, laborer
49 Cornelius Doxey, boilermkr

Florence-st, north side from 72 Bay north to west of Dundurn

4 Mrs A Tomes
6 D McDonald
8 Vacant
14 Mrs Hy Westfall
16 Lewis J Constable, supt Rolling Mills
20 Wm Armstrong, laborer

Pearl-st intersects

30 Wm Mitchell, mason
36 W Lockman, carpenter
40 Wm H Lockman, contractor
42 Geo S Board, blacksmith
44 Hugh W Corry, laborer
46 Wm Nex, carpenter
48 Robt Rolston, upholsterer
50 James Watson, moulder
52 Peter Wright, laborer
54 Mrs Wm Potter

Locke-st intersects

56 Stephen Carter, blacksmith
58 Robt Caine, coremaker
60 Isaac Rigg, moulder

Inchbury-st intersects

Semmens' factory

Sophia-st intersects

86 Robt Britton, machinist
88 John T Scharp, laborer
90 John Attle, tinsmith
94 Wm Beckman, laborer
96 C Neighorn, marblecutter
98 Geo S Thompson, laborer
102 Richard Gray
104 Chas Wedge, tobaccoroller
106 Kristan Scharp, laborer
110 John Craig, carpenter
112 Thos Jackman, fitter
118 Ed Housego, fireman
120 Wm Herbert, tinsmith

Dundurn-st intersects

Mrs Elizabeth Burns, nurse

Breadalbane-st intersects

Florence-st, south side

1 J W Norman, laborer
3 John Trotman, polisher
5 John Ceasar, teamster
7 Wm Moffat, laborer
7½ Wm R Dyer, laborer
9 Wm J Millgan, baker
13 Joseph Robbins, compositor
13 Joseph Robbins, shoemaker
15 John Marshall, wire rope mkr
17 John Henry, boilercleaner
19 John Fox
21 George T Collett, machinist

Pearl-st intersects

25 Alex Anderson, blacksmith
27 Thos Farmer, photographer
29 Wm Westfall, laborer
31 John Carston, laborer
33 John Westfall, laborer
35 Robt Leslie, shoemaker
37 Jos Jocelyn, plasterer
39 Ed Reiger, driver
41 James Symmers, clerk
43 Robt Pollard, carpenter
45 Geo Kerr, timekeeper
47 James Gavey jr, scalemaker
49 Chas Plater, shoemaker
51 Wm C Allen, fireman

Locke and Sophia-sts intersect

86 John Meiler, tailor

95 James P Judd, soap manf
99 Geo Belling, carpenter
105 John Nelson, hackman
107 Samuel R Hancock, laborer
109 John McMahon, shearsman
115 Peter McCullough, laborer

Dundurn-st intersects

Garth-st, east side, from end of King w to Mountain

1 Chas A Blunden, laborer
Ed Cooper, laborer
Frank Duley, laborer
Thos Packman, laborer

Main-st intersects

Wm Cassford, melter
John Milligan, stovemtr
John Philips, laborer

Herkimer-st intersects

Fred Richards, wood worker

Concession-st intersects

Wm Shawcross, traveler

Garth-st, west side

Chas Lest, laborer
Thos Kelly, laborer
Bristol Barber, laborer
E New, brickyard

Main-st intersects

Fred Childs, brickmaker
Jos Walker, dairyman

Herkimer-st intersects

Mrs Jos Fielding

Concession-st intersects

Wm Gillaland, moulder
Hugh McDougll, mason
Alex Thomson, patternmkr
Wm Y Dow, moulder
W H Nicolls, farmer

George-st, north side, from 6 Bay s to Locke

2 G D Hawkins & Co, manfr

12 Geo Stewart, laborer
14 Peter Snider, laborer
16 Wm Russell, laborer
18 Wm Pegler, laborer
20 W H Chilman, merchant

Caroline-st intersects

26 John Gillard, merchant
28 John H Herring, traveler
30 G G Hacker, merchant
32 Robt Wright, merchant
34 Wm H Finch, merchant
36 Miss Mary, Robinson
40 Vacant
42 Chas Lemon, barrister
44 P B Barnard, merchant

Hess-st intersects

54 Chas Tolmie, agent
56 Chas O Jolley, manfr
56 Mrs Wm Richardson

Queen-st intersects

70 John Thomson
   Wm Nicholson, wood dealer

Ray-st intersects

78 Wm Malcolm, manfr
80 Francis D Boyes, clerk
82 John Wallace, tinsmith
86 Wm Pearce, engine driver

Pearl st-intersects

92 David Bates, teamster
94 Richard McBride, packer
   Robt A Ross, cigarmaker
   John Atkinson, machinst
108 Chas Coleman, laborer
110 James Robins, butcher

Locke-st intersects

George-st, south side

3 Samuel Bennett, turner
5 Joseph Tavener, tinsmith
7 James Dryden, driver
9 Thos Beckett, driver
11 Chas Shields, pedler
13 Geo Case, blacksmith
15 Dewey & Sons, ice dealers

Caroline-st intersects

35 Henry Blue, laborer
39 F C Bruce, seedsman
41 C Cooper, carriage painter
43 D McKenzie, engineer
45 Edmund Brown, builder
47 Ephraim Coombs, plater
49 Mrs Fryburger

Hess-st intersects

59 Henry Duncan, merchant
61 Mrs Arch McDearmid
61 J I Mackenzie, license insp
63 Thos B Greening, merchant
65 Adam Zimmerman, tailor

Queen-st intersects

69 Geo M Hunt, ins agent
71 Wm F Findlay, accountant
73 Geo H Mills, barrister

Ray st intersects

77 Girls' Home
79 Wm Somerville jr, merchant
81 Jos Prentice, serj police
83 And Higgins, confectioner
85 Wm H Woodhouse, timeke'r

Pearl st intersects

93 Thos Shea, laborer
95 Thos C Jackson, laborer
103 Geo Rosbrook, laborer
109 Richard Packham, cigarmak'r

Locke-st intersects

Gore-st, north side, from 90 James n, east to Catharine

2 D T Baxter, dentist
6 Grand Opera House
8 Garrick Club
14 G L MacKelcan, M D
16 Wm McCargow, M D
18 E H Dilliabough, M D

Hughson st intersects

   Lutheran Church
28 Mrs Mary Bates
30 Moss Freeman, laborer

John-st intersects
44 James Kelly, grocer
50 John Burkholder, laborer
52 Wm Gell, broker
54 Wm McMeekin, carpenter
56 Mrs Joseph J Myles
60 John Temple, livery keeper

Catharine-st intersects

Gore-st, south side

5 Hamilton Bottling Co
7 Thos Young, saloon
13 Mrs John Shaw, boarding
15 John Gilbert, machinist
17 Vacant
19 Mrs Arthur Goring
21 Geo Caldwell, machinist

Hughson-st intersects

23 Mark Mossman, shoemaker
29 Alex Thomson, cabinetmak'r
31 Aaron Mann, clerk
33 Rev C O Johnson
    Methodist Church

John-st intersects

51 Vacant
53 R Lord, tailor
55 Henry O'Brien, gunsmith
57 Lewis Bennett, waiter
59 Benj Lewis, wool sorter

Catharine-st intersects

Greig-st, east side, from Queen north

2 Cornelius Murphy, catcher
4 — Cox, carpenter
6 Mrs Jos Hunter
8 Geo Brettingham, fitter
10 Wm D Curry, engineer
16 Ed Flynn, laborer

Greig-st, west side

1 Patrick Williams, boilermkr
3 John Murphy, laborer
5 Patrick Sullivan, laborer
7 John J Rourke, bricklayer
9 L N Vail, carpenter

11 John B Clark, puddler
13 Fred Pearson, tobaccoroller
15 John Cardwell, laborer
19 Thos Foulton, laborer

Grove-st, north side, from 3 Liberty east to Wellington

1 Wm Stewart
7 David Little, barber
9 Wm H McGaw
11 Wm Geiger
13 Mrs Peter Freeman
15 John Farthing, machinist
17 J Redding, gardener
19 Jacob Gould, carpenter

Wellington-st intersects

Grove-st, south side

2 Geo Canning, plasterer
4 Thos Hager, stovemtr
8 Thos Davis, traveler
10 Leslie Wright, baggage masr
12 Wm H McKay, laborer
14 Peter Sinclair, laborer
10a Robt Stewart, bailiff
12a Mrs Alex Rutherford
16 Wm Shuttleworth, salesman
18 Mrs E B Shaw
24 Alex McKay

Wellington-st intersects

Guise-st, north side, from 383 James n to the Bay

23 Hy Foule, teamster
25 Stephen Dunn, foreman
31 Richard Scott, teamster

John-st intersects

Myles' coal yard
Murton & Reid's coal yard

Guise-st, south side

10 Patrick Bennett, laborer
12 Jos Thompson, laborer
14 Margaret Callahan
16 Thos Cross, laborer
18 Thos Lawson, laborer
20 Wm Berryman, painter

24 Arch McCoy, watchman
26 Mrs Mary Munro
28 Mrs McVeigh
30 Richard Green

Hughson-st intersects

34 James Berry, grocer
38 Vacant
40 Hy Gagan, laborer
42 James Ferguson, cigarmaker
44 Patrick Earl
46 Vacant
48 T Reardon, sailor
50 Vacant
56 Vacant
58 Samuel Berry, carpenter

John-st intersects

House of Refuge

Hannah-st e, north side, from 137 James south to Wellington

Hughson-st ends

Ch of Ascension S School

John-st intersects

25 Wm G Strathdee, engineer

Catharine-st ends

29 Rev H Birkenthal
31 Mrs Maria Wyllie
33 Vacant
35 Mrs Henry Whately
37 Martin Hanley, blacksmith
39 Geo Campbell
41 John Bingham, laborer
43 John Painter, bread pedler
45 David McLean, carpenter
47 James Shea, leather cutter
51 John Fisher, cigarmaker
53 Vacant
55 Ralph McCormick, teamster
59 John Williams, laborer
61 Vacant
63 Michael Dwyer

Walnut-st ends

67 Patrick Connell, laborer
71 Mrs Mary Cusha

77 James McCarthy, nursery
79 James Adams, mechanic
81 Leo Blatz, tailor

Cherry-st intersects

93 Patrick Dillon, laborer
95 Arthur O'Neil, tailor
99 Adam Milne, shoemaker
101 Wm Nugent, laborer

Aurora-st intersects

113 Michael Wickham, laborer
119 Timothy Foley, laborer
121 Alexander Anderson, teamster

Wellington-st intersects

Hannah-st e, south side

4 R A Pringle, barrister
6 W A Robinson
8 John J Stuart, merchant
12 Dennis Moore, founder

John-st intersects

22 Joseph Hancock
24 Donald Manson, merchant
26 Mrs R N Taylor
28 R L Gunn, clerk 9th division court

Catharine-st intersects

46 Mrs John Bartley
56 Chas H Martin, laborer
58 John W Fox, gardener
60 Alex Sutherland, carpenter
62 David Towler

Walnut-st intersects

64 Michael Boyle, boilermaker
r 64 Mrs Electa Wild
66 Timothy Cashman
84 Chas Locke, stovefitter
86 Daniel Mahoney, stovemoun'r

Cherry-st intersects

120 D Northey, engineer
122 Geo Chandler, stovemounter
126 Thos Byron, broommaker
126½ Peter Mulholland, laborer
128 Michael Lahey, bricklayer

Wellington-st intersects

Hannah-st west, north side, from James south to Locke

8 Morton W Murdoff, mercha't
10 Henry Martin, artist
12 Edward Noyes
14 A W Leitch, com merchant
16 Adam Burns
18 Arch McKellar, sheriff

Macnab-st intersects

Joseph Jeffrey

Park-st intersects

44 John H Pipon, clerk
46 Wm Vallance, merchant
48 Mrs I C Chillman
   Donaldson & Patterson, builders

Bay-st intersects

Peter Balfour sr
62 James P Johnson, manager Express Co
   Mrs Edith Bullen
44 A Boyle, shoemaker
46 Wm J Kingdon, printer
48 Mrs Martha Rogers
50 John T Irwin, manf
   John McAllister, laborer

Caroline-st intersects

54 Daniel Henry, grocer
60 Alex Crooks, dairyman
62 Wm Kaye, laborer
64 John Rackley, laborer
66 James Smith, gilder
68 T A Aitchison, bookkeeper
70 Mrs Hannah Pim
72 Geo McKeand, ins agent
74 Martin Sammons
74 S W McConochie, M D

Hess-st intersects

76 John M Dixon, chemist
78 John B Nicholls, clerk
80 Hugh Gorman, porter
82 J B Kitchen, photographer
84 Chas A Zwick, attendant

Queen-st intersects

37

96 Levi Woodcroft, laborer
102 Chas H Holdsworth, warehouseman

Locke and Garth-sts intersect

Hannah-st west, south side

Private grounds

Macnab-st intersects

Rev Hartley Carmichael
25 Robt H Parke
27 Thos C Haslett, barrister
   H P Coburn, manfr

Park-st intersects

33 John B Young, bookkeeper
37 W R Davis, jeweler
39 Robt S Topping, engineer
41 Rev John Morton
43 J S Hossack, builder
45 Hy Northey, speculator
47 Wm McBeth, machinist

Bay-st intersects

49 Ed Appleby, stovemtr
53 Chas Sayer, shipper
41 Samuel Cottrell, bricklayer
43 C W Mulligan, architect
45 James Lockhart
47 Vacant
49 Fred Hutty, gardener
51 Vacant

Caroline-st intersects

65 Mrs Richard Rowe, florist
67 John Riviere, laborer
   — Miller

Hess-st intersects

Methodist Church

Queen-st intersects

89 Wm S Scott, porter
93 Abraham White, machinist
93 M E Gilbert, traveler
103 Vacant
105 Geo Swanton, broommaker

Kent-st intersects

125 Philip Viedenheimer, baker
127 Morris Hendershot, driver

F S Morrison, bookkeeper
John Bridgewood, teamster

Locke and Garth-sts intersect

Harriet-st, north side, from 115 Caroline north, west to Hess

2 Lawrence McCormick, condr
4 John Campbell, fireman
14 John Carroll, engineer
14½ Erancis Brohman, maltster
15 Richard McCarthy, hackdrivr
18 Geo Childs
20 C McCarthy, hackman

Hess-st intersects

Harriet-st, south side

1 Patrick McCarty, laborer
3 John Coppins, laborer
5 Wm Alderman, blacksmith
7 John Whitney, laborer
9 Fred Pfeiffer, laborer
11 Vacant
13 Vacant
15 Vacant
17 John Henderson, blacksmith

Hess-st intersects

Head-st, from Sophia

Hand & Co, fireworks
John Lyons, shipper
John McLean, tailor
Alfred Barnard, bookkeeper

Dundurn-st intersects

8 John Cotter, carter
Geo Sharkay, caretaker

Herkimer-st, north side, from James west to Queen

10 Mrs James Osborne
12 W R Macdonald, barrister

Argyll Terrace { J M Burns, banker
Mrs Richard Thomson
Mrs Fanny Chapman

Park-st intersects

36 Miss Sarah Bowes
38 Wm S Duffield, bookkeeper
44 John L Stoney, ins agent
46 J B Browne, com traveler

Bay-st intersects

52 Geo Morton
54 R v C A Johnson
58 Thos Meston, bookkeeper
58½ A E Jarvis, banker
60 Geo Jelfs, barrister
62 James Davidson, jeweler
64 A H Baker

Caroline-st intersects

70 Adolph Egener, exciseofficer
72 W M Goodwin, inspector
74 Chas Bremner, grocer

Hess-st intersects

110 Thos Hedley, upholsterer

Queen-st intersects

James Rowe, gardener
Mrs Ellen Ward
John Bond, coachman

Kent & Locke-sts intersect

G W Collins, mason
Thos G Harper, plater
Baptist Mission Church
A F Drew, carpenter
Vacant
D Dolman, teamster
Thos King, laborer
C Clark, laborer

Garth-st intersects

Herkimer-st, south side, James west to limits

Burlington Terrace { 1 Chas M Counsell
3 H C Baker
5 Thos H Stinson
7 F W Gates, pres Gas Co

Macnab-st intersects

11 John E Parker, manf

13 Vacant
21 A Gaviller

Park-st intersects

Judge Sinclair

Bay-st intersects

53 Thos Irwin, manf
55 David McLellan, ins agent
57 J G McIlwraith, merchant
59 D Henderson, salesman
61 Geo E Jones, clerk
65 Richard Raycroft, grocer

Caroline-st intersects

Geo Hunt, grocer
69 E E W Moore, clerk
71 Fred R Buscome, traveler
73 John Crossley, merchant
75 Samuel Rogers, manf
77 Rev Joseph Gdery
79 Mrs Wm Gage

Hess-st intersects

107 James Muckersie, fitter
109 J B Gunmo, harnessmaker
111 Mrs M P Coston, dressmaker
Richard Graham, dyer
113 G Murison, health inspector
Vacant
Geo Nicholson, wood dealer

Kent & Locke-sts intersect

Presbyterian Mission Ch
Wm Harvey, grocer
Henry Henderson, machinist
Albert G Durling, brickmak'r
212 Fred Notz, painter
St Mark's Mission Church
Thos J Taylor, machinist
Stephen Summers, shoemak'r
John Smith, laborer

Garth-st intersects

Wm Boswell, clerk

Henry-st runs north from Cannon east

4 Adam Beltz, cutter

6 **Samuel** Lucas, carpenter
8 John Gotte, jeweler
10 Mrs John White
12 Alex McGregor, tailor
14 Ethelbert Knapp, shoemaker
16 Ed Hall, carpenter
18 Fred Johnston, moulder
20 Wm Hurst, carpenter
Henry Young, **carpenter**

Hess-st n, east side, from 183 King w to Stuart

8 Nicholas McKeegan, plaster'r

Market-st intersects

26 P McCarty, teamster
28 John McMurray, driver
30 Lewis McDonald, machinist
32 Alfred Rieger, blacksmith
34 Patrick Fitzgerald, moulder

Napier-st intersects

44 James H Cooper
46 Mrs James R Foster
48 Wm Simpson, railroader
50 Roland Hill, merchant
52 Wm Brooks, bookkeeper
54 Jas B Rutherford, moulder

York-st intersects

Central Drug Store
56 Wm Philip, M D
58 Miss Elizabeth Galbraith
60 Mrs Thos Bridgewood
60 Postal Newyear
62 Mrs Wm Wyllie, dressmaker
64 Mrs Hattie Kappelle
66 Woalf Cohen, deal**er**

Cannon-st intersects

68 Wm **J Bruggie,** grocer
70 John **Dowe,** cooper
72 James Brugge, cabinet
82 Mrs Susan Malamphy

Mill-st intersects

84 Danford Evans, traveler
86 James Bowen, tobaccoroller
88 Wm McDonald, moulder

90 F E Roderick, lather
92 Mrs Wm McCartney
92½ Mrs Wm McCartney
98 Mrs Charlotte McNeil

Harriet-st ends

100 R E Williams, roller
104 James Lloyd, laborer
106 Maurice Devine, moulder
108 S J Whitehead, manfr
120 John Connors, conductor
122 Thos Stewart, cellarman
124 Wm Fennell jr, laborer
126 Mrs T McCoumb
128 Vacant

Barton-st intersects

140 Wilmot Wilson, switchman
142 Geo Manders, heater

Stuart-st intersects

Hess-st n, west side

1 Wm Reeves, baker
5 Geo Clark, machinist
7 Jas Hamilton, tobaccowork'r
9 Wm Vint, tobaccoroller
11 Mrs Mary Doran
13 Patrick Hanlon, grocer

Market-st intersects

25 G C Archer, cutter
29 Wm Richardson, hackman
31 Vacant

Napier-st intersects

45 Abe A Reid, bookkeeper
51 Mrs Margaret Rymal

Peter-st intersects

53 John W Thornson, traveler
55 Mrs Alex Macdonald

York-st intersects

  M O'Grady, marble works
  Public School
75 Vacant
77 Arch McGowan, machinist
79 Robt T Brown, machinist
81 John L Brown, machinist
83 Arthur Goulding, caretaker

85 D Sheehan, baker
87 Wm McGovern, laborer
89 James Falls, swichman
89½ Geo Copely, clerk
91 Hy Tuck, caser
91½ W H Thompson, nailer
93 Geo Knox, engineer
95 J McIntosh, conductor
97 Joshua Brundle, letter coll'r
99 Amos Cassidy, carpenter
103 John Jones, mechanic
105 Maurice Connell, laborer
107 John Peden, merchant
109 Andrew Cameron, GTR
111 J H Wilson, pork butcher
113 John Anderson, heater
115 Julius M Williams, druggist
117 Wm M Crossman, painter
119 Wm Thompson, machinist
121 John Taylor
123 Geo Green, laborer
137 James Brass, watchman

Stuart-st intersects

Hess-st s, east side, from 185 King w to Mountain

1 Geo Harper
3 John Kinleyside, manf
5 J H Killey, manf
9 James D Wilson, merchant
11 Mrs Samuel Olmsted

George-st intersects

13 W B Webber
15 Andrew Dalton, moulder
17 James Logie

Main and Jackson-sts intersect

41 John Dow, wood dealer

Hunter-st intersects

45 Wm Horspoole, clerk
47 John Fahey, shoemaker
49 Chas Male, laborer
51 C H Sandford, sausagemaker
43 Gellert Hummel, bricklayer

Bold-st intersects

  Vacant lots

Duke & Robinson-sts intersect
99 J C Stacey, upholsterer
101 Geo Graham, tailor
Hannah-st intersects.
117 Wm Flitcroft, blacksmith
Herkimer-st intersects
127 John Hislop, blacksmith
Markland & Concession-sts intersect
Wm Poland, engineer
James M Williams, manf

Hess-st s, west side

2 John Patterson
4 Herbert A L Dixon, customs
6 James Fraser, moulder
12 C Carpenter, merchant
George-st intersects
14 Wm McBride, laborer
16 Vacant
Main-st intersects
20 Wm H Ryckman, grocer
22 Miss Margaret Colville
Jackson-st intersects
W D Booker, sec Vic ins Co
42 Peter Knight, broommaker
44 Wm Scott, packer
46 Frank Lipkle, laborer
Hunter-st intersects
Wm Smye, wagonmaker
Vacant lots
Bold, Duke and Robinson-sts intersect
Andrew Robb, engineer
Hannah and Herkimer-sts intersect
Vacant
Markland-st intersects
Wm Irving, carpenter
Chas Clark, bricklayer

Wm Lane, bricklayer
John Price, carpenter
Concession-st intersects
Alex H Moore, banker

Hilton-st, east side, from Markland s to Concession

2 Daniel A Bedwell, cutter
4 Vacant
6 Wm S C Hazell
Concession-st intersects

Hilton-st, west side

3 Wm Miller, shoemaker
5 Vacant
Concession-st intersects

Hughson-st n, east side, from from 34 King e to Guise

4 Wm Peace, barber
6 Jeremiah McAuliffe, saloon
8 Wm Somerville & Co, com agents
10 Stinson's bank
12 Hover & Hoyle, tailors
12 Alfred Irving, picture framer
14 Alex Mars, bookbinder
16 H C Duval, barber
18 John Clayton, painter
20 David Mitchell, shoemaker
22 James E Halloran, livery
24 Frank Ireland, engraver
24 J Adam, plumber
26 A S Hill, hotel
King William-st intersects
28-30 James Sweeney, stoves
34 Central Fire Station
42 Mrs Ann Drinnon
r 42 James Davis, blacksmith
44 Mrs John Elrington
44 Mrs Thos Hartley
46 Mrs Jos Taylor
48 Wm Blake, butcher
50 John Leitch, machinist

Rebecca-st intersects

54 John Bartlett, blacksmith
56 John H Chadwick, manfr
58 John Faustman, cooper
60 Mrs Andrew Goddard
64 J W Simpson, com agent
66 Edgar Myers, cooper
68 Frank Johnson, barber
70 Geo Watt, teamster
72 Thos Bale, machinist

Gore-st intersects

74 Rev Gustave De Zocher
78 Geo H Denison, clerk
80 John T Steel
82 Ed Cleary, shoemaker
84 Thos Buttle
88 Albert S Vail, merchant
Congregational Church

Cannon-st intersects

120 Samuel Purnell, painter
122 Ephram Taylor, pressman
124 Miss Annie O'Malley
126 Chas Robertson, teacher
128 Albert Roberts, U S Consul
130 Alex McAdams, lumber
132 A R Morrison, agent
134 Wallace Zimmerman, clerk
136 Allen Land, bookkeeper

Robert-st intersects

138 J W McArthur, manfr
140 Wm Omand
142 H M Coates, letter carrier
144 Miss McCully, tailoress
146 Alex McCully, shoemaker
Vacant lot
152 Freeman Johnson, pipemkr
154 John W Baker, laborer
156 Thos Applegate, laborer
158 Jos Carroll, salesman
160 James Martin, laborer
162 Mrs Alex Dingwall
164 Mrs Catharine Riddell
166 Daniel Newington, gunsmith
168 Mrs Thos E Fawcett
170 Thos Applegate, hackman
172 Mrs Smith
174 David Robson, laborer

176 James Mitchell, porter
178 — Hannon, laborer
180 Mrs Hy Hill

Barton-st intersects

182 Geo Carmichael, cab driver
188 Wm Russell, traveler
190 John Dunn
192 Wm Gillespie, patternmaker
196 Thos Hutchison, engineer

Murray-st intersects

202 John McCarthy, laborer
205 C Quinlan, laborer
206 Geo Towers, laborer
208 John Brennan, carpenter
210 Thos O'Neil, laborer
212 Geo A Warren, puddler
214 Wm Gray
216 Jos Nolan, laborer

Stuart-st intersects

222 Hy Owens, melter
224 John Pinch, fitter
226 Wm Jones, driver
228 Mrs E Griffiths
230 Mrs Ann Reid, grocer

Strachan-st intersects

238 Geo Johnson, carpenter
242 Wm Jamieson, moulder
242 Wm Mathieson, moulder

Simcoe-st intersects

248 Patrick Harte, clerk
250 Mrs M Monihan
252 Michael Duffy, moulder
256 Mrs L Adley
258 Thos Grace, wood dealer
260 Donald McKay, laborer
264 John Pearson, cab driver
266 Thos Williamson
268 Robt Williamson, sailor

Ferrie-st intersects

270 Thomas Lawley
272 James Hurley, moulder
274 John Wild, dyer
274½ Ed Jobborn, gardener
276 John Milligan, laborer
278 John O'Connor

STREET DIRECTORY.

280 Elijah Corey, mariner
282 C Whitley, helper
284 Mrs C McGroggan
286 John McKinley, laborer
288 Robt Gray, laborer

Picton-st intersects

294 H H Walker, woodworker
296 Vacant
300 Thos Beatty, boilermaker
302 Robt Finch, bricklayer
304 James Ellis, laborer
306 Jos Cahill, glassblower
310 Robt Ball, laborer
312 John Roach, laborer

Macauley-st intersects

326 Geo Johnson, carpenter
328 Joseph Pauley, carpenter
330 John Blake, laborer
332 George Strampel, laborer
334 Daniel Tracey, teamster
336 Mrs Ann Smith
338 Mrs Margaret Colvin

Wood-st intersects

342 W J McFadden, grocer
348 James Black, laborer
350 A Robitaille, laborer
352 Daniel Sullivan, laborer
354 Mrs Joseph L Wetherall
356 John Reardon, boilermaker
360 Michael Reardon

Burlington-st intersects

368 J H Thompson, boatbuilder
370 John Thompson, grocer
374 F N Farmer, carter
380 Wesley Lee, carpenter

Guise-st intersects

Hughson-st n, west side

J A Clark, druggist
1 *Times* editorial rooms
5-11 *Times* Printing Co
13 Gore Coffee Tavern
15 J Matthews & Son, painters
17 James Mackie, carpenter
19 Wm J Brush, St James' saloon

21 Vacant

King William-st intersects

33 Wm H Weston, manf
35 Frank Crooks
49 James H Williams

Rebecca-st intersects

55 Dr Alex C Reid
55 J W Simpson, merchant
J M Williams & Co, manfs
71 Mrs Thos Mitchell

Gore-st intersects.

77 Mrs E Clark
85 Robt Bow, tinsmith
87 Mrs John Godden
r 87 Wm Robertson, tailor
89 Thos Greenan, moulder
91 Jas Jackson, sailmaker
93 Thos Carling, machinist
95 D M Oliver, mariner
97 John Stewart, builder

Cannon-st intersects

Public school
105 John Cole, bookkeeper
107 Jas Chisholm, barrister
109 David McKean
111 A E Carpenter, contractor
113 J W Sutherland, lumber
117 Peter Ruthven

Robert-st intersects

143 Thos Gribben, carpenter
145 Alfred Bissonette, moulder
147 Mrs Robt McCulloch
161 D J Kelly, wood dealer
163 Vacant
165 James E Doyle, grocer
167 Robt B Murray, silverplater
169 Geo Bartman, tailor
171 L Roehm, tailor
173 David Findlay, moulder
175 Emile Wolliung, pork butcher

Barton-st intersetcs

183 Jas Bartholemew, laborer
185 James Gray, helper
187 Mrs John Duffy

189 Walter Long, painter
193 Jas H Stannard, carpenter
195 John Gillespie, machinist
197 Wm Burrow, founder
199 Mrs Wm Ambrose

Murray-st intersects

203 Mrs M Cartney
205 Louis Burnett, laborer
207 Wm O'Toole, cigarmaker
r 207 Mrs Margaret Dyne
209 James McDonald, machinist
211 Anthony Bowker, laborer
215 Chris Clark, hatter

Stuart-st intersects

Geo Mills, grocer
GTR bridge
225 Wm Fowler, laborer
225 Matthew Sexton, burnisher
227 Jos Kerslake, cabinetmaker

Strachan-st intersects

231 Mrs John Hannon
233 Jacob Young, wheelwright
235 Thos Brady, coal inspector
237 Wm Roe, moulder
239 T Horn, carpenter
241 Geo Horn, carpenter
243 John Noonan, mariner
245 Thos W Laird, machinist
249 Vacant

Simcoe-st intersects

251 J A Ball, brassfinisher
253 David Sinn, porter
255 Mrs David Creighton
259 Primary School
261 Patrick Dalton, laborer
263 M Nelligan, wagonmaker
365 Mrs M Nelligan

Ferrie-st intersects

275 Andrew Hay, carpenter
r 275 — Evans, painter
277 Patrick Donnelly
279 Vacant
281 Robt Wilson, laborer
283 James Begley, fireman
285 James Vallance, carpenter

Picton-st intersects

305 Hamilton Glass Works

Macaulay st intersects

315 Vacant
317 Vacant
329 Wm Richardson, bricklayer
331 J Hodson, laborer
335 Thos O'Neil, laborer

Wood st intersects

351 Moses Blondin, engineer
353 James Henderson, teamster

Burlington-st intersects

367 Hy Gillam, laborer
369 Thos Doyle, laborer
373 Mrs Chas Lee
375 Chas Blackburn
381 Vacant

Guise-st intersects

Hughson-st s, east side, from 117 King e to Hannah

Hamilton Provident and Loan Society Chambers {
  Bell Telephone Co
  1 Cameron & Witherspoon, barristers
  1 Crerar, Muir & Crerar, barristers
  Parkes & Macadams, barristers
  3 Dun, Wiman & Co, mercantile agents
}
5 Vacant
7 Fred H Lambe, assignee
7 A F Forbes, stock broker
Thomas Myles & Son, coal dealers

Main-st intersects

Court House
Prince's Square
Registry Office

Jackson-st intersects

J & R Kilgour, organ manfrs
R T S Powell, florist

Hunter-st intersects

51 Union hotel

STREET DIRECTORY.

Wood Market

63 James Wilson, clerk
65 Miss Mary Wilson
67 H B W Western, clerk
69 W H Perriton, upholsterer
71 S S Ryckman, grocer

Augusta-st intersects

79 Synagogue
79 John Buscombe, bricklayer
83 Alex Turner, merchant

Young-st intersects

85 Rev R J Laidlaw
87 Harold Lambe, broker
89 Rich H Greene, merchant
Vacant lots

Maria and Hannah-sts intersect

Hughson-st south, west side

Bank of Commerce
4 John Labatt, bottler
8 Gage & Jelfs, barristers
10 Harold Lambe, broker

Main-st intersects

Chancery Chambers {
18-20 Jno Pearson, accountant and ins agent
L H Patten, barrister
D G Ellis, broker
}

Equity Chambers {
12 Charles Lemon, barrister
12 R Bull, ins agent
14 Walter Ambrose, insurance agt
A W Leitch, agent
}

14 Lyman Lee, barrister
16 Club Chambers
28 E S Collins, sign painter

Jackson-st intersects

30 Z B Choate, carpenter
32 Joseph Plastow, caretaker
  Wm G Leitch, manf
  Alex Milne, builder
  David Roach, livery

Hunter-st intersects

5 Myra Hodgins
38

52 Thos Evans
54 John Burrows, laborer
56 H J Hampton, machinist
58 Angus Reid, teamster
60 Wm Reid, teamster
66 James Gay
68 Vacant
70 Mrs Francis **Mandelbaum**

Augusta-st intersects

76 Mrs Owen Kennedy
78 Miss Janet Addison
78½ Mrs Alex Dickman
80 Richard Pray

Young & Maria-sts intersect

98 John Calder, merchant
102 W H Glassco, merchant

Hannah-st intersects

Hunter-st e, north side, from 61 James s to Emerald

1 Mrs Mary Carr
3-7 Salvation Army barracks
9-11 James Cheyne, builder
15 Chas Hill, carpenter
19 James Jolley, merchant

Hughson-st intersects

Hotel stables

John-st intersects

39 W H Olmsted, merchant
41 James H Shouldice, agent
43 Nelson Cornell, clerk
45 John Vannater, policeman
47 Mrs Herbert Andrews
49 Robt Bland, machinist
49½ Geo Sharp, builder
51 Wm Warwack, carpenter
51 Mrs Geo Sinclair
53 John Stephenson, grocer

Catharine-st intersects

55 Mrs Michael Allen, grocer
59 Wm Stevenson, carpenter
61 John Tuckett, tobacconist
63 J S Ralston, land agent

65 Miss M Jones, dressmaker
67 R W Hynds, bookkeepr
69 James Dunlop, merchant
71 Levi Stewart, traveler
73 Mrs Wm McKee
75 Mrs Thomas Atkinson
77 Vacant
79 Mrs Wm Traill
81 Smith Will carpenter
83 John Burgess, music teacher

Walnut-st intersects

93 Ernest Fischer, manf
95 Vacant
97 Joseph Black, wagonmaker
97½ Jonathan Pottruff, salesman
99 R J Howard, blacksmith
101 Chas Oder, laborer
103 Mrs James E Keats
105 Mrs Sarah Brick, grocer

Cherry-st intersects

107 Edw Moshier, stovemounter
113 Mrs J C McCarthy
115 Job B Jeffs, machinist
117 Mrs John Sullivan
119 Mrs James Twomey
121 John Richmond, butcher
123 Peter Nielsen, engineer

Spring-st ends

129 Robt Moore, tailor
131 Mrs Patrick Gorman
133 Vacant
135 Peter Adams, tailor
137 James Peer, cutter

Wellington-st intersects

Vacant lots

West-ave intersects

161 Vacant
Vacant grounds

Victoria-ave intersects

Vacant grounds to Emerald street

Hunter-st e. south side

4 G Stevenson, baker

6 Robt Burnet, laborer
8 Vacant
12 Augustus Leighton, laundry
14 Richard Bull, ins agent
16 Mrs M Adams
18 John Barry, barrister
20 James Sellar, laborer

Hughson-st intersects.

22 J W Rattenbury, wagonmakr
24 Mrs Amy Disher
26 P Moore, shipper
32 Geo N Hughson, carpenter
32½ Simeral Doak, blacksmith
34 Misses Cross & McConnell'

John-st intersects.

40 Mrs Barnard Jacobs
42 Levi Potruff, clerk
44 Mrs Levi Pottruff
46 Wm J Myers, painter
48 W B Mitchell, tailor
50 Wm Cosgrove, agent
50½ Robt D Cowan
52 Wm Bews

Catharine-st intersects.

54 Felix O'Neil, hackman
58 James Didman, butcher
60 M Stonehouse, shoemaker
60½ W Truman, bookkeeper
64 Jacob Voelker, tailor
66 Geo Jackson, shipper
68 Mrs Addie Sayers
68½ Jas Strous, messenger PO
70 James B Blair, exciseman
70 Peter Nichol, machinist

Baillie-st intersects

74 Geo Matthews, clerk
76 Wm Strongman, policeman
78 Wm Stoneham, plasterer
80 Wm Hillyard, shoemaker
82 Thos Sylvester, coppersmith
84 Neil McKay, winemaker
86 Rudolph Rissman
88 Thos Healey

Walnut-st intersects

88 Mrs Donald Stuart

88½-90 Vacant
92 Vacant
94 Geo Magill
94½ S B Hummill, teamster
104 Long's wood yard

Cherry-st intersects

St Patrick's school

Liberty-st intersects

120 P Stuart, wood inspector
124 Vacant
126 Vacant
130 S S Rolls, carriage trimmer
132 Thos Old, laborer
134 Mrs Wm Gow
136 Mrs John McKenzie
138 Vacant
138½ Mrs Esther Smith
140 Alex McLaughlin, salesman
142 Hy McNeiley, salesman
144 Donald Dawson, tax col

Wellington-st intersects

154 Alex McFarlane, merchant
Primary School

West, Victoria and East-aves intersect

Hunter-st w, north side, to Garth

Private grounds

Park-st intersects

St James R E Church
32 J C Burrows, builder
34 Thos McBride, supt
36 O S Hillman, accountant
38 E McLoughlin, civil engineer
40 Alex Gillies, com trav
42 Alex Anderson
44 Wm Acres, furrier
46 Mrs Wm Troup
48 John Kerner
50 Geo Vallance
52 Peter Brass, architect

Bay-st intersects

52 James T Braston, bricklayer
152 E V Orme, clerk
54 John Knox, merchant

56 Wm Bowman, merchant
58 James Walker, agent

Caroline-st intersects

78 Hy Turnbull, sexton
80 D D Campbell, clerk P O
82 J B P Stacy, mattrasmaker
90 John Gilmore jr, pianomkr
94 Mrs J S Smith
96 Vacant
98 Jos King

Hess-st intersects

100 Vacant
104 Arthur Fell, machinist
106 James Thompson, shoemkr

Queen-st intersects

116 Wm E Cook, plumber
118 Wm Scott, laborer
124 John Male, laborer
126 Wm Cooke, laborer
128 John E Wing, machinist

Ray-st intersects

134 Jos Tomkins, shoemaker
136 James Glass, shoemaker
138 Vacant
140 Richard Herod, bricklayer
142 Thos Winfield, grocer
146 John D Virgint, tanner
150 John Mostyn, tinsmith

Pearl st-intersects

160 Fred Beckman, laborer
162 Ed J Ram, carpenter
164 A G Ram, printer
166 Vacant

Locke-st intersects

176 Geo Barker, driver
178 Mrs Mary Milligan
180 Rudolph Thatcher, laborer
184 James Vint, carpenter
186 Vacant
190 Wm Randall, laborer
192 Mrs Margaret Relph
194 — Boden, bricklayer

Poulette-st intersects

Arthur McFarlane, laborer

Ed Wild, laborer

Hunter-st w, south side

1 Wm A Howell, druggist
5 J J Tulk, moulder
7 Thos W Bryant, upholsterer
9 John Shields, laborer
11 Michael Donovan, hackman
15 R Chisnell, moulder
17 Geo Ward, machinist
19 Hart Emery Wheel Co
21 Mrs P McHenry
25 Wm C Stewart, founder

Macnab-st intersects

Presbyterian Church

Charles-st intersects

31 R R Waddell

Park-st intersects

Central School

Bay-st intersects

49 Rev R G Sutherland
51 Mrs R Marlatt
53 David Graham, hatter
55 M Newman, traveler
59 Daniel LeMessurier, painter
61 A Maclean, merchant
63 J J Mason, accountant
65 Mrs Jessie Kennedy
67 Alex Lockie, pressman

Caroline-st intersects

69 James Dodman, agent
71 Mrs Frank Harrison
73 T Scott, clerk
75 — Russell, ins agent
77 Thos Hardiman, confectioner
79 John Russell, laborer
81 Mrs J Duggan, laundress
83 Mrs Thos Kelly
85 Thos Milligan, packer
87 James Cutt, cutter
89 B Dickson, laborer
91 Vacant
95 Geo Feasel, gardener

Hess-st intersects

99 W J Nex, laborer
103 Robert Paton, laborer
105 Thos Stephens, machinist
107 John Plank, grocer

Queen-st intersects

Congr'l Sabbath School
121 Jacob Johnston, tailor
123 John Lavelle, laborer
125 Geo Bond, grocer
127 Mrs S A Conklin

Ray-st intersects

137 Thos Young, porter
139 Duncan McDonald, mason
141 Wm Male, laborer
143 Thos Thomson, shoemaker
145 A C Best, salesman
147 Wm A Renwick, porter
151 Wm McFedries, salesman

Pearl-st intersects

155 Wm Lanceley, engineer
157 Chas Lovejoy, plasterer
159 James Pinkett, laborer
166 John Cruickshanks, mason
169 Francis Kittyle, sailor
171 Thos Exley, printer

Locke-st intersects

175 James T Reynolds, painter
Geo Fitzgerald, lamplighter

Poulette-st intersects

John Ripley, carpenter
Vacant

Inchbury-st n, east side, from 296 York to St Mary

6 Robt Binnington, laborer
8 J Lamplough, watchman
14 Thos Adam, carpenter
22 Wm Taft, packer
24 Joseph Neville, machinist
24½ John Barlow, helper
26 Michael Gleason, boilermakr
28 Wm Sandercock, boilermkr
30 A D McDougall, brakeman

STREET DIRECTORY. 301

32 T Daley, laborer
48 Jacob Williams, laborer
50 Thos Blackburn, engineer
52 Ed Buscombe, bricklayer

St Mary's Lane-st intersects

Inchbury-st n, west side

5 Thos J Hughes, fitter
7 John McKenzie, carpenter
9 David Randall, nailer
11 Wm Hawkins, machinist
13 Thos Hall, fitter
15 Wm Bankes, artist

Kinnel-st intersects

25 C Mitchell, broommaker
27 Chas Morris, machinist
29 John Patterson, cutter
31 Richard Buscombe, bricklay'r
33 Thos Stokes, wood dealer
35 Wm Johnson, painter
37 Geo Gallagher, boilermaker
39 Mrs Jane Hilder
41 James Honeyford, fitter
43 Chas Athawes, bookkeeper
51 Michael Reardon, driver

St Mary's Lane intersects

Inchbury-st s, east side, from 305 York to Florence

8 Vacant
10 James McMurray, agent
14 John Ross, blacksmith
16 Thos G Gaston, wireweaver
18 Wm Broughtan, fireman
20 James Robinson, brickmak'r
22 Geo Scragg, moulder

Florence-st intersects

Inchbury-st south, west side

3 Wm J Harris, carter
5 John Birkle, carpenter
7 John Scragg, moulder
9 Timothy Winter, fireman
21 Walter Nisbet, carpenter
23 Mrs Joshua Audette
25 Mrs Thos Oliver

Jackson-st e, north side from James s to Wellington

7 Hy Kronsbein, tailor
9 Imperial Mineral Waterwrks
11 Silver Creek Brewery

Hughson-st intersects

Court House

John and Bowen-sts intersect

37 Michael Murphy, hotel

Catharine-st intersects.

43 Miss Annie Harvey
45 Mrs Margaret Rudell
47 Hy Limebald, tailor
55-57 Robt Cruickshank & Co, planing mills
59 James Findlay, laborer
r 61 Mrs Ann O'Neil
r " Jeremiah Kenny
r " Geo Davidson, laborer
r " Mrs Jane Wilcox
r " Mrs M Burns
r " Stephen Donohoe, laborer
Mrs Frederick Wilcox
61 John T Trafford, laborer
63 Mrs Mary Ann Niblock
65 Mrs Gabriel Ottobin
69 James Nichol, teamster
71 F Jarvis
73 Vacant
75 John West, baker
r 75 Jeremiah Leegrice, blacksm'h
79 Mrs Peter Spence
81 Hamilton Dairy Co
83 Thos Stone, baker

Walnut st intersects

91 Walter Chapman, teamster
93 Ed Sevier, letter carrier
95 G H Thomas, messenger
97 Alex Penny
99 Isaac Levi, tailor
101 John Webb, carpenter
105 Mrs Samuel Graham
105½ Moses Cross, carter

Cherry-st intersects

107 Robt Gimblett, shoemaker

111 Thos Beatty, laborer
117 Frank Osler, filecutter
119 Patrick Meegan, tanner
125 Humphrey & Newberry, tanners

Spring-st intersects

133 A McIsaac, teamster
135 James McCreath, blacksm'h

Wellington-st intersects

Jackson-st e, south side

2 Mrs Alex Strachan
4 Geo Slater, salesman
12 John McGinnis, stovemtr

Hughson-st intersects

14 Geo Moore, laborer
16 R J Howard, horse shoer
18 Bell Telephone Co's storehouse
20 Geo Bridgewood, carriagemaker
24 Jas Wall, blacksmith
26 M H TenEyke, V S

John-st intersects

32 Mrs Theo, Stafford
34 Frank McGuire, plumber
36 Benjamin Treiter, cigarmkr
38 Henry Griffin
40 Mrs Mary J Warner
42 Mrs Sarah Hart

Catharine-st intersects

44 Wm Shields, laborer
46 Joseph Taylor, bartender
48 Lawrence Griffin
50 James Cleary, laborer
52 Colin Campbell, tailor
54 John Burns, assessor
56 Chas H Thompson, engineer
58-60 Cruikshank's lumber yard
68 Mrs James Ruach
70 Edward Morton, painter
72 Geo Dennis, teamster
78 Christopher Lee, clerk
80 Mrs John Oliver
82 John Spiers, teamster
84 James Robinson, moulder

86 Peter McKay, porter

Walnut-st intersects

88 Mrs Daniel Barry
90 Joseph Royall, laborer
92 Wm Hover, tailor
92½ Mrs James Walker
94 Mrs Jane Wells
96 Rev James Black
98 James Walsh, screwmaker
100 Chas J Smith, laborer
102 John Cron, laborer
104 John Brick, inspector
106 Thos H Wakeham, tinsmith
108 Richard Crozier, laborer
108½ Mrs Thos McSherry
110-112 Mrs John Butterfield grocer

Cherry-st intersects

116 John Plant, wood dealer
118 Thos Barret, parper hanger
120 Thos Bolton, porter
122 John O'Neil, printer
124 Miss Eliza Barr
126 John McCann, moulder
128 Thos Wm Gilpin, lumber

Spring-st intersects

134 J Langton, painter
136 James Wall, blacksmith
140 Mrs Geo Armitage

Wellington-st intersects

Jackson-st west, north side, from James s to Garth

St. Paul's Church
4 Palace Roller Rink
10 Samuel McKay, livery
 Wood yard

Macnab-st intersects

Central Presbyterian Church
20 Rev Samuel Lyle

Charles & Park-sts intersect

28 Charles Limin, butcher
30 R Hills, sec Canada Life
30½ Mrs David Clark

32 W E Brown, bookkeeper
34 Robt Sterling, merchant
36 Thos McIlwraith, merchant
38 Jas Turpin, com trav
40 Mrs Margaret Harris
42 John T Atkinson, traveler
44 Mrs Joseph C Bowman
46 Mrs James F McClure

Bay-st intersects

50 John Connors, dairyman
52 Mrs David McCulloch
54 Michael Klager, bricklayer
56 Wm Kennedy, clerk
58 S H Lambe, accountant
60 H F Witherby, jeweler
62 T D Walker, inspector
64 N H Davis
66 Joseph T Wallace, clerk
68 Miles A Pennington, ins agt
70 John McCullough, builder
74 John Thom
74 Lestock W Cockburn M D

Caroline-st intersects

76 Murray A Kerr
80 Henry A Eager, clerk P O

Hess-st intersects

88 W D Booker, sec Vic Mut Ins Co
90 Richard Coleman, traveler
92 Thos Marsden, merchant

Queen-st intersects

100 C J Dixon, clerk
102 Wm Bremner, traveler
104 John D Clarke, editor *Times*
106 Chas Mills
108 R Campbell, potter
112 J E Hampson, traveler
114 Vacant
116 Vacant
12. Colin C Campbell, bookkeepr
122 Wm Marsden, manf

Ray-st intersects

124 Mrs C M Schierstein
126 Henry H Craft, butcher
128 Fred Hebner, laborer

130 Ed Bridges, laborer
132 John Holmes, painter
134 H Hopper, cabinetmaker
136 Joseph Embling, laborer

Pearl-st intersects

138 David New, potter
140 Vacant
142 Lew Lepslietz, rag dealer
144 Wm R Barker, fireman
146 Wm Knapman, laborer
r " James Maria, whipmaker
148 Joseph Long, laborer
    Vacant
150 Noah Pollington, laborer

Locke-st intersects

156 Wm Ridler, shoemaker
160 Miss Maggie Burke
162 Mrs Michael Keagan
164 Miss R Cresswell

Poulette-st intersects

170 Daniel Sullivan, laborer
172 Mrs Deborah Douse
176 Ed Downing, carpenter
178 James Garner, dealer
184 Thos Ellis, laborer
186 John Donald, laborer
    Campbell Sewer Pipe Co

Garth-st intersects

Jackson-st w, south side

3 John Billings
5 Chas Magill

Macnab-st intersects

1 B McQuesten, barrister

Charles-st intersects

German Roman Catholic Church

21 James S Pearson, manfr
23 Vacant
25 Samuel Slater, banker

Park-st intersects

27 Mrs Geo Pierce
29 Mrs Maltyward Simpson

31 Mrs E Dewar
33 Lyman Moore
35 John J Scott, barrister
37 Mrs Hugh McInnes
39 Mrs Christina Aiken
41 F F Dalley, manf
43 John Hoodless, manf
45 Wm Young, manf
49 Samuel Woodley, shoemaker

Bay-st intersects

51 Robt T Steele, merchant
51 David Steele, barrister
53 Mrs Daniel Campbell
55 John Campbell, merchant
57 Miles Overend, deputy registrar
65 W E Sanford, merchant

Caroline-st intersects

75 Mrs T B Fuller
77 Geo H Bull, clerk P O
79 Robt Armor, C E
81 Angus Sutherland
83 Richard Brierley, druggist
85 Vacant
87 Edmund Hudson, clerk

Hess-st intersects

87½ Miss Mary Ann Briggs
87½ H H Willard, manfr
89 G S Counsell, Co clerk
90 Edwin Van Allen, bookkpr
95 J R Thompson, wood carver

Queen-st intersects

109 M G R Locke
111 P L Scriven, engraver
113 Mrs Alex F Kemp
115 August Huebner

Ray-st intersects

121 Thos Connors, carpenter
129 Vacant
131 Vacant
139 Alfred Defour, wireworker
141 Wm Ford, salesman

Pearl-st intersects

145 James W Webb, shoemaker
147 Alfred Canhem, laborer

147½ Geo Leavers, painter
149 Vacant
151 Ed Neal, brickmaker

Locke-st intersects

165 James Harman, laborer
167 Wm King, fireman

James-st n, east side, from King to the Bay

2 Geo M Barton, barrister
2 T LeP Filgiano, dentist
4 E L Schwartz, tobacconist
6 G G Hacker, hatter
6½ The Hub Saloon
8 Mrs M C A Hinman, milliner
10 Oak Hall, clothing
12 McIlwraith & McMaster, dry goods and millinery
14 S Thorne & Co, dry goods
14½ Donald Smith, merch tailor
16 Pratt & Watkins, dry goods
18 A S Vail & Co, clothiers
20 J K Applegarth, dry goods
22 S Woodley, boots and shoes
24 C P Edwards, boots and shoes
26 W P Giles & Co, clothing

King William-st intersects

28 Irving Crossley, dry goods
30 John W Gerrie, druggist
32 Sewell Bros, grocers
34 J G Currell, barrister
   Anderson & Bates, occulist and aurists
36 E F Robinson, druggist
38 Ferres & Co, hardware
40 John McCoy, dry goods
42 Lazier & Monck, barristers
42 R D Kennedy, surveyor
42 Jos Lister
42 Misses Graham, hair jewelry
44 Wm Bell & Co, musical instruments
46 Thos Marsden & Son, gilders
48 Temperance Dining Rooms
48 Louis Schwarz, tobacconist
50 A Zimmerman, tailor
52 A Hood, bookseller

54 Wm Battram, fruiterer
56 Mrs E Hubbard, millinery
58-60 J E Lister & Co, clothiers hatters and gents' furnish's

Rebecca-st intersects

62 Vacant
65 St Charles Restaurant
66 Thos Clappison, stationer
68 Vacant
70 Old Post Office
72-74 Carl Blaase, hotel
76 J R Hesse & Co, auctioneers
78 Thos Burrows, auctioneer
80 A & S Nordheimer, pianos
82 Vacant
84 David McLellan, ins agent
86 Masonic Hall
88 J J Mason, grand sec grand lodge, A F & A M
88 W J O'Brien, grocer
90 Vacant

Gore-st intersects.

92 Gardner & Thomson, gents' furnishers
Grand Opera House
J M Chapman, hotel
98 Wm Carroll, barber
96 Mrs Hannah Bradfield, confr
96 Mrs M Jost, hair works
96 J C Pronguey, coachmaker
98 Andrew Jeffrey, auctioneer
100 Wm Dryden
100 Fitch Bros, fish dealers
102 Mark Hill, baker
102½ John H Hall, confectioner
104 Jos Davis, butcher
106 Harry Ing, watchmaker
106 A Fleck, painter
108 W J F Gordon, coal and lime
108 Foresters' Hall
110 Mrs Isabella Dodds, fancy goods
Cumming Bros, grocers
112 Samuel Shannon, restaurant
110 Wm Farmer, plumber
112 Mrs Richard Brockelsbey confectioner
114 Martin Manf Co

116 Hord & Co, druggists
118 A Bismarck, tobacconist
120 Isaac Stevens, fancy goods
122 Mrs Esther Edwards, millin'y
124 James Dwyer, undertaker
126 Geo Ellis, grocer

Cannon-st intersects

Knox Church
122 G M Shaw, M D
122½ James Lafferty, M D
124 Dr John A Mullin
126 Stephen Willcock, watchmkr
128 Mrs M Hussell, fancy goods
130-132 Aarn Sanders, barber
134 Anthone Moran, hotel
136 J Colvin, grocer
138 Wm McKeever, baker
146 Drill Shed

Robert-st intersects

152 Daniel O'Neil, tobacconist
152 Miss Hannah Lawson
156 Geo Richardson, watchmak'r
158 J McCartney, plasterer
160 Ed Pope, cabinetmaker
162 D H Gould & Son, boots
164 Thos Adams, mariner
164 Mrs Sophia Hillman
166 T B Paine, bookkeeper
Christ Church Cathedral
Jesse Linger, sexton
168 Mrs M Morrow, confection'r
170 Mrs Ann Dallyn
172 Geo Midgley jr, bookseller
172½ Geo Midgley, shoemaker
174-6 John Field, crockery
178 Mrs Phoebe Morris, fancy goods
180 Mrs C Nelligan, fancy goods
182 L Hemmings, cabinetmaker
184 Hy Collingwood, tripe dress'r
186 J Gant, hairdresser
188 H C Chappel, tinsmith
190 Mrs Jas Meakins, dry goods
192 John Hunter & Son, grocers

Barton-st intersects

194 Mrs O'Neil, grocer
196 Chas Stein, betcher

198 John Kelly, hotel
200 John Huxtable, shoemaker
202 John M Teeter
204 A P Williamson, stationer
206 Wm Magee jr, flour dealer
208-10 A Simon, confectioner
212 Thos Clarke, butcher
214 Jos Marck, barbar
216 Mrs Sarah Gilmore
218 Jeremiah McCoy, carpenter
220 James E Doyle, grocer
222 Jos Cook, butcher
224 Jos Morin, boots and shoes
226 Wm McLaren, dry goods
228 M J Dake, hotelkeeper

Murray-st intersects

230 A Vincent & Co, druggists
232 G & B Nelligan, gents' furnishings
228 Jos Allis, laborer
230 Wm Halcrow, mason
232 L A Edick, spinner
234 Maurice Carroll, hairdresser
234½ Stephen Pollitt, plumber
236 Miss Welsh, dressmaker
240 Fred Larkin, weaver
244 P J Kirby, grocer

Stuart-st intersects

248 M D Nelligan, wagonmaker G T R bridge
250 Mrs Oliver Gagnier

Strachan-st intersects

252 Thos Dickinson
254 Jeremiah Shea, machinist
256 Henry Kirkpatrick
258 Thos Armstrong, mariner
260 Alfred Nash, expressman
262 Adam Clark, fitter
264 Mrs Grace Clarkson
266 Mrs Alex Miller
268 John W Watson, checker
270 John Hafner, glassblower
272 James Young, carriagemaker
274 Mrs Catharine Moran
274½ John Holt, engineer
274 Harrison Bros, druggists

Simcoe-st intersects

276 Wm Buckingham, butcher
278 Vacant
280 John Day, shoemaker
282 J Roland, basketmaker
284 Vacant
286 Theo Le P Filgiano, dentist
288 S Malcolmson, mariner
288½ Dominick Wynn, cotton dyer
290 Mrs Emily Hamburg
292 Philip Wennesheimer
296 Richard Williamson, ice dealer

Ferrie-st intersects

298 A E Bessey, butter dealer
300 Oliver Beatty, hotel
304 John Jackson, carpenter
306 Chas Guttridge
308 Vacant
312 Wm B Williamson, icedealer
314 Richard Williamson, tinsmith

Picton-st intersects

Hamilton Glass Works

Macauley-st intersects

326 Henry Free, engineer
328 Thos Davidson, laborer
330 John Irvine, fireman
342 Wm Burnette, glassblower
344 Isaac Blowes, laborer
346 Neil Kirkpatrick, engineer
348 John Harold, glassblower
348½ Mrs Eliza Kinsler
350 Jos P Harvey, hotel

Wood-st intersects

356 James Hyde, loomfixer
358 Wm McGahey, loomfixer
364 Mrs James Blowes
366 Daniel Mahoney, teamster
368 Miss Rosanna Routh
370 John Gorman, laborer

Burlington-st intersects

376 Hugh Guy
378 John Campbell, packer

382 Mrs Geo Mullin
390 Morris Reardon, hotel

Guise-st intersects

394 James Johnston, laborer
Mackay's wharf

James-st n, west side

1 A Hamilton & Co, druggists
3 David Graham, hatter
5 Thos Lees, watchmaker
7 Joseph Mills & Son, hatters
9 W A Edwards, architect
9 Wm White, engraver
9 Smith & Farmer, barristers
11 C E Morgan, broker
13 Thos Mason, hatter
15 Mrs T F Walker, saloon
17 Robt Duncan & Co, books, etc

Market Square

City Hall
21 Andrew Lay, saloon
23 Samuel Easter, saloon
25 John Morris, oyster parlors
27 A C Quimby & Co, tobacconists
29 Kellogg & McKenzie, hotel
31 Jas Smallwood, tobacconist
33 *Globe* (Toronto) Agency
Alexandra Arcade
Canada Business College
Alexandra Hall
Caledondia Hall
33 Wm J Grant, ticket agent
35 Chas Dallyn, hairdresser
35-41 St Nicholas Hotel
43 John Smith, saloon
45 Frank England, barber
47 P Grossman, music dealer
47½ Grossman Hall
49 Kennedy & Co, tailors
51 Alex McPherson, printer
51 Pennington Printing Co
53 Alhambra Saloon

Merrick-st commences

55 Vacant

57 G McKeand, ins agent
57 R F Keays, real estate agent
57 Ontario Mutual Life Asso'n
57 O S Hillman, accountant
59-61-63 Royal Hotel
65 Vacant
67 Walter Urry, barber
69 John Harvey & Co, wool brokers
69 Strathroy Knitting Co
71 James Eyers & Sons, dyers
73 Geo A McCully, shoemaker
75 J H Aussem, confectioner
77 S J Sheffield, pawnbroker
79 John Holman, gunsmith
81 Thos Lawrence, druggist
83 James Atkins, barber
85 Jacob Lewis, broker
87 Chinese Laundry
89 Thos Appleton, pawnbroker
91-93 Ed Murphy, sign painter
95 T Richter, saloon

Vine-st commences

97 Federal Life Association
Elford G Payne, ins agent
Royal Templars' of Temperance office
99 John Gorvin, shoemaker
99 F F Dalley & Co, patent medicines
99½ James Somerville, signptr
101 John McCann, shoemaker
103 R W Yaldon, hotel
107 Frank Rouse, fruiterer
109 Queen's Laundry
111 Thos Reid, machinist
113 Geo R epp, tailor
115 Miss G Rodgers, fancy goods
117 Richard Henry, butcher
119 A Almas, hair dresser
Wm Noble, hotel

Cannon-st intersects

119 Hy Harding, plumber
121 John Morrow, policeman
123 Mrs Chas McLeod, dyer
125 Mrs Andrew McPherson
127 Morris G Cornish, flour & feed
129 John E Taylor, confectioner

131 Mrs S Hartley, knitter
131 John M Middleton, moulder
133 C Morris, tailor
133 James Hannah, contractor
133½ James Morris, tailor
135 D J Kelly, wood dealer
137 Mrs Marshall

Mulberry-st commences

139 Robt Jackson, plasterer
141 James Greer, shoemaker
143 M C Dickson
143 James Smith, moulder
145 Turkish Baths
147 Aaron Sayman, cutler
151 Miss Æ Edson
153 Dr A Woolverton, coroner
155 Geo Membery, renovator
157 Mrs Barbara Kramer, saloon
159 J S Lightfoot, shoemaker
159 W D Griner, glassblower
163 Miss M B Fiset, milliner
165 R J Dunstan, com trav
167 Jos W Loemas
169 W A Freeman, coal & wood
173-5 H D Baker, whip manf
175 John A Chadwick, metal spinner
173 A M Forster & Co, brass founders

Colborne-st commences

177-183 Gurneys & Ware, scale manf
185 Mrs Johnston
187 John Nixon, laborer
189 Thos Walsh, machinist
191 Mrs Mary Smith

Barton-st intersects

193 Vacant
203 Robt Deary, mechanic
205 Andrew Harron, hackman
207 Wm Jewell, laborer
211 Buckley Whitehead, hotel

Murray-st intersects

213 James Armstrong
215 Frank Sturdy, steward
217 Robt Dawson, baker

219 John Tremiet, shoemaker
221 Fred Cookman, grocer
223 Mrs Martha Smith, grocer
225 John Carroll, stovemounter
227 Dunn Bros, butchers
229-331 Francis Salavie
235 James Gibbons, laborer
239 John McHendrie, hotel

Stuart-st intersects

243 Police Station No 2
245 B J Connolly, brakeman
247 Alfred Richmond, grocer

Strachan-st intersects

249 Daniel Croyne, carter
253 James Burkholder, laborer
255 Patrick Walsh
259 Peter Commerford
261 James Hutton, pedler
263 John Griffin, laborer
265 Mrs Edward McIntosh
267-9 Hugh Monro, grocer

Simcoe-st intersects

Ontario Cotton Mills

Ferrie-st intersects

281 James Rutherford, barber
283 Thos Bard, glassblower
289 Mrs Ellen Curtin
293 John Walls, cotton weaver
297 D P Le Valle, dry goods
305 E Cherrier, butcher

Picton-st intersects

307-9 R Quinn, hotel
311 Wm Cole, hair dresser
313 Fred Wilbee, laborer
315 C Jobbon, broker
317 Mrs M Barr
319 Thos Smith, grocer
321 James McEntee, laborer
323 Mrs Bridget Kelly
325 Wm Cook, weaver
327 Thos Kenney, glassblower
331 Mrs Amelia Carron

Macaulay-st intersects

345 Thos Nixon, policeman

STREET DIRECTORY.

347 Mrs John Arthur
Wood st intersects
351 John Knox, policeman
355 Robt Simpson, laborer
357 Holden Barker, laborer
359 John Walwork
363 Vacant
369 Thos Richmond, grocer
Burlington-st intersects
379 Mrs Æ D Mackay
381 R O Mackay, warfinger
Mackay's wharf

James-st s, east side from King to Mountain

Canada Life Chambers
1 Canada Life Assurance Co
  Osler, Teezel & Harrison, barristers
  Kilvert & Biggar, barristers
  Bruce, Burton & Culham, barristers
3 Landed Banking & Loan Co
5 Brown, Balfour & Co, wholesale grocers
7 G F Glassco & Co, hatters

Wentworth Chambers
  Victoria Mutual Fire Ins Co
  W F Findlay, ins agent
  Martin, Kittson & Martin, barristers
  James Balfour, architect
  Bell & Thomson, barristers
  Geo H Mills, barrister
  Wm Stewart, architect

Main-st intersects

Victoria Chambers
  McQuesten & Chisholm, barristers
  W A H Duff, barrister
  W C Livingston, barrister
  R A Pringle, barrister
  John W Jones, barrister
33 W R Macdonald, barrister
33 G S Papps, barrister
37 Edwin B O'Reilly, M D
39 Dr Hillyer

Jackson-st intersects

41 Ed McGrath, blacksmith
52 Hy Harrison, butcher
53 Ed Kidner, printer
Hunter-st intersects
61-73 Vacant
75 John Denew, engineer
77 Wm Worrall, cabinetmaker
79 Vacant
r 79 Pennington & Baker, furniture manfs
81 Easter & Purrott, painters
81 Frank Miller, carpenter
81 Miller & Pitcher, manfs
85-87 Hamilton Vinegar Works
89 Herman Levy, merchant
91 Vacant
93 John S Hendrie, contractor
95 Mrs Agnes Buchanan
Augusta-st commences
97 W J Ballentine, grocer
99 Thos Snider, baker
99½ James Thomas, shoemaker
101 J M Rousseaux, grocer
103 Mrs S E Nimmo
105 Mrs E Hamilton
107 Rev S J Hunter, Methodist
Young-st intersects
Vacant lots
Maria-st intersects.
133 Mrs L H Brooks
137 Æmelius Irving, Q C
Hannah-st intersects.
139 Wm Griffith, merchant
141 John Riddle, broker
143 Mrs Thos G Chesnut
147 John Armour
149 P D Crerar, barrister
151 A T Wood, merchant
153 Hy McLaren
155 Mrs McLaren, Oak Bank
157 A G Ramsay, Canada Life
159 T D Beddoe, manf
161 Mrs S B Freeman
161 K J Dunstan, Bell Tel Co
Richard Russell, jeweler

James-st s, west side
2 Molsons' Bank
2½ Hamilton Business College
" Martin Malone, barrister
" David Blackley, accountant
" P L Scriven, wood engraver
" John McMeekin, ins agent
" A Davidson, accountant
" License Commissioners' Office
" Carscallen & Cahill, barristers
" John Proctor & Co, hardware
" W H Zwick, real estate
" Robt Clohecy, architect
" Furlong & Beasley, barristers
4 James Osborne & Son, grocers
6 J B Fairgrieve, coal merchant
" Seneca Jones, ins agent
" N H Davis, issuer Marriage licenses
6½ Sherman E Townsend, accountant
" Rutherford & Lester, ins agents
8 C P R Telegraph Co
10 Walker, Scott & Lees, barristers
12 H T Bunbury, clerk 1st Div court
12 D R Dewey & Co, coal dealers
12 R W Suter, ins agent
14 C M Counsell, banker
16 J T Routh, ins agent
" Wm Herman, com agent
" *Mail* Newspaper office
" MacKelcan, Gibson & Gausby barristers
18 Great Northwestern Tel Co
" American Express Co
" *Spectator* Printing Co
" Howell Lithographic Co
" Staunton & O'Heir, barristers
" C F Abraham, grain broker
20 Haslett & Washington, barristers

Commercial Chambers { Fuller, Nesbitt & Bicknell barristers
Oaklands Jersey Dairy
D G Greer, real estate agt
22 Ont Sewing Machine Co
22 F M Willson, accountant
26-8 W C Baker, fruiterer
30 Alex Seymour, dairyman
32 Wm Scott, shoemaker
34 W S Hicks, carver
36 Adam Clark, plumber

Main-st intersects

Bank of Montreal
Wm Angus, sexton
St Paul's Church

Jackson-st intersects

Baptist Church
50 Mrs Dougall McCallum
52 Dr John W Rosebrugh

Hunter-st intersects

Wm A Howell, druggist
60 Mrs E H Davidson
62 Geo Cushen, butcher
66 J M Webber
68 Mrs E Malloch
70 Dr A E Malloch
72 F S Malloch
74 Mrs Geo Lees
78 Dr Elias Vernon
80 Mrs Mary Howard

Bold-st intersects

82 John A Orr, merchant
84 J E P Aldous, B A
86 S W Cornell, merchant
88 James Noyes
90 James Ferres, merchant
92 Geo Taylor, clerk
94 Horace Long, merchant
96 Mrs Andrew Stuart
98 Mrs Geo Marshall
100 Richard Mackay
102 Sherman E Townsend, accountant

Duke-st commences

Vacant

STREET DIRECTORY.

Robinson-st commences

134 Hubert Martin, merchant
136 Thos Lawry, merchant

Hannah-st intersects

140 C Stiff, supt GTR
144 Wm J Waugh, merchant

Herkimer-st intersects & Markland commences

    Edward Martin, Q C, barrister

Concession-st intersects

    John Stuart, merchant

John-st north, east side, from 70 King east to the Bay

2 Geo James, dry goods
4 Robt Parker & Co, dye wks
6 Vacant
8 Larkin Hall
8 C R Smith, grain dealer
8 Willson & Gates, stock brok's
8 Ed Adamson, grain inspector
10 Ed Barker, printer
12 Vacant
14 W H Kerner, saloon
16 H Longhurst & Co, stained glass
18 Fairley, Stewart & Co, plumbers
20 Vacant
22 Vacant
24 Vacant
24 Odd Fellows' Hall
26 Orr & Laird, perfumes, etc
28 Cuttris Engraving Co
28 John F Jagoe, customs brokr
30 Robt Raw Co, printers

King Wm-st intersects

32 James Reed, hotelkeeper
34 Mrs Wm Pease, dealer
36-42 E & C Gurney, founders

Rebecca-st intersects

44 Murton & Reid, coal dealers

46 James Coleman, laborer
48 John Bromley, laborer
50 Mrs Hy Magill
52 Mrs O Springer
54 G H Bisby, wood dealer
56 Geo Leith
58 B E Charlton

Gore-st intersects

62 Thos Greenaway, moulder
64 Thos Young, saloonkeeper
66 John Beckerson, teamster
68 J E Halloran, livery
76 Mrs James Musgrove
78 W P Campbell, printer
80 B M E Church
82 Rev J A Johnson
84 Mrs Geo Allan
88 Hugo Oder
90 Wm Tallman
96 Vacant
98 W H Tallman, wood dealer
100 Wm Bellknap, tinsmith

Cannon-st intersects

1.2 Mrs Nora Westbrook
106 Wm Miller, cigarmaker
108-114 Waterworks Yard
116 Fred Brown, laborer
122 Chas Stewart, founder
124 Chas J Silver, traveler
126 Peter Templeman
128 John Caffery, moulder
128½ Geo Hogarth, carpenter
130 Mrs M McCardle

Robert-st intersects

132 J H Myrick, picture framer
136 John Roderick, tailor
138 Mrs Wm O Eastman
r " J T Middleton, marble
140 Robt Acland, patternmaker
140½ Alex McPherson, printer
142 John McMullan
144 Wm Verral, butcher
146 Alfred H Myles, coal mercht
148 John Seitz, telegraphist
148½ Hy Robinson, bricklayer
150 Gage & Jones, wood dealers
152 J O Downing, whitewasher

154 Vacant
154½ Ed Hawkes, collector
156 James Houlden, carpenter
158 Thos P Bates, clerk
160 J Warner, carpenter

Barton-st intersects

164 M A Broderick, grocer
166 Wm Allberry, shoemaker
r " Henry Tucker, laborer
168 Wm O'Brien, grocer
174 Mrs J Johnson
174 Philip Long
176 Lawrence Kehoe, hackman
178 Vacant
180 Wm Rigg, car inspector
182 Miss Murton, private school
182 Wm Murton, clerk
184 Nelson Humphrey, manf
186 Alex Maver, asst supt G T R
188 Martin Malone, barrister
190 Mrs Catharine Jones
192 R W Witherspoon, barristsr
194 Miss Armstrong
196 W L Waterman, clerk

Murray-st intersects

202 Mrs James Brennan
208 Hugh Kelly, laborer
r " — Boyle, blacksmith

Stuart-st intersects

210 H M Dwyer, traveler
214 James Lynch, switchman G T R bridge
216 Wm Yates, riveter
220 J F McBride, grocer

Strachan-st intersects

224 John McCracken, tailor
226 Patrick Gray, laborer
228 Mrs Jane Cranston

Simcoe-st intersects

Simcoe St Methodist Church
260 St Lawrence Catholic School

Ferrie-st intersects

280 Joseph Gormley, glassblower
282 Walter Gordon, moulder

284 Mrs Margaret Sullivan
286 Wm Grant, reporter
290 Mrs Mary Geddes

Picton-st intersects

292 John Hotrum, carpenter
294 Edmund Neff, stovepolisher
296 Henry Shaw, laborer
300 Wm Dermody, porter
304 Hiram Walsh, constable
306 St Luke's Church

Macauley-st intersects

306 John Sheehan, teamster
308 Francis Smyth, glassblower
308½ Jos Collins, glassblower
310 Samuel Smith, glassblower
312 Geo Bolton, laborer
314 John Malloy, glassblower
314½ John McNichol, laborer
316 Luke McNamara, laborer
320 Chas McNichol, glassblower

Wood-st intersects

324 John Campbell, boilermaker
334 John Kelly, laborer
336 Vacant
    Daniel Flynn, laborer

Burlington-st intersects

350-2 Geo Calback, hotel
354 Vacant
356 Geo Dick, laborer
358 — Begley, laborer
r " Mrs Margaret Connors
r " Mrs John Brown
360 John Gompf, brewer
    Corporation weighing house

Brock-st intersects

368 Patrick Harley, laborer
    House of Refuge

Guise-st intersects

Murton & Reid's wharf
Myles' wharf

John-st north, west side

3 W Pratt, barber
5-7 Jimmie's Restaurant

STREET DIRECTORY.

9 Fraser Johnson, & Co, saddlery
11 Mrs P T Evan's restaurant
13 H A Martin, printer
15 J Wallace & Son, tinsmiths
17 Young & Bro, plumbers
19 Robt Lavelle, stoves, tins
21 Andrew Dillon, hotel

King William-st intersects

23 Vacant
27 Vacant
29 B McCauley, cigar manfr
29 Wm Dodson, painter
31 Eppstein & Zidersky, rags
37 E & C Gurney's pattern shop
39 Chas Powell, machinist
41 Sylvester Jones, farmer
43 Abraham Belifoy, bricklayer

Rebecca-st intersects

Wesley Church
45 Ernest Faustman, cooper
47 Andrew Mackie, moulder
49 Geo Forman, moulder
51 James Hall, moulder
55 Vacant
57 Mrs Geo Trumbull
59 Mrs Julia Higby
Gore Street Meth Church

Gore-st intersects

65 John Walker, blacksmith
67 Miss Sarah Easterby
69 J Harris whitewasher
71 Thos McDonald, teamster
73 James Wagner, tailor
75 Thos Jones, cutter
77 James Wilson, dyer
79 John Monteith, moulder
81 Hy Kerley, weaver
79 Mrs Jas Pulkingham
79½ O Biglow, carpenter
81 John Williams, stovefitter
83 Neil McLaughlin, miller
85 Mrs James Harris
87 John McManus, com trav
89 Vacant
91 Thos Hill, cabinetmaker
93 Samuel Harris, teamster

95 Geo Heilig, builder
97 Mark Keane, laborer
98 Mrs H McStravick
101 James Munn, laborer
103 Mrs Marr, nurse
103 Mrs Wm Smith, grocer

Cannon-st intersects

Malleable Iron Works
121 Bishop of Niagara
127 Thos G Peat

Robert-st intersects

126 Philip Morris & Sons, grocers
131 Thos Ireland, traveler
133 Mrs Michael Dolan
135 Wm Carlyon, painter
137 Wm Bradfield, laborer
139 John Bird, machinist
141 Dennis Buckley, laborer
143 Wm Fraser, porter
145 Thos K Foster
147 C A Sandburg, brassfinisher
149 Wm Strong, ins agent
151 Mrs Geo Otto
153 Stiles Stevens, moulder
155 Vacant
157 Mrs John Pringle
159 James O'Brien, manager
161 S E Whitehead, watchmkr
163 Byron Smith, Can Business College
165 Chas Wilson, sr
167 John Hall, patternmaker
169 Peter Lynch, mason
163a Martin Guth, cabinetmaker
165a John Zoeller, tailor

Barton-st intersects

167a James Main, grocer
169a Nicholas Cook, moulder
169½ Angus McKay, machinist
169b Wm Durden, engineer
173a Jos Zingsheim, manf
175 Arthur Cross tea dealer
177 Colin Munro, traveler
179 Donald Crerar, tailor
181 Ed Armstrong
183 Ed Marks, moulder

Murray-st intersects

195 James Lister
197 Geo Moore, clerk
199 Chas Bolton, carpenter
201 Mrs Wm Bleeze
201½ James W Johnson, sailor
203 Vacant
205 Wm Linstead, laborer
207 James Kelk, tinsmith
209 Geo Lewin, grocer
Stuart-st intersects
211 Vacant
215 Ed Passmore, blacksmith
G T Bridge
217 James Whalen, laborer
219 Hy Searle, machinist
219½ Vacant
221 Thos Stirton, stonecutter
Strachan-st intersects
223 John Legaire, blacksmith
227 Wm Copham, moulder
229 Wm Murray
233 Patrick Hanley, bricklayer
235 John Thorpe, laborer
237 Mrs Margaret McLaren
237½ Alfred Mayo, laborer
241 Andrew O'Brien, laborer
Simcoe-st intersects
243 Vacant
245 Patrick Donnely, laborer
247 Stephen Wilson, laborer
249 Alex McNab, stonecutter
249 Vacant
251 John Vance, weaver
257 — Cornell, laborer
259 Wm Wilson, spinner
261 J S Dillon, hotel
Ferrie-st intersects
265 Ed Crofton, grocer
267 And Bard, glassblower
269 James Ford, health inspector
273 Henry Smith, laborer
275 Wm Hanley, laborer
277 Fred Hoskins, laborer
279 James Sullivan, laborer
281 James Smith, blacksmith
283 Patrick Malloy, laborer

Picton-st intersects
287 Mrs Bridget O'Neill
289 Michael O'Neill, moulder
291 Ed Murphy, laborer
293 John Hickey, laborer
295 Wm McCarthy, laborer
297 John Crosslin, laborer
299 Thos Drever, carpenter
301 Thos Fallihee, checker
Macauley-st intersects
305 James Unsworth, dyer
309 A H Phoenix, carpenter
311 James F Malcolmson
Wood-st intersects
325 Patrick Connors, laborer
329 John McFadden
337 Chas F Riche, harnessmaker
339 Thos Routh, teamster
341 Wm Hutton, teamster
Burlington-st intersects
349 Thos Dreaver, carpenter
351 Jacob Strumble, teamster
353 Jas Hammond, weighmaster
355 Wm Dryden, agent
367 John Whalen, laborer
Brock-st intersects
375 Wm Snowden, blacksmith
379 Vacant
383 Vacant
385 John Doyle, packer
Guise-st intersects

John-st s, east side, from 43 King e to Mountain

Merchants' Bank
13-15 W E Sanford & Co
17 Geo Goering, hotel
19 Richard Magen, butcher
21 W G Townsend, custom br'r
23 Vacant
25-7-9 Morgan Bros, millers
Ralston & Irwin, real estate agents
33 Germania Hall

35 R N Taylor & Co, druggists

Main-st intersects

37 John Stuart, Son & Co
39 Frank Squibb, plumber
42 John Patterson & Co, tailors
43 Geo M Ryerson, agent
45-7 Jas Jolley & Sons, saddlers
49 Joseph I Blumensteil, broker
51 Mrs M Moses, broker
53 J R Wolf, pawnbroker
55 Vacant
55 ½ H J Halford, barber
57 Court House hotel
61 David Little, hairdresser
63 Thos Backus, barber
65 Matthew High, hotel

Jackson-st intersects

67 John McPherson & Co
71 Geo Elliott, hotel
73 Jacob M Tunis, grocer
75 Mrs Eliza Peacock, fancy goods
77 M W Attwood & Son, watchmakers
79 Lendrum Irvine, dry goods
79½ Geo B Ryckman, jeweler
81 Mrs Mary Stein, confection'r
83 C J Bird, dry goods
83½ James Barker, fruiterer
85 Mrs P Dowling, dry goods
87 Geo Morton, barber
89 Arch McDonald, hotel

Hunter-st intersects

91 Ashbourne Flour Mills
93 Geo C Hunter, tinsmith
95 Vacant
97 R N Taylor & Co, druggists
99 H Goodwin, watchmaker
101 Vacant
101½ H Strauss, grocer
101a Chas Hitzroth, shoemaker
103 C A Bridgewood, boots and shoes
103 Mrs Caleb Johnson
105 Hunt B & Bro, carriagemkrs
105 Alex Morrison, grocer

107 Wm Mallory, broker
107½ John McDonald, shoema'r
107-9 James Dunlop, merchant
109 J Jacobson, butcher
109½ Vacant
111 A Tyson, feather renovator
115 Geo Ashby, furniture
117 Fred Miller, butcher
119 Ballantyne Bros, grocers

Augusta-st intersects

121 Fred Landau, agent
123 Mrs Wm Morrison
125 James S Farmer, blacksmith
127 Samuel Willer, pork butcher
129 Hy Davis, tailor
131-33 Harry Bryant, grocer

Young-st intersects

135 Vacant
137 James Wills, shoemaker
139 Geo W Brooks, laborer
141 Wm Francis, pedler
141 James Inches, merchant
143 Robt Griffith, com traveler
145 Hy Vernon, manager W H Irwin & Co
147 H A Ambridge, accountant
149 H G Greig, bookkeeper

Maria-st intersects

151 Wm Newcomb, laborer
151½ Jos Way, gardener
153 Mrs Isabella Alexander

Hannah-st intersects

167 G W Johnson, teacher
169 Alex McInnes, merchant
    Mrs Richard Martin
    Col C C Grant
    Richard Tew, merchant
    Thos Robertson, barrister

John-st south, west side

2 Post Office
2 Custom House
2 Inland Revenue
2 Weights and Measures Office
2 Gas Inspector's Office

14 Hamilton Coffee and Spice Co
4 Gillesby & Barnes, flour and feed
6 Wm Gillesby, grain dealer
8-10 J R McKichan, paper bags
12-14 D H Long, hotel
16 Hugh Pierson, tailor
18 Fraser & Inches, grocers
20 2 Robt Jahn, hotel

Main-st intersects

Court House

Jackson-st intersects

48 Thorley Cattle Food Co
50 T M Kelly, grocer
52 J T Bronson, hotelkpr
54 Mrs Wm Forrest
56 Mrs Geo T Allen, confec'r
58 Mrs E B Caldwell, tobaccon't
60 Robt Smith, baker
62 W H Ryckman & Co, grocrs
64 J & R Kilgour, organ manfs
64 W B Mitchell, tailor
66 Andrew Martin, butcher
68 Mrs Geo Shaw, confectioner
70-72 Hugh McKeown, saddler
    Mrs Hugh McKeown, grocr
74 Edwin Gordon

Hunter-st intersects

76 W H Olmsted, grocer
78 David Dunlop, harnessmak'r
82 F Franey, gardener
84 Chris Loney, shoemaker
86-8 J Morrison, grocer

Wool Market Square {
13 Mrs Mark Aldrean
12 Peter Bowman, board'g
8 D Jackson, retinner
7 N Norris, hay dealer
Union Hotel
Jas Priestman, butcher
}

90 Thos S Hill, jeweler
92 Wm Rossell, coachman
94 Samuel White, shoemaker
96 Isaac Raphiel, tailor
98 Thos Morrison
102 Robt George, tailor

Augusta-st intersects

104 Vacant
106 Wm Sharp, baker
110 Fred Meinkle, stovemtr
112 Louis Geisel, tailor
114 R Ralston & Co, stovepolish
116 Wm J Bordley, upholsterer
118 Vacant
122 Wm H Homer, confectioner

Young-st intersects

124 Robt Gallagher, tailor
126 Jas Garson, carpenter
128 Thos Paradine, sexton
130 David West, laborer
132 Mrs Edmund Dalley
134 Chas H Webber
136 C W G Schwartz, bookkeeper

Maria-st intersects

Church of Ascension

Hannah-st intersects

Edward Browne, wharfinger
Samuel Barker
Mrs Edward Gurney
Chas Gurney

Jones-st, north side, from Dundurn w to city limits

2 S S King, mover
4 Miss Lizzie McIlroy, tailoress
6 James Jarvis, engineer
8 Thos Nelligan, laborer
10 Mrs H G VonHoxar
12 Harvey Hill, laborer
14 Elgin Bezanson, artist
16 James A Agutter, carpenter
18 Vacant
20 James Ryerson, carpenter
22 Samuel Coombs, mechanic
24 John Gibbon, mechanic
26 Thos Johnston, boilermaker
28 James Hamilton, laborer

Jones-st, south side

Wm Maddocks, blacksmith
3 Joseph Taylor, machinist
5 James Gaskin, laborer

Kelly-st, north side, from 82 Mary, e to Wellington

Laidlaw Manfrg Co, founders
4 M J Paterson, custom officer
6 Edw Dunnett, clerk P O
8 G E Mills, bricklayer

Elgin-st intersects

20 James Williams, teamster
22 Arthur Keeble, teamster

Ferguson-ave intersects

42 Mrs Lewis Marter
44 Geo A Peterson, laborer
46 Robt J Harte, teamster
48 Vacant
50 David Cox

Cathcart-st intersects

J & H Mulholland, wd dlrs
56 Hy Buchanan, sausagemaker
58 A T James, shipper

Wellington-st intersects

Kelly-st, south side

3 Robt Laceley, moulder
5 Chas Carter, scalemaker
7 Michael Pletz, tailor
13 James Connelly, grocer

Elgin-st intersects

17 Mrs Daniel Downs

Ferguson-ave intersects

31 Samuel Beeston, laborer
33 Michael Givey, shoemaker
35 James Potter, laborer
37 Henry Hunting, fireman
39 Marion Lewis, machinist

Cathcart-st intersects

53 Vacant
53 Hugh Cassidy, moulder
55 Hy Cartmell, tailor
57 Alex Strachan, bookkeeper

Wellington-st intersects

Kent-st, from Hannah w, to Concession

No houses

King-st e, north side, from James to Delta

2 S G Treble, gents' furnishings
4 Mrs F McLean, fancy goods
6 Garland & Rutherford, drugs
8 W E Mayhew & Co, dry goods
8½ C S Chittenden, dentist
" Thos Farmer, photographer
" C Oddfellows' Hall
" Mrs J R Greenwood, dress cutter
" Miss Alice E Jones, caligraphist
10 D A Hyslop & Co, carpets
12 Wm Acres, hatter
14 Richard Brierly, druggist
14½ Wm Bruce, patent agent
16 J Eastwood & Co, books, etc
18-20 A Murray & Co, dry goods
22 I O F Hall
22 J G Sinclair, dentist
24 R P Leask, gents' furnish's
26 Arland Bros, boots and shoes
28 J D Climie, boots and shoes
30-32 Thomas C Watkins, dry goods
34 John A Clark, druggist

Hughson-st intersects

36 Traders' Bank
38 J Zimmerman, dentist
38 Y M C A
4 . J F Shea, boots and shoes
42 James Shea, dry goods
44 Wood & Leggat, hardware
46 Vacant
48 McKay Bros, dry goods
50 Hy Blandford, gilder
52 Canada Glass House
54 Bowman & Moore, hardware
56 Robt Wilson, boots & shoes
58 Geo Gage, boots and shoes

60-62 Pratt Bros boots and shoes
64 Chas Israel, confectioner
66 Murphy & Murray, grocers
68 Davis & Burt, dentists
68 W J Waugh, gents' furnisher

John-st intersects

70 Geo James, dry goods
72 Mrs F Mandelbaum, fancy goods
74 Bews Bros, tailors
76 J M Rosseaux & Co, grocers
78 John B Gay, stationer
78 James Davidson, jeweler
78½ E S Whipple, land agent
" Richard Sheehan, cigar manf
" John Sintzel, tailor
" J W Stainton, ins agent
80 Chas Huton, tailor
82 Jos Heron, merchant tailor
84 Globe Hotel
86 J C White, fancy goods
88 D J Peace, tobacconist
90 Miss L Rowe, milliner
92 A S Brunt, hairdresser
94 A S McKenzie, shoemaker
96 W J Walsh, plumber
98-100 D Moore & Co, stoves
102 Adam Hope & Co, hardware

Catharine-st intersects

104 Reid, Birely & Co, general merchants
104 McMahon, Broadfield & Co crockery
104 N D Galbreaith, grocer
106 John Staunton, hotel
108 James Hennigan, hatter
112 B Cauley, tobacconist
114 J A Zimmerman, druggist
118 Geo Webster, merchant tail'r
120 Smart's Tea Co
122 Dominion Furniture Co
116 J Happle Hutchison, tailor
120 Mrs Jos Towersey
122 Mrs E Tremlett, boots and shoes
122 E Battram, fruiterer
124 C S Cochrane, photographer

124 Hy Schuhl, bookseller

Mary-st intersects

126 P D Carse, gents' furnis's
128 Vacant
130 V B Whipple, printer
" Hunter & Ross, tailors
" Geo Webster, machinist
" Storm Bros, teas
" James Wagner, tailor
" Boothman & Hutchison, painters
134 Alex Wetherall, dry goods
134 Thos L Stevens, picture dealer
136 J Pecover, cabinetmakr
138 Vacant
140 J Finagin, mercht tailor
142 J K C McGregor, drug't
144 H S Williams, stationer
146 C Black & Co, hardware
148 Alfred H Baylis, grocer
150 Mrs W H Bilton, tobac't
152 Miss H Carr, millinery
152-4 J Scott, fancy goods
156 Mrs E Stewart, milliner
158 F Claringbowl, jeweler
160 S Thorne & Co, dry goods
162 F E Moody, fancy goods
164 M Mundy, druggist
166 Frank E Walker & Co, housefurnishings

Walnut-st intersects

M Nesbit, hatter
170 Dennis Kerrigan, tailor
172 John B Lovell, tobacconist
174 W T Bell, confectioner
176 W H Coddington
178 Misses Harrison, milliners
180 E Newport, confectioner
182 China Arcade
184 James Gow, shoemaker
186 Robt Stewart & Co, grocers
188 John Riach, general dealer
190 Brethour & Co, tailors
190 John Peebles, watchmaker
192 Herman Stephany, barber
194 Mrs Chas Israel, confection'r
196 Hy Martin, hotel

198 Robt B Spera, dry goods
200 H S Hooper, confectioner
202 Thos O'Brien, barber
204 Ontario Pharmacy

Ferguson-ave intersects

208 Walker House
210 Mrs S C Robbins, tobacconist
212 Thos Spellacy, broker
214 J E Riddell, stoves
216 Mrs Janet Grigg, confectioner
218 Mrs Eliza Roe, fancy goods
218 Geo Roe, tailor
220 G W Powell, window shades
220½ Robt Corner, shoemaker
222 R Spence & Co, file cutters
224 S R Roos, watchmaker
226 Frank Truman, barber
228 Abraham Swayzie, flour
230 Fred W Truman, bookseller
232 Michael Sullivan, hotelkeepr
234 John Ellicott, plumber
236-8 Miss N A Jarvis, fancygoods

Upper Cathcart commences

240 Jos Precore, grocer
242 Geo Phillips, tailor
244 R M Cline, fish dealer
246-8 Alex McFarlane, flour, etc
250 E W Bateman, baker
252 Wm Hill, butcher
254 Miss Addie Morton
256 Geo Biggar, M D
258 C Hayhoe, fruiterer
260 Dominion Hat Co
270 R Leslie, fruiterer
272 John McMillan, grocer
274 A W Smith, fancy goods
276 D D Smith, M D, druggist

Wellington-st intersects

Corporation lumber yard
226 Wm Haskins, city engineer

West-ave intersects

228 W F Burton, barrister
240 Rev Canon W B Curran
242 John Tunstead, manf
244 Rev J J Craven

Victoria-ave intersects

246 B Winnifrith, grocer
250 T Arthur, carpenter
254 Thos Kilvington jr, florist

East-ave intersects

256-60 Samuel Mann, fancy goods
262 W Javis, confectioner
264 John B Turner, teacher
266 Andrew Patterson, teacher
268 D W Campbell, M D
270 Mrs Alexander Mitchell
272 John W Lowes, traveler
274 Mrs S M Healey
276 J H Johnson, upholster
278 W D Bews, merchant
280 Wm A Spera, fruiterer
282 Edment Hill, grocer
284 Samuel Chapman, druggist

Emerald st intersects

Bowes, Jamieson & Co, founders

Tisdale-st intersects

272-4 Frank Quinn, patternwkr
276a Geo Kerr, laborer
274 Vacant
276 Wm Campbell, shipper
278 Arch McKillop, health ins
280 W W Boughner, ins agent
282 Mrs Chas Renner
282½ Mrs Patrick Gallivan
284 Henry Taylor, grocer

Steven-st intersects

286 Wm Mills, carpenter
288 Jos Chapman, chair repairer
292 George Mills
302 Vacant

Ashley-st intersects

304 Arthur Peacock, butcher
306 Joseph Myers, laborer
308 H P Bonny, clerk
324 Alex McLean, clerk GTR

Wentworth-st intersects

Mrs Wm Tindill, tavern
Moses Niblock, laborer

H Smith, crockery
Thos Fitzgerald, laborer
Timothy Kelly, stovemountr
Thos Howard, laborer
Mrs M Sullivan, rag dealer
Richard Curran, laborer

Burlington-st intersects

Thos Small, butcher
Louis Morris, butcher
Samuel Burner, gardener
Wm J Anderson, butcher
Jos T Ross, painter
Alex Grover, dairyman
Robt Hopkin, merchant

Toll Gate

A C Case, farmer
George Gage, farmer
Anthony Webb, gardener
James Gage, farmer
Delta, Simon James

King-st e, south side

1-3 Canada Life Assurance Co
5 Bank British North America
7 Knox, Morgan & Co, wh dry goods
9 J A Skinner & Co, crockery
11 China Palace
13 Vacant
15 Canadian Bank of Commerce

Hughson-st intersects

17-19 Hamilton Provident and Loan Society
21 Alex Harvey & Co, wholesale grocers
23-25 J Winer & Co, wholesale druggists
27 Levy Brothers, wholesale jewelers
29 Vacant
31 Gillespie & Powis, brokers and ins agents
31 Canadian Pacific Railway offices
31 Park & Lee, custom brokers
33 Dixon Bros, wh fruiterers
35 Atkinson Bros, stationers
39 Post office

John-st intersects

45 Merchants' Bank
47-9 W E Sanford & Co, wholesale clothiers
51-53 J McPherson & Co, wholesale boots and shoes
55 E J Thompson & Co, wholesale jewelers
57 A W Gage & Co, wholesale jewelers
57 Wesleyan Ladies College
65 Singer Manf Co
67-69 McPherson, Glassco & Co, wholesale grocers
71 Duncan Bros, wh grocers
73 Blumensteil & Karsten, cigar manf

Catharine-st intersects

75 VanNorman & Co, agents
77 Geo Stevenson, plumber
77 Palladium Office
77 Hamilton Brush Co
77 J D Mills & Co, paper boxes
79 Victoria Hotel
81 Wah Sing, laundry
81½ Wm Dicker, shoemaker
83 Fred Langberg, cabinetmkr
87 Robt Coulter, shoemaker
89 Chas T Tomlinson, saddler
91 Thos Evans, varieties
93 D McPhie, plumber
95 Mrs Caroline Moore
97 John R Cambden, butcher
99 H D Bassett, machinist
101 James Cahill, police magistrate
113 W I A Case, M D
113 Wm H Case, M D

Walnut st intersects

115 Chas Bremner, grocer
117 Patrick Taafe, butcher
119 F E Woolverton, M D
121 Julius L Mandelbaum salesman
123 Francis Beer, butcher
125 James Amos, builder

127 Mrs Geo Robertson
131 Geo Whyte, carpenter
135 Central Hotel
    N & N W Station
143 Cook & Seaver, wood dealers
149 Hy Fell, fireman
153 Simcoe Hotel
155 Ed Breheny, shoemaker
167 A Ross, carriagemaker
169 Thos Baxter, wireworker
171 Geo Way, tailor
175 Jos Ross, blacksmith
177 Mrs Elizabeth Kingdon
179 Vacant
181 Vacant
183 Vacant

Spring-st commences

185 Culp & Tinling manf Co
187 Mrs Robbins, laundress
187½ Fox & Work, confectioners
189 James Garrick, mason
191 Geo A Truman, plumber
195 John A Macaulay, huckster

Wellington-st intersects

    First Methodist Church
207 Geo Fisher, porter
209 Chas Irish, shoemaker
211 T J Steward, ornamenter
213 Robt Hopkins, weaver
215 John Leitch, manf
221 Chas Peters, teamster
223 Mrs Jane Nelson
225-29 Meakins & Sons, brush
    manfs
231 Geo Buckingham, painter
233 Frank Volland, machinist
235 Geo Swallow, mason
237 Fred J Isard
241 James Laws, bill poster
243 John Irving, laborer
245 Mrs P Cummings, grocer

Victoria-ave intersects

    St Patrick's Catholic Church

East-ave intersects

267 W H Nichols, butcher
271 Thos C Watkins, merchant

41

Emerald-st intersects

273 Louis N Soper, salesman
275 Wm C Campbell, teacher
277 Chas Cutler, carpenter
193 A J Heath, dairyman
295 Chas Stillwell, manager
297 Mrs Peter Grant

Wentworth-st intersects

John Little, carpenter
James Nichol, machinist
B F Barber, clerk P O
Wm Windham, packer
John Fowler, tailor

Burlington-st intersects

James Gosnay, file cutter
Colin Arthur, butcher
F W Watkins, merchant
John Proctor, cedar grove
Robt Ward, Boys' Home
Mrs John Hart, toll gate kpr

King-st w, north side, from James to city limits

2 A Hamilton & Co, druggist
4 Wm Collier, restaurant
6 Dixon Bros, fruits
1-10 Farmer Bros, photographrs
10 H O Sonntag, tobacconist
10 Francis Fitzgerald, barrister
10 Drs R J & T H Husband, dentists
12 Davis & McCullough, jewelers
14 N A McLean, restaurant
16 John Moodie, fancy goods
18 Finch Bros, dry goods
20 J M Henderson & Co, tailors
22 W F Wood, boots and shoes
24 James Angus jr, hatter
24½ E Overell & Co, booksellers
26 Vacant
28 W G Simpson, boots and shoes
30-32 H Blachford & Co, boots and shoes
34 A R Kerr & Co, dry goods
36 Barnard, Murdoff & Co, dry goods

38 J Crawford, confectioner
40 A J Taylor, gents' furnishings
42 Mrs Joseph Taylor, jeweler
44 Wm Wilson & Son, tailors

Macnab-st intersects

48 Thos MacKay, grocer
50 H S Case, druggist
52 Wm Morton, fruiterer
54 James Slater, tailor
56-58 J B Browne, grocer
60 Richard Haigh, bookbinder
62 W Applegath, gents' furnisher
64 Robt Steven, boots
66 Thos Armstrong, hotel
70 H J Geiger, watchmaker
72 W R Fish, tobacconist
74 Mrs S Murphy, fancy goods
76 J B Kitchen, photographer
78 N Wolfe, varieties
82 Dominion hotel
82½ James Cooper, barber
84 T J Baine, organ manf
86 Edwin Green, furniture
88 M W Attwood & Son, watchmakers
88½-90 Hamilton House Furnishing Co
92 C L Thomas, piano manf
94 Franklin House

Park-st intersects

96 Wm McIver, hotel
98 R Elliott, mattrass maker
100-2 B Edwards, confectioner
104 Chas P Edwards, boots
106 Jas Lawrie, crockery
108 Miss E Johnstone, millinery
108 Vacant
108½ Wm Harvey, grocer
108½ E Britt, labor agency
110 Oliver Hancock, tobacconist
112 Reddall & McKeown, tins
114 Matthew Kouber, hatter
114½ B Martin, cabinetmaker
116 Richard Allen, bootmaker
118 Tuckett & Son, tobacco manfrs
124 R Buskard, carriagemaker

Bay-st intersects

130 T B Fairchild, hotel
132 Samuel Crawford, grocer
134 Mrs Wm Hudson, fancy goods
136 Ed Bates, upholsterer
140 Winslow & Webber, carriage hardware
142 John Mayhew, knitter
144 Miss Mary Marks, dressmakr
146 James Watt, gardener
148 J Murray, rag carpet weaver
150 A Pastine, fruiterer
152 Frank O'Reilly, plumber
156 J McDonnell, flour and feed
158 Thos E Nichols, wireworks
160 T O'Connor, carriage painter
162 Peter Gorman, blacksmith
164 T & G Broadbent, machinery brokers

Caroline-st intersects

168 Mrs Wm Armitage
170 Thos H Orton, M D
172 R L Featherstone, salesman
176 John Dixon, patternmaker
178 Troy Laundry
178½ Nathaniel Goddard, fruit'r
180 Vacant
182 John Johnstone, china, etc
184 Ross R Wilson, traveler
186 J K Applegath, merchant
188 John S Reid, traveler
190 Justus Griffin, printer
202 Mrs J Chambers, dressmaker
202½ Jacob W Smith, shoemkr
204 Miss A Smith, confectioner
206 J W Sutherland, druggist
208 Thos Pillman, butcher
210 Alex Cuthbertson, grocer

Hess-st intersects

190 A L Reeves, baker
192 G H Hill, butcher
194 L H Patten, barrister
196 W G Scott, traveler
198 John Walsh
200 Mrs David Almond, dairy
204 A Tshaan, butcher
206 J J Bigelow, grocer

79 John Skinner, watchmaker
81 Ed Stockwell, dye works
83 Miss Emma Pargeter, hair worker
85 Mrs E Woolverton, homœopathic
87 A M Theal, sewingmachines
87 Mrs E King, laundry
89 Bowering & Pain, butchers
91-3 E & D Carr, flour and feed
95 Mrs F McGuire, broker
97 Chas H Winckler, cutler
99 Richard Catchpole, china
103 Vacant
95 James Crisp, locksmith
101 R J Hamilton

Bay-st intersects

103 Wm L Wilson, boarding
105 James Carson, boarding
111 Wm Nicholson, wood dealer
113 Wm Cole, butcher
115 Geo Read, carpenter
117 J H Young, architect
119 I C Chilman, confectioner
121 John Cumming, cutter
123 James Thornton, manfr
131 Geo H Geldart, gilder
139 Wm Cox, pork curer

Caroline-st intersects

141 Pioneer hotel
143 T & G Broadbent, brass founder
145 Ham Piano Stool Co
149 Wm G Stark, M D
151 Mrs Alex T Loemans
159 B Osborne, manf
181 Thos Miller, M D
185 Alfred J Taylor, merchant

Hess-st intersects

All Saints Church

Queen-st intersects

207 Geo T Tuckett, manf
215 D McGregor, carriagemaker
217 G E Tuckett, manf

Ray-st intersects

229 Wm Terryberry, clerk P O
233 Wm Kavanagh
235 John Henry
237 C G Fortier, col in revenue
241 W H Ballard, school insp
243 John J Thomas, piano mkr
245 Arthur Doherty, grocer

Pearl-st intersects

267 Jefferson Stevens, carpenter
269 John Hurrell, carpenter
271 C McDonnell, basketmaker
277 Wm Trevaskis, blacksmith
279 Thos H Semmens, painter
281 Theo Myers, laborer
r " Mrs Fred Beckman
283 J Brundle, tinsmith
287 Wm Howick, grocer

Locke-st intersects

289 Edward Tompkins, laborer
289½ Geo Cooper, laborer
291 Vacant
293 David J Jennings, carver

Margaret st commences

295 John Eydt, teamster
303 C F Thomas, piano manfr
307 Ed New, brickmaker
309 Edwin Longhurst, moulder
311 Geo A White, bricklayer

New-st intersects

317 Vacant
319 Wm Travaskis, blacksmith
321 John Kitchen, pedlar

Garth-st intersects

337 John Bridges, laborer

Main-st intersects

Andrew Gerrard, dairyman

King William-st, north side from 28 James north to Wentworth

2 Moore & Davis, estate agts
2 Thos Marshall, tailor
2 Chas G Booker, merchant tailor

STREET DIRECTORY. 323

208 Wesley Keller, foreman
210 James Lithgow, laborer
212 P T Robertson, grocer

Queen-st intersects

216 John H Geiger, hotel
218 Albert Geiger, baker
220 John E Geiger, flour & feed
226 Alex Harvey, merchant
230 Mrs Sarah Smith
232 John Donaldson, carpenter

Ray-st intersects

238-246 Loretto Convent

Pearl st-intersects

248 John Morrisey, grocer
250 James Bremner, com agent
256 Vacant
258 C E Richardson, tobacconist
r 258 Dan Lehann, laborer
260 Matt Richardson, shoemaker
278 Lucian Hills, architect
280 Wm Randall, laborer
282 David C Beasley, broommkr
284 Mrs Sarah Haines
286 John Travaskis, blacksmith
288 Arch Wilson, hotel

Locke-st intersects

Crystal Palace and grounds

Sophia-st intersects

298 Wm Bradley, blacksmith
300 Mrs Mary J Taylor
302 Vacant
304 Mrs James Keith
306 Geo S Howick, salesman
308 Geo Fraser, driver
310 Hand & Co, fireworks
314 A K Smith, teamster
318 Wm Baker, laborer
320 Wm H Holmes, tinsmith
322 Wm Taylor, laborer

Dundurn-st intersects

330 Thos Cheeseman, brickmkr
338 John Cheeseman, brickmkr
Old Cemetery
Arthur Duggan, brickmkr

King-st w, south side

5 Richard Russell, manf
5 Geo A Young, ins agent
5 Star Box Factory
7 Vacant
9 Vacant
9 E Freeman & Son, real estate
9 Vacant
13 John Alexander, leather
13 Colin McRae wh Boots
17-19 Bank of Hamilton
21 Orr, Harvey & Co, boot and shoe manfs
23 T B Greening & Co, teas
25 G C Briggs & Sons, patent medicines
27 Jas C Taylor, coal oil, etc
29 R Pray & Son, undertakers
31 Willson & Gates, woodenware
33 Hendrie & Co, cartage agts
35 Wm Farmer, photographer

Macnab-st intersects

37-9 J A Bruce & Co, seeds
41-3 Buntin, Gillies & Co, wh stationers
45 Vacant
47 Blachford & Son, undertakrs
49 Jesse Chapman, funeral emporium
51 Joseph Hoodless & Son, furniture
53 Halloran Bros, carriage supplies
55 Vacant
57 Wm Griffith, wholesale boots and shoes

Charles-st intersects

59-63 American hotel
65 J Elliott, barber
67-69 Malcolm & Souter, furniture

Park-st intersects

71-73 Z Pattison, confectioner
75 Geo Walker, grocer
77 Photoglyptic Co

2 Philip Waddelton, tailor
2 St George's Hall
2 Charles Sylvester, tailor
4 China & Japan Tea warehouse
4½ G W Counihan, barber
6 W H McLaren, grocer
6½ Hyslop, Cornell & Co's shirt facrory
8 Vacant
10 G H Hopkins, boots
10 John Bartman, tailor
12 John Heritage, tailor
12 Joseph Greenfield, auctioner
14 Robt Allen, furniture
16 John Wright, stoves
18 A W Wright, broker
20 E Nixon, saloon
22 Robt Smyth, tinsmith
26 Edison Lamp Co
28 W T James, hotel

Hughson-st intersects

James Sweeney, tinsmith
30 Thos Cooper, fruiter
32 Mrs Ed Rosenstadt, broker
36-40 Geo Richardson, broker
42 Mrs Elida Demun, broker
44-46 Fire engine station
48 John Wright, locksmith
54 Vacant

John-st intersects

56 James Reed, hotel
66 E & C Gurney, pattern shop
66½ Mrs Mary Hall
68 Andrew Watson, tailor

Catharine-st intersects

A Hope & Co, store houses
Police Station

Mary-st intersects

110 Vacant
112 Vacant
124 Stamp & Franks, painters
116 W H Stamp, painter
r 116 W J McDonald, carpenter
122 Alex Gibb, paper boxes

124 Geo Winn, shoe manfr
126 Mrs T Booth, milliner
128 Jos Horton, rag merchant
130 Thos Bogges, furniture dlr
130½ Fred Grainger, expressman
132 Wm Fairley, plumber
134 Mrs E Munson
136 Wm Allan, carpenter
138 Mrs Soloman Simons
140 Robt Reid, carpenter
142 Mrs John Hubbard
r142 John Kemp, laborer
144 Daniel Hutchinson, laborer
146 David Parks, shoemaker
148 Mrs E Hartnett
150 Geo Potter, carpenter
152 John McGoff, machinist
154 James Bryer, lather
156 Hiram King
158 James Spence, carpenter
160 Alex McPherson, teamster
162 Samuel Hunter

Ferguson-ave intersects

164 Chas Philips, carpenter
166 John Smith, tinsmith
168 Walter Potter, machinist
170 Brennan's lumber yard
178 James Neville, laborer
180 Chas Wilkin, laborer
182 Hy Fowler, shoemaker
184 Phillips & Mottashed, build's
186 Robt Aldrige, teamster
188 Anthony Murray
190 Jeremiah Donovan, moulder
192 Alfred Emberson, coal oil
194 Wm Sommers, packer
r194 Mrs John Doyle
196 Arthur TenEyck, fireman
198 Geo Hooper, blacksmith
200 Mrs M Maitland
202 Mrs Wm Wilkinson
204 Ed Lavis, pork buyer
206 Andrew Linklater, porter
208 Bryan Doyle, detective
210 Thos Morris, flour and feed

Wellington-st intersects

212 Wm Miller, tinsmith

212 Robt G Robinson, cutter
214 Wm Foster, foreman
216 James Kingdom, blacksmith
226 Peebles & Hamilton, carpenters
228 Robert Stewart, bottler

West-ave intersects

230 Nathaniel Hurd, laborer
232 Timothy Sullivan, laborer
234 Mrs Elizabeth Tulk
236 Vacant
238 Mrs Thos Hoag
240 Geo Walker, machinist
S J Moore's Factory

Victoria-ave intersects

Public School

East-ave intersects

Vacant grounds

Emerald st intersects

Vacant lots

Tisdale st intersects

Robt Warren, butcher
290 John Gardiner, postman

Steven-st intersects

294 Hugh McPhail, agent
302 E C Fearnside, gardener

Ashley-st intersects

312 James Riddle, laborer
314 John P Kirwin, shipper
318 John Homes, gardener
328 Robt Bennet, blacksmith
330 Thos Johns, carpenter

Wentworth-st intersects

King Wm-st, south side

Stinson's Chambers {
  T H Stinson, solicitor
1 Samuel McNair
1 William Shawcross, tea dealer
}
3 H Martin, leather dealer
9 James Crooks, hotel
11 Thos Fowkes, dry goods
13 Robt Allen, broker

15 John Carruther, merchant
17 Wm Gell, broker
19 T Bogges, broker
21 Mrs John Kilroy, broker
23 Vacant
25 Vacant

Hughson-st intersects

33 Anchor Hotel
41 Wood & Leggat warehouse
47 H W Judd, fruit canner
47 Geo Dempsey, manfr
47 Griffin & Kidner, printers
47 E C Jones, iron fencing
49 Ham Wrought Iron Works
49 Robt B Murray, whip feriles
49 W C Barnes & Son, stained glass works
55 Andrew Dillon, saloon

John-st intersects

57 Edward Bolus, pattern fitter
r 57 Chas James, machinist
r 57 James Wishart, blacksmith
63-67 M Brennen & Sons
69 John Strathdee, salesman

Catharine-st intersects.

85 G T R stables
87 Geo Forbes, stableman
89 John Lewis, shoemaker
91 Thos Edwards, huckster
93 — Heriot, laborer
95 Joseph Horton, rag dealer

Mary-st intersects

101 Arthur Weir, hotel
105 David Nash, laborer
107 Esau Carter, harnessmaker
109 John Chapman
111 Wm H Taylor, laborer
113 Wm Harper, shoemaker
115 Vacant
117 Mrs Geo N Henderson

Walnut-st intersects

125 Matt C Cooper, glassblower
127 Geo Nott, butcher
129 James Nichol, laborer
131 Mrs Catharine Campbell
133 John Rigsby, builder

135 Young & Bro, manfs
145 Fred Wurst, carpenter
147 Mrs Jas Cox, dressmaker
149 Hy Reid, machinist

Ferguson-ave intersects

151 John Wurst, bricklayer
153 W Carruthers, clerk
155 Wm Berry, stock fitter
157 Wm Swallow, carpenter
161 John Hampson, shoemaker
163 Mrs Eliza Allen
165 Vacant
167 James Mortimer, moulder
169 John Close
171 James Ainslie, tanner
173 Wm Smith, traveler
175 Lewis Cook, moulder
181 Mrs Martin Duggan
185-89 S F Hopkins, pickle manf

Wellington-st intersects

Robt Harper, florist
209 Wesley Tice, salesman
211 Wm Fraser

West-ave intersects

241 Geo C Holden

Victoria-ave intersects

247 John McNeil, laborer
249 John Trebilcock, carpenter
251 Geo Smith, painter
255 Thos Long, laborer

East-ave & Emarald-st intersect

259 Chas Karsten, cigarmaker
261 Wm Aldridge

Tisdale-st intersects

279 Mrs James H Wright
281 S F Hopkins, manf
283 Robt J Hopkins, carpenter
283½ Mrs Richard Wodell
285 David Love, carpenter
287 Thos Byrrows jr, auctioneer
289 Adolphus Hinds, printer
291 James Bracken, shoemaker
291 Geo J Rayner, grocer

Steven-st intersects

293 Dennis Kelly, laborer
295 Mrs Reid
315 Wm Wilson, laborer

Wentworth-st intersects

Kinnell-st, north side, from Inchbury

6 James P Weatherston, clerk
8 Wm Lambert, mechanic
10 Wm Hyndman, blacksmith
14 John McBean, patternmaker

Kinnell-st, south side

9 G H Snider, miller
11 Robt Allen, carter

Leeming-st, runs from Cannon to Barton

Frank Ling, pickle manf

Liberty-st, east side, from 120 Hunter east, south to Young

3 Mrs Wm Costie

Grove-st intersects

17 Mrs Wm Anderson
19 Mrs John Mellon
21 Vacant
23 Bradford Mitchell, engineer
25 Pirie LePage, shoemaker
27 Wm Flynn, clerk. P O
31 Donald Work, quarryman
33 Patrick Booth, shoemaker

Young-st intersects

Liberty-st, west side

Grove-st intersects

4 J R Hesse, merchant
6 James Armstrong, painter
8 Mrs I Reid
10 Peter Reid, carpenter
12 Mrs Harry Gillard
14 J Johnson, music teacher
16 Mrs Wm Foreman

18 John Sintzel, tailor
20 Ed W Loosley, cutter
22 John C Smyth, merchant
24 Henry Hutton, bookkeeper
26 Ebenezer P Barnes, merch't
28 C S Cochrane, photographer
30 Robt Keefer, traveler
32 D S Jaquith, salesman
34 Patrick Jones, laborer
22a Vacant
26a Wm Brantford, plasterer

Young-st intersects

Ontario Canning Co

Little Market-st, north side, from Pearl north, west to Locke

2 E R Williams, laborer
4 Rich Batterton, bricklayer

Little Wellington-st intersects

8 W J Weller, porter
10 Felix Joice, engineer
12 Wm Goodram, pedler
20 James Dore, laborer

Little Peel-st intersects

22 Ed Makies, machinist
22½ Ed Milligan, engineer
24 Patrick Doyle, tailor

Locke-st intersects

Little Market-st, south side

21 James Weller, laborer

Locke-st intersects

Little Peel-st, e side, from 20 Little Market to Napier

4 Vacant
8 Robt Edgar, laborer
10 Wm A Smith

Napier-st intersects

Little Peel-st, west side

3 John Semmens, carpenter

5 John Sheehan, com agent
7 John Dyke, laborer
9 Donald Fraser, tailor
15 Sameel R eeves, baker

Napier-st intersects

Little Wellington-st, from Little Market to Napier

1 James Potter, brickmaker
3 Michael Nolan
5 Wm Tyson, builder
7 John Dean, laborer

Napier-st intersects

Little William-st, east side from Barton e north to G T R Track

2 Harry Headland, laborer
12 J W Sinclair
14 Christain Rehder, plater
22 Francis King, mechanic
32 Wm Dodge, laborer
34 Alfred Cheeseman, laborer
Wm Woodley, staves

South-st intersects

Little William-st, west side

3 Wm Garvin, machinist
13 John Graham, machinist
15 Thos Jones, moulder
21 Jos Halter, butcher
25 Oscar Wilcox, carpenter
27 Herbert Brown, machinist
29 Geo Western, watchman
31 Thos Feaver, butcher
33 Hugh Robinson, plasterer
37 John Burns, laborer
37 John Old, laborer
39 A W Darby, laborer
41 James Catlin, laborer
43 Ed Buckingham, polisher
45 Thos Smith, laborer
47 John Pointon, laborer
49 Arch McKenzie, laborer
51 Louis Covener, pedler
53 Mrs Mary Ann Wass

55 John Ellis, laborer
57 Seymour Skinner, laborer
59 John Lyne, shoemaker

South-st intersects

Lockearne-st runs from Dundurn to Breadalbane
Mrs E Burns

Locke-st n, east side, from 228 King w to G T R work shops

6 John Sullivan, laborer
8 Wm H Rendell, blacksmith
10 Chas A Hall, brickmaker

Little Market-st ends

26 Wm Potter, machinist
28 Geo Skuse, laborer
32 Hy Weaver, teamster

Napier-st ends

42 Francis Kelly, laborer
Crystal Palace View Hotel

Peter-st ends

62 James D Park, asst inspector
62 John Kerran, carpenter
64 James Tracie, brakeman
Vacant lots

Florence-st intersects

70 Wm Gray, laborer
72 Andrew Hennerberry
74 Geo Dorman, laborer
76 John Durphey, carpenter
78 Chas Blackman, porter
80 Wm Hollingrake, engineer
82 Fred Ball, moulder
84 Richard Smith, laborer
88 Wm Peel, machinist
90 Gilbert Hutton, machinist

York-st intersects

110 James McCue, enginedriver
112 Frank Evans, blacksmith
114 Arthur Weir, machinist
114½ Jos Taafe, moulder
42

116 Jos Wm Reid, carpenter
116½ John R Burns, trimmer
118 Jos Foster, engineer
120 Donald Campbell, carpenter
122 Thos W Milligan, huckster
124 James Merriman, checker
126 John Minnes, blacksmith
130 Wm Sayers, laborer
132 Wm McDaid, laborer
134 Mrs Elizabeth Watts
136 Mrs Elizabeth O'Leary
138 Wm J Hamill, laborer
140 John Jackson, shipper

Barton-st ends

Locke-st north, west side

Crystal Palace and Grounds
Geo Kerr, caretaker
Engine House

Florence-st intersects.

71 Peter Dingman, shoemaker
73 Mrs John Nicholson
75 John Marshall, polisher
77 **Vacant**
81 G Cook, machinist
83 John Houghton, carpenter
85 Thos H Garner, cooper
87 Thos Gordon, distiller
89 Wm Monk, bookkeeper
91 John T Hall, cabinetmaker
91½ John Croft, teamster
93 Thos K Hall, blacksmith

York-st intersects

99 Samuel Morrison, agent
101 John Daly, railroader
103 James Barry, clerk
105 John Quirk, finisher
111 Thos James, roller
113 Vacant
115 Samuel Ryckman, conduct'r
117 Geo McHattie, wiper
119 Daniel McCarthy, rougher
121 Thos Milne, laborer
123 Wm Milne, shipper
125 Robt Conway, moulder
127 Duncan Davidson, laborer
129 Loyal Davis, carpenter

133 Wm McDougall, machinist
135 Arthur Cline, hackman
139 Michael Frayley, laborer
141 Thos Lewis, laborer
143 John W Peace, iron worker
r " Thos King, fireman
147 Michael Carroll, heater
149 Jas O'Connor, dairyman
153 Anthony Gorman, rougher
155 Claude S Sala, draughtsman

St Mary's Lane-st intersects

Locke-st s, east side, from 287 King w to the Mountain

3 David Hall, blacksmith

George-st ends

15 H L Martin, foreman
17 Robt Heydemann, helper
19 West Campbell, potter

Nelson st intersects

21 Elijah Wright

Main, Jackson and Canada-sts intersect

55 Adam Sachs, grocer
61 Adolphe Muntz, laborer

Hunter-st intersects

Vacant lots

Bold-st intersects

71 Geo Metcalfe, painter
71½ John N Rowe, stonecutter

Pine st intersects

65 John Moore, laborer
67 Wm Wright, machinst

Oak and Hannah-sts intersect

Wesley Vollick, cabinetmakr

Herkimer-st intersects

James Burns, machinist
165 K McLennan, builder

Concession-st intersects

Locke-st s, west side

2 Geo Trenwith, blacksmith
8 Mrs Ellen Audley
10 Wm Finchamp, moulder
12 Vacant
16 John Elwell, moulder
18 G Morris, butcher
20 James Farrell, laborer
20½ James Snaudee, printer
22 James Watson, carpenter
26 Wm Davidson, tailor

Main-st intersects

42 J C Boligan, grocer
44 John Levy, pedler

Jackson-st intersects

46-52 R Campbell's pottery

Canada-st intersects

58 Mrs Emily A Miller
60 John Doherty, stonemason
62 John Fuller, gardener
64 Wm Mars, laborer

Hunter-st intersects

66 Geo Baxter, driver

Duke-st intersects

66 Thos Coil, laborer
68 Michael Fanning
70 Mrs Wm Frid
72 Mrs Christian Marshall
74 John D Moore, brickmaker
76 John Hockbush, laborer
T Fanning, grocer

Robinson-st intersects

J W Blasdel & Co, grocers
S C Smith, teamster
Miss Margaret Macklem

Maple st intersects

98 Wm H Mattice

Herkimer-st intersects

108 John Knapman, laborer
Vacant lots

Concession-st intersects

Locomotive-st east side, from 230 York n to Barton

4 Patrick O'Reilly, laborer
6 Hugh Walker, machinist
8 D Edgar, lumber merchant
10 Jos D Reed, conductor
16 Mrs Hugh Young
18 John Daly, gardener
20 Vacant
22 Wm A Emory, hat manf
24 T R Honeycomb, bricklayer
26 John W Clifton, engineer
28 Nicholas F Randall, feeder
32 James M Grassie, yardsman
34 Ed Egan, fitter
36 Wm Burt, boilermaker
38 John Collins, cutter
40 Sidney H Brown, laborer
44 Ed Daniels, cutter
46 Harry Tomlinson, fireman
48 Mrs Peter Dick
50 Vincent Raglin, laborer
52 Alex Young, iron worker
54 Wm Jenkins, laborer
56 R W England, boarding
58 J J B McCallum, laborer
60 Michael McDonough, rough'r
62 Wm Bell, laborer
64 Donald Mathieson, laborer
66 Adam J Grotz, nailer
68 Wm Clunas, machinist
70 David Cashon, moulder
72 James M Latimer, machinist

Barton-st intersects

Locomotive-st, west side

Vacant lots
9 D O'Connell, laborer
11 K McKenzie, porter
15 Vacant
19 J W Horning, coffin finisher
21 John Sandercock, tinsmith
23 Alex Grant, brakeman
27 Wm Hancock, contractor
29 Duncan McDougall, contrac'r
31 Geo Taylor, laborer
33 Herman Prillipp, laborer
37 C S Griggs, policeman

39 James Harris, policeman
47 Ed Makins, boilermaker
49 Wm Connelly, laborer
51 Robt Fenton, laborer
53 John W Herbert, messenger
55 John Jamieson, painter
57 W H Tribute, machinist
59 M A McEachern, boilermkr
61 B Salisbury, saddler
67 Herbert R Hall, fireman
69 J W Ronald
71 Wm W Wills, draughtsman
73 Vacant
75 James Enright, clerk
81 Wm Hamilton, carpenter
83 Vacant

Barton-st intersects

Macnab-st n, east side, from 40 King w to the Bay

6 American Suspender Co
8 John Riach, gen dealer
10 Mrs Jas McDougall, oil and lamps
12 Wm Turner jr, shoe manf
14 Vacant
16 McCallum & Hall, cabinet-makers
18 Canadian Oil Co
20 G M Bell, machinist
22 Wm Wholton, lunch rooms
24 Vacant

Market Square

Merrick-st intersects

56 W H McWaters & Co, teas
58 Long & Bisby, wool dealers
60-62 Walter Woods & Co, wooden ware
64 Lumsden Bros, grocers
74 Thos Johnston, blacksmith

Vine-st intersects

76 R Peters, machinist
78 G Schumacher, cabinetmak'r
80 Adam Bartman, tailor
82 Vacant
84 R Gwyder, whitewasher

86 Mrs Mary Dunn
86½ A Buckingham, plasterer
88 Matthew G Meek, bookkpr
92 Dodson Bros, brass founders
94 H E Bucklen & Co
Cannon-st intersects
104 Vacant
r " Hy Aconib, laborer
r " Isaac Stephens
106 Baptist Church
r " Mrs Epps, laundress
108 Isaac Buckingham, plasterer
110 Wm Britt, shoemaker
112 Mrs Margaret Wood
114 James Chisholm, builder
116 Central Carriage Factory
120 David Cobb, laborer
122 Mrs Emily Mullings
Mulberry-st commences
124 S H Metman, laundry
126 Wm Hunt, butcher
128 John J McAllistar, builder
130 C Delorme, carriagemaker
130½ Mrs Wm Pitt
132 Chas Barnhart, barber
r " Vacant
134 Chris Halliday, laborer
136 Vacant
138 Mrs Chas Bennett
140 Capt J Malcolmson
140 John McKenzie, lumber dealer
150 H Twohy, collector
152 Mrs V Howells
154 W Woods, manf
156 Rev C H Mockridge, D D
158 A A Wyllie, customs clerk
160 G H Richards, moulder
160½ John Finagin, merchant
Colborne-st intersects
162 Robt Grames, laborer
164 Robt McKay
168 Wm Cumbers, bookkeeper
170 Wm Warren, machinist
172 Wm T M Crowther, music teacher
174 Geo W McKay

176 Chas E Weaver, hotel
Barton-st intersects
182 Wm Dummer, glassblower
184 Miss Agnes Young
r " Humphrey Hodges
186 Wm A Hull
188 J M Young, foreman
190 A E Drake, foreman
192 Mrs M E Baillie
194 J T Routh, ins agent
196 John A Ward, clerk GTR
198 Wm Yaldon, tavern
Murray-st intersects
204 Sam'l Young, timekeeper
206 Harry Keymer, boilermkr
208 Wm Lowe, machinist
Stuart-st intersects
Weigh Scales
218 H March, baggageman GTR
GTR Track
220 John Breheny, shoemaker
222 Albert Case, car driver
Strachan-st intersects
226 Robt Archibald, fireman
228 Mrs Susan Kerr
230 Richard Dowle, clerk
232 Rev Vernon H Emory
234 John B Nelligan, clerk
236 Arthur McCamis, laborer
244 Mrs Wm Montgomery
Simcoe-st intersects
250 Ontario Cotton Mills Co
256 Thos Thompson, laborer
r " Thos McKenna, laborer
r " James Clark, carpenter
" Vacant
262 James M Dillon, hotel
Ferrie-st intersects
264 James Andrews, carpenter
266 Mrs Geo Malcolmson
268 Fred Held, teamster
270 John Flockton, fireman
272 Hiram Backhouse, weaver
274 Arthur Talbot, teamster
276 C J Holland, machinist

278 Thos Smith, dealer
280 Henry Dean, laborer
282 Wm Robinson, salesman
286 James McGowan, laborer

Picton-st intersects

290 Elijah Bowen, engineer
292 Mrs J M Lister, dressmaker
294 Hugh Doherty, engineer
296 Dennis Donahue, laborer
300 James Hill, grocer

Macauley-st intersects

302 Thos Clark, laborer
304 Ralph Lewis, carpenter
306 Wm Naff, traveler
308 Robt Barclay, laborer
310 Wm Turk, laborer
312 Robt Smith, laborer
314 Vacant

Wood-st intersects

320 John Slater, carter
324 Simon Ferris, mechanic
326 Robt Douglas, glassblower
328 James Havers, glassblower

Burlington-st intersects

334 Oliver Dobbie, watchman
    Wm Cunningham, teamster
    Thos McIlwraith, Cairnbrae

Macnab-st n, west side

1-3 Thos McKay, grocer
5 S Zimmerman, M D, dentist
7 M Shine, barber
9 Harry Green, stoves
11 E J Furnivall, tailor
13 J P Kelly, shoemaker
15 Jno Watt & Son, meht tailors
17 F W Fearman, provisions
19 Archdale Wilson & Co, wh druggists
21 Willard Bros, harness
23 Stuart Bros, wh grocers
25 Vacant
27 Vacant
29 Andrew Ruthven, hotel

Market-st commences

31 R C Cooper, grocer
33 Robert Evans & Co, seed merchants

York-st intersects

35 John A Barr & Co, druggists
37 John S roud, hotel
39 C H Peebles, grocer
41 John A Dressel, hotel
43 Campbell & Pentecost, dry goods
45 John W Schram, boots and shoes
47 Mrs Thos Bradfield, restaurant
49 Clyde hotel
51 John N Davis, china and glass
53 Mrs E Duffy, fancy goods
55 Peter Duffy, hotel

Merrick-st intersects

57 John Calder & Co, wholesale clothiers
59 Lucas, Park & Co, wholesale grocers
61 Vacant
75 Jas Stewart & Co, foundry

Vine-st intersects

77-9 Chas Freeman, rag dealer
79 Abraham Levy, rag dealer
83 Vacant
85 James L Hill, baggageman
87 A H Henry, expressman
89 Daniel Doyle, wagonmaker
91 M A Pigott, builder
95 J W James, bookkeeper

Cannon-st intersects

97 J W Biggar, livery
99 Mrs Maria Bond
101 Vacant
103 Frank Burdett, brushmaker
105 Thos Clochecy, harnessmkr
107 Miss Margaret Clifford
109 David Hurley, engineer
" Chas Bradfield, laborer
111 Wm J Wright, moulder
113 Robt Chisholm, builder
115 W A D Baby, excise officer

117 John Cummings, maltster
Mulberry-st intersects
119 Walter Bruce, brakeman
121 James Chambers, conductor
123 Geo Moore
127 Hy Fernihough, laborer
129 Francis Edgar, carpenter
131 Arch McEachern, teller
139 Mrs S J Evans
141-7 R C Model School
149 Jno McKenzie, wood dealer
151 Chas Jenkins, engineer
153 K nneth McKenzie, painter
155 Mrs M Browne
157 Ed Joy, laborer
Colborne-st intersects
163 Andrew Nicholson, laborer
165 Mrs Ellen Delanty
167 Vacant
169 Hy Creel
171 Ed Hardy, collector
173 Geo Hall, mechanic
Barton-st intersects
179 Peter O'Reilly, brushmaker
181 Capt Wm Wood, mariner
183 John Wark, clerk
185 John McDougall, car check'r
187 Matthew Wilson, manf
189 Wm Doran, manf
191 C E Morgan, ticket agent
193 Allison Wyllie, foreman
195 John C Goodenough, clerk
197 Casper Teiper, C E
Murray-st intersects
209 Wm Massie, machinist
Stuart-st intersects
 T & R Williamson, wood dls GTR Bridge
221 Samuel Church, laborer
Strachan-st intersects
221 James Morris, grocer
227 John Harris, contractor
231 John McLaren, agent
233 Wm Sutherland, laborer
235 James Inch, machinist

Simcoe-st intersects
251 Chas Beatty, custom broker
253 Vacant
255 John Corrigan, laborer
257 Thos Elliott, engineer
259 Mrs Jos James
261 Daniel Husted, glassblower
263 Hugh Gillespie, grocer
Ferrie-st intersects
263½ Wm G Fairweather, grocer
265 John Kerr, moulder
267 Matthew Carroll, lumberman
271 Mrs Mary Doody
273 Ed Hancock, carpenter
275 Robt Cowie, carpenter
283 Patrick Burk, laborer
285 Ed Brennan, tinsmith
Picton-st intersects
287 Jos Paquin, grocer
289 John Stewart, clerk
293 Arch Irvine, sailor
295 Moses Furlong, hackman
299 Lawrence Kelly
303 Thos Jones, glassblower
Macauley-st intersects
309 Robt Arrol, second hand dlr
311 Jos Fritzman, glassblower
313 Eby Taylor, laborer
313½ Mrs Patrick Murphy
Wood st intersects
315 Geo Mullin, glassblower
317 James Arrol, moulder
319 Mrs Mary Armstrong
321 Vacant
323 Vacant
327 Vacant
Burlington-st intersects
 Burlington Glass Works
Brock-st intersects
 Browne's Wharf

Macnab-st s, east side, from King w to Markland

7 Chas Makinson, driver

9 Mrs Ann Murphy
13 Wm Richardson, laborer
15 Hy Turner, gardener
19 Thos Hedley, upholsterer
21 Mrs Wm Storrer

Main-st intersects

27 Benj Coombs, laborer
29 Ed Parker, harnessmaker
   S McKay, livery

Jackson & Hunter sts-inersect

53 R R McCleave, shoetrimm'r
55 Mrs Alex Lawson
61 J B Fairgrieve, coal merch't

Bold-st intersects

63 O S M N Fraser
65 J D Macdonald, M D

Duke & Robinson-sts intersect

91 James M Young, manf
93 A H Hope, manf
95 Mrs Adam Hope

Hannah-st intersects

John Crerar, barrister

Herkimer-st intersects

113 John H Bradley, cabinetm'r
115 Wm F McGivern, bookkeep'r
117 Cameron Bartlett, accounta't

Macnab-st s, west side

John A Bruce & Co, seedmen
6 Joseph Miller, artist
8 Mrs Ann Thatcher
10 Francis Waters, driver
12 Thos Irwin & Son, tinsmiths
14 A O U W Hall
16-20 Thos Lawry & Son, pork packers
22 F M McGowan, artist
" *News* office
" David Bewicke, printer

Main st-intersects

24 Mrs Horace Aylwin
   Central Presbyterian ch

Jackson & Hunter-sts intersect

   Macnab st Presbyterian ch
58 Rev D H Fletcher
60 Lloyd Mewburn
62 Wm A Howell, druggist
64 David Newton, broker

Bold, Duke, Robinson & Hannah-sts intersect

Vacant

Herkimer-st intersects

114 Luther D Sawyer, manf
116 John T Glassco, merchant

Markland-st intersects

Macauley-st c, north side, from Glass Works, James n, to Wellington

Hughson-st intersects

25 — O'Neil, laborer
27 Joseph Volk, moulder
31 Patrick Kelly, laborer
33 Mrs Knowles
35 James Cowie, wagonmaker

John, Catharine and Mary-sts intersect

75 John Jones, bricklayer
77 Hugh Churchill, laborer
79 Thos Harrison, stonecutter
81 Hiram Jones, bricklayer
85 John Voll, glassblower
87 Mrs Ellen Jordan
89 Mrs H Wheeler
91 Geo Maxwell, laborer
93 Pat Conlon, laborer

Ferguson-ave intersects

129 W H Bodden, bricklayer
131 Timothy Murphy, laborer
133 Ed Newman, tinsmith
135 James Stevens
137 James Sweetlove, carpenter
143 John Laurie, carpenter
145 --- Rodgers, laborer

Wellington-st intersects

Macauley-st e, south side

Hamilton glassworks

Hughson-st intersects

28 James Kelly, laborer
30 Mrs Jane Miller
32 Wm Simple, laborer
34 Edward Ball, laborer
36 Michael Daley, laborer
38 Thomas Hayes, shoemaker

John-st intersects

John O'Neil, tinner

Catharine & Mary-sts intersect

80 Michael Conway, laborer
82 Michael Bullen, laborer
84 Mrs Mary Taylor
84½ Patrick Wickham, stovemtr
86 James Russell, laborer
90 Robt Nuttell
92 Wm Keegan, glassblower
96 John Wickham, laborer

Ferguson-ave intersects

122 James Maxwell, fireman
124 Moses Morris, laborer
126 John Madgett, machinist
128 Robt Gill, machinist
130 Robt Wooley, spinner
132 James Shuttle, machinist
134 Geo Hopkins, tinner
136 Wm E Carless, carter
138 David Hutton, wood worker

Wellington-st intersects

Nacaulay-st w, north side, from 331 James n to Bay

7 Thos Treavar, laborer
11 John Christie, blacksmith
13 Ed Daley, laborer
15 Ed Maloney, laborer
17 J Mahoney, laborer

Macnab-st intersects

29 Robt McWilliams, machinist
33 John Phillips, sailmaker
35 John Thornton, mechanic

37 James White, laborer
41 Peter Davis
43 Geo Rutley, machinist
45 Rev Wm Massie
47 John Fell machinist
49 — Betzner, glassblower
51 Wm Reid, carpenter

Bay-st intersetcs

Macauley-st w, south side

5 Edward Murphy, laborer
7 Thos Dreaver, laborer

Macnab-st intersects

32 Isaac Leblanc, laborer
36 Mrs Jessie Brown
40 Thos Beavers, laborer
42 Geo Foster, glassblower
44 Robt P Leslie, bookkeeper

Bay-st intersects

Macklin-st runs north from King west

Hy Eland, rag dealer
— Ross, rag dealer

Magill-st, east side, from 250 York north to Barton

4-6 John C Cooper, baby carriage manf
8 Thos Sandercock, fitter
10 Thos Grant, carpenter
15 Geo J Lazarus, turner
18 Chas Thomson, carpenter
22 James A Snider, miller
24 Mrs Wm Flock
28 James Sloan
30 C W Smith
30½ John McAulay, millwright
32 James Flynn, laborer
36 Geo C Byrnes
38 Chas B Brown, roll twiner
40 Jas Baines, fitter
42 John G Morton, fitter
44 Mrs Thos Ritchie
46 Miss Martha Laycock
50 Chas A Hopkings, hooker
52 Donald Campbell, detective

Barton-st intersects

Magill-st, west side

Arthur Boyle, chemist
11 G Soby, com traveler
13 Jas Nickling, laborer
15 Robt Martin, engineer
17 John D Morden
19 Daniel Jack, engineer
21 John Work, laborer
23 W Wagstaff, tinsmith
25 Wm Hornby, engineer
27 Wm Hunter, collector
35 Geo Dawe, blacksmith
37 Chas C Booth, heater
39 Jas R Allen, agent
45 Mrs Helen Hendry
47 Robt Gowanlock, engineer
51 Wm Newcomb, engineer
53 Wm Walker, brakeman
55 John Lawson, laborer
Barton-st intersects.

Main-ste, north side, from 25 James-st to city limits

11 J Turner & Co, wh grocers
Hughson-st intersects.
Thos Myles & Son, coal dealers
J Winer & Co
29 G H Lees & Co, mfg jewelers
29 John Quarrier, millers' agent
31 Wm Lees & Son, bakers
33 N & N W R R offices
r 33 Ham Coffee & Spice Mill Co
35 Landing warehouse
39-41 Robt Jahn, hotel
John-st intersects
43 R N Taylor & Co, druggists
49 Morgan Bros, flour mills
Royal Roller Rink
Catharine-st intersects
61 Fred Woodward, upholsterer
71 Isaac Ryall, M D
73 Samuel McKay, livery
43

77 Alexander Hay, traveler
79 Matthew Backerson, driver
81 Mrs Peter Sinnett
83 Mrs Jacob Curran
85 Wm Johnson, brushmaker
89 S H Ghent, dep clerk crown
Walnut-st intersects
101 Vacant
103 R S Beasley
107 Chas Black, merchant
109 John R Rule, cutter
115 Vacant
Cherry-st intersects
117 E Lepatourel, engineer
123 Mrs Mary Mullin
129 James Whelen
131 Wm J Reid, carpenter
131½ Wm Halliday, carpenter
133 Mrs Joseph Forde
135 Thos H Sterling
137 P W Froude, shipper
139 Isaac Culp, manf
141 Miss Isabella Lamond
143 Miss Augusta Choate
145 Wm Elliott, shoemaker
147 Wm Rodwell, painter
149 Chas Raslow, painter
151 Mrs Patrick Dermody
153 Thos O'Neill, baker
155 Thos Crawford, hat worker
Spring-st intersects
165 Wm Stewart, architect
167 Marshall Feelay, traveler
169 G S Bingham, M D
171 H S Case, druggist
173 H W Woodward, accountant
175 Wm Woods, merchant
177 H A Mackelcan, barrister
179 Wm G Proctor, manf
Wellington-st intersects
First Methodist Church
179a Rev John Kay
181 Alex Drysdale, agent
183 Edward Davis, porter
185 Mrs Mary Bain
187 Mrs Jane Christian

191 Chas Wilkes, carpenter
193 John G Cloke, merchant
195 James Macpherson, merch't
205 Mrs J T Geddes
207 Mrs Thos Jackson

Victoria-ave intersects

St Patrick's Church

East-ave intersects

219 P W Dayfoot
221 A A Stewart, bookkeeper

Emerald-st intersects

225 A I Mackenzie, surveyor customs
227 Wm S Morgan, merchant
239 J G Davis
241 W P Moore, estate agent
243 Hy Carscallen, barrister
245 Joseph Hannon

Wentworth-st intersects

Chris Magen, butcher
Jas Iredale, blacksmith
Henry Hall, traveler

Burlington-st intersects

Frank Squibb, plumber
David Snody, plumber
W J Lavery, solicitor

Toll Gate

Warren Holton, nursery
Josiah S Huntoon
Thos Beasley, city clerk
Donald Smith, tailor
Thos Barnes, farmer
M W Franey, gardener
Franey Bros, gardeners
Wm Henstridge, painter
Thos Hyland, laborer
J A Bruce & Co, seed farm

Main-st e, south side

2 Hamilton Club House
4 John Riddle, stockbroker
4 P H Simpson, barrister
4 W J Lavery, solicitor
  T S Bell, civil engineer
  R Benner, broker

6 David Newton, agent
8 C A Sadlier, barrister
10 Miss M May
12 John W Bickle, broker
14 Mrs Hy Bauer, wine mercht
16 Hamilton & Dundas R'y Co
Albert Chambers {
20 Mackelcan & Mewburn barristers
20 James Walker, ins agent
22 J Simpson & Son, brok's
}
24 Ennis & Cook, printers
24 Harold Lambe, broker

Hughson-st intersects

Pince's Square
Registry office
Court House
Æ Irving, Q C
Robertson & Robertson, barristers
Miles O'Reilly, Q C, Master's office
J E O'Reilly
G S Counsell, county clerk
John Stock, Co treasurer
Hon A McKellar, sheriff
S H Ghent, dep clerk of the crown
Waddell & Waddell, barristers
H Stevens, accountant
C W Mulligan, architect
Ninth Div Court
Hamilton Homestead Loan and Savings Society
Matthew Broadbent, engin'r

John-st intersects

John Stuart, Son & Co

Bowen-st intersects

52 Sullivan & Reddy, livery
54 T McIlwraith, coal dealer

Catharine-st intersects.

62-64 Joseph Hoodless & Son, mattrass shop
72 Casey & Sons, planing mill
76 Stables
80 Fred Boehm, tailor

86 Wm Casey sr, manf
88 Hugh Murray, customs
90 W H Rowe, printer
96 John Winer

Walnut-st intersects

102 Wm Orr, carpenter
104 W A Edwards, architect
116 D B Galbraith, customs

Cherry-st intersects

118 James McKay, grocer
120 Daniel Hunt
124 Arch Davis
126 Daniel Galvin, tanner
132 Geo W Kerry
134 Vacant
136 Freeman Slaght, porter
138 Mrs Mary A Cuttriss
138½ Mrs Catharine Haines
140 Vacant
142½ James Holmes, shoemaker
142-4 Chas Mills, grocer

Spring-st intersecss

146 Wm Gilmore, butcher
154 T H Wilson, M D
158 J Cummings, tax collector

Wellington-st intersects

St Thomas' Church

West-ave intersects

166 J B House. agent
168 P Grossman, music **dealer**
170 C W **Meakins**, brush **manfr**

Victoria-ave intersects

172 Wm Turner
174 W G Moore
178 N D Galbraith, grocer

East-ave intersects

182 Alex McLagan
184 Mrs N F Bireley

Emerald st intersects

186 David Morton, soap manfr
188 Wm Barr
192 M Brennan, merchant
194 Jonathan Davis

196 W R Reasnor

Erie-ave intersects

198 Daniel Kelly
200 Mrs Daniel Kerrie
208 John Porter, gardener
214 Alex **Bain, hackman**
220 Wm Blair

Wentworth-st intersects

Henry Blanford, gilder
Thos Marshall, laborer
John Lamont, gardener

Burlington-st intersects

Mrs Andrew Harper
Fred Thorne, moulder
Maurice Begley, brakeman
Geo S Herne, farmer
John Meinn, laborer

Argo-st intersects

Albert McNair, clerk
Mrs Osborne Allan
Mrs Maria Quinn
Wm Smith, gardener
Robt Powell, butcher
Mrs E Crockett, toll-keeper
Mrs Andrew Skinner
Geo Rutherford, druggist
Ed Mitchell, banker

Blake-st intersects.

John Eastwood, bookseller
J W Murton, coal dealer

Springer-ave intersects

Lewis Springer
J T Middleton, marble dlr
Anthony McDonagh, gard'r
Arthur Nugent, dairyman
Philander Barnes
Geo Willcock, farmer
R R Gage, barrister
The Children's Home
Simon James, Delta hotel

Main-st w, north side, from 36 James s to city limits

2 Jas Hiscox, chimney sweep
4 Jas Beardwell, carpenter

6 Vacant
8 A W Noble, chair caner
  Centenary Church
10 Geo Read, hackman
12 Mrs Chas Magill
14 Mrs A Henderson
16 Vacant

Macnab-st intersects

18 C VanNorman Emory, M D
20 Mrs Wm McDonald, board'g
22 John H Caddy
24 Mrs John W Pounden
26 Mrs Thos Connolly, board'g
28 Alfred Bowditch, clerk
30 Wm King, merchant tailor
32 Henry King, hostler

Charles-st intersects

36 Miss Lucy Bautz
38 E A Gaviller, M D

Park-st intersects

40 Thos Cook, founder
42 Daniel V Mott, canvasser
44 Mrs John Davis
46 Jas H Davidson, traveler
48 John H Fernside, clerk P O
50 W W Summers
52 Thos Kirby, painter
54 Wm A Venator & Son, turners
56 58 Aitchison & Co, planing mill
60 Joseph Jeffery city laundry
62 Wm B Stuart, merchant
64 Miss H A Wilkins, music teacher
66 John Morrison, grocer

Bay-st intersets

68 Wm Herman, merchant
70 George Sharp
72 Vacant
74 Vacant
76 Vacant
78 Cyrus King, grocer
80 Wm P Robarts, bank Ham
80½ Colin McRae, traveler
82 E Martin, cabinetmaker

84 Vacant
  Collegiate institute

Caroline-st intersects

100 Thos C Livingstone, surveyor
102 John M Gibson, barrister
104 Alex Hamilton, druggist
108 Peter C Blaicher, druggist
112 Geo Dempsey, agent
114 W J Lindsay, clerk

Hess-st intersects

116 Alex Murray, merchant

Queen-st intersects

138 Duncan Fitzgerald, collector
140 John Skerritt, warehouseman
142 Adam Clark, plumber
144 Fred Hooper, ins agent
148 T C Mewburn, insp customs
150 Vacant
152 Fred W Tribute, collector

Ray-st intersects

154 Henry New, manf
156 John Stuart, merchant
158 Wm Somerville sr, merchant
160 Vacant
162 D J Campbell, ins inspector
164 John Lennox, merchant
166 Wm F Mann, carpenter
168 Chas H Sutherland, C E
174 John Montgomery, grocer

Pearl st-intersects

  Vacant lots
  Ed Harrison, coal dealer

Locke-st intersects

184 E H Wands, carpenter
186 Hilton Loucks, harnessmkr
188 — Wilson, laborer
190 John Pausell, laborer
192 Mrs Isaac Page
196 Carl Kreiger, laborer

Margaret st intersects

226 Geo H Richardson, miller
228 John Ripley, carpenter
228 Mrs Eliza New

New-st intersects
250 Samuel New, carriage manf
Garth-st intersects

Main-st w, south side

1 Ross Bros, painters
1 Wm Johnston, carpenter
7 Wm C Harvey, merchant
11 W H Gillard & Co, grocers
15 Julius Winckler, machinist
17 Ed Evans, laborer

Macnab-st intersects

21 Albert Pain, merchant
23 Mrs Mary J Field
27 C K Domville, loco supt G T R
31 Dr Henry T Ridley

Charles-st intersects

35 James Robertson, merchant
37 James Leslie, M D

Park-st intersects

39 John Guggisberg, manf
41 Alfred Clark, accountant
43 Mrs C E Bateman
45 H & J Dow, wood, etc
55 Mrs Alexander Wright
57 W G Dunn & Co, spice mills

Bay-st intersects

67 Geo Lavelle, broommaker
67 John Foote
69 Henry Death, laborer
69 Chas Hurton, caretaker
71 Mrs Wm Leith
73 Miss Sarah A Feast, dressm'r
75 Dr Geo E Husband
79 Wm E LaChance, traveler
81 Mrs E Wilson, dressmaker
83 G Nielson, clerk
85 R D Kennedy, architect
87 Walter Spencer, organ buildr
89 Theodore Rutter, stove moulder
91 Wm Diack, miller
93 Vacant

Caroline-st intersects

101 Vacant
103 Fred G Snider
105 R Thos Steele, music teacher
107 Rev Jos W A Stewart, B A
109 Geo H Armstrong
111 Robt Campbell
113 James H Mills

Hess-st intersects

127 Vacant
   Primary school

Queen-st intersects

141 John McCaffie, merchant
145 Thos Lees, merchant
147 Robt Laidlaw, photographer
147½ James Slater, merchant
149 G W Baker, agent
131 Wm H Mills

Ray-st intersects

155 Geo Bible, contractor
157 W B Palmer, com trav
159 Mrs Eliza Land
161 O Hudson, cabinetmaker
163 John Maxwell, painter
167 Thos Keane, grocer

Pearl-st intersects

169 John N Barnard, manf
171 Benj Swenerton, com trav
175 W S Lumgair, agent
177 Wm C Brend, fitter
179 Geo Kennedy, carpenter
181 Ed Harrison, wood merch't
183 Robt Jones, plasterer
181 Chas Mann, mason
183 Ered Schadel, blacksmith
185 Geo N Webb, shoemaker

Locke-st intersects

   John C Bolegan, grocer
189 Fred Linas, laborer
191 Vacant
193 John Davis, brickmaker
197 Thos Frowley, laborer
199 Geo Hempstock, butcher
201 Andrew Miller, laborer
203 Wm Cox, engineer

CITY OF HAMILTON.

205 Chas A Plastow, carpenter
207 Mrs I Hume, seamstress
209 Thos Leivington, laborer
211 Thos Mapham, plasterer
211½ Mrs Andrew Muir

Poulette-st intersects

213 Stephen Bull, laborer
215 — Taylor, laborer
217 Philip Saunders, laborer
219 Jos Jackson, blacksmith
221 Geo W Frid, brickmaker
221 Mrs Thos Riley
223 Matthew Murphy, polisher
227 Lawrence Ruppell, driver
229 Geo R Alladice, stonecutter
231 Mrs James New

Garth-st intersects

Leonard Foster, potter
Geo Frid's brick yard
Geo Brannigan, brickmaker
Geo Jenkins, cabinetmaker

Maple-st, north side, from Locke south to Garth

Public School
Ed Walters, potter
Wm Penny, machinist
Vacant
Ed Stephenson, laborer
John T Laing, fitter
Vacant
Andrew S Peters, laborer
John Fair, laborer
Wm Sealey, laborer

Maple-st, south side

Chas Bevan, laborer
John Bell, machinist
Thos Dunford, laborer
David Duncan, machinist
Wm Lavers, carpenter
Patrick Conners, teamster
Ezekiel Morton, laborer
D Messer, tailor
Vacant
David Hobbs, laborer

Maple-ave from Stinson to Mountain

Jos O'Donnell, clerk P O
James Carson, moulder

Margaret-st, east side, from 293 King w to Main

1 James Perrin, laborer
3 Joseph Shipley, potter
5 Mrs M Brand
9 Thos Fee, hackman
15 Mrs James Walsh
17 C J Kemp, fireman
19 John Morley, blacksmith
23 Robt Wade, laborer
25 Wm Smith
27 Michael Gallivan, laborer
29 Vacant
31 Lemuel Haines, potter
33 Michael Gallivan, laborer
35 — Madden, laborer

Main st-intersects

Margaret-st, west side

2 Richard Ailles, bricklayer
4 Wm T Manser, brickmaker
6 Thos Keller, agent
8 Mrs Adam Logan
10 R E Woodruff, piano tuner
12 Jeremiah King, potter
12½ Wm Hearn, watchman
14 Vacant
16 A E Smith, mason
18 W B Sheridan, blacksmith
20 John Gentle
22 Vacant
24 Mrs Wm Gillespie
26 John Modlin
28 Geo Williams, plasterer
30 Vacant
32 Vacant
34 Vacant
36 Kennedy Connor, shoemaker

Main-st intersects

STREET DIRECTORY. 343

Maria-st, north side, from James s, east to Wellington

Vacant lot

Hughson-st intersects

19 J W Jones, barrister
23 Geo French, gardener
25 Mrs A L Meikle
27 Mrs Chas Ambrose

John-st intersects.

31 Thos J Watson, policeman

Catharine-st intersects

47 Robt Cruickshank, manf
49 Mrs Wm Harris
51 Wm Mahony, laborer
55 Alex Anderson, laborer
57 Wm Kell
59 Michael Whelen, laborer
61 Chas Williams, carriage trimmer
63 Mrs Ann Lavelle
65 Robt Hunter, watchman

Walnut-st intersects

75 Vacant
77 Albert Ryan, shoemaker
79 Mrs C Munn
81 Mrs Connell Smith

Cherry-st intersects

93 Thos Curtis, tailor
97 Vacant
99 Mrs Michael Sullivan
101 Martin Rowan, carter
103 Geo Stacey, laborer
105 Alfred Hildreth, laborer

Aurora-st intersects

111 A Doyle, laborer
115 Geo D Rioch, printer
117 Joseph Dillon, laborer
119 Mrs Thos Kerruish

Wellington-st intersects

Maria-st, south side

8 Mrs Robt McKay

Hughson-st intersects

20 Mrs H C Davis
22 F J Rastrick, architect
Church of Ascension

John-st intersects

Vacant

Catharine-st intersects

40 Mrs Thos Hockady
42 Mrs Isabella Webber
44 John A Webber, clerk
52 Miss Minnie O'Kelly
56 Wm Macfarlane, machinist
58 John McDonald, laborer
60 Hy Wooldridge, coachman
60 Wm F Mills
62 Vacant
64 Alfred F Webber, builder
66 Robt Carr, laborer
68 Nelson Walton, butcher
70 Wm Kelk, music teacher

Walnut st intersects

72 John Shea, machinist
74 C Donovan, inspector
76 Robt Rowan, teamster
78 Hy Callowhill, tinsmith
80 John B Lewis
82 Wm Hallisey, policeman
Wm Morris grocer

Cherry-st intersects

86 Patrick Padden, laborer
88 Daniel Barrett, fireman
90 Samuel Coulston, blacksmith
92 Mrs Eliza Murray
94 Wm Burgess, laborer
96 Timothy Sheehan, laborer
104 D O'Connor, laborer
106 Patrick Connell, laborer
108 Wm C Wilde, printer
110 Fred Clark, laborer

Aurora-st intersects

112 P Hayes, laborer
114 Vacant
116 Patrick Kennedy, moulder
118 Wm Aspell, agent
120 Jos Mortimer, stove fitter
122 Ed Collyer, miller

124 Mrs P F Madden
126 Hiram Burges, pedler

Wellington-st intersects

Market-st, north side, from 31 Macnab n to Ray

4 Philp & Son, saddlers
6 E Gorman, barber
8 C Kerner, saloon
10-14 Simon Lalor, hotel
16 Hiram E Bush, pumpmaker
18 Market Stables
20 J H Craig, V S
24 S H Pocock, saw manf
26-28 Imperial Straw Works

Park-st intersects

34 J H Craig, vet surgeon
36 Mrs M O'Herron, boarding
38 John H Kennedy, buyer
40 Mrs Jane Smith
42 Siegmond Loewy, confectio'r
44 Geo Pyle, machinist
46 John Anderson
48-54 John Roger, blacksmith

Bay-st intersects

58 Dr Anderson
62 Washington Tufford, driver
64 Samuel Aikins, driver
66 Thos McCall, driver
68 Matthew Whitney, driver
70 Hendrie & Co, shops
72 Geo Goodale, laborer
74 Napoleon Guillett, tobacco roller
76 John Baxter, driver
78 Vacant
80 Dennis Gleason, agent
82 Fred Swarz, tobacconist
84 Mrs James Gilchrist
86 David Searlett, tobacconist

Caroline-st intersects

88 John Wilmot, scalemaker
90 Neil Johnson, laborer
92 Wm Brass, carpenter
94 Jacob Lowery

96 Primary School
98 Rev August Spies
    Evangelical Church
100 T S Bell, civil engineer
102 James Flett, mason
104 John Brundle, tinsmith
106 Matern Obermeyer, piano maker
108 Hy Phillips, machinist
110 James Fulton, teamster

Hess-st intersects

114 Walter Anderson, bookkeep'r
116 Wm P Giles, merchant
118 J B Cook
120 R E Gallagher, principal Canada Business College
122 Mrs Ellen McKenzie
124 Mrs James Horsburg
126 Rev D W Snider, Methodist
128 Wm Harper, printer
130 Jas Stewart, plumber
132 John Stewart, bookkeeper

Queen-st intersects

140 James F Holland, boilermakr
142 Joseph Gibson, driver
144 John Shields, laborer
150 Patrick O'Neil
154 Miss Maggie Collins
156 Wm Harper, engineer
158 James Fairclough, carpenter
160 Hugh McLauchlan, horse trainer
162 Mrs Annie Bailey
164 Thos Shields, blacksmith

Ray-st intersects

Market-st, south side

1 Robt Berryman, wool dealer
3 T H McKenzie, wool dealer
5 N Bowman, commission
7 John D Carroll
7½ Vacant
11 Russell & Dunn, gen agents
13 Donald Campbell, livery
    Snider, Lake & Bailey, millers

Park-st intersects

29 Rich Morgan, carriage trim'r
31 Robt N Lucas, moulder
33 Matthews' livery stabl
35 Miss Minnie Matthews
37 Geo H Mathews, livery
39 Joseph Quarry, traveler
41 Tuckett's warehouse
43 Thos Wilson, city foreman

Bay-st intersects

63 Geo Schadel, brewer
69 Hendrie & Co's stables
71 Robt Spencer, driver
73 Arch Whyte, foreman
75 John Marriott, packer
77 Thos Moffat, mail carrier
79 Vacant
81 Geo Brock, driver
83 Robt Robson, driver
87 Thos Clappison, bookseller
89 Hiram E Bush, pump maker

Caroline-st intersects

91 Mrs James Caldwell
93 John Billington, shoemaker
95 I Armstrong, grain buyer
97 Thos E Leather, traveler
99 Chas Judd, clerk P O
101 Z Hemphill, agent
103 Chas Huton, tailor
105 Mrs Patrick McAuliffe
107 Wm T Brown, machinist
109 Hamilton Cooper, manf
111 Mrs John McMillan

Hess-st ends

117 Mrs Benjamin H Scriver
119 John Morty, laborer
121 David J Fenton, plater
123 David Souter, carpenter
125 Mrs Olivia Daley
127 James F Harper, mail clerk
129 H T Drope, printer
131 J W Taft, fireman
133 Wm Smith, packer

Queen-st intersects

Market Sqare, from 17 James north to Macnab

1 McGregor & Parke, druggists
2 P Ronan, flour and feed
3 Laut Tea Co
4 Wm Fell, engraver
5 J & C J Brennan, grocers
6 R Evans & Co, clothiers
7 London China House
7 W & J Morden, produce and commission
8 W F Webster, flour and feed
6 Carpenter Bros, grocers
10 Cyrus King, grocer
10 Ontario Shirt Co
11 J Lucas, restaurant
12 Mrs Benj Lester, hotel
13 Eli Rymal, hotel
14 Harris Bros, bakers
15 F L Cherrier, grocer
16 Thos W Scott, EmpireHouse
17 Patrick Crilly, tailor
18-19 M D Healey & Co, dry goods
20 Hugh McKeown, harness maker

Macnab-st intersects

Markland-st, from James s to Garth, south side

Mrs D Nicholson

Ontario-st commences

J H Park, merchant
Mrs M R Logie

Bay-st intersects

25 Wm Ainslie, trunk maker
27 Benj Brass, carpenter

Hilton-st intersects

W R Job, shoemaker
E E Taylor, clerk
Philip Waddleton, tailor

Caroline-st intersects

W J Locke, salesman
Geo Jones, carpenter

Thos Briers, painter
Bruce-st commences
David Philip, machinist
Wm Lennox, laborer
Hess and Queen-sts intersect
Locke-st intersects
John Unsworth, painter
Cyrus Oliver, cutter
Peter Balfour jr, ins agent
John Heritage, tailor
Kent and Locke-sts intersect
Dennis Kelly, machinist
Mrs Thos Watts
G E Russell, harnessmaker
Ernest Smith, baker
Geo Collis, coppersmith
John Hahan, mason
Chas Bishop, carpenter
Wm Marsh, blacksmith
Mrs J W Korn, furrier
Wm Coombs, moulder
Geo Coombs, moulder
Garth-st intersects

Markland-st, north side
2 Ernest Door, coachman
Macnab-st ends
Miss Agnes Irvine
Park-st ends
Wm Wallace
Bay-st intersects
30 John Walford, packer
36 James C Taylor, merchant
38 Thos Copeland, carpenter
40 Wm Dillon, coachman
Caroline-st intersects
38 David Morton sr
40 John Mills, builder
42 Wm Beare, dairyman
44 A W Semmens, manf
46 P J Thomas, contractor
Wm C Burrows, carpenter
Richard Graham, dyer

Miss Mary B Miller
Hess-st intersects
Mrs Robt West
Queen-st intersects
Geo J Williams
Joseph Mason, caretaker
John Nicholson, wood dealr
Kent-st intersects
John Bradley, carpenter
Locke-st intersects
John J Fitzpatrick, painter
N Power
— Howard
Thos Towers, carpenter
H Reinholt carpenter
Mrs C Reinholt
Mrs Geo Butler
Peter Hillman, carpenter
Garth-st intersects

Mary-st, east side, from 124 King e to the Bay
8 G B Smith, wood yard
10 Burn & Robinson Manf Co
16 Vacant
18 Vacant
20 James Arthur
A Weir, hotel
King Wm-st intersects
26 James Way, painter
34 C C Baird, merchant
38 Wm Smye, collarmaker
Rebecca-st intersects
46 Chas Wagner, shoemake
Public School
Wilson-st commences
68 Bain & Colville, machinists
68 John Radigan, tinsmith
68 John B Freed, manf
70 Vacant
72 J A Laidlaw, bookkeeper
74 Chas F Gallagher, traveler

76 J Carruthers, flour dealer
78 John C Henry, teamster
80 Wm Harell, baker
82 Ferdinand Weimer, japanner

Kelly-st intersects

84-88 Laidlaw Manf Co

Cannon-st intersects

106 Geo Bilton, soda water
108 W J F Gordon, merchant
110 Hy Magee, saddler
112 Geo Dench, freight agent
114 Mrs Wm Wagner
116 Wm McAndrew, printer
118 Vacant
122 Guether **Voelker**, laborer
124 Chas Holland, agent
128 James Kingdon, tailor
134 James Ennis, printer
136 Mrs Geo McKay
138 Alex McKay
140 J Brown, foreman
140½ Vacant
142 Richard Pearce, grocer

Robert-st intersects

148 John Stevens, baker
148½ Maurice McKenna, labor'r
152 Mrs Daniel McCallum
154 James Sturdy, foreman
156 E T Richards, packer
158 Michael Turnbull, manf
160 John Home, tinsmith
162 Thos Gully
166 Jos Hopkins, weaver
r 166 Thos Love, shipper
168 R T Smith, baggageman
170 Wm Rymal, teamster
172 Ed Fearman, plasterer
172 F L Cherrier, grocer

Barton-st intersects

180 Wm McDonald, timekeeper
184-206 Hamilton Cotton Co
   John Holt, carder
210 Jos Fairley, carpenter
   G T R Bridge
238 Alex Main & Son, rope manfs

Strachan-st intersects

240 James Gordon, clerk
242 T H Buckingham, mechanic
244 Peter Gorman, blacksmith
246 Wm Thompson, blacksmith
252 Alex Hunter, laborer

Simcoe-st intersects

254 John Lynch, laborer

Ferrie-st intersects

264 C J Kerr, machinist
266 Mrs Thos Davis
270 Alfred Bates, carpenter
272 Wm Gray, weaver

Picton-st intersects

276 Peter Carroll, carpenter
278 Thos Mullins, carpenter
280 Samuel Mines, moulder
282 Chris Conley, boilermaker
284 Wm Wickham, stovefitter
288 Geo Kiernan, agent
290 James McDonald, carpenter
292 — Riddell, carpenter

Macauley-st intersects

   Albert Westmore, grocer

Wood-st intersects

   Timo hy Holland, laborer

Mary-st, west side

15 Geo Garson, wood dealer

King Wm-st intersects

25 John Watson, cattle doctor
27 Thos Stevenson, cabinetmkr
29 Mrs Hy Dixon
31 Isaac Stevenson, polisher
33 P Armstrong, carriagemaker
   J H Smith, hotel keeper

Rebecca-st intersects

   H Hill, butcher
43 Wm Limage, cutter
45 Geo H Milne, builder
47 Thos J Holland, hay dealer
49 Amos Johnston, huckster
51 Jos Chine, laborer
53 Harvey Haller, laborer

348   CITY OF HAMILTON.

55 W W Holden, clerk
57 Fred Gerbrand, tailor
57½ Geo Buckingham, tanner
59 Mrs Susan Sweeney
61 Mrs Jane Daniels
63 Hugh Hennessey, blacksm'h
67 Thos Holland, hay dealer
75 James Hunter, porter
77 Fred Green, merchant
79 S D Biggar, barrister
81 Hamilton Whip Co, limited
83 James Adams, packer
85 Mrs Wm Mowat
87 John W Noble, messenger
89 Thos Laidlaw, clerk
91 Patrick Kennedy
93 John Morris, laborer
95 James Fitzgerald, laborer
97 Fred C Locke, mechanic
99 Wm Critchley, teamster

Cannon-st intersects

111 Richard W Seldon, grocer
115 Vacant
117 Mrs E Barrett
119 John A Riche, druggist
121 Peter Fitzpatrick, carpenter
123 John Marcham, moulder
125 Mrs Wm Johnson

Robert-st intersects

143 Mrs Francis King
145 David Gilbert, baker
147 Donald Warren, sexton
149 Hy Mathews, moulder
151 David Coulter, policeman
153 Thos Bale
157 Duncan Brown, bookkeeper
159 Stephen Searle
161 Alfred Crowe, machinist
163 Vacant
165 John Farr, teamster
167 John Hayes, stovemounter
169 Wm Buttenham, teamster
171 Vacant
173 James Sims, moulder
175 Geo T King
177 Alex Ogg, grocer
179 H Little, grocer

Barton-st intersects

179 Mrs Alice McLean
181 John Halloran, merchant
183 Mrs Janet Roag
185 Ed Mines, traveler
187 James Mines, moulder
189 Vacant
191 E J Thompson, traveler
193 John Maden, spinner
195 Thos Burns, bookkeeper
197 Martin Byrne, machinist
199 James Dalton, laborer
201 John Bain, laborer
203 Miss Mary Grace
205 John Marshall, flax dresser
207 Robt Leitch, blacksmith
209 Eugene Haliot, foreman
211 Vacant
213 Wm Quinlan, tinsmith
215 John Connor, teamster

Murray-st intersects

225 J Zingsheim, cabinet manf
227 Arthur Board, stovemounter
229 Wm Dundon, laborer
233 Peter Connor, teamster
   G T R Bridge

Strachan-st intersects

243 Samuel Holt, carder
245 Fred G Johnson, mechanic
245½ Francis X King, ropemaker
247 Thos Kelly, shoemaker
249 P Crotty, carpenter

Simcoe-st intersects

255 James Blake, grocer
257 Geo Askew, shoemaker
259 John Pomford, loom fixer
271 Vacant
273 Robt Filkin, laborer
275 Vacant

Ferrie-st intersects

273 John M Ferguson, laborer
275 Mrs Wm Jones
277 James Ryan, track layer
281 John Wright, agent

Picton & Macaulay-sts intersect
   Vacant lots

Wood-st intersects

Merrick-st, north side, from 55 James n to Bay

2 Vacant
6 John Rowan, barber
8-12 Royal Hotel
14 City Directory Office
14 The Trade Association
16-18 W Goering & Co, wine and spirits
20-22 James Johnston, auction'r
24 Robt Hunter, auctioneer
26 James A Harvey, printer
26 Chas Lawry, hide dealer
28 Market View Hotel
30 Canada Furniture Co
32 Hamilton Laundry
34 Wm J Gilmore, furniture
36 Hy Simon, cigarmaker
Gospel Hall
36 Vacant
38 Vacant

Macnab-st intersects

62 James Simpson

Park st intersects

72 A G Miles, plumber
74 Geo Bicknell, feather dyer
76 Hannaford Bros, plasterers
78 Mrs Malcolm Munro
80 Abner Fraser, bookkeeper
82 John Faillie, bookkeeper
84 Geo Henderson
86 R A Allardice & Co, **furniture**
90 Alex Calder, druggist
92 D G Storms, M D
94 John W Sangster
96-98 Hurd & Roberts, **marble** works

Bay-st intersects

Merrick-st, south side

1-7 Billiard rooms
Market Hall

Macnab-st intersects

47-9 Thos Robinson, hotel
53 Flamboro House
57 Wm B Garner, blacksmith

57 Samuel Howard, carpenter
59 Thos Clohecy, harnessmaker
61 Mrs Ann Roman
63 Mrs Catharine Murray
67 G & J Shoots, painters

Park-st intersects

71 Webber Ressey, **produce**
73 Jos Bigar, livery
75 John Walsh, shoemaker
77 Geo Reid, carriagemaker
79 Thos Evans, pedler
81 Robt Weston, shoemaker
83-5 Alex Campbell, grocer
87 Vacant
89 A Calder, druggist

York-st intersects

Mill st, north side, from 95 Caroline n west to Hess

2 Daniel McGowan
4 Mrs John Ellis
6 W Sterrett, policeman GTR
8 Elijah Beckerson, teamster
12 Solomon Frank, laborer
10 Wm Coutts, teamster
14 Fred Dauberville, scalemkr
16 Wm **Williamson, teamster**
18 Sam Walsh, tobacco **roller**

Hess-st intersects

Mill-st e, south side

1 Daniel Durham, axemaker
1½ Patrick Fahey, laborer
3 Wm Wheaton, mechanic
5 Robt L Cook, mechanic
7 Wm H Childs, machinist
9 Wm Ede, clerk
11 Mrs John Mount
13 John Ellat, laborer
15 Mrs John Dryland
17 Wm Butler, brakeman
19 Wm Laing, conductor

Hess-st intersects

Mulberry-st, north side, from 159 James n to Railway

6 Adam Irving, picture dealer
14 David Brown, builder

16 E Wright, supt
18 J Madigan, foreman
18½ — Garrety, laborer
20 Vacant
22 Philip Crier, shoemaker
24 Felix Guimet, shoemaker
26 Henry S Metman, laundry

Macnab-st intersects

30 Walter Bruce, brakeman
32 Vacant
34 Horace Ringrose, stovemou'r
38 John Slaughter
40 John Dingman, carpenter
44 James Somerville, painter

Park-st intersects

62 Edmund Lane, carpenter
64 Thos Enwright, stoker
66 Jos Champagne, harnessmkr
   New gasometer
82 Henry Waybrant, machinist
84 James Wright, mariner
86 David Betzner, laborer

Bay-st intersects

P Grant & Son's brewery

Railway-st intersects

Mulberry-st, south side

7 John Moriarty, laborer
9 John Moriarty, laborer
11 Mrs M J Cusick
13 John Bradley, contractor
15 Arch Coutts, hackman
17 Frank Kavanagh
19 Alex F Hendry, accountant
21 Wm H Margetts, lithograph'r

Macnab-st intersects

29 Thos Meegan, moulder
33 John Couture, shoemaker
35 Vacant
37 Mrs W J Taylor
39 Geo Mansfield, engineer
41 Ed Kavanagh, moulder

Park-st intersects

66-67 Hamilton Gas Light Co

Bay-st intersects

103 Wm Goodyer, malster

Railway st intersects

Murray-st east, north side, from 228 James north to Wellington

7 Robt Walker, car driver
9 Thos Littlewood, brakeman
15 Geo Anderson, carpenter
17 Patrick Dillon, laborer

Hughson-st intersects

25 Robt Jackson, weaver
27 Wm Silver, manf
29 Wm Forsyth, tinsmith
31 Wm Omand jr, machinist
33 Vacant
35 Isaiah Beer, builder

John-st intersects

Vacant lots

Catharine-st intersects

87 James Daly
91 A M Forster, manf
93 James Copley, carder

Mary-st intersects

93a Mrs Ellen Harvey
95 Wm Seaton, machinist
91 John Webb, builder
101 John Smiley, teamster
103 A J Cox, cork cutter

Wellington-st intersects

Murray-st e, south side

10 Wm Potter, ropemaker
12 Andrew Andrews
16 James Greenless, moulder

Hughson-st intersects.

20 Geo Burton, engraver

John-st intersects

74 James Blair, train despatch'r
76 Louis Fraser, traveler

STREET DIRECTORY. 351

80 Wm Conley, laborer
82 Mrs Wm Seelbach

*Catharine, Mary & Ferguson-ave
intersect*

J Pett, sheepskins
96 Vacant
98 Geo Niblock, teamster
100 Patrick McBride
102 Geo Maxstead, laborer

Wellington-st intersects

Murray-st west, north side, from 213 James north to Bay

12 H B Witton, canal inspector
16 Mrs Capt Ed Zealand

Macnab-st intersects

28 Wm Omand, machinist
30 Wm Fardy, printer
32 John Edmunds, stableman
Primary school
42 Vacant
44 H A White, electric instrument maker
46 J G McIntyre, boilermaker
48 Robt Archibald, machinist
50 David Porteous

Bay-st intersects

Murray-st w, south side

7 Vacant
9 Mrs John H Greer
11 Walter Urry, barber
13 Fred H Hoffer, traveler
15 Mrs Robt Hanning
23 Wm Yaldon, hotel

Macnab-st intersects

41 Geo Moore, restaurant
45 Philip Peer, carpenter

Park-st intersects

Napier-st, north side, from 43 Bay n, west to Locke

8 T J Derrick, tobacco roller

10 Vacant
14 Patrick Moran, laborer
16 Robt Holmes, machinist
18 Robt Edwards, tinsmith
20 Hy Bennett, foreman
22 Hugh Callaghan, pavior
30 Chas Drew, tinsmith

Caroline-st intersects

48 Geo Thatcher, laborer
50 Jas Connell, tobacco roller
52 Benj Myers, engineer
54 I McMichael, whip maker
58 J Edmonstone, conductor

Hess-st intersects

Mrs Edwin B Feast, grocer
74 Mrs John Hardiker
76 Mrs Hannah Johnson
78 Geo H Lees, merchant
80 Peter McBeth, contractor
82 James Thompson, moulder
88 James Young, bookkeeper

Queen-st intersects

112 Mrs Jos Fletcher
114 Julius Breternitz, tailor
116 James Grice
118 Sinclair McBeth
120 Alfred Hipkins, printer
122 David Lowe, wire worker
124 Geo Daniels, engineer
126 Mrs James Hobson

Ray-st intersects

150 Donald McKenzie
152 James Murdoch, policeman
154 Wm Doran, carter
156 Mrs Elena Gourlay
158 Robt Ferguson, printer
160 James Brennan, grocer
162 Mrs Douglas Lawrason
164 John Memory, machinist

Pearl st-intersects

172 Zion Sunday School
174 S Eckbrusch, weaver
178 Geo Small, potter
180 Mrs Gilbert Henderson
182 Mrs Mary Ackworth

186 Hy T Lovell, fireman
188 John Bayne, moulder
Locke-st intersects

Napier-st, south side

9 John McLeod, printer
11 No 4 Police station
17 John Hall, laborer
19 Chris Rieger, laborer
21 Mark Pulling
23 Mrs Caleb Fonger
31 Ed Kinsella, engineer
33 Mrs John Hagerty
35 John Leepine, laborer
37 Thos Moylan, shoemaker
Caroline-st intersects
45 Robert Woods, cabinetmak'r
47 James Steedman, machinist
53-55 James Baker
59 Thos I Dixon, manf
61 Robt F Keays, land agent
63 Mrs T C Webber, dressmkr
65 Thos Cuff, engineer
67 Thos Fraser, butcher
69 Edward Dryland, painter
Hess-st intersects
71 H Fisher, machinist
73 Jacob S Rymal
75 Vacant
77 Mrs James Horan, laundress
79 James Weir, baker
87 Vacant
89 Aaron Carr, messenger
91 John O Carpenter, merchant
93 J M Dingwall, fitter
95 Thos P Lovell, marbleizer
Queen-st intersects
103 Robt Wilson, fireman
105 Daniel Wrigley, machinist
107 Thos Cookson, machinist
111 Wm Cole, butcher
113 Wm Payne, nailer
117 G Hilderbrandt, laborer
119 Chas Eikoff, cigarmaker
121 Rev F Coleman
125 James McDermott, laborer

127 Elias I Foster
129 Vacant
131 Wm Crawford, laborer
135 Vacant
137 Geo Larmer, tinsmith
139 Andrew Keenan, laborer
Ray-st intersects
157 Joseph Faulknor, builder
Pearl and Little Wellington-sts intersect
173 H Welsher, carpenter
175 Geo Mitchell, machinist
179 Mrs Frederick Elley
181 James Smith, rougher
183 Mrs Wm J Debus
185 Stephen Hurd, laborer
Little Peel & Locke sts intersect

Nelson-ave, north side, commences at Queen s, and runs west to Locke

2 John Harrison, barrister
2½ Irving Crossley, merchant
4 E E Kittson, barrister
8 L C Smith, barrister
18 Joseph R Mead, manf
Kent-st intersects
26 Henry J Healey, collector
28 Egerton Healey, traveler
30 Geo Catchpole, salesman
38 Vacant
Locke-st intersects
1 Vacant
3 T L Whatley, **clerk**
5 Vacant
7 Geo N Hobbs, excise officer
9 Daniel McCarthy, steward
11 Thos E Horne, spice miller
19 John Rankine, teller
23 Mrs J Stuart
25 Joseph Kent, contractor
Kent-st intersects
31 Jas Bicknell jr, accountant

43 Vacant

Locke-st intersects

Nelson-st, commences at 20 Pearl south, runs west to Locke

2 Frank McCusker, merchant
4 J Taylor, laborer
6 Thos H Taylor, bookkeeper
9 Vacant
11 John W Frid, brickmaker

New-st, from King west to Main

7 Frank Osborne, laborer
8 Bristol Barber, laborer
9 Wm Wheaton, laborer
10 Chas Beveridge, carpenter
11 Geo Southworth, laborer
12 Thos Pumfrey, laborer
13 Geo Harrison, machinist
15 Robt Neil, laborer

Nightingale-st, north side from 31 Steven to Wentworth

4 Mrs Wm Woodall
6 John Mellon, builder
8 James H Dunn, mechanic
  Thos Kerr, moulder

Wentworth-st intersects

Nightingale-st, south side

5 Geo Duncan, laborer
7 Wm White, blacksmith
9 Wm Ralph, glass stainer
11 Hy Longhurst, glass stainer
13 John H Smith, clerk
15 Samuel Harvey, carpenter
17 James Goodale, laborer

Wentworth-st intersects

B Anson, laborer
Mrs John Draper
John Landers, laborer

Oak-ave (formerly Chisholm street) east side, from 225 Cannon e, north to South

Wm Blair, grocer
2 Mrs Wm Long
2½ Mrs Catharine Gage
4 Michael Dunbar, carpenter
8 Thos Anderson, baker
10 Oliver Simons, laborer
12 Wm Woodhall, builder
14 John Smith, stonemason
16 Jos Cole
18 Fred Arnedt, tailor
20 Wm Seal, laborer
22 Wm Klingbeil, butcher
30 Wm Eaves, laborer
32 Mrs Adolphus Lewis
58 Fred Hunt, stovemounter
60 Townsend Lyons, laborer
60½ Wm Sullivan, shoemaker
62 Frank Deeley, poulterer
64 Thos Irwin, laborer
66 Wm Lewis, plasterer
68 Mrs James Lamrock
70 Mrs Francis McGargle
72 Sandford Casey, laborer
74 Frank Campaign, blacksmith

Barton-st intersects

Oak-ave, west side

1 Wm J Moore, painter
3 Patrick Dunbar, carpenter
3½ Ed Flannery, moulder
5 Erskine Smith, bricklayer
5½ John Smith, machinist
7 Wm McCoomb, moulder
9 John Connor, sawyer
11 Hy Myers, engineer
21 Thos Mullens, carpenter
23 Jos Smith, teamster
25 John Arthur, polisher
27 Roderick McMillan, carpen'r
29 Robt Menary, milk dealer
31 Jas Millman, carpenter
33 Jas Lyng, carpenter
37 Thos Beardmore, brassfinishr
39 Chas Berry, patternmaker
41 Wm McCarty, carpenter

47 Andrew Locke, moulder
51 Richard Hammond, plaster'r
53 Stephen Freeman, laborer
57 Jas Fisher, stovemounter
59 David Monger

Barton-st intersects.

Thos Howard, bricklayer
Samuel Howard, contractor

Oak-st, from Locke south to Pearl

2 Geo Green, laborer
4 Thos Lang, laborer
6 John Young, engineer
8 John Harrison, machinist

Ontario-st, from Markland south

5 Geo D Barr, salesman
6 Mrs John Wardlaw
7 John McKeown, moulder
8 Benj Fowler, scalemaker
9 Hugh McKellar, carpenter

Oxford-st, east side from York between Queen and Locomotive to Barton

G E Tuckett & Son's warehouse
40 S G Catchpole, bookkeeper
42 Vacant
44 Vacant
46 Vacant

Oxford-st, west side

1 David Vent, laborer
3 Peter Smith, carpenter
5 Ralph Fiderington, boltmkr
7 Jas Harris, engineer
9 Alex Campbell, policeman
11 John McBride, policeman
13 Thos Dawes, mechanic
15 Wm Mapplebeck, shearsman
17 P B Hennessey, locksmith
19 Alfred Ried, machinist
21 Samuel Watt, machinist

23 G S Findlay, traveler
25 Thos W Lannin, moulder
27 Albert Newman, heater
A M C Fox, carpenter
Wm Wharry, blacksmith
Timothy Corbett

O'Reilly-st, north side, from west of Walnut to Cherry

1 Leo Blatz, tailor
3 Wm Neighorn
5 Robt Magnus, cutter
7 Wm Anderson, boot crimper

Walnut st intersects

17 Jas Webster, mason
19 John Spence, carpenter
21 Jas Rathitoy, barber
24 Thos Murray, carpenter
25 Mrs Jas Robertson
29 Michael Sullivan, laborer

Cherry-st intersects

O'Reilly-st, south side

2 Thos Hilliard
4 Mrs David Stalker
6 Alex Fleck, painter
8 C W Simpson, carpenter
10 Jas J Murphy, cigarmaker
12 Mrs Anson Mills

Walnut-st intersects.

16 Mrs Richard Harper
18 Chas Morris, locksmith
20 Jas Johnson, laborer
22 Hy Smith, locksmith
24 John Brady, laborer
26 Jas Keating, machinist
28 Vacant
32 Michael Kelly, laborer
34 Thos Kirkpatrick, laborer
36 Geo Honeyborne, carpenter

Cherry-st intersects

Park-st north, east side from 94 King w to Murray

Franklin House
6 Little & Linfoot, livery

10 Vacant
Market-st intersects
28 Samuel Groves, blacksmith
York-st intersects
34 John Hyslop, blacksmith
Merrick-st intersects
50 Jas Stewart & Co, warehouse
52 Lenton Williams, millwright
54 A G Miles, plumber
56 Robt Miller, boarding
Vine-st intersects
64 E J Townsend, florist
68 Mrs Geo Stull
70 Thos Parry, builder
72 Wm Clark, carriage builder
74 Vacant
Cannon-st intersects
84 Vacant
86 John Callahane
88 Jas Connor, machinist
90 Ed Baker, gas fitter
92 Wm Crawford, bridge ins
94 Robt Raw jr, printer
96 Wm Mundy, letter carrier
98 Miss Byrne, dressmaker
100 Thos Evans
Mulberry-st intersects
St Mary's School
Roman Catholic Cathedral
Sheaffe-st intersects
126 Jas Wall, hatter
128 John Allen, machinist
130 Mrs Sarah Armstrong
132 Mrs John Harte
134 Alex McDowell, laborer
136 John McKeown, moulder
138 St Joseph's Orphan Asylum
Colborne-st intersects
152 Chas Jamieson, operator
154 Mrs John Pollitt
Barton-st intersects
162 Edward Treganza, grocer
164 Lawrence Murphy, laborer

168 Mrs Riddle
170 James Hanrahan, moulder
Murray-st intersects

Park-st n, west side

1-5 Columbia hotel
7 N Stevens, tobacco roller
9 Dominion Carriage Factory
13 Chas Morgan, trimmer
15 James Austin, blacksmith
17 Henry W Pierce, painter
Market-st intersects
21 J B Bagwell
29 Mrs Thos Duffy
29½ James Garland, painter
31 Commercial hotel
York-st intersects
33 Vacant
35 Wm Daily, tailor
Merrick-st intersects
45 Mrs Robt Wm Blamey
47 J H Hogan
49 O M Johnson, traveler
51 Mrs W H Hammond
53 Wm Webster, flour and feed
55 Wm Harris
Vine-st intersects.
57 Joseph Jeffrey
61 Wm Riach, general dealer
63 Wm Edgar, carpenter
65 Wm Mullins, laborer
67 Hy Arland, shoemaker
69 Henry Bradford, laborer
73 Geo Brown, packer
75 M E Bessey, butcher
Cannon-st intersects
77 Mrs Martin Fitzpatrick
79 Augustus Taufkirch
81 Mrs Mary Scully
83 Michael A Pigott, contractor
87 Mrs John Matches
89 Miss M L Bruce
91 Gas Works office
99 T Littlehales, manager gas works

Mulberry-st intersects

105 Mrs James Ivory
109 Jas Clark, stovemounter
111 Thos Early, salesman
113 Daniel Caughlin, carpenter
119 Vacant
121 Vacant
123 Mrs Daniel Gilmore
125 Angus Mundy, grocer

Sheaffe-st intersects

129 Thos McKinty, laborer
131 Albert Campbell, moulder
133 Francis Sheppard, customs
133½ Bart Conway, inland rev
135 Geo Gardner, brakeman
135½ Thos A Duggan, clerk
137 John O'Brien, railroader
139 Thos G Priestland,
141 Chas Ranger, carpenter
143 Mrs Patrick Merin
145 James Cottar, tailor

Colborne-st intersects

147 Rev Mungo Fraser
153 J Midwinter, carpenter
155 Geo H Stiff, clerk
157 John Garry, weaver
159 Mrs James S Laing
161 Wilson Barr, clerk

Barton-st intersects

163 G C Morrison, machinist
171 James F Egan, traveler
173 Wm Hyndman, blacksmith
179 Frank O'Callahan, inspector

Murray-st intersects

Park-st s, east side, from 69 King w to Markland

1-5 Malcolm &Souter, furniture
7 J E Berryman, shoemaker
9 Mrs Mary J Wilkinson
9½ Francis Leckenby, travel'r
11 Wm Morris, expressman
13 Lewis Edworthy, patternmkr
17 Chas F Abraham, merchant

Main st-intersects

29 Wm Evans, foreman Bell Tel Co
31 Geo Hughes, laborer
33 Samuel J Vint, marblecutter
35 Jas Hirst
37 John Banbrick, foreman
39 Walter Turnbull, painter
41 Wm Preston, laborer
43 Calvin Campbell, cook

Jackson-st intersects

Vacant lots

Hunter and Markland-sts intersect

Park-st s, west side

2 Z Pattison, confectioner
6 H G Cooper & Co, coach factory
8 Mat Wright, cotton broker
10 James T Barnard, manf
12 Mrs M W Browne
14 L Garland, druggist
16 F Armstrong, station agent

Main-st intersects

Vacant lots

Jackson-st intersects

Reformed Episcopal Ch

Hunter-st intersects

Central school

Bold and Duke-sts intersect

Samuel Briggs, manf
Geo F Glassco, furrier

Robinson-st intersects

Skating rink

Hannah-st intersects

102 Robt F Wallace, clerk
104 C S Scott, merchant
106 J V Teetzel, barrister

Herkimer-st intersects

110 Hy T Bunbury
114 W L Smart, barrister

Patrick-st, runs w from the head of Walnut

Albert Blackstone, sawyer
Frank White, stovemounter
James Leonard, laborer

Pearl-st n, east side, from 264 King w to York

14 Wm Newson, trunk maker
16 Wm H Hobbden, tailor
18 Wm Brown, tailor
20 H Mann, laborer

Napier-st intersects

38 Mrs John Rush
40 Thos Kennedy, mechanic
42 Samuel Crawford, grocer
Primary school

Peter-st intersects

52 Jas W Rushton, boilermaker
54 F F Greenway, artist
56 Adam Turnbull, laborer
58 A W Sievert, joiner

Florence-st intersects

68 Jas Greenley, carpenter

York-st intersects

Pearl-st n, west side

5 Jacob Hiles, agent
7 Wm A Spera, grain buyer
Erskine church

Little Market-st commences

17 John McIndoe, machinist
" Thos Butler, hackman
21 Philip Lowry, laborer
23 Wm Payne, engineer
25 Thos G Furnivall, tailor

Napier-st intersects

Zion Tabernacle
41 Geo Tristam, clerk
41½ Jas Gould, marblecutter
43 John Crawford, moulder

Peter-st intersects

51 Jas Heath, blacksmith
53 Geo Southworth, laborer
55 H Stokes
57 Wm Stewart, laborer
59 Isaac Hodgins, engineer
61 Wm Coiley, lithograph r

Florence-st intersects

65 Monk Bros, grocers
67 A Hendrie, ward foreman
69 F H Taylor, foreman
71 Wm B Robson, miller
73 Wm W McKee, nailor
75 Jas D Hinchliffe, machinist
77 Thos Faulknor, bricklayer
79 Mrs Wm Lynd
r " Thos Ford, biscuit baker
81 Egbert Barwell, saw filer
83 Mrs John Brown

York-st intersects

Pearl-st south, east side, from 241 King w to Bold

George-st intersect

17 J A Attwood, watchmaker
19 Duncan Robertson, machin't
23 Rowland Patten, builder
25 John Cox, spice manf
29 John Hover, boilermaker
35 John Montgomery, grocer

Main-st intersects

41 W J Blackbrough, carpenter

Jackson-st intersects

51 Geo T Kent, city foreman
53 Alex Faird, shoemaker
55 John Lutz, teamster
Hy G Park, teacher

Canada-st intersects

Vacant lots

Hunter-st intersects

Pearl-st south, west side

6 Wm O'Brien, shoemaker
8 Geo Duncan

George-st intersects

14 A Polucco, cabinetmaker
16 Robt Wright, driver
18 Wesley Kirkendall, painter
21 Hy Barnes, moulder
20 Wm Hull, bookkeeper

Nelson-st intersects

St Vincent R C School

Main-st intersects

40 James Harrison, hackman
44 John Donovan, blacksmith

Jackson-st intersects

46 Wm T Fell, porter
48 Thos Heddon, blacksmith
52 Vincent Edwards, baker
54 John Dent, driver
56 Wesley Daniels, millwright

Canada-st intersects

62 Ramsay Will, machinist
64 Geo Fleck, laborer

Hunter-st intersects

L D McAllister, agent

Bold-st intersects

Peter-st, north side, from 53 Hess n to Locke

6 Hy Knowles, salesman
8 Peter Corridi, bookkeeper
10 John Thomson
12 John McKeown, carpenter

Queen-st intersects

26 Chas Rieger, bartender
28 Wm Dickson, driver
30 James O'Laughlan, baker
32 Mrs Jane Wheeler
34 James A Cox, salesman
36 James Turnbull, laborer
40 W H Thomson, traveler
42 Thos Ford, baker
44 Thos Hayes, laborer
46 Robt Burns, heater
48 J W Halloran, grocer

Ray-st intersects

58 Wm Dean, shoemaker

62 Geo Milens, shipper
64 Mrs Mary Jackson
68 John A Hanes, laborer
72 Mrs Wm Snodgrass
74 Mrs Annie Bailey

Pearl-st intersects

82 Mrs Dennis Reardon
84 Alex Martin, laborer
86 John Robertson, fireman
88 Mrs Christina Archibald
90 Mrs Peter McArthur
92 Joseph W Knight, base ball player

Locke-st intersects

Peter-st, south side

5 Fred A Ashbaugh, traveler
7 John Hall, loco foreman
9 Joseph Herald, piano maker
21 Leitch & Turnbull

Queen-st intersects

27 John Burton, carpenter
29 Mrs Alice Williams
31 Felix Russell, laborer
33 John Scott, laborer
35 Ed Oakes, tobacco roller
37 Arthur Buggy, tobacco roller
39 Fred Foster, tobacconist
41 Stephen Balmer, laborer
43 Alonzo P Wyman, carpenter
45 Hy Knight, laborer
47 Mrs C Bailey
53 Henry T Cook, baker

Ray-st intersects

59 Mrs Catharine Corcoran
61 Samuel Burchill, laborer

Pearl st-intersects

71 Wm F Ryan, shoemaker
r71 Arthur J Miller, carpenter
73 Thos Duncan, laborer
75 Mrs John Andrews
79 James McKenna, engineer
81 Alex McKerlie, traveler
83 Mrs John Duffy
85 Harry Bawden, hotel

Picton-st e, north side, from 314 James north, to Wellington

21 J C Malcolmson, foreman

Hughson-st intersects

33 John Walwork
37 Andrew Richardson, checker

John-st intersects.

Vacant lots

Catharine & Mary-sts intersect

92 Geo Cooper, laborer
94 James Fielding, engineer
96 Joseph Jackson, glassblower
98 Jos Williams, machinist
102 John Keating, laborer
104 Michael Roach, laborer
114 John Bailey, blacksmith
116 Vacant

Ferguson-ave intersects

124 Francis Maxwell, boilermaker
126 Wm Culm, laborer
128 John Histead, laborer
130 Thos Lucas, blacksmith
132 John Kennedy, boilermaker
134 Thos Finn, laborer
136 Wm Philips, laborer
138 Jos Humphreys, laborer
140 Michael O'Grady, **laborer**
142 Wm Topp, engineer
144 John Place, laborer
146 Robt Lucas, teamster

Wellington-st intersects

Picton-st e, south side

10 James Burnett, **laborer**
14 James Vallance, carpenter
20 James Green, laborer

Hughson-st intersects

32 Geo Wing, loomfixer
34 A Bloomer, laborer
36 Wm Duston, weaver
38 Horatio Chappel, tinsmith
40 Joseph Perno, grocer

John and Catharine-sts intersect

81 James Kennedy

Mary-st intersects

89 Wm Caldwell, laborer
91 Hy Alexander, machinist
93 John Jackson, heater
95 T W Jutton, carpenter
97 John Kirkwood, laborer
99 Vacant
101 Robt Epstein, rag dealer
103 Michael Moran, laborer
  Oscar Matthews, carpenter

Ferguson-ave intersects

123 Wm Ferguson, fitter
125 Arthur Screeton, shoemaker
127 Enoch Taylor, file grinder
129 James Taylor, polisher
133 John Taylor, laborer
135 Vacant
139 A J Anthony, plasterer
143 Geo King, painter

Wellington-st intersects

Picton-st w, north side, from 307 James to Bay

6 Robt Campbell, carpenter
10 Geo Watson, engineer
12 Peter Callaghan, laborer
14 Lawrence Fitzgerald boilermaker
16 John Culican, laborer
20 Peter **Cullican**, carpenter

Macnab-st intersects

26 Mrs Ann Murphy
32 Michael O'Neil, glassblower
34 Hy Hale, laborer
42 Alex McCallum, moulder
44 John Reid, glassblower
46 James Cloney, laborer

Bay-st intersects

Bastien's boat house

Picton-st w, south side

3 Hy Mullen, carpenter
5 Thos Balsh, fitter

7 Mrs Annie Andrews
r " Michael Burke, laborer
9 Miss Ann Bloomer
11 Cyrus Weaver, laborer
13 Robt Williamson, laborer

Macnab-st intersects

35 Geo C Morrison, machinist
37 Geo Kingston, laborer
39 Mrs J Robinson
43 Geo A Barr, glassblower

Bay-st intersects

Pine-st, north side, from 71 Locke s to Cricket Ground

4 J Bertram, laborer
8 Wm J Pratt, barber
12 H W Judd, manf

Pine-st, south side

1 Daniel McDermott, painter
3 Mrs Mary A Robinson
7 John Clapham, plasterer
11 Albert Peart, machinist

Poulette-st, east side, from end of Main w, to Hunter

1 Hugh Toner, laborer
3 Chas Mietzner, laborer

Poulette-st, west side

2 Fritz H Hoth, laborer
4 Harvey A Holmes, painter
30 E Bellville, laborer
32 John Logan, watchman
34 John J Symington, laborer

Queen-st n, east side, from 212 King w to Stuart

8 Alex H Wingfield, customs
10 Hugh Malcolmson, carpent'r
12 Hy Marris, cutter

Market-st intersects

32 Thos Crooks
34 John Clifford, machinist

Napier-st intersects

Crockett, Muirhead & Co
Leitch & Lurnbull, machint's

Peter st-intersects

James Skimin, foundry

York st intersects

100 Mrs Col McGiven
102 Wm Tribbeck, packer
104 Geo W Kemp, tinsmith
106 John Crooks, laborer
108 Patrick McGeabe, laborer
98 Thos Jinks, heater
100½ J A McLardy, train despatcher
102 Adam Clark, machinist
104 —Lumstead, coal weigher
106 John T Johnson, mechanic
108 Robt Jarrett, engineer
110 Mrs Thos Shaw
112 Alex Hamilton, clerk
114 Wm Michael, laborer
116 Elijah A Middlemiss, check'r
120 Michael Ritchie, machinist
114 John McCabe, laborer
116 John Kavanagh, laborer
118 James Pemberton, laborer
120 Michael Brady, laborer
122 Jos Wilson, pork dealer
122½ Wm T Mayo, fireman
124 Geo D Stapleton, rougher
r124 Thos Furlong, laborer
126½ John Jinks, heater
130 Chas Littlejohn, inspector
132 Mrs Mary Sullivan
134 Stephen Jenkins, machinist

Barton-st intersects

Hamilton Forging Co
146 John W Macdonald, lumberman

Stuart-st intersects

Queen-st n, west side

Chas D Mills, hackman
13 Thos L Horning, driver
15 Wm Amor, excise officer

Market-st intersects

17 Henry Harvey, plumber
19 Vacant
21 W Carlyon, blacksmith
23 Robt J Seriver, boilermaker
25 Peter Bayne, carpenter
27 John Malcolnison, carpenter
29 Thos Johnston, marblecutter
31 John Kennedy, carpenter
33 Wm Hutton, laborer
35-7 F B Howard, butcher

Napier-st intersects

41-3 Greening's wire mill
45 Jas Alexander
47 John Firman, laborer

Peter-st intersects

57 Jas Skimin, founder
59 Chas A Herald, manager
61 Mrs Wm Herald
63 S O Greening, wire manf
67 David Ross
69 Geo Anderson, carpenter
69 Jas Boston, spice manf

York-st intersects

West Lawn

Greig-st intersects

119 John Greig, bookseller
121 Wm Kennedy, tender
121½ Walter Murray, saddler
123 Alex Johnson, machinist
123½ Alex Johnston, machinist
125 Henry St J Dance, laborer
127 John Sinker, laborer
129 L Pollard, laborer
131 Thos Higham, blacksmith
133 James Mason, fruiterer
161 James Thurling, laborer
163 Francis Sommerville, laborer
167 Vacant
169 Jarvis Abey, boilermaker

Barton-st intersects

Rolling mills

Stuart-st intersects

Queen-st s, east side, from 207 King w to Mountain

All Saints Church
1 Hy Scharlach
1½ Mrs M Taylor
1½ Ernest A Collett, engineer
3 Mrs James Amor
r " Robt Hill, cabinetmaker
5 Wm Sharp, assessor

George and Main-sts intersect

29 Chas Roantree
31 Wm Myers, coachman
33 Vacant
35 Chas Stoneman, stonecutter

Jackson-st intersects

37 T Mitchell
41 Mrs Wm Campbell
43 James Bicknell, bookkeeper
45 Chas J Woolcott, engineer
47 Daniel Sullivan, livery

Hunter st intersects

57 R J Faulknor, bricklayer
59 Wm Dowrie, carpenter
61 David Dowrie, contractor

Bold-st intersects

67 Hy Mansergh, clerk
69 Hy Lowe, salesman
71 Geo F Harris, pressman

Duke & Robinson-sts intersect

127 Thos C Searles, turner
129 John Sutton, huckster

Hannah-st intersects.

Wm Murray, bookkeeper
Alex Murray jr, bookkeeper

Herkimer-st intersects

Wm Lord, dairy
Asylum Engine House

Markland-st intersects

Vacant
Jos Pearce

Concession-st intersects

Vacant
Andrew J Patton, mail clerk
J H Farmer, photographer
H R Williams, foundryman
J M Williams, county regist'r

Queen-st s, west side
Private grounds

George-st intersects

12 Mrs John Ferrie
　W G Dunn, manf

Main-st intersects

24 Alonzo Lutes, salesman
26 Alfred H Taylor, painter
28 Wm Stewart, carpenter
30 Wm H Fisher, laborer
32 Geo McVittie, coachman

Jackson-st intersects

34 V E Fuller, barrister
42 Miss H Mills

Canada-st commences

　John Marshal, carpenter
46 Mrs David Bowman
48 T Shadbolt, cabinetmaker
54 T Gilmore, cabinetmaker

Hunter-st intersects

56 P Costello, baker
　Vacant lots

Bold st intersects

64 Mrs Thos S Allen
66 Thos Allen, shirt cutter
68 James McC Patterson, trav'r
70 J B Maclean, cabinetmaker
72 J G Kelk, paper bag manf
74 John Langford, carpenter
76 Hugh McLean, baker
78 Robt Wade, baker

Duke-st intersects

80 C B Izzard, traveler
82 David Coombs
84 Daniel M Glover, carpenter
88 Richard Tomlinson, clerk
90 Walter W Greenhill
96 Wm L Robertson, salesman

Robinson-st intersects

L McAdams, mason
Rich Avis, driver

Hannah-st, Nelson-ave and Herkimer-st intersect

Vacant lots

Markland-st intersects

A M Theal, agent

Concession-st intersect

Isaac Coomb, patternmaker
John A Studdard
Robt Forbes
Thos Wilson, carpenter
Wm McFarlane, laborer

Railway-st, east side, from 100 Cannon w north to Mulberry

10 Thos Addlay, laborer
12 Robt Bryce, stovemounter
14 Thos Elwell, laborer
16 Patrick Lawlor, carter
18 T Sullivan, cooper
22 Albert Newman, mechanic
28 Geo Mathieson, wool buyer
30 Jos P Kelly, shoemaker
32 Samuel Astle, machinist

Mulberry-st intersects

Railway-st, west side

13 John Kavanagh, blacksmith
15 Mrs Patrick Mooney
15 Rice Carson, laborer
19 Wm Ibbetson, tailor
21 Wm Ibbetson jr, painter
23 James Gartland, laborer
25 Joyce Tilley, patternmaker
29 Mrs John Doyle
31 Thos Lyon, mariner
33 John M Brown, machinist
35 John Morton, laborer
37 John W Coffee, lather

Mulberry-st intersects

Ray-st n, east side, from 234 King w to York

Private grounds

Market-st intersects

12 Mrs Marion Ward
14 Thos Shields, blacksmith
16 Samuel Garity, baker
18 Mrs Geo Fox
20 Capt I. B Barr
20½ Geo Harper, printer
22 Mrs Elizabeth Beck

Napier-st intersects

26 Mrs M Metcalf
30 Mrs I Parkinson
32 Thos A Martin, laborer
34 Chas Swinton, laborer
36 Sam Heath, blacksmith
38 James Burns, messenger
40 Daniel McDougall, blacksmih
42 James E Mills, laborer
46 Wm E Haughey, machinist
48 John H Jarvis, laborer
48½ Hy T Cook, baker

Peter-st intersects

48 Jas Halleran, grocer
50 Chas H Hines, butcher
52 Ed Smith, mechanic
54 Jas Hennessey, carpenter
56 Wm J Swinton, carpenter
58 John Martin, laborer
" Samuel Gariety, customs
60 Thos Garrow
62 Mrs J Laskie
64 Wm Morris, moulder
66 Chas Smith, polisher
68 John Duffy, traveler
70 Patrick Duffy, blacksmith
72 Mrs Maria Montgomery

York-st intersects

Ray-st n, west side

Loretto convent

Napier-st intersects

33 John Howard, stonemason

35 R J Hope, printer
37 Wm Gunner, tea dealer
37½ Robt Currie, carpenter
39 Mrs Wm Sallaway
41 Wm Boylan, laborer
43 Mrs Alex Bell
45 Jas Thomas, stonecutter
47 John Orr, laborer
49 Jas Owen, laborer

Peter-st intersects

53 Joseph Fletcher, carpenter
55 W H Cliff, printer
57 H N Thomas, marblecutter
59 Jas Tickle, engineer
61 M McLaughlin, blacksmith
63 Mrs John McCowell

Florence-st intersects

71 Wm Royal, woodworker
75 G E Wilson, provis'n dealer

York-st intersects

Ray-st s, east side, from 217 King w to Hunter

49 John Wilson, tinsmith
51 Jas Bardwell, machinist

Canada-st intersects

61 John Springate, boilermaker
63 Adam Miller, stovemounter
67 Mrs Elizabeth Mepham

Hunter-st intersects

79 Hiram De Witt, porter
  Wm Scott

Ray-st south, west side

6 T B Griffith, ticket agent
8 R Æ Kennedy
14 Mrs Robt B Ferrie

George-st intersects

16 S F Ross, dep col in rev
20 Robt Chisholm, builder

Main-st intersects

34 John W North, letter carrier
36 Robt Dow, plasterer

40 Hugh Hunter, fitter
42 Frank Smith, porter
Jackson-st intersects
44 Geo Drewett, butcher
48 Thos May, laborer
50 Geo Burke, agent
Canada-st intersects
62 Robt Reinholt, presser
64 Harry Hedge, shoemaker
66 John Paterson, machinist
68 Thos Brooks
70 John Newman, cigarmaker
72 James Spencer, tinsmith
74 Wm Bridgewood, laborer
Hunter-st intersects
86 John Cameron, shipper
88 Mrs Wm E Clayton
   James Munroe, laborer
   John Mitchell, laborer
Bold-st intersects

Rebecca-st, north side, from 62 James n to Wellington

6 Vacant
8-10 J Harvey & Co, wool dlrs
12 Andrew F Post, livery
Hughson-st intersects
16 Chas Post, livery
18 Wm Waldhoff, hay dealer
40 Wesley Church lecture room
John-st intersects
64-68 Victor Engine Works
70 Geo Sillett, cooper
Catharine-st intersects
82 Wm Gordon, cooper
84 Mrs H E Harrison, boarding
86 Louis Rubin, buttonholemkr
88 John Stacey, sawyer
90 Israel Todd, whitewasher
92 Wm Gilmore, shoemaker
98 Hy Hill, butcher
Mary-st intersects

100-2 D Sutherland, grocer
104 T J Carroll, brass worker
108 John W Ball, baker
112 Mrs Mary Farmer, dressmkr
114 Fred J Domville, GTR
116 D B Smith, tailor
118 Robt Wilson, merchant
120 A Winckler, cooper
122 Wm Gugel, shoemaker
124 James Robertson, moulder
126 Fred Abel, tailor
128 Wm Blackburn, patternmkr
130 John McVittie, cooper
138 Mrs Alford
140 John Nolan, laborer
142 James Hugill
142 Hamilton Oliver, collector
144 Jabez Saunders, carpenter
146 Vacant
Ferguson-ave intersects
148 Jos Horton, rag dealer
150 Mrs Hy Hewitt
150 Mrs Hymes, dressmaker
152 Robt Bogges, merchant
152¾ Hy Campbell, porter
154 C W Olmstead, laborer
156 Robt Campbell, laborer
158 Robt Pringle, bookkeeper
160 James Sherman
162 Wm Burrows, tailor
164 Mrs Geo Glass
Cathcart-st intersects
166 Chas Mason, gardener
170 Thos Chapple, butcher
172 Mrs H Pettigrew, dressmkr
174 Mrs Basquill
176 Mrs Chas Ward
178 John Kivell, mason

Rebecca-st, south side

1 Reliance Hall, IOGT
1 J B Smith, teacher
1 John Hendry, patent agent
3 Hy Jost, hatter
5 H Barnard, rubber stamps
7 Vacant
7½ Hy Martin, artist
9 Vacant

11 Fred J Ricketts, painter
13 Robt H LeFever, weaver
15 Geo Catchpole, umbrellas
17 W H Howard, tailor

Hughson-st intersects

27 Vacant
29 Central Iron Works
33 Vacant
35 O Nowlan
37 Mrs A E Hamilton

John-st intersects

43-63 E & C Gurney manf Co
65 S Kidd, fruiterer

Catharine-st intersects

73-75 E Wright & Co, japanners
83 Miss Louisa Schaffer
85 Nicholas Davis, bellman
87 Dan Collins, laborer
89 Mrs Mary E Nicholson
91 Hy Ireland, fruiterer

Mary-st intersects

97 Wm Smye, collarmaker
101 Alex A McDonald, traveler
103 Mrs James Walker
105 Ed Lavis, carpenter
107 Mrs James Green
109 John H Murden, driver
111 M Williams, harnessmaker
113 Mrs John Addison
115 Robt McHaffie, traveler
115½ Mrs Jenny Hobbs
117 James Shearer, joiner
119 Geo Coumbs, bricklayer
121 Hy Cowing, machinist
123 Wm J Locke, agent
125 Thos Guthrie, poultry dealer
127 Mrs John Trampkowski
129 Wm J Crankshaw, bookkpr
131 Wm Godfrey, baggageman
133 Vacant
135 Mrs Wm Bernger
137 Mrs Elizabeth Oxley

Ferguson-ave intersects

Lumber yard
Pork factory

177 Wm Joy, shoemaker
179 Geo King, saw filer

Wellington-st intersects

Robert-st e, north side, from James n to East-ave

7 Miss Mary A Gorman
9 Chas E Sexton, patternmkr
17 C B Snow, manf

Hughson-st intersects

35 Wm Givin, accountant
37 Mrs Josiah Blanchford
39 Samuel Parish, book dealer
41 Philip Morris, grocer

John-st intersects.

45 Mrs M Ledgerwood
47 Wm McLaughlin, laborer
49 Frank Ike, moulder
51 Thos Johnson, stovemounter
53 James Munn, farmer
57 Hy Smith, shipper
59 Thos S Dalton, boat builder
61 Chas Reid, fireman
63 Mrs E Witherspoon
69 Sylvester Nelson, brakeman

Catharine-st intersects

73 Wm Edwards, laborer
75 James Farr, bricklayer
77 John Shea, machinist
79 Alfred Wright, storekeeper
85 Hiram Olmstead, laborer

Mary-st intersects

89 Kenneth McKenzie, checker
91 Jos Noyes, scalemaker
93 Chas Kingdom, plater
95 Wm Robins, tailor
97 R Dynes, moulder

Elgin-st intersects

109 David White

Ferguson-ave and Cathcart -sts intersect

135 W C Toye, clerk
137 James Murray, finisher

139 John O'Grady, moulder
Wellington-st intersects
141 J McMeekin, agent
143 Mrs Jane Reid
145 R Darche, conductor
147 Richard Hunt, moulder
West-ave intersects
167 John Kellner, tailor
Victoria and East-aves intersect
Mrs Thos Brydges
Emerald-st intersects

Robert-st e, south side

Drill shed
Hughson-st intersects
Private grounds
John-st intersects
50 James McNab, jeweler
52 John Cunninghan, teamster
54 Robt Curry, dyer
56 Samuel Gardiner, lineman
58 Julian Ardini, image maker
58½ Mrs Maria Kelly
60 Mrs Maggie Allan
62 Mrs John Kirkham
64 Mrs Britton, laundry
66 Geo Williams, laborer
Catharine-st intersects
Moore's foundry
80 C E Newberry, tanner
Mary-st intersects
90 Jas Gibbons, gardener
92 Miss Helen Servos
94 Mrs John Stephenson
Elgin-st intersects
N & N W Sheds
Ferguson-ave intersects
134 Jas Sharples, collector
136 Vacant
Cathcart-st intersects

138 Jas Proctor, boilermaker
140 Geo Burges, laborer
Wellington-st intersects
Vacant lots
West-ave intersects
176 Arch Martin, moulder
178 Jas O'Grady, moulder
182 Patrick O'Brien, laborer
184 Samuel Scott, grocer
Victoria-ave intersects
186 Mrs Frank Arnold
188 Arch Cutler, polisher
190 Wm O'Neil, laborer
192 Mrs Mary Keenan
194 Oliver Christopher, laborer
196 Henson E Smith, hatter
198 Nelson Clark, carter
200 Jas Wedge, carter
204 Joseph Brown, stonemason
East-ave intersects

Robert-st w. from Garth east between Hunter and Bold

1 Benj Brown, laborer
4 A Walter, laborer

Robinson-st, north side, from James s, west to limits

Private grounds
Macnab-st intersects
John Harvey, merchant
J M Henderson, merchant
Park-st intersects
Vacant lots
Bay-st intersects
36 Harmon Kartzmark, mach't
38 Jas Malcolm, accountant
40 M Kartzmark, blacksmith
42 Patrick McGrath, laborer
44 Edw Burdett, brushmaker
44½ Robt Mundt, laborer
46 John Driscoll, laborer

STREET DIRECTORY.

48 John Timson, policeman
50 Alfred Ram, carpenter

Caroline-st intersects

52 Wm Burns, laborer
54 Donald McMahon, laborer
56 Andrew Provost, barber
60 John T Laing, bricklayer
62 Joseph Lambert, teamster
64 Wm F Birnie, miller
66 Wm O Crawley, salesman

Hess and Queen-sts intersect

88 Mrs Munro
90 James Speight, laborer
94 Vacant
96 James Martin, baker
98 Fred L Whately, accountant
100 Alfred Hannaford, plasterer
102 Robt Hannaford, plasterer
104 Mark L Tew
106 C A Carlson, tailor
Cricket grounds

Locke-st intersects

Thos Fanning, grocer
Thos O'Connor, laborer
Stephen Sweerey, laborer
Geo Reynolds, butcher
E B Santee, stamper
Robt Chanter, laborer
John W Frid, engineer
Geo Norwood jr, brickmakr
Wm Smith, dyer
Geo Jackson, laborer
Thos Wilson, laborer
James Lemmond, laborer
Wm Hempstock, laborer
Geo Porter, machinist
Owen Neaney, laborer
James Napier, machinist
Mrs Thos Wyatt
Wm S Russell, driver
Oscar Hendershott, driver
Robt Scott, iron planer
Mrs Adcock

Garth-st intersects

Robinson-st, south side

1 Mrs W Mundie
3 Geo S Papps, barrister
5 Wm Osborne, founder

Macnab-st intersects

Francis H Mills

Park-st intersects

Curling rink
29 Geo M Bagwell, printer
31 John A Beattie, clerk

Bay-st intersects

39 Wm Kemp, laborer
41 Robt Murray, shoemaker
43 Joseph Shields, laborer
45 Mrs Thos Jones
47 A H McKeown, merchant
49 Matthew Armstrong, clerk

Caroline-st intersects

51 Henry Feist, gardener
53 Jas Turnbull, cabinetmaker
55 Joseph Bailey, shipper
57 Mrs Wm D Jermyn
59 Jacob Gebhard, shoemaker
61 Jas A McKeown, carriagmkr
63 James Bridgwood, teamster

Hess-st intersects

73 Rich Tope, mason
75 Chas Imboden, foreman
79 Mrs Mary Crawford

Queen-st intersects

93 Edwin Layland, driver
95 Wm Porter, machinist
99 S W Fraser, watchman
101 Hy Bustin, pianomaker
103 H Kleinsteiber, pianomaker
Vacant

Locke-st intersects

J W Blasdell & Co, grocers
Mrs S Cornell
Robt Patrick, laborer
Henry Hall, laborer
Wm Waldren, foreman
Jas Newlands, machinist

Jas Kerney, tobacco roller
Wm Auld, laborer
Mrs Eliza Brown
109 John Hummel, bricklayer
111 Chas Mundt, laborer
111 Wm Cuseck, laborer
115 Robt Crowe, machinist
115 John McLean, boilermaker
115 Francis Dean, brickmaker
115 C Vaughan, driver
115 Christopher Russell, laborer
117 Wm Bell, machinist
121 Alfred Green, laborer

Garth-st intersects

St Mary's Lane, from end of Locke n to Inchbury

2 John Cousins, carpenter
4 James G H Rhynd, fireman

Shaw-st, from 200 Victoria-ave n, running east

Anson Dean
Jos Servos, fireman
Richard Kiedby, laborer
John Morrison, woodworker
Philip Langley, watchman

Sheaffe-st north side, from St Mary's Cathedral, Park n, west to Caroline

Dewey's ice house

Park-st intersects

16 Ed Rickerson, machinist
18 Jos Heitzmann, cigarmaker
20 Thos B Spence, watchman
22 Rev Hy Langton
24 Alfred S Peene, contractor
26 Geo Steele, dancing master
28 D J O'Brien, music teacher

Bay-st intersects

34 Mrs John Spanton
36 Samuel Spencer, laborer
38 James Melody, laborer
40 Geo Friday, laborer
44 Mrs John Hilliard

Sheaffe-st, south side

1 John McKenzie, wood dlr
3 David McDeod, moulder
St Mary's Cathedral

Park-st intersects

17 John Coyne, laborer
19 Wm H Gray, stonemason
21 Jacob Morden, laborer
25 Bishop's Palace
27 Miss Sarah Bigley
29 Mrs C Reardon
31 Michael Moriaty, laborer
33 John Latremouille, confr
35 Miss McCowell, seamstress
37 David Nutley, laborer
39 Chas Wilson, laborer

Bay-st intersects

41 Mrs Wm Gully
43 T G Gully, soda water manf
45 Malcolm Robertson, pedler
47 Thos Cook, engineer
49 Wm Patterson, teamster
51 Patrick Kelly, laborer
53 Alex Donald, bottler

Simcoe-st e, north side, from 276 James n to Wellington

5 David Terryberry, butcher
7 James Rake, shoemaker
9 John McDonald, inspector

Hughson-st intersects

25 Martin Kennedy, glassblowr
27 G H Kennard, helper
27 Wm V Inch, moulder
29 Mrs Eliza Cresswell
31 Alfred Buskard, carriagemkr
33 Vacant

John-st intersects

Simcoe-st Church
39 Mrs John McLean
41 James Trainor, laborer

Catharine-st intersects

69 Arthur Cullon, laborer
71 Wm McQuinn, moulder

Mary st intersects

83 R Partridge, engineer
85 Patrick Cosgrove, laborer
87 John O'Dowd, laborer
89 John Kinsella, laborer
91 Richard Terner
95 James Begley, laborer
99 Hiram Siddall, teamster
101 Timothy Hanley, laborer
103 James Talbot, laborer
105 Isaac Swallow, mason
107 Drury Harper, polisher
107½ Sydney Brenton, polisher
109 Thos Fursdon, laborer
113 M Quinlan, laborer

Ferguson-ave intersects

119 Francis Saxton, laborer
121 James McCallum, laborer
125 Daniel Mulcahay, laborer
129 Mrs Elizabeth Lewis
129 Wm Symons
131 Peter Clark, laborer

Wellington-st intersects

Simcoe-st e, south side

2 Hugh Torrance
2 David Torrance, tailor
8 Jeremiah Behan, glassblower
10 Thos Allen, machinist
12 Geo Clark, stableman
14 — Boyd, blacksmith
16 Martin Nolan, glassblower
18 Francis Smith, moulder

Hughson-st intersects

18½ H F Dunne, fireman
22 David Hardy, moulder
24 John Eustice, laborer
28 Hy Allan, boilermaker
30 Lawson Hamburg, laborer
32 P Ryan, shoemaker
34 Patrick Hanley, laborer
36 Hy Hanley, laborer
38 Andrew O'Brien, laborer

John-st intersects

47

Vacant lots

Catharine & Mary-sts intersect

84 Michael Canary, laborer
86 Patrick Dowd, laborer
88 Fred A Allan, laborer
90 Wm Inglis, laborer
92 Richard Simons, laborer
94 Fred Newman, moulder
96 Arthur Garrick, laborer
100 Andr w Larkin, machinist
102 Thos Garrett, moulder
102 Robt Batty, moulder
106 Thos Maloney, laborer
108 Vacant
108½ Peter Doherty, laborer

Ferguson-ave intersects

Richard Sheldrick, carter
120 John W Woodcock, laborer
124 Wm White, laborer

Wellington-st intersects

Simcoe-st w, n side, from 261 James n to Bay

Ontario Cotton Mills Co

Macnab & Bay-sts intersect

Simcoe-st w, south side

13 Stephen O'Toole
15 David Jackson, laborer
17 David McIlroy, machinist
19 Wm Kirkpatrick, carpenter
21 Stephen O'Donnell, glassblo'r
23 Thos Burbeck, teamster
25 Fred Willis, moulder
27 Mrs Eliza Cross
29 Jas Campaign, laborer

Bay-st intersects

Smith-ave, e side, from Barton to Cannon, between Emerald and Wentworth

14 Thos Bayley, carpenter
22 Matthew Lourie, builder
26 Ephraim Jeffrey, plasterer

28 Felix Legault, shoemaker
28½ Vacant
30 Jacques Legault, shoemaker
32 James Anderson, bricklayer
36 Thos Griesley, gardener
38 Elzear Sirois, shoemaker
40 Sidney Foster, wood turner
42 Vacant
44 Wm H Fagan, teamster
48 Robt Somerville, carpenter
50 Steven Land, machinist
54 Andrew Cowan, clerk
60 G K Jones, roof painter

Smith-ave, west side

5 John Pottinger, laborer
35 Napoleon Morin, shoemaker
37 Hy Johnson, merchant

Sophia-st n, east side, from 319 York

12 Chas Howson, engineer
14 Mrs Julia Hobson
16 Ernest G Rumple, cabinetmkr
16 Alonzo Tufford, carriagemakr
18 David Craig, machinist
   Ontario Planing Mill

Florence-st intersects

Sophia-st n, west side

   Geo H Davey, news agent
13 John Stevens, painter
15 James Gee, fitter
17 Geo H Andrew, laborer
19 Wm Smith, moulder

Tom-st intersects

   Private grounds
   John Armstrong, wire weavr

Florence-st intersects

Sophia-st s, from 298 King w north to Palace Grounds

3 John Larmer, laborer
5 Ed Dowling, boilermaker
9 James Wales, miller
13 Michael Hayes, carter

South-st w, north side, from Locke to Garth

   Richard Bolt, machinist
   Edwin Peard, caretaker
   James Falconer, carpenter
   Robt Patterson, patternmkr
   Wm Wallace, machinist
   John McIntosh, machinist
   — Mitchell, carriagemaker
   Peter Crerar, carpenter
   James Carter, plasterer
   Geo Hudson, marble polish'r

South-st w, south side

   Alfred Wells, porter
   Hy A Booker, machinist
   Geo Simkins, painter
   Wm Jones, polisher

South-st e, from 199 Wellington n east to Wentworth

1 John Webb jr, bricklayer
3 Jos Erwood, carter

Victoria ave intersects

21 Robt McVinnie, shipper
22 Vacant
23 Wm Martin, blacksmith
24 James H Jackson, laborer
28 Alfred King, painter
   Vacant
   John Herman, laborer
   J B Golden, teamster
   Vacant
   Mark Lampshire

Oak-ave intersects

Spring-st, east side, from 183 King e south to Hunter

1 Pilgrim Bros, soda water mfs
   N H Tabb, traveler

Main-st intersects

   Wm Gilmore, butcher
7 Hy Pearson, cutter
9 John McCauley, lithographr
11 Thos Bateman, baker
13 Wm Jarvis
15 Mrs Walter Locke

STREET DIRECTORY. 371

17 Alex Stewart, tailor
19 Andrew Bain, clerk

Jackson-st intersects

21 Wm E Burtshall, hatter
23 Evan McKenzie, carpenter
25 James A Harvey, printer
27 Thos Lewis, cigarmanf
31 Stewart Maitland, painter
33 Miss Mary Smith
33a Chas VanEvery, painter
35 Vacant
37 Jacob Lewis, blindmaker

Hunter-st intersects

Spring-st west side

2 Chas Mills, merchant
6 Douglas Shaylor, laborer
8 James Fox

Jackson-st intersects

22 Mrs Wm Chambers
24 Jos Livernois, fruit dealer
26 Wm McClelland, spice manf
30 G H McMahon, contractor

Hunter-st intersects

Steven-st, east side, from 286 King east to Cannon

6 Louis Kretschman, brushmkr
r 6 Richard Mantle, laborer
8 Vacant
12 John Anders, brushmaker

King Wm-st intersects

14 Mrs Jos Hunter
16 Richard Himes, laborer
24 Benj Parrett, carter

Nightingale-st intersects

34 Samuel Cook, carpenter
36 James Page

Wilson-st intersects

46 Geo W Carr, plater
47 F L Ross, shoemaker
50 R Henderson, carpenter
52 Chas Cripps, bricklayer

54 Albert Smith, polisher
56 Robt Mellon, bricklayer
58 Christian Klingbeil, laborer
60 James Ditty, tinsmith
64 Thos P Haines, machinist
66 David Sinclair, laborer
68 Geo Truesdale, teamster

Cannon-st intersects

Steven-st, w side

9 G J Rayner, grocer

King William-st intersects

13 John B Reid, burnisher
15 Bernard McCully, machinist
17 John P Gardner, cutter
19 Mrs Ann Gainey
21 James Fallahee, laborer
23 James G Weir, grain buyer
25 J J White
27 Geo Rutley, machinist
29 Geo Maslin, laborer
31 James Miller, porter
33 Thos O Veale, gardener
35 C Piercy, printer

Wilson-st intersects

37 John Rouse, porter
37½ Alfred Rouse, fireman
39 J S Smyth, polisher
41 Chas Stevens, carpenter
43 Frank Lewis, moulder
45 Chas E Farr, plasterer
47 Fred Lentz, laborer
49 Ernest Wolter, laborer
51 Wm Stewart, carpenter
53 James Kenny, carpenter
53½ James Thomson, laborer
55 James Husted, moulder
57 John Jones, moulder
59 Chas Libke, brushmaker
61 Robt Acland, carpenter
63 Louis Johnson, contractor
65 Joseph Cripps, laborer
67 Alfred Bourque, burnisher
71 Ferdinand Albrecht, machin't
75 Michael Ryan, laborer

Cannon-st intersects

Stinson-st, north side from 81 Wellington south, east to Wentworth

9 Vacant

West-ave, Victoria-ave, East-ave & Emerald-sts intersect

75 Hy Tinling, merchant
77 Edwin Cuckow, shipper
79 W S Hicks, carver
　Boys' Home

Wentworth-st intersects

Stinson-st, s side

8 E Gillet
20 John F Jagoe, custom broker
22 Mrs John Fraser

Victoria-ave intersects

　Joseph Lister
58 F W Fearman, pork dealer

Maple-ave intersects

64 W P Sturt, traveler
66 Raymond Blandford, bookkeeper
70 L Eckerson, photographer

Emerald and Blythe-sts intersect

82 Spencer Furniss, marble dealr
82½ Jas Bovaird, carriagemakr
84 Mrs Samuel Maslen
84 Arthur Fish, painter

Erie-ave intersects

86 John Noble, bricklayer
88 Isaac Christian, pressman
90 F E Dallyn, bookkeeper
100 Jas Patterson, carpenter

Wentworth-st intersects

Strachan-st e, north side, from 252 James north to Wellington

9 Mrs Andrew Begley
11 David Farr, constable GTR
13 Patrick Carroll, laborer

Hughson-st intersects

31 Hugh Cassidy, laborer
33 Leonard Marshall, laborer
35 Fred Skerrow, laborer
37 John Ford sr, painter

Jackson-st intersects

45 Wm Jessop, shipper
47 Martin Harvey, laborer
51 Mrs Mary McGowan
53 James Carry, laborer
55 Michael Kerr, moulder
61 John Fred Foster, plumber

Catharine-st intersects

Vacant lots
67 Pat Canaty, laborer
69 John Lawlor, cabinetmaker
41 John Gray, laborer
73 B McMahon, policeman

Mary-st intersects

83 Patrick Warren, laborer
85 Patrick McInerney, watchman
89 Mrs Bernard McDonald
91 James Madigan, laborer
97 Michael O'Brien, laborer
99 Michael Sunderland, laborer
101 M Shaughnessy, laborer
103 John O'Toole, sealemaker
107 Mrs Ellen Erkert
109 Anthony Bonney, laborer

Wellington-st intersects

Strachan-st e, south side

Hughson-st intersects

24 Mrs Margaret Bowers
26 Wm Johnson, stovemounter
28 James McMahon, laborer
32 Peter Anderson, laborer
34 Vacant
36 Mrs John Shea
38 Mrs Ann Armitage

John-st intersects

46 Robt Patton, laborer
48 John Weir, clerk
52 Uriah Leaver

54 Mrs Charlotte Wilson
60 James Fallahee, laborer

Catharine-st intersects

68 Mrs Mary Warren

Mary-st intersects

96 James Steele, laborer
98 James Miller, fireman
102 Wm Parker, tinsmith
106 John O'Neil, laborer
108 Wm Green, laborer
110 Hugh Hawthorne, laborer
112 Lewis Bonney, laborer
114 Peter Austin, carpenter

Ferguson-ave intersects

Jos White, carpenter

Wellington-st intersects

Strachan-st w, north side, from 249 James n to Bay

16 Chas Cameron, laborer
18 John Ames, laborer
20 Geo Joiss
r 20 Fred Alexander, laborer
22 Geo Harris
24 Geo Frazer

Macnab-st intersects

28 Wm Dummer, glassblower
30 Francis Hislop, laborer

Bay-st intersects

Thompson's boat house

Strachan-st, south side

5 Wm Carlisle, weaver
7 James Delaney, laborer
23 Wm Williamson, carpenter
27 Thos Fuerd, laborer
29 Jas Wilson, laborer

Macnab-st intersects

37 Hy Gray, customs officer
39 Jas McLean, freight agent

Bay-st intersects

Gillesby's warehouse

Stuart-st e, north side, from 244 James n to Catharine

19 Samuel Crist, glassblower
23 Daniel Flynn, stovemounter
25 Mrs Rachel Fleming

Hughson-st intersects

27 Fred Childs, brickmaker
29 Vacant
31 Vacant
33 Vacant
35 Vacant
37 Vacant
39 John Coutts, patternmaker
39½ John Galtrey, laborer
41 Joseph Davis, butcher
43 Mrs B Hammond

John-st intersects

51 Wm Cooper, laborer
53 John Sherdon, laborer
55 Daniel Nelson, laborer
57 Vacant

Catharine-st intersects

Stuart-st e, south side

4 Mrs Mary Ann O'Brien
6 Geo Stry, laborer
10 John Gray, laborer
12 Jno O'Callaghan, cigarmak'r
16 Samuel Grove, laborer
18 Mrs Daniel Langdon
20 Vacant
24-26 Geo Mills, grocer

Hughson-st intersects

30 Mrs Louisa Leonard
32 Joseph Lappin, brakeman
34 Wm Smith, laborer
36 Mallack Doyle, baggageman
38 Robt Aikins, scalemaker
42 A J Case, dairyman
44 Ichabod Sharp, agent

John-st intersects

48 Thos Duffy, carpenter
50 Patrick McAndrews, laborer
52 Chas Coy, harnessmaker
54 Geo Armstrong, laborer

Catharine-st commences

Stuart-st w, north side, from 239 James n to Queen

- 14 Sylvester Nolan, laborer
- 16 James O'Donnell, glassmak'r
  City Weigh Scales

Macnab-st intersects

G T R general offices

Bay-st intersects

GTR station
J B Fairgrieve, coal office
T Myles & Son, coal dealers

Stuart-st w, south side

- 5 John McHendrie, tavern
- 7 James McHendrie, carpenter
- 9 Hy Horton, laborer
- 11 Wm Jones, laborer
- 19 H E Wood, baker
- 21-3-5 S Taylor, hotel

Macnab-st intersects

- 31 Doran Bros, vinegar works
- 35 Old Custom House
  Street Railway stables
- 49 Metropolitan hotel

Bay-st intersects

- 51 Allison house
- 59 Hy Smith, laborer
- 61 Lorenzo Patton, dyer
- 63 R England, fruiterer
- 65 M J Wolf, hotel
- 67 Roach's hotel
- 69½ Wm Moriarty, restaurant
- 73 John Boyle, hotel

Tiffany-st intersects

- 79 J Steanger, temperance hotel
- 81 John Callanane, hotelkeeper
- 87 Immigrant sheds
- 89 Robt Thomson, lumber dlr

Caroline-st intersects

A Gartshore & Co

Hess and Queen-sts intersect

Tiffany-st, from 73 Stuart w to Barton

- 2 Mrs John Hardman
- 4 E Connor, conductor
- 6 Chas Meakins, laborer
- 8 Joseph Lomes, laborer
- 10 Geo Knott, laborer
- 12 Thos Griffin, laborer
- 14 Arthur Shaw, farmer
- 13 Wm Bradley, cooper
- 19 John Johnston, fireman

Barton-st intersects.

Tisdale-st, east side, from 272 King e north to Barton

- 2 Thos Howes, coachman
- 4 A E Cann, traveler
- 6 Jos Day, porter

King Wm-st intersects.

- 16 Robt Warren, butcher
- 18 Wm Mallins, carter
- 20 Wm Spence, laborer
- 22 John H Blackburn, watchm'n
- 24 Thos Donohoe, shoemaker
- 26 Thos Costello, printer
- 28 Alex Robertson, stonecutter
- 30 Geo Hamilton, stonecutter
- 32 Vacant
- 34 Albert Jaggar, gardener
- 36 Wm D Broatch, engineer
- 38 Thos J Haygarth, stovemtr
- 40-40½ Vacant
- 42 R W Randal, carpenter
- 44 Wm Giles, moulder
- 46 Wm H Martin, machinist
- 48 Robt Lucas, moulder
- 50 Robt F Drake, packer
- 54 Francis Booth, bookkeeper
- 56 Geo Sweetlove, watchman

Wilson-st intersects.

- 58 Samuel Buscombe, shoemkr
- 60 Mrs Patrick Knight
- 60½ Thos Woodcock, laborer
- 62 James Connors, builder
- 64 Geo Hunter, tailor

68 Arthur Smith, laborer
70 John Walker, moulder
72 Patrick Fitzgerald, laborer
74 Samuel Griffith, porter
76 David Murray, gardener
78 D H C Roberts, clerk
80 Wm Howard, builder
82 Jos Richards, traveler
84 Chas Truscott, carpenter

Cannon-st intersects

Tisdale-st, west side

Vacant lots

King William-st intersects

17 Chas Renner, teamster
19 Smith McNeil, laborer
21 Wm Smith, machinist
25 Robt Smith, laborer
25½ Vacant
27 R I Smith
27½ Mrs Andrew Wilson
29 James Osborne, engineer
31 Robt Reynolds, baker
33 Robt Herring, polisher
33½ John Gee, laborer
35 Ed Steer, painter
37 Walter Butler, turner
39 Mrs Martin Karsten
41 Hans Andurp, tinplater
43 Andrew Schau, laborer
45 James W Stewart, carpenter
47 August Lenz, laborer
49 L W Keil, grocer

Wilson-st intersects

51 J D Burkholder, carpenter
53 Vacant
55 Mrs James Hodd
57 John Clushman, moulder
73 James Cameron, moulder
75-77 Vacant

Cannon-st intersects

Tom-st north side, from Sophia to Dundurn

10 Hy Fitt, cabinetmaker

Devonport-st intersects

26 John Pickard, miller
28 Robt Robertson, mason
30 James McCulloch, engineer

Dundurn-st intersects

46 Vacant
50 Wm Buscomb, moulder
56 Wm Ashborne, laborer

Tom-st, west side

1 Matthew Hunter, carpenter
3 J Semmens
5 Dennis Mahoney, shoemakr
9 Alex Begley, blacksmith
11 Thos Burrell, fireman
1 " Chas Alderman, laborer
15 Samuel Marsden, machinist
17 John Clegg, laborer
21 John A R Lawrence, salesm'n
25 Geo Maddox, blacksmith
29 H N Thomas, marble dealer
33 Samuel Fiddler, saddler
37 Thos S Chessum, painter
39 Wm Furnis, marble cutter

Dundurn-st intersects

57 Wm Hull, coffin trimmer
59 John Foreman, expressman

Victoria-ave n, east side, from 244 King e to the Bay

8 J H Stone
10 Chas C Foote, plater

King Wm-st inersects

Public school
20 John Robinson
22 Wm Marshall, salesman
24 W H Jones, bookkeeper
28 Samuel Atkin, salesman
26 Samuel Heard
30 S K McIlroy, bookkeeper
32 L McKellar, traveler
34 Jos S Brennan, manf
36 John McCoy, inspector
38 J T Bampfylde, ale bottler
40 Hy Bennett, printer
42 Vacant

Wilson-st intersects

44 Alex Hayes, grocer
48 Hy Glebe, tailor
50 Wm Hazell, porter
52 John Carr, patternmaker
54 Vacant
58 Samuel Medley, stonecutter
60 Moses Overholt, tailor
64 David R Gibson, mason
66 Mrs Wm Findlay
70 Benj Temple, machinist

Evans-st intersects

72 J R Jackson, carpenter
74 Frank Mesle, brushmaker
74½ John Wise, machinist
78 Mrs Samuel Bradt
80 James Ecclestone, tailor

Cannon-st intersects

86 Frank Stinson, porter
90 Mrs Wm West
92 Peter McKay, builder
94 Samuel B Longhrae, traveler
94 Mrs Catharine Merrick
96 Simon Elliott, watchman
    Jacob Strahler, traveler
98 Fred Adams, machinist
100 Vacant
102 John DeVine, moulder
104 Peter Thompson
106 Robt Blakeley

Robert-st intersects

110 Wm Riddell, moulder
112 Benj Bothwell
114 Emory Chagnon, metal spin'r
    Walter Bale, bookkeeper
118 James Farmer
124 Wm Farmer, photographer
128 Abraham Ripley, moulder
130 Jos Bale, shipper
132 David Dick, fireman
134 Peter Burshaw, laborer
136 Thos Gillespie, laborer
138 John O'Neil, cutter
140 Walter Holden, engineer
142 Edmund Webster, machinist
142 John R Hore, painter

Barton-st intersects

146 Wm McKittrick, moulder
148 Wm Smith, ropemaker
154 Mark Thomson, carpenter
156 Wm Elliott, packer
158 Abraham Ripley, moulder
160 Robt Johnson, carpenter
162 Thos Ballantyne, plumber
164 Hy Berry, laborer
166 Thos Johnston, blacksmith
168 Wm Hay, scalemaker
170 Wm G Beers, clerk
172 James Shoots, trimmer
174 Robt T Dickenson
174½ Edgar N Lucas, shoelaster
176 A G Nie, machinist
178 James Green, laborer
180 A W Small, shipper
182 John Wilson, engineer
184 John Shannon, laborer
186 Wm J McKenzie, melter
190 C P Moore, file cutter

South-st intersects

202 Mrs Hugh Shaw

Shaw-st intersects.

206 Wm Barclay, carpenter

Barton-st intersects

208 Michael Flannigan, laborer
210 John Stark, stovemounter
210½ H Munsie, accountant
212 Ed B Tarbox, solderer
214 Geo Stroud, tanner

Ferrie-st intersects

220 Vacant
    H & N W R'y wharf

Victoria-ave n, west side

3 Hy Bedlington, traveler
5 J M Little, merchant
5½ Jas Brown, hide insp
7 John B Rousseau, detective
9 Walter Oaten, salesman
11 Miss Fitzpatrick, dressmaker

King Wm-st intersects

13 H S Williams, stationer
   S J Moore, manf

Victoria-ave s, east side, from 246 King east to the Mountain

St Patrick's Church

Main-st intersects

29 Thos McKay, grocer
31 Wm G Reid, merchant
37 Jas Matthews, painter
43 Wm Edgar, lumber dealer
49 Alfred Morgan, merchant
55 J F Stewart, manf

Hunter-st intersects

57 Thos Myles, coal dealer
65 Fred J Howell, lithographer
67 Vacant
67½ Vacant
69 Vacant
71 Vacant
73 Thos D Wanzer, manf

Stinson-st intersects

Joseph Lister, Wood Lawn

Victoria-ave s, west side

10 Geo Pearson, carter
12 Mrs Michael Morrisey
14 Thos Morgan, tanner

Main-st intersects

28 Moore A Higgins
30 John M Lester
38 John A Barr, druggist
Walder Park, druggist
42 Vacant
44 Egerton DeCew, treasurer
46 S J Moore, machinist
48 Mrs Phoebe McGregor
50 M Cohen, ins agent
52 Mrs Mary Slater
54 W E Glennie, traveler
56 Alex Stuart, chamberlain

Hunter & Stinson-sts intersect

82 F L Wanzer, manf
88 J M Stewart, clerk
90 W L Billings, M D
94 Frank Miller, carpenter

96 Thos Burns, P O
100 James Keenan, sectionman

Vine-st, north side, from 95 James n to Bay

Federal Life Building
16 Mrs A C Quimby
18 Alex S Cruikshank, teacher
24 Rudolph Peters, machinist

Macnab-st intersects

34 Mrs Sophia Hill
42 J B Rousseaux, watchman
44 Frank Kaiser, machinist

Park-st intersects

58 Levi Dean, traveler
60 Hiram F Inglehart
62 W Stroud, hide dealer
66 Geo J Reid, messenger
68 Mrs Richard Barrett
70 Wm Birrell, foreman
" Farmers' Dairy Co
" Walton Ice Co
72 Wm Kirk, baker
74 Mrs Anthony King

Bay-st intersects

Vine-st, south side

1 Vacant
5 Robt Chatto, teamster
9 E A Ware, scale manf
15 McKeever Bros, coal & wood
17 George Brown

Macnab-st intersects

Stewart's foundry
43 Mrs John Corey

Park-st intersects

65 John Glasgow
67 D J Peace, tobacconist
69 James Anderson, carpenter
71 Wm Gillies, watchman
73 John Green, traveler
75 John Mathieson, porter

Bay-st intersects

15 Rev E Lounsbury
17 Wm Heeney, accountant
19 Engine house
21 J E Hutchings, bookkeeper
23 Jas C Fairgrieve, coal mcht
25 W D Bewes, merchant
27 E W Bateman, baker
29 Wm Wilson
31 Jas Johnston, auctioneer
33 John Weatherston
35 John Hooper, traveler
39 John Ross
41 Wm Farrar, mangr Oak Hall
43 John Stoneman, traveler

Wilson-st intersects

49 Chas Howard, carpenter
51 Philip Gee, laborer
53 B D Bowron, tinsmith
55 Andrew Will, shoemaker
57 James Charteris, letter carrier
59 Samuel Shaddock, moulder
61 C E Miner, cabinetmaker
63 J H Carpenter, milk dealer
65 Wm Dodson, painter
67 David McMurtrie, traveler
69 James Hooper, traveler
71 Thos Rumsey, polisher
73 Mrs L Cooper
75 Chas J Newman, music tchr
77 John Quinn, patternmaker

Evans-st intersects

81 Robt S Miller, clerk P O
83 Jas Johnston, caretaker
85 Jas F Bryant, plasterer
87 Hy Johnson, fitter
89 Edwin A Dewitt, grocer
91 Hugh Logan, salesman

Cannon-st intersects

91 Thos M Williamson, grocer
91½ Geo Richmond, printer
93 James E Mathews, painter
95 Thos Sharp, bookkeeper
97 Wm Anderson, machinist
99 James Anderson, laborer
101 Stephen M Russell, polisher
103 Wm Anstey, shoemaker

105 Robt Bagnall, roadmaster
107 Mrs D I McGee
109 Wm Robertson, **clerk**
111 Vacant
115 Wm Macdonald, scalemaker
119 Patrick Doherty, moulder
127 Samuel Scott, grocer

Robert-st intersects

131 John Linfoot, agent
137 Hugh C Bracken, spinner
139 Wm Burns, tailor
141 Alex Wetherall, merchant
143 A T Filgiano, bookkeeper
147 Mrs F W Hore
155 F W Hore, manf
159 Robt Robinson, mason
161 Mrs Wm Hardstaft
City hospital

Barton-st intersects

183 Thos W Turner, engineer
185 E Hill, laborer
189 Thos Lyons, laborer
191 Wm Michael, laborer

South-st intersects

195 Patrick Nelson, road master

G T R Track intersects

213 Thos Patterson, machinist
215 Patrick McCartney, carter
217 Hy Hincks, machinist
217 Robt Davis, car checker
219 Wm Nelson, yard foreman
221 John Carmichael, conductor

North-st intersects

225 Wm H Finch, iron founder
227 David Fawcett, machinist
229 James Purvis, carpenter

Albert Road intersects

231 Geo Welby, patternmaker

Ferrie-st intersects

James Durne
James Walker, soap factory
Michael Coughlin, laborer

Walnut-st north, east side, from King to King-Wm

4 F H Sharpe, barber
6 John Burke, laborer
12 Geo McCullough, blacksmith

Walnut-st north, west side

1 Joseph Wilson, painter
5 Burn & Robinson, Manf Co
7 John Armstrong, carpenter
9 John Chapman, machinist

Walnut-st south, east side, from 113 King e, south to Hannah

1 Geo Bartman, tailor
1 Thos Ferguson, shoemaker
3 Mrs Thos Derrington
5 Mrs Robt Walker
7 Miss Jessie Lane
7½ Wm Breheny, shoemaker
9 Samuel White, news agent
11 Mrs Peter Sinclair

Main-st intersects

15 H D Griffin, M D
17 Richard Ellicott, assessor
19 A W Robertson, bookkeepr
21 Roderick McDonald, clerk
23 Fire Engine House
25 H S Laribet, shoemaker

Jackson-st intersects

27 John O'Neil, laborer
31 Wm Stern, traveler
33 Geo Moyes, moulder
35 F S Ryckman, contractor
37 Chas James, machinist
43½ Nelson Walton, butcher
45 Nelson Keefer, grocer

Hunter st intersects

45 Vacant
47 Mrs Emily Keele
49 Chas Knott, manf
51 Chas Gurney jr, clerk
53 John Flynn, laborer
55 Mrs Margaret O'Brien
55a John O'Brien, cigarmaker

53a Michael Flynn, clerk
55½ M Birrell
" Geo Hewson, cabinetmkr
57 Hugh Flook, salesman
59 Chas L Ennis, tuner
61 Vacant
63 Robt C Bland, machinist
65 Vacant
67 Vacant
69 Mrs M Hamilton
71 D Sullivan, grocer

O'Reilly-st intersects

73 Wellington Tice, teamster
77 Wm Ferguson, tailor
79 Geo Spence, shoemaker
81 Thos Baker, baker

Young-st intersects

95 Hy Lavery, bookkeeper

Maria-st intersects

105 Mrs John Fitzgerald
107 M Foley, moulder
109 Michael Gallagher, shoemkr
113 M J Forster, carpenter
113 James Gallagher, watchman
117 Owen Connell, laborer
121 James Mulholland, laborer

Hannah-st intersects.

Walnut-st s, west side

Wm I A Case, M D

Main-st intersects

John Winer
18 Jos Conian, conductor
18½ Mrs M R Smith
20 C B Sweet, teamster
24 Thos Wilson

Jackson-st intersects

30 Peter Awrey, farmer
32 Robt Taylor, shoemaker
1 " John Fuller, laborer
34 Jas Burge, agent
36 Ed Schwarz, shoemaker
38 Frederick Wakelin
40 John C Williams, gardener

Hunter-st intersects

44 Geo Spence, carpenter
46 Vacant
48 Vacant
48½ Richard Beckerson
50 Michael Flynn
52 Albert Roney, tailor
54 Edwin J Case, laborer
56 John Cousins, bank messengr
58 John Bayley, salesman
60 Edward Stewart, hatter
62 Joseph Tinsley, printer
66 Mrs E Sarginson, tailoress
68 David Dunlop, harnessmak'r

O'Reilly-st intersects

80 John Coltrust, laborer
82 John Halliday, laborer
84 James Flaherty, laborer

Young-st intersects

92 Jas O'Reilly, laborer
94-96 Wm Myles, laborer

Maria-st intersects

106 Mrs M Eltz
110 Thos Coughlin, laborer

Hannah-st intersects
Patrick-st intersects

Wellington-st n, east side from 216 King e to Burlington Bay

2 Chas Smith, messenger
4 Mrs Alex McDonald
6 James Foster, plater
8 H H Martin
10 Wm Connell, finisher
12 Wm McCurdy, carpenter
14 Mrs Thos Baine
16 Mrs James Smith
18 Robt Harper, florist

King Wm-st intersects

24 John Hancock, builder
26 Thos Morris, flour and feed
28 Vacant
30 Wm Dewart, laborer
32 Miss Nancy McDermid
34 Wm Aiken, blacksmith

36 John Baldwin, carpenter
38 W Hunter, brass founder
40 Mrs Alexander Boyd
42 Albert Hayman, laborer
44 John Pearce, laborer
46 Mrs Wm Hanna
48 Arthur Moore, watchman
50 Hy Vanderbilt, moulder
52 A Bowron, tinsmith
54½ James Dennis, shoemaker
56 Walter Tallman, moulder

Wilson-st intersects

54 John Willcocks, butcher
56 Vacant
58 Thos Torrance, harnessmkr
60 Vacant
62 Hy McStravick, shipper
64 John Earley, driver
66 R M Ross, painter
68 Frank J Nelson, reporter
68½ E Barker, printer
70 W R Powell, builder
72 Wm S Nixon, printer
74 Emerson Gage
82 Hy Jaeger, bricklayer
82½ Mrs Jas McManus
84 Jas Redfield, burnisher
88 Wm R Dingle, machinist

Evans-st intersects

Meriden Britania Co

Cannon-st intersects

Octave Legarie, wagonmaker
122 Alex Durand, carpenter
124 Andrew Ross, commission
126 Mrs Abe Neff
128 Brent Johnston, carpenter
130 John Savage, machinist
132 Lumber yard

Robert-st intersects

136 S Cunningham, conductor
138 John Lowery, policeman
140 Mrs Francis E Boan

Wellington terrace {
1 Nicholas Carrier, shoemakr
2 Mrs Sidney Jackson
3 Vacant
4 Hugh S Wallace, tinsmith
5 Geo Senn, foreman
6 J Fenton, policeman
}

- 1 John Caldwell
- 2 Vacant
- 3 Wm Stokes, clerk
- 4 Frank Irving, machinist
- 5 R VanOrder, conductor

Barton-st intersects

102 Robt Reader, moulder
104 C S Copeland, ropemaker

South-st intersect

G T R Crossing
L D Sawyer & Co, agr implements

Ferrie, Wood & Macaulay sts intersect

City Crematory

Wellington-st n, west side

1 D Day Smith, M D
3-9 Hamilton Vinegar Works
11 Swimming Baths
15 Alex Zitonsky
19 M Steinberg, rag dealer

King Wm-st intersects

21 Thos Morris, flour and feed
25 Mrs W W Reid
27 Mrs Elizabeth Abell
29 Wm Boisfeuillet, electrician
31 Thos Lawless, journalist
27a Wm Horsfield, laborer
29a Hy Burrows, bookkeeper
31 Geo Millward, engineer
33 Thos Nevills, laborer
35 Arch McMaster, painter
37 Jas O'Neil, wood worker

Rebecca-st intersects

39 C C Baird, grocer
41 James Miller, butcher
43 John H Foster
45 Thos Martin, mail clerk
47 Mrs Wm Dixon
49 Jas Randall, traveler
45 John Burt, moulder
47a Walter Stanley, porter
49a Alex McPhie, biscuit pedl'r
51 Mrs H Gildon, grocer

Wilson-st intersects

53 Chas W Stillman, mechanic
55 Herbert B Whipple, agent
57 Vacant
59 John Campbell, machinist
61 F W Lawrence, builder
63 Geo Cuttriss, engraver
65 Wm Gilmore, shoemaker
69 Mrs Jas Robertson
71 John Ronan, grocer

Kelly-st intersects

75 Chas Walker, confectioner
77 John C McCoy, merchant
79 Geo Russell, soap maker
81 Alex Kerr
83 John Ross, teacher
85 Wm Robinson, foreman N & N W R
87 Willis Yeager, carpenter
87 John McDonald, shoemaker
89 J H Cummer
91 John Acheson
93 W P Crawford, excise officer
95 Alfred Hearce, telegraphist
97 Robt Gondon, clerk
99 Vacant
99½ Richard Atkinson, shoemkr
101 Thos Wilson, hotel keeper

Cannon-st intersects

103 Miss Nora Ronan
Primary school
109 Mrs J Truscott
111 Thos McCallum, merchant
113 John Cook, painter
115 Thos J Symonds, laborer
117 Mrs Alexander Campbell
119 Thos Campbell, moulder
121 Wm Rowland, measurer
123 Alfred Robbins, engineer
125 Wm T Sheill, shoemaker
127 Mrs Warren Davis
131 Byron Ketcheson, moulder

Robert-st intersects

133 Thos Renwick, engineer
135 Vacant
137 Ed Robertson, carpenter
139 Michael Quigley, moulder
141 Chas Goring, carpenter
143 Vacant

145 Miss Kate Johnston
147 Chas Erdman, grocer
149 John Dow, buffer
151 Albert Dowling, machinist
153 Thos Fair, machinist
155 Andrew Kennedy, stonemasn
157 Alfred Cox, cork cutter
159 Hy Hyatt, shoemaker
161 Simon Lawrie, agent
163 Horace Green, millwright
165 Thos O'Grady, moulder
167-9 E Ecclestone, grocer
177 Mrs John Forbes

Barton-st intersects

167 J Kirkpatrick, grocer
171 Jonathan Lilly, messenger
175 Thos Sisman, shoemaker
177 Ed Halloran, carriage goods
179 Guy Munson, foreman
179½ Joseph Grace, shoemaker
181 Alex Forbes, potash manf
187 Hy Foot, laborer
189 John Brodie, clerk
191 Wm Lee, mason
193 John A Cameron, fitter
193½ Wm Wilson
195 Robt Arkinson, shoemaker
197 Wm Robinson, laborer
199 John Truscott, painter
2.1 T Kennedy, cotton operator
203 Nelson Seaver, laborer
205 Murray Seaver, carpenter
205 Mrs H Marigold
207 Robt Barker, carriagemaker
209 Duncan McKenzie, wood dlr

Murray-st intersects

219 Thos Wallington, painter
219 John Cameron, boilermaker
221 John McKenzie, wood dealer
    D R Dewey & Co, coal
    Railway crossing
231 Markham Phillips, laborer

Strachan-st intersects

237 Wm McMenemy, baggagemn
239 John Conway, machinist
245 Patrick Noonan, laborer

Ferrie and Picton sts intersect

Matthew Quigley, laborer

Macauley-st intersects

Kenneth McGillivray, carpntr

Wood-st intersects

Alfred Wragg, plasterer
John Rutley, stovemounter

Wellington-st s, east side, from 191 King e to the Mountain

First Methodist Church

Main-st intersects

19 Wm Hunter, brass moulder
23 Edmund Pinch, machinist
25 Hy Dallas, traveler
27 Wm Hyslop, merchant
29 H N Kittson, merchant
31 T D Murphy, mangr WhipCo
33 Vacant
37 Alex F Sutherland inspector
45 J X Randall
47 Gotlieb Haas, nurseryman
49 Geo Canning, plasterer
51 F T Day, traveler
53 Mantagu Raymond, pianotunr
55 Peter Ferres, policeman

Hunter-st intersects

61 John A Kennedy, merchant
63 Frank E Walker, merchant
65 Raymond Walker, merchant
67 Joseph Herron, tailor
71 P S Bateman, blacksmith
73 Mrs Andrew Stevenson
75 Wm J Barclay, pianomaker
77 Wm Claringbowl, gardener
79 Hy Gayfer, mangr A Murray
    & Co
81 John Isbister, contractor

Stinson-st intersects

Thos Gillett
101 Fred Kellond, bookbinder
105 Peter McCandlish, shipper
    Railway Crossing
    Aged Women's Home
    Hamilton Orphan Asylum

Hannah-st intersects

Wellington-st s, west side
Private grounds

Main-st intersects

28 Robt Peebles, carpenter
30 John Miles, carpenter
36 W S Champ, paymaster GTR

Jackson-st intersects

38 J E Bull, salesman
44 John Wilson, painter
46 C H Stevenson, inspector
48 Luke Harrison, butcher

Hunter-st intersects

54 Peter O'Heir, customs Offic'r
56 John H Tilly, clerk
58 Hy D McBrien, plumber
64 D G Ellis, broker

Grove-st intersects

72 Robt Gordon, carpenter
84 Geo Wm Bartman, tailor
86 Wm N Blakeley
90 Wm Addison, jr, builder
92 James Piercy, bookkeeper
94 Wm Addison, sr, builder

Young-st intersects

98 David Heddle, mason
102 C Doyle, moulder
104 Mrs Wm Barton
106 Thos Sullivan, laborer
110 Fred Wilson, carpenter
112 George Paine, salesman
Church of Ascension Mission

Maria-st intersects

118 Richard Plant, manf
122 Hy Nixon, quarryman
124 John Prike

Hannah-st intersects

Wentworth-st n, east side, from King e to the Bay
Street Car Inn
John Baylis, gardener
Mrs A Donohoe

Nightingale-st intersects

John Gully, shoemaker

Wilson-st intersects

Robt Burns, blacksmith
Mrs Agnes Eaglesham
Mrs John Goodman
John Walker, moulder
Hy Smith, shoemaker
M B Burkholder

Cannon-st intersects

Wm Milne, wine manf
Mrs E G Brown, gardener
C Whitehend, gardener

Barton-st intersects.

Col John Land
Chas Hewitt, laborer
Thos Nelson, oil refiner
P H Land, brickmaker

Railway Crossing

Hamilton Sewer Pipe Works
Thos Lawrey, pork factory
John Duffy, gardener
Wm T Carry, ice dealer

N & N W Crossing

James Webster, florist
Geo Webster
James Weir, boat builder
John Morris, boat builder

Wentworth-st n, west side
Francis French, grain buyer
Wm M Rousseuux, carpenter

King Wm-st intersects.

Baptist Mission Church
5 Thos Burgess, laborer
7 Wm Sutherland, garden.r
9 Samuel Smith, laborer
11 Jos Wilson, watchman

Nightingale-st intersects

15 Green Sranton, tobaccoroller
17 John Cropper, stovemounter
19 Wm Nelson, laborer

Wilson-st intersects
Ed W Cuttriss, carpenter
John Cardwell, plasterer
John Eden, laborer
Cannon-st intersects
Peter Taylor, grocer
Barton-st intersects
Rev Robt Miller
John Marshall, foreman
Mission Sabbath School
John M Arthur, porter
Alex Miller, car cleaner
I Lessard, brushmaker
Wm J Tout, machinist
Elijah Whittaker, machinist
James Stein, laborer
South-st commences
G T R crossing
Thos Seal, brickmaker
Wm J Nott, butcher
Michael Gerrie, butcher
Thos Hodgson, laborer
Alfred Bailey, gardener
Wm H Eaglesham, gardener
N & N W crossing
Rev Geo Anderson
Lansdowne Park

Wentworth-st south, e side
Mrs Geo Wilds
Hy Marshall, gardener
Aikmans'-ave intersects
Chas R Wilks, carpenter
Joseph Hooker, gardener
Chas Armstrong, N W R
Alex Fraser, merchant
Main-st intersects
Jacob T Nottle
E L Kraft, harnessmaker
Ida-st intersects
Wm Bell, barrister
J H Davis, merchant
Geo Billington, machinist

Wentworth s, west side
Robt Hall, inspector
Main st intersects
Arthur Woodhouse
Wm Gillesby, merchant
Vacant
Stinson-st intersects
Andrew Alexander

West-ave n, e side, from 238 King e to Barton
2 John Cotton, carpenter
8 John F Kievell, carpenter
10 Asher Holmes, agent
12 Wm Nunn, blacksmith
14 Matthew Forster, wood wkr
16 Mrs James Govier
18 Sylvester Battram, grocer
King William-st intersects
20 John Scollard, butcher
26 John Williams, shipwright
28 Mrs Thos Griffin
32 Wm Snaith, butcher
36 Vacant
38 Mrs John Essex
40 John White, laborer
42 David Ross, bricklayer
42½ Mrs Wm Watson
44 Robt Rogers
46 Ithamar Smuck
48 Thos Burrows, auctioneer
50 Joseph Mearce, teamster
52 Geo Barr, contractor
54 D Kapelle, tailor
56 John McComb, tailor
62 Hy McCann, confectioner
Wilson-st intersects
64 Samuel Challice, butcher
66 M J Barry, shoemaker
68 Albert Vaughan, clerk
70 James Babb, melter
74 Mrs Mary Shea
76 David Barton, bookkeeper
78 J P Steedman, clerk

80 Mrs Andrew Lyle
82 John Lyle, plumber
84 Thos Parkhill, salesman
84½ Wm Myers, tinsmith
86 James Campbell, moulder
90 John W Yeager, carpenter
90 Mrs S Rodgers
94 John M Carroll, moulder
96 Philip A A Brooking
98 Frank C White, lock shipper
98½ James Springstead, laborer

Evans-st intersects

100 James Robinson, moulder
102 Hy Beare, moulder
104 Albert Dalton, flagman
110 Robt McQuillan, teamster
112 John Watt, merchant

Cannon-st intersects

116 Michael Donohoe, tinsmith
118 Thos Lewis, carter
124 Samuel Knight, laborer
126 Mrs John Mulholland
128 Robt Stuart
130 John Townsend
132 Mrs James McMenemy
134 Richard Haigh, bookbinder
136 James Forman, brakeman
138 James Groves, blacksmith
140 Edgar Montgomery, blacks'h
142 Mrs John Whitelock
146 Alex Campbell, druggist

Robert-st interects

154 Wm C Southwell, fitter
156 Alex Beddie, mason
158 Wm Wolton, tinsmith
164 John B Freed, manf
166 Chas Dallyn, barber
168 Hy A Clark, publisher
170 J G Muir, bricklayer
172 Wm R Leckie, bookkeeper
174 John Glassford, laborer
176 James Martin, laborer

Barton-st intersects

West-ave n, west side

3 James Boyd

49

5 Wm G Wright, machinist
7 Mrs Stephen James
11 James Phillips, builder
13 Ed J Moore, clerk
15 A W Aitchison, chief fire brigade
17 Chas Mottashed, builder
19 James M Davis, machinist
21 Wm J Hall, porter
23 E H Blockley, civil engineer

King William-st intersects

27 Robt Stewart, grocer
29 Shadwick L Seaman
31 M McFarlane, machinist
33 Jos Wilson, grocer
35 Arch Wilson, moulder
37 James Qua, sawyer
39 Alfred M Walters, marblec'r
43 Alex Morrison, laborer
45 Philip Hastings, carpenter
47 Robt Proctor, sawyer
49 John Henry, carpenter
51 Geo Magill, moulder
53 John R McKichan, manf
59 Chas Stickle, letter carrier
61 James Anderson, blacksmith
63 Alex Quinn, moulder
65 Allen Trail, porter
67 John Kenrick, grocer

Wilson-st intersects

69 R C Pettigrew, wood & coal
71 John Pettigrew, carpenter
73 Jesse L Kramer, cigarmaker
73½ Lenord H Futtrey, finisher
75 Fred Burrows, clerk
77 Max Steinberg, rag dlr
79 Thos Murray, porter
81 Josiah Beare, moulder
83 Geo Watson, shoemaker
85 Jas C Pinch, sergt police
87 Vacant
89 Sam McNair, court crier
91 Thos Mulhuron, moulder
93 Mrs John Mulaney
95 John Peacock, health insp'r
97 Ed Smith, clerk
99 Wm McLaren

Evans-st intersects
101 J W Smith, foreman
103 Mrs Ann Evans
105 Wm Crockett, bookbinder
107 Mrs Allen Armstrong
109 Herbert Linton, laborer
111 Geo Blake, laborer
113 Theo Barth, cigar packer
115 Alfred Tory, clerk GTR
Cannon-st intersects
129 Hy Williams, teamster
131 Patrick Henry
133 Mrs Wm Perkins
135 Mrs Richard Hales
137 Walter Fricker, machinist
139 David Murray, blacksmith
Robert-st intersects
143 Thos Allen, contractor
145 Mrs Samuel Perry
147 Emory Chagnon, spinner
149 Jno Trimble, bridge repairer
151 J D Baine, machinist
153 R Armstrong, patternmaker
155 John Glassford, fireman
157 Geo Phillips, tailor
159 Alfred Conde, fireman
161 J R Dodson, brassfinisher
163 Wm L Cook, machinist
165 J J Bennett, engineer
167 James Sime, plater
169 Vacant
171 Vacant
173 Thos Hall, engineer
175 Vacant
177 Chas L Smith, builder
179 Fred Moore, builder
    Public school
Barton-st intersects

West-ave s, east side, from St Thomas' Church, Main e to Stinson

1 S J Treble, merchant
2 E G Payne, ins agent
  R Mathews, artist
3 Alex Davidson, accountant
5 Mrs E Dallas

7 Thos C Stewart, traveler
9 James Stuart, merchant
9½ S M Kenny, ins agent
11 Chas R Smith, merchant
13 Hugh Angus, bookkeeper
15 Ed Overell, merchant
17 G P Harrison, traveler
19 Rev Thos Goldsmith
21 Mrs Frederica Burns
23 Mrs Mary Patton
25 E C Murton, merchant
27 J W Morden
31 C W Burns
Hunter-st intersects
47 R M Wanzer, manf
Stinson-st intersects

West-ave s, west side

Main-st intersects
  St Thomas' Church
6 Jonathan Ames, manf
10 F E Kilvert, collector customs
12 R L Whyte, custom officer
22 Julius Grossman, merchant
24 A Grossman, merchant
26 Mrs Ann Fox
26½ Hy Beckett, clerk
28 Hugh H Stevens
Hunter-st intersects
42 Jas E Pointer, traveler
44 G Hutchinson
46 J J Upfield, traveler
48 Thos M Kelly, grocer
50 Mrs Jas Campbell
54 Mrs J W Goering
54 Wm Goering, merchant

Stinson-st intersects

West-st runs north from end of King w

Samuel Cheeseman, brickmkr
Wm Nichols, brickmaker
John Rankin, laborer
John Ollman, brickmaker
— Williams, gardener

Wilson-st, n side, from 56 Mary to east of Burlington

4 Mrs Bella Turnbull
4 Jas Mahaffy, machinist
6 Chas Colville, machinist
10 Wm Turnbull, assessor

Elgin-st intersects

16 Chas Duncan, merchant
18 T H Butler, manf
20 Alfred Jenkins, machinist
22 Miss Mary Golden
24 Samuel Robbins, tinsmith
26 Vacant
28 Wm Robbins, carpenter
30 Mrs M Lemon, dressmaker
32 Joseph Atkinson, painter

Ferguson-ave intersects

John W Goodson, shoemakr
34 Mrs Thos Griffin
36 Miss Margaret Walker
38 Miss Ross
40 Tanis Osier, foreman
42 Thos Lawlor, machinist
44 John Radigan, tinsmith
50 Thos Lormie, machinist
52 Mrs Wm Rowe

Cathcart-st intersects

54 Fred Cork, steam fitter
56 Jos Wilson, letter carrier
58 Chas Morrow, bricklayer
58 Geo Wilson, filecutter

Wellington-st intersects

68 to 74 Vacant
76 Mrs Alex McLeod
78 R C Pettigrew, coal & wood

West-ave intersects

84 John Knowles, salesman
86 Mrs Hugh McCawley
88 Thos Appleton, gardener
90 James Brock, whipmaker
92 Geo Forbes, fireman
94 A G Russell, jeweler
96 J McCarthy, messenger
98 Geo Hazan, tailor

Victoria and East-aves intersect

118 J C N Jenkins, machinist
120 Saml B Fuller, policeman
122 Robt J Taylor, cabinetmaker
124 Geo Dunnett, moulder
126 Edgar Teeter, butcher
   Geo Barlow, grocer

Emerald-st intersects

Vacant lots

Tisdale-st intersects

148 Alex Thomson, proof read'r
156 Geo Collins, carpenter

Steven-st intersects

162 John Underhill, laborer
164 Albert Karsten, laborer
r " Thos Smith, butcher
168 John Cox, carpenter
170 Jos Vandusen, carpenter
174 Chas Bourque, brushmaker

Ashley-st intersects

176 Fred Frewing, plasterer
178 Wm Wilson, laborer
180 John O'Hara, laborer
190 Vacant
192 Thos H Herbert, stonecutter

Wentworth-st intersects

Wilson-st, south side

3 Miss Ann Eadie
7 Mrs Wm Roberts
9 Alex L Phillips, blacksmith
11 Stephen Millon, plumber
17 Adam Laidlaw, founder
19 Hugh Hennessey, blacksm'h
21 Fred W King, traveler
23 Mrs J McVicar
27 John McMahon, dairy

Ferguson-ave intersects

33 Wm Elvin, traveler
35 John Quarrier, millers' agent
37 John Finlayson, saddler
39 J A Walterhouse, engineer
41 Geo Begg, clerk
43 Chas Smith, box maker
45 Stanley Arnold, cabinetmakr
47 Albert E Storm, tea dealer

49 Ed Hodgkiss, piano tuner
51 Geo W Kappele, bookkeepr

Cathcart-st intersects

53 Ed Williams, engineer
57 Mrs Matthew Bell

Wellington-st intersects

77 F G Shearsmith, carpenter

West-ave intersects

91 Mrs James Wright
93 Jas W Buckingham, painter

Victoria-ave intersects

97 Mrs Alfred Feast
99 John Smith, baker

East-ave intersects

117 J J Smith, cigar manf

Emerald-st intersects

L W Keil, grocer

Tisdale-st intersects

149 Geo Axford, butcher
151 Geo Nash, carpenter
153 James Waynard, painter
155 John McKnight, engineer

Steven-st intersects

163 G McLaughlin, laborer
167 Mrs Mary Lynch
169 Mrs Robt Tansley
169½ John Mulholland
171 Wm Holmes, brushmaker

Ashley-st intersects

177 W Shaughnessy, laborer
185 Wm Hannah, stonecutter
187 Mrs Eliza Harris
191 Jeremiah Gregg, laborer

Wentworth-st intersects

Geo Smith, laborer
Edmund Hunt, blacksmith
Hy East, bricklayer

Burlington-st intersects

Wood-st e, n side, from foot James n to Wellington

7 Wm Miles, laborer
9 John Lawrence, painter
11 — McKay, coal dealer
13 Patrick Cahill, boilermaker
13 Philip Doyle, laborer
17 Robt McKay, coal merchant

Hughson-st intersects

25 Wm McFadden, grocer
27 Geo Points, moulder
29 Mrs Hughine Wright
31 John Blake, laborer
33 Patrick Curran, laborer
35 Mrs Mary O'Neil
37 John Dunn, laborer
39 John Smith, laborer
41 Richard Fuerd, laborer
43 Jas Wickham, stovemounter

John-st intersects

55 Robt O'Neil, laborer
57 John McCarthy, driver
57½ Dennis Mulcahy, stovemo'r
59 Jesse Stibbs, glassblower
61 Thos O'Connor, glassblower
63 John M Nealson, laborer

Catharine & Mary-sts intersect

105 John E Miller, moulder
107 Arthur Stevenson
107½ Thos Ward, laborer
109 Thos Wilson, laborer
111 Joseph Hardy, carpenter
113 Joseph Oddy, carpenter

Ferguson-ave intersects

129 Vacant
133 Geo Fielding, warper
135 Ed Allan, blacksmith
137 Ed Fuller, laborer
139 Robt McKenzie
141 Wm Aldrich, laborer

Wellington-st intersects

Wood-st e, south side

6 Samuel Blowes, sailor

8 Arthur Miller, fireman
10 John McNichol, glassblower

Hughson-st intersects

24 Mrs Patrick Colvin

John-st intersects

50 Wm Daly, tailor
52 Laurence Dunn, laborer
54 Vacant
56 Patrick Burns, laborer
60 Augustus Fickel, packer
64 Joseph Gilligan, laborer

Catharine and Mary-sts intersect

100 Thos Pearson, glassblower
108 James Turner, machinist
110 John Phillips, stovemounter
114 Wm Parker, blacksmith
116 Walter Chapman, laborer
118 Stephen Saxby, laborer
120 Vacant

Ferguson-ave intersects

122 Geo Woods, laborer
124 James Stevens
126 Thos Moore, laborer
128 Wm Walton, laborer

132 James Nolan, laborer
136 Wm Greenway, laborer
142 Mrs P McKeever

Wellington-st intersects

Wood-st w, north side, from 239 James n to Macnab

8 Michael Hamilton, laborer
10 Robt McManus, laborer
12 Martin Mahoney, sailor
16 Dennis Kavanagh, laborer
20 Mrs Mary Lawlor

Macnab-st intersects

24 Jacob Burrowhuff, laborer

Wood-st w, south side

11 Patrick Roach, laborer
13 John Mahoney, teamster
15 Wm Braidwood, clerk
17 Dennis McAuliffe, laborer

23 Mrs John Doyle
25 Chas Moody, weaver

Macnab-st intersects

37 John Holmes, carter
39 James Dilworth, laborer

Burlington-st intersects

York-st, north side, from Macnab n to City limits

2 John Greig, stationer
4 Hy Magee, harness
6 Geo W Carey, groceries
6a John Davis, crockery
6½ Mrs Bradley, fancy goods
8 Kraft & Son, saddlery
10 A Lawson & Co, printers
12 Geo Luxton, flour, feed, etc
14 Mrs Wm Bangerth, confect'r
16-18 D Murray, flour and feed
20 John P McLeod, printer
20 Wm Ronald, grocer
22 J Henry, boots and shoes
24 John Kerrigan, tailor
26 O'Connell & Evans, marble
    dealers
28 Chas Drew, tinsmith
30-2 Albert Brunke, furrier
34 Wm Scott, laundry
36-38 Geo Kramer, saloon
40 John Taylor, flour and feed

Park-st intersects

Cheapside Block {
Carl G Carlson, tailor
Philp Muter, patternmaker
Mrs Elizabeth Moore
Thos Bowker, fruiterer
Mrs Wm Sangster
Vacant
}

50 Wm Kraft, pork butcher
52 Vacant
54 Alex Campbell, grocer
56 Wm F Farmer, watchmaker
58 Vacant
60 A Calder & Co, druggists

Bay-st intersects

Copp Bros, founders

390   CITY OF HAMILTON.

100 F G Beckett Engine Co
102 Samuel Mathers, rag dealer
106 Vacant
110 J & G Nicholson, wood dlrs
114 Wm J Crowley, dealer
116 John Browne, blacksmith
118 Fred Gottorff, marble dealer

Caroline-st intersects

124 Ed Green, furniture dealer
126 Miss Jennie Hill
128 John Fitzpatrick, clerk
130 Adam Hunter, stationer
132 Alex McKay, machinist
134 Geo Kellond, shoemaker
136 F W Wodell, journalist
144-146 John Duff, grocer
146½ Wm Britt, merchant tailor
148 Vacant
150 John Lewis, grocer
152 John DeVine, shoemaker
154 James H Rodgers, baker
156 J Philp, druggist

Hess-st intersects

160 James Mason, confectioner
162 British American Laundry
166 M O'Grady, marble works
168 Wm Cook, painter
172 Donald Dallas, rubber
174-6 Geo Scott, wood dealer
178 James Allen, laborer
180 Vacant

Queen-st intersects

West Lawn, A Copp

Oxford-st intersects

226 Jas Haydon, tinsmith
228 James Porteous, machinist
230 Otis Hines, butcher

Locomotive-st commences

242 Chas R Nex, laborer
244 Wolf Goldberg, rag dealer
246 J A Malcolm, carriagemkr
250 National Hotel

Magill-st commences

254 Arthur Boyle, druggist

256 Wm Phillips, butcher
258 Patrick Shea, laborer
260 Matthew Flynn, engineer
262-4 Percy A Wynn, shoemaker

Crook-st commences

27- Geo R Snider, grocer
276 Arthur Richmond, butcher
278 Wm B Robson, miller
    Dennis Mahoney, shoemaker

Locke-st intersects

286 John Wright, butcher
288 Mrs Mary Ann Stroud
290 Wm Armstrong, tailor
292 F W Hunter, bookkeeper
294 Geo Dodd, piano finisher
296 Richard Pentecost

Inchbury-st intersects

300 Thos Tribute, machinist
320 Isaac Mills, electrician
324 Robt P Leask, gents' furnish'r
326 J B Smith, laborer
    Dundurn Castle
    Mrs N M Wheeler, hotel
    Wm Cross, toll keeper
    Wm Cross sr, trackman
    — Ross, detective
    Michael Pender, laborer
    — McGrath, trackman
    Malcolm McFee, trackman
    Patrick Crana, trackman
    James Everett, trackman
    — Burwell, gardener
    Michael O'Neill, gardener
    Mrs Kean
    Valentine Flood, trackman
    Daniel Young, gardener
    James Sayers, laborer
    — Hutchison, shoemaker
    Dennis Sullivan, trackman
    Edwin Fairbank, finisher
    Mrs Hy Fairbank
    Alfred Fagan, painter

York-st south side

1 R Evans & Co, seedsman
3 Philp & Son, saddlers
5 E Gorman, barber

7 C Kerner, hotel
9 J H Carmichael, shoemaker
11 Mrs Mary Walker, milliner
13 Mrs Annie Bowen, fancy good
15 Jas Cuzner, shoemaker
17 Ham & Edwards, tinsmiths
19 H Brazier, barber
21 J Belling, watchmaker
23 J M Munzinger, bookbinder
23½ Ed Bird, gunsmith
25 Robt Arroll, broker
27 Chris Moody, watchmaker
29 Julius J Goodhart, clothes cleaner
31 Jas Kirk, barber
33 P S Bateman, blacksmith
33½ K J Scully, painter
35 John Wilson, tinsmith
37 S Groves, blacksmith
39 John F Kavanagh, grocer

Park-st intersects

41 Commercial hotel
43 John Walsh, shoemaker
45 Michael J Fitzgerald, laborer
47 James Wilson, broker
51 E M Furniss & Son, marble
53 L Tufford, tobacconist
53 C Carpenter & Co, hardware
55 Joseph Watson, shipper
57 Peter Carnegie, tailor
57 Alex Hannah, bricklayer
57½ Alex Dingwall, stonecutter
61 Vacant
63 H Goering, hotel keeper
65 Wm H Connor, fruiterer
67 John Spriggs, shoemaker
69 F Oxley, grocer
71 W H C Harrison, herbalist
73 Mrs Thos Platts, fancy goods
75 T C Jackson, butcher
77 David McDonald, grocer

Bay-st intersects

79-83 Vacant
85 Vacant
87 Jos Holdsworth, broker
89 Geo Bradshaw
91 J Andeason, barber

93 Mrs Arthur, broker
95 Geo Millward
97 Geo C Potter, painter
99 Robt Snodgrass
99½ Saml J Coulter, shoemaker
101 John O'Hope, agent
103 Wm Fulton, laborer
105 C J Lancefield, trimmer
107 Rose & Makins, hair dressers
107 Thomson & Wright, lumber dealers
113 H Pearson, hotel
115 John Dixon, knitter
117 Wm Radford, baker
119 Vacant
123 J & H McAllister, grocers

Caroline-st intersects

127 Vacant
129 Thos G Applegath
131 Wm Evans, carpenter
133 Samuel Thorne, merchant
135 John Billington, shoemaker
137 Samuel McGell, carpenter
139 Vacant
141 Mrs W H Duffield,
147 James Naylor, fancy goods
149 Thos Viner, fruiter
151 Wm McKay, conductor
153 John Cameron, moulder
155 Duncan Cameron, traveler
157 Vacant
159 Wm Gillies, jr, grocer

Hess-st intersects

161 Geo Edmonson, butcher
167 Franklin Krum
169 Geo A Young, manf
171 Robt Thompson, builder
173 T S Atwater
183 James G Wilson, moulder

Queen-st intersects

189 Wm McDonald, packer
207 Robt Walker, grocer
209 John Burrows, laborer
213 Philip H Sutton
215 James Patton, carpenter
217 Thos Walsh, grocer
219 Richard May, laborer

221 James Martin, scalemaker
227 G Beaver, hotel
Ray-st intersects
229 Vacant
237 Vacant
241 James Stevenson
245 Samuel Burns
253 Wm Kench, confectioner
Pearl st-intersects
255 Mrs E Renwick, grocer
257 John Dawson, laborer
261 E Wyth, carpenter
263 Geo Ellis, machinist
265 Wm Mitchell, machinist
267 Wm Lackie, piler
269 Wm Greenman, machinist
271 Geo Morris, grocer
285 James McHarg, agent
287 Dundurn Hotel
Locke-st intersects
291-3 Geo Steele, grocer
299 James Hinchliffe, grocer
301 Jos Hancock, saw grinder
305 Vacant
Inchbury-st intersects
307 Geo J Smith
309 R C Cuff, butcher
311 Robt Howat, butcher
315 Wm Quinn, fitter
317 Ed Collins, painter
319 Mrs John Boyle, dairy
Sophia-st intersects
327 Vacant
333 Thos F Smith, artist
335 Thos Young, heater
337 Samuel Collyer, laborer
Devonport-st intersects
Ed Winter, blacksmith
Dundurn-st intersects
James Browne
C Moss, shoemaker
H N Thomas, marble works
Wm Jarritt
Burlington Cemetery

Fred Morrison, hotel
Peter Colvin, grocer
Alex Craig, caretaker cemetery
Burlington Cemetery
Adam Rutherford, laborer
Alex Reid, gardener
Alex Burgess, hotel

Young-st (formerly Catharina) n side from 105 James s to Wellington

1 Bernard Daniels, pedler
3 Mrs Joseph Murphy
5 F M Willson, manf
Hughson st intersects
11 Geo A Young, ins agent
13 Chas H Dempster, manfr
John-st intersects
21 Geo A Filman, salesman
23 — Ballentine, merchant
27 Vacant
Catharine-st intersects
37 Thos Loney, shoemaker
39 Robt Pilgrim
41 A L Reeves, jr, merchant
43 Andrew Martin, butcher
43½ Chas Fitzgerald, laborer
45 Wm Fitzgerald, cab builder
47 Vacant
47 Benj Whitling, gardener
49 Wm G Smith, laborer
51 Dennis Corcoran, carpenter
r " Mrs John Riddle
r " Chas Evans, lamplighter
r " Miss Mary Kidney
r " James Ennis, cabinetmaker
r " Mrs Elizabeth Baikie
r " Robt Barrett, laborer
53 Mrs Eliza Murphy
55 Mrs Wm Cox
57 James Lewis, machinist
59 Mrs Francis Dicker
61 Michael Thorne, laborer
65 G F Townsend, printer
67 Vacant

SUBSCRIBERS'
CLASSIFIED BUSINESS DIRECTORY

ACCOUNTANTS

Blackley David, 2½ James s
Findlay W F, 25 James s
Herman Wm, 16 James s
Lamb Fred H, 7 Hughson s
Mason J J, Masonic hall
Pearson John, 18-20 Hughson s
Townsend Sherman E, 6½ James s
Willson F M, 22 James s

AGENTS—COLLECTING (RENTS, DEBTS, ETC)

Moore & Davis, 2 King Wm
Pearson John, 18-20 Hughson s
Ralston & Irwin, 31 John s
Whipple E S, 78½ King e

AGENTS—LAND AND ESTATE

Bull Richard, 12 Hughson s
Freeman E & Son, 9 King w
Ghent & Staunton, 17-19 Arcade
Mills J B & Co, 26 Merrick
Moore & Davis, 2 King Wm
Pearson John, 18-20 Hughson s
Ralston & Irwin, 31 John s
Strong Wm, 15 Arcade
Whipple E S, 78½ King e

ARCHITECTS

Balfour J, 25 James s
Brass Peter, 50 Hunter w
Clohecy Robt, 2½ James s
Edwards W A, 9 James n
Mulligan C W, court house
Rastrick F J & Son, 22 Maria
Stewart Wm, 25 James s

AUCTIONEERS AND APPRAISERS

Burrows Thos, 78 James n
Hesse J R & Co, 76 James n
Hunter Robt, 24 Merrick

BABY CARRIAGES

Cooper John C, 4-6 Magill

BAGGAGE AND PARCEL EXPRESS

Henry A H, Arcade

BAKERS

Bateman E W, 200 King e
Chilman I C, 119 King w
Geiger H, 214 King w
Harris Bros, 14 Market Square
Lees Wm & Son, 31 Main e

BANKS

Bank of British North America, 5 King e
Bank of Hamilton, 17 King w
Bank of Montreal, cor James and Main
Canadian Bank of Commerce, cor King and Hughson
Merchants' Bank, King cor John
Molsons Bank, cor James and King
Stinson's Bank, 10 Hughson n
Traders' Bank, 36 King e

BANKERS, EXCHANGE STOCK AND SHARE BROKERS

Forbes A F, 7 Hughson s
Morgan Chas E, 11 James n

Walnut st intersects

69 Thos Harlow, grocer
71 Mrs James Kearman
73 Patrick O'Brien, laborer
75 Daniel Shea, laborer
77 John Cauley
79 Thos Freeborn, laborer
81 Vacant
81 Vacant
83 Miss Ann Merriman
85 Andrew Swayzie, laborer
87 Geo Mowat, bricklayer
89 Mrs John Ankertell
91 Mrs Johanna Teehan
93 Wm Edgecomb, carpenter
95 Michael Feeley, laborer

Cherry-st intersects

97 Patrick Doyle, moulder
99 Nicholas Engel, tinsmith
    Ontario Canning Co

Liberty and Aurora-sts intersect

117 Alex Finlayson, clerk
127 Michael Ryan
129 Emile Deronde, laster
    Addison's Planing Mills

Wellington-st intersects

Young-st, south side

Vacant lots

Hughson-st intersects

8 Mrs David McKean
10 Rev T J Macfadden
12 Thos Meade, builder
12½ Wm Hunt, laborer
14 Vacant
16 Alex Walker, carpenter

John-st intersects

18 J G Buchanan, journalist
20 Benj Hunt, carriagemaker
22 Mrs Thos Warner
24 Richard Crawford, coachman
26 Miss Mary Carey
28 Miss Ann Thompson
30 Mrs Taafe
50

32 A Blakemore, mechanic

Catharine-st intersects

40 James Philp, harnessmaker
44 Edmund Smee, shoemaker
46 Samuel A Moore, clerk
48 W Meyers, grocer
50 Ninian McAdams, broommkr
50½ James Hancock, whipmkr
50½ James O'Brien, laborer
52 Philip K Fenton, salesman
54 John McGurk, carpenter
56 John Myers, laborer
58 John Gerrie
60 Thos Dunnieg, teamster
62 Chas Watson, laborer
62½ Fred Hirst, carpenter

Walnut-st intersects

64 Anthony Rowan, laborer
76 Mrs Robt Judge
78 James Pierce, polisher
80 Michael Carroll, shoemaker

Cherry-st intersects

100 A L S Ainsworth, poultry dlr
102 Mrs John Smith
102 Wm Moore, stovemounter
104 Wm Warnick
106 Peter Metz, shoemaker
108 Chas Gracey, laborer
110 John Fleming, laborer
r " Wm Stokes, laborer
r " John Hughes, laborer

Liberty-st intersects

116 Mrs Wm Montgomery

Aurora-st intersects

120 Vacant
122 John O'Neil, laborer
124 Mrs John Sheehan
126 Wm Stevens
128 Emile Deronde, laster
130 Michael Dwyer, shoemakr
132 Robt McClellan
136 John Walsh, shoemaker

Wellington-st intersecs

PROFESSIONAL CARDS.

McQuesten & Chisholm,
Barristers and Solicitors,

VICTORIA CHAMBERS.

31 James St. South.

HAMILTON, ONT.

I. B. McQuesten, M.A., James Chisholm, M.A.

LAZIER & MONCK,
Barristers and Solicitors.

42 JAMES ST. NORTH,

S. F. Lazier, M.A., L.L.B.   J. F. Monck.

PARKES & MACADAMS,
Barristers and Solicitors,

In the Supreme Court,

ATTORNEYS & NOTARIES

OFFICES—Hamilton Provident Building, 1st flat; entrance on Hughson Street.

J. PARKES,   A. H. MACADAMS.

Mackelcan, Gibson & Gansby,
BARRISTERS, ETC.

16 James St. South,

HAMILTON, CANADA.

F. Mackelcan, Q.C., J. M. Gibson, M.A., LL.B.
J. D. Gausby,   Geo. E. Martin.

ROBERTSON & ROBERTSON,
BARRISTERS,

Solicitors, Notaries, Etc.,

COURT HOUSE,

HAMILTON,   ·   CANADA.

Thomas Robertson, Q.C., H. H. Robertson.

Money to lend at lowest rates of interest.

BARTON, GEORGE M.,
Barrister, Solicitor, Notary,

CONVEYANCER.

Money Loaned on Lands at Lowest Rates

OFFICE

4 James St. North, Cor. King

SHERMAN E. TOWNSEND,
Accountant, Auditor, Assignee and General Attorney

6½ James St. South, Hamilton.   27 Wellington St. East, Toronto.

REFERENCES BY PERMISSION.

Frederick Wyld, of Messrs. Wyld, Grasset & Darling, Wholesale Dry Goods, Toronto; Messrs. Foster & Macabe, Wholesale Fancy Goods, Toronto; Messrs. Bain, Laidlaw & Co., Barristers, Etc., Toronto; Edmund Scheuer, Esq., Wholesale Jeweller, Toronto; Alex. Turner, Esq., of Messrs. James Turner & Co., Wholesale Grocers, Hamilton; Adam Brown, Esq., of Messrs. Brown, Balfour & Co., Wholesale Grocers, Hamilton; John W. Murton, Esq., of Messrs. Murton & Reid, Coal Merchants, Hamilton; Messrs. Fuller, Nesbit & Bicknell, Barristers, Etc., Hamilton; Messrs. Long & Bisby, Wool Merchants, Hamilton; James Watson, Esq., President of Strathroy Knitting Co., Hamilton; Messrs. Mackelcan, Gibson & Gausby, Barristers Etc., Hamilton; Edward Mitchell Esq., Manager Canadian Bank of Commerce, Hamilton; Geo. H. Gillespie, Esq., President Hamilton Prov. and Loan Society, Hamilton; A. G. Ramsay, Esq., President Canada Life Assurance Co., Hamilton, Messrs. Orr, Harvey & Co., Wholesale Boots and Shoes, Hamilton; Waterous Engine Works Company, Brantford.

BARRISTERS AND SOLICITORS

Barton Geo M, 4 James n
Bell & Thompson, Wentworth Chambers, 25 James s
Biggar & Lee, 1 James s
Bruce, Burton & Culham, Canada Life Chambers, 1 James s
Cameron & Witherspoon, 1 Hughson s
Carscallen & Cahill, 2½ James s
Haslett & Washington, 20 James s
Crerar & Bankier, 24 Main e
Crerar & Muir, 1 Hughson s
Curell J G, 34 James n
Duff W A H, 31 James s
Fitzgerald Francis, 10 King w
Fuller, Nesbitt & Bicknell, 20 James s
Furlong & Beasley, 2½ James s
Gage & Jelfs, Hughson s
Jones John W, 31 James s
McQuesten & Chisholm, 31 James s
Lavery W J, 4 Main e
Lazier & Monck, 42 James n
Lemon Chas, 10-12 Hughson s
Livingston W Churchill, 31 James s
Macdonald Walter R, 33 James s
MacKelcan, Gibson & Gausby, 16 James s
MacKelcan & Mewburn, 20 Main e
Malone Martin, 2½ James s
Martin, Kittson & Martin, 25 James s
Mills Geo H, 25 James s
Osler, Teetzel & Harrison, Canada Life Chambers, 1 James s
Papps Geo S, 33 James s
Parkes & Macadams, 1 Hughson s
Patten L H, 18-20 Hughson s
Pringle R A, 31 James s
Robertson & Robertson, Court House
Sadlier C A, 8 Main e
Smith & Farmer, 9 James n
Staunton & O'Heir, 18 James s

Stinson T H, cor James and King Wm
Waddell & Waddell, court house
Walker, Scott & Lees, 10 James s

BIRD CAGES, JAPANNED WARE, ETC

Burn-Robinson Manufact'g Co, 12 Mary
Wright E T & Co, 26-8 Catharine n

BOOKSELLERS AND STATIONERS

Buntin, Gillies & Co, wholesale 41 King w
Clappison Thos, 66 James n
Duncan Robt & Co, cor Market Square and James
Eastwood John & Co, 16 King e
Hunter A, 52 James n
Midgley Geo jr, 172 James n
Overell E & Co, 24½ King w
Williams H S, Copp's Block, King e

BOOKBINDERS.

Duncan Robt & Co, cor James and Market Square
Eastwood J & Co, 60 King e
Haigh Richard, 60 King w
Mars Alex, 14 Hughson n

BOOTS AND SHOES.

Arland H & Bro, 26 King e
Blachford H & Co, 30-32 King w
Climie J D, 28 King e
Edwards C P, 104 King w
Gage Geo, 58 King e
Griffith William, wholesale, 57 King w
McPherson John & Co, wholesale 51-3 King e
Schram John, 45 Macnab n
Turner Wm jr, manf, 12 Macnab n

Martin, Kittson & Martin

Barristers & Solicitors

WENTWORTH CHAMBERS,
25 James St. South
HAMILTON, CANADA

Edward Martin, Q. C. E. E. Kittson,
Kirwan Martin, B. A.

MACKELCAN & MEWBURN

Barristers

Solicitors of Supreme Court of Ontario

NOTARIES, ETC.

NO. 20 MAIN ST. EAST

HAMILTON, ONTARIO

H. A. Mackelcan. Sydney C. Mewburn

FRANCIS FITZGERALD

Barrister, Etc

10 KING STREET WEST,

HAMILTON, - - ONTARIO.

W. A. H. DUFF,

BARRISTER, SOLICITOR,

NOTARY PUBLIC, ETC.

VICTORIA CHAMBERS,

31 James Street South,

HAMILTON, - - ONTARIO.

CAMERON & WITHERSPOON

Barristers,

Solicitors *in Supreme Court of Ontario*

NOTARIES, ETC.

Offices—Hamilton Provident Building, 1st flat entrance on Hughson street.

A. D. Cameron, LL.B., R. W. Witherspoon

WALKER, SCOTT & LEES

Barristers, Etc.

10 James Street South

HAMILTON, ONTARIO

W. F. Walker, M. A., LL. B., John J. Scott
Wm. Lees, Thos. Hobson.

FURLONG & BEASLEY

BARRISTERS, ETC.

COR. KING AND JAMES STS.,
Next Molsons' Bank,

Hamilton, - Ontario

CHARLES LEMON,

Barrister and Solicitor

NOTARY PUBLIC, ETC.

Money to Loan on Real Estate Security.

Collection of Accounts and Agency promptly attended to.

Office *No. 14 Hughson Street South,*

HAMILTON, - ONTARIO.

BREWERS

Gomph John, 360 John n
Spring Brewery, P Grant & Sons, 119 Bay n

BROKERS

Broadbent T & G, machinery, 164 King w
Gillespie & Powis, teas, sugars, etc, 31 King e
Ralston & Irwin, 31 John s
Townsend W G, customs, 21 John s

BROOM MANUFACTURERS

Willson & Gates, 31 King w
Woods Walter & Co, 62 Macnab

BRUSH MANUFACTURERS

Meakins & Sons, 225-9 King e
Willson & Gates, 31 King w

BUILDERS AND CONTRACTORS

Addison Wm & Sons, Wellington cor Young
Beer Isaiah, 35 Murray e
Chisholm Robert, 174 Macnab
Clucas Wm, 123 Cannon w
Cruickshank Robt, 55 Jackson e
Hancock Wm, 27 Locomotive
Hannaford Bros, plasterers, 76 Merrick
Isbister John, 81 Wellington s
Meade Thos, 12 Young
Miller F, 81 James s
Pigott M A, 95 Macnab n
Patterson Bros, ft Lower Cathcart
Phillips & Mottashed, 184 King Wm
Sharp Geo, 147 Park n
Smith Thos, 74 Catharine n
Whyte Geo, 131 King e

BUILDERS' SUPPLIES

Freeman W A, 169 James n

Gordon W J F, 108 James n

BUTCHERS

Bowering & Pain, 89 King w
Harrison Henry, 51 James s
Duff John & Son, 146 York
Hill Wm, 252 King e
Lawry Thos & Son, James st market, and 18-20 Macnab s
Limin Chas, 26 Jackson w

CABINET MAKERS AND UPHOLSTERERS

Allardice R A & Co, Merrick
Hoodless & Son, 51 King w
McCallum & Hall, 16 Macnab n
Malcolm & Souter, 67-9 King w
Pecover Joseph, Copp's Block, King e
Zingsheim Jacob, Mary, near Murray

CANNING COMPANIES

Crockett, Muirhead & Co, Queen cor Peter

CARPETS AND HOUSE FURNISHINGS

McKay Bros, 48 King e
Walker Frank E & Co, King cor Walnut n

CARRIAGE MAKERS

Cooper H G & Co, 6 Park s
Malloy & Malcolm, 9 Park n

CARTAGE AGENTS.

Armstrong Chas (N & N W R) 33 Main e
Hendrie & Co (G W R), 35 King w
Shedden Co (G T R) Catharine cor King Wm

CHINA, GLASS AND EARTHENWARE

Canada Glass House, 52 King e

J. W. JONES, LL. B.
Barrister, Etc.

OFFICE:
VICTORIA CHAMBERS,
31 James Street South

N. B.—Money to Loan at Lowest Current Rates.

L. H. PATTEN
Barrister, Solicitor

Conveyancer, Notary Public, Etc.

Office, Chancery Chambers,
18-20 Hughson St. South, cor. Main

HAMILTON, - - - ONTARIO

WILLIAM BRUCE
Solicitor of Canadian and Foreign
PATENTS,
Draughtsman and Engrosser,

14½ King St. East, opposite the Gore

HAMILTON, CANADA.

T. S. BELL
Civil Engineer
AND DRAUGHTSMAN

Draining, Bridging, Road Constructing Surveying, etc., County and Township Engineering

Office, 4 Main St. East, Hamilton, Ont.

R. D. KENNEDY
Provincial Land Surveyor
AND CIVIL ENGINEER

42 JAMES ST. NORTH

HAMILTON.

ROBERT CLOHECY
Architect and Building Surveyor

Designer, Valuator, Etc.

NO. 2½ JAMES ST. SOUTH

MONTAGU RAYMOND
PIANOFORTE TUNER, VOICER AND REGULATOR

From John Broadwood & Son's, Piano Makers to the Queen, London, England

REFERENCES FROM EMINENT MUSICIANS.

Orders left at A. Hamilton & Co.'s Drug Store, or Robert Duncan & Co.'s Book Store.

53 WELLINGTON STREET SOUTH, HAMILTON

London China House, 9 Market Square
McMahon, Broadfield & Co, 104 King e
Skinner J A & Co, 9 King e

CIGAR BOX MANUFACTURER.

Scharlach & Co, 2 Caroline s

CIGARS, TOBACCOS, ETC.

Pattison Z, 65 Cannon w
Reid, Birely & Co, cor King and Catharine
Schrader J C, cor Bay and Cannon

CIVIL ENGINEERS.

Bell T S, 4 Main e
Kennedy R D, 42 James n

CLOTHIERS.

Calder John & Co, wholesale, Macnab cor Merrick
Giles W P & Co, 26 James n
Oak Hall, Wm Farrar, manager, 10 James n
Lister J E & Co, James cor Rebecca
Pratt & Watkins, 18 James n
Sanford W E & Co, wholesale, 47 King e
Vail A S & Co, 18 James n

COAL OIL, LAMPS, ETC.

Canada Glass House, 52 King e
Farmer Wm, 114 James n
Taylor J C, 27 King w
Williams J C, manf, 18 Macnab n
Young & Bro, 17 John n

COAL AND WOOD.

Browne E, foot Macnab n
Dewey D R & Co, 12 James s, and Wellington cor G T R

Dow Bros, 45 Main w
Fairgrieve J B, 6 James s
Freeman W A, 169 James n
Harrison Ed, Main cor Locke
Jones & Gage, 150 John n
Kelly D J, 135 James n
McIlwraith Thos, cor Main and Catharine
McKenzie John, 149 Macnab n
Murton & Reid, cor John and Rebecca, and Main cor Charles
Myles Thos & Son, cor Main and Hughson
Nicholson Wm, 111 King w
Payne W, Cannon cor Cathcart
Smith G B, 8 Mary

COFFEE AND SPICE MILLS.

Canada,—W G Dunn, 59 Main w

COFFEE TAVERNS.

(Hamilton Coffee Tavern Co propietors)
Arcade Coffee Room, Arcade adjoining the market
East End Coffee Room, King e adjoining N & N W R Station
Gore Coffee Tavern, 13 Hughson n

COMMISSION.

Benner Richard, 6 Main e
Gillespie & Powis, 31 King e
Morden W & J, 7 Market sq
Somerville W & Co, 8 Hughson n

CONFECTIONERS.

Aussem J H, 75 James n
Chilman I C, 117 King w
Edwards Benjamin, 102 King w
Newport E, 180 King e
Pattison Z, wholesale, cor King and Park s and 65 Cannon e

CITY OF HAMILTON. 401

CONSULS

Hawaii Kingdom, Adam Brown, 5 James s
Norway & Sweeden, S E Gregory 55 Catharine s
United States, Albert Roberts, G T R station

COTTON FACTORIES

Hamilton Cotton Factory, Mary
Ontario Cotton Mills Co, 250 Macnab n

DAIRY

Oaklands Jersey Dairy, 20 James s
Seymour Alex, 30 James s

DENTISTS

Chittenden C S, 8½ King e
Husband Drs R J & T H, 10 King w
Zimmerman S, M D, King cor Macnab

DINING ROOMS

Tocher's Temperance Dining Rooms, 48 James n

DRUGGISTS

Barr John A & Co, 33 Macnab n
Boyle Arthur, York cor Magill
Brierley Richard, 14 King e
Calder A & Co, 58 York
Central Drug Store, York cor Hess
Doherty Arthur, 245 King w
Gerrie John, 30 James n
Hamilton A & Co, cor King and James
Ontario Pharmacy, John W Yeomans, King cor Ferguson ave
Robinson E F, 36 James n
Smith D Day, King cor Wellington

Sutherland Jas W, 206 King w
Vincent A & Co, 130 James n
Wilson Archdale & Co, wholesale, 19 Macnab n
Winer J & Co, wh, 25 King e

DRY GOODS, MILLINERY, ETC

Barnard, Murdoff & Co, 36 King w
Campbell & Pentecost, 43 Macnab n
Crossley Irving, cor James and King Wm
Finch Bros, 18 King w
Kerr A R & Co, 34 King w
Knox, Morgan & Co, wh, 7 King e
McCoy John A, 40 James n
McIlwraith & McMaster, 18 James n
McKay Bros, 48 King e
Mayhew W E & Co, 8 King e
Murray A & Co, 18-20 King e
Pratt & Watkins, 16 James n
Shea James, 42 King e
Thorne & Co, 14 James n and 160 King e
Watkins Thomas C, 30-2 King e

DYERS AND CLEANERS

Howard W H, 17 Rebecca
Parker Robt & Co, 4 John n
Roe G, 218 King e

ELECTRIC INSTRUMENTS

White Hy A, 44 Murray w

ELECTRIC LIGHT CONPANIES

Edison Lamp Co, C T Stillwell mangr, 26 King Wm
Hamilton Electric Light Co, W H Boisfeuillet, mangr, 1 Catharine s

ENGRAVER

White Wm, 9 James n

51

ENGROSSER

Bruce Wm, 14½ King e

EXPRESS COMPANY

American Express Co, 18 Jamess

FANCY GOODS

Hinman Mrs M C A, 8 James n
Levy Bros, 17 King e
Maclean Mrs F, 4 King e
Moodie John & Sons, 16 King w
Moody Miss F E, 162 King e

FELT AND GRAVEL ROOFERS

Irwin Thos & Son, 12 Macnab s

FILE MANUFACTURERS

Spence R & Co, 176½ King e

FISH DEALER

Cline R M, 244 King e

FLORISTS AND NURSERYMEN

Foster Fred G, 53 Charles
Hamilton Nursery, W Holton, Main e
Harper Robt, 18 Wellington n

FLOUR AND FEED

Carr E & D, 91-93 King w
Dunlop Jas, 107-9 John s
McFarlane Alex, 196-8 King e
Morgan Bros, 25-9 John s
Morris Thos, 21 Wellington n
White John E, 220 King w

FOUNDERS, MACHINISTS, IRON WORKS, ETC

Beckett F G Engine Co, York cor Bay
Bowes, Jamieson & Co, King cor Tisdale
Brayley & Dempster (wrought iron, etc), 47 King Wm
Burrow, Stewart & Milne, cor Cannon and John
Copp Bros, Empire Foundry, cor York and Bay
Gartshore Alex, end Stuart w
Gurney E & C Co, 36-42 John n
Hamilton Bridge & Tool Co, ft Caroline n
Hamilton Iron Forging Co, cor Barton and Queen
Hart Emery Wheel Co, Samuel Briggs, mangr, 19 Hunter w
Hart Machine Co, S E Rogers, mangr, 19 Hunter w
Laidlaw Mant Co, Mary cor Kelly
Leitch J & Son, 27-29 Rebecca
Moore Dennis & Co, Catharine n
Morrison Geo, ft Caroline n
Ontario Rolling Mills, ft Queen
Osborne, Killey Manufacturing Co, Barton e
Sawyer L D & Co, foot Wellington n
Stewart J & Co, cor Macnab and Vine

FORWARDERS

Browne Edwd, Browne's wharf
Mackay R O, Mackay's wharf

FRUIT, FISH, OYSTERS, GAME, ETC

Dixon Bros, wh, 33 King e
Dixon Bros, retail, 6 King w
Hayhoe C, 204 King e
Leslie Robt, wh and retail, 270 King e

GENTS' FURNISHINGS, ETC.

Hacker G G, 6 James n
Hennigan James, 108 King e
Leask R P, 24 King e
Lister J E & Co, cor Rebecca and James
Taylor A I, 40 King w
Treble S G, 2 King e
Waugh W J, 68 King e

GILDERS.

Blanford Hy, 50 King e
Marsden T & Son, 46 James n

GROCERS.

Bremner Chas, 115 King e
Brennan J & C J, 5 Market Sq
Brown, Balfour & Co, wholesale, 5 James s
Carpenter Bros, 9 Market Sq
Cherrier F L, 15 Market Sq
Cooper Robt C, 31 Macnab n
Cumming Bros, 108 James n
Doherty Arthur, 245 King w
Duff John & Son, 144 York
Duncan Bros, 71 King e
Galbraith N D, 104 King e
Gillard W H & Co, wholesale, 11 Main w
Harvey A & Co, wholesale, 21 King e
Hayes Alex, 44 Victoria ave n
King Cyrus, 10 Market Sq
Lucas, Park & Co, wholesale, 59 Macnab n
Lumsden Bros, wh 64 Macnab n
Macpherson, Glassco & Co, wh 67-9 King e
McLaren W H, 6 King Wm
McMillan John, 210 King e
Main Jas, John cor Barton
Mann Samuel, 256 King e
Morrison Alex, 105 John s
Murphy & Murray, 66 King e
Osborne Jas & Son, 4 James s
Peebles C H, 39 Macnab n
Robertson P T, 112 King w
Seldon R W, 86 Cannon e
Sewell Bros, 32 James n
Stuart John, Son & Co, wh, cor John and Main
Turner Jas & Co, 11-13 Main e
Winfield Thos, 142 Hunter w
Winnifrith B, King cor Victoria ave

GUNSMITHS.

Hamilton Gun Works, J Holman, 79 James n

HAIR WORKS.

Pargater Miss E, 83 King e

HARDWARE, PAINTS, OILS, ETC.

Ferres & Co, 38 James n
Hope Adam & Co, wholesale, 102 King e
Kraft E & Son, saddlery, 8 York
Winslow & Webber, carriage, 140 King w
Wood & Leggat, 44 King e

HARNESS, SADDLES AND TRUNKS.

Jolley Jas & Sons, 57 John s
Kraft E & Son, 8 York
Philp Jas & Son, 3 York

HAT MANUFACTURERS.

Dominion Hat Co, John Tunstead, 210 King e

HATS AND CAPS.

Acres Wm, 12 King e
Hacker G G, 6 James n
Leask R P, 24 King e
Lister J E, cor Rebecca and James
Mills Jos & Son, 7 James n
Nisbet Matrhew, King cor Walnut
Taylor A J, 40 King w
Treble S G, 2 King e
Waugh W J, 68 King e

HOT AIR FURNACES

Copp Bros, **cor York and Bay**
Gurney E & C Co, 36-42 John n
Irwin Thos & Son, 12 Macnab s
Stewart Jas & Co, cor Macnab and Vine

HOTELS, SALOONS AND RESTAURANTS

Allison, Wm Y Allison, 51 Stuart w

American, F W Bearman, cor King and Charles
Atlantic House, Andrew Ruthven, 29 Macnab n
Bliase Chas, 72 James n
Central, Neil McLean, 135 King e
Columbia, Wm McIver, King cor Park
Commercial, cor York and Park
Continental Hotel, Wm Proper, 162-4 Bay n
Continental, J McHenry, corner Stuart and James
Cosmopolitan, John G Geiger, 214-6 King w
Court House, Wm Gowland, 55-9 John s
Crystal Palace View, Harry Bawden, cor Peter and Locke
Dominion, Caughell & Weaver, 80 King w
Dundurn, Jas Little, cor York and Locke
Fairchild T B, cor King and Bay
Franklin, Daniel Poole, King cor Park
Germania, Robert Jahn, 20-22 John s
Goering Hy, 61-3 York
Grand Opera House restaurant James A T, 28 King Wm
Jimmie's Restaurant, Jas McKeown, 5-7 John n
McLean N A, 14 King w
Noble W, cor James and Cannon
Pioneer John D McLean, 141 King w
Richter T, James cor Vine
Royal, Hood & Bro, 61-63 James
Russell, T Armstrong, 66 King w
St Charles Restaurant, H C Hicock, 64 James n
St James' Saloon, Wm J Brush, 19 Hughson n
St Nicholas, Alex Dunn, 37 James n
Victoria, Richard Irwin, 79 King e
Walker House, R H Kretcshman, 166 King e
White Elephant Saloon, Andrew Lay, 81 James n

HOUSE FURNISHINGS

Martin Manufacturing Co, J E Martin, prop, 114 James n

ICE DEALERS

Dewey D & Son, 15 George
Walton Ice Co, 70 Vine

INSURANCE CO'S AND AGENTS

Accident of North America, Seneca Jones, 6 James s
Ætna of Hartford, fire, W F Findlay, Wentworth Chambers, 25 James s
Agricultural of Watertown, fire, M A Pennington, 51 James n
British America Assurance Co, fire and marine, A F Forbes, 7 Hughson s
British American Assurance Co, Wm Strong, 15 Arcade
British America Assurance Co, Elford G Payne, 97 James n
British & Foreign Marine Insurance Co (Liverpool) W F Findlay, 25 James s
British Empire Mutual Life, Wm Strong, 15 Arcade
Canada Life, A G Ramsay, F I A, manager, head office, cor King and James
Canadian Millers' Mutual Fire Co, Seneca Jones, 6 James s
Citizens Insurance Co, James Walker & Co, 20 Main e
Citizens Insurance Co (Accident branch) Richard Bull, 12 Hughson s
City of London Fire Co, Richard Bull, 12 Hughson s
City Mutual Fire, Walter Ambrose, 14 Hughson s
Commercial Union Assurance Co [London, Eng]. Elford G Payne 97 James n

INSURANCE AND SHIPPING DIRECTORY.

The following are among the Principal Companies represented in the City. See also Insurance and Steamship agents

SENECA JONES,
General Insurance Agent

COMPANIES REPRESENTED:

Fire—Northern Assurance Co. of London, Eng.
" Royal Canadian Insurance Co. of Montreal.
" Waterloo Mutual Ins. Co. of Waterloo.
" Canadian Millers' Mutual Ins. Co.
Life—Confederation Life Association of Toronto.
Accident—Accident Insurance Co. of North America, of Montreal.
Guarantee—Guarantee Co. of North America, of Montreal.
Plate Glass—The "Lloyds" of New York.

OFFICE—6 JAMES STREET SOUTH,
HAMILTON.

W. F. FINDLAY,
Public Accountant and Adjuster

Financial and Estate Agent.

—AGENT FOR—

Ætna Insurance Co. (Fire).
London and Lancashire Fire Insurance Co.
British and Foreign Marine Insurance Co.
Western Assurance Co. (Marine).

Private Funds to Lend at Current Rates.

NO COMMISSION.

Wentworth Chambers,
25 James St. South, - Hamilton.

WALTER AMBROSE,
14 Hughson St. South,
HAMILTON, ONT.

REPRESENTS THE FOLLOWING COMPANIES.

Norwich Union Fire Insurance Society, (of England).
Established 1797. Capital, $5,500,000.

Mutual Accident Association, (limited), of England.
Guarantee Fund, $500,000. Dominion Deposit $35,000. Plate Glass Insurance effected by the same Company.

London Mutual, and City Mutual Fire Insurance Companies.
Of London, Ontario.

Special agents for Ontario Mutual Life Assurance Co.

WM. STRONG,
Insurance, Real Estate and Financial Agent.

Economical Mutual Fire Insurance Company of Berlin.

British American Assurance Co. of Toronto.

British Empire Mutual Life Assurance Co. of London, Eng.

Real Estate Bought and Exchanged.

Money to Lend on any Good Security.

15 ALEXANDRA ARCADE,
HAMILTON, ONT.

Commerc'l Union Assurance Co
OF LONDON, ENG.

Fire, Life, Inland and Ocean Marine.

British American Assurance Co.
Gore District Mutual Fire Ins. Co.
Perth Mutual Fire Insurance Co.
Federal Life Assurance Co.

ELFORD G. PAYNE, Agent
97 JAMES ST. NORTH.
HAMILTON, ONT.
TELEPHONE NO. 90.

GEO. McKEAND,
57 James-st N., Royal Hotel Buildings

—AGENT FOR—

Richelieu and Ontario Navigation Co to Montreal, Quebec and Intermediate Ports.

Anchor Line, to Glasgow, via Londerry.

Hartford Fire Insurance Company.

R. & O. Steamers, run in connection with Intercolonial Railway to Maritime Provinces.

GEO. McKEAND,

57 James Sreet. North, Royal Hotel Buildings

Confederation Life Association, Seneca Jones, 6 James s
Connecticut Fire, J T Routh, 16 James s
Dominion Plate Glass Insurance Co, David McLellan, 84 James n
Economical Mutual Fire, Wm Strong, Arcade, 33 James n
Federal Life Insurance, David Dexter, managing director Elford G Payne, agent, James cor Vine
Fire Insurance Association, J T Routh, 16 James s
Glasgow and London Insurance Co, Wm Strong, Arcade
Gore District Fire, Elford G Payne, 97 James n
Guarantee Co of North America, Senaca Jones, 6 James s
Guardian Fire and Life Assurance of London, [Eng] Gillespie & Powis, 31 King e
Hartford Fire, George McKeand 57 James s
Insurance Co of North America, [the] Marine, Gillespie & Powis 31 King e
London & Lancashire Fire Insurance Co, W F Findlay, 25 James s
London Guarantee & Accident Co, Geo A Young, 5 King w
London & Lancashire Life Co, J T Routh, 16 James s
London Mutual Fire, Walter Ambrose, 14 Hughson s
Lancashire Fire and Life, Geo A Young, 5 King w
Life Association of Scotland, A F Forbes, 7 Hughson s
Lloyd's Plate Glass Insurance Co, Seneca Jones, 6 James s
Mutual Accident Association, Walter Ambrose, 14 Hughson s
Mutual Plate Glass Association, Walter Ambrose, 14 Hughson s
New York Life Co, Jas Walker & Co, 20 Main e
New York Mutual Marine Insurance Co, A F Forbes, 7 Hughson s
North American Life Assurance Co, J McMeekin, 2½ James s
Northern Fire Assurance Co, Seneca Jones, 6 James s
North, British & Mercantile, fire and life, J T Routh, 16 James s
Norwich Union Fire Insurance Society, Walter Ambrose, 14 Hughson s
Ontario Mutual Life Assurance Walter Ambrose, 14 Hughson s
Pearson John, general agent, 18-20 Hughson s
Perth Mutual Fire, Elford G Payne, 97 James n
Phœnix Ins Co, marine, J B Fairgrieve, 6 James s
Phœnix Fire of London [Eng] Gillespie & Powis, 31 King e
Providence & Washington Insurance, David McLellan, 84 James n
Quebec Fire Assurance Co, J T Routh, 16 James s
Quebec Fire Assurance, M A Pennington, 51 James n
Queen, Fire and Life, R Benner, 6 Main e
Queen, Fire and Life, George A Young, 5 King w
Royal Canadian Marine, J B Fairgrieve, 6 James s
Royal Canadian, fire, life, Seneca Jones, 6 James s
Royal, Fire and Life, David McLellan, 84 James n
Scottish Union and National Ins Co, Jas Walker & Co, 20 Main e
Standard Life Assurance Co, David McLellan, 84 James n
Star Life, E Freeman & Son, 9 King w

Temperance and General Life, M A Pennington, 51 James n
Travelers' Life and Accident, J T Routh, 16 James s
Victoria Mutual, Fire, W D Booker, sec-treas, 25 James s
Waterloo Mutual, Fire, Seneca Jones, 6 James s
Watertown Agricultural, Fire, M A Pennington, 51 James n
Western Assurance Co, (ocean and inland marine, Toronto) W F Findlay, 25 James s
Western Assurance Co, Fire, Geo A Young, 5 King w
Western, Marine, J B Fairgrieve, 6 James s

IRON FENCING WORKS

Nichols Thos E, 158 King w

LAND COMPANIES

Hamilton House Building Co, R L Gunn, Court House

LAUNDRIES

City, J Jeffrey, 60 Main w
Royal, Mrs S Robbins, 187 King e
Troy, W H Clarke, mangr, 178 King w

LEATHER AND FINDINGS

Alexander John, 13 King w

LIVERY AMD SALE STABLES

Craig Joseph, 24 Market
Matthews G H, 33 Market
Temple John, 20 Catharine n

LOAN COMPANIES

Hamilton Provident and Loan Society H D Cameron, treas, King cor Hughson s
Landed Banking & Loan Co, Samuel Slater, treas, 3 James s

LUMBER MERCHANTS

Brennen & Sons, 63-67 King Wm
Flatt & Bradley, Barton corner Wellington
Patterson Bros, ft Lower Cathcart
Thomson Robert, 89 Stuart w
Thomson & Wright, 107 York

MARBLE WORKS

Hurd & Roberts, wholesale, 86-100 Merrick
O'Connell & Evans, 26 York
Thomas Hy N, York cor Dundu n
Victoria Marble Works, E M Furniss & Son, 51 York

MARRIAGE LICENSES

McKeand J C, Landed Banking and Loan Co, 3 James s, h s s Concession between Locke and Garth
McLellan David, 84 James n, h 55 Herkimer
Whipple E S, 78½ King e

MERCANTILE AGENCIES

Dun, Wiman & Co, 3 Hughson s
Merchants' Protective and Collecting Association, J B Mills & Co. 55 James n
Trade Association (wholesale and retail) Mercantile Agency, M B Rymal, local manager, 14 Merrick

MERCHANT TAILORS AND CLOTHIERS

Bartmann Geo, 1 Walnut s
Bews Bros, 74 King e
Booker Chas G, 2 King Wm
Carlson Carl G, 44 York
Evans & Co, 6 Market Sq
Furnivall E J, 11 Macnab n
Howard Wm H, 17 Rebecca

THE COOK'S FRIEND BAKING POWDER.

FOR many years the favorite of the people, is now much improved. Superior in every essential point to any other in the market. Guaranteed Pure and Healthful. Forty per cent. saved by careful housekeepers by the use of the

☞ COOK'S FRIEND. ☜

SOLD BY ALL FIRST-CLASS GROCERS.

Manufactured only by

W. D. McLAREN, 55 College Street, MONTREAL.

North American Life Assurance Co.

HEAD OFFICE,—TORONTO, ONT.

HON. ALEX. MACKENZIE, Ex-Prime Minister of Canada, - - *President.*
HON. ALEX. MORRIS, Ex-Lieut.-Gov. of Manitoba, ⎱
JOHN L. BLAIKIE, Pres. Can. Landed Credit Co., ⎰ - - *Vice-Presidents.*
WILLIAM McCABE, LL.B., F.I.A., Eng., - - *Managing Director.*

JOHN McMEEKIN, District Agent,

2½ James Street South, Hamilton.

WM. GOERING & CO.,

Wine and Spirit Merchants,

AND DEALERS IN FINE CIGARS.

16 & 18 MERRICK STREET, HAMILTON.

ESTABLISHED 1854.

W. H. HOWARD

CLOTHING MADE TO ORDER,

Dyed, and Cleaned in Superior Style,

No. 17 Rebecca Street, Hamilton.

Henderson J M & Co, 20 King w
Herron Joseph, 82 King e
Hutcheson James Happle, 118 King e
Huton Chas, 80 King e
Kennedy & Co, 49 James n
Roe George, 218 King e
Slater James, 54 King w
Smith Donald, 14½ James n
Watt John & Son, 15 Macnab n
Webster Geo, 118 King e
Wilson Wm & Son, 44 King w
Zimmerman A, 50 James n

MILLINERS.

Hinman Mrs M C A, 8 James n
Stewart Mrs E, 156 King e

NEWSPAPERS.

Canadian **Live Stock** Journal, Thos Shaw, proprietor, 48 John s
Globe [daily and weekly] J H Mattice, correspondent and agent 33 James n
International Royal Templar, monthly, W W Buchanan, managing editor, James cor Vine
Mail [daily and weekly] Julian R F Boyd, agent, 16 James s
News [Toronto] daily and weekly, Main cor Macnab
Palladium of Labor [daily and weekly] King cor Catharine
Spectator [daily and weekly] 18 James s
Times [**daily** and weekly] 3 Hughson n
World [daily] Toronto, R S Beasley, agent, Arcade

OPTICIANS.

Claringbowl Fred, 158 King e
Lees Thos, 5 James n
Peebles John, 190 King e

ORGANS, PIANOS, MUSIC AND MUSICAL INSTRUMENTS.

Baine T J, manf, store, 84 King w
Bell Wm & Co, R A Hutchison, manager, 44 James n
Grossman Peter, 47 James n
Nordheimer A & S, 80 James n
Thomas C L, manf, 92 King w

PAINTERS AND PAPER HANGERS.

Dodson Wm, 29 John n
LeMessurier Daniel, 17 Charles
Mathews James & Son, 15 Hughson n
Ross Bros, 1 Main w

PATENT SOLICITORS.

Bruce Wm, 14½ King e
Young John H, 117 King w

PHOTOGRAPHERS.

Farmer Bros, 10 King w
Farmer Thos, 8½ King w
Farmer Wm, 35 King w
Kitchen J B, 76 King w
Photoglyptic Co, 77 King w

PHYSICIANS.

Anderson James 25 Bay n
Anderson & Bates, 34 James n
Bigger G W, 204½ King e
Bingham G S, 169 Main e
Case Wm I A, 113 King e
Case W H, 113 King e
Cockburn Lestock W, n e cor Jackson and Caroline
Cochrane J M, city hospital
Emory C VanNorman 18 Main w
Gaviller E A Main cor Park
Griffin H S, Walnut cor Main
Higgings Ed M, 54 Catharine n
Hillyer E S, 37 James s
Husband Geo E, 75 Main w
McConochie Saml, cor Hannah and Hess

Macdonald John D, 10 Duke
Mackelcan G L, coroner, 14 Gore
Malloch A E, 70 James s
Miller Thos, coroner, 181 King w
Montgomery J W, Asylum
Mullin John A, 124 James n
O'Reilly Ed B, 37 James s
Orton Thos H, 170 King w
Osborne A B, hospital
Philp W, coroner, cor York and Hess
Reid Alex C, 55 Hughson n
Reynolds Thos W, Asylum
Ridley H T, 31 Main w
Rosebrugh John W, 52 James s
Ryall Isaac, 71 Main e
Smith Daniel Day, cor King and Wellington
Shaw Geo M, 122 James n
Stark W G, 149 King w
Storms D G, 92 Merrick
Vernon Elias, 78 James s
Wallace J McL, Asylum
White James, coroner, 8 Cannon w
Wilson T H, 154 Main e
Woolverton Algernon, coroner, 153 James n

PIANOS [SEE ORGANS, PIANOS, ETC]

PIANOFORTE TUNER.

Raymond Montagu, 53 Wellington s

PLANING, SASH, DOOR, BLINDS, ETC

Aitchison & Co, 56-58 Main w
Allardice R A & Co, 86 Merrick
Brennen M & Sons, 63-67 King Wm, and cor Mary and Cannon
Casey & Sons, 72 Main e
Cruickshank Robt, 55 Jackson e

PLATED WARE AND SILVER AND METAL PLATERS.

Moodie & Sons, 16 King w

Meridan Britannia Co, cor Wellington and Cannon

PLUMBERS, SMEAM AND GAS FITTERS.

Adam James, 22 Hughson n
Clark Adam, 36 James s
Fairley & Stewart, 18 John n
Farmer Wm, 110 James n
Harding Henry, cor James and Cannon
Miles Alex G, 72 Merrick
Squibb Frank, 39 John s
Walsh W J, 96 King e
Young & Bro, 17 John n

PORK PACKERS.

Fearman F W, 17 Macnab n
Lawry Thos & Son, 18 Macnab s

POTTERS.

Campbell Robt, cor Locke and Canada
Campbell Sewer Pipe Co, Henry New, sec-treas, end Jackson w
Hamilton Sewer Pipe Co, Wentworth, near G T R Track

PRINTERS—BOOK AND JOB.

(See also Newspapers.)

Canada Ready Print Co, 3 Hughson n
Caxton Printing House, 22 Macnab s
Griffin & Kidner, 47 King William
Harvey Jas, 26 Merrick
McPherson Alex, 51 James n
Martin H A, 13 John n
Midgley Geo jr, 172 James n
Pennington Printing Co, 51 James n
Raw Robt & Co, 28-30 John n
Rowe W H, cor Catharine and King

PUBLISHERS
(See also Newspapers).

Irwin & Co, Directory, 14 Merrick

RAG CARPET MANUFACTURER

Murray John, 148 King w

RAILWAYS AND AGENTS

Canadian Pacific, W J Grant, 33 James n
Grand Trunk Ticket Agency, C E Morgan, 11 James n
Hamilton & Dundas Street Railway, John Weatherstone, lessee and manager, 16 Main e
Hamilton & Northwestern Railway, 33 Main e
Michigan Central, W J Grant, 33 James n
New York Central & Hudson River Railroad, W J Grant, 33 James n
Northern & Northwestern, W J Grant, 33 James n

SCALE MANUFACTURERS

Burrow, Stewart & Milne, Cannon cor John
Gurneys & Ware, cor James and Colborne
Osborne & Co, Barton e

SEEDSMEN

Bruce J A & Co, 37 King w
Evans Robt & Co, cor Macnab and York

SEWING MACHINE MANUFACTURERS AND DEALERS

New Raymond, John Pearson, 8 Hughson s
Ontario Sewing Machine Co, 22 James s

Singer Mfg Co, Joseph Hargrove, manager, 65 King e
Wanzer R M & Co, 91 Barton e
Wanzer Sewing Machine, Van-Norman & Co, agents, s e cor King and Catharine

SHIRT MNNUFACTURERS

Mead Joseph R Co, 10½ Market Square
Treble S G, 2 King e

SLATERS

Findlay J, 12 Macnab s
Irwin Thos & Son, 12 Macnab s

SOAP MANUFACTURERS

Judd & Bro, 73 Bay n
Walker James, 19 Bay s

SPRING MATTRASSES

Martin J E, Manfr Co, 114 James n

STEAMSHIP LINES AND AGENTS

Allan, J B Fairgrieve, 6 James s
American, Chas E Morgan, 11 James n
Anchor, Geo McKeand, 57 James n
Bremen, Wm Herman, 16 James s
Canada Transit Co, W J Grant, 33 James n
Carr's Direct Hamburg Line, Wm Herman, 16 James s
Cunard, W J Grant, 33 James n
Dominion Steamship Line, David McLellan, 84 James n
Dominion Steamship, Chas E Morgan, 11 James n
Georgian Bay Transportation Co, W J Grant, 33 James n
Guion, Chas E Morgan, 11 James n
Hamburg, Chas E Morgan, 11 James n

Inman, G McKeand, 57 James n
Inman, Chas E Morgan, 11 James n
Muskoka Lakes, W J Grant, 33 James n
National Steamship Line, Chas E Morgan, 11 James n
Red Star Steamship Line, W J Grant, 33 James n
Richelieu & Ontario Navigation Co, Geo McKeand, 57 James n
Rotterdam Steamship Line, Wm Herman, 16 James s
States Steamship Line, Chas E Morgan, 11 James n
White Star, Chas E Morgan, 11 James n

STAINED GLASS WORKS

Longhurst H & Co, 16 John n

SURVEYORS

Bell T S, 4 Main e
Kennedy R D, 42 James n
Staunton F H Lynch, Arcade

TANNER

Brown John E, 9 East ave n

TEA COMPANIES

Laut Tea Co, 3 Market sq
McWaters W & Co, 56 Macnab n

TELEGRAPH AND TELEPHONE COS.

Canadian Pacific Railway's Telegraph Co, 8 James s
Great Northwestern Telegraph Co, 18 James s
Bell Telephone Co, 1 Hughson s

TINSMITHS AND STOVE DEALERS

Bowes, Jamieson & Co, cor King and Tisdale
Gurney E & C Co, 35-42 John n
Irwin Thos & Son, 12 Macnab s

Laidlaw Manufacturing Co, Mary
Lavelle Robt, 19 John n
Moore Dennis & Co, 98-100 King e
Reddall & McKeown, 112 King w
Riddell John E, 214 King e
Sweeney James, King Wm cor Hughson
Stewart Jas & Co, cor Macnab and Vine
Wallace J & Son, 15 John n
Williams J M & Co, Hughson n
Wilson John, 35 York
Wholton Wm jr, 162 West ave n

TOBACCO MANUFACTURERS

Tuckett George & Son, 118-124 King w

TURNERS, WOOD AND IVORY

Venator Wm A & Sons, 56-58 Main w

UNDERTAKERS

Blachford & Son, 47 King w
Chapman's Sons, 49 King w
Pray R & Son, 29 King w

VINEGAR MANUFACTURERS

Doran Bros, Stuart w
Hamilton Vinegar Works Co, (limited) Wellington n and James s

WASHING MACHINES

Eagle Steam washer
Joseph Peart, 13 Arcade

WATCHMAERS AND JEWELERS

Belling James, 21 York
Claringbowl F, 158 King e
Davis & McCullough, 12 King w
Goodwin Wm, 99 John s
Ing Hy, 106 James n

CITY OF HAMILTON. 413

Lees Thos, 5 James n
Levy Bros, importers, 27 King e
Peebles John, 190 King e
Russell Richard, manf'g, 5 King w
Skinner John, 79 King w
Thompson E J & Co, wholesale, 55 King e

WHIP MANUFACTURERS.

Brown John E, whip lashes, 9 East ave n
Hamilton Whip Co, 81 Mary
Morgan Bros, 25-29 John s

WINES AND SPIRITS.

Goering W & Co, 16-18 Merrick
Reid, Birely & Co, 102 King e

WIRE MILLS.

Greening B & Co, 41 Queen n
Nichols Thos E, 158 King w

WOODEN AND WILLOW WARE.

Willson & Gates, 31 King w
Woods Walter & Co, 60-2 Macnab n

WOOL MERCHANTS.

Harvey John & Co, 69 James n
McKenzie T H, 3 Market

WRINGERS AND WASHERS.

Hamilton Industrial Works, cor Bay and Murray
Martin Manufacturing Co, J E Martin, 114 James n
Peart Joseph, 13 Arcade

THE
Hamilton Galvanized Iron Works
ESTABLISHED 1863.

THOMAS IRWIN & SON, - - Proprietors,

12 McNab Street South,

HAMILTON, ONTARIO.

MANUFACTURERS OF ALL KINDS OF

GALVANIZED IRON WORK.
TIN AND COPPER WARE.

Iron, Tin and Gravel Roofing a specialty. Also, sole manufacturers of the celebrated Acme Chimney Top, which has proved such a grand success—warranted to cure any smoky chimney

COUNTY OF WENTWORTH.

COUNTY OFFICERS.

J S Sinclair, Judge; Hon A McKellar, Sheriff; John Crerar, Clerk of Peace and County Attorney; G S Counsell, Clerk; John T Stock, Treasurer; S H Ghent, Clerk of Court, Deputy Clerk of the Crown and Registrar Surrogate Court; J M Williams Registrar; A B Wardell, Warden.

ALBERTON—Six miles from Lynden, thirteen from Hamilton.

Kerr Jas A, P M, merchant

ALDERSHOT—[Waterdown Station, G T R] 5 from Hamilton

Brown Alex W, P M, coal
Dickson H B, station agent

ANCASTER VILLAGE—Stages twice daily between here and Hamilton. Hamilton distant 7 miles. Population about 400

Ancaster Carriage Co
Ancaster Sulphur Springs Co
Bradshaw Abraham, blacksmith
Brandon James, M D
Clark Edwin, P M, grocer
Clark Rev W R, Episcopal
Donnelly Bolton W, druggist
Dyer Rev Jas E, Methodist
Egleston E F, manf
Filman John H, hotel keeper
Findlay Samuel A, merchant
Gurnett L A, Division Court, Clerk
Gurnett L A & Son, merchants
Henderson Ed, hotel
Heslop John, township clerk
Hyslop David A, merchant
Irwin James S, blacksmith
Johnston Rev T T, Presbyterian
Kenrick Ed, barrister
Lowry Morris, hotel
O'Neil Hy, tinsmith
Orr Jos, harnessmaker
Richardson Hy, M D
Smith J H, public school inspector
Thompson Geo, shoemaker
Wilson James, shoemaker

BARTONVILLE—4 miles e of Hamilton

Gage John W, P M, grocer

BINBROOK VILLAGE—Eleven miles southeast of Hamilton

Alway Enoch A, M D
Bailey Edward, saw mills
Barlow A, wagons
Bush Geo, harness
Harris Rev S G, Baptist
Henderson Jas, shoemaker
Henderson John, tinsmith
Hildreith Jas, merchant
Laidman S W, hotelkeeper
Ogilvie & Harrison, carpenters
Russell Jas, M D
Taylor Jas T, clerk 8th Division Court
Wickett Robt, hotel
Wright Wm, P M, merchant

BLACKHEATH P O

Bain A, P M, merchant

COUNTY OF WENTWORTH.

BULLOCK'S CORNERS—
2 miles from Dundas
Bullock Wm, P M, grocer
Burns Thos, hotelkeeper
Clark A & J, woollen manfrs
Cochenour Jacob, saddler
Davidson A T, blacksmith
Lyons Michael, hotel

CARLISLE—12 miles west of Hamilton
Hawes John, tinsmith
Koella Mrs R, P M, general store
Sullivan Bart, hotel keeper
Whitley Daniel, blacksmith

CARLUKE—11 miles south of Hamilton
Calder·John B, postmaster
Chisholm T C, merchant
Mayhew R, merchant
Somerville Adam, miller
Wilson Wm, blacksmith

CLYDE P O—Tp Beverly, 5 miles from Galt
Mulholland J D, postmaster

COPETOWN—Station GTR, 10 miles west of Hamilton
Bowman Joseph, sawmills
Head Thos, drover
Horning John E, agent
Howell C W, P M, storekeeper
McCarty Mrs C, hotel
Williams Wm, shoemaker

DUNDAS—A town and station on the G T R, 5 miles west of Hamilton. Population 4,000.
Allen James, watchmaker
Bain Thos, M P
Barrett T J, exciseman
Barton G M, barrister
Batty Benj, watchmaker
Begue T H A, barrister
Bell & Watson, props *Standard*
Bennett Alfred, hotel

Bertram & Sons, tool works
Bertram T A, M D
Bickell G, grocer
Bowman Jos H, lumber
Brady Patrick, tinsmith
Brady Peter, tinsmith
Brinkworth Wm, watchmaker
Brooke R S, photographer·
Burns Mrs Mary, boots and shoes
Burton J F, cabinetmaker
Byrne Thos, saddler
Cain A S, grocer
Cain Patrick, hotel
Campbell Wm F, butcher
Canada Screw Co
Canadian Bank of Commerce
  Wm Smith, manager
Cantwell James, dry goods
Coote Geo, auctioneer
Cowper Willoughby, coal dealer
Cronin D S, news dealer
Dixon J C & Bro, woolens
Doidge Bros, grocers
Dominion Card Clothing Co
Dundas Cotton Mills Co
Dundas Curling and Skating Rink
  R T Wilson, proprietor
Dundas Drug Co
Dundas Foundry, T Wilson
Dundas Gas Light Co
Dundas Stove Manf Co
Dundas Horse Shoe & Drop Forging Co
Dundas Standard, Bell, & Watson, proprietors
Dundas Tannery, C Lawry
Dundas True Banner, R V Sommerville, editor
Duggan Michael, tailor
Dunn Wm, wood dealer
Durant C H, grocer
Elliott Mrs, hotel keeper
Enright John & Bro, livery
Fisher John & Sons, paper mills
Freeman Mrs A, confectioner
Fry C & John S, wagonmakers
Goold Hy, hotel keeper
Grafton T B & J S, dry goods
Graham Wm, grocer

COUNTY OF WENTWORTH.

Gray Wm R & Sons, card clothing
Gurney E & C, agri implements
Gwyn H C, barrister
Hamilton & Dundas Railway, E W Kelk, agent
Hardy Wm, saddler
Knight C F, dentist
Knowles W E S, barrister
Keough Rev, Roman Catholic
Kerwin John, grocer
Kew Geo, freight agent, GTR
Laing Rev John, Presbyterian
Laing P & R, grocers
Latshaw Fred A, cabinetmaker
Lawson James, blacksmith
Lees Geo, baker
Lennard & Sons, hosier manfs
Lucas Benj, boots and shoes
Lumsden W W, baker
McCardle James, hotel
McLaughlin Da'l sewing machine
McMahon James M D, MPP
McMillan D, photographer
McQueen James jr, postmaster
Maddigan Rev P J, R S
Mallett Wm, hotel
Mason Wm & Sons, tanners
Maw & McFarlane, machinists
Montgomery G M, plumber
Mordon W J, grocer
Moss Mrs Joseph
Munro Rev J M, Baptist
Nelson Bros, carriagemakers
Niblett W C, druggist
Powell H F, grocer
Riach Joseph, grocer
Roderick James, hotel
Ross James, M D
Ross Miss J A, fancy goods
Shackleton G, tobacconist
Skelly J C, tobacconist
Smith & Co, dry goods
Smith J F, hardware
Smith Wm, mangr Bank Comm'e
Smyth Wm G, grocer
Somerville Jas, M P
Somerville Roy V, *True Banner*
Spittal L P, boots and shoes
Stock Thos, customs collector

Suter F D, clerk 2nd Div Court
Suter R W, ins agent
Taylor E, cutler
Thomas M B, gass works
Tunis W E, dentist
Walker & Bertram, M D S
Walker Frank E & Co, furniture
Wardell A R, solicitor
Watson David A, druggist
Webster James, flour and feed
Wilson Mrs J, mill owner
Wilson R T, axe manfr
Wilson Thos, founder
Witherspoon David, boots & shoes
Woodhouse Edwin, town clerk

ELFRIDA—10 miles south-east of Hamilton

Edmunds E, blacksmith
Swayze Mrs H, P M, merchant
Walker Rev W P, Presbyterian

FLAMBORO' CENTRE P O

Geo Church, postmaster

FREELTON—16 miles west of Hamilton

Hirst Edward, merchant
Hourigan John T, hotelkeeper
Kirk P, hotelkeeper
Laking Wm, miller
McManus Mrs M G, grocer
Metherall Geo, M D
O'Leary, Rev J S
Ross John, P M, gen merchant

GLANFORD VILLAGE—7 miles south of Hamilton

Armstrong Bros, blacksmiths
Atkinson Mrs Susan, P M, grocer
Carroll N, hotel
Case D G, storekeeper
Farewell A, M D
McClemont J, clerk 7 div court
Neal John & Son, wagonmakers
Smith W L, M D
Terryberry Chas, hotel keeper

GREENSVILLE—2 miles from Dundas

Bear Fred, tailor

Black And, M P, gen merchant
Brennan John, gen store keeper
Green Wm, blacksmith
Morden J M, miller
Snasdell Joseph
Steele J & Son, maltsters

HANNON [Rymal Station]—
6½ miles south of Hamilton

Cowie Mrs Thos, P M, merchant
Degear David, saw mills
Long Sylvester, hotel keeper
Pottruff Philip, blacksmith
Wilson James, hotel Keeper

HAYESLAND P O—11 miles west of Hamilton

Green Patrick, merchant
Hayes Michael, P M
Washington Mrs, grocer

JERSEYVILLE—4½ miles from Lynden Station, G T R

Grant Rev W, Baptist
Hendershot A, postmaster
Howell Levi, merchant
Howell W H, merchant
Pitcher P, M D
Swartz John L, pumps

KIRKWALL—20 miles west of Hamilton

Carruthers, Rev S, Presbyterian
Christie Geo, P M, store keeper

LYNDEN—A station of the G T R, 16 miles w of Hamilton

Baker John, hotel
Bennett Mrs E A, grocer
Berrington John, station master, G T R
Foster Geo, M D
Hagerty Meno, merchant
Hanes Rinear, postmaster
Nichols & Johnson, tinsmiths
Pitton John, hotel
Thompson R, saw mill
Vansickle B, general store

MILLGROVE—8 miles west of Hamilton

Berney Wm H, P M, gen store
Cummings Chas S, saw mills
Cummings T J, grocer
Flatt John Ira, lumber merchant
LeBarr & Lewis, fruit dryers

MOUNT ALBION P O—7 miles southeast of Hamilton

Cook J R, miller
Davis Herbert, merchant
Martin Henry, merchant
Mason James, postmaster
Pottruff James, hotel keeper

MOUNTSBERG P O—
Revell Chas, P M

NORTH GLANFORD P O—6 miles s of Hamilton

Choate Thos, tp clerk
Dickenson Ed & Sons, PM brickmakers

ORKNEY P O—3 miles from Copetown

Fisher Rev W S, Presbyterian
Robinson R, hotel
Thompson Adam P P M, grocer

RENFORTH P O—9 miles south of Hamilton

Mayhew R, P M, gen store

RENTON STATION P O

Thos Wilkinson, P M

ROCKTON—15 miles west of Hamilton

Cornell Benoni, P M
Halberstadt Fred C, hotelkeeper
Jackson Daniel, wagonmaker
McDonald Wallace, J P, tp and div court clerk

Patrick Geo, miller
Plastow J B, gen merchant
Wood Wm, gen merchant

RYCKMAN'S CORNERS—3½ miles south of Hamilton

Carr John, hotel keeper
Tice James, P M, grocer

SHEFFIELD—19 miles west of Hamilton

Bond Edwin & Son, P M, and produce dealers
Laing C W & Co, storekeepers
Smith John W, M D

SINCLAIRVILLE P O

Wilson James R, P M, gen store

STONEY CREEK—7 miles east of Hamiton

Carpenter C, tinsmith
Grieves Walter, saw mills
Howitt Rev F E, Church of Eng
Hull Fred, hotel
Jones Alva G, P M, clerk 5th div court, township clerk
Moore J, grocer
Rogers Wm, builder
Russel T, builder
Springstead A C, wagon maker
Wodehouse, Arthur, hotel
Wodhouse W H, merchant

STRABANE—12 miles west of Hamilton

Cathcart Rev J W, Presbyterian
McIntosh Donald, hotel keeper
Peebles Matthew, postmaster

TAPLEYTOWN—11 miles s e of Hamilton

Harris John C, P M, dry goods
Smith Rev Thos, Church of Eng
White Wm, merchant

TROY—18 miles s w of Hamilton

Clark Geo, P M, merchant
Misener Sidney, storekeeper
Roelofson John, cabinetmaker

TWEEDSIDE P O—3 miles from Winona station

Johnson S, P M, blacksmith

VALLENZ, P O—

Wm Cook, P M

WATERDOWN—An incorporated village and station on the G T R, 7 miles Hamilton

Baugh J, M D
Bremer John, township clerk
Brown & Baker, cradles, rakes, etc
Crooker W H, grocer
Docking W, agri implements
Doyle Michael, hotel
Eager J C & Co, gen merchant
Francis Rev J, Church of Eng
Green Samuel, hotel
McGregor J O, M D
McMonies James jr, auctioneer
Munson Rev J C, Episcopal
Otway-Page Thos, teacher
Robertson Rev W, Presbyterian
Robson Bros, millers
Ryckman Wm, builder
Seeley W O, merchant
Thompson J B, postmaster
Vanfleet A P, harness
Whittemore W H, merchant
Yenny Rev John, Lutheran

WIER P O—

E Williamson, P M

WEST FLAMBORO'—Distance from Hamilton, 8 miles

Clark Wm, woolen mills

COUNTY OF WENTWORTH. 419

Durrant A J, P M, merchant
Fisher Rev S, Presbyterian
Rivers Ed, hotel keeper
Shaver A W, M D
Stutt Albert, M D
Stutt James & Son, paper manfs
Sweet Geo, grocer

WESTOVER—15 miles west of Hamilton

McDonough Jas, saw mills
McIntosh Benj, post master
Mills James, merchant

WINONA STATION, G T R —12 miles from Hamilton

Carpenter Jos, P M
Secord W K, merchant
Smith R R, township clerk
Smith & VanDuzen, nurseryman
Whittaker J G, station agent

WOODBURN—15 miles s e of Hamilton

Jarvis James E, merchant
McEvoy Wm, P M
Ptolemy Wm, township clerk

CITY AND COUNTY DIRECTORIES

The following are now ready, and will be sent on receipt of price :

City of Hamilton $2 50
City of Kingston, including Frontenac County.................... 2 00
City of St. Catharines, incuding Lincoln and Welland............ 2 00
City of Brantford, including Brant County...................... 2 00
County of Simcoe... 2 00
County of Wentworth.. 2 00
County of Waterloo... 2 00

WE ARE ALSO AGENTS FOR THE

City of Guelph..$2 00
County of Wellington... 3 00
City of Quebec 2 50
City of Ottawa 2 50
City of Montreal... 3 00

All books are recent editions.

W. H. IRWIN & CO.,

12 MACNAB ST. SOUTH, HAMILTON, ONTARIO.

A. McPHERSON,
Fine∴Book∴&∴Job∴Printer,

51 JAMES STREET NORTH,

HAMILTON, - - ONTARIO.

Fine Commercial and Society Printing a Specialty.

MISCELLANEOUS DIRECTORY.

CITY COUNCIL, 1887.

Regular Meetings 2nd and last Monday, at 7.30 p. m.

Alexander McKay, Mayor.

Ward No. 1—Wm Morgan, H A Mackelcan, Thomas Brick. Ward 2—P C Blaicher, R Cruickshank, Wm Griffith. Ward 3—C L Thomas, J J Mason, W Nicholson. Ward 4—Jas Stevenson, W J Morden, W H Judd. Ward 5—John Field, Wm Doran, Wm Kavanagh. Ward 6—John Carruthers R K Hope, A H Moore. Ward 7—Thomas Patterson, James Dixon, John Kenrick.

COMMITTEES.

Board of Works—Ald. Morgan, chairman, Ald. Brick, Cruickshank, Thomas, Kavanagh, Carruthers and Patterson.

Market, Fire and Police—Alderman Kenrick, chairman, Ald. Morgan, Cruickshank, Nicholson, Stevenson, Doran and Carruthers.

Hospital and House of Refuge—Ald. Moore, chairman, Ald Mackelcan, Blaicher, Thomas, Stevenson, Field and Patterson.

Jail and Court House—Ald. Mason, chairman, Ald. Mackelcan, Blaicher, Morden, Kavanagh, Moore and Patterson.

Waterworks—Ald. Stevenson, chairman, Ald. Morgan, Griffith, Nicholson, Field, Hope and Kenrick.

Parks, Crystal Palace and Cemetery—Ald. Kavanagh, chairman, Ald. Morgan, Griffith, Thomas, Judd, Hope and Dixon.

Sewers—Ald. Doran, chairman, Ald Brick, Griffith, Nicholson, Morden, Hope and Dixon.

Finance, Printing, Railway, Assessment and Legislation—Ald. Blaicher, chairman, Ald. Mackelcan, Mason, Judd, Doran, Moore and Dixon.

Board of Health—Ald. Carruthers chairman, Ald. Field, Mr. Lillis, Ald. Judd, Cruickshank, Kenrick, and Messrs Billings and McPhie.

Auditors—R L Gunn and S E Townsend.

BOARD OF EDUCATION.

Public Schools.—Rolland Hills, chairman; W H Ballard, inspector; Thos Beasley, secretary; A Stuart, treasurer; Charles Smith, messenger.

Ward 1—Jas Cummings, B J Morgan. Ward 2—S F Lazier, John Muir Ward 3—Rolland Hills, Angus Sutherland. Ward 4—John Greig, William Clucas. Ward 5—F F Dalley, A M Ross. Ward 6—Alex McPherson, H S Brennen. Ward 7—Thos Morris, W F Burton.

COLLEGIATE INSTITUTE.

David McLellan, Louis Garland, Alex Turner, Wm Young, C R Smith, Wm Bell.

CHAIRMEN OF COMMITTEES.

Finance.—Louis Garland.
Internal Management.—Wm Bell.
Building.—B J Morgan.

BOARD OF TRUSTEES SEPARATE SCHOOLS.

Very Rev E I Henan, chairman; C J Bird, secretary; P Ronan, treasurer; Messrs A C Best, Rev Father Craven, Patrick Duffy, J O'Brien, Chas Leyden, J Zingsheim, J T Routh, Alfred Bates, J Ronan, Patrick J Bateman, Andrew Dillon.

CITY OF HAMILTON.

CHAIRMEN OF COMMITTEES.

Finance.—Charles Leyden.
Internal Management.—A C Best

CITY HALL.

Mayor's Office—Alex McKay, mayor; Charles Smith, city messenger.

Waterworks Department.—William Haskins, manager and city engineer; William Monk, first assistant; W A Kerr, second assistant; W R Campbell, third assistant; William Anstey, general foreman.

Collector's Office—James Cummings, collector; Andrew T Neill, assistant collector; Robert V Matthews, assistant collector; Donald Dawson, assistant collector.

Treasurer's Office.—Alex. Stuart, sr, treasurer; Alex Stuart, jr, assistant treasurer.

City Clerk's Office—Thos Beasley, city clerk; S H Kent, assistant city clerk.

Assessor's Office.—Peter Balfour, supervisor. Wards 1—John Burns; 2, Wm Sharp; 3, Joseph Kent; 4, J B Nelligan; 5, Lucian Hills; 6, Wm Turnbull; 7, R Ellicott.

Board of Health Office—Isaac Ryall, M D, medical officer; George Murison, inspector; James Ford, assistant inspector; John Peacock, assistant inspector; Archibald McKillip, assistant inspector; Charles Foster, food inspector.

James Cahill, police magistrate; Hugh McKinnon, chief of police; Geo Murison, building inspector.

POLICE.

The force consists of **45 men all told**: One chief, three sergeants, four acting sergeants, four detectives, 33 constables. There are four stations: No 1 at City Hall; No 2, corner James and Stuart streets, No 3, corner King William and Mary streets; No 4, 11 Napier street, which is also the patrol wagon station. The department is govered by Hugh McKinnon, chief, under the direction of the board of commissioners, which consists of mayor, police magistrate and county judge.

FIRE BRIGADE.

A W Aitchison, chief; Thos Wilson, assistant chief.

LOCATION OF SIGNAL BOXES.

2	Corner	Catharine and Jackson
3	"	King and John
4	"	Park and King
5	"	Hess and King
6	"	Locke and King
7	"	Macnab and Picton
8	"	Inchbury and York
9	"	{ Queen and York
	"	{ Magill and Barton
12	"	Bay and York
13	"	Bay and Mulberry
14	"	James and Mulberry
15	"	James and Gore
16	"	Hughson and Barton
17	"	Stuart and Macnab
18	"	Guise and John
19	"	Barton and Mary
21	"	Catharine and Cannon
23	"	Cathcart and Cannon
24	"	Wilson and East Ave
25	"	King and Steven
26	"	Stinson and Victoria Ave
27	"	King and Wellington
28	"	O'Reilly and Cherry
29	"	Catharine and Young
31	"	James and Hannah
32	"	James and Hunter
34	"	Park and Hunter
35	"	Bay and Robinson
36	"	Hunter and Queen
37	"	Pearl and Jackson
38	"	Main and Caroline
42	Brennen's Planing Mill	
43	Central Fire Station	
45	Corner	Rebecca and Ferguson Ave
46	"	Emerald and Cannon
47	"	Stuart and Caroline
51	City Hall Police Station	
52	Corner	John and Simcoe
53	"	Ferguson Ave and Ferrie

LICENSE COMMISSIONERS.

John W Murton, John Proctor, Nelson Humphry, John I Mackenzie, inspector. Office, 4 James street south.

HAMILTON POST OFFICE.

2 John street south
H N Case, post master; H Colbeck, assistant postmaster

CITY OF HAMILTON.

Clerks.—H A Eager, T Burns, G H Bull, G Ross, A C Crisp, J S Matthews, E H Dunnett, B F Barber, W R Ecclestone, H Dinsee, P J O'Donnell, R M Fitzgerald, W Flynn, D D Campbell, W L Waterman, H F Hill, J A Webber, H E J Filgiano, C Judd, O Beatty, J R Morden, J E B McKay, J O Mc Culloch, R J Harron, W P McCawley, R S Miller, G Smith, J H C Dempsey.

Letter Carriers.—J Murphy, superintendent; J H Fearnside asst-supt; J Gore, T B S Austin, W G Flooks, H M Coats, C W W Fielding, J Gardiner, R Stratton, J Wilson, W Angus, W Rennie, C Anstey, D C Dowery, A Griffin, W Dawe, W H James, E Frank, J W North, C H Stickle, G Springate, M Dawson, E Sevier, W A Munday, W Strongman, W Lawrence, Jas Carters.

D Walsh, J Strauss, messengers; J Brundle, street-letter box collector.

Letter Boxes are placed at the corner of the following streets—Mulberry and Park, Murray and James, Picton and James Simcoe and Mary, Barton and Mary, Barton and East Ave, Nelson and Emerald, King and Tisdale, Hunter and Emerald, Stinson and Victoria Ave, O'Reilly and Cherry, Young and John Hannah and James, Herkimer and Park, Hannah and Caroline, Bold and Bay, Main and Bay, King and Caroline, Main and Queen, Canada and Locke, King and Pearl, York and Pearl, York and Hess, York and Bay, Rebecca and James, Cannon and James, Cannon and John, Kelly and Mary, Cannon and Ferguson Ave, Cannon Wellington, Wilson and West Ave, King and Wellington, King and Ferguson Ave, Opp Copp's Block, King and John, Court House, Hunter and John, Hunter and James, Main and James, King and Macnab, York and Macnab, Market and James, Opp Eastwood's.

HAMILTON BOARD OF TRADE.

W H Gillard, president; J W Morton, vice-president; R Benner, secretary.

CUSTOMS.

Custom House, 2 John south.

F E Kilvert, collector; John Thompson, appraiser; A A Wyllie, assistant; A I Mackenzie, surveyor; R L Whyte, chief clerk; F Shephard, H W Woodward Andrew Alexander, Hugh Murray S W Townsend, D B Galbraith, clerks; H A L Dixon, chief landing waiter; M J Patterson, J McKinty, P O'Heir, A Wingfield, landing waiters; Stephen Cleary, searcher; James Halcrow, locker and guager; Gray, locker; Michael Malone and Samuel Garrity, porters; Alex Ferguson, messenger.

INLAND REVENUE.

2 John street south.

C G Fortier, collector; S F Ross, deputy collector; J B Blair, B J Conway, S Grecy, W P Crawford, T J Barret, A Egener, G W Brown, G N Hobbs, G W Mackay, J Logan, Wm Amor, J F O'Brien, W A D Baby, excise officers.

INSPECTOR OF WEIGHTS AND MEASURES.

T H Mackenzie, inspector; Wm McDonell, John McDonell, Chas E S Black, L Park, Thos Beatty, asst inspectors.

GAS INSPECTOR'S OFFICE.

2 John street south.

Donald McPhie, inspector.

CHRCHES.

Diocese of Niagara—Right Rev Chas Hamilton, M A, Lord Bishop.

Christ Church Cathedral, Rev Chas A Mockridge, D D, rector. Divine service on Sundays at 11 a m and 7 p m, and Wednesday evenings at 8 p m. Sunday school at 3 p m. Baptism second Sunday in every month at 2.30 p m. Holy communion every Sunday; first and third Sundays at 11 o'clock service, and second, fourth and fifth (when occurring) at 8 a m.

St Luke's Church, cor John and Macauley streets. Rev Wm Massey, M A, curate in charge. Services on Sundays at 11 a m and 7 p m.

Church of Ascension, John street south—Rev Hartley Carmichael, M A; R L Sloggett. Divine service each

Sunday at 11 a m and 7 p m. Holy communion celebrated.
1st Sunday in each month, 11 a m
3rd   "   "   11 a m
Last   "   "   7 p m
Sunday school, 3 p m. Divine service every Wednesday at 8 p m

All Saints' Church, corner Queen and King streets. Rev Geo Forneret, rector. Services at 11 a m and 7 p m

St Thomas Church, corner Main and West ave—Rev W B Curran, rector. Services at 11 a m and 7 p m

S Mark's Church, cor Bay and Hunter streets—Rev R G Sutherland, B A, rector. Services at 8 a m, 11 a m, 4 p m and 7 p m.

REFORMED EPISCOPAL.

St James', cor Hunter and Park sts. Rev T James Macfaddin, rector. Sunday services are held at 11 a m and 7 p. m.

St Stephen's, Canada near Pearl. Rev Wm Myers rector. Services 11 a m and 7 p m

PRESBYTERIAN CHURCHES.

Hours of service 11 a m and 7 p m

Central Church, corner Jackson and Macnab streets. Pastor—Rev Samuel Lyle.

Macnab Street Church, corner Hunter and Macnab streets, **Pastor—Rev** Donald H Fletcher

St Paul's Church, corner James and Jackson streets. Pastor—Rev R J Laidlaw

Knox Church, corner Cannon and James streets. Pastor—Rev Mungo Fraser

St **John's** Church, **corner King and** Emerald streets. **Pastor—Rev Thos** Goldsmith

Erskine Church, Pearl cor Little Market

METHODIST CHURCHES

Hours of service, 11 a m and 7 m, except otherwise stated. Sunday school at 2 30 p m.

Centenary Church, Main street west. Rev S J Hunter, D D, pastor

Wesley Church, John street, **corner** of Rebecca. Rev W J Hunter, **D D,** pastor.

First Methodist Church, corner of King and Wellington streets. Rev John Kay, pastor.

Zion Tabernacle, **Pearl street north.** Rev D W Snider, **pastor**

Simcoe Street Church. **Rev Vernon** H Emory, pastor.

Hannah Street Church. Rev Joseph Odery, pastor.

Gore Street Church, corner John and Gore streets. Rev C O Johnson, **pastor.**

Emerald Street **Church, Rev J H** White, pastor.

American **M E Church,** 80 John st **north.**

BAPTIST CHURCHES.

James street Baptist Church. Hours of service 11 a m and 7 p m.

Baptist Church (colored) Macnab st north. Hours of service, 10.30 a m and 6 30 p m.

Baptist Mission, **Wentworth street north.** Sabbath **school, 2.30 p m. Preaching** service **every Sunday at 7 p m**

SALVATION ARMY.

Burracks, 3-7 Hunter **e.** Services every evening at 8 p m. Sundays, 7 and 11 a m, 3 and 7.30 p.m

EVANGELICAL ALLIANCE

Rev Thos Goldsmith, president ; Rev John Kay, vice-president , Rev D H Fletcher, recording sec ; James Walker, treasurer.

CONGREGATIONAL AND OTHER CHURCHES

Congregational Church. Hours of

service, 11 am and 7 p m. **Rev J Morton,** Hughson st north

Brethren of the One Faith, corner of James and Rebecca. Each first day at 11 a m. Lecture on Bible subject at 7 p m.

Believers, cor Merrick and Macnab. Hours of service, 11 a m, 3 p m, and 7 p m.

St Paul's German Evangelical **Lutheran,** Gore cor Hughson Streets. **Rev** Christopher De Zücher, pastor.

Evangelical Lutheran Congregation, **Market street.** Hours of service, 10.30 a m and 7 p m. Sabbath School at 3 p m

New Jerusalem Church, Rev J S David, minister. 14 King street east. 7 p m.

Mountain Mission. Meeting at 2 p m. Supplied by the pastors of the city.

Jewish Synagogue—Hughson street south. Services, Friday evening and Saturday at 10 a m. Rev Dr H Birkenthal, rabbi.

ROMAN CATHOLIC CHURCHES.

St Mary's Church—Pro Cathedral Right Rev J J Carbery, D D, Bishop; O P, S T M; Very Rev E I Heenan, Vicar-General of Hamilton Rev Fathers E M Carre, P McCann, and M S Halm. Hours of service, 1st mass, 7.30 a m, 9 a m; high mass, 10.30 a m, vespers 7 p m. Mass every day at 6.30 and 7.30 a m. Cor Park and Sheaffe streets.

St Patrick's Church, King street, east. Rev P Cosgrove, J J Craven. **Mass 7.30 a m** and **10.30 a m ; vespers 7 p m.**

St Joseph's Church, Rev Father R Bergman. Mass 10 30 a m Sundays; Mass every day, 7.30 a m ; vespers 7 p m Corner Charles and Jackson streets.

EDUCATIONAL

SCHOOLS AND COLLEGES.

PUBLIC SCHOOLS

W H Ballard, M A, inspector For school purposes the city is divided into four districts, in each of which there is a district school. Over each district is placed a head master, who has supervision not only of his own school, but also of the primary schools attached to the central scool of the district.

District I includes Wards **1 and 7 ;** head master, John Ross.

District II includes Wards **2** and **3 ;** head master, G W Johnson

District III includes Ward 4 ; head master, A S Cruickshank.

District IV includes Wards 5 and **6 ;** head master, W C Morton.

There are 14 schools, 100 teachers, and a regular attendance of between 5.000 and 6,000 **pupils.**

There **is a Kindergarten in each of** the four districts.

COLLEGIATE INSTITUTE.

P S Campbell, B A, principal ; P S Campbell, B A, classical master ; Chas Robertson, M A, modern languages and English master ; J B Turner, 1st A, science **master ;** R A Thompson, B A, mathematical master ; O J Brown, M A, assistant classical master ; Andrew Paterson, history ; Mrs M Davidson, **upper** second form; Miss L C Bell, lower second form; H G Park, B A, upper first, N E ; G W Johnston, B A, lower first, N E ; H Birkenthal, Ph D, German ; James Johnson, music ; W C Forster, drawing.

WESLEYAN LADIES' COLLEGE.

King street east, incorporated 1861. Rev A Burns, DD, LL D governor. Prof C W Harrison, M A, natural science and latin ; Prof Henry Martin, O S A, drawing and painting ; Prof R S Ambrose, music ; Prof L H Parker, singing and **vocal** culture, **and** eleven lady **teachers**

CANADA BUSINESS COLLEGE.

Established 1862. Alexandra Arcade Building, 31, 33, 35, 37 and 39 James street north. R E Gallagher, principal and proprietor ; Byron Smith, vice-principal ; and a staff of four assistants and lecturers in commercial law, custom of trade, finance, coommercial ethics, etc., etc.

HAMILTON BUSINESS COLLEGE.

2½ James street south. Rattray & Geiger, proprietors. M L Rattray, principal ; E A Geiger, vice-principal ; E A Geiger, penmanship, phonography, telegraphy. Miss M Smith, oil painting.

ROMAN CATHOLIC SCHOOLS.

St Mary's Model School, Sheaffe street—Charles J Macabe, principal ; number of pupils on the roll, 200

St Mary's Central and St Mary's Training Schools, Mulberry street.

St Patrick's School, Hunter street ; St Lawrence School. John st, and St Vincent, Pearl street s, conducted by the sisters of St Joseph

The number of pupils attending these schools (not including the Model School) is about 2,000

Convent of Mount St Mary, King street west—under the direction of the Ladies of Loretto ; M Francis, lady superioress.

LITERARY AND SCIENTIFIC ASSOCIATIONS.

Hamilton Association. Instituted 1857, incorporated 1883. Meets second Thursday of the month.—President, Rev C H Mockridge, D D ; 1st Vice-pres, Rev Samuel Lyle, B D ; 2nd vice-pres, Matthew Leggat ; rec-sec, A Alexander, F S C ; cor-sec, Harry B Witton ; treas, Richard Bull ; curator and librarian, Alexander Gaviller ; council, I Alston Moffatt, W Milne, Samuel Slater, S Briggs and James Leslie, M D. Museum and library, Alexandra Arcade

Hamilton Art School, Canada Life buildings. J M Gibson, pres ; B E Charlton, vice-pres ; S J Ireland, principal.

Hamilton Law Association, 70 members—Æ Irving, Q C, pres ; Thos Robertson, Q C, vice-pres ; A Bruce, treas ; R R Waddell, secretary

Hamilton Cricket Club Company,—E Martin, pres ; F L Whately, sec-treas.

Hamilton Medical and Surgical Society, meets 2nd Tuesday of the month at Royal hotel—Wm McCargow ,president ; F E Woolverton, sec-treas.

Hamilton Business College Alumnae Association—E A Geiger, pres ; M L Rattery, sec-treas.

St Thomas' Church Literary Society —Rev W B Curran, pres ; E Bethune, secretary.

Young Men's Christian Association, 38 King st east—F W Watkins, president ; Frank Lonsdale, sec. A free reading room. Meeting Sundays at 4.15, and Tuesday and Saturday evenings. Ladies' Auxiliary in connection with above. Mrs Dennis Moore, pres ; Mrs Bidwell Way, sec.

Garrick Club, Gore street—W F Findlay, pres ; Alex Ramsay, sec.

Grand Opera House Co—C M Counsell, president ; James H Mills. sec-treasurer.

CHARITABLE INSTITUTIONS.

City Hospital, cor Barton and Victoria ave—A B Osborne, resident physician ; E Easterbrook, steward.

Asylum for the Insane, mountain top —J McL Wallace, medical supt ; J W Montgomery, M D, assistant supt ; Thos W Reynolds, M D, assistant physician ; Bidwell Way, bursar.

House of Providence, Dundas—Sisters of St Joseph.

House of Refuge foot of John street north. Frank Sturdy, steward

Boys' Home—Mrs M Shaw, matron, 59 Stinson st.

St Mary's Orphan Asylum, Park st north—Under the supervision of the Sisters of St Joseph.

Aged Womens' Home. 115 Wellington s Miss Margaret McFarlane

Hamilton Orphan Asylum, 115 Wellington south—Miss J McFarlane, matron.

Home of the Friendless, 72 Caroline street south—Miss Helen Mair, matron.
Girls' Home, 77 George street—Mrs Mary A Scott, matron.

Ladies' Benevolent Society, Roman Catholic—Mrs J T Routh, president ; Miss A Hogan, treasurer.

NATIONAL AND BENEVOLENT INSTITUTIONS.

St George's Society—Wm Hancock president ; B Winnifrith, secretary

St Andrew's Society—Instituted December 29th, 1835. John Greig, president ; D McLellan, treasurer ; John I Mackenzie, secretary

Caledonia Society—Ian McKenzie, chief ; Wm Murray, secretary ; Mark Patterson, treasurer ; meets 1st and 2nd Friday in Caledonia Hall, Arcade

Sons of Scotland, Dunrobin Camp, No. 7—Dan McQueen, chief.

Irish Protestant Benevolent Society —Established in 1869. John Alexander, president ; Geo Ross, secretary ; H A Eager, treasurer. Meets in A O U W Hall, Macnab street, second Thursday of each month.

St Jean Baptiste—J B Lattremouille president ; W Pothier, vice-president ; A Bourque jr, secretary ; A Bourque, treasurer. Meets 2nd and last Wednesdays in the month in Emerald's Hall.

Catholic Mutual Benefit Association No 37—John Byrne, president ; James F O'Brien, rec sec.

Emerald Beneficial Association Hall, 74 James n, Sarsfield Branch, No. 1, Ont—James Henigan, president ; P Dowd, secretary Stated meetings, 1st and 3rd Wednesdays of each month.

Shambrock Branch, No 16—M Malone, president ; James Ball, secretary ; meets 1st and 3rd Mondays.

St Vincent de Paul's Society—H Arland, president ; M Higgins, vice president ; A C Best, secretary ; Francis Burdett, treas.

German Benevolent Society—Hall, John cor Main. Geo Bartmann, president ; L Roehm, secretary ; E Faustman, treasurer.

Germania Club—L Roehm, president ; — Schelling, secretary. Hall, John cor Main.

SONS OF ENGLAND.

Britannia Lodge, No 8—W Hover, president ; J Fisher, secretary

Acorn Lodge, No 29—Jesse Linger, president ; Hedley Mason, secretary

MILITARY.

Drill Sheds, James cor Robert

Hamilton Field Battery—Major H P VanWagner, commanding ; Capt J S Hendrie, Lieuts Bankier and Duncan ; Instructor, Kerlie.

XIII BATT. A. M.

Lieut-Col John Morrison Gibson, M P P, commanding ; Majors Alex H Moore and Henry McLaren ; Surg-Major, Isaac Ryall ; Asst-Surgeon, H S Griffin ; Hon Major Chas Armstrong, Pay Master ; Hon Major J J Mason, Quarter Master ; Capt J J Stuart, Adjutant ; Captains, Peter Benjamin Barnard, James Adam, John Stoneman, Wm Gilgen Reid, Edward Gibson Zealand, Geo McLaren Brown, Edmund Evelyn Wentworth Moore ; Lieutenants, Robt B Osborne, John C Gillespie, Sidney C Mewburn, J W Gordon Watson, Fred B Ross, James W Hendrie, Robt Hobson, W O Tidswell, Chas A Chapman, A D Cameron John W Bowman.

TEMPERANCE SOCIETIES.

Gospel Temperance Reform Club, Edward Shepherd, secretary. Meetings at the Foseter's Hall every Saturday at 8 p. m. and Sundays at 9 a m and 3 30 and 8.30 p m.

Gospel Temperance Reform Mission meets in the Royal Templar's Hall, 97 James n. Saturdays 8 p m, Sundays 9 a m and 3.30 p m. J B Watson, president.

Hamilton Gospel Prohibition Society

No 1—Meets at 60 King w. Meetings at 9 a m, and 3.30 p m, on Sunday. J E Berryman, president.

Women's Christian Temperance Union, Mrs Pratt, secretary.

INDEPENDENT ORDER GOOD TEMPLARS

Hamilton City Temple—Meets 1st Friday in each month, 22½ King st e

Excelsior Lodge No 6—Jas Weller, L D; meets Tuesday, King Wm, cor James

Rescue Temple, No 222—J G Wilson, L D; meets every Thursday evening, James cor King Wm.

Burlington Lodge No 470—M Smith L D; meets Monday evening in the hall, 22 King street east

Reliance Lodge No 518—T LeMessurier, L D; meets Wednesday evening in St Georges' Hall.

Ambitious City Lodge No 586—Peter Armstrong, L D; meets Monday evening, James cor King Wm

Under the jurisdiction of the Right Worthy Grand Lodge of the World.

Crown of Life Lodge, W Myers. Meets Tuesday evening in school room Reform Episcopal Church

International Lodge No 1—D Hunt, L D, meets every Tuesday evening at 8 o'clock in the Foresters' Hall, 110 James n

Unity Lodge No 5—J Freeman L D, meets every Wednesday evening at 8 o'clock in school room A M E Church.

Public meeting under the auspices of the city lodges held every Sunday afternoon at 4 o'clock in Forsters' Hall, 22½ King e

ROYAL TEMPLARS OF TEMPERANCE.

Hall, 97 James street north

District Council—Dr C V Emory, D C; Edward F Smith, D S.

Imperial Council No 5—J G Y Burkholder, S C; E F Smith, sec; meets every 2nd and 4th Thursdays in hall, 97 James north.

Sovereign Council No 9—E Williams, S C; Dr E Emory, R S; meets 2nd and 4th Fridays.

Regina Council No 67—J M Warner, S C; C W Bradfield, R S; meets 1st and 3rd Tuesdays.

Wentworth Council No 149—H A Ray, S C; Andrew Devine, R S; meets every Thursday King cor Emerald n

Sceptre Council No 187—Meets Tuesday. Geo H Lees, S C; A Dingwall, R S.

Empire Council No 190—F G Shearsmith, S C; Robt Gordon, R S.

Clarmont Command No 1, meets 2nd Monday in each month. J H Land, Ex-com; G H Lees, Adjt.

League of the Cross—Pres, — Earley; sec, John Hennessy. Meets 1st and 3rd Thursdays in each month in Emeralds' Hall.

SOCIAL ORGANIZATIONS.

MASONIC.

Hamilton District—W Kerns, D D G M.

Barton Lodge No. 6—John Hoodless, W M; Colin McRae, sec; meets second Wednesday.

Strict Observance No 27—W F McGiverin, W M; T H Husband, sec; meets 3rd Tuesday.

St John's Lodge No 40—W R Job, W M; Wm Birrell, sec; meets 3rd Thursday.

Acacia Lodge No 61—Alex Smith, W M; J D Clark, sec; meets 4th Friday.

Temple Lodge No 324—H A Mackelcan, W M; G S Bingham, sec; meets 2nd Tuesday.

Doric Lodge No 382—J J Mason, W M; Geo Purrott, sec; meets 3rd Monday.

Mount Olive Lodge—G H Hughes, Wm; L Bennet, sec.

Hamilton Masonic Hall Association—Edward Mitchell, pres; Jas Robertson, treas; J J Mason, sec.

Hamilton Masonic Mutual Benefit Association—R Brierley, pres; J J Mason, sec-treas.

The Hiram, R A C, No 2—E Comp H Sweetman, Z; Oliver Hillman, Scribe E; meets 1st Monday in each month.

St John's R A C, No 6—E Comp E Mitchell, Z; W McGiverin, S E; meets second Thursday in each month.

Harington Conclave, No 22—Kts R C R and C—Sir Kt H A Mackay, M P S, Sir Kt W Gibson, recorder; meets February, May, August and November.

The Godfrey de Buillon Preceptory—Em Comp J Malloy, E P; A Doherty, registrar; meets 1st Friday.

Murton Mo lge of Perfection, No 1—Ill Bro John W Murton, 33°, T G P M. Ill Bro Davi l Dexter 32°, secretary; meets 1st Tuesday.

Hamilton Sovereign Chapter Rose Croix No 1—Ill B o D vid McLellan, 33°, M W S; Ill Bro J M Little, 32° reg strar. Meets 4th Tuesday.

Moore Sovereign Consistory, S P R S 32°,—Ill Bro Hugh Murray, 33°, com chief; Ill Bro W H Ballard, 32°, grand secretary; meets 2nd Friday in January, April, June and October.

Royal Order of Scotland for the P ovinces of Ontari) and Quebec—Ill Bro H A Mackay, 33°, Prov G M; Ill Bro J W Murton, 33°, Sr Gr Warden; Ill Bro W Reid, 33°, Jr Gr Warden; Ill Bro Hugh Murray, 33°, Prov Gr Secretary.

ODD FELLOWS.

INDEPENDENT ORDER.

Hamilton Canton, Patriarch's Militant—Meets 1st Monday; R J Faulknor, captain; J C Buligan, lieut; F R Hutton, ensign; Alfred Tory, clerk.

Burlington Encampment, No 7—F R Hutton, C P; H H Rleinsteiber, scribe; 2nd and 4th Mondays.

Royal Encampment No 36—A Tory, C P; Wm Brooks, R S; 1st and 3rd Monday.

Excelsior Lodge, No 44—G Smith, N G; Dr F E Woolverton, R S. Meets every Thursday.

Unity Lodge, No 47—E Egan, N G; S S McCandlish, R S.

Victoria Lodge, No 64, Wm Wurst, N G; G E Heming, R S. Meets every Wednesday.

Crescent Lodge, No 104—S S King, N G; R J Faulknor, R S.

Oak Leaf Lodge, No 159—Askew N G; T McBride, R S. Every Tuesday.

Minerva Lodge, No 197—R McDonald, N G; Geo W Kappele, R S; meets every Tuesday.

CANADIAN ORDER, MANCHESTER UNITY.

Loyal Hamilton Lodge, No 7—Robt Fauks, N G, Thos Parry, P S; meets every other Wednesday.

Loyal Commercial Lodge. No 9—J Daley, N G; J Philp, P S; meets every second Wednesday.

Loyal Strict Observance, No 48—John Kennedy, N G; John A Morrison, P S; meets every other Monday each month.

Royal Purple Encampment, No 1—John Wilson, N G; Thomas Parry, P S; meets last Tuesday.

KNIGHTS OF PYTHIAS.

Red Cross Lodge, No 3—G W Dunnett, C C; W H Tribute, K of R & S; meets at the Odd Fellows' Hall, John street north, Mondays at 8 p m.

Alpha Division, No 1—D J Peace, Sir Kt Commander; Thos Knott. rec; meets Wednesdays at 8 p m for drill, and 1st Monday at 8 p m.

Grand Orient, No 1—D J Peace, I S ; Alex W Aitchison, H S ; meets last Monday, at Odd Fellows' Hall, John street north.

Endowment Rank, No 774—John L Brown, president ; G D Phibbs, sec,

ANCIENT ORDER OF UNITED WORKMEN.

Hall 14 Macnab south.

Hamilton Lodge, No 49—John Donaldson, M W ; A McPherson, recorder ; meets 2nd and 4th Fridays.

Gore Lodge No 88—Geo Croal W M; E Hawkes, recorder; meets 1st and 3rd Fridays.

Dixon Lodge No 237—Andrew J Diamond, M W; J Ross, recorder. Alternate Wednesday.

Wentworth Legion No 3, Select Knights of A O U W—Robt Crowe, C W H Woodhouse, S R; meets 1st and 3rd Tuesdays.

Mystic Legion No 46—James H Shouldice C; Geo Elmslie, recorder; 2nd and 4th Tuesday in A O U W hall.

HOME CIRCLE.

CANADIAN ORDER.

Circle No 18—Meets 4th Thursday in A O U W, Thos Paradine, leader ; G H Gilbert, R S.

CANADIAN LEGION OF HONOR.

Grand Lodge office, 169 Main e. H A Mackelcan, G C; Dr G S Bingham, sec.
Hall, James cor King Wm.

Parthenon Lodge No 1—Wm Noble, commander ; P Corridi, sec. Meets 2nd Friday in each month.

Monarch Lodge No 1—Dr G S Bingham, commander, H N Kittson, secretary. Meets 4th Friday in each month.

CHOSEN FRIENDS.

Maple Leaf Council—S Heath, C C; M G Meek, sec. Meets alternate Monday.

ROYAL ARCANUM

Hall, 14 Macnab st s

Kanawha Council, No 681—M Richardson, regent; W S Duffield, sec; meets first and third Mondays.

Regina Council No 757—R McRae, regent; Alex Finlayson, sec; meets 2nd and 4th Mondays.

KNIGHTS OF MACCABEES.

Barton Tent No 2—Meets 1st and 3rd Thursday, at 22 King street e. Sir Kt J W Madigan, C; Sir Kt Joseph Rousseaux, R K.

ANCIENT ORDER FORESTERS.

Hall, 110 James north.

Court Pride of Ontario, No 5,640—James Baines, C R; J B Buckingham, sec. Alternate Thursdays.

Court Excelsior, No 5,743—C McMillan, C R; W J Vale, sec. Alternate Thursdays.

Court Maple Leaf, No 5,690—T Partridge, C R; R Davis, sec. Alternate Thursdays.

Marquis of Lorne, No 6,490—W G Guthrie, C R ; J W Buckingham, sec. Alternate Tuesdays.

Sanctuary, A O S—T G Priestland, P; Jas Barry, scribe. Third Fridays.

KNIGHTS OF SHERWOOD FOREST.

Pioneer Conclave. No 21—J Madgett, commander ; W R Tribeck, Ad; meets 4th Wednesdays

INDEPENDENT ORDER O F.

Court Oronhyateka, No 23—Geo Shambrooke, C R; Alex Munro, R S. Meets first and third Fridays in each month, at 22 King st e

Court Amity No—T B Spence, C R ; A P Nichol, secretary. Meets 1st and 2nd Tuesday

Court Hamilton No 170— Dempster, C R, J Johnston, R S.

LOYAL ORANGE ASSOCIATION

DISTRICT OF HAMILTON.

County Lodge—Wm Nicholson, W C M; H Hamill, R S.

Hamilton District Lodge — E T Richards, W D M; Wm H James, D S.

Royal Scarlet Chapter—E T Richards. W C in C ; Wm E Armstrong, Scribe.

De Schomberg Commandery, Royal Scarlet Knights No 1—Edward Morton, commander ; W C McAndrew, adjutant.

Royal Black Preceptory, No 148, G R I Encampment—Richard Ailles, W Sir Kt in command ; E T Richards, registrar. Meets on the third Monday in the month, in the Orange Hall, King st east.

LOYAL ORANGE LODGES.

No 71—Jno W Johnstone, W M ; Wm McFarlane, R S. Meets on the 1st and 3rd Tuesday in each month.

No. 286—Wm Burwell. W M ; Edward Morton, R S. 1st Wednesday.

No. 312—Richard Ailles, W M ; James Irwin, R S. 1st Monday.

No 554—John Noble, W M ; John R Krug, R S, 2nd Monday.

No 779—Chas Hamilton, W M ; S R Hammond, R S ; 1st Monday.

No 1,019—Wm Hover, W M ; W H Coddington, R S. 4th Thursday.

BANKS.

Bank of British North America—D G McGregor, manager; Chas Moore, accountant ; A W Hanham, teller ; W Graham, discount clerk ; J Cant, ledger Keeper ; W Kennedy, Jos Bencelle clerks ; T Wilson, messenger.

Bank of Hamilton—E A Colquhoun, cashier ; H S Steven, assistant cashier; C Bartlett, accountant ; J H Stuart, assistant accountant ; W J Lindsey, teller ; Geo W Brent, receiving teller ; E Ambrose, teller ; F Bennett, messenger.

Canadian Bank of Commerce—E Mitchell, manager ; S Read jr, accountant ; O G Roy, assistant accountant ; G A Holland, paying teller ; W H Dunsford, receiving teller ; C J Noble, ledger keeper ; John Cousins, messenger.

Bank of Montreal— J N Travers, manager; J H Pipon, accountant ; Jno Rankine, teller ; J W G Watson, ledger-keeper ; C L Benedict, receiving teller ; James J Rankin, assistant accountant ; G Thomas, messenger.

Merchants' Bank of Canada—J S Meredith, manager ; A B Patterson, teller ; W A Bellhouse, accountant ; A R Cabill, ledger keeper ; A H Devitt, discount clerk ; J R Little, P G Heming, clerks ; J Johnston, messenger.

Molson's Bank—J M Burns, manager ; H A Ambrose, accountant ; F G Peto, teller ; A W Hartt, discount clerk ; J R Wainswright, collection clerk ; A W Barnard, ledger keeper. W Havercroft messenger.

Stinson's Bank, 10 Hughson street north—Jas Stinson, prop ; A H Moore, manager ; A Leith, teller ; Walter G Harvey. ledger keeper.

Traders' Bank of Canada, 36 King east—Æ Jarvis, manager ; A W Clark, teller ; N Booker, ledger keeper ; David Muir, collection clerk ; P J Carroll, discount clerk.

LOAN AND BANKING.

Hamilton Provident and Loan Society ; corner King and Hughson, Incorporated in 1871—H D Cameron, treasurer ; A F Sutherland, inspector ; John McCoy assistant inspector ; Campbell Ferrie, accountant ; A McEachern, teller.

Hamilton House Building Co—R L Gunn, sec. Court House.

Landed Banking and Loan Co—Samuel Slater, sec-treas, 3 James street south

CITY OF HAMILTON. 431

DIVISION COURTS AND CLERKS

Wentworth—1st, H T Bunbury, Hamilton ; 2nd, F D Suter, Dundas; 3rd, J McMonies, jr, Waterdown ; 4th, W McDonald, Rocton ; 5th, Alva G Jones, Stoney Creek ; 6th, L A Gurnett, Ancaster ; 7th John McClemont Glanford ; 8th, J T Taylor, Binbrook ; 9th, R L Gunn, Hamilton.

RAILWAYS

Grand Trunk Railway—General Offices, Montreal—Joseph Hickson, general manager ; L J Seargant. traffic manager; Wm Wainwright, assistant manager ; Chas Percy, general manager's assistant. J Stephenson, superintendent. E P Hannaford, chief engineer. Herbert Wallis, mechanical superintendent. R Wright, treasurer. Thomas Tandy, general freight agent. W Edgar, general passenger agent. T B Hawson, auditor. H W Walker,

accountant. John Taylor, general storekeeper.

Great Western Division. G T R—Offices, Hamilton—Chas Stiff, superintendent, Joseph Hobson, chief engineer. C K Domville, mechanical superintendent W S Champ, paymaster. E R Baines, storekeeper, London

Hamilton and Northwestern Railway—John Stuart, president. John Proctor, vice-president. Maitland Young, secretary

Northern and Northwestern Railway—Head office, Toronto. S Barker, general manager. Jas Webster, superintendent. Robt Quinn, general passenger agent. W C Schreiber, purchasing agent, Toronto Hamilton City offices, 33 Main st east. W J Grant, city freight and passenger agent. Chas Armstrong, cartage agent. David Murray, clerk.

W. H. IRWIN & CO.

Directory Publishers and Publishers' Agents

The oldest established Directory publishing firm in Ontario, and excepting Messrs. Lovell & Son, of Montreal, in the Dominion. During our long experience we have compiled this class of work for all the cities of Ontario and Quebec with the exception of Montreal; a large number of the counties of Ontario ; the Eastern Townships of Quebec, and compiled the Messrs. Anderson's Ontario Directory published in 1869. This experience authorizes us to state that our compilations are as complete as any of the publications of this kind can be. While avoiding all redundancy; cramming the book with matter foreign to the character of this class of books, nothing is omitted that should be included in the legitimate contents of the Directory. Please see list of our publications on page 247.

☞ To avoid the confusion and mistakes resulting from subscribing to Directories of the City of Hamilton, or our other publications, which may be undertaken by outside parties, please observe that all orders bear the name of W. H. Irwin & Co. ☞ We are permanent residents of the city, all our agents reside here, the book is printed here and is essentially a local work.

Address—12 Macnab Street South, Hamilton, Ontario.

Counties of Wentworth and Waterloo

Directories and Gazetteers

For 1887, including Postal Addresses of the Farmers, Numbers of Lots and Concessions, Etc.

PRICE, EACH $2.00.

CITY OF KINGSTON and COUNTY OF FRONTENAC Directory, third tri-ennial edition, will be ready in July, 1887.

PRICE, EACH, $2.00.

W. H. IRWIN & CO., PUBLISHERS
12 McNAB ST. SOUTH, HAMILTON, ONT.

SLATING! SLATING!

The undersigned take this opportunity of informing

Builders, Contractors and the Public Generally

That in connection with their GALVANIZED IRON WORKS, GRAVEL ROOFING, ETC., they are now prepared to do all kinds of **SLATING** at the very LOWEST PRICES, and in the most workmanlike manner.

Thos. Irwin & Son
12 McNAB STREET SOUTH.

JOHN MACDONALD & CO.,

WHOLESALE

IMPORTERS OF DRY GOODS,

CARPETS, WOOLLENS & FANCY GOODS.

TORONTO,

BEG to call the attention of the Trade that by the combined efforts of expert departmental buyers, going to Britain twice a year, and a resident buyer and staff there, they are enabled by watching the home markets thoroughly to contract and purchase lines of goods not obtainable elsewhere. They can confidently assert that no house in the Dominion has elaborated and systematized their business to such an extent as this firm. The effect and consequence are that year by year the trade constantly and uniformly increases. The stock is always large and varied, and is continually being supplemented by new purchases of the latest novelties and value.

They solicit an inspection at all times. Letter orders or orders through our travelers receive careful and prompt attention, but personal inspection is solicited.

DEPARTMENTS:

GROUND FLOOR—Woolen Department
Canadian Woolens, Rubber Goods, Carriage Cloths, Tailors' Trimmings, etc.

FIRST FLOOR—Staple Department
Linens, Cottons, Etc., Etc., Etc.

SECOND FLOOR—Staff Department
Dress Goods, Etc., Etc., Etc.

THIRD FLOOR—Mantle Department
Silks, Crapes, Jackets, Etc.

FOURTH FLOOR—Haberdashery Department
Sewing Silks, Etc., Etc.

FIFTH FLOOR—Carpet Department
Carpets, Etc., Etc.

NEW WING—(Second Floor)
Imported Woolens.

NEW WING (Third Floor)
Canadian Tweeds.

NEW WING (Fourth Floor)
Gents' Furnishings.

21, 23, 25, 27 Wellington Street East, } TORONTO.
30, 32, 34, 36 Front Street East,
31 Major Street, Manchester, **England**.

ROYAL INSURANCE CO'Y
OF ENGLAND.
FIRE AND LIFE.

Assets, - - - $29,000,000.

The Royal Insurance Company has the Largest Surplus of Assets over Liabilities of any Fire Insurance Co'y in the World.

STANDARD LIFE ASSURANCE CO.

Total Risk - - - - - - - - - $100,000,000
Invested Funds - - - - - - - 32,000,000
Investments in Canada - - - - 3,000,000

Rates Liberal and Losses Promptly Settled.

DOMINION PLATE GLASS INSURANCE OFFICE.

Insurance on Plate Glass Windows, Show Cases, etc. Stock held on hand for immediate replacement in case of breakage

Sun Accident Ins. Co.

Insurances against all classes of Accident.

DOMINION LINE OF STEAMSHIPS,

From Quebec or Portland every week.

ISSUER OF MARRIAGE LICENSES

For City of Hamilton and County of Wentworth. Good for any part of the Province of Ontario.

Money to Loan on Real Estate,

At Liberal Rates of Interest and Easy Terms of Payment.

DAVID McLELLAN,

House 55 Bay Street. Office 84 James Street North.